SWEDES IN

Invisible Immigrants

Since 1776, more than 100,000 Swedish-speaking immigrants have arrived in Canada from Sweden, Finland, Estonia, Ukraine, and the United States. Elinor Barr's *Swedes in Canada* is the definitive history of their experience. Active in almost every aspect of Canadian life, Swedish individuals and companies are responsible for the CN Tower, ships on the Great Lakes, and log buildings in Riding Mountain National Park. They have built railways and grain elevators all across the country, as well as churches and old folks' homes in their communities. At the national level, the introduction of cross-country skiing and the success of ParticipACTION can be attributed to Swedes.

Despite this long list of accomplishments, Swedish ethnic consciousness in Canada has often been very low. Using extensive archival and demographic research, Barr explores both the impressive Swedish legacy in Canada and the reasons for their invisibility as an immigrant community.

ELINOR BARR has written extensively about Northwestern Ontario and Scandinavian immigrants in Canada. She is a research associate of the Lakehead Social History Institute at Lakehead University.

The Old Country bonded them
even when it was not the same
old country. They had exile
as their common heritage.
Mary Frost, "Planting in Northwestern Ontario,"
STRAIGHTLINES, Penumbra Press, 2003.
Excerpt reprinted with permission.

Swedes in Canada

Invisible Immigrants

ELINOR BARR

Including a new article "The Swedes in Canada's
National Game: They Changed the Face of Pro
Hockey" by Charles Wilkins

UNIVERSITY OF TORONTO PRESS
Toronto Buffalo London

© University of Toronto Press 2015
Toronto Buffalo London
www.utppublishing.com
Printed in the U.S.A.

ISBN 978-1-4426-4494-6 (cloth)
ISBN 978-1-4426-1374-4 (paper)

Printed on acid-free paper

Library and Archives Canada Cataloguing in Publication Data

Barr, Elinor, 1933–, author
Swedes in Canada : invisible immigrants / Elinor Barr.

Includes new article "The Swedes in Canada's national game: they
changed the face of pro hockey" by Charles Wilkins.
Includes bibliographical references and index.
ISBN 978-1-4426-4494-6 (bound).   ISBN 978-1-4426-1374-4 (pbk.)

1. Swedish Canadians – History. 2. Swedes – Canada – History.
3. Canada – Emigration and immigration. 4. Sweden – Emigration
and immigration. I. Title.

FC106.S8B37 2015   971.004'397   C2015-901337-2

 Sponsored by Lakehead Social History Institute,
Thunder Bay, Ontario.

The research material for *Swedes in Canada: Invisible Immigrants* has been donated to
University of Manitoba Archives in Winnipeg.

University of Toronto Press acknowledges the financial assistance to its publishing
program of the Canada Council for the Arts and the Ontario Arts Council, an agency
of the Government of Ontario.

 Canada Council   Conseil des Arts
for the Arts   du Canada

University of Toronto Press acknowledges the financial support of the Government
of Canada through the Canada Book Fund for its publishing activities.

This book has been published with the help of a grant from the Canadian
Federation for the Humanities and Social Sciences, through the Awards to Scholarly
Publications Program, using funds provided by the Social Sciences and Humanities
Research Council of Canada.

To my dad, Tony Berglund of Ignace, Ontario, who embodied the best of both countries. He loved his daughter and two sons, and worked two jobs, sometimes three, to give them the educational opportunities he never had. He loved the wilderness and took delight in sharing it with others. He loved to laugh, to play the piano, and to dance.

He was born Anton Berglund (1898–1966) in Skog, Ångermanland, and immigrated to Northwestern Ontario with his family at age nine.

Contents

Contents

Maps and Illustrations

Acknowledgments

First of all, I would like to thank Don Sjoberg, who made the Swedes in Canada project possible by offering to raise funds to make a published history a reality, and for his continued commitment and support throughout. I am grateful to A. Ernest Epp for associating the project with the Lakehead Social History Institute, which allowed Lakehead University to accept donations and to issue income tax receipts. He also received a Human Resources Development Canada grant to pay for summer students to check census statistics, leading to publication of his book *Nordic People in Canada: A Study in Demography 1861–2001*. We were "The Three Musketeers," as it were, who started the ball rolling.

And did it roll! That so many individuals "caught the spirit" and helped in various ways was a wonderful inspiration to me. The project was carried out in three phases: researching, cataloguing the research material, and writing the history. The volume of research material eventually filled 12.5 metres of shelf space, the length of a large room, so that the original five-year project had to be extended to eight years. This research material has been donated to University of Manitoba Archives in Winnipeg.

During the research phase I visited British Columbia, Alberta, Saskatchewan, Manitoba, Toronto, Ottawa, and Halifax, as well as Swenson Center and Vasa Archives in Illinois and various repositories in St Paul and Minneapolis. I also spent six weeks researching in Sweden. To those who assisted with research, who offered billets and transportation, and who arranged public meetings, I am deeply grateful. Thanks are also extended to those individuals who donated family histories, memoirs, photographs, articles, newspaper clippings, and other material in various formats.

Several people donated personal research material to the project, including Michael Brook of Nottingham, England, Viveka Janssen of Victoria, British Columbia, Irene Howard of Vancouver, British Columbia, and Lucille Szumutku of Stockholm, Saskatchewan. These significant collections are much appreciated and a welcome addition to the research material. I would also like to thank Helen Deachman for carrying out research at Library Archives Canada, and Carin Routledge for researching the William Wonders Collection at the University of Alberta Archives.

The amount of correspondence was daunting at times. For example I received a hundred responses to an early blurb about the project, which appeared in a genealogical journal in Sweden. Most of these letters had to be answered in Swedish, and my language skills were rudimentary. One of the correspondents, retired teacher Bertil Nyström, kindly offered to help via e-mail, and the considerable improvement in my fluency is thanks to him and to the local self-help group Svenskaspråket.

I would also like to thank the volunteers who translated letters, articles, and parts of books on request. They include Lars-Ove Carlson, Joanna Daxell, Siv Ek, Kerstin Guillemaud, Irina Hedman, Houdeh Houshangi, Eeva Isaksson, Tove Malmqvist, Marianne Pfister, Tina Reid, Sigrid Rishor, Eva St Jean, Maria Sandberg, and Carl Widstrand. A special thank you is due to Eva Grenier, who translated our website www.swedesincanada.ca to make it bilingual in English and Swedish, and to Elisabeth Thorsell for translating my newsletters and updates, and other additions. For the website's design and maintenance I am grateful to Tricia Littlefield, then, after her twins were born, to Donna Brown and her crew at PC Medic, and finally to Neil Sideen of Vancouver. A study of the website in May and June 2003 recorded 960 hits, of which 40 per cent opted for the Swedish version. The project's mailing list has remained consistent at 500 to 600 e-mail addresses.

For significant donations of books I would like to thank Swenson Center in Rock Island, Illinois, Släktforskarnas hus in Leksand, Sweden, and Viveka Janssen in Canada. The names of individuals who donated or loaned books, and photocopied the sections in local histories and published articles where Swedish residents are named, can be found below. An important part of the project was indexing local histories, and for this labour-intensive task a huge bouquet is due to Verner Loov, Ann-Mari Westerback, Annette O'Brien, and Carol Barry, and to Sylvia Nordstrom for photocopying relevant articles from *Swedish Press* for the years 1986 to 2009. I would also like to thank the more than 200 "new" immigrants who responded to our online questionnaire, as well as Linnea Lodge, Ted Simonson, and Barbro Baker for being consistent supporters in ways too numerous to relate.

Two research assistants, Terry Rizzo and Pat Lamminmaki, were hired consecutively to help catalogue the research material, for a total of one year. During this time three databases were compiled, one for published and unpublished materials (almost 2,300 entries), one for immigrants before the Second World War (6,164 entries), and one for immigrants after the Second World War (213 entries). The headquarters for the Swedes in Canada project was my basement, where a second computer and research material were installed in the recreation room. Visitors who toured the facility included Ambassador Lennart Alvin. I would also like to thank Pat Lamminmaki and Beth Boegh for compiling "Honour the Pioneers," and Ann-Mari Westerback for compiling the database of Sweden's ambassadors and consular representatives in Canada.

After completion of the draft manuscript it was submitted to readers who recommended significant changes. I am grateful to the following persons for suggestions: Phil Anderson, Don Sjoberg, Carl Widstrand, Don Wilson, and especially my adviser, Tory Tronrud, whose concise remarks helped a great deal in tailoring the manuscript to its present form. I would also like to thank Beth Boegh and her co-director, Michel Beaulieu, of the Lakehead Social History Institute, as well as the institute's board of directors for their ongoing support behind the scenes.

It is significant that the project itself has been totally funded by Swedish organizations and individuals. The chief organizational donors follow, in no particular order: District Vasa Lodge Central Canada #16, District Vasa Lodge Alberta #18, Strindberg Vasa Lodge #259 in Winnipeg, Branting Vasa Lodge #417 in Calgary, Skandia Vasa Lodge #549 in Edmonton, Bethel Lutheran Church in Camrose, Augustana Lutheran Church in Edmonton, Don Sjoberg for a memorial to Bethlehem Lutheran Church in Scandinavia, Manitoba, Swedish Embassy in Ottawa, SWEA Toronto, Norrskenet Swedish Society of Thunder Bay, Swedish Cultural Association of Manitoba, Swedish Club of Victoria, Swedish Council of America in Minneapolis, and the Arvid Lundbäck Award in Sweden. The chief individual donors were Neil Carlson, Enid Edwards, Luella Lind, Linnea Lodge, Ted Simonson, and Don and Trudy Sjoberg, although many others donated lesser amounts, including those who participated in "Honour the Pioneers." Although Canada Council is responsible for allotting funding to Canadian authors to allow worry-free time to write, successive juries missed the opportunity to support this, the first history of Swedes in Canada.

For valued assistance I would like to recognize Alfred Adamson, George Bailey, Anette Rosberg Arnäs, Byrna Barclay, Dolores Bellamy, Eric Bengtsson, and Lisa Bengtsson. Thank you also to Lasse and Margareta Berg, Karmen Blackwood, Rocklee Bogseth, Sonja Boyce, Rolf Brodin, Michael Brook, Joanna Daxell, Ken Domier, Enid Edwards, Kaa Eneberg, Donna Englund, Sven Eriksson, Per and Rayhni Ersson, Lars Fahlstrom, Hälle Flygare, John Freed, Eva and Dale Grenier, Art Grenke, Sylvia and Gunnar Gullnäs, Bo Gustafsson, Chris Hale, Ida Hallin, Vi Hautala, Irina Hedman, Jörgen Hedman, John Hoas, Elaine Hogg, Richard Gottfrid Larsson Holt, Hans Hornfeldt, Irene Howard, Viveka Janssen, Christina Johansson, Sven Johansson, Vera Johnson, Ruth Kizlyk, Erik Kjellberg, Helen Kletke, Birgit Kostenius, Maureen Landine, Verna Larson, Julie Lawson, Bernice Lever, Betty Lewis, Eva Loader, Alma Macdonald, Elizabeth Mårald, Denis Marshall, Lila Martinson, Jane Mattisson, Father William Maurice SJ, Mary McIntosh, Myron Momryk, Leif Mörkfors, Helen Moseson, John Munro, Martha Neilson, Greta Nelson, Anders and Hamida Neumüller, Lyn Niemi, Eva-Lena Nilsson, Gunnar Nilsson, Verna Nystrom Nichols, Adolf Nordin and Arlie Nordin, Sylvia Nordstrom, Gunnel Nyström, Irene Olljum, Lennard Olson, Norman Olsson, Inga and Evert Olsson, Nick Pappas, Lorne Pearson, Lennart Petersson, Stenåke Petersson, Stig Petersson, Mildred Rasmussen, Mats Rehnström, Tina Reid, Cliff Reinhardt, John Richthammer, Ruth Wahlgren Rinaldo, Gloria Roberton, Carin Routledge, Per Anders Rudling, Tim Sandberg, Eleanor Sander, Brent Scollie, Alan Sideen, Lena Sillanpaa, Vernon Silver, Deanna Summy, Walter Syslak, Per Talgoy, Tom and Doreen Thomeus, Leah Tourond, Karen Trygg, Rena Utterstrom, Bev Valvasori, Heather Walker, Richard Williams, Linnea Wilson, and Bertil Wockatz.

I would also like to thank the following people for contributing family information used in this book: Lars Anderson, Margaret Anderson, Olga Anderson, Pat Angus, Doug Barber, Connie Bjorkquist, Jean Blaine, Howard Blaxland, Leif Bloomquist, Harriet Boman, Della Dixon Brunskill, Roxann Buskas, Sheila Callen, Ed Carlson, Florence Carlson, G. William Carlson, Harriet Lee Carlson, Denis Cartwright, Anna-Greta Edlund, Allen Eng, Don Erickson, Margit Fredrickson, Jim Galley, Eleanor Gardiner, Amanda Gellman, Nels Granewall, Diane Harri, Bev Haug, Margaret Hewitt, Fay Hicks, Ken Holmberg, Ahlan Johanson, Annelie Jönsson, Isabel Johnson, Irene Johnstone, Maureen

Landine, Bob Lilja, Luella Lind, Ernest Lindholm, Kay Lindholm, Ally Malmborg, Ingalena Marthin, Susanne Martin, Christina Matyczuk, Mary McIntosh, Ernie Melville, Linda Michaud, Ben Nelson Jr, Jason Ness, Verna Nichols, Malte Nilsson, Carl John Nordstrom, Ralph Ohrn, Norman Olsson, Kenneth Palmgren, Dan Pearson, Jim Pearson, S.G. Pearson, Katherine Peebles, Marion Petersson, Alma Pippy, Jerry and Nils Pokrupa, Selma Reid, Bertha Risbey, Lillian Rodke, Perry Rydman, Lasse Schulze, Edith Shiells, Stig Söderberg, Stuart Stevenson, Ted Stone, George Sward, Jean Tavanee, Clarence Tillenius, Erik Tornblom, Rolf Tornblom, Ingrid von Rosenbach, and Esther Williams.

Because of the enthusiastic response the project lasted longer than expected, and my husband, Peter Barr, deserves special mention as chief cook and bottle washer to allow me uninterrupted time to work on the project throughout its eight years' duration. A special thank you is due to Don Sjoberg, Tory Tronrud, and Beth Boegh for their unfailing support, which made possible the project's successful completion. For all who participated, including those who have not been mentioned through oversight, rest assured that your contributions have helped to broaden my understanding, to raise the profile of Swedes in Canada, and to give descendants a sense of their place in contemporary Canada.

Canada

ELLESMERE ISLAND

Beauton Sea

Baffin Bay

DEVON ISLAND

MELVILLE ISLAND

BANKS ISLAND

SOMERSET ISLAND

PRINCE OF WALES ISLAND

VICTORIA ISLAND

PRINCE CHARLES ISLAND

BAFFIN ISLAND

Davis Strait

SOUTHAMPTON ISLAND

NUNAVUT

Great Bear Lake

Yellowknife ★

Great Slave Lake

NORTHWEST TERRITORY

YUKON

Whitehorse ★

Pacific Ocean

BRITISH COLUMBIA

Vancouver

VANCOUVER ISLAND

Victoria ★

ALBERTA

Edmonton ★

Calgary ★

Lake Athabasca

SASKATCHEWAN

Saskatoon ●

Regina ★

MANITOBA

Lake Winnipeg

Lake Winnipegosis

Winnipeg ★

Hudson Bay

James Bay

ONTARIO

Lake Nipigon

Thunder Bay

Lake Superior

Lake Michigan

Lake Huron

Toronto

Lake Erie

Lake Ontario

Ottawa

Montreal

Quebec ★

QUEBEC

Labrador Sea

NEWFOUNDLAND

NEWFOUNDLAND

St. John's

Gulf of St. Lawrence

Prince Edward Island

NEW BRUNSWICK

Fredericton ★

Saint John ●

NOVA SCOTIA

Halifax ★

Map courtesy of Bruce Jones Design.

SWEDES IN CANADA

Invisible Immigrants

Sweden

The counties (*län*) as they were before 1991.   The provinces (*landskap*).

Note: The counties are the administrative districts of Sweden.

Used with the permission of *Swedish American Genealogist*.

Chapter One

Under an Invisibility Cloak

The low profile of the 100,000 Swedish immigrants to Canada has rendered them almost invisible, as though they never existed. This chapter examines the reasons for such a phenomenon, some of them affecting different parts of the country at different times, and others more far-reaching. An important factor is the lack of a comprehensive history, an issue being addressed by publication of this book. Curious descendants and others will be interested in peeking under the invisibility cloak to discover what kind of place this minority group carved out for itself in the larger Canadian society, and where they fit into the puzzle as individuals.

The question of why Canada's Swedes are not better known as a group was posed in 1977 by the Swedish-American historian Arnold Barton.[1] As editor of the Swedish-American Historical Society's quarterly journal, he put out a call for articles, but there were no takers. Finally in 1982 he devoted an entire issue to Canada, explaining that the word "American" in the title really meant "North American."[2] The emigration scholar Harald Runblom of Uppsala University wrote the lead article, "The Swedes in Canada: A Study of Low Ethnic Consciousness."[3] He thought that Swedes were themselves to blame, that they had assimilated so thoroughly that they no longer cared about their heritage. Contributing factors were racially mixed marriages resulting from wide dispersal of Swedes and uneven sex ratios, and diverse origins, not only in Sweden, but also in Finland, Estonia, and Russia.

Lars Ljungmark, the scholar of Winnipeg Swedes, cited a number of reasons gleaned from the newspaper *Svenska Canada-tidningen*, including the suggestion that Swedish-American migrants had left their initial Swedishness behind in the United States, and that the radical politics of the

1920s newcomers made the homeland less appealing for earlier immigrants. He emphasized that the level of ethnicity was not static, but fell during the First World War and rose with the attention received by Sweden's Middle Way,[4] the name given to the reform policies of the Social Democratic Party and publicized in a 1936 book titled *Sweden: The Middle Way*.

While the concept of low ethnic consciousness may be a factor in the lack of a published history, the relatively small number of Canada's Swedes cannot be blamed. According to the 1931 census, residents of Swedish origin formed 0.78 per cent of Canada's total population of 10,376,786. Those of British origin made up more than half; and French, more than one-quarter, leaving less than one-quarter – that is, 2,067,725 people – in all other categories. Germans led at 4.6 per cent, followed by Ukrainians, Jews, Netherlanders, Poles, First Nations, Italians, Norwegians, and finally Swedes. The percentage of Norwegian origin was 0.9 per cent; Finnish, 0.42 per cent; Danish, 0.33 per cent; and Icelandic, 0.1 per cent. Yet, all these Nordic immigrant groups have written histories except for Danes, who have channelled their energies into establishing a museum.[5]

More recently a new generation of scholars returned to the intriguing question of a Canadian mosaic in which Swedes are virtually invisible. Carina Rönnqvist of Umeå University carried out an in-depth study, published with the clever title *Svea People in the Land of Babel*.[6] According to Canadian scholar Gerald Friesen, "the map of the southern half of the western interior was a giant checker-board of culturally and linguistically distinctive settlements."[7] After Rönnqvist considered the impact on immigrants of the homeland, Sweden, the United States, Canada's Scandinavians, and Anglo-Saxon Canadians, and how they affected the construction of identity at the individual, organizational, and official levels, she concluded that "Sweden represented their glorious past, and Canada their prosperous present and future ... [The Swedish nationalism felt by Canadian Swedes] did not negate Canadian nationalism. Rather it functioned as [a] complementary identity within the Canadian national framework,"[8] effectively reducing their visibility.

It is interesting to compare the Canadian situation to Dag Blanck's 1997 doctoral dissertation at Uppsala University,[9] a study of the development of Swedish ethnic identity in the United States. He argues that the American Revolution established the country as a "new nation": "This new nation was founded on a set of abstract political and philosophical ideas, codified in such central documents as the Declaration of

Independence and the Constitution, and the U.S. was thus what Wilbur Zelinsky has called an 'ideological construct,' making it different from other 'old' nations in that it lacked 'strong historical or territorial tradition' or common 'cultural bonds' such as a common religion or language."[10]

Swedish immigrants, many with former allegiances to small communities rather than to the national entity, were introduced to a much larger nationalism based on the American political ideals of liberty, equality, and republicanism. Commitment to these ideals left Swedes and other ethnic groups free to follow their own culture and religion, resulting in hyphenated Americans.

If this paradigm were transferred to Canada, Swedish immigrants came to a colony of Great Britain in which the political philosophy was "peace, order, and good government." Most immigrants expected to conform to the language and customs of the English-speaking majority, but they were unprepared for the impact on their lives of official Anglo-conformity, and, later, the ethnic discrimination they experienced during the First World War. As a result they suppressed their Swedish identity and became Canadians of Swedish descent rather than the hyphenated variety.[11]

Anglo-conformity permeated every aspect of life during the first three waves of immigration. Schools played a crucial role in creating Canadians out of ethnic children. Geographer William Wonders explained: "From the viewpoint of culture there is, strictly speaking, very seldom any second Scandinavian generation."[12] Similarly Swedish author Gunnar Nilsson found that the second- and third-generation Swedes he met in Canada during the 1970s had only a rudimentary knowledge of the Swedish language.

Blanck went on to study the Augustana Synod, the most influential institution among Swedish Americans. Until the 1890s this Lutheran synod encouraged immigrants to become good Americans, but after this time promoted a Swedish-American history in which the Vikings, the New Sweden colony on the Delaware, and cultural icons, such as the Swedish king Gustavus Adolphus and Civil War hero John Ericsson, figured prominently.[13] These ideas spread to Canada through the synod, and resulted in three place names: Monitor and Lindbergh in Alberta, and Lindbergh Island in British Columbia. Monitor, named in 1913, commemorates the fiftieth anniversary of the Civil War battle with the ship John Ericsson designed, and Lindbergh and Lindbergh Island honour Charles A. Lindbergh's historic flight across the Atlantic in 1927.

Despite the concentration of American Swedes in certain areas of Canada, I have been unable to find evidence that they showed more interest than other Swedes in Canada in the 300th anniversary of the establishment of New Sweden in 1938. In Washington the New Sweden Monument sculpted by Carl Milles was presented, with President Roosevelt and Prince Bertil as guest speakers. The delegation from Sweden included the Crown Prince and Crown Princess, cabinet ministers, church dignitaries, a select choir of seventy voices, and the Swedish Royal Horse Guards Band. Sweden even struck a Tercentenary Memorial coin to mark the occasion.[14]

In Canada Esse Ljungh of Winnipeg coordinated a very modest contribution as secretary of Canada's Delaware Committee.[15] In Port Arthur and Fort William (after 1970, Thunder Bay) a Scandinavian picnic was arranged, complete with speeches, races, and music, which, it was hoped, would become an annual event. However, the second annual picnic in 1939, held in honour of the royal visit of King George VI and Queen Elizabeth, was the last.[16]

The Swedish Pioneer Centennial in 1948 commemorated the first Swedish immigrants to the American Midwest. Among the celebrations was a gathering of 18,000 people in Chicago Stadium to hear speeches by President Truman, Prince Bertil, and author Carl Sandburg. The high-profile centennial inspired the founding of the Swedish Pioneer Historical Society, which in 1983 changed its name to the Swedish-American Historical Society. The occasion excited little interest in Canada, except for ten entries to an essay contest sponsored by the Swedish American Line.[17]

Eva St Jean's study of Swedish immigrants in British Columbia found that everyday life was more influential in shaping identity than the cultural baggage carried from home: "Swedish immigrants created a new world and culture that depended not only on strength of body and character, but also on the solidarity and welcome they found among kinsmen and among fellow workers of all nationalities."[18]

Although her approach to assimilation is from a different perspective from those of other scholars, she leaves no doubt that Canadian identity overshadowed Swedish ethnicity. Per Rudling of the University of Alberta blamed the overpowering presence of the United States.[19] Although the reasons differed, scholars agreed with Runblom's generalization that Canada's Swedes had a low ethnic consciousness.

What caused this phenomenon? Perhaps it was the lack of a national organization. In his study of Winnipeg, Ljungmark pointed out how strong differences of opinion in religious, political, and temperance matters weakened any positive impact that Swedes might have had as a group. The competition for members between Lutheran and Mission Covenant denominations split communities and families, the cause of temperance was even more divisive, and the socialist ideas immigrants began bringing from Sweden before the First World War resulted in deep schisms. The only national organizations, the elitist Svenska förbundet i Canada (Swedish Canadian League) founded in 1917 and its grassroots successor of the same name, were both short-lived.

Another possibility is the relative dearth of scholarly studies, caused in part by a lack of reliable statistics for the first and second waves of immigrants. The official designation "Scandinavian" lumped Swedes together with Norwegians in the Canadian census from the very beginning. Although their political alliance ended in 1905 it was not until 1921 that statistics were collected for Swedish immigrants and their descendants. More recently, funding agencies geared research grants to Scandinavian projects rather than to individual Nordic groups, so that researchers added a token example to projects in order to conform to the "Scandinavian" requirement.

Or perhaps Rudling is right. Perhaps Canada's Swedes were so heavily influenced by the culture and settlers emanating from the United States that they became overwhelmed by all that its much larger Swedish population represented. Prime Minister Trudeau described Canada's relationship with its only neighbour as being "a mouse in bed with an elephant." According to 2008 statistics Canada's total population came close to 11 per cent of that of the United States. About 1.1 per cent of these 33,212,696 Canadians were of Swedish heritage, whereas the proportion in the United States was higher at 1.6 per cent in a population of 303,824,640. Up to 1.25 million emigrants left Sweden up to 1930,[20] the period of heaviest emigration. A million or more are estimated to have migrated to the United States and 100,000 to Canada. Without a person-by-person analysis these numbers remain arbitrary. However, it is clear that Swedes in the United States have always vastly outnumbered those in Canada.

During the 1850s and 1860s almost 47,000 Scandinavians had poured into the United States through the St Lawrence River corridor.[21] By 1873 thousands of Swedes had passed through eastern Canada, but only 257 individuals are known to have remained as settlers, and they were quickly absorbed. When the government began its campaign to populate the Prairies, immigrants from Europe were steered westward to Winnipeg, bypassing eastern Canada.

Canada was officially a colony until 1926, when the Imperial Conference gave it equal status with Great Britain, and only that year began appointing representatives abroad with full diplomatic status. Sweden began appointing trade representatives to Canada in the 1920s or a little earlier, so that the two countries had little opportunity to build a relationship until the fourth wave of immigration after the Second World War. It is significant that Canada appointed its first diplomatic representative abroad to the United States.

The decision of the United States to name its country, its citizens, and its language after two continents has been termed "linguistic imperialism,"[22] and with good reason. The confusion has contributed to rendering Canada invisible – not just Swedes – through the labelling of both countries as the single entity of "America." Canada has since come into its own, but annoying hold-overs from the past continue to occur.[23]

In 1971 Consul Rudolph Zoumer of Calgary wrote a polite letter about the Swedish word "*Amerika*" to the bilingual magazine *Bryggan/The Bridge*, published by the Emigrant Register in Karlstad, Sweden: "There are the United States of America and there is Latin America, but for us here there is, above all, a country called Canada. Swedish achievements in Canada and especially in the western provinces of Saskatchewan, Alberta and British Columbia are unknown. [Also] they have, as far as I know, no awareness of the emigrant research being done in Sweden."[24] He called for articles that Canadians would be interested in, and noted that the publication did not list the cost of a subscription to Canada, only to the United States.

Recently *Bryggan/The Bridge* has published several of Alf Brorson's articles about Canada, but in May 2009 the magazine's name changed to *Sweden and America*, and the Emigrant Register's new building became the Swedish American Center. The new names suggest that Canadian subscribers and clients are not welcome, since "Swedish American" refers only to residents of the United States. To include Canada, the appropriate terminology would be "Swedish North American." In 2013 the name was changed to the Swedish Migration Center, more accurately reflecting emigration from and immigration to Sweden.

No pastor from the Augustana Synod was willing to establish residency until 1892 because of negative stories about Canada, its weather and its wildlife, spread by shipping agents and other officials stationed in Sweden. The legacy of these commercial strategies lingers on; for example, in the joke about summer tourists coming to Canada for a skiing holiday, and in American weather reports warning of a cold front coming down from Canada. The concept of an international boundary separating the United States from the frozen North has been ingrained into the American subconscious.

But perhaps Swedish humility is partly to blame. The quality of humility had been reinforced throughout Scandinavia for centuries as a form of social control in tightly knit rural communities. The Danish author Aksel Sandemose called it "Jante's Law" in his 1933 novel *A Fugitive Crosses his Tracks*. The book details life in the small Danish town of Jante, where nobody wanted to be at a higher social or financial level than his neighbour. Those who broke this social code could expect retribution through a form of "shunning." Although Jante's Law has never been codified, it is accepted as a reality in the Nordic countries.

In his book *The Swedish Mentality* Åke Daun credits Jante's Law for outward shyness and humility: "Personal worth is gained not least as a reward for being [able, skillful], industrious, hard-working, but one is admonished not to forget that 'pride goes before a fall' ... [and reminded] that 'you have nothing to be proud of.'"[25]

Swedes were expected to be capable and to work hard. If one happened to rise above the rest, his/her success was due to luck in one form or another. A proper response to congratulations for an accomplishment would be "It was nothing," or "I was lucky." The American humorist Josh Billings wrote, "It is a great art to be superior to others without letting them know it." For Swedes, it came as second nature.

When I asked artist Clarence Tillenius why his name was not on the plaque beside his spectacular diorama of a buffalo stampede at Winnipeg's Manitoba Museum,[26] he explained that many other people had taken part, not just him. Similarly the contribution of Swedes to the unique built heritage at Riding Mountain National Park seems to be a well-kept secret. And although most Canadians know the hymn "How Great Thou Art" few realize that the lyrics were composed in Sweden by Carl Gustav Boberg in 1885 and set to a Swedish folk melody.[27] Another popular tune for skaters, "Life in the Finland Woods," was composed by Sweden's famous accordionist, Carl Jularbo.[28] The title commemorates the Forest Finns who migrated to the Swedish province of Värmland in the 1600s.

Another example is *smörgåsbord*. Although the word is included in Canadian dictionaries,[29] meaning "a buffet meal featuring a large variety of meats, salads, etc.," it is difficult to find a Swedish smörgåsbord in any Canadian restaurant. Meanwhile, other ethnic groups routinely refer to their buffet fundraisers as "smorgs," even though the menu might be Polish or Ukrainian.

Still another example is the disappearance of trolls from the Canadian mindscape. "[During the 1920s] Dad and Mom would tell us stories in the evenings. Dad always told us about the little elves in Sweden ... [Granny] too always spoke about the little men in Sweden. If someone had a woodpile to move the little men (elves) would move it overnight!"[30]

In Sweden the popularity of trolls never seems to wane. Examples are Jenny Nyström's Christmas illustrations and the 1991 reprint of the illustrated book *John Bauers sagovärld*. No doubt, the Swedish-American commercial artist Haddon Sundblom was quite familiar with them, too. Our modern version of Santa Claus derived from his annual paintings from 1931 to 1986 advertising Coca-Cola.

Canadian scholar David Delafenêtre examined the dual behaviours of public assimilation and private ethnicity in a 1995 article titled "The Scandinavian Presence in Canada." He suggested that Nordic immigrants assimilated voluntarily:

> These immigrants expected that the Old World would have to be left behind and that the primary identification would be with Canada ... Furthermore, immigrants would take part in a fusion that would lead to the consolidation of a new North American culture. It was to be distinctly Canadian and the adoption of English was not regarded to be a step towards Anglo-conformity.
>
> The first generation tried to retain what they deemed worthy to blend with the existing Canadian culture. At the same time, they adopted what was considered positive among the host country's ways. One of the main features of the Scandinavian adaptive process was that the homeland traditions which were selected would become part of the Canadian setting.[31]

Delafenêtre named the values transmitted to the Canadian mainstream as skiing and building homes for the elderly, to which can be added the Swedish smörgåsbord. He further claimed that the ready assimilation of Nordic immigrants was a success story, and that multiculturalism discouraged scholarly research of these groups. Instead, attention was directed towards visible minorities because their experience supported the separateness inherent in the multicultural policy.

At the same time the generalization of low ethnic consciousness cannot be applied to all of Canada's Swedes. Arthur A. Anderson of Winnipeg was visibly upset when back issues of the newspaper *Canada posten* were destroyed by fire after the office closed in 1952. "Fifty years of work went up in smoke," he raged, and then stated resolutely, "We must get an archives."[32] Yet, even with his connections as a leading businessman and Swedish consul, no arrangements were made to preserve Swedish documents. Instead, they are scattered in private collections, archives, and ethnic institutions across the country, and even outside the country in repositories such as Sweden's national archives and Vasa Archives in Bishop Hill, Illinois. Fortunately a set of *Canada posten* survived at Winnipeg's Legislative Library, and has been microfilmed.[33]

In 1973 Erik Kjellberg of Stockholm tried to interest Canadian individuals, organizations, and governments in funding a study of Swedish people in Canada. His first letter of inquiry was addressed to collector Olof Seaholm of Vancouver: "I feel that Canada, in this respect as in so many others, has been overshadowed by its big brother in the south. When Swedes discuss, write or read about Swedish people in North America, it is nearly always the Swedes in the U.S. I would like to try to inform the Swedish public more about the Canadians of Swedish descent."[34]

Kjellberg lived in Canada from 1975 to 1986, during which time he earned his master's degree at McMaster University, and McClelland and Stewart published several ethnic histories in its Generations series. Unfortunately, like Arthur A. Anderson's hope for an archives, his dream failed to materialize. He returned to Sweden with his Canadian wife and family.[35]

Irene Howard recognized the importance of research material when she decided to write about Swedes in Vancouver. She was inspired by two significant collections at the University of British Columbia Library. The first was the Matthew Lindfors Fonds,[36] and the second was the Olof Seaholm Collection. During the 1960s Seaholm[37] had received a federal New Horizons grant of $2,000 to write a history about Swedish immigrants, and began by collecting research material. The book never materialized, but his collection takes up more than a metre of shelf space and includes a subject index to articles in *Nya svenska pressen* from 1933 to 1970. After publication of *Vancouver's Svenskar* in 1970 Howard donated her research material[38] to the same repository.

Olof Seaholm was a first-generation Swede, and Irene Howard's parents came from Sweden and Norway. Admittedly Matthew Lindfors was an exception who made a career of promoting Swedish culture, but both Seaholm and Howard had mainstream careers and Anglo-Saxon spouses. Similarly, of the research materials donated to the Swedes in Canada project by hundreds of individuals, most were family histories and memoirs featuring their Swedish heritage. Perhaps Delafenêtre was right about individuals keeping their ethnic feelings to themselves while giving the impression of complete assimilation. In this case the impression of a low ethnic profile was inevitable.

I first became aware of the scattered nature of Swedish documents during research for my dissertation, an annotated bibliography published in 1991 as *The Swedish Experience in Canada*.[39] Official sources turned up 162 published articles and books in the English language, but only a handful were written by Canadian authors. The possibility of a published history seemed remote. "Clearly Canadian scholarship stands in a disadvantaged position. No university or discipline specializes in Swedish studies after almost two decades of official multiculturalism. And no single repository has a mandate to collect either published works, documents, or artifacts reflecting the Swedish experience in Canada."[40]

Don Sjoberg of Winnipeg, who read my dissertation during a visit to Sweden, was unwilling to accept my gloomy prediction. One evening he phoned, a stranger to me, and asked if I would consider writing such a history if he raised funding for it. I agreed, and the Swedes in Canada project was launched in 2001 with the Lakehead Social History Institute as sponsor.

The research material that surfaced filled 12.5 metres of shelf space, a veritable mountain compared to the less than half a metre garnered for my dissertation. It included Swedish language materials, unpublished works, photocopies from general histories, photographs, various media, and new publications. This treasure trove had existed all the time; it needed only to be gathered together to provide the building blocks for writing a comprehensive history.

Issues addressed include the reasons immigrants left Sweden and what enticed them to choose Canada over other destinations, how they managed to learn English without the benefit of organized classes, and the impact they and their descendants have had on our country's development. Basic questions, such as the number of immigrants who came and where they settled, are discussed, along with religious, political, and cultural affiliations, and relationships with immigrants from other countries, including England. Also explored are Swedish contributions to both world wars, the people behind their newspapers, and an unexpected literary genre.

High-profile Canadians who made light of their Swedish heritage include Pamela Wallin,[41] appointed to the Senate in 2008 after a successful career as broadcaster and diplomat, and Ralph Gustafson,[42] recognized as one of Canada's finest poets. While it is true that the Swedish heritages of only a few people are well known, it is also true that a great many have made significant contributions at the grassroots level. The casual observer might see the men as hewers of wood and carriers of water,[43] but closer inspection would reveal inquisitive minds and strongly held opinions beneath an exterior that might seem stern and uncommunicative at first. An example is the group of nameless Swedish fallers who risked losing their jobs by giving union organizers safe entry into British Columbia's logging camps during the Depression.[44]

A common trait of Swedes on both sides of the Atlantic was helping others less fortunate, such as establishing the Scandinavian Hospital in Wetaskiwin, Alberta, and the Scandinavian Home Society in Port Arthur, Ontario. The lives of Frank Eliasson and Emil Berg, who championed the co-operative and labour movements, respectively, exemplify this trait on an individual basis. The same strict moral code based on fairness can be discerned in the politics of Rolf Bruhn, and, more recently, by Sweden's returning its Haisla totem pole to British Columbia.

The above overview of possible reasons for the long delay in publishing a history of Swedes in Canada has left out a key factor: lack of opportunity. In the United States a relatively small group of individuals, usually connected with a university, have been responsible for recording the nation's Swedish-American history from documents held in their own archives and libraries as well as Sweden's. None of these exist in Canada. Instead, the Swedes in Canada project was conceived and carried out by Canadians with a relatively high degree of ethnic consciousness, and financed by Swedish individuals and organizations with similar feelings. After the project is completed the research material will be donated to a Canadian repository to ensure that future researchers have the necessary resources at hand to continue raising the profile of Canada's "invisible" Swedes.

Chapter Two

Emigration from Sweden, Immigration to Canada

In 1860 the population of Sweden was 3,859,728, and by 1914 the population had swelled by almost two million to 5,679,607. Population growth continued up to 1930, by which time more than 1.25 million citizens had emigrated. Calculating an accurate percentage of the total population is therefore impossible because their numbers kept growing despite emigration. Most came to North America, but others ended up in such diverse places as Argentina, Australia, Brazil, Egypt, England, Germany, Ghana, Mongolia, New Zealand, St Petersburg (later Leningrad), South Africa, and Saint Barthélemy in the West Indies. It is estimated that about 100,000 Swedes immigrated to Canada, and more than a quarter of a million Canadians (282, 760 persons) claimed Swedish descent in the 2001 census.

What made them leave? At the beginning of emigration, the main reason was the lack of hope for breaking the cycle of poverty that affected many families. Later came labour unrest, when participants were blacklisted and unable to find work. Other push factors included Sweden's compulsory military duty for young men, degrading class distinctions, restrictions on the right to vote, the lack of a democratic spirit, the dominant position of the church,[1] and personal reasons, such as escaping from a debt or an unhappy marriage.

Most Swedes came to the New World with the hope of improving their lot, prodded by stories of successful immigrants and stock phrases that suggested the streets were lined with gold waiting to be scraped off with a knife. They were more likely to believe tried-and-true homilies embroidered and hanging on their walls, such as "Easy come, easy go" and "All that glitters is not gold." But there was also the saying that "Even a blind hen can find a kernel of grain now and then," and it was this slim hope that drove many people to leave their homes and loved ones.[2] Individuals who emigrated were said to have 'America fever' or the 'wanderlust,' suggesting that forces beyond their control were at work.

What attracted them to Canada? Beginning in 1884 the Canadian government embarked on a campaign for Swedish immigrants, with free land and ready employment as the most popular drawing cards. Immigration agents were appointed, and brochures and other promotional material were sent to Sweden and distributed by shipping agents. Ships brought immigrants to England to board ocean liners crossing the Atlantic, and immigrant agents met the boats at Halifax, Montreal, and Quebec City to guide travellers to trains for the last leg of their journey westward. But the most important pull factor by far was satisfied immigrants visiting Sweden and writing letters, encouraging friends and relatives to join them.

Immigrant Database

From its research material the Swedes in Canada project compiled a database of 6,164 immigrants up to 1979, a little more than 6 per cent of the estimated 100,000 newcomers.[3] Since this percentage qualifies as a reliable statistical indicator, the following numbers can be considered reasonably indicative of the population as a whole. Of the total number of 6,164 immigrants, 56 per cent were males and 23 per cent females, with 21 per cent children, confirming the patterns of family orientation and gender imbalance. Those born in Sweden numbered 5,834, with 330 persons born in other countries. Of the 95 per cent born in Sweden, only 67 per cent specified their province of birth. Of these, 45 per cent came from northern Sweden,[4] 36 per cent from southern Sweden,[5] and 19 per cent from middle Sweden,[6] with all twenty-five provinces represented.

Royal Commission on Emigration

Emigration had become politically important by 1907, when the Swedish parliament appointed a Royal Commission (*Emigrationsutredningen*) to carry out an historical-statistical study. The reasons given for this surge of patriotic fervour among the ruling classes were the twin blows of losing not only its citizens through emigration, but also Norway.[7] However, the official view of the Swedish government was "the combination of the persistent population drain and the continuing discontent in society ... [which] threatened Sweden's self-respect and, some thought, its very existence."[8]

As part of the study, more than 300 men and women were interviewed that summer at Hull, England, of which 14 were bound for Canada.[9] Another part of the study printed brief biographies written by immigrants already living in North America. Of the 119 letters received, 15 came from Canada.

The letters were not without criticism of their adopted country, including the weather. One of them described working on railway construction in the mid-1880s: "People from Skåne [Sweden's southernmost province] never dreamt of such cold as I experienced beside Lake Superior. My face froze solid before I knew it. We had to sleep in tents, and our knives froze to our lips when we ate."[10] Another suggested that Canadian homes would be warmer if wood was burned in Sweden's more efficient tiled stoves (kakelugnar),[11] in which hot smoke travelled up and down a series of vertical passages to provide a gentle heat through the masonry.

The Royal Commission also compiled statistics to show the amount of money transferred from 1899 to 1907 from the United States to Sweden through postal money orders. The figure amounted to 95 million kronor ($24,700,000), whereas 16 million kronor ($4,160,000) had flowed in the opposite direction. The money received in Sweden through postal money orders from 1886 to 1906 was triple the value of Swedish exports to the United States during the same period.[12] Obviously emigration was having a positive impact on Sweden's economy.

The Royal Commission did little to check emigration. The last of its twenty-one volumes was published in 1913, the year before the First World War began. Far more effective was the National Society against Emigration (Nationalföreningen mot emigrationen), founded in 1907. Through its agencies for home loans and land acquisitions, and its lobbying for social and economic changes, Sweden became a more attractive place to live. Lectures and publications with photographs, statistics, and factual accounts of life in North America enabled Swedes to become more aware of what they would experience if they emigrated.[13]

Adrian Molin spearheaded the promotion of the Own-Home movement and wrote pamphlets and books as a counterbalance to the extravagant claims of emigration agents, shipping lines, and "Yankees" home on a visit. One of his books dealt with Canada,[14] specifically Wetaskiwin and Sedgwick in Alberta, and Fleming and Young in Saskatchewan. When asked which they would rather have, 160 acres (64.7 hectares) of free land in Canada or a much smaller farm on credit in Sweden, farmers answered with the question, "Who in Sweden wants to give a worker, who owns nothing, that amount of land on credit?"[15] The implication was that they would rather have stayed in Sweden, and that lack of opportunity was a major push factor.

Push Factors

There were many reasons why they left,[16] but the main ones were economic. When large-scale emigration began in the 1860s, Sweden was a poor country, in which 90 per cent of the population earned its livelihood from agriculture. Pauperization of the countryside reached its peak during this decade, ending with two consecutive years of famine. Many of those who emigrated were living with poverty and hunger.[17] At least 257 of them ended up in eastern Canada,[18] scattered among immigrants from Great Britain, the provinces' primary target group.

Their names were plucked from among those listed as Scandinavians in the censuses of 1851, 1861, and 1871 by Sten Aminoff, consul general of Sweden in Ottawa from 1972 to 1974.[19] Aminoff's compilation reveals, through the nationality of their children, that Swedes began trickling in much earlier than once thought. For example, Catherine Wood (her married name) was born in Ontario ca. 1798, and Thomas Johnsen in Quebec ca. 1809.[20]

In some ways these 257 Swedes were a microcosm of those who would follow. First, men were in the majority, at 162 persons, with only 45 women and 50 children, and, second, they were widely dispersed. One hundred thirty-four of them lived along transportation routes in Ontario, with eighty-six in Quebec, eighteen in New Brunswick, thirteen in Nova Scotia, and six in Newfoundland.[21] Swedes were clearly in the minority among the 1,623 Scandinavians listed in the 1871 census; that is, those born in Denmark, Iceland, Norway, or Sweden, and their descendants.[22] Scattered settlement and marriage into other traditions resulted in rapid assimilation so that the language, food, and customs did not survive more than a generation or two. Poverty in Sweden would continue to be a significant push factor.

Another reason Swedes emigrated was labour unrest. When the pace of industrialization increased in the 1870s, industries moved to the towns, providing jobs for displaced rural residents, both male and female. Sweden's first major strike, which took place in 1879 in the sawmill district near Sundsvall on the Baltic coast, resulted in 1,000 workers dispossessed and their leaders imprisoned.[23] However, continuing unrest throughout the country, including the Norberg Strike of 1891–2 and, above all, the Great Strike of 1909, which involved 300,000 workers,[24] eventually led to major economic and social changes. They also encouraged, and sometimes forced, emigration as the only alternative.

August Palm introduced socialism to Sweden in 1881.[25] Five years later the Stockholm newspaper *Socialdemokraten* (The Social Democrat) was founded; in 1889 the Swedish Social Democratic Labour Party; and in 1898 the Swedish Federation of Trade Unions (*Landsorganisationen*).[26] It was these political ideas that caused a schism in Canada between immigrants with a conservative farm background and those who had worked in industry.

An example is the Swedish Construction Association, founded by Winnipeg's 'old guard' to build a hall for social gatherings. The 300 workers who attended a 1912 meeting overturned the original idea in favour of a meeting place for workers' organizations. Before the evening ended a new society had been formed, the Scandinavian People's Hall. At the incorporation celebration the new society's radical spirit was emphasized by the singing of "Sons of Labour" before dancing began. Unfortunately neither organization succeeded in building a hall.

Similarly, the Swedish Liberal Club, founded by the old guard in 1908, never really got off the ground, and neither did the Scandinavian Liberal Society formed in 1913, although both had the unstinting support of *Svenska Canada-tidningen*. At the same time the Scandinavian Social Democratic Club was founded at Winnipeg's Scandinavian Temperance Café. The club held regular meetings and sponsored a lecture by Carl Bergström, formerly a journalist for the social democratic newspaper *Jämtlands folkblad*. Although Winnipeg's weak labour movement allowed very few opportunities for Swedes to be heard in the political arena, the political split divided the Swedish community.[27]

The Swedes who settled in Kipling, Ontario, came from Sundsvall's sawmill district during the decade from 1892 to 1902, as did many of C.O. Swanson's Swedish maids. Similarly more than 200 people left neighbouring Hälsingland after the 1905 announcement that the German-owned sawmill in Ljusne would close. Fifty of them came to Haileybury and North Cobalt, Ontario, some because of silver finds at Cobalt and construction of the Ontario Northland Railway. An important part of *Socialdemokraten*'s mandate was to provide dependable information about North America's labour market.[28]

Lars Jansson[29] was one of the workers blacklisted in the iron mines of Malmberget and Kiruna in northern Sweden, before he came to Canada in 1905. As a labour leader during the 1890s and early 1900s he helped to found the union *Gruv tolvan*, which continues today.[30] As a result one of the main streets in Kiruna is named Lars-Janssons-gatan in his honour. It is said that he knew the father of Swedish socialism, Hjalmar Branting, long-time editor of *Socialdemokraten*, president of the Social Democratic Labour Party, and, later, prime minister.

Jansson and six other Swedes filed on homesteads in Magnolia, 130 kilometres west of Edmonton.[31] His wife, Amanda, their four-year-old son Herbert, and Amanda's grown daughter, Agnes, joined him the following spring. In 1911 the sale of his homestead to the Canadian Northern Railway[32] allowed him to return to Sweden as an independent person. Agnes had married[33] and remained in Magnolia. When she died in 1918 Amanda and Herbert came from Sweden to help care for her children.[34]

The first Swedish immigrants to Silverhill, east of Vancouver, had been blacklisted in northern Sweden after the Great Strike of 1909.[35] Rönnqvist's study of these mining districts showed a steep rise in emigration to Canada from 1909 until 1914. She also looked at the coastal areas, where agriculture and forest industries predominated, and was able to establish a direct link between the economic downturn that began in 1922 and the considerable emigration that followed until 1930. Until these dates neither agriculture nor forest areas were a significant source of immigrants to Canada.[36]

The Great Strike of 1909 also inspired emigration from southern Sweden, including Albin Plym, who hid his identity for the transatlantic journey: "I boarded a ship in Esbjerg, Denmark. I got a false passport for two crowns from the emigrant agent in Denmark. Everything went as planned and after a couple of weeks I arrived in Montreal and spent the first night on the basement floor in the railway station."[37]

Plym was horrified by the brutal behaviour and disregard for human life that he encountered as a labourer in Canada. He expressed his socialist ideas by saying that the nameless immigrants who built the railways, cultivated the soil, and opened roads to mines were the real heroes. It was they who opened the safe, so to speak, from which the millionaires stole their riches. After nine years he returned to Sweden and wrote about his experiences.

Another push factor was the threat of legal action. In 1923 Johan Ståhl[38] had been sentenced to prison for his part in a labour demonstration in

Jämtland. The family ended up on a homestead in Fosston, Saskatchewan. Johan's wife, Maria, clothed and fed their eight children with difficulty, and things got worse as six more children came along. However, each child left home to work at the age of fourteen, and in this way contributed to the family's support. Johan became a Jehovah's Witness and moved to Prince George, British Columbia, in 1951.

Axel Wallgren[39] fled Sweden in 1890 rather than face charges of embezzlement. He changed his surname to Bruhn and became a farmer in Malakwa, near Revelstoke, British Columbia. He had been well respected as the royal sheriff (*kronofogde*) in charge of an administrative district in Bohuslän, where he lived in the official residence in Resteröd with his large family and several servants. After his departure the family was left homeless, penniless, and fatherless, with a cloud of shame hanging over their heads. Nevertheless, one of the sons, Åke Wallgren, became a famous opera singer. Another, Rolf Wallgren Bruhn, immigrated to Canada and became a millionaire.

People seldom think of a learning disability as a reason for emigration, but it was dyslexia that drove Erik Giöbel[40] to Canada in 1927. He received no help for his problem and failed to pass the entrance exam for high school, a necessity for his social class. His jobs as a poorly paid bush worker fulfilled neither his parents' expectations nor his own.

In Canada Erik was bitterly disappointed to discover that his glowing letters of recommendation were worthless, even though he had spent a year in England learning the language. Once again he turned to bush work, and in 1941 moved from Kapuskasing, Ontario, to British Columbia, eventually landing a steady job in a sawmill in Fort Alberni. His dyslexia did not prevent him from writing to his sister Ingrid, and after his death she was surprised to receive a legacy of 38,000 kronor, more than $8,000.[41] Erik's lonely and frustrating years in Canada had earned him the self-respect that comes with having money in the bank.

After the Second World War some residents left Sweden for political reasons. Nils Granevall[42] brought his family to Victoria, British Columbia, in 1951 because he feared a Communist invasion of Sweden. He was a prime target as a former high-ranking Communist who turned against the party when the Soviet Union invaded Finland, and author of two books against Communism. The family settled in Victoria, earning a living through market gardening. Other political immigrants included some of the 9,000 Estonian Swedes who had sought refuge in Sweden when their country was overrun by the Soviet Union.

Pull Factors

The most powerful pull factor was free land on the Prairies under the *Dominion Lands Act* of 1872, based on the *American Homestead Act* passed ten years earlier. The civil engineer Harald Fegræus[43] was one of thirty surveyors working for the Canadian Pacific Railway (CPR) Lands Department in 1884. In August he wrote a letter home from Qu'Appelle in Saskatchewan: "We arrived here yesterday after an 8-day march and will break camp again tomorrow. This place is very beautiful for us, who haven't seen a single green tree during the whole summer. It is a future town consisting at the moment of some 20 houses that are located in the middle of an aspen forest ... One can't walk a thousand steps without finding buffalo skeletons, but there are no more living on these prairies ... It is sad to see the devastation that has taken place."[44]

Systematic land surveys were a necessary prelude to transforming the open prairies into farmland. The 49th Parallel marking the international boundary became the first baseline for the Dominion Lands Survey System, which divided arable land into square townships of thirty-six sections, each measuring 259 hectares. A typical township would reserve eighteen sections for free homesteads and two for schools, with fourteen granted to the railway and two to the Hudson's Bay Company.[45] Title to a quarter-section or 64.75 hectares (in Swedish terms of the time, about 130 *tunnland*) could be had from the government for $10 plus settlement duties that included building a suitable residence and cultivating a specified area. Railway lands, on the other hand, were purchased outright at the going rate.[46]

In preparation for completion of the prairie section of the railway the federal government appointed immigration agents to advise immigrants where to settle. The immigration agent for Scandinavians was Emanuel Öhlén,[47] a tall blond from Stockholm, who worked as assistant to the Dominion immigration agent in Winnipeg, W.C.B. Grahame. Öhlén's appointment in late 1884 marked the beginning of Scandinavian immigration to the Canadian Prairies. His official designation was "interpreter," and his annual salary was $800.[48]

Öhlén returned from an official visit to Sweden, Norway, and Denmark in 1886 with a bold plan of action. First, he requested a grant of land for Scandinavian settlement, the New Stockholm colony in present-day Saskatchewan. Then, he formed the Scandinavian National Society to sponsor a brochure,[49] with Prime Minister John A. Macdonald as patron, W.C.B. Grahame as first honorary member, and himself as president.

Leading Swedes, including the Winnipeg pioneer M.P. Peterson,[50] numbered among the executive, and immigration agents in Ottawa, Quebec, Halifax, and Göteborg were listed as honorary members.[51]

Ten thousand copies of the resulting twenty-page brochure were distributed in Sweden, Norway, Denmark, and the United States.[52] It promoted the Canadian Prairies by prominently displaying the society's emblem and Macdonald's name. Not only was Canada larger than the United States, but it also had the longest railway in the world. As for climate, Manitoba's southern boundary was on the same parallel as Paris and southern Germany. In addition to practical details, such as a township sketch with its thirty-six sections showing free land, the brochure focused on the colony of New Stockholm in today's Saskatchewan.

While he was in Sweden Öhlén had printed a smaller brochure about the colony,[53] complete with a map showing the nearest railway. He had a personal interest because he and M.P. Peterson had chosen the location the previous September 1885, and he had named it after the capital city of Sweden. When Öhlén sent Nils Johanson,[54] who worked at the experimental farm in Selkirk, Manitoba, to confirm its fertility, he responded by filing on a homestead. The colony, located twenty-one kilometres north of Whitewood on the CPR, consisted of four adjoining townships and offered 160 acres (64.7 hectares) of land to every person, male or female, over eighteen years of age.

In June 1886 Öhlén accompanied the first group of immigrants to New Stockholm,[55] which was then empty prairie and wooded hills. One of his most successful strategies was to send a satisfied immigrant back home, at government expense, in order to attract others, just as he had done himself in 1886. These "return men" always brought friends and relatives, and sometimes strangers, back with them in what is called "chain migration." Known return men were M.P. Peterson and Andrew Hallonquist of Winnipeg in 1887, and, from New Stockholm, Zakris Bergman[56] in 1888, and Nils Johanson and Mr von Holstein-Rathlow, a Dane, in 1893.

In six short years Öhlén had set the wheels in motion for Scandinavian immigration to the Canadian Prairies. He initiated the Swedish colony[57] in New Stockholm, promoted it through a well-distributed brochure and "return men," and oversaw its development. He founded the first Scandinavian newspaper, *Den skandinaviske canadiensaren* (The Scandinavian Canadian), which the Canadian government distributed in the Old Country and the United States as a monthly "immigrant brochure." When Öhlén resigned in 1890 Winnipeg had become not only a destination, but also an information centre for those venturing further west.

Just as Öhlén sought immigrants from the Old Country, so the mission field of C.O. Swanson[58] was the United States. An 1871 immigrant to Waterville, Quebec,[59] Swanson was appointed Dominion immigration agent in 1892. That year the CPR completed a railway from Calgary to Strathcona, now part of Edmonton, and homesteads were opened southeast of Siding 16, the early name for Wetaskiwin. Swanson advertised Alberta's free homestead land through personal visits along the Atlantic seaboard, supplementing his powers of persuasion with kits of print information and free guided tours.

The quest for farmers from the American Midwest, not necessarily Swedes, had already begun. In 1892 a typical poster in Aberdeen, South Dakota, boasted in large print: "Seeing is believing – Products of Alberta – Grains, Grasses, Roots Grown on Free Homestead land where you can get 160 acres free. The richest soil on earth. Healthiest climate in the world. No taxes except school taxes. No McKinly [sic] Bill."[60] By the turn of the century Canada was budgeting up to a million dollars each year to maintain recruiting offices in sixteen American cities, distribute literature, and pay agents a commission of $3 per farmer.[61]

In 1895 Swanson's duties increased to cover the entire United States. He continued his earlier method of personal visits throughout the Midwest and also advertised in Scandinavian newspapers in Boston, Chicago, and Minneapolis. These tactics got results, judging from 1899 statistics, which showed that 473 of the 764 Scandinavian immigrants that year came from the United States.

In 1904–5 he guided ten tours from St Paul, also recommending the new Canadian Northern Railway, which dipped into Minnesota south of Lake of the Woods before continuing on to Winnipeg. Railway access was important. Most migrants brought with them at least one railway car loaded with effects, animals, and equipment.[62]

Swanson felt a growing commitment to the Westaskiwin area. He had a house built, and in 1900 his wife and children moved to Alberta to join him.[63] By 1905 his monthly tours from St Paul, Minnesota, had become weekly events,[64] causing him to remark that his home was in Wetaskiwin, but his office was in St Paul. A landmark near his home came to be called Swanson's Corner,[65] suggesting that his home also served as an office. Swanson's death in 1906 marked the end of federal promotion in the United States for the Wetaskiwin area.

In 1894 Swanson had initiated a scheme with the federal government to encourage young women to emigrate as domestic help in private homes. His sister, Christina Swanson of Waterville, assisted and after his death carried on alone. The heyday of the popular Swedish maid[66] gave unattached women an unprecedented opportunity to emigrate on their own. Jobs were guaranteed on arrival, so that they could start paying back the cost of the ticket right away. However, some girls took advantage of the system and left for the United States, leading to the scheme's abandonment in 1909.[67]

In 1898 a group of twenty-three Swedish maids from the Waterville area wrote a promotional letter, no doubt at Swanson's request, published in Winnipeg's Swedish newspaper under the headline "What the Girls Say about Canada": "Mr. Swanson did not get a commission on our tickets, we got them for the same price as if we had paid cash. We earned six crowns [$1.56] a week for the first six months, and after learning English ten crowns [$2.60] more or less, depending on circumstances ... You don't have to worry that they are slave tickets, as many told us when we left. One more thing we want to point out, and that is that Mr. Swanson solemnly swears to you that you can depend on being well taken care of. He has helped more than 192 girls to emigrate from Sweden and Norway over the past four years."[68] Addresses were given for the twenty-three girls and also C.O. Swanson's government address in Ottawa.

Christina Swanson made at least three trips to Sweden to bring girls back to Canada.[69] Others came on their own with tickets provided by the Dominion Line to the ports of Quebec, Halifax, or Portland, Maine, where Christina met them. The federal government paid her $4 for each girl who stayed in Canada. In 1907 the *Canadian Magazine* of Toronto published the article "Swede Girls for Canadian Homes: A Class of Imported 'Canadians' Whose Presence Is Regarded in This Instance as Mutually Beneficial."[70] The article's condescending tone, with dialogues in pidgin English, tells a great deal about the attitudes Swedish maids met in urban Anglo-Saxon homes.

Signe Olson[71] worked from 1911 to 1918 in Port Arthur, Ontario, for the widow of a former mayor. The two women lived alone in an impressive, three-storey, brick house with a circular, bell-topped tower and multiplicity of windows.[72] Signe's thoughts worked best on Monday mornings, doing laundry in the basement, and she admitted stealing time now and then to write them down.[73] One of her poems, "The Letter Started On," reflects the immigrant experience, probably her own:

Her road was the coldest she had ever known,
Barren and empty was the world she saw,

For all her trials she had to bear alone,
There was no place where comfort she could draw.
When at last she reached the goal that she had set,
And had done her best then it was she heard,
What many poor people in their lives have met,
They would be repaid with but a cruel word.[74]

Those who worked for widowers with small children were more appreciated. Another pull factor was the abundance of jobs. Immigrants from Långasjö, Småland, in southern Sweden, had their own version of "return men." Of the 364 persons who immigrated to Canada from 1882 to 1930, more than 100 were migrant workers who returned to Sweden with savings earned as section foremen or labourers on the spiderweb of railway lines between Vancouver and Field in southeastern British Columbia.[75] Friends and relatives already in Canada sent money or prepaid tickets, to be repaid. The cost of a steerage ticket ranged from $54 to $70 (206 to 263 kronor).[76] The CPR roadmasters, quite often Swedish, did the hiring.[77]

Eighteen per cent of the men returned to Sweden and bought a farm with the money they had saved from a starting wage of fifteen cents an hour. Some came back to Canada temporarily to earn money to improve their farms or to pay debts, but they always returned home. A detailed analysis of 10 per cent of the returnees showed that "during their years in America they had, on the average, sent home 3,580 kronor [$947] each and upon their return brought home an average of 8,500 kronor [$2,249] apiece."[78] These amounts represented a considerable transfer of capital.

Örkened in the neighbouring province of Skåne followed a similar pattern, and probably lost more residents to emigration than Långasjö did.[79] The main industry, quarrying, had suffered crippling strikes in 1907, 1909, and 1912,[80] and 121 adults emigrated to Canada from 1909 to 1929.[81] Many of them, like Karl Bengtsson,[82] ended up working along the Canadian National Railway's (CNR) northern railway line between Sioux Lookout and Hearst, Ontario, to populate Canada's longest Swedish community.[83] An added incentive was a succession of roadmasters from Örkened, and some from over the border in Småland, who spoke the area's distinctive "göinska" dialect.[84] An earlier, smaller group had worked for the CPR between White River and Chapleau, Ontario,[85] and they continued coming during the 1920s.[86]

Companies requiring specialized workers sometimes set up

immigration schemes. Workers were required to sign contracts for a specified period, during which time they paid back the cost of their transportation through wage deductions. Swedish authorities discouraged immigration schemes. In 1903 the Davison Lumber Company built a sawmill at the mouth of the Miramichi River, with O.W. Nordin from Sweden as manager. In September 1905 a New Brunswick government representative asked Mr Carrick, the British vice consul at Gävle in Sweden, to assist Nordin in hiring workers experienced in sawmill and woods operations. In all 114 men were hired. Subsequently the Swedish government successfully sued Carrick for having illegally acted as an emigration agent. This judgment was later overturned.[87]

Lewis Miller, an entrepreneur from Crief, Scotland, who had owned sawmills in northern Sweden, organized the only other documented immigration scheme. Believing his timber limits to be in jeopardy, in 1900 he transported the entire operation across the Atlantic. Scottish and Swedish employees, as well as the mill manager, a Norwegian named Hanson, signed three-year contracts in return for passage to Millertown in central Newfoundland. At least sixty workers came from northern Sweden, not all of them former employees.[88]

The setting for the new company town was ideal. The sawmills, jetties, booming grounds, and jack ladders were located at the south end of historic Red Indian Lake, a former Beothuk encampment.[89] Lining the sandy point above the industrial complex were eighty two-room family cottages, with the Mary March River on the other side. But the Swedes were unhappy with their wages from the beginning. The $1.10 they earned each day had the purchasing power of only 30¢. Some left right away, but the majority stuck out their contracts.[90]

Among those who stayed was O.G. Johnson,[91] who had married a Newfoundland girl. At work he introduced the use of snowshoes for horses hauling timber in the winter, evidently a custom in Jämtland. His career path followed that of Newfoundland's pulp and paper industry, and he retired after many years as woods manager.

Another reason that young men and women gave for coming to Canada was to seek adventure. John Hagglund[92] chose Fort William as his destination in 1907 because of a book he had read about the fur trade. He did not become a trapper, as planned. Instead, a hospital stay allowed him time to take a correspondence course in architectural drawing and design. This knowledge led to the founding of Hagglund Lumber and Fuel in the mid-1920s. Coal sales sustained his company during the Depression, and the building boom after the Second World War assured its survival during these years.

Many immigrants came in family groups over a period of several years. This chain migration resulted from the first immigrants writing letters home, telling of local opportunities, and from personal visits. Those who returned to Sweden, either on a temporary or permanent basis, were called "Yankees" because of changes in their habits, talk, and clothing.[93] Some Swedes viewed them with interest and others with jealousy, but most were ready to listen to their stories and consider emigrating themselves. Letters were eagerly awaited in Swedish homes, where photos of those who had emigrated were often prominently displayed.

Märta Jansson, who was single when she immigrated to Newfoundland, made her letters home more interesting by writing them on birchbark.[94] The letters of Gottfrid Larsson[95] of St Mary's, Ontario, were so eloquent that they formed a bridge across the ocean between his son and his father. Gottfrid announced the arrival of a second son: "Last Friday there arrived a fine little boy, who claims that you, Pappa, are his grandfather. Due to such circumstances we must of course let him stay ... Little Oskar does not think we should keep him but wishes we would send him back to the store, where he claims he came from. Anyway he is well and strong, has good lungs and knows how to use them when he is not sleeping. He has blue eyes, blond hair and weighs 8 English pounds. Laura is recovering."[96]

Besides family matters, his garden, and his work, with his father Gottfrid discussed politics and the war as if they were in the same room together.

Development of an Immigration Policy

The earliest immigrants to western Canada did not have the benefit of immigration agents or other official assistance. The first Swede to live in Manitoba and the only known Swede to immigrate via Hudson Bay was Jacob Fahlstrom,[97] who served a six-year apprenticeship in the Canadian fur trade from 1811 to 1817, its most volatile period. He had signed a five-year contract before boarding the Hudson's Bay Company ship at Stornaway, but how he got from Sweden to the Outer Hebrides at age seventeen remains a mystery.[98] After five years at York Factory his contract expired, just after the bloody incident at Seven Oaks in June

1816. He then hired on with the rival North West Company, leaving their employ at Sault Ste Marie[99] to join the American Fur Company. Because he is recognized as Minnesota's first Swedish resident, Prince Bertil of Sweden unveiled a plaque in his memory in downtown St Paul in 1948.[100]

Another unofficial point of entry was the British Columbia coast. Eric Anderson[101] worked on a British sailing ship that anchored near present-day Vancouver in the summer of 1872. He decided to jump ship, walked up the Fraser Valley, and settled within the present city limits of Surrey. Today, the first log cabin he built stands beside Surrey Museum, preserved as an historic monument.

The first point of entry to Winnipeg from the United States was the Red River. In 1874 M.P. Peterson travelled that route, and four years later his fiancée, Annie Nelson, arrived on the first train from St Paul.[102]

Before Confederation the eastern provinces of Quebec and Ontario (Lower and Upper Canada) had acted together to promote immigration, mostly from the British Isles and other Protestant countries but also from French Catholic districts in France, Belgium, and Switzerland. Northern Europeans were preferred immigrants, next to those from Great Britain, because they were literate, Protestant, accustomed to a northern climate and constitutional monarchy, and similar in appearance to Canada's existing Anglo-Saxon population. Ontario distributed brochures in English, French, German, and Norwegian, and placed agents in England, Germany, and Norway. Resident agents appointed in Quebec City, Montreal, Toronto, and Kingston helped direct incoming immigrants to the United States, and sometimes succeeded in redirecting them to Canadian destinations. Ontario's previous experience and errors from earlier campaigns were a great help to the Canadian government after 1867 when the *British North America Act* came into effect with immigration as a joint provincial and federal responsibility.[103]

In 1873 the federal government appointed retired politician William McDougall[104] as Special Agent for the Scandinavian Kingdoms, soon to be replaced by the Swedish-American Hans Mattson,[105] who had achieved great success in encouraging Swedish immigration to Minnesota. Representatives of the Allan Line were appointed as emigration agents, working on commission. Canada's goal was to encourage satisfied immigrants to attract friends and relatives through letters home.

North Americans first became acquainted with Sweden on a large scale in 1851 when Jenny Lind, "The Swedish Nightingale," toured the United States. She spent several weeks vacationing in Niagara Falls,

Ontario, and during this time Anna Jameson's 1838 travel book *Winter Studies and Summer Rambles* inspired her trip by steamer to the Detroit River, as well as up the Thames. She also gave concerts at local hotels[106] and in Toronto's Lawrence Hall.[107] Jenny Lind's popularity helped to establish her countrymen as immigrants worth courting.

Swedish-language brochures were printed and distributed, and articles and advertisements were published in the daily press and in Göteborg's emigration weekly, *Nya Verlden* (The New World) but results were disappointing. When Hans Mattson finished his contract as agent at the end of 1875 he had to admit defeat. He was responsible for neither the agency's single success, the 1875 transplanting of Icelanders to Gimli, Manitoba, nor its most publicized failure, the importing in 1873 of Norwegian iron workers to Moisie, Quebec.[108]

One of the reasons for not making headway was the fierce competition for immigrants in all but Iceland. As for Sweden, most prospective emigrants had their sights already set on the American Midwest, where settlement had begun in the 1840s. To them the destination of hope was "Amerika," and it was not until the 1880s that this term began to include Canada.

It was Prime Minister John A. Macdonald who in 1881 revived official interest in Scandinavian immigrants. During a visit to Liverpool, home of Canada's immigration agent John Dyke,[109] the Scandinavians he met impressed him a great deal. He directed Dyke to travel to the Scandinavian kingdoms and report on the emigration situation there.[110] Dyke's survey showed the main problems to be "a great deal of hostility to everything Canadian" arising from competition issues, including the allegation that Canadian steamship lines were subsidized by the government.[111] An example of negative propaganda was the map printed by an American steamship line in Norway, showing the St Lawrence River as frozen year-round, with the admonition that skates would be needed to reach the mainland. As a result Dyke introduced Manitoba as a northern part of the American Midwest rather than as a Canadian province, and agents of American and English lines, rather than Canadian lines, distributed his first brochure.[112] In 1884 Dyke recommended Emanuel Öhlén as Canada's first immigration agent for Scandinavians. With completion of the prairie section of the Canadian Pacific Railway in 1885, the federal government began its campaign to attract homesteaders. Immigrants from Europe were steered westward to Winnipeg, bypassing eastern Canada and the previous Swedish immigrants who had established residence there.

Government Incentives

Several organizations were founded ostensibly to help immigrants. In 1919, the non-profit Canadian Colonization Association (CCA) had been jointly formed by the federal government, the CPR, and the CNR as a subsidiary of the Department of Immigration and Colonization, with responsibility for recruiting immigrants and securing their placement. By 1923 the CPR was in charge with a head office in Calgary. The CCA founded the Swedish Colonization Board of Alberta in 1925, appointing Axel R. Mellander[113] as colonization agent. Problems arose almost at once because the fares on Canadian Pacific steamships were much higher than on the Swedish-owned Swedish American Line.[114] As a result the board had limited success and was discontinued in 1927.[115]

Much more effective was the department's own aggressive campaign, begun in 1923 with distribution in Sweden of the Winnipeg newspaper *Svenska Canada-tidningen*. The same year the Swedish American Line initiated direct service between Göteborg and Halifax, and the following April established an Information Office in Winnipeg. The office would be a coordinating agency to help Scandinavian immigrants find work on the Prairies. In 1925 the government appointed as manager Albert Hermanson,[116] a Swedish immigrant who had just completed two terms as Liberal representative for the provincial riding of Canora, Saskatchewan.

In 1924 the number of Swedish immigrants soared from 948 to 3,536, the highest annual figure ever recorded. The reason was twofold: the federal campaign noted above, and an annual quota imposed by the United States. But even after 1927, when the quota was reduced from 9,000 to a little over 3,000, immigration to the United States rarely reached this plateau because conditions in Sweden had improved. Those who wanted to emigrate increasingly turned their attention to Canada.[117] From 1921 to 1931 the Swedish-born population increased by 18,498 persons.[118]

In 1925 Ottawa and Washington jointly hosted the twenty-third interparliamentary conference. A participant from Sweden, Ivar Vennerström,[119] made some interesting observations following a Canadian tour that fall: "The Swedish-Canadian Information Office [in Winnipeg] is meant to serve Swedish immigrants, but others too may get free information there. During its first working year [March to November 1925] it had arranged employment to 239 Swedes, 75 Norwegians, 14 Finns,

8 Danes and 3 others. Most of them had immigrated with the Swedish America [*sic*] Line ... No other shipping line has such an information and contact service."[120]

In December Albert Hermanson sailed to Sweden to promote immigration of farmers to Canada. His audience with government officials in Stockholm was one of the first, with coverage by Sweden's leading newspapers.[121] The following year the Canadian National Railway, a Crown corporation, which after the First World War brought together five financially troubled lines, opened an office in Göteborg (which is also called Gothenburg). In 1926 the office published an attractive book of seventy-two pages, including a pull-out map titled "*Världens största transportsystem*" (The World's Largest Transportation System).[122] Two years later the CPR published a similar brochure of fourteen pages, listing offices in Göteborg, Stockholm, and Malmö.[123] A network of railway lines had been built throughout the Prairies to transport grain to terminal elevators in Port Arthur, Fort William, and Vancouver. Alas, with the onset of the Great Depression in 1929 immigration ground to a halt and did not begin again until after the Second World War ended in 1945.

Crossing the Atlantic

In 1850, after England repealed her restrictive navigation laws, Norwegian sailing ships began to carry passengers to Quebec City for the equivalent of $8 each, returning to Europe with a cargo of Canadian timber. In eleven years, from 1854 to 1865, almost 47,000 immigrants from Norway, and some from Sweden, arrived in these ships on their way to the United States.[124] They continued by steamboat to Hamilton, where the newly opened Great Western Railway offered transportation as far as Windsor for another $8.[125] These immigrants could not afford the safer and much more comfortable American vessels cleared for ports along the Atlantic seaboard. Only 257 of the Swedes are recorded as remaining in Canada.

Sweden opened its first Canadian consulate in Quebec City in 1850[126] for the Norwegian timber trade. A temporary consul filled in until 1855, when King Oscar I appointed Alfred Falkenberg,[127] who held the post for eighteen years. One of very few immigrants from high-ranking Swedish nobility, he was always addressed as Baron Falkenberg. Perhaps because of his rank, he received an invitation to the 1864 official dinner following the Quebec Conference, along with the consul general of France.[128] The other guests were the politicians who hammered out the resolutions that led to the creation of Canada in 1867.

Baron Falkenberg was responsible for handling breach-of-contract and similar matters concerning the timber trade rather than assisting destitute immigrants. Vice-consuls with English-sounding names were appointed to postings along the coastline, wherever river drives could bring logs from the interior to dockside. The first was Montreal, followed by Saguenay, then around the south shore and Nova Scotia to Saint John, New Brunswick. The capital cities of St John's, Newfoundland, and Halifax, Nova Scotia, were also represented. By 1871 there were seventeen vice-consuls, all under Baron Falkenberg's supervision. During his term of office he was decorated for his services by both Sweden and Norway.[129]

The break with Norway in 1905 led to the establishment of separate consular offices.[130] The Swedish government dropped most of the early vice-consulates in the Maritimes and Quebec, leaving only seven.[131] Also continued were those in Ottawa and Toronto in Ontario, Winnipeg in Manitoba, New Stockholm in Saskatchewan, Calgary in Alberta, Vancouver in British Columbia, and Dawson in Yukon Territory. The consular headquarters moved from Quebec City to Montreal in November 1906, with the promotion of Montreal's vice-consul, Gustaf Erik Gylling, to consul. Two years later new coats of arms were issued to all consulates and vice-consulates.[132]

By 1870 steamships had replaced sailing vessels for the most part, and transporting immigrants to the New World had become a thriving and competitive business. So-called feeder lines brought passengers to Hull on England's east coast, then they travelled by train to Liverpool. Those bound for Quebec City or Montreal boarded the transatlantic steamships of the Allan Line, Beaver Line, and Dominion Line. On the Anchor Line, steerage accommodation from Göteborg to New York cost about $39, second class cost $49, and first class cost $100. Other major lines between Liverpool and New York were the American Line, Cunard Line, Guion Line, Inman Line, National Line, and State Line. The Wilson Line came to dominate as a feeder line to England. The Norwegian American Steamship Company offered direct passage from Bergen to New York from 1871 to 1876.[133]

A very limited number of immigrants avoided commercial transportation altogether. Around 1887 James Akerstream[134] and a chum crossed the Atlantic in a homemade boat, following the Viking route via Iceland and Greenland, then past Newfoundland and up the St Lawrence River to Montreal. Akerstream was knowledgeable about ships and sailing, having apprenticed as a patternmaker. He thought the ocean voyage would be a great adventure, and brought along a Swedish-English dictionary so that he could learn the language en route.

Clifford Sifton's vigorous immigration policy from 1891 to 1905, while he was minister of the Department of the Interior, included a clandestine arrangement with the North Atlantic Trading Company in Amsterdam. An umbrella organization for European steamship lines, the company received a bonus of $3,571 from Ottawa,[135] and distributed the Swedish version of *Canada, the Land of Opportunity* from offices in Stockholm and Göteborg. The Sundsvall area was singled out for special attention. For every farmer, farmhand, or domestic servant who emigrated, the company received an additional $5. By the time Sifton agreed to the scheme in 1899, all the European steamship companies were locked into a vast syndicate that fixed the cost of steerage tickets and directed Swedish passengers to their English steamship according to a quota system. Although this monopoly continued in some form until the Second World War, the Canadian government ended its involvement in 1906.[136]

Crossing the Atlantic had become a week-long pleasure trip by the 1920s, although some lines still crammed as many passengers as possible into their ships. The Swedish-owned Swedish American Line put comfort ahead of profit. Their fleet of ocean liners – *Stockholm, Drottningholm, Gripsholm, Kungsholm* – even hired physiotherapists to offer massage to passengers.[137] Pier 21, which included an immigration shed, opened in Halifax in March 1928. Among its early clients was Erick Carlson, who emigrated with a buddy: "We got into Halifax on the 21st of April 1929 at 4 p.m. It was very late before we could get off the boat and it was dark. There was a Swedish man there. He gave out Swedish bibles to all the Swedes. I had that bible for many years and I had it out on the homestead. We were herded like livestock from the boat to the train. We left that evening by train for Winnipeg."[138]

One million immigrants, half of them during the Second World War, passed through Pier 21 before it closed in 1971. By this time the great ocean liners had been replaced by air travel. The building is now a national historic site and houses Canada's Immigration Museum.[139]

Immigration from Sweden had a slow start, mainly because Canada did not exist as a country until 1867 and official efforts to promote immigration were not successful until completion of the CPR in 1886, almost twenty years later. Whether immigrants wanted to farm or to work as labourers, the most powerful magnet was personal contact with those already here. The grand sweep of the Prairies beckoned as farmland, and for the most part work was plentiful. Building a nation was labour-intensive, and many hands were required to construct and maintain its transportation systems, to build and enlarge its cities and pioneer communities, and to extract and process its natural resources.

Chapter Three

Immigrants

It could be argued that the first Swedes in Canada arrived at L'Anse aux Meadows with the Vikings in 1,000 A.D. National boundaries in the Nordic countries did not exist until several centuries later, and the exact location of Viking places of origin has not been determined. L'Anse aux Meadows in Newfoundland is the only archaeologically verified site of Norse settlement in North America. Discovery by the Norwegian Helge Ingstad and excavations directed by his wife, archaeologist Anne Stine Ingstad, verified in 1968 that it was indeed a Norse settlement.

That year L'Anse aux Meadows was named a National Historic Site by Parks Canada, and in 1978 UNESCO declared it a World Heritage Site. Confirmation of the date, 1,000 A.D., and the circumstances under which L'Anse aux Meadows was constructed, proved once and for all that Norsemen had "discovered" North America five centuries before Christopher Columbus. Their short stays are the only documented Viking visits to North America.[1]

However, the great trans-Atlantic migration did not begin until the mid-1800s. Swedish immigrants to Canada arrived in an undulating flow of four major waves. The very first immigrant arrived in 1776 and newcomers remained a trickle until 1884, when the newly founded country appointed a Scandinavian immigration agent. The first wave continued until the turn of the century, the second lasted until the First World War in 1914, the third embraced the 1920s, and the fourth began after the Second World War. The first wave consisted mainly of couples with children and single men, the second added Swedish maids, and the third were mostly young men seeking work and adventure. Not until the 1950s was there a substantial number from the middle class, so that the fourth wave included refugees, transferred employees of

Swedish companies, and individuals seeking opportunities unavailable in Sweden. Most arrived directly from Sweden or via the United States, but a significant number came from Swedish-speaking districts in Finland, Estonia, and Ukraine.

Early immigrants, both families and individuals, were mostly young and from poor families. They came from an agricultural tradition,[2] and the Lutheran religion left them with more than their share of the Protestant work ethic. Almost all were literate, the women having experience as homemakers, and some of the men having experience as tradesmen and artisans.[3] They settled wherever opportunities for jobs and land presented themselves. Timing was of the essence. Latecomers were left with marginal land.

Learning English and paying back their boat ticket were priorities, but proximity to relatives and other Swedes was also important, especially at first. Immigrants were generally law-abiding and willing to please. Nevertheless, the existing urban population on the Prairies, mainly from Ontario and Great Britain, viewed them as intruders. Such an exclusive attitude by those who held key positions in politics and business, as in Winnipeg, for example,[4] limited opportunities for urban immigrants and forced them into ethnic enclaves such as the one along Logan Avenue. Others, for various reasons, settled voluntarily in Swedish communities such as New Stockholm, Silverhill, and Kipling, but the majority lived among other working-class people of various origins.

Culture shocks included Canada's immense size, the heterogeneity of its population, and the prairies, a landform that does not exist in Sweden. The Setterlund family from Torsby, Värmland, was surprised when they visited a relative's farm near Wetaskiwin: "We had expected to see a manor house, because anyone in Sweden who owned so much land would have had a very large house, instead we came to a small log cabin, on a very barren land, or so it seemed as we had come from a forest area."[5]

The main complaint in letters home was homesickness, especially at first. In 1929, a year after immigrating to Manitoba, Anna Nilsson wrote to her cousin in Sweden: "I am starting to feel homesick for Sweden now when I think of those at home and how far away I am from my nearest and dearest ... [Then four years later] Please ask Karin if they have a photo that she can give me. I have such a longing to see all my relatives."[6]

Jon Persson left his birthplace in Fryksände, Värmland, in 1876 to work in northern Sweden, then in 1892 immigrated to New Stockholm,

Saskatchewan, with his wife and children. Seven years later he waxed poetic in a letter to a niece in Värmland whom he had never seen: "Fly away O spring wind to that comfortable humble abode, to the home of my childhood which I cannot forget ... Hardly a day has gone without my going back in thought to the old home where I tramped out my childhood shoes. I see a cottage in the shelter of the woods by Fryken's [Fryken Lake] pretty shore among green spruce trees. I there my first gladness enjoyed, there my first pain experienced. When May is dressed in flowers around the world, I long constantly for this home."[7]

Letters home, and from home, were often the only link with friends and relatives, and with their past.

Statistics

Canadian government records were woefully inadequate until 1921. In addition to the Scandinavian designation, until 1925 statistics excluded migrants from the United States. No records at all were kept on out-migration. In an effort to deal with this statistical nightmare, at least in part, a detailed study of census data was carried out for Nordic people; that is, Danes, Finns, Icelanders, Norwegians, and Swedes. The following tables have been excerpted from the resulting publication prepared by historian Ernest Epp.

The total does not include those naturalized in Canada, a necessity for homesteaders in order to receive title to their land. Clearly the overwhelming majority of Swedish nationals lived in western Canada, from northern Ontario to British Columbia and the Yukon, with only 11 per cent in southern Ontario and eastwards. Growth of the Prairie population at the turn of the century can be traced to four major events: the easing of the depression that had begun in 1893, the vigorous immigration policy of the Liberal government since 1896, the development of fast-maturing wheat, and the push factors in the American Midwest of prolonged drought and high prices for good agricultural land.

The 1911 census recorded the country of birth and therefore cannot be compared with the 1901 census. Nevertheless, it is clear that immigration had sped up considerably with more than 28,000 Swedish-born residents, although their descendants born in Canada had not been included. As in Sweden, many turned to the cities for employment and others to small towns and frontier areas. In British Columbia 1,376 Swedish-born lived in Vancouver, 338 in Nanaimo, and 131 in Victoria,

Table 3.1 Swedish nationals living in Canada, 1901

Alberta	564
British Columbia	850
Manitoba	512
New Brunswick	15
Northwest Territories	1
Nova Scotia	58
Ontario	454
Prince Edward Island	0
Quebec	146
Saskatchewan	53
Yukon	254
TOTAL	2,907

Source: Epp, *Nordic People in Canada*, table 7.

Table 3.2 Swedish-born living in Canada, 1911

Alberta	6,345
British Columbia	7,118
Manitoba	3,858
New Brunswick	155
Northwest Territories	3
Nova Scotia	132
Ontario	3,660
Prince Edward Island	8
Quebec	499
Saskatchewan	6,229
Yukon	239
TOTAL	28,246

Source: Epp, *Nordic People in Canada*, table 8.

while 1,088 swelled the burgeoning lower mainland. In Quebec 113 lived in the Waterville/Sherbrooke area, while 267 chose Montreal and its suburbs. In Ontario 231 Swedish-born lived in Toronto, 83 in Ottawa, and 51 in Hamilton, but almost four-fifths (2,789) could be found in

Table 3.3 Number of Swedish-born and of Swedish heritage, 1921 and 1931

Provinces	Sw-born	Sw heritage	Total	Sw-born	Sw heritage	Total
	1921			1931		
Alberta	6,535	9,408	15,943	7,431	12,397	19,828
British Columbia	5,735	3,931	9,666	9,333	6,775	16,108
Manitoba	3,948	4,075	8,023	4,138	5,311	9,449
New Brunswick/ Nova Scotia/Prince Edward Island	254	820	1,074	254	867	1,121
Ontario	3,302	3,411	6,713	4,708	5,836	10,544
Quebec	455	453	908	860	798	1,658
Saskatchewan	7,381	11,683	19,064	7,580	14,878	22,458
Yukon/Northwest Territories	90	22	112	111	29	140
CANADA	27,700	33,803	61,503	34,415	47,161	81,576

Source: See Epp, *Nordic People in Canada*, tables 11 and 12 for the totals; for the 1921 Swedish-born, see Helge Nelson, *Nordamerika: Natur, bygd och svenskbygd*, Del 1 (Stockholm: Magn. Bergvall, 1926), 135; for the 1931 Swedish heritage, see his "Kolonisation och befolkningsförskjutning inom Kanadas prärieprovinser," *Ymer* (1934): 173.

northern Ontario, more than half of them in the region of Northwestern Ontario.[8]

The 1921 census, the first to focus on ethnic origin, shows that most Swedes lived in Saskatchewan, followed by Alberta and British Columbia.

According to geographer Helge Nelson's statistics, based on unpublished material provided to him by Dominion statistician R.H. Coates, from 1921 to 1931 the Swedish-born population increased from 27,700 to 34,415; that is, by 6,715 persons. However, *The Canada Yearbook* records that 18,498 Swedish immigrants entered Canada during the same period, so that almost two-thirds of them have disappeared. It is possible that migration to the United States, those returning to Sweden, and natural decrease through death could account for the disappearance of 11,783 Swedish-born persons over a decade, but hardly likely. Even harder to explain is the increase of 13,358 persons of Swedish heritage. The influx of Swedes from the United States had long since passed, and natural

Table 3.4 Number of immigrants from Sweden
1921–1931 according to *The Canada Yearbook*

1921	715
1922	442
1923	948
1924	3,536
1925	2,138
1926	1,076
1927	1,966
1928	2,552
1929	2,636
1930	2,020
1931	469
TOTAL	18,498

Source: As excerpted from *The Canada Year
Book.* The figures do not include Swedes entering from the United States or Swedish-speakers
from Finland.

increase through births would be much lower. Despite the confusion in details, it is clear that the number of people of Swedish heritage, including those born in Sweden, increased by more than 20,000 persons during the decade; that is, from 61,503 to 81,576.

When the Second World War ended in 1945 there had been virtually no immigration for fifteen years. Nevertheless, the 1941 census recorded an increase of 4,000 persons, bringing the population of Swedish origin up to 85,396. At the same time there had been considerable migration within Canada itself. British Columbia's population had risen by 1,900, with half the total located in the lower mainland, and some of Ontario's 2,600 Swedes had spilled southward into the golden horseshoe area. The most striking feature between 1951 and 1961 was the move to urban centres.[9]

The sharp drop in the 1971 totals, from 121,757 to 101,870, contrasts sharply with the growth among Norwegians, from 148,681 in 1961 to 179,290 ten years later. The 1971 census was the first to allow declarations of Nordic ancestry, and the author of *Nordic People in Canada* drew the following tentative conclusion: "Declarations of Nordic ancestry were not made by everyone who should have done so, although the Norwegian pride in their ancestry certainly stands out. The extent of

Table 3.5 Population of Swedish Heritage by Province, 1941 to 1971

	1941	1951	1961	1971
Alberta	20,505	22,399	28,654	24,380
British Columbia	17,979	26,012	33,251	31,390
Manitoba	9,547	9,438	10,382	8,955
New Brunswick	642	858	1,099	465
Newfoundland		135	328	260
Nova Scotia	738	1,017	1,489	835
Northwest Territories	72	105	151	180
Ontario	13,146	17,178	23,610	17,880
Prince Edward Island	19	48	58	35
Quebec	1,605	1,922	2,856	2,005
Saskatchewan	20,961	18,474	19,641	14,635
Yukon	182	194	238	310
TOTAL	85,396	97,780	121,757	101,870

Source: Epp, *Nordic People in Canada*, tables 13, 14, 16, and 18.

the reticence is impossible to know but, if the Swedish population had grown like the Norwegian (as it did in the previous decade), the 1971 census would have reported 146,839 persons of Swedish origin."[10]

The reliability of census figures comes into question when such major variations occur.

The 1991 census showed 236,655 Swedes, with 43,345 of them having two Swedish parents, or one in every 5.5 persons. The latter represent immigrants or children of immigrants, and the former indicates a high rate of intermarriage. By 2001 the count had risen to 282,760 Swedes, but only 30,440 had two Swedish parents, or one in every nine persons. These figures indicate that new immigration was not keeping pace with the death rate. Still, Swedes were coming in respectable numbers, especially to British Columbia and Alberta. Like their predecessors, many would marry individuals from another ethnic background.

Because the Census of Canada registered residents by country of birth rather than by language, the above figures do not include Swedish-speakers born outside Sweden. The numbers of those from Finland, Estonia, and Ukraine are difficult to assess from official sources. At the unofficial level most gravitated to existing Swedish religious and social organizations unless their numbers allowed for separate groups. For

Table 3.6 Population of Swedish Heritage by Province, 1991

	Both parents Swedish	Swedish included in ethnic heritage	Total
Alberta	11,175	49,160	60,335
British Columbia	14,880	62,925	77,805
Manitoba	3,035	14,765	17,800
New Brunswick	225	1,235	1,460
Newfoundland	145	500	645
Nova Scotia	260	1,950	2,210
Northwest Territories	80	455	535
Ontario	7,320	37,330	40,650
Prince Edward Island	40	225	265
Quebec	890	3,070	3,960
Saskatchewan	5,175	20,880	26,055
Yukon	115	820	935
TOTAL	43,345	193,310	236,655

Source: Epp, *Nordic People in Canada*, table 21.

the purposes of this book Swedish-speakers have been integrated into the text as Swedes.

Finland Swedes[11]

Sweden ruled and colonized Finland for more than 600 years before ceding the country to Russia in 1809. During this time Finland, including its westward archipelago, the Åland Islands, was integrated politically and economically into the Swedish realm, and Swedes who had settled along the southern and western coasts became a ruling class. Swedish continued as the language of government until 1863, when the czar decided to give Swedish and Finnish equal status. A bitter controversy followed between advocates of the two languages. Before 1900 a policy of Russification was imposed and Finland Swedes lost much of their privileged position.

Emigration is cited as one of four reasons why their numbers have continued to drop from almost 13 per cent of the total population in 1900 to just below 6 per cent in 1990. The other reasons are a lower birth rate, language shifts, and intermarriage.[12] However, Finland remains officially bilingual, and communities in Swedish-speaking districts have two names, one Swedish and the other Finnish.

Finland took advantage of the Russian Revolution in 1917 to become an independent country, and in 1921 the League of Nations confirmed the Åland Islands as an autonomous state within Finland. As a result the Åland Islands has its own flag and a single language, Swedish, whereas the rest of Finland is bilingual and flies the Finnish flag. Finland Swedes who came to Canada were caught between their linguistic and national identities so that early immigrants generally called themselves Swedes, even in the censuses, whereas those who immigrated after Finland became independent were often proud to be called Finns.[13] Although social relations between Finland Swedes and Swedes from Sweden could be strained, individuals from both groups often joined the same organizations. On the other hand, Finland Swedes hardly ever associated with Finns.[14]

They settled mainly in Ontario and British Columbia. Statistics for 1931 show a total of 2,485 Finland Swedes – 1,350 in British Columbia, 799 in Ontario, and 105 in Quebec, with less than 100 in each of the Prairie provinces.[15] However, the Swedish Finn Historical Society of Seattle, Washington, claims that 6,000 Finland Swedes were included among the 50,000 Finns who immigrated to Canada.[16]

Among celebrated Finland Swedes are Jean Sibelius (1865–1957), composer of the tone poem "Finlandia," and poet Johan Ludvig Runeberg (1803–1877), creator of Finland's Swedish national anthem, "Vårt land" (Our Land); in Finnish, "Maamme laulu." Another countryman, the botanist Pehr Kalm,[17] was the first-known Swede to set foot in what is now Canada. He was one of the nineteen students Linnaeus sent throughout the world to discover plants that might benefit Sweden's economy. During the summer of 1749 Kalm visited Quebec City and Montreal, and the following year became the first person to write a reliable eyewitness description of Niagara Falls.[18]

Three of Kalm's North American diaries were published during his lifetime, in whole or in part. Almost a quarter of them are about Canada, everything from plants and trees to the Eskimo (Inuit) language and ladies' fashions. Kalm was a keen observer, interested in everything. His candid and wide-ranging notes provide a glimpse of metropolitan life in New France a decade before its fall, perhaps the only such account written by a foreigner.[19]

Estonian Swedes

Estonia's Swedish-speaking population began arriving from Sweden and Finland in the 1200s, settling in the coastal areas and islands of northern and western Estonia. Swedish was an official language from 1561, when Sweden established the Dominion of Swedish Estonia, until the territory was ceded to Russia in 1721. Estonian Swedes prospered during this time, but conditions deteriorated under Russian rule. When the independent Republic of Estonia was created in 1918, the constitution granted certain rights to minority groups, including Swedes.

A few Estonian Swedes immigrated to Canada before Estonia was overrun by the Soviet Union during the Second World War, and more arrived afterwards. During the occupation most of them fled to Sweden as refugees. They became understandably nervous in 1947, when Swedish authorities registered all Baltic refugees as Soviet citizens.[20] Emigration began that year. Many ended up in Toronto, where in the 1960s they founded a Swedish Estonian Lutheran Church with 100 members.[21]

Anne Zoumer[22] grew up on her parents' farm, Mattsgården, on the island of Muhu. In 1944, like countless others, she fled from Estonia to Sweden under dramatic and dangerous circumstances. In 1952 Anne and her husband Rudolf followed her parents to Alberta. They settled first in Edmonton, then in Calgary. Both served as Swedish consuls, Rudolf from 1970 to 1983 and Anne for the following decade. "For me," she told a reporter, "it meant that I could say thank you and return a little of the generosity Sweden had shown me." Like other Swedish consuls after eight years' service, they were both honoured with the Swedish Order of the Polar Star (*Nordstjärneorden*).[23] Rudolf was also awarded the Gold Medal for Exemplary Foreign Service.

Christian von Rosenbach[24] worked as an engineer west of Stockholm. On the way to spend Christmas with his parents he stopped at the Canadian embassy to check on the family's application. The embassy was crowded with people from the Baltic countries, all hoping to obtain the coveted visa. Almost without thinking Christian entered the elevator marked "For employees only" and was whisked directly to the visa office. There, he met the chief immigration officer, and quickly explained his situation. After reviewing his file the officer said, "I like your initiative, attitude and spirit of enterprise. You are the kind of guy Canada needs." The family sailed on the *Empress of France* in January 1951, and settled in Hamilton, Ontario.

Ukrainian Swedes

Swedes from the Estonian island of Dagö founded the agricultural community of Gammalsvenskby, on the Dnieper River in Ukraine, in 1782. They had been forced to relocate under Catherine the Great of Russia, and over that winter of 1782, 1,000 people made the 1,931-kilometre trek on foot, via Moscow. Only half of this number survived.[25]

By the late 1800s land in the immediate vicinity of Gammalsvenskby was becoming scarce. In addition Russia imposed heavy new military duties – six years of active service and nine in the reserve – for all young men except a family's eldest son. Because of their pacifist beliefs, some German-speaking Mennonites from nearby communities left for North America. The Swedes were not pacifists, but when information about free land in Canada filtered across the Atlantic in 1886, they began leaving, too.

Hindrik Utas, his German wife, Beata, and their five young children were the first to leave. Hindrik farmed in Alberta's Cypress Hills, then sold his farm and, with the money, bought a hotel in Wetaskiwin.[26] Many of those who followed settled thirty-seven kilometres southeast of Wetaskiwin, near Red Deer Lake, and near Vernon, British Columbia.

Emigrants usually left through a German port to Halifax or New York, then travelled westward by rail. Andreas Sigalet, his German wife, Walba, and their seven children were the first to settle in the Vernon area in 1889.[27] In 1904 Victor Hugo Wickström, a journalist from Sweden who had visited Gammalsvenskby five years earlier, interviewed members of the group.

By chance Wickström found Johan Andreasson Utas[28] in Vernon for the day, and they had a long talk about the sixty Ukrainian Swedes who lived more than nine kilometres away over an impassable road. Altogether, the Albers, Sigalet, and Utas families owned 1,813 hectares, where they grew apples and pears, also oats, wheat, and timothy. Each family kept an average of fifteen cows and nine horses, in addition to pigs, chickens, and geese. They spoke Swedish and German, and attended Vernon's German Lutheran church. The children were learning English in school.[29]

The surnames of those who chose their 160 acres (64.7 hectares) between Red Deer Lake and Battle Lake in Alberta included Albers, Malmas, Sigalet, Tennis, and Utas. Of the thirty-four charter members of Svea Lutheran congregation, twelve were Ukrainian Swedes. For many years their children dominated the confirmation classes.[30]

Like some of the others, newlyweds Johannes and Katarina Malmas spent time in Gretna, Manitoba, a Mennonite community, to earn
money to pay back their tickets. In 1891 they filed on a homestead near
Red Deer Lake. A son was born while they were building a place to live.
"Their home, like the first home of many settlers, was a dugout; it was
also called a soddie. A dugout home consisted of sod walls and a sod
roof built over an excavated two-foot-deep hole in the dry hard prairie
ground. A dugout tended to be warm and comfortable in the winter
but come spring the water-laden sod roof drained into the building.
For every day it rained outdoors, it rained two days indoors, much to
the discomfort of the occupants."[31] Later immigrants discovered how
to make a leak-proof roof by using a base of wheat straw and sod taken
from the heavy soil around Battle Slough, coated with white-mud
gumbo.[32]

Johannes walked to Calgary to work for a lumber company in order
to earn much-needed money. He bought a team of horses and a lumber wagon, and was driving them home when a man stopped him. He
claimed that the team had been stolen from him and he wanted it back.
Johannes protested, but in vain. He had been "slickered" by a pair of
crooks. The growing family survived this scam, a prairie fire, and a hail-
storm, and by 1904, when Victor Hugo Wickström visited, they owned
130 hectares of land, a two-storey frame house, and a field of horses
and sheep.[33]

As a group the Ukrainian Swedes stand out because of their distinctive surnames and dialect, and their commitment to Lutheranism. Like
other Swedes they were hard-working and frugal, and realized the
value of education. Wickström noted that they subscribed to Swedish
newspapers and sometimes had a home library in addition to bibles
and psalm books. Many kept in touch with Gammalsvenskby, and a
few returned to encourage others to emigrate. Their willingness to relocate as far afield as Vancouver and Toronto is singular for a group that
came from such a closely knit community. By 1929 more than 200 Ukrainian Swedes had immigrated to Canada[34] and a handful had gone to the
United States.

The Swedish Lutheran Immigration Aid Society of Canada was first
mentioned in 1928 in connection with Swedes in Gammalsvenskby. Stalin's collective agricultural policy marked the end of their communal
lifestyle, and they were actively seeking options. Pastor Kristoffer Hoas
had contacted the society through Pastor O.H. Miller of Wetaskiwin,
enquiring about the possibility of re-establishing the Gammalsvenskby

community in Canada. Pastor Miller replied that he could guarantee enough land and also help from the government.[35] The society received federal letters patent under the *Companies Act* in January 1930, with a head office in Winnipeg. The mandate was broad, and included cooperating with government and other corporations as well as acquiring money and property in order to assist immigrants to establish themselves in Canada.[36]

Early in 1929 Pastor Hoas travelled to Uppsala University to participate in a study conducted by the Institute of Dialect and Folklore Research. While in Sweden he presented government officials with a request from his flock that they be allowed to resettle there. The same year, with aid from the government and the Swedish Red Cross, 885 immigrants set out for Sweden with joyful hearts. However, their dream of founding a new Gammalsvenskby in Sweden failed to materialize. Not only were they separated from each other by being allotted menial jobs throughout Sweden, but they also suffered from the culture shock of moving from an isolated communal society based on Lutheranism to a different and much larger Swedish-speaking milieu. In addition some felt they had to learn high Swedish because of their dialect, a variant of the Swedish spoken on Dagö centuries ago.

As an alternative, Pastor Hoas formed a fact-finding committee to look into the possibility of settling in Alberta.[37] They set off for Canada in February 1930, but the trip proved to be a disappointment.[38] They had been promised land right away and also the right to their own school, but neither was feasible. Immigrants had to work to pay for their transportation before they could secure land. The agent for the Swedish Lutheran Immigration Aid Society of Canada, Charlie Johnson, guided the committee during their stay in Alberta. However, their relationship deteriorated. Later, at the annual meeting of Augustana Synod's Canada Conference that summer, he reflected the contemporary political climate against Russia by describing his charges as "a bunch of bolsheviks and communists."[39]

The Canadian Pacific Railway, through agent J.A. Hägglund in Göteborg, had promised a loan of $150,000, but did not specify that this would be in the form of land purchases and transportation rather than cash. "Before leaving Sweden they had been promised that settlement possibilities were available for them at Rose Valley, north of Wadena, Wetaskiwin, Lloydminster and the Peace River country. Upon arrival at Wetaskiwin they were informed that they could only secure land that the CPR had for sale. Realizing that it was impossible to accept the

terms under which the Lutheran Emigration [*sic*] Aid Society in con-
junction with the CPR was offering them, they decided to sever all connections with them."[40]

They telegraphed Sweden for money to pay the CPR for their fares
and returned via the Candian National Railway and the Swedish American Line.[41] After the committee delivered its report there was general
agreement that creating a new Gammalsvenskby in Canada would be
impossible. By 1931 forty families had returned to Ukraine, despite
Pastor Hoas's passionate pleas that they remain in Sweden, where the
church bells brought from Gammalsvenskby hung in the bell tower of
Roma church on the island of Gotland.

One of the committee members, Andreas Malmas,[42] believed that
Canada offered the best hope, and remained in Alberta to help those
who wanted to try it, despite each family's having to pay the Swedish
government $17,000 for bringing them to Sweden and housing them
there.[43] A dozen families arrived in Wetaskiwin in May 1930, sponsored
by John and Ted Malmas, with tickets advanced by the CPR.[44] The following year Andreas Malmas led nine of the families to Meadows, about
forty-six kilometres west of Winnipeg. With Emil Hallonquist acting
as interpreter for the Scandinavian Landseekers Company in Winnipeg, arrangements were made to purchase an abandoned 1,518-hectare
industrial farmstead along the CNR at Meadows, Manitoba, for $42,000
plus 7 per cent interest.[45] They named it Lilla Svenskby (Little Swedish
Village). Because of the large mortgage and heavy payments to Sweden,
the families formed a collective.[46]

Through hard work and cooperation they not only survived the
Depression, but also paid off their debts. Everybody did his or her share
without shirking, at the same time keeping the Sabbath holy. The pastor from St Mark's Lutheran Church in Winnipeg held services in one
of their homes every second Sunday. After Andreas Malmas died, Peter
Hoas[47] became leader. In 1953 the collective was dissolved and its assets
divided amicably among the participants.[48]

Sweden has shown great interest in the Svenskbyborna in Meadows.
Radio Sweden sent Sven Järfeldt to interview Peter Hoas around 1962,
and then in 1966 Folke Hedblom, sent by the Institute of Dialect and
Folklore Research at Uppsala University, interviewed his son John:
"Our visit in John and Kristina Hoas' home ended with song. Those
present formed a chorus and they sang in parts as they had done in
the church on the banks of the Dnieper. They sang hymns out of both
the 1695 *Psalmbok* and the "new" hymnal of 1819. They also sang "Vänta

efter Herren" [Await the Lord] and "Signe och bevara" [Bless and Keep]. 'These,' they said, 'are not written, but are in our memory only.'"[49]

John Hoas,[50] who was only seventeen when he became a shareholder in the collective, often represented the community as spokesperson. In 1988 he and his wife Kristina were presented to King Carl XVI Gustaf and Queen Silvia in Winnipeg. It is fitting that the cairn commemorating the colony, dedicated in 1996, is located at the entrance to the Hoas farm.

However, the unique Swedish dialect, which survived for generations in Ukraine, died out in a single generation,[51] and there was no organized contact among the various groups. In 2005, Alberta's centennial year, descendants arranged a seventy-fifth-anniversary jubilee in Wetaskiwin, and the Svenskbyborna Cultural Society was incorporated the following year. Its website is linked to that of Sweden's Föreningen Svenskbyborna, which holds a gathering in Roma, Gotland, 1 August every year to commemorate the day in 1929 when Svenskbyborna first stepped onto Swedish soil. In 2007 a Canadian group travelled to Gammalsvenskby, and in 2010 the Svenskbyborna Cultural Society hosted the eightieth-anniversary jubilee in Wetaskiwin.

American Swedes

Migrants from the United States were also a minority ethnic group living in another country, but they had already experienced the culture shock of living on the North American continent. They were also able to bring more belongings with them than were the immigrants from Europe. In the days before fences they could travel overland, sending their furniture, farm implements, and livestock by train. In March 1906 Andrew and Anna Bloomquist[52] and their children rode in a covered hayrack from Bowbells, North Dakota, to Trossachs in southern Saskatchewan, a distance of 162 kilometres. The journey took one week.

In his landmark book *The Swedes and the Swedish Settlements in North America*, Helge Nelson made the misleading statement: "Up to 1920 inclusive the greatest immigration of Swedes into Canada took place indirectly, via U.S.A., and not direct from Sweden."[53] Repetition of this unfortunate error has lent it a certain credibility, but Nelson's remark would have been acceptable if he had specified the Wetaskiwin area. A Canadian geographer, William Wonders, carried out a study of nine townships southeast of Wetaskiwin, the area targeted by immigrant agent Swanson.[54] Of the 324 Swedes who took up homesteads, 48.5 per cent came from the United States and 37.5 per cent from Sweden,[55] with 1.6 per cent from other places in Canada. The remaining entries for previous residence, 12.4 per cent, had been left blank.[56]

The Immigrant Database compiled by the Swedes in Canada project, which covers all of Canada, showed only 17.0 per cent arriving via the United States – 17,000 persons – and a third of them did not stay.[57] Provinces chosen for settlement, in descending order, were Alberta (36.6 per cent), Saskatchewan (22.8 per cent), British Columbia (18.5 per cent), Ontario (11.4 per cent), Manitoba (8.3 per cent), Quebec (1.4 per cent), and the remaining 1.0 per cent in Yukon, Nova Scotia, and New Brunswick. Clearly Wonders's study was carried out in one of the areas most densely populated by American Swedes.

The American Swedes form an interesting subgroup. Of the 1,033 persons in the Immigrant Database, the ratio of men, women, and children is similar to that of immigrants from Sweden. The approximate year of entry of 911 persons is known. Fully 88 per cent arrived during the period from 1870 to 1919, with the peak years between 1900 and 1909. Many had lived in at least two different states before trying Canada, and some had stayed less than a year. Most worked as farmers, labourers, railway workers, gold seekers, carpenters, miners, and trappers, and many had held an assortment of jobs. There were several pastors, civil engineers, hotel owners, and store owners, as well as a chiropractor and a dentist, but very few of the "longer established families with maturing sons wanting farms"[58] who have formed a large part of scholarly rhetoric.

Immigration agent Swanson was active at the height of Canada's aggressive campaign for farmers from the American Midwest, from 1895 to 1906. From his office in St Paul, Minnesota, he encouraged immigrants to settle in Alberta, southeast of Wetaskiwin, but some chose other farming areas, especially if friends or relatives had located there. Most hoped to better their lot by selling or renting their farms in the United States in order to buy much cheaper land on the Canadian Prairies, but those who had suffered drought or other calamities had to take homesteads if they were available.

Except for professionals who chose urban life, most migrants from the United States settled on farms, preferably near relatives or friends, after finding their expectations were not being realized on their American farms. In 1911 John Anderson,[59] a dairy farmer in Minot, North Dakota, shared his problems in a letter to his sister in Sweden:

We have had another year of crop failure. Last year I did not get anything. Not even hay or straw. Had to get into new debt of $400 for seed grain and feed for horses and cows. This year I got enough hay and straw and also grain for both seeding and feed. I also sold wheat for about $55, which was not enough to pay interest on the debt. Besides that I had to buy a pair of horses as I lost two last winter, probably from old-age weakness, so I had to get into further debt of $400. So if you have anything for me I could surely use it if you will send it here ... I have also moved my house this summer ... The well I had where the house stood lost its water, so instead of carrying water 600 ft I moved the house over to the well I have had since I first came here ... I have during this last week thought of selling out here and maybe go to Canada and take a new homestead.[60]

The following spring he sold his farm for $5,500 and chose a homestead forty-five kilometres west of Battleford, Saskatchewan, adjoining those of his English-speaking wife's brother and brother-in-law. By acquiring a homestead for $10 he was able to use his capital to rent 64.7 hectares from the Hudson's Bay Company for $30 a year to use as pasture, and to buy animals. He had cleared twelve hectares the previous summer and seeded half of it in wheat, oats, and potatoes, and the other half in flax. He owned five horses, four dairy cows, a Jersey bull, three heifers, and four calves.

Did John Anderson find a better life in Canada? His family was happier because they disliked Minot's windstorms, which he claimed were a daily event. However, the problems a homesteader faced in Saskatchewan, as he told it, seemed insurmountable:

There will not be any crops the first year, very little the second and third years. However, the debts grow and prosper amazingly. After a few years (in most cases the 5th or 6th year), one has cultivated enough to start thinking of getting free of the debts, but then they are so high that one can barely look over them. There is also another difficulty, maybe worse than the above mentioned. All debts are due for payment between October 15 and November 1, a couple of weeks before threshing starts ... [It would be different] if one is lucky enough to find a homestead near a town, then one can work and earn some money.[61]

A school opened in 1916, eliminating one of his worries, and he must have fared pretty well on the homestead. In 1925 he built a motor home on a Model T chassis so that he could drive his family to Florida and back. He also lived to fulfill a personal dream, to own a Harley Davidson.

Canada's campaign for farmers was not lost on American speculators. There was money to be made by buying up parcels of land and selling it to their countrymen, including Scandinavians. The Scandinavian Canadian Land Company, based in Chicago, offered 50,000 acres (20,234 hectares) in the Preeceville/Buchanan area from its office in Canora. The poster read, "Buy while land is cheap. Five families in 1903. 800 families in 1906. Buy your tickets to Canora, Saskatchewan. Free livery to land buyers." Agents named were Mr Lageson and D.M. Frederiksen.[62]

Land developer Victor J. Wallin, a Mission Covenant pastor from Minnesota, hoped to establish religious colonies, and in this he was quite successful. Along with his brother, a realtor, he founded the Swedish Canadian Colonization Company based in Winnipeg from 1904 to 1910, where he served one year as pastor of the Mission Covenant Church. He sold land in Kamsack,[63] near Duck Mountain, and also in the Hyas-Norquay area, which he called Wallinberg. Both Hyas and Norquay founded Mission Covenant congregations.

In 1907 Wallin advertised 5,000 acres (2,023 hectares) south of Minnedosa, Manitoba, with a map showing the sections available. He called the property Småland after the birthplace of pioneer Charles Johnson, who had settled in Minnedosa in 1871.[64] Wallin's asking price was $12 to $16 an acre for 160 acres, with $400 to $500 down and the rest within seven years. He noted that similar land in the United States was worth $50 to $150 an acre. Other selling points were fertile soil, good water, and proximity to Minnedosa for shopping and to Brandon's experimental farm. He also claimed that hurricanes and violent snowstorms were unknown.[65]

Wallin arranged for Pastor J.E. Bjorklund of Winnipeg to organize what became Smoland Mission Covenant Church in 1908, in the home of John Berg.[66] By 1912 a number of other Swedes had become members as a result of in-migration and religious revivals.[67] He also sold land in Alpine in the Swan River valley, south of Benito. The Mission Covenant pastor A.T. Carlson began holding services in Alpine schoolhouse in 1910.[68]

In contrast to the relatively smooth integration of farmers who bought land from American companies, the heartless behaviour of a Canadian corporation towards those who bought CPR land in Scandia, Alberta, stands out as an isolated incident. The federal government had granted the Irrigation Block to the CPR in 1903 on the condition that the company develop irrigation systems. (The southeastern corner of Alberta and the southwestern corner of Saskatchewan form what is known as Palliser's Triangle because of its low rainfall. Irrigation was necessary, and the government designated areas into irrigation blocks.) The Augustana Colonization Association began recruiting Swedish farmers from the United States in 1914, evidently without much success. The CPR launched a second drive in 1917, which attracted a handful of settlers. Advertisements had read "Scandia, an oasis in the desert," and the agent promised a railway and irrigation water. However, the ditches, which had been dug several years earlier, were overgrown with grass and filled with debris. Just before the railway finally came in 1927 the CPR renegotiated its land contracts, and they were not in the settlers' favour.

The same year the Swedish Colonization Board of Alberta received a letter from John Bengtson[69] of Scandia on behalf of Salem, an Augustana Lutheran congregation: "I have been instructed by our church to write to you and ask you to help us to resettle our colony. We prefer Augustana Synod Lutherans from the States. Lutherans from Sweden's state church are not church loving, not as they should be ... We do not insist on getting such as speak Swedish only. English speaking Lutherans are all right."[70]

Pastor Elving, the Augustana promoter from Omaha, Nebraska, had organized the Salem congregation in 1919. Several settlers left Scandia two years later, after being hailed out. The departure in 1927 of four founding families who refused to sign the CPR's new contracts prompted Bengtson's letter. According to the daughter of postmaster John L. Johnson, "Those who stayed were those who couldn't afford to leave." In 1929 Charles J. Anderson[71] of Scandia began spearheading negotiations with the CPR, and the farmers were finally allowed to take over the Eastern Irrigation District in 1935. With this change, "land prices became realistic and the settlers were able to pay for their farms." The long-awaited construction of Salem church began two years later.[72]

It is likely that the Swedish Lutheran Immigration Aid Society of Canada helped with negotiations. The unsympathetic attitude of the CPR's colonization department in Calgary was made clear in an official letter dated 1929: "The only way to get on in this country is for the immigrant to take whatever work he can get, and do his best ... It is true that he has a hard time at first, and therefore, is liable to meet with discouragement, but if he persists and gains farming experience together with some knowledge of English, he will eventually find a way of getting on his feet. In Canada there are innumerable opportunities and it is up to the immigrant to fit himself for them."[73]

Most of the settlers in Scandia were experienced farmers and well versed in the English language.[74] They had been kept in bondage to the CPR for eighteen years through unfair land contracts and broken promises.

Many American Swedes assumed leadership positions on the Canadian Prairies, not only because of their facility with English and with North American ways, but also because of their higher status through ownership of property. It is not surprising that of the thirty-one Swedish place names in Alberta mentioned in Appendix 1, sixteen either were named by American Swedes or commemorate American events.

Survey of Immigrants since the Second World War

The Swedes in Canada project also carried out a survey to supplement the sparse information available about more recent Swedish-speaking immigrants. The questionnaires, available online through the website www.swedesincanada.ca, and as handouts at Swedish Women's Educational Association (SWEA) Toronto's Christmas Fair, resulted in 213 random responses covering a period of fifty-seven years. Although an official survey would require a larger number of responses, the results suggest an interesting demographic profile of Swedish immigrants to Canada from 1948 to 2005 and how they differed from earlier immigrants.

Most of them, 66 per cent, came during the first half of this time period, up to the end of the 1970s. In contrast to earlier immigrants, 59 per cent were female with only 41 per cent male. Sixty-two per cent were married, 5 per cent divorced, and the rest single. The overwhelming majority, 92 per cent, were born in Sweden, with 2 per cent born in Finland, Germany, England, Estonia, or Tehran. The rest did not specify. Of those born in Sweden, most (47 per cent) came from southern Sweden, with 38 per cent from the middle provinces, and less than 15 per cent from the north. Forty respondents were born in Sweden's three largest cities, twenty-four in Stockholm, thirteen in Göteborg, and three in Malmö.

More than half, 52 per cent, settled in Ontario, with 21 per cent each in British Columbia and Alberta, and 3 per cent in Manitoba, and the rest in Saskatchewan, Quebec, and Prince Edward Island. Of the reasons given for emigrating, pull factors included adventure (thirty-three), love or marriage (thirty), employment (thirty), joining relatives (nine), and a better future (six), while push factors were a dislike of Sweden's political system (ten) and difficulty finding housing or inexpensive farmland (six). Forty couples had brought ninety-one children, while others had come themselves as children. Several had arrived in Canada as students or *au pairs* and returned as immigrants. Fully fifty-seven had university degrees, and thirty-seven had post-secondary training, mainly in the fields of health, education, or business. Employment varied from truck driver to professional skier, from minister to marine surveyor, from equestrian to violin teacher, from landscaper to designer of ski wear.

Ten of the respondents experienced some form of discrimination, from immigration officials, from Norwegian war survivors who mistook their accents for German, from people making snide remarks about sexy Swedish women, or from workmates who resented "foreigners" having supervisory positions. One person felt that their accent had an adverse effect on being promoted. Only two people experienced ethnic derision, and three did not feel welcome. Forty-nine admitted being homesick.

Seventy people had taken advantage of the dual citizenship law introduced in 2001, while thirty-three retained their Swedish citizenship and twenty-four chose to remain Canadian citizens only. Permanent residents numbered 164, with the remaining 48 keeping their options open. The children of ninety-two respondents spoke Swedish to some degree. Most kept in contact with family in Sweden, and exchange visits were fairly common. The trend towards secularization was confirmed, with only 23 per cent specifying a religion, the majority being Lutheran. Those who had joined Swedish organizations numbered eighty-eight, with the sixty-six who belonged to other groups sometimes overlapping.

This survey of recent immigrants shows both similarities and differences with their predecessors. Major differences were the sex ratio in favour of women, northern Sweden sliding from first to last place as a source of immigrants, and more than half settling in Ontario, with more than a fifth each in Alberta and British Columbia. The similarities were that immigrants came from many places in Sweden, travelled in family groups, and avoided the Far North and the far eastern provinces as places of settlement. Unlike most earlier immigrants, who received training at home, on the farm, or through apprenticeship, many recent immigrants were well educated, lived in urban areas as white-collar workers, and had fewer children. Learning English was not a problem for those who had attended school since 1962, when that language became a compulsory subject. Closer contact with relatives and friends was possible through improved communication and transportation systems. For many people, modern technology reduced the culture shock experienced by all immigrants.

Chapter Four

Settlement Patterns

Both Canada and Sweden have similar landscapes: in the north built upon earth's most ancient bedrock, the Precambrian Shield; and in the south built upon younger sedimentary rocks. Both countries benefited from glaciation through sedimentary deposits suitable for farming and an abundance of water, so that lakes cover 8.5 per cent of Sweden's surface and 7.6 per cent of Canada's. Many immigrants chose the more familiar wooded areas on the Precambrian Shield, preferably near a lake or river,[1] but the majority settled on the Prairies, within the fertile bow extending from the Red River Valley to the Rockies.[2]

In 1905 Alberta and Saskatchewan became provinces, rendering obsolete the former mailing addresses of Athabaska and Assiniboia in what was originally called the North-West Territories. Athabaska became part of present-day Alberta, and Assiniboia became part of Saskatchewan. Edmonton became Alberta's capital, and Regina became Saskatchewan's. Their new status put the provinces firmly in control of their own destinies rather than trying to absorb a population explosion under the paternalistic hand of a distant federal government.

The Immigrant Database compiled by the Swedes in Canada project showed that 21.0 per cent made their homes in Alberta, 20.6 per cent in Ontario, 16.4 per cent in British Columbia, 15.6 per cent in Saskatchewan, 13.5 per cent in Manitoba, and 2.9 per cent in Quebec, leaving 9.2 per cent who settled in other provinces, moved to the United States, or returned to Sweden.[3] Among the Swedes sent to investigate Canada was the geographer Helge Nelson,[4] whose book *Swedes and the Swedish Settlements in North America* offers a glimpse of the centres of population in 1931, as Canada slid into the Depression.

This chapter outlines the geographic distribution of the Swedes, moving from east to west. At the same time an explanation is given for their choice of settling in certain areas and not in others, with special attention to one of Canada's first Swedish colonies, Scandinavia in Manitoba, and to the country's only Snoose Boulevard, Winnipeg's Logan Avenue.

Maritimes and Newfoundland

In 1871 there were five watchmakers from Sweden living in St John's, Newfoundland, and one of them, John Lindberg, is said to have become wealthy.[5] The eighteen Swedes in New Brunswick were male, one of them, lumberman John Fred, being the first to match the stereotype of the Swedish logger. Two of the thirteen Swedes in Nova Scotia were women. Charlotte Warren kept a boarding house in Halifax, but her children were born in Prince Edward Island. The men included three mariners and three seamen, as befits a maritime province.

In 1962 the Swedish company Stora Enso opened a paper mill at Port Hawkesbury on Cape Breton Island. The company had acquired extensive timber limits in 1957 under the name Nova Scotia Pulp Limited, which were harvested on a sustained-yield basis. Swedes filled a number of management positions through the years, but all returned to Sweden except for Lars and Dagmar Anderson.[6] Although Halifax became a major immigration port, only a few Swedish immigrants settled in the Maritimes or Newfoundland unless they had employment.

Quebec

In 1871 there were eighty-six Swedes living in Quebec, almost a third of them in Montreal, at that time Canada's fur-trade centre. The earliest furrier, Peter Martin Petterson, arrived in 1824. In Quebec City, in addition to Baron Falkenberg, were a tobacconist, a male servant, a tailor, a watchmaker, an agent, and the wife of the Anglican minister, R.G. Plus. The rest included scattered farmers north of Ottawa, and two miners in Beauce. Immigrants learned the local language quickly because they dealt primarily with people who were not Swedish. Helge Nelson noted that few Swedes settled in Quebec because they did not feel at home among Catholic French-Canadians.[7]

Most of those living in the Sherbrooke area, east of Montreal, came after 1871. Their lives in the Eastern Townships were much different

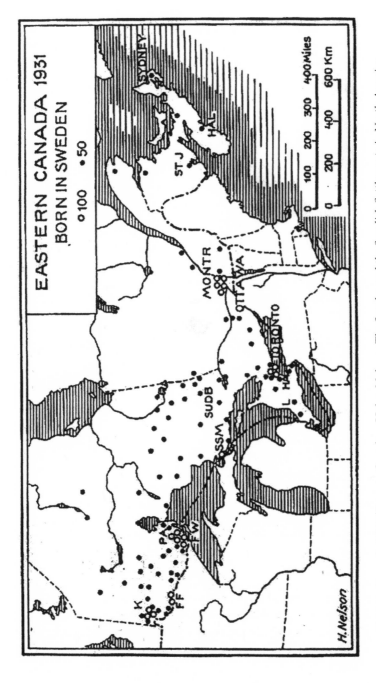

Eastern Canada 1931/Born in Sweden, Helge Nelson, *The Swedes and the Swedish Settlements in North America* (1943), 1:340.

from those of Prairie homesteaders, partly because of their relatively small numbers and partly because they were living in established communities. Existing public transportation to farms, businesses, churches, and schools as well as a welcoming attitude from the Anglo-Saxon majority cushioned culture shock. Interaction with English speakers was common, and those who chose to marry one of them could, like C.O. Swanson, look forward to upward social mobility.

In 1906 the consular office and its staff moved from Quebec City to Montreal as a result of the break with Norway the year before. By 1917 Montreal was home to the Swedish Steel & Importing Company and several engineers. In addition paper mills in Three Rivers, Shawinigan Falls, Chandler, and East Angus had Swedish engineers on their payrolls.[8] By 1988 the province of Quebec had established its own foreign ministry in Montreal, home of the Swedish Consulate General and a Swedish Trade Office. Swedish businesses in the city included ASEA-Brown Boveri, Ericsson, Sandvik, Alfa-Laval, Atlas Copco, Pharmacia, and IKEA.[9]

In 1931 about 60 per cent of the province's Swedes, or more than 1,000, lived in Montreal,[10] and there the favourite gathering place was Krausman's Café on St James Street.[11] Montreal had been a mecca for Scandinavian designers since the 1920s, most of them from Denmark, but Sigrun Bulow-Hube[12] was a Swede who spearheaded modern furniture design. Her projects included the executive offices at Air Canada and McGill University, and a model suite at Habitat for Expo '67. Evidently it was the presence of an artistic community that inspired the Swedish author Lars Forssell to write the play *Flickan i Montréal* (The Girl in Montreal).[13]

Ontario

Ontario is Canada's most populous province, with a pronounced urban-rural and north-south split. Most residents live in the heavily industrialized south, which depends on northern Ontario for resources in the mining and forestry sectors. Few Swedes followed agricultural pursuits in southern Ontario's orchards and market gardens, instead gravitating to the cities and towns. In 1931 more than half of Ontario's 4,708 Swedish-born lived in Northwestern Ontario, where they earned a living through resource extraction, railway work, and farming in the Slate River and Rainy River valleys and the clay belt near Dryden. Another 23 per cent of the Swedish-born lived in the northeast, mainly in Kipling, the Lake Timiskaming area, and along the railways, while 22 per cent called Toronto home.[14]

Swedes made up 16 per cent of Kenora's population of 6,776, and 6 per cent of the 5,470 living in Fort Frances, with very high concentrations in the farming townships of McCrossan (53 per cent) and Tovell (82 per cent) in the Rainy River valley. About 1,000 Swedes lived in the Lakehead cities of Port Arthur and Fort William, with the rest scattered throughout the area in small communities, bush and mining camps, and along railways.

Swedish speakers in the Lakehead included immigrants from both Sweden and Finland, in roughly equal numbers. In 1879, when Andrew Johnson opened Manitoba House in Port Arthur to service railway workers, he became the first Swedish hotel owner in Canada.[15] His wife, Katie, was a colourful Laestadian evangelical who promoted establishment of an Apostolic Lutheran church. Another hotel owner, Finland Swede Andrew Wadson,[16] advertised his Kimberley Hotel rooms at a dollar a day in 1906. The hotel had fifty bedrooms, hot-water heating, and an electrically lit bar. Wadson also owned the Park Hotel and other property at nearby Stanley, a farming and railway community.

All travellers had to pass through the Lakehead, whether they came by rail or by boat, until the 1920s, when the northern railway line began offering passenger service. About twenty-five families lived on marginal land in Flint and Ellis on the Grand Trunk Pacific Railway and in adjoining Finmark on the CPR, sixty kilometres west of the Lakehead. They supported their farms through seasonal jobs on the railway, in the bush, or on construction.[17] Further west, a number of Swedes operated tourist camps after Highway 17 opened in 1935.[18]

It is almost impossible to keep track of the bush workers who cut pulpwood for paper mills and sawlogs for sawmills, but mill workers settled in a single location. The Shevlin-Clark sawmill in Fort Frances covered just over four hectares on the east side of town. A wide-angle photo of employees in 1929 included sixty Swedes.[19] There was foreman C.M. Carlson and his brother John, president of the Vasa Lodge. There was Axel Johnson, whose son Art "Doc" Johnson helped the Fort Frances Canadians win the Allan Cup in 1956, and Adolf Carlson, whose daughter Lois played the organ in the Lutheran Church. And there was the Norrlund family – dad Eric and sons Art, Gene, and Marvin – who loved to fight. Not included in the photo were Bertil Forsberg[20] and Sigurd Lindberg,[21] partners in a clothing store.

In 1896 an immigration agent in Montreal enticed Swedes to Haileybury,[22] near the Quebec border, relying on a pamphlet promoting the Lake Timiskaming area as an agricultural centre. The Swede August Peterson confirmed the area's fertility, saying it was "just like Sweden."[23] Erik and Karin Persson[24] had three children, and Johan Oslund[25] and his wife, Christina Fernholm,[26] brought ten, one of them married with a baby. Their intended destination had been the Prairies, but the Atlantic fare for nineteen persons, $30.15 each, stretched their finances to the limit. Three daughters went to Quebec as domestic servants, and the rest crossed Lake Timiskaming by steamboat to Haileybury. Johan Oslund noted that it was not quite within the clay belt, as advertised. The land was mainly rock and swamp, just like Sweden, as August Peterson had said. Nevertheless, by 1901 fully 3.7 per cent of the population spoke Swedish as a first language, more than those who spoke French.[27]

Godfrey Hammarstrom[28] headed a family group who came from Ljusne, Hälsingland, from 1906 to 1909. Along with the Youngbergs[29] they settled along West Road in Bucke Township, near Haileybury. Like the others they supplemented their incomes by working in C. C. Farr's limestone quarry and the Frontier mine at Silver Centre.

Another group settled in North Cobalt, which became known as Swedetown. They included the Hedmans[30] and Mannerstroms[31] from Ljusne, and also the Bybergs, Isabrands, Jacobsons, Magnussons, Petersons, and Westbergs. They attended the Swedish Presbyterian church in Haileybury.[32]

Relatively few Swedes were able to find work in urban centres because they lacked the necessary educational credentials or because Anglo-Saxons were given priority for steady employment.

In 1917 only three Swedes worked for federal government departments in Ottawa, two for pulp and paper companies in Hawkesbuty and Merritton, and one for the Canadian Boving Company in Lindsay.[33] In Toronto Miss Ida Wallberg left a bequest of a million dollars to the University of Toronto in 1933 to construct an engineering building in memory of her brother, Emil A. Wallberg. An industrial engineer and designer, he was also president of several large companies, including Canada Wire and Cable. Ida had been his sole beneficiary.[34]

Joseph Ander[35] served as consul in Toronto from 1939 to 1957. He had come to New Brunswick in 1907, representing a Swedish forestry firm, and by the 1920s worked as Swedish Trade Consul out of Newcastle. In 1938 in Toronto he founded the Atlas Polar Company Limited, which continues today. Björn Leyner[36] came in 1954 to establish Astra Canada as a subsidiary of the Swedish pharmaceutical giant. He became the first president of the Swedish-Canadian Chamber of Commerce (SCCC), founded in 1965 by Ander's successor as consul, Nils Kallin,[37] to promote trade between Canada and Sweden. Kallin was the director of the ball-bearing company SKF, one of the first Swedish companies to establish in Canada, followed by the electrical firm ASEA during the First World War. With the founding of SCCC in 1965 Toronto joined Montreal as a Swedish business centre.

Toronto's Nordic business community had taken its first step towards acting as a group in 1960, with the formation of the Scandinavian Canadian Businessmen's Association (SCBA) with Severus Persson as president. With increasing trade Birgitta Westin founded the Scandinavian Centre in 1985 to provide professional corporate services to companies like Scandinavian Airlines and IKEA, and organizations like SCBA. Her travel agency also operated out of the Scandinavian Centre.

The office of the Swedish Canadian Chamber of Commerce (SCCC) works in tandem with the Canadian Swedish Business Association in Stockholm, founded in 1994. The Scandinavian Canadian Businessmen's Association, in Toronto, which in 1996 established a Canadian chapter in Halifax, provides a forum for Swedish and Canadian businesses to meet through conferences and seminars, and also arranges for exchange programs between university students and companies on both sides of the Atlantic. Toronto was already functioning as a gateway to the United States market in 1994, when the signing of the North American Free Trade Agreement enhanced Canada's position.[38]

Manitoba

Most Swedes came to Winnipeg as part of the immigration process, to receive information about opportunities further west. However, some stayed in the city or in the province. In 1931 almost half the Swedish population in Manitoba lived in or near Winnipeg, while the rest spread westward to Scandinavia/Erickson/Hilltop and Smoland, eastward to the Lac du Bonnet/Riverland area, and northward to Teulon/Norris Lake and Eriksdale/Lillesve in the Interlake region. The most northerly settlements were Alpine, west of the Duck Mountains, Minitonas/Birch River to the north, and The Pas.[39]

Scandinavia had been established as a colony in July 1885 in response to a request from N.D. Ennis of Minnedosa. Ennis was agent for the Allan Line and brother of the line's manager, one of the first steamship officials in Europe to champion Swedish immigration to Canada.[40] The land around Scandinavia was marginal and heavily wooded, with several lakes and sloughs,[41] and was originally named New Sweden.[42] Access was via the Manitoba and Northwestern Railway to Minnedosa, then overland through 32.2 kilometres of dense forest.[43] Controversy

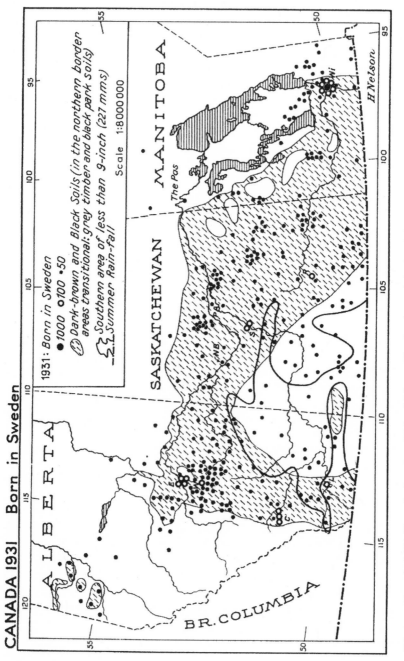

CANADA 1931   Born in Sweden

1931: Born in Sweden
● 1000 ○ 100 • 50

🖉 Dark-brown and Black Soils (in the northern border
areas transitional; grey timber and black park soils)

〰 Southern area of less than 9-inch (227 mms)
Summer Rain-fall

Scale 1:8000000

ALBERTA

SASKATCHEWAN

MANITOBA

BR. COLUMBIA

The Pas

H. Nelson

Western Canada 1931/Born in Sweden, Helge Nelson, *The Swedes and the Swedish Settlements in North America* (1943), 2:72.

over the issue of temperance[44] resulted in the founding of the Scandinavian Colonization Society of Manitoba to oversee settlement.[45] John H. Noreus,[46] who had filed on shoreline property on Otter Lake as well as two adjacent homesteads, was elected as president.

In January 1886 Ennis discovered to his horror that Noreus was nothing but a swindler. Forty-four homesteaders had been lured by false promises, and another twenty-two had given him the $10 government homestead fee, on request.[47] He had paid neither the labourers who built the immigrant house nor the suppliers of building materials.[48] Ennis was particularly upset over the improvements made on his shoreline property: "He [Noreus] has not paid one cent. This land is now surveyed into town lots. By this you will see the Noreus object must have been to get a large slice of the colony lands in the centre of the settlement, 480 acres, houses erected. The nucleus of a town and all without expending one dollar of his own money."[49] A deputation of angry homesteaders travelled to Winnipeg in April to deliver Ennis's letter to railway and government officials. After being assured that Noreus did not have official backing they returned to their homesteads.[50] Noreus was not heard from again.

James Hemmingson,[51] a Dane, had already bought the community's sawmill, and in September 1886 the Dominion Lands Commission turned over Noreus's property to him.[52] He was appointed postmaster and named the post office Scandinavia,[53] perhaps to reflect the homesteaders' origins. In addition to his own house and a shingle mill, Hemmingson replaced the original immigrant house, which had burned.[54] Postmaster, welcoming committee for newcomers, employer: small wonder he became known as "King" Hemmingson![55]

In 1893 Pastor Johan Fremling[56] waxed eloquent about Scandinavia's beautiful spruce trees, tasty lingonberries, and fragrant twinflowers, or *Linnea borealis*, named by the botanist Linnaeus after himself. "At least one hundred Swedish families could be counted last August [1892] in Scandinavia. Their number is constantly being increased by immigration from Sweden. They do not go to a great deal of work to develop the land. The most of them occupy themselves with stock raising. During the winter they cut wood and haul it to Minnedosa and trade it for all manner of household goods."[57]

His remarks confirm the reasons some Swedes settled in familiar landscapes. Picking berries, raising grazing animals, and selling forest products met their personal needs.

Their milk pails full of saskatoon berries, an unidentified Thompson girl, Vera
Nordin, Gladys Thompson, Maria Nordin, and Margot Nordin pose at the
Nordin farm in 1927. Courtesy of Nordin Heritage Farmstead.

Immigration to Lac du Bonnet began in the early 1900s when immigration officials suggested it as an alternative to Tyndall, where work
was available in the Garson quarries. The CPR linked Lac du Bonnet to
Winnipeg in 1901, with the result that J.D. McArthur, who owned the
Lac du Bonnet townsite, brickyard, sawmill, and all the timber limits
on the lake, could ship to Winnipeg markets. Job openings increased
in 1903 with construction of Pinawa, the first of several dams built
on the Winnipeg River to generate hydroelectric power for the city
of Winnipeg. Helge Nelson claimed that the Swedes' greatest contribution to Canada was the back-breaking task of reclaiming land for
agriculture. He chose as an example Eric Gustaf Anderson of Lac du
Bonnet, who had to blast or chop out 256 stumps in every acre that he
cleared.[58]

Edwin Nordin, Charlie Bjork, and Clarence Nordin dip into the snuff after a
hard day's work of picking the rocks behind them on the Bjork farm, 1927.
Courtesy of Nordin Heritage Farmstead.

The Interlake offered a similar landscape. After the railway reached
Teulon in 1898 thirteen Winnipeg families decided to move to nearby
Norris Lake.[59] A homestead offered a base where they could build a
house and stables, cut cordwood, and clear land while they were unemployed during the winter, and work in Winnipeg during the summer.
By 1907 Township 17 was almost entirely settled by Swedes, so that
they overflowed beyond Inwood to the northwest.[60]

The land, described as "very poor with sloughs and stony ridges covered with shrubs," produced only enough hay and grain for dairying
and stock raising. Per and Maria Nordin[61] homesteaded in 1904, and
Nordin eventually owned a prize herd of Ayrshire dairy cattle. In 2002
the farm took on a new life as Nordin Heritage B&B Inn and Cottage.[62]

Norris School was built in 1904, and a Baptist church was organized
three years later with homesteader P.M. Meyer as pastor from 1909 to

1917.[63] In 2004 a plaque attached to a huge rock was unveiled at the Norris Lake Pioneer Cemetery to commemorate sixty-one Swedish pioneer families and the forty-two people buried there from 1904 to 1923. The work of refurbishing included placing markers of marble and Tyndall stone on unmarked graves.[64]

By 1901 Winnipeg had 511 Swedish residents,[65] more than any other Canadian city. That number had almost tripled to 1,403 by 1911.[66] At the same time the total population had more than tripled from 42,000 to 136,000, making Winnipeg the third-largest city in Canada, after Montreal and Toronto. The Scandinavian-born were now in fourth place, behind Anglo-Saxons, Galicians (born in Russia, Poland, Austria, Hungary, and the Balkans), and the American-born.

Logan Avenue[67] paralleled the railway tracks to the south. The area between Fountain and Laura streets was especially Swedish, with the Lutheran, Mission Covenant, and Baptist churches, the Scandinavian Salvation Army, and several rooming houses. The monumental CPR station was on Main Street, which cut across Logan. Nearby were Hallonquist's grocery store, the provincial immigration office, the immigrant hall,[68] and two Scandinavian hotels.[69]

Logan Avenue was well on its way to becoming a Snoose Boulevard, the name designated for Swedish enclaves in North American cities.[70] Although Swedes were not the only ones who chewed tobacco or snuff (*snus* in Swedish), snoose came to be identified with Swedes more than any other group.[71] Hotel lobbies always had at least one spittoon, a metal bowl with a wide rim sloping inwards, sitting on the floor. Outside, the men spat on the sidewalk. Winnipeg Swedes claimed, tongue-in-cheek, that in winter there were more snuff chews than snowflakes on Logan Avenue.[72]

Oscar Sundborg[73] of Chicago established the Canada Snuff Company in Winnipeg in 1906, then opened a factory in Vancouver two years later. His products were sold under the Lion Swedish Snuff brand and included Sundborgs Rappe, also known as Copenhagen. Copenhagen, still a well-known brand of snuff, was memorialized in the dialect song "The Battle of Copenhagen":

Ten tusen Svedes ran through the veeds [tobacco fields]
At the Battle of Copenhagen,
And the [leaves] from the veeds made snus for the Svedes
At the Battle of Copenhagen.[74]

This Winnipeg sign was painted on the wall of the Sproule Block, later
the Savoy Hotel, in 1891. It advertised the Main Street location of the
Manitoba immigration agents in the English, French, Swedish, and
German languages, with the grocer A. Hallonquist on the bottom.
Courtesy of Gunvor Larsson.

Norwegians took great delight in teasing Swedes with another version, "Ten tusen Svedes ran through the veeds chased by vun Norveg-
ian," followed by howls of laughter.

On Logan Avenue could be found cheap accommodation, bathing
facilities, Old Country cooking (*husmanskost*), traditional foods like
hardtack and pickled herring, patent medicines, reading rooms, card
games, and companionship. Although the temperance hotel did not
sell booze, it carried reading material, snoose, cigarettes, Läkerol cough
drops, and the popular alcohol-based tonic Kuriko.[75] For the newly
arrived Logan Avenue offered the most important commodity of all –
contact with other Swedish speakers.

Jack Bogseth, centre, was manager of the Stockholm Restaurant and Lunch Room on Logan Avenue in 1908. Standing beside him is the cook, his future wife, Martha Jansson. Her best friend, Hilma Gryte, is on the right, with co-workers Anders and Olga on the left. This photo, although imperfect, captures the spirit of Logan Avenue. Courtesy of Rocklee Bogseth.

In addition to residents there was a significant floating population of new immigrants, the unemployed, and those with seasonal jobs, and people from the surrounding area who came to visit or to shop.[76] Winnipeg, through its Snoose Boulevard, was fast becoming a full-fledged service centre for Swedes throughout the Prairies as well as a comfort station for those with broken dreams. For many, stepping off the train and walking along Logan Avenue was like coming home because the buildings were familiar, Swedish was in the air, and you always met someone you knew.

In 1915 John A. "Snus" Gustafson[77] established Swedish Canadian Sales at 208 Logan Avenue to import high-quality tools, Swede saws and files, handled knives for stripping logs, and Dala knives and Mora knives for wood carving. Since customers included non-Scandinavians such as the City of Winnipeg and Manitoba Hydro, it was one of the last Swedish businesses on Logan Avenue to close.[78]

In addition to the concentration of Swedes on Logan Avenue, a residential district sprang up across the Red River in Elmwood (formerly Louisebridge). By 1901 it was supporting a Mission Covenant congregation. Swedes had also begun moving into Anglo-Saxon Winnipeg in the south and west ends, but they continued coming to Logan Avenue for their social life, which included church activities such as youth groups, sewing clubs, choirs and orchestras, auctions, concerts, lectures, and soirées.

Cafés, restaurants, and barbershops also offered meeting places, but it was impossible to satisfy all the shoppers' needs with grocery and hardware stores, bakeries, and tradesmen. For ready-made clothing, furniture, and other services, they turned to Main Street. There, by 1909 American Swedes had set up an insurance company, bank, music store, goldsmith, realtor, travel agent, lawyer, several doctors, and a dentist.[79]

Ed Carlson,[80] who became Winnipeg's Swedish consul, was only eighteen when he arrived in 1929.

My first summer in Winnipeg is one I would like to forget. The odd day's work for 25 cents per hour did not seem to last. Many were the days when I spent my last nickel on a glass of milk and a cupcake. When I had enough for a meal, I could buy one at the Exchange Restaurant on Main for 15 cents. Just for the record, I made friends with the Swedish grocer Algot Wessberg. He had a store in the Hallonquist Block on Logan and Ellen St. Wessberg would give me 50 cents to deliver some groceries. I would walk all the way to Elmwood with one or two parcels. Fifty cents was a lot of money in those days. Thank God for the Danish Bakery on Logan and Laura, sometimes they would hand out some one day old Danish pastries, and that I never forgot.

When I had a nickel to spare, some of us boys would walk down to a dairy on Logan and Sherbrook, where we could buy a jug of buttermilk for 5 cents; and don't think that was not a life saver many times over. When fall came in 1929, some of my new acquaintances and I, who lived in the duplex on Logan Ave. rented by Anders Anderson and his wife Karin from Leksand in Dalarna, were facing a bleak and horrible prospect of winter. As luck was smiling on us, we were able to hire out as bush workers in

Ontario. Cutting pulpwood was not the easiest kind of work for me, but I could learn. With an axe, a file and Swede saw bought at Gustafson Hardware store on Logan Ave. I was keeping up with the rest of them.[81]

When he returned in the spring he had enough money to pay his back rent, but Snoose Boulevard itself was on a down-slide.

With unemployment rampant the flood of immigrants abated, and those who could return to Sweden did so. Nevertheless, Logan Avenue had its finest hour helping the poor with both organized and spontaneous aid. "It was to 'Tailor Nilson,' 'Old man Meyer,' 'the Rich Peterson' or 'Mr. Hallonqvist' one went for help, or to the organizations they led. Once again the crowded rooming houses were the salvation for those who had nowhere to live. Once again the six restaurants with 'Norden' and 'Sverige' in the lead were gathering places, now combined with distribution of free bread. Once again the three churches and the Salvation Army were meeting places, now with the holy message combined with free food."[82] The employment office of the Swedish American Line closed in 1936, and Tailor Nilson[83] died the following year.

One by one, boarding houses, restaurants, barbershops, and stores were forced out of business. No longer could one easily find patent medicines such as the laxative Pirico, the liniment Oleoyd, the tonic Magvigori, Swedish Bitters, or even Kuriko.[84] No longer could one separate Swedes from their money by playing poker, as Alfred Thorin had done in 1929.[85] By 1942 a dozen different ethnic groups were represented on Logan Avenue,[86] and before the decade ended the three Swedish congregations had moved to other parts of the city. The Depression had claimed Canada's only Snoose Boulevard.

Saskatchewan

Saskatchewan's total population increased fivefold during the decade between 1901 and 1911, but the number of Swedish-born increased even more dramatically, from only 452 persons to 6,229.[87] They came as serious growers of grain. By 1931 there were 22,458 people of Swedish origin living in Saskatchewan, more than any other province, but they were outnumbered two to one by Norwegians, who often settled in the same rural communities.[88]

Both the New Stockholm colony and Canwood west of Prince Albert became focal points for Swedish settlement. Clustered around New

Stockholm were Broadview, Dubuc, Percival, and Whitewood. Communities near Canwood included Kilwinning, Parkside, Shell Lake, and Shellbrook, all on the prairie fringe and needing to be cleared before cultivation could begin.[89]

Settlement of New Stockholm began on 1 July 1886, the day the first immigrants arrived. Karolina Johanson was a twelve-year-old and remembered it well.

> They shipped their belongings on freight from Winnipeg, but that train must have gone astray so we had to wait in Whitewood almost a week ... The first settlers got a loan of $250 to start with oxen, cow, wagon, plow, and what was left of the money was set in at Nolens Store [in Whitewood] for groceries, windows, doors and some lumber. So father bought an iron pot and a few necessary things and so they started out to this wild place – no roads so it was hard to get here and lots of mosquitoes to fight ... They lived in tents the three first months. They had to break some land and haul logs to build a house before it got too cold. Oh how nice it felt to walk on a floor again![90]

The house was built of squared timbers, vertical for the first storey and horizontal for the second, the exterior plastered with white lime.[91] For the first little while Karolina's mother used the iron pot over an outdoor fire for all her cooking, including baking bread.

Every week her dad walked or skied to the Hungarian colony of Esterhazy to pick up mail until 1889, when the CPR began dropping the mailbag off at Whitewood station. The Johanson home became an immigrant house and meeting place, not just for mail, but also for community events and meetings. The Scandinavian Colonization Society of New Stockholm, for example, campaigned tirelessly for a road to Whitewood, including a bridge over the Qu'Appelle River.[92] After the original colony had been settled the CPR sold its adjacent land, which had risen in value "by the reclaiming work of the Swedes on homestead lands," to the highest bidder.[93]

Canwood was incorporated as a village in 1917, but settlement had begun with the coming of the railway. Little did Alfred Nordstrom[94] know when he filed on a homestead in 1909 that it would become part of Canwood. He sold the land to the community in 1914 and opened a blacksmith shop on the main street. There, he sharpened ploughshares, fashioned grub hoes and brush axes, welded machinery, and shod horses.

Aside from these two centres, Swedes were pretty evenly distributed throughout the province, including the arid regions to the southwest. It was the railway that spawned Shaunavon there in 1913, three years after the Anderson brothers filed on adjoining homesteads. Zion Lutheran congregation was founded in the Erik Anderson[95] home in 1914. The couple welcomed Sunday worshippers for many years because no church was built.

The Andrew Andersons[96] on the adjoining homestead also enjoyed visitors, especially young people, who were fascinated by Aunt Mela:

[She wore] old fashioned high-necked wasp-waisted dresses over layers of petticoats. She had golden earrings in her pierced ears and carried a small silver snuff box from which she would take little pinches of snuff and sniff up her nose. She also had a good supply of white peppermints quite strong ... [The outhouse] was a grand place, the walls covered with pretty calendars and when you sat down you faced a large one of Whistler's Mother.[97]

Twenty-two members of the Young People's Society met at the Anderson home in 1914.

Other communities with significant Swedish populations in 1931 were scattered over a large area east of Saskatoon. To the southeast lay Colonsay and Young, and, to the northeast, Beatty and Kinistino. Extending eastward towards the Manitoba border were Hendon, Wadena, Margo, and Buchanan, with Hyas and Norquay north of the latter and Kelliher directly south of Wadena.

Two unusual structures commemorate Saskatchewan's Swedish pioneers. In Verwood Cemetery, 100 kilometres south of Moose Jaw, stands an iron cross erected under the direction of August Dahlman[98] when he was almost 100 years old. It has four horizontal bars, curled at the ends, with iron leaves hanging from them to symbolize the tree of life, topped by a small cross.[99] It was modelled after crosses he remembered in Värmland.

When the original Faith Lutheran church in Buchanan was replaced, lumber from the old church was used to build a replica one-quarter of the size in the cemetery. Inside the building were placed a pump organ, three pews, pulpit, entry-steeple, and a visitors' book. Adolf Nordin[100] fashioned the wrought-iron arch at the entrance, with cairns on each side. The property offers a pleasant and inviting wayside stop.

Although Saskatoon may not have had many Swedish residents, the city twinned with Umeå in 1975 through Project Sweden. The event began with a three-day walking competition inspired by ParticipACTION's sixty-year-old Swede, and continued with cultural exchanges among schools, Boy Scouts, industries, and civil service departments. Visits by dignitaries resulted in the legacy of Saskatoon Park in Umeå and Umeå Park in Saskatoon.[101]

Alberta

Like Saskatchewan's, Alberta's population increased fivefold during the decade between 1901 and 1911, and the Swedish-born population grew almost as fast. From a starting point of 1,641 persons in 1901, their numbers quadrupled to 6,345, more than any other Scandinavian group. By 1931 the Swedish population had almost reached 20,000,[102] most of them farmers attracted to the corridor between Lethbridge and Edmonton and along the railway line extending eastward from Wetaskiwin. The rest were scattered throughout the province, from the arid southeast to the Peace River country in the far northwest.[103] Almost all had been attracted by the province's fertile farmland.

Alberta's earliest known Swedish settler, John Hallgren,[104] came to Winnipeg in the late 1870s, ran a small hotel, then contracted with the North-West Mounted Police to freight supplies to Battleford, Saskatchewan. He continued freighting as he and his wife followed CPR construction westward, first to Regina, then to Calgary. In 1886 he filed on a homestead in the Springvale district, near Red Deer, and there raised twelve children.

Wetaskiwin became a service centre for its hinterland after immigration agent C.O. Swanson started bringing Swedes from the United States in 1892. The following description was written twenty years later: "Wetaskiwin is an almost exclusively Swedish town with a population of roughly 2,000. It is the center of a significant farming area cleared and cultivated largely by Swedes. The older settlements are situated to the east, the more recent ones to the west. The farms are well built and the sod houses, which were used to house the animals during the first years, have been replaced with modern buildings."[105]

Wetaskiwin's population in 1931 was 2,125. Of this number 97 were Swedish-born and 203 of Swedish heritage, or more than 14 per cent of the total. The surrounding townships of Bigston and Montgomery had considerably more Swedes, as did townships near the Norwegian community of Camrose: Lloyd George, Cornhill, Evergreen, and Lakeside. At the same time the populations of Calgary and Edmonton each included 100 Swedes.[106]

Consular services began in Calgary in 1893, but not until 1920 in Wetaskiwin and Edmonton. Emil Skarin[107] served as vice-consul in Edmonton from 1920 to 1945, and as consul from 1945 to 1950. His is an immigrant success story. He had arrived in 1902 not knowing any English and with $1.47 in his pocket. By 1920 he had earned a civil engineering degree from the University of Alberta and co-founded the construction company Crown Paving and Alberta Concrete Products. He had the ability to overcome obstacles, and helped many immigrants to do the same.

His nephew, Lars Fahlstrom, counted himself lucky to have Emil as a mentor:

> Many would describe him as an eccentric person and I can easily under-stand why. Take a wealthy person, dress him in worn old clothes, never hear him brag, see him drive an old beat-up pickup truck ... [but] every-thing Emil did had a purpose. As he became old and shaky, I wrote all Uncle Emil's cheques, while being a guest in their home. If he, for exam-ple, donated $1,000 to a particular charity, I had to make the cheque for $1,000.14 and I asked, of course, why the 14 cents? "So I know that I have donated to that charity for 14 years." It took me awhile to grasp the logic. I have since adopted the simplicity of letting the bank do my accounting, that is, while paying off a car loan, I deposited $100.01 then $100.02 and so on, and I knew that when I made the payment of $100.36 – the car was mine![108]

Before being appointed vice-consul J.P. Johnson[109] had grown up in Winnipeg and established a real-estate office in Wetaskiwin. In 1929 the Swedish community was shocked to discover that he had been arrested for embezzling $20,000 from a Canadian colonization concern. As a result Skarin took responsibility for Wetaskiwin as well.[110]

Edmonton was home to only eleven Swedes in 1906, but by 1914 the growing population could eat at the Stockholm Café, room at Scandia House, and shop at Swea Fruit Store.[111] Therefore, Gus Rydman[112] was a very early city resident in 1908 when Swift's in St Paul transferred him to Edmonton. The following year his brother Axel joined him at the meat-packing plant.

Rural communities with a significant Swedish population before 1914 included Amisk, Battle Lake, Bawlf, Bittern Lake, Buford/Glen Park, Burnt Lake, Camrose, Cherhill, Clive, Czar, Donalda, Ferintosh,

Fridhem, Gwynne, Hardisty, Hay Lakes, Hayter, Hughenden, Magnolia, Mecca Glen, Meeting Creek, Metiskow, New Hill, New Norway, Stavely, Sylvan Lake, Viking, Wainwright, and Water Glen. Of existing communities with official Swedish names, Alsike, Calmar, Lindale, Thorsby, and Warburg are located northwest of Wetaskiwin; Falun and Westerose to the west; and Edberg to the southeast.

Two houses and two plaques commemorate Alberta's Swedish pioneers. The Ohrn Family Home stands in the Alberta Heritage Exposition Park west of Leduc, having been donated to the Leduc West Antique Society by Donald and Ralph Ohrn. The elegant two-storey structure has been restored and furnished with additional items handcrafted earlier by Andrew Kvarnberg,[113] with the official opening in 1995. It had been built seventy-six years earlier by homesteader Herbert Ohrn,[114] part owner of the Strawberry Sawmill Company, which sawed the lumber.[115]

Emanuel Cronquist[116] owned such a spacious home overlooking Red Deer River that in 1985 it was moved to Red Deer, restored, and dedicated as the community's Multicultural Centre. Built in 1912, the stately three-storey brick house was commercially designed with a circular tower, a large porch supported by sturdy columns, and a complicated fusion of peaks and gables on the roof. Cronquist made his money operating a limestone quarry, selling life insurance, and dealing in real estate, livestock, and machinery, in addition to farming and ranching.

In 1993 the Alberta government purchased part of the Loov homestead on Battle Lake, west of Wetaskiwin, for a park. The plaque reads: "The Mount Butte Natural Area is dedicated to the memory of William and Asta Loov. This Swedish couple settled here in June 1933 because the lakes and birch-covered hills reminded them of their native homeland. In naming this Natural Area, the Loov children, Solveig, Verner, Bob and Bill along with the province of Alberta, pay tribute to the spirit, endurance and stewardship shown by these pioneers. June 1993."

William Loov[117] immigrated in 1927 and soon sent tickets for his wife, Asta, and two children. After a series of misunderstandings and bad luck the family ended up on their homestead in June 1933 with no house, no work, and no credit. When twin children were born in October the family was living in a house built of slabs from a nearby sawmill, and enough hay had been cut by hand for the cows William had bought with money borrowed from Asta's sisters. The family survived these hard times through ingenuity and hard work.

Charlie Sahlström, right, stands in front of the family's log home in 1910. Postmaster August Sahlström named the community after his hometown of Torsby in Sweden. The post office was located in the lean-to addition at the back, with the name Thorsby over the door. Courtesy of Bob Sahlstrom.

In 1978 a more inclusive plaque was erected four kilometres south of Meeting Creek, southeast of Wetaskiwin, to recognize the contribution of Swedish immigrants to central Alberta:

Swedish Settlement
From 1892 to 1920 the dream of being independent landowners attracted hundreds of Swedish families to central Alberta, both from the old country and from the northern United States. These pioneers homesteaded the new land, and mixed farming settlements grew and prospered at Thorsby, Calmar, Malmo, Falun, and Edensville (Meeting Creek). Sound farming practices and dedication to church and family have perpetuated these Swedish-Canadian communities.

Svensk Bebyggelse
Mellan åren 1892 och 1920 drog drömmen om egna marker hundratals svenska familjer från både Sverige och norra US till mellersta Alberta. Deras nyodlingar blomstrade och mångsidigt jordbruk växte upp runt Thorsby, Calmar, Malmo, Falun, och Edensville (Meeting Creek). Sunda jordsbruks metoder samt hängivenhet till kyrka och familj lade en god grund för dessa svensk-canadensk bevarande.

Initiated by Meeting Creek's Norden Vasa Lodge No. 513, coordinated by Linnea Lodge of Alberta Cultural Heritage, and assisted by Historic Site Services, Alberta Culture, the plaque was unveiled in the presence of Swedish Ambassador Per Anger,[118] Alberta Minister of Culture Horst A. Schmid, Swedish Consul Lars Fahlstrom, MLA Gordon Stromberg,[119] and 400 other interested individuals. The event marked the fiftieth anniversary of Norden Lodge.

British Columbia

In 1931 there were 16,108 residents of Swedish heritage living in British Columbia, 57 per cent of them born in Sweden. More than half lived in the southwest corner of the province, in and around Vancouver and the east coast of Vancouver Island. The other half was scattered throughout the southern part of the province, with a few in the middle and northern sections. Most were attracted by the mild climate, but there were also jobs on the railways and in the forest industry, in mining in the Kootenays and the Rossland district, and in fishing along the coast. Mixed farming and fruit growing were carried

British Columbia 1931/Born in Sweden, Helge Nelson, *The Swedes and the
Swedish Settlements in North America* (1943), 1:362.

out in Evelyn, Hilltop, Malakwa, Matsqui, the Peace River block, Silverhill, Smithers, the Prince George area, and the Kootenay Lake and
Arrow Lake districts.

Helge Nelson called British Columbia "the country of short-lived
lumber camps and mining places," because it was impossible to keep
track of the 1,000 Swedes who made up 8 per cent of the labour force
in the lumber industries. Prince George claimed a population that was

8 per cent Swedish, but most of them were lumberjacks and labourers going to and from work camps.[120]

The rate of growth in British Columbia's Swedish population between 1961 and 1991 was 134 per cent; that is, from 33,251 to 77,805. Of the latter, 14,880 had both parents born in Sweden, indicating that they arrived after the Second World War. The only province to come close to this number was Alberta, with 11,175.[121]

In 1889 the entrepreneurial Thulin brothers founded the Swedish community of Lund on the mainland coast about 100 kilometres north of Vancouver. That year Charlie[122] had welcomed his brother Fred[123] to Lund, and the two agreed to change their surname from Peterson to Thulin and to become business partners. They built a wharf and sold cordwood and fresh water to passing tugs, processed cod livers for oil, and salted salmon to ship to the Orient. Lund's post office was established in 1892, the second on British Columbia's mainland coast. Other business enterprises included a shipyard for tugs and small boats, a sawmill, and a palatial hotel built in 1905 and restored in 2000, when it was advertised as "the gateway to Desolation Sound."

In 1904 the Thulins founded Campbell River, across Georgia Strait on Vancouver Island, by building the Willows Hotel and buying 1,012 hectares of land. Charlie is regarded as the key figure in promoting sports fishing. He also established a dairy farm with purebred cattle and in 1918 built the Lillelanna dance pavilion named for his daughters Lillie, Elin, and Anna.[124]

In 1897 Rolf Wallgren Bruhn[125] joined his father, Axel Wallgren Bruhn, in Malakwa, where the two men farmed together. Rolf's life of poverty in Sweden had changed course when he won the lavish sailboat *Norve*[126] in a yacht-club lottery. He sold it for 1,800 kronor ($468), then bought a boat ticket and gave the rest to his mother. In Malakwa he supplemented his income with government roadwork, and in 1902 married Anna Treat from Missouri. When his father returned to Sweden in 1909 he sold the farm and moved to Salmon Arm. After winning a contract to provide cedar poles to the B.J. Carney Pole Company the family moved to Sicamous. Within a decade this initial venture led to the development of a diversified forest company centred on Shuswap Lake, and made him a millionaire.[127] However, by 1926 he had lost so much of his first language that he had difficulty conversing with a newspaper reporter in Sweden. Fortunately his travelling companion, author Harry Macfie, was able to help out.[128]

Rolf Wallgren Bruhn began his career in provincial politics in 1924, representing the new riding of Salmon Arm as a Conservative.[129] After

visiting Sweden again in 1936, he shared with the legislature his enthusiasm for the new "middle way" of socialized capitalism being developed there. As a politician he was fiercely independent, paying his
own campaign expenses and voting as he saw fit. He also maintained
personal friendships across party lines; in fact, he helped to draft the
platform of the Social Reconstructive party in 1937.[130] The *Vancouver
Province* paid him a high compliment in its final tribute: "[he was] a
very good politician ... because mainly, in the old party sense, he was
hardly a politician at all."

The main employer in Revelstoke was the CPR, which provided job
opportunities that had attracted Swedes ever since the railway was
built, including those from Långasjö. Mayor Arvid Lundell, who served
as MLA for twelve years, wrote the following report in 1966: "Some
60 years ago there was a Scandinavian Society in Revelstoke composed
mostly of Swedes. They owned their own hall and many outstanding social events were held there. A similar society in Malakwa still
functions but with greatly reduced numbers."[131] Locomotive engineers
included the brothers Jack and Ole Johnson, and Alf Holm, who organized the occasional Swedish concert.

The growth of the logging industry was reflected in the number
of Swedish boarding houses in Vancouver. Each spring lumberjacks
descended upon the city with money to spend and time on their hands
until they returned to their cutting camps in the fall. Each fall construction workers and other itinerants took over their rooms for the winter's coldest months. The hotels on Cordova and Carrall streets did
a roaring trade as gathering places, not only for the sale of beer, but
also for snoose, candy, patent medicines, newspapers, and other small
items. The places of business and accommodation were scattered so
that Vancouver never developed a full-blown Snoose Boulevard, as in
Winnipeg.[132]

Frank Hart,[133] a second-generation Swede from Illinois, was Vancouver's first merchant. He was on the scene on 4 July 1886 when the first
transcontinental train steamed into Port Moody, and moved his furniture business to Vancouver when the railway extended its line. He built
a welcome arch and, at the mayor's request, presented a bouquet to the
first lady who alighted from the train.[134] He is best known for building Hart Opera House. The name was grandiose for a rough shed 15.2
by 39.6 metres, reconstructed from Port Moody's roller-skating rink,
but it served the purpose. There was a small stage on the long side,
with chairs and benches in the middle and bleachers at each end. There,

Vancouver's pioneers enjoyed concerts, dances, and church services, and occasionally roller skating.[135]

Pete Larson[136] became Vancouver's leading hotel man. A carpenter on a sailing barque, he jumped ship during railway construction. His first establishment, Hotel Norden, was open for business when the first train pulled in to Vancouver in 1887. The next one, Union Hotel on Abbott Street, catered to sailors. Larson married Gerda Peterson, one of five siblings to come to Vancouver from southern Sweden.[137] These five young families formed the nucleus of the early Swedish community in Vancouver, together with Emil and Marie-Louise Peterson[138] from Kristinestad, Finland.

By the end of the Second World War Vancouver was gradually replacing Winnipeg as Canada's Swedish centre, but with major differences. Although many loggers and other itinerants gave Vancouver as their mailing address, the city never became a distribution centre for immigrants, and after the Second World War the Anglo-Saxon majority became more welcoming. In 1987 Mayor Gordon Campbell declared Sweden's Flag Day, 6 June, as "Sweden Day," with events that included five major exhibitions at the Media Centre with videos and lectures, a Midsummer pole with folk dancers, instrumental musicians and singer Titti Sjöblom from Sweden, and Minneapolis's Snoose Boulevard balladeer Anne-Charlotte Harvey,[139] with nearby restaurants serving Swedish food and baked goods. In addition the Royal Swedish Ballet performed at the Queen Elizabeth Theatre, and Pacific Cinematheque showed Swedish films, five of them premieres.[140] The previous year the Scandinavian Midsummer Festival had celebrated Vancouver's centennial. A memento of this event is the granite rune stone in Vanier Park. The stone came from Sweden but the carving was done on-site.[141]

The sixtieth anniversary of *Swedish Press* in 1989 was one of the last events to be held in the Swedish Hall before its sale. The Sweden House Society was incorporated in 1991 as a non-profit group to raise funds to replace it,[142] and the first fundraiser was the musical *Värmlänningarna*, performed by an ensemble from Sweden. The Sweden House Society bought the Roald Amundsen Centre in Burnaby in cooperation with the Norway House Society and the Finland House Society, and the Scandinavian Community Centre opened in 1996 with Lennart Osterlind[143] as president.[144] Soon the Denmark House Society joined them, all four holding meetings, festivals, and midsummer and other events there.

In 1996 Heritage Day was dedicated to Canadians of Nordic descent. The teaching material prepared by Heritage Canada was based on the

poster "A Nordic Saga" created by British Columbia artist Patricia
Guttormson Peacock, of Icelandic heritage. The package was sent to
80,000 teachers and leaders of children throughout Canada, with all five
embassies assisting.

A high-profile event that took place on the property was the British
Columbia Viking Ship Project, which was to build a Viking ship as close
to the original as possible. *Munin* was launched in 2001 as a twelve-
metre replica of the twenty-three-metre *Gokstad* on display at the Viking
Ship Museum in Oslo, Norway. Munin, one of the ravens that sat on the
shoulder of the Norse god Odin, represents memory. The ship docked
at the Vancouver Maritime Museum Heritage Harbour in Vanier Park
from May through September so that members of the museum as well
as the general public could enjoy the experience of rowing and sailing
in a real Viking ship.[145]

Far North

Although the Klondike gold rush was long past, by 1931 there were
still 112 Swedes living in the Yukon. Some were temporary residents,
others had found steady employment, and a few were still hoping to
strike it rich. The Nordling family came to Dawson in 1914. The eldest
son, Otto Nordling,[146] would become Yukon's chief booster, founding
the International Sourdough Club in Ottawa and Vancouver, and starting the ball rolling for a Yukon coat of arms, which Governor General
Vincent Massey presented in Whitehorse in 1956. Nordling retired from
the army in 1957[147] but never stopped promoting the Yukon, its university fund, and the territorial flag, and writing letters advocating such
changes as indexed pensions and a minimum wage.

Barbro Baker[148] lived in Whitehorse for twelve years while her husband, a civil engineer, was posted there. In 1979 she welcomed Ulf Beijbom from the Emigrant Institute in Växjö, who was promoting his book
about the gold rush.[149] While in Dawson Beijbom presented the mayor
with six lithographs of Klondike maps from 1896 to 1899, by artist Willy
Läth.[150] The following year Läth[151] arrived to try to trace the Klondike's
Swedes. He stayed with Emil and Lilly Dahlgren,[152] who had come to
the Yukon in 1941, thereby qualifying as members of the Yukon Order
of Pioneers, which required thirty years' residence.

In 1962 the government of Canada hired Sven Johansson[153] to super-
vise its reindeer herd on the recommendation of Al Oeming of the
Alberta Game Farm. Because it was felt that reindeer could offer an

alternate source of income, food, and clothing for the Inuit, and because the Mackenzie River delta offered suitable lichen for browse, the government decided in 1929 to establish a reindeer industry in the Northwest Territories. A herd of more than 2,000 animals arrived in 1935, after a six-year trek from Alaska. Reindeer are not native to North America; these had originally been brought from Russia across the Bering Strait.

Introducing the farming of reindeer to an economy based on hunting and trapping presented problems, despite the presence of Sami herders as instructors. The government decided on a five-year program of research and practical experiment. Johansson, who had twelve years' experience with reindeer husbandry in northern Sweden, was chosen as manager with headquarters at Reindeer Station. The results, as noted in his 1965 report, were positive: "Conditions were very favourable for efficient reindeer husbandry in the Canadian Reindeer Reserve. The reorganization to high efficiency can be done in a short time because there are no cultural or social problems involved in the reindeer industry here, and that the Canadian Reindeer Industry is now in an advanced position in the western world and might become a pattern of modern efficient reindeer industry."[154] This did not happen. Instead, the industry stagnated, and in January 2008 Canada's only herd of 3,000 animals strayed from Richards Island near Tuktoyaktuk. Only 400 were found, and there was concern that reindeer diseases could endanger the already fragile caribou population.[155]

During the summer of 1972 the mystique of Canada's Barrens attracted a group of Swedish adventurers who canoed from Wood Buffalo National Park to Baker Lake near Hudson Bay, a ten-week journey covering 1,620 kilometres. Their trip was documented on film and slides, in sound recordings and diaries. Along the way they spotted wolves, black bears, muskoxen, moose, caribou, buffalo, bald eagles, Canada geese, a whistling swan, and sandhill cranes, proving to their satisfaction that the Northwest Territories were not barren after all.[156]

The first immigrants settled in eastern Canada, but with the introduction of a federal immigration policy the first, second, and third waves were directed westward as homesteaders and labourers. Thus, the prairie provinces, British Columbia, and northern Ontario became important places of settlement with Winnipeg as a distribution centre and home of Canada's only Snoose Boulevard. The fourth wave chose to live in cities because of employment opportunities and urbanization. With this shift Vancouver replaced Winnipeg as a population centre and Toronto established itself as the heart of the Swedish business community.

Chapter Five

Religion

Many Swedish immigrants were devout, but for various reasons only about half of them attended church.[1] Religious services were not available, for example, to workers in shifting construction, mining, and logging camps, or in communities where the number of immigrants was too small to support a Swedish church. In addition, some believers may have been overwhelmed by the responsibility of building and maintaining a church, since these services were provided by the state in Sweden. Others may have found the church of their choice unavailable where they lived, or too far away to attend regularly. There were three Swedish-speaking denominations to choose from: Augustana Lutheran, Mission Covenant, and Swedish Baptist.

But communities with a substantial number of potential members usually had at least one driving individual to mobilize a congregation, and to arrange for construction of a church, for lay readers, and for a pastor to preside at baptisms, marriages, and funerals, and sometimes to hold services as well. For these immigrants, going to church offered an opportunity to share their faith with others and with their children, without experiencing the class distinctions practised by some of its clergy in Sweden. Since pastors came from the United States until 1946, uniquely Canadian interpretations did not develop.

Background in Sweden

All immigrants had been members either of the state Church of Sweden or one of the free churches that broke away from it. The Lutheran structure, which had been emerging since the 1520s, became official in 1593 with formalization of the Augsburg Confession. The Church of

Sweden retained much of the liturgy from the Roman Catholic Mass, which was translated into Swedish, as was the Bible, catechism, hymnal, and devotional writings. Financial support for church buildings, cemeteries, and salaries and residences of clergy came from the state until disestablishment in 2000, when much of that support began shifting to the congregations.

Lutheran discipline and beliefs were woven into the very fabric of life, which was overwhelmingly rural. However, it took a long time to replace the pagan gods Odin, Thor, and Freija. Traces of this religion linger today and will continue as long as Swedes call Wednesday *onsdag*, Thursday *torsdag,* and Friday *fredag*. Most Christian holidays in Sweden, except for those associated with Easter, stem from pagan celebrations, and believing in trolls was not considered inconsistent with Lutheranism.

Sweden was divided into more than 2,000 parishes, each with its own church. Until 2000, the pastors were responsible for keeping civil records such as births, deaths, and marriages, as well as noting parishioners' movements into, out of, and within the parish, including the certificate (*flyttningsbetyg*) required to immigrate to other countries.[2]

Since Sweden's church records are among the best in the world, they are a boon to genealogical researchers.[3] However, their collection was thoroughly disliked by those who chafed under the church's authority. Many immigrants who chose not to attend church were in this category, while others felt unwelcome because their lifestyle did not meet the expectations of church members or other personal conflicts. Overly religious parents had adversely affected others. It was not unusual, for example, for a father to quote the Fifth Commandment, "Thou shalt honour thy father and thy mother," to force the youngest daughter to remain at home to care for her aging parents.

The Swedish government introduced compulsory education for children in 1842, but before that the church had instituted a drive towards reading literacy so that adult parishioners could draw comfort from the Bible. Therefore, the vast majority of immigrants to Canada were literate in Swedish, which many regarded as the language of heaven,[4] and their luggage included bibles and other religious books. All had been influenced by the Lutheran view of Christianity with the result that they were generally hard-working, serious, rational, and humble.[5] These traits were often passed on to their children.

The free churches formed as part of the evangelical revival movements that swept Sweden beginning in the early 1800s. Until the repeal of the *Conventicle Act* in 1858 they met strong opposition from the Church of Sweden. Some broke away at once while others founded their own denominations over a period of time. Baptist, Methodist, and Mormon missionaries from similar revival movements in England and the United States also influenced Sweden,[6] so that the early immigration period was a time of great religious ferment both in Sweden and in North America as new faith groups sought to establish themselves.

In Sweden Baptists built a church in Göteborg in 1861, becoming the first among free churches to do so, and also organized the first Sunday schools. Because they were the first to break away, and because the religion was imported from abroad, they bore the brunt of persecution and many immigrated to the United States.

The Evangelical Covenant Church, formerly called Mission Covenant, sprang from the indigenous Svenska Missionsförbundet (Mission Friends), which was founded as a denomination in Sweden in 1878 and in the United States in 1885. Its doctrines were influenced by the Swedish theologian P.P. Waldenström,[7] whose atonement theory held that the cross reconciled man to God rather than God to man.

The three major denominations in Canada were Augustana Lutheran, Evangelical Covenant, and Swedish Baptist. Although administered by counterparts in the United States at first, by 1914 all had formed Canadian administrative bodies. Still, for many years they continued to rely upon American seminaries and publishing houses for pastors and print materials.

Lutheran

The Augustana[8] Evangelical Lutheran Church was organized in the United States in 1860.[9] At the same time the state churches of Sweden and England had been holding lengthy negotiations for intercommunion, so that the Episcopalian (Anglican) Church felt justified in actively recruiting Swedish migrants as members. The scene was set for an antagonistic relationship between the two American denominations, the one established and the other fledgling: "This included sporadic Episcopalian efforts to form Swedish Episcopalian congregations in the United States that would directly compete with Augustana congregations, as well as efforts to bring the Augustana Synod into the Episcopalian denomination ... The Church of Sweden itself was initially weak in its own support of the Augustana Synod, as Swedish Church leaders were suspicious of the Synod's low-Church, pietistic orientation, and lack of Episcopal structure."[10] By the 1890s the Church of Sweden had begun to support Augustana, but the memory of the Episcopalian challenge lingered for a long time, even crossing the border into Canada.

The controversy manifested itself in Port Arthur, Ontario, in 1906 when St John's Anglican Church established the first and last Swedish mission in Canada. Swedes and Norwegians had been registering their baptisms, marriages, and funerals in the parish records for more than a quarter-century without organizing their own congregations. The change began in 1905 with organization of the Swedish Baptist Church, followed the very next year by the Anglican mission. It was called St Ansgarius after Ansgar (801–865), who built Sweden's first Christian church. The pastor, a charismatic Finland Swede named Knute S. Tottermann,[11] had been ordained by the Episcopal Church even though he was a Laestadian believer.[12] Before coming to Port Arthur in April, he had served St Peter's Swedish Mission in Duluth. The Anglican chancellor of the diocese described his Port Arthur ministry this way: "His first service was interrupted by the determined opposition of representatives of the American Swedish Lutherans, and he never regained his congregation. He set to work, however, to collect funds for the building of a church in which he was very successful, and without the authority of the Bishop and contrary to his advice he pushed forward, until the work was barred for lack of funds, and when Mr. Tottermann left [in 1908] there was a tangle of debts, an unfinished edifice, and no congregation."[13]

In 1912 St John's sold "Tottermann's church," as the property was called, to the Norwegian Lutheran congregation founded five years earlier.[14]

Augustana pastors from Kenora, Ontario, and Two Harbors, Minnesota, had visited the Lakehead cities irregularly since 1903, but discussions about organizing a congregation had not led to action. Finally in February 1906 a group of nine women met at the home of Mrs Ida Stone[15] and organized a Ladies' Aid, probably at the suggestion of Ida's brother-in-law, who was an Augustana pastor. It was these ladies who mounted the "determined opposition" at Tottermann's service, perceiving the mission as an Episcopalian threat. In July 1906 the Swedish Immanuel Evangelical Lutheran Church was organized by the newly ordained Augustana pastor P.N. Sjögren, who formally accepted from Mrs Stone the presidency of the Ladies' Aid, which now included the men. Ida's husband became secretary.

A gender controversy followed. Despite their key role in founding the congregation, the women were not allowed to vote on church matters until 1917.[16] Few congregations could survive on givings alone. They relied upon additional money raised by the Ladies' Aid through the sale of baking and handwork, draws, teas, bazaars, and the like,[17] but evidently this source of funds had been withdrawn. Immanuel was able only to pour a basement church in 1912, and did not erect the sanctuary above it until 1957. In contrast, Immanuel's sister congregation, Zion in Fort William, built its church in 1909 and the manse next door in 1912.[18]

During the late 1870s the Augustana Synod and the Covenant Church in the United States viewed each other as serious threats, and as a result participated in acrimonious name-calling in their respective publications.[19] This antagonism manifested itself a decade later in New Stockholm, Saskatchewan, where in 1888 the Covenant Church had established its, and Canada's, second Swedish congregation.[20] A Mr A.G. Sahlmark[21] had attended services since his arrival from Minnesota the year before: "[He was described as] an orderly man in every way [who] wished to organize Sunday in the Colony. He set it that there should be a prayer meeting every Sunday from house to house in turn. He himself read a portion of the Postilla and Mrs. S. sang from a hymn book."[22]

He contacted the Augustana Synod in 1889 after objecting to certain readings from a prayer book. A newcomer from Sweden, possibly A.P. Sjöström, had carried out the service and made no secret that he felt offended by Sahlmark's criticism. The meeting ended on a sour note and resulted in the founding of Augustana's first Canadian congregation.[23] Active support for one denomination or the other split not only families, but also the community itself.

The rift between the two local congregations had not been reconciled by 1894, when the Covenant pastor C.O. Hofstrand[24] called an outdoor meeting, with Pastor A.G. Olson[25] representing the Augustana congregation, to discuss the questions: "Is it necessary in such a small colony as this one that there should be two active Church denominations? What are the primary causes of this state of affairs? What would be the best way to remove these hindrances to co-operation?"[26] Sven Svedberg, who claimed to support neither group, described the meeting wryly as "more Christian and harmonious than usual,"[27] but the hoped-for compromise did not take place. With dedication of the New Stockholm Augustana Lutheran Church by Pastor Erik Norelius[28] in 1896, the two buildings stood as silent witnesses to the awesome power of religion to divide believers into separate camps.

New Stockholm's schoolteacher from 1899 to 1901, W.J. Sisler, commented on the Lutheran congregation ten years after its founding: "The members were strict as to formality but rather lacking in carrying the religion into everyday life. Dancing, drinking and swearing were no great sins provided that they performed their religious duties on the Sabbath."[29]

Sisler, who often attended services in the Mission Covenant church, may well have been biased. However, his comparison of the two buildings leaves little doubt about the priorities of each congregation. The Covenant church was "a small square wooden building with no spire, no pictures, statues nor ornaments of any kind," whereas the Lutheran church was "an impressive building with a high steeple and stained glass windows."[30]

The financial status of A.G. Sahlmark and his wife Kate represented the Lutheran church as described above. Both had been born in Sweden but grew up in the United States. When they arrived in New Stockholm with seven children they brought "considerable farming equipment ... [also] furniture for their home and sufficient money to allow them to begin homesteading under very favourable circumstances."[31] Unlike other women who shared in the farm work, Kate could devote all her time to home, family, and church. Her husband and his brother Charles, who were experienced in civic affairs, played leading roles in the church, school, and community. If New Stockholm had an élite, then the Sahlmarks headed the list.

But there were also doctrinal differences. The Augustana Synod followed a confessional and liturgical order similar to the Church of Sweden, though without state connection, and the ecclesiastical head was called president rather than bishop. The Evangelical Covenant, on the other hand, held firm convictions not only about Christian beliefs based on their interpretation of the Bible, but also about how people should behave. Since revivalism was closely associated with the temperance movement,[32] Covenanters and Baptists were usually more persistent in the crusade against alcohol than Augustana Lutherans.

All three denominations tried to influence the lifestyle of members. The Baptist constitution forbade dancing, drinking, card playing, gambling, and clothing that was too colourful. In the 1990s a parishioner offered a shrewd comment about such restrictions in a changing society: "In the early church days cosmetics were frowned upon and powder and lipstick a real sin since only actresses used those. Smoking, however, was accepted and nearly all the men smoked, even in the church basement. Hannah Norden was very vocal when disapproving of this practice. However, now cosmetics are accepted as part of a woman's dress and used everywhere in daily life, but smoking is all but banned!"[33]

Augustana, unlike the Church of Sweden,[34] was against lodges that practised forms of religion in their rites, like the Vasa Lodge and the Masonic Lodge. This attitude was not officially relaxed until the 1962 merger that founded the Lutheran Church in America.[35] Although Lutheran pastors continued to arrive from Sweden, the establishment of Augustana College and Theological Seminary in Rock Island, Illinois, ensured an indigenous clergy.

Geographical groupings, called conferences, provided support and supervision for congregations and for pastors. Before Canada Conference was organized in 1913 the closest conference in the United States assumed responsibility for the work in Canada. A man named T.N. Hasselquist, who became a patriarch of the Minnesota Conference, visited Winnipeg in June 1883.[36] He did not meet any Swedes, and expressed surprise that the weather was so warm. Wasn't Canada a "world of ice and bears"?[37]

The following winter Pastor L.A. Hocanzon[38] found the very opposite: cold weather but a very warm welcome. A staunch Covenanter, M.P. Peterson, introduced him to interested Swedes and arranged with the English Methodist church for him to hold Sunday services there. After three visits Hocanzon recommended that a pastor be sent to Winnipeg, but these early calls were refused.[39] The notion that Canada was cold and dangerous was obviously widespread.

In 1890 Pastor L.G. Almén[40] presided over the organization of Augustana's second congregation, Zion (later St Mark's) in Winnipeg, and of Bethlehem in Scandinavia the following year.[41] Itinerant pastors[42] served all three congregations irregularly before and after 1892, when Svante Uddén[43] accepted the call to become Canada's first resident Augustana Lutheran pastor. A year earlier, when he had arrived in Winnipeg as an itinerant pastor, he was horrified to discover that the Zion congregation was considering joining the Anglicans because of their mounting debt and feeling neglected by the synod.[44] Losing Winnipeg as headquarters for the fledgling Augustana mission would have been unfortunate indeed.

Pastor Uddén was an indefatigable worker. During his six-year stay he managed to put Augustana's Canadian mission on a firm footing with headquarters in Winnipeg. The church was located on Logan

Avenue, near the CPR yards and shops, the city's main employer of Swedes. By 1900 almost 800 members in ten congregations in Minnesota Conference had built five churches and were being served by three resident pastors in Canada.[45] At the same time the Mission Covenant had grown more slowly with four congregations, three churches, and two resident pastors.[46]

Uddén's letters to his superior, Erik Norelius, reveal some of the challenges he faced. The need for pastors was paramount, either students or ordained, in order to further the work in Canada and to keep Baptists and Covenanters from gaining the upper hand.[47] Lack of money posed a major problem, especially in Winnipeg, where Uddén had personally backed nearly $500 in church debts. "Next Thursday a large I.O.U. is due and what shall I do?" he asked plaintively in October 1894. He felt the conference was not supporting his mission the way it should and, at one point, threatened to quit.[48]

Uddén had visited three times previously. The reason for his second trip in 1888 was a six-week tour for Minnesota Conference.[49] As a result several pastors agreed to act as itinerant missionaries, like Uddén himself in 1885 and 1891. By example, Uddén transformed Canada from a call Augustana pastors refused out of hand to one they might consider. His memoir, *Från Canada* (From Canada), the first book about Canada in the Swedish language, was published in 1898 by the Augustana Book Concern.

Ten years earlier, when Uddén took the train to Rat Portage, now Kenora,[50] he found a pioneer community nestled around the outlet of Lake of the Woods, a former fur-trade centre. There, fifty Swedes worked in the flour mill and in sawmills. By the time the Bethesda congregation[51] was founded in 1894, a Swedish community called Lakeside had been established on the spruce-laden hills in the eastern part of town. Members built the church within this enclave on land donated by Western Lumber Company, evidently a major employer.[52]

Canada's second resident Swedish Lutheran pastor, Axel Helander,[53] arrived in Kenora in 1895. The following year he was appointed Swedish vice-consul, as were his successors Gustaf Severin Larsson (from 1898 to 1901) and Bernt Olai Berg (from 1901 to 1902). Kenora's vice-consulate then closed. Uddén's comment to Minnesota Conference that "Rat Portage may soon be as important as Winnipeg"[54] may have had something to do with the community's getting not only a permanent pastor, but also the services of a Swedish-speaking vice-consul.

Pastor Fremling[55] of Minnesota Conference brought Uddén along on his 1893 trip to Alberta. Among the welcoming committee at the

Wetaskiwin station were Ukrainian Swedes who had settled to the southeast, near Battle Lake. Their community of 200 included Germans and Englishmen, but mostly Swedes.[56] The first two congregations in Alberta were founded in 1898, Bethlehem in Wetaskiwin[57] and Svea[58] by Battle Lake, named for Svea, Minnesota, home of the presiding pastor, Olof Lindgren.[59] He would be the first Augustana pastor to remain in Canada for his entire career.

Instrumental in organizing both Svea Lutheran Church and Star School was Olof Save,[60] formerly a politician in Sweden. He and his wife arrived in 1892. Their home, built of squared timbers with a shingled roof, served as the first school and venue for the founding meeting of the church. Save also arranged for a donation of 16.2 hectares of CPR land, which allowed the congregation to work the land to help pay for the construction of a church.

In 1902 Bethlehem Church in Wetaskiwin welcomed Pastor Per Almgren,[61] who also served as field missionary for Alberta. He held services at Battle Lake and organized congregations at Falun (Dalby) to the west, Calmar to the northwest, Camrose (Fridhem)[62] to the east, and Meeting Creek to the southeast. He also organized the Fryksende congregation at Archive, south of Moose Jaw. The name honoured the imposing Fryksände Church in Torsby, Värmland.[63]

All the above congregations mourned when Pastor Almgren was killed in 1906 by a tree falling on the wagon in which he was riding. He was buried in Fridhem churchyard.[64] His widow, Anna Margreta, remained in Wetaskiwin, continuing as the church's organist and choir director and also active in the Ladies' Aid of the Scandinavian Hospital Society.[65]

Pastor G.A. Anderson of LaConner, Washington, organized the Swedish Lutheran congregation in Vancouver in 1903, as part of Columbia Conference.[66] The original building was replaced in 1910 with a handsome structure costing $60,000, with stained glass windows and oaken pews from Sweden. Paying the debt became almost impossible during the 1913 Depression when more than half the membership left the city to look for work, but Mrs Frida Engblom[67] inspired the remaining members with her forceful personality. At a general meeting called to discuss the church's fate, she stood up and declared, "The Church shall remain open ... even if I have to keep it open all by myself!" Augustana Church, as it was called, survived the crisis to celebrate its centennial in 2003.[68]

In Alberta Pastor Olof Lindgren presided over the founding meeting of the Wilhelmina congregation in 1908. Choosing a name was easy because most of the founding members came from Vilhelmina, Lappland.[69] Selecting a building site was another matter: "Feeling was running very high at this meeting and tempers were near the breaking point. The group in the eastern part of the community known as the "*Östren*" [the east] had used underhanded means of obtaining enough votes to carry a majority. This created a split in the congregation and seven confirmed members and fourteen children left the congregation in a group."[70]

Pastor Lindgren came once a month to preach in members' homes until the church was built in 1913, with the bell tower and spire being added six years later. The landmark building, originally designed after its namesake in Vilhelmina, sits like a beacon on a hilltop not far from Miquelon Lake Provincial Park.

In 1954 Anna Greta Lofgren[71] donated a large album of correspondence and photos to the local museum in Sweden. *Alberta-pärmen*, as it was called, became a symbol of the historic relationship between Vilhelmina and Wilhelmina, and inspired further research. In Alberta publication of *Each Step Left its Mark: A History of Hay Lakes and Surrounding Area* gave the final impetus to the exhibition "Vilhelmina to Wilhelmina," produced by Västerbottens Museum, Umeå, and brought to Edmonton in 1984 by the curator, Per-Uno Ågren.[72] The church, which had acted as a catalyst to bring the communities together, celebrated its centennial in 2008.

Most church buildings became vibrant centres in their community, but not always. John P. Ocklin[73] organized the Augustana congregation in Eriksdale, Manitoba, in 1913, but the church built in 1917 was never completed, nor was a stove installed. The congregation's indifference was attributed to Ocklin himself, whose personality was said to be reminiscent of long-winded and pompous pastors back in Sweden. The last function held in Nyland Church was his eightieth birthday celebration in 1932.

The sites of Swedish Lutheran congregations in 1914 were Mabel Lake, New Westminster, and Vancouver in British Columbia; Brightview, Burnt Lake, Calgary, Calmar, Camrose, Clive, Czar, Edmonton, Falun, Hay Lakes, Hughenden, Kingman, Meeting Creek, Water Glen, Westerose, and Wetaskiwin in Alberta; Admiral, Archive, Assiniboia, Beatty, Buchanan, Dubuc, Fleming, Goodwater, Gull Lake, Kelliher, Kinistino, Kipling, Marchwell, New Stockholm, Parkman, Percival, Scotsguard, Shaunavon, Theodore, Wadena, Waldeck, and Young in Saskatchewan;[74] Eriksdale, Inwood, Lac du Bonnet, Lillesve, Scandinavia

(Erickson), Whitemouth, and Winnipeg in Manitoba; and Fort William, Kenora, and Port Arthur in Northwestern Ontario.[75] Covenant congregations also existed in Calgary, Meeting Creek, New Stockholm, Winnipeg, and Young.

In Montreal an Augustana Lutheran church had been organized in 1919 with ninety-four parishioners, under New England Conference. The Gustavus Adolphus Lutheran congregation did not thrive and was discontinued in 1942. The reasons given were the transience of the Swedish community and its overriding interest in Swedish culture rather than the Word of God.[76] However, a Vasa Lodge founded in 1927 did not flourish, either.

When the Augustana Lutheran church in Edmonton was organized in 1929, the Society for the Preservation of Swedish Culture in Foreign Lands sent a communion chalice and paten as a gift. The congregation began as First Swedish Evangelical Lutheran Church of Edmonton, but changed its name to the more manageable one in 1941, and dedicated the present building in 1953. Five years later, Pastor Don Sjoberg broke tradition by allowing Skandia Lodge to conduct a Vasa memorial service in the church. An earlier congregation had met in homes from 1914 to 1923, and possibly attended the Norwegian church.

The decline of Logan Avenue in Winnipeg forced its churches to locate elsewhere. Noting Zion's drop in membership the Home Mission Board decided in 1948 that the congregation should relocate to a residential area and drop "Swedish" from its name. The final service was held in 1950 and the new name chosen was St Mark's Evangelical Lutheran Church. After a period of homelessness, the current building in River Heights was dedicated in 1955.[77]

Canada Conference of the Augustana Lutherans, organized in New Stockholm in 1913, was divided into three districts: Alberta, Saskatchewan, and Manitoba/Northwestern Ontario.[78] The impetus was a call by Minnesota Conference for a Canadian Lutheran publication and school, inspired by the success of *Canada posten*, the Mission Covenant newspaper, and the Baptist-run Scandinavian Department at Brandon College. Neither Augustana initiative lasted longer than three years. The high school operated out of a parsonage and a private home in Percival, Saskatchewan, from 1912 to 1914, and plans to erect a school building in Yorkton fell through. The publications were *Canada härold* (1914–15) and *Canada nyheter* (1919–20).[79]

Luther Leagues for young people began in 1921, and in 1933 Canada Conference published the annual minutes in Swedish for the last time.[80]

However, attracting pastors from the United States presented a major problem. In 1930 there were forty-seven congregations with only fourteen pastors to service them.[81] Therefore, in 1945 Canada Conference began to support the Lutheran College and Seminary in Saskatoon by supplying a professor who doubled as pastor for the local church, Gilbert T. Monson. His predecessor, Anton Nelson, had paved the way for Augustana participation when the seminary invited him to teach the English Bible.[82]

Pastor Nils Willison,[83] who was born in Sweden, served as president and dean of the seminary in Saskatoon from 1936 to 1949. When he graduated from the Lutheran Seminary in Waterloo in 1914, he was the very first Swedish graduate of any Canadian Lutheran college or seminary. His career included being chosen as the Canadian delegate to the Lutheran World Convention in Denmark (1929) and Sweden (1947), editing *The Canada Lutheran* for seventeen years, and chairing the Canadian Lutheran Commission for War Service during the Second World War. He also published the choicest of his poetry in the chapbook *Muskoka Echoes*.

Among early Augustana graduates at Saskatoon were Bernhard Bengston in 1946; Paul and Harold Eriksson in 1952; Alf Sander,[84] Don Sjoberg,[85] and Vern Sundmark in 1953; Vincent Eriksson in 1957; and Ferdinand Baglo in 1958. Pastor Baglo is best known for adapting his Bachelor of Divinity thesis into the history book *Augustana Lutherans in Canada*.[86] Pastor Sjoberg was director of Canadian Missions from 1960 to 1970, then until 1985 served as bishop of both the Western Canada Synod and the Evangelical Lutheran Church in Canada. Pastor Sander became executive director of Luther Village on Dogtooth Lake near Kenora.

A Lutheran merger in 1962 brought together four ethnic Lutheran churches to found the Lutheran Church in America (LCA). Canada's three synods became LCA's Canada Section, with authority to form an indigenous Lutheran church with other Lutherans. This materialized in 1986, and the merged church became known as the Evangelical Lutheran Church in Canada (ELCIC) with some 190,000 members. The ELCIC owns and operates the Lutheran Theological Seminary in Saskatoon, the Waterloo Lutheran Seminary, Luther College in Regina, and the Lutheran Collegiate Bible Institute in Outlook, Saskatchewan.

The need for Swedish-speaking pastors surfaced again during the 1950s wave of immigration, especially in Vancouver and Toronto. Estonian Swedes displaced by the Second World War had started emigrating

from Sweden in 1947, many of them from Estonia's capital, Tallinn,
including Pastor Söderlund. His son, Sven Söderlund, moved to Vancouver in 1991 as associate professor of Biblical Studies at Regent College. Every Christmas he conducted the early morning *julotta* service
for Vancouver's Swedes at the Danish Lutheran Church.[87]

Toronto's existing Swedish Lutheran congregation, which always
rented church facilities, benefited from lengthy terms by Swedish Estonian pastors August Raidur and Tönnis Nömmik. Margit Paulson[88]
and Sigrid and Bertil Reilitz had founded the congregation during the
1930s, with Pastor Josef Sjoberg holding services in a building owned
by the United Church of Canada, called the Church of all Nations. In
1953 the expanded and still growing congregation joined the Evangelical Lutheran Church in Canada as an ethnic group. Swedish services
were held at First Lutheran Church in downtown Toronto, later at the
Danish church in Willowdale, and finally at Agricola Finnish Lutheran
Church.

Difficulty finding a Swedish-speaking pastor led to discussions with
the Swedish Church Abroad (*Svenska kyrkan i utlandet*, or SKUT), which
in 1990 admitted the Toronto church into its fold. In 1991 SKUT sent
Pastor Lars Frisk, followed in 1996 by Pastor Per-Olov Carvell for two
years, and Pastor Gunnar Prytz for one year. Due to financial difficulties
SKUT then withdrew its economic support,[89] but helped the congregation to find Pastor Jan Janson, who took over from 2003 to 2005 on a
part-time basis. The present pastor is Anna Runesson, whose husband,
Anders Runesson, is a professor of religious studies at McMaster University in Hamilton.[90]

It was Pastor Frisk who began travelling to Vancouver at least once a
year to hold services in Swedish, a tradition being upheld and expanded
by Pastor Runesson. In addition to regular visits to Vancouver she has
officiated at well-attended services in Ottawa, Winnipeg, Calgary, and
Edmonton.

Evangelical Covenant

Canada's first Swedish congregation,[91] the Evangelical Covenant, was
organized in 1885 in Winnipeg, at the home of Immigration Agent
Emanuel Öhlén. It was M.P. Peterson, who had hosted weekly prayer
meetings and Bible study since 1875, who arranged for Pastor John Rod-
man of Minnesota to be present. He also donated a small building for
use as a church, and in 1887 Andrew Johnson became the first resident

pastor. The congregation held its first picnic on 1 July 1885, Dominion Day, and dedicated its stately new building on Logan Avenue in 1897.

In 1904, with the establishment of several more congregations, the Evangelical Covenant Church of Canada was instituted as both a denomination and as a Conference of the Evangelical Covenant Church, with headquarters in Chicago. Malcolm Magnuson, a student at Chicago's North Park College, was the first home missionary, and in 1914 J.E. Bjorklund, pastor in Winnipeg, became the first superintendent.[92] The sites of congregations in 1914 were Calgary, Highland Park, Malmo, Meeting Creek, and New Sweden in Alberta; Brockington, Hyas, New Stockholm, Norquay, and Young in Saskatchewan; and Smoland in Manitoba, with Winnipeg as the mother church.[93]

The church buildings in Hyas and Norquay were completed in 1912. After many years of sharing a pastor the two congregations joined in 1979 under the name Evangelical Covenant Church of Norquay. Since the early 1950s the Norquay Covenant Church Women have kept Swedish food traditions alive by hosting a smörgåsbord every November as a fundraiser. They serve more than 300 individuals the traditional Swedish flatbread, brown bread, potato sausage, pickled herring, corn pudding, brown beans, and fruit soup.[94] What an inspired tribute to the area's Swedish pioneers!

Church members had to make difficult decisions about switching to English. Some women's groups refused to give up their Swedish, with the result that the younger women usually started their own English-speaking group. In time non-Swedish speakers replaced secretaries for business meetings, and minutes began being written in English.[95] It was not an easy transition for either side. The final blow came when the only pastors available were English-speaking.

The Covenant Church kept young people in its fold through annual Bible camps, the first on Minnedosa Lake in July 1919.[96] In 1951 a permanent camp was built on Clear Lake in Riding Mountain National Park, called Covenant Heights Bible Camp. Alberta's Covenant Bay Bible Camp is located on Pigeon Lake, near Westerose.[97] The tradition continues today, with an additional site, Kootenay Covenant Bible Camp, at Harrop, British Columbia.

The Covenant Bible Institute began in 1918 as a three-month experiment, an attempt to fill the need for Canadian-trained Covenant pastors. Revived in 1927 under Superintendent A.G. Quarnstrom[98] as short-term Bible Institutes,[99] winter classes were held in various churches until 1941, when the Covenant Bible Institute was established in Norquay.

Four years later the institute moved to Prince Albert, Saskatchewan,[100] where it flourished for more than forty years before moving to Strathmore, Alberta. This school, Canada's only Swedish Bible Institute, closed in 2007 because of financial overreaching. Campuses also existed in Colorado and Equador.[101]

Soon after the Covenant Bible Institute moved to Prince Albert the urgency for its founding became apparent. In 1946 a doctrinal dispute over Waldenström's theory of atonement[102] resulted in fifteen of its twenty-five pastors' resignations, seven taking their congregations with them. This episode had a profound effect not only on the denomination's growth, but also on its Swedish roots. The Evangelical Covenant Church of Canada was incorporated as a legal entity in 1966, and in 2003 had twenty-two congregations located from Surrey, British Columbia, to Toronto, Ontario. Only a few started out as Swedish.

After ninety-nine years of service the Winnipeg church quietly closed its doors in 1984.[103] The original building still stands at the corner of Logan and Ellen, a provincial and municipal heritage site restored as the offices of Boge & Boge Consulting Engineers.[104]

Baptist

Canada's first Swedish Baptist congregation was organized in 1892 in Waterville, Quebec, where prayer meetings had been held in homes since 1885. Eventually this Swedish group became the nucleus for an English Baptist Church, marking the end of Swedish Baptist missions in eastern Canada.[105]

Although the first Swedish Baptist service on the Prairies was conducted by Pastor S.P. Ekman in 1883, in the home of Mrs M. Peterson of Winnipeg,[106] a Scandinavian Baptist congregation was not founded until 1894. Pastor Martin Bergh, a Norwegian from North Dakota, organized the Winnipeg group with fourteen charter members including couples from Denmark, Norway, and Sweden.[107] That fall Pastor Bergh held a "Love Feast" for Christians of all denominations. Participants spoke in Swedish, Norwegian, Danish, Icelandic, French, and English, interspersed with musical numbers, and ended the evening by singing together "Blest Be the Tie that Binds."[108] However, the tie that bound Norway and Sweden together came undone in 1905, and in 1914 Norwegians founded their own Baptist congregation.[109]

But before that, in 1897, the Scandinavian congregation had built a church on Logan Avenue. Pastor Alexander Grant of First Baptist

Church (now Broadway First Baptist) supported them from the beginning by attending services, learning Swedish hymns, and offering assistance to immigrants getting off the train at the CPR station. When he drowned in a boating accident that summer, the money raised in his honour went to help finance construction of a church. The grateful congregation changed its name to Grant Memorial Baptist Church, which today, although no longer Swedish, is one of Winnipeg's largest and most active congregations.[110]

Like most early congregations Grant Memorial's members were highly mobile. When some of them moved to Kenora in 1897, Pastor Stolberg came from Winnipeg to organize the Lakeside Baptist congregation.[111] Ten years later, when some of them moved to Norris Lake,[112] Pastor Fred Palmborg, known as Canada's Apostle, organized the congregation there.

In 1896 a congregation had been organized south of Scandinavia, but still within the colony's original four townships, which became known as Hilltop Baptist. The following year the men cut enough logs to saw into lumber and shingles to build a church, which they whitewashed inside and out.[113] During services the men sat on one side of the church, with women and children on the other, until one of the women objected to caring for her children alone. With the threat that she would no longer attend under these conditions, the seating arrangement changed so that families could worship together.[114]

The farming community of Kipling, midway between Sudbury and North Bay, was founded by Swedes from Svartvik and Alnö parishes, near Sundsvall on the Baltic coast. Many residents were Baptists, and in 1901 decided to join the Baptist Convention of Ontario and Quebec. The following year Rev H.L. Thomas of First Baptist Church, North Bay, organized the Kipling Scandinavian Baptist congregation and baptized several people in Deer Lake. The log church built beside the lake doubled as a meeting place, community hall, and school. The tight little community carried on Swedish customs and language for many years, mostly connected with the church.[115]

In 1907 Swedish Baptists divided themselves into two conferences, one called Central Canada (Saskatchewan, Manitoba, and northern Ontario) and the other Alberta (British Columbia and Alberta). At this time there were seventeen congregations with 372 baptized members.[116]

In 1914 Swedish Baptist congregations were located at Matsqui, Metiskow, Vancouver, and Victoria in British Columbia; Camrose, Crooked Lake, Edmonton, Ferintosh, Hughenden, Meeting Creek,

New Norway, Water Glen, and Wetaskiwin in Alberta; Biggar, Canwood, Earl Grey, Govan, Killam, Midale, Regina, Saskatoon, Stockholm, Verwood, Wadena, and Weyburn in Saskatchewan; Brandon, Hilltop, Teulon, and Winnipeg in Manitoba; and Kenora, Kipling, and Port Arthur in Northwestern Ontario.[117] Of these, Meeting Creek, Stockholm, and Winnipeg supported Lutheran and Covenant congregations as well.

In 1925, because they had become suspicious of the orthodoxy of Brandon College graduates, Swedish Baptists held their first Bible Institute in Wetaskiwin in an attempt to train young people for the ministry. Within seven years the initiative had grown to become the Alberta Baptist Bible Academy. Courses were in English, of nine weeks' duration, and based on a four-year high school program that allowed credits towards a degree from Bethel Seminary in Minneapolis. However, the school did not last. By 1929 Swedish Baptists were already voting to join English-speaking congregations, and it was not long before the Canadian conferences dropped the word "Swedish" from their names.[118] Despite the fact that the annual report for 1942–3 listed twenty-one Swedish Baptist congregations from Alberta to Northwestern Ontario,[119] the writing was on the wall. Today there are no active Swedish Baptist congregations in Canada.

Other Religions

Although most immigrants who attended religious services chose from among the three Swedish-speaking churches, some adopted the religion of their spouse. Others turned to existing English-language denominations, the Anglican Church and the Congregationalist and Presbyterian churches. Baptist congregations were the first to adopt English officially in 1929, with Augustana following suit in 1934, although many congregations chose a more gradual change. Some Lutheran churches maintain a Swedish link today, especially in those cities that experienced immigration after the Second World War, but in many other congregations the ethnic focus has been diluted over time.

Canada's first known Swedish immigrant, Rev Paulus Bryzelius,[120] was a minister. He came from the United States to Lunenburg, Nova Scotia, in 1767, the year of his ordination in London by the Church of England. Formerly ordained both as a Moravian and a German Lutheran, he came originally to serve Lunenburg's German Lutherans. However, they found him too "high church" and sacked him.

St John's Anglican Church caught him on the rebound. The congregation was very pleased, and his sermons in English and German "moved
many to shed tears."[121] He died on Good Friday, 1773, and was buried
beneath the pulpit.[122] His American wife and nine children remained in
Lunenburg, and numerous descendants still live in Nova Scotia.[123] Even
so, the surname of Canada's first Swedish immigrant has not survived.

Another Swedish Moravian, Johannes Lundberg,[124] lived in Labrador
from 1811 to 1850 as a missionary. The Moravian Church had begun its
mission to the Inuit at Nain in 1777. Lundberg was ordained in 1821,
and seven years later became Moderator of Missions with headquarters
in Nain. In Labrador he served on the Okak Islands from 1816 to 1819,
and during this time Lundberg Island began appearing on maps, only
to be replaced later by the original Inuit name. Moravian congregations
are still active in Labrador.

Early Lutheran congregations without a pastor sometimes called on an
Anglican minister for special occasions. In 1897 Canon Wharton Gill of
Minnedosa arrived in Scandinavia to officiate at a wedding. A subdued
congregation overflowed the church while the canon intoned a prayer and
delivered a short sermon in English, interspersed with Swedish hymns,
before the solemn ceremony.[125] After the benediction everybody moved
outside, and the mood changed to one of gaiety. Rows of linen-covered
tables beneath the trees were spread with a "bountiful yet simple repast."
As the canon was leaving, after performing several baptisms, he could hear
in the distance "sounds of laughter and faint strains of [dance] music."

Swedes in Haileybury, Ontario, registered their official acts in the
Anglican Church at first, but in 1915 marriage entries began appearing in the records of the Cobalt-Haileybury Scandinavian Presbyterian
Mission. The congregation had acquired a Presbyterian church built at
the turn of the century, which became known as the Swedish Presbyterian Church. The building was destroyed by fire in 1922[126] and there
is no further information about the congregation. In 1923 mainstream
Presbyterians, at least some of them, joined with Methodists and Congregationalists to form the United Church of Canada.

The Chicago Theological Seminary (Congregational) had a Swedish
department from 1885 to 1916, so that Swedes in Waterville, Quebec,
were able to attend Swedish services and Sunday school in the existing
Congregational church.[127] Mr C.O. Swanson had already held positions
as church trustee and as municipal councillor by 1892 when he was
appointed Dominion immigration agent, with the Wetaskiwin area as
a major destination.

Like his predecessor, immigration agent Öhlén, Swanson had a religious colony in mind from the beginning. He asked Anton Andreason, a lay preacher with a good command of English, to gather together a group large enough to start a church in Alberta.[128] As a result the nucleus for New Sweden Mission (Covenant) Church, built in 1896, came from the Swedish Congregational Church in Worcester, Massachusetts,[129] the rest from neighbouring communities and also directly from Sweden. Through Swanson's influence the Canada Congregational Missionary Society paid part of the pastor's salary.[130] The church building doubled as a school for two winters, when the congregation sat on benches provided by the school board. Shortly afterwards Swanson donated pews from the Congregational church in Waterville, which had replaced its small church with a larger one.[131]

The New Sweden Church served members on both sides of the Battle River, although there was no bridge. A visitor in 1896 described the ford crossing: "Even though the water reached up to the sides of our kind horses and produced a strong current, there was no other choice. Into the river we must go and thanks to these patient draught animals the journey went well. But the robust Newfoundland dog which faithfully followed us had a much harder time to cross."[132] In 1903 those living on the east side of the river built a sister church, which became Malmo Mission Covenant Church.

Pastor G.A. Sanden was the glue that held these congregations together during the early years, along with Bethel in Highland Park.[133] It is fair to say that Swanson achieved his goal of founding a religious colony southeast of Wetaskiwin. Although New Sweden, Malmo, and Highland Park no longer exist as place names, the region has become part of Alberta's Bible Belt. It is also fair to say that Öhlén accomplished his goal in New Stockholm. The community became home to three Swedish congregations instead of just one.

Pentecostals held services under several names. Ed and Augustine Hallgren[134] are credited with founding the Pentecostal Gospel Chapel in Sylvan Lake, Alberta, along with two other couples. Pastor C.O. Nordin[135] served from 1916 to 1957, and in 1935–6 was the first Canadian to attend an early conference of the Fellowship of Christian Assemblies in the United States. At that time he came from Amisk, Alberta.

The Salvation Army began serving Logan Avenue in Winnipeg in 1908 from a new and impressive two-storey brick building with the Swedish words "SKAND. FRÄLSNINGS ARMÉN" (Scandinavian Salvation Army) prominently displayed on the façade.[136] Members included Einar Walberg,[137] drummer in the Salvation Army Swedish Corps Band, who married in a Salvation Army ceremony in 1924. Currently the Salvation Army offers an international Family Tracing Service, with more than twenty offices in Canada alone.[138] This service is widely used in Sweden.

Swedish immigrants also became Mormons, Jehovah's Witnesses, Seventh Day Adventists, and Buddhists. In 1887 Charles Ora Card was sent to Canada to establish a Mormon colony along Lee's Creek in southern Alberta, and it was named Cardston in his honour. The Church of Jesus Christ of Latter-day Saints, as it was called, had actively recruited members in Sweden to come to Utah, and some eventually crossed the border into Canada. Among them was homesteader Johannes Anderson,[139] a member of the church's High Council, and Hjaldermar Ostlund of the second generation,[140] who studied law at Osgoode Hall in Toronto and became the first Mormon in the British Empire to be made king's counsel. Cardston functioned as the Alberta headquarters until 1895, when a second headquarters was established in Raymond. A temple built in Cardston in 1913 still stands.

Some of the Swedish families who settled near Calmar, Alberta, belonged to the International Bible Students Association or Watchtower movement, now known as Jehovah's Witnesses. They met weekly in each other's homes until erecting a meeting house in 1912. A new Kingdom Hall was built after the first one was destroyed by fire in 1945.[141]

The first settlers in Bergland, Ontario, M.A. Andersson[142] and his wife, Kristina, were Seventh Day Adventists and held services in their home every Saturday. Andersson had emigrated from Värmland to Minnesota during the 1880s, married there, and in 1901 brought the family to Bergland. There he homesteaded, operated a store, and cut and sold firewood to the steamboats plying the Rainy River, an occupation that cost him a hand. He lived his last years in the Seventh Day Adventist Home in Winnipeg.

In 1966 seventy-one-year-old John Bergenham[143] was invited to attend a special event at the Buddhist Church in Taber, Alberta, despite the long journey from his home in Moberly, British Columbia. He and his sister Caroline lived in the family home, making regular donations to the Buddhist cause. After serving in the First World War John returned to the homestead, where he and his sister cared for their widowed mother until her death in 1965 at age 104. Both siblings would also live to that ripe old age.

In 1973 John and Caroline Bergenham donated 202 hectares of land to the province, to be used as a wildlife sanctuary, in return for being able to live out their lives in the squared timber house built by their father in 1913. "The animals brought up my family on this place," explained John, "so what's left of the family is giving the land back to the animals – that's only fair."[144] The family would have starved had they not put wildlife on the table during the hungry pioneer years. Today Kootenay Management Unit's Region 4 cares for the Bergenham and Moberly Marsh Wildlife Sanctuary.

Emanuel Swedenborg,[145] who founded Swedenborgianism during the 1700s, is better known in other countries than in his birthplace of Sweden. Credited as having one of the highest intelligence levels in the world, he spent the first half of his career in Europe as a leading scholar, statesman, and scientist. A prolific author, he published his findings in Latin, one of the eight languages he spoke and wrote fluently, and in many more volumes after he developed a new form of Christianity in 1752. By the time he died thirty years later he had devoted followers in Sweden, France, the Netherlands, and England. Those influenced by his writings include August Strindberg, Charles Beaudelaire, and Elizabeth Barrett Browning. In contemporary Canada there are Swedenborgian congregations in Dawson Creek, Kelowna, Vancouver, Calgary, Edmonton, Grande Prairie, Rosthern, Saskatoon, Winnipeg, Kitchener, and Toronto.

The early Lutheran and Covenant churches, and to a lesser extent Baptist churches, were bastions of the Swedish language and culture, and therefore helped to cushion the culture shock felt by all immigrants. On the other hand, because they depended upon the United States for pastors and religious publications, parishioners were affected by the politics and procedures of both countries instead of just one. In the United States the Society for the Preservation of Swedishness in America, an offshoot of the Society for the Preservation of Swedish Culture in Foreign Lands, was founded in 1910 to work through the Augustana Synod.[146] It never became a strong movement, partly because Swedish nationalism already existed in the United States, but in a different form.

However, a surge of Swedish-American pride had flowed into Canada through the Augustana Synod already in 1904. That year Winnipeg's Zion Church organized three festivities to commemorate first the Old Country and the Delaware colony, then Gustav II Adolf, who reigned at the beginning of Sweden's Age of Greatness, and finally the death of Karl XII in 1718, which marked its end. The Mission Covenant Church, following Zion's lead, also arranged a memorial celebration. However, Canada's contribution to the Delaware Jubilee in 1938 can only be described as "meagre." At this point in time Canada's Swedes were more interested in surviving the Depression than in celebrating another country's past.

Swedish immigrants founded congregations and built churches in a hundred or more communities, despite being a scattered and mobile population living in an area much larger than Sweden, and with limited means of transportation. One cannot help but admire their dedication, especially at a time when they were busy establishing their own homes and farms. Those early churches still in existence provide a living testimony to their faith, which helped them to survive the drudgery and deprivations of pioneering and allowed them to enjoy a social life. Some of these churches still celebrate Swedish traditions, allowing modern descendants to experience the flavour of their religious heritage.

Chapter Six

World Wars

Swedish immigrants came from a country that had been at peace since 1815. A century later those who had been naturalized in Canada were asked, and later forced, to enlist in a European conflict. The reason was not easy for immigrants outside the Commonwealth to understand. Although many intellectuals, industrialists, and the upper class in Sweden were pro-German, most Swedish immigrants in Canada felt little or no sympathy one way or the other. Only a few showed pro-German feelings during the First World War (1914 to 1918), and virtually none during the Second World War (1939 to 1945).

First World War

Canada entered the First World War along with the rest of the British Empire on 4 August 1914, when Great Britain declared war on Germany and the Austro-Hungarian Empire. The economic depression of 1913 continued, with poor grain crops in 1914 and 1915 caused by droughts, resulting in railway layoffs and cutbacks in construction, which affected both rural and urban residents. Whether for economic reasons or because of the war some men returned to Sweden and even more crossed the international boundary to the United States.[1] In British Columbia, where the ratio of males to females was highest of all the western provinces at 4.55, a veritable flood crossed into Washington State.[2] Even in Manitoba, which had the lowest ratio at 1.33, Winnipeg's Swedish population dropped noticeably.[3] However, it is virtually impossible to determine the number of young men who returned to Sweden because of the war.[4]

Other Swedes had begun enlisting as soon as war was declared. Whether for economic, patriotic, or other reasons, more than 1,680 men born in Sweden signed up, 1,233 as volunteers and 447 as conscripts, and 122 of them made the supreme sacrifice.[5] Total enlistment in Canada was 600,000 men, of whom 60,000 lost their lives.

On the home front, Winnipeg Swedes demonstrated their loyalty by attending a meeting of naturalized citizens in November 1914, and by replacing the Swedish national anthem with Canada's "God Save the King," and even "Rule Britannia," at religious and secular events. Midsummer festivities were cancelled the first summer of the war due to "difficult times,"[6] likely a response to the torpedoing of the passenger ship *Lusitania* by a German U-boat in May 1915. Of the 1,959 people aboard, 1,198 died.[7] Immigration from Sweden continued, but in greatly reduced numbers.[8]

By 1916 the economy had recovered and there was a shortage of manpower. The Imperial Munitions Board had become Canada's largest employer with a quarter-million workers in a total population of eight million people.

For some reason, perhaps to emphasize the patriotism of Scandinavians in a public way,[9] the minister of Public Works in Manitoba, an Icelander named Thomas H. Johnson, took the initiative earlier that year to create a Scandinavian battalion under the command of Colonel Olaf Albrechtson, a Dane. The goal was to recruit 1,100 Scandinavian officers and men. Shortly afterwards three Norwegians lobbied the federal government to set up a Scandinavian battalion under Lieutenant-Colonel A.G. Fonseca, a Spaniard. For some reason Ottawa gave Fonseca's 197th Battalion the nod and turned down the Honourable T.H. Johnson's application. The ensuing furor resulted in the official sanction of a second Scandinavian battalion, Albrechtson's 223rd, in March 1916.[10]

Among those who joined the 223rd Canadian-Scandinavian Overseas Battalion was Lieutenant Charles Avery Nord,[11] a veteran of the Boer War and a fifteen-year resident of South Africa. Of the 507 men and 17 officers who enlisted, only 69 were born in Sweden. The 197th Infantry Battalion "Vikings of Canada" raised 306 men and 9 officers, including 144 born in Sweden. The cap badge of the 197th was a Viking ship and a scroll bearing the words "Vikings of Canada," while the 223rd chose a Viking wearing a horned helmet superimposed on a maple leaf, with the words "Canadian Scandinavians" printed underneath.[12]

Other than those born in the other Nordic countries, North America, and the British Isles, recruits entered such birthplaces as Argentina, Bohemia, France, Galicia, Greece, Italy, Montenegro, Moravia, New Zealand, Russia, Serbia, Switzerland, and Tasmania,[13] suggesting that some were adventurers. One reason may be that Canadian soldiers

Cap badge of the 197th Battalion.

were considered well paid at $1.10 per day.[14] After basic training the men embarked from Halifax, the 197th in January 1917, and the 223rd the following May. Soldiers from both so-called battalions (neither was up to strength, either separately or combined) were absorbed into the Canadian Expeditionary Force upon arrival in England, and before the year was out both had been disbanded by Order-in-Council.

First- and second-generation Swedes are represented in cemeteries at the Somme, Vimy, and Ypres,[15] Canada's major battlegrounds, and in other places as well. Svea Stenberg received the dreaded telegram about her son Fritz, who was twenty-four, just as the war was ending:

Ottawa, Ont; Oct 11/18

Mrs. Alex Stenberg,
Gen. Delivery, Stockholm, Sask;
11159. Deeply regret inform you 1069249 Private Fritz Rangnard Stenberg, Mounted Services, officially reported killed in action, Sept 29th.

Director Records.[16]

Stark and impersonal. Not even signed with a name. Fritz Stenberg had joined up 19 December 1916 and spent a furlough at home in the fall of 1917. At this time he wrote in his diary, "Shot eleven ducks with 5 shells. Darn good shooting. Ducks very plentiful"; and "Hauled in my first three loads of hay, almost played me out"; and finally "Went down to the Lake and picked cranberries." His body lies in Raillencourt Communal Cemetery Extension in France, along with 187 other Canadian soldiers.

The renowned Swedish soldier of fortune, Ivor Thord-Gray,[17] touched the Canadian forces briefly as information officer in the fall of 1918 before heading off to the Siberian front. His tour in the British army from 1914 to 1917 earned him the rank of major, and he retired from the Russian front in 1919 as a major general. He had lived a charmed life, fighting in successive war zones since 1897, finally being wounded after more than twenty years in combat.

In 1914 Canada had invoked the *War Measures Act*, which gave the federal Cabinet unprecedented powers. "Foreigners" continued to be suspect, especially German immigrants who were classed as enemy aliens. Shortly after the declaration of war rowdies attacked the German and Austrian consulates in Winnipeg, vandalized the premises of the German club, and beat up German-speaking citizens. In response German immigrants maintained a low profile and banded together to help each other survive difficult times. Some lost their jobs; others presented themselves as Russians or Poles in order to keep working. Residents who were not naturalized were sent to internment camps, while the rest had to report monthly to a registration bureau. As enemy aliens all had to register their firearms, give prior notice of bank withdrawals, and submit to official searches of their clubs, churches, and bookstores.[18]

A Swedish visitor to Winnipeg wrote his impressions from the early war years: "War fever ... is running high among the English and French-Canadians. So much so that it is a risk to one's life to dare utter a pro-German opinion ... Patriotism, really it is hating Germany, is egged on and supported by the [English language] newspapers with words and posters ... In one window there was a German helmet on display and a notice signed Canuck soldier, as the Canadian soldiers were called. The Notice read 'This helmet belonged to one of the Huns [Germans] who I had the pleasure of killing.'"[19]

The anti-German hysteria even affected sauerkraut, which could be purchased only under the name "victory cabbage."[20] And in 1916 the city of Berlin, Ontario, felt compelled to change its name to that of Great Britain's secretary of state for war and a veteran of the Boer War, Lord

Kitchener, who died that year. Despite the hysteria, no German resident in Canada was ever found guilty of sabotage. When all was said and done they had never posed a significant military threat.[21]

Germans were subjected to official discrimination, but all immigrants suffered the unofficial kind from acquaintances and strangers, businesses and employers, because of war hysteria. Swedes were targeted because they were considered pro-German and therefore disloyal. Individuals, groups, and families often met with suspicion, either overt or hidden. In January 1915 Swedes and Norwegians in Winnipeg banded together to form the Scandinavian Central Committee to help the poor and sick. Funds were raised through annual folk festivals, and food and clothing through public appeals. Evidently discrimination was already being felt, causing *Svenska Canada-tidningen* to remark, "The time of affliction has not been wasted because it has awakened the feeling of kinship and responsibility in our hearts."[22]

Sweden's wartime politics and trade policies gave critics good reason to label the country "pro-German." Highly placed German sympathizers included members of the ruling Conservative party, the military élite, and King Gustaf V.[23] The queen, Victoria of Baden, was a granddaughter of Kaiser Wilhelm I and honorary colonel of a German regiment. Openly pro-German, she wielded considerable influence over her husband.[24] In addition the Luxburg affair of September 1917 received a high profile in the English-language press, for political reasons. The British had intercepted and deciphered a diplomatic cable, sent with permission over Swedish lines, in which the German minister in Argentina suggested that two Argentinian ships en route to Europe with supplies should be sunk without a trace.[25] The fallout from this and other press reports spilled over onto Swedes in Canada.

Censorship officials kept a close watch on Independent Order of Good Templars (IOGT) members, supporters of temperance, because many were socialists and embraced pacifism.[26] The book *War, What For?*, published in Ohio in 1913, was prohibited as "a [Socialist] tirade against all things military and particularly detrimental to the progress of recruiting." The Royal North West Mounted Police supervised investigation of Saskatchewan residents Severt and Thomas Swanson[27] for distributing the book, despite a letter from the chief press censor describing it as "most objectionable but nothing to justify taking action." After being under investigation for more than two years the brothers were finally cleared of "alleged sedition," but only after their premises had been entered under a search warrant.[28]

In another instance the commissioner of customs forwarded one of 760 copies of foreign-language material to the chief press censor for clearance in 1918. "It may not be in an enemy language," he wrote, "but does it contain objectionable matter?" The shipment was clearly addressed to Rev L. Heiner, Camrose, Alberta. The publication in question was the minutes of the previous Swedish Lutheran conference held at Dubuc, published by Augustana Book Concern in Rock Island, Illinois.[29]

The postmaster general was responsible for censorship of mail, with investigations carried out by the chief commissioner of Dominion police in Ottawa, Sir Percy Sherwood. The following excerpt translated from a letter from James Olson of Tanglefoot, British Columbia, to Nils Olson, Offerdal, Jämtland, merited official correspondence in January 1918: "Here is lots of trouble now, as they take people to France to fight the Germans. England has all it can do now; it is only England that gets licked as they have done nothing else than make trouble for others. England wants to be regarded as the best country on earth, but it is the poorest, because here one cannot talk much about England."[30] Olson's letter languished in the Dead Letter Office, pending Sir Percy's review.

The above examples were hardly treasonous, yet they illustrate the overbearing and pompous attitude of officials, who were often inept, and the intimidating nature of investigations carried out under the *War Measures Act*. Obviously the harassment affected immigrants adversely, especially those who were not yet fluent in English. In 1916 a Saskatchewan police inspector wrote in a report that "Swedes and Danes are all pro-German and utterly disloyal to this country."[31] That his basic premise was widespread seems likely, given the tenor of the times.

Socialists and members of IOGT were among those who opposed the conscription law passed in July 1917. Some Swedes moved to the United States in protest, even though that country had entered the war the previous April. For his part editor Brown ran an article in *Svenska Canada-tidningen* on how to regain Swedish citizenship[32] because citizens of Sweden were not subject to call-up. In at least two instances a consular official wrote a letter confirming a young man's Swedish birth to keep him from being conscripted. One young man was seventeen and would be of recruitment age on his next birthday.[33] The other was twenty-six, with a wife and child still in Sweden.[34]

Swedes were highly indignant over the disenfranchisement of Germans and Austrians naturalized since 1902, a draconian law passed under the *War-time Elections Act*. The timing, just prior to the federal election of 17 December 1917, seemed to favour the return to power of Borden's Conservatives.[35] The openly discriminatory ban also affected Swedes who went to vote, many of them Liberals, as noted earlier. Brown justified his paper's response in a letter to the chief press censor:

> The authors of these articles, Mr. K.R. Jonson of Buford, Alberta, and Mr. A. Nylund of Shaunavon, Sask. are respectable Swedish farmers and far from pro-German ... Regarding Mr. Jonson's article entitled "The Rights of Foreigners," it criticizes the "War time Election Act" [*sic*] and especially the way that Canadian citizens of Swedish origin were treated during the last Dominion election, this has also been criticized in several other papers. In many places everything was done to keep the Swedes from voting and it even occurred that old, highly esteemed Swedes was refused to vote, and their Canadian citizen papers were treated as "scraps of paper."[36]

It seems clear that individual discrimination was based for the most part on Sweden's wartime relationship with Germany, and that the Canadian government did not target resident Swedes as a group.

Public opinion against Swedes manifested in violence after peace was signed on 11 November 1918. Soldiers came home to find few jobs available. This was partly because of the Imperial Munitions Board's factories being shut down, but hotheads hyped on aggressive Canadian nationalism blamed "foreigners." Canada's Swedish heartland, Logan Avenue in Winnipeg, became the first target of a mob of hooligans who destroyed property, overturned street cars, and broke into homes and assembly halls, forcing immigrants to kiss the Union Jack, the flag of Great Britain and Canada. The wartime sacrifices of individual Swedes did not matter; they had been condemned as a group, and police did not intervene.

The riot lasted two days, Sunday and Monday, 26 and 27 January. To Winnipeg Swedes this was the major happening of 1919, not the dramatic course of events played out during the General Strike that spring, in which Swedes were not centrally involved. The riot became a symbol of their "time of affliction" during the war.[37] Through no fault of their own Canada's Swedes had become a target for unaccustomed violence and derision.

By September 1918, when newspapers published in enemy alien languages were summarily banned, the government was already worried about a perceived Bolshevik (Communist) threat. The following month an

Order-in-Council prohibited meetings in the languages not only of countries Canada was at war with, but also of Ukraine, Russia, and Finland. In addition it named thirteen left-wing political groups as "unlawful associations." Their supporters, mostly immigrants, could be arrested without a warrant and imprisoned. The extraordinary power of the *War Measures Act* could now be wielded against both enemy aliens and Bolsheviks. The two had become synonymous. The *War Measures Act* continued in force until June 1920, more than a year and a half after the armistice, in order to deal with the post-war "Red Scare" that swept across North America. However, Canada's worst nativist riots against immigrants took place in Winnipeg,[38] starting with the incident on Logan Avenue.

The Spanish flu epidemic that followed the war was a disaster of staggering proportions. The flu claimed 50,000 lives in Canada, only 10,000 less than the number of military casualties. Most of the victims were young and healthy.[39] In Calmar Andrew and Sarah Westlund[40] lost their youngest daughter, Elvina, nineteen, and their only son, Albert, twenty-three, who was home on furlough. In an effort to keep the second death from the seriously ill mother downstairs, neighbours lowered Albert's body on planks from an upstairs window. They also restrained the grief-stricken father from shooting himself.

Eric and Minnie Lundstrom[41] died on their homestead near Battleford, Saskatchewan, leaving five children aged three to fourteen. The eldest, Carl, and Minnie's mother, fifty-nine, cared for them until they were grown. The Lindgren family[42] was decimated when the parents and eldest son died near Mulvihill, Manitoba. The four children, ages three to twelve, were separated and raised by different families. The epidemic lasted from September 1918 until late 1919, a time of fear and turmoil when the few who did not contract the disease tried to care for the sick and dying. As illustrated above, for some families the effects of the flu lasted far beyond the epidemic itself.

The war left its own legacy. Federal income tax, introduced as a temporary measure to fund the war effort, became a permanent fixture. The Royal Canadian Mounted Police owes its beginnings to shortcomings uncovered by the pressure of war. The force, formed in 1920 with the merger of the Royal North West Mounted Police and the Dominion Police, expanded former responsibilities to include federal law enforcement and national security. The federal government, having discovered its power under the *War Measures Act*, built on wartime methods of repression to counteract labour militancy and socialism. The crushing of Canada's first significant nation-wide challenge by the working class, the Winnipeg Strike of 1919, is a good example. Similar tactics would continue throughout the 1920s and 1930s.

Swedes were no more affected than the rest of the population by the war and the flu epidemic, grim as they were, but the ethnic discrimination and intimidation they experienced left lasting scars. Their "time of affliction" had culminated in a frenzied attack on Canada's Swedish heartland with no police protection for either people or property. For the first time, Swedes as a group were made to feel ashamed of their origin. Individuals responded by not openly opposing government restrictions, but instead, learning strategies to keep clear of compromising situations. They became defensive, avoiding contact with officialdom whenever possible. The immigrants who flooded into Canada during the 1920s would find countrymen with attitudes unlike any they had met in Sweden, although they themselves would not be significantly affected.

Spanish Civil War

A few idealists would volunteer in the Mackenzie-Papineau Battalion, "Mac-Paps" for short, to fight in the disastrous Spanish Civil War from 1936 to 1939. This conflict pitted the existing Spanish government, assisted by the Soviet Union and Mexico, against the rebels, who were supported by Germany, Italy, and Portugal. The conflict was seen as a struggle between the communist Soviet Union and fascist Italy and Germany, and ended with the fascist General Francisco Franco in power. An estimated 30,000 foreign nationals, most of them communists or trade unionists, fought in the International Brigades on the losing side.[43]

Of the 1,300 Canadians who joined the Mac-Paps, more than 400 died. Among the casualties were several Swedes, including Pete Nielson, one of the eight delegates for the On-to-Ottawa Trek. Osborn Johnson and Sten Udden of Port Arthur were wounded and returned to Sweden. Elis Frånberg was named as a potential spy for the Spanish government's secret police, but he deserted and escaped to Sweden before his spying career could begin.[44]

Harry Anderson, a steelworker from Quebec, joined the Communist Party in 1930, and the following year helped to organize the miners' strike in Estevan, Saskatchewan. He was among those who returned to Canada. Without pay he had fought on the side of a democratically elected government, yet received no official welcome home. Instead, in 1940 he was removed from his job as business manager for the Meat

Packers Union in Winnipeg and interned in Kananaskis, Camp Petawawa, and Hull jail.[45]

For veterans of the Spanish Civil War there was no Book of Remembrance, no Department of Veterans Affairs hospital, and no army pension. Communists raised money to repatriate survivors to Canada, where authorities interrogated them closely to make sure no aliens slipped into the country.[46] It was not until 2001 that a national monument to the Mac-Pap veterans was erected in Ottawa, although an earlier memorial existed in Victoria, British Columbia.

In retrospect the Spanish Civil War, with Germany providing airplanes, bombs, and tanks, was viewed as a rehearsal for the Second World War. Ironically, the reason for Canada's declaration of war 9 September 1939 was to continue the struggle against fascism, but on a much larger scale.

Second World War

The Second World War is generally credited with ending the Depression. Hungry men who had been riding the rods only a few months earlier in search of work were now in demand as soldiers. Rather than having to buy their own work clothes, and sometimes tools, they were given uniforms, guns, and enough money for tobacco with a bit left over. After basic training they rode to the east coast in comfortable passenger coaches, eating three square meals a day in the diner. These seasoned veterans of hardship were on their way to war, along with fresh-faced youths who had grown up in Canada. Immigration during the past decade had been negligible, yet 1,305 of those who joined the armed forces were Swedish-speaking, as seen in Table 6.1 on next page. The total would have been much higher if second- and third- generation Swedes who did not speak the language had been represented.

While Canadian troops were facing the enemy in Italy and France, on the North Atlantic and in the air, the Nordic countries were fighting battles of their own. Finland suffered invasion twice, first during the bitter Winter War with Russia from 1939 to 1940, and second during the Continuation War from 1941 to 1944, in which Germany provided troops and material support in its thrust against Russia. As a result Great Britain declared war against Finland, and Canada followed suit, severing diplomatic relations with that country. During the Winter War Sweden provided 8,000 volunteers for service and large quantities of arms and ammunition. Although Sweden did not support the Continuation War,

Table 6.1 Swedish speakers in the army, navy, and air force, according to province of enlistment.

	Army	Navy	Air Force	Total
British Columbia	152	17	27	196
Alberta	207	7	29	243
Saskatchewan	311	7	44	362
Manitoba	158	9	33	200
Ontario	229	24	22	275
Quebec	7	2	3	12
Maritimes	12	–	2	14
Outside Canada	–	–	3	3
Total	1,076	66	163	1,305

Source: LAC, B2, volume 13A; "Canada totals from 551,273 Hollerith cards punched from occupational history forms coded to date to show by province of residence at enlistment, the languages other than English (and-or) French spoken by men in the Navy, Army and Air Force," and "Tabulations ... men in the army," "Tabulations ... men in the navy," and "Tabulations ... men in the air force." Thanks to archivist Myron Momryk for bringing these files to my attention.

it accepted 70,000 Finnish children who moved to relative safety across the Baltic to live in private homes.

Sweden became an oasis in the midst of chaos in April 1940, when Germany invaded Denmark and Norway. In June the Norwegian government fled to London, England. Sweden was pressured to allow German goods and soldiers on leave to travel on its railways to and from Norway, and in 1941 permitted an entire German division to pass through on its way to Finland, among other concessions. At the same time Sweden helped its neighbour by supplying food, hospital supplies, and other necessities. Hundreds of young Norwegians were trained as post-war police, or sent to Camp Little Norway near Toronto to learn to be fighter pilots. By 1943 there were 400,000 German troops in Norway, but as the tide of war began to turn Sweden tightened control over both its railways and its trade with Germany in ball bearings and iron ore.

Although Sweden's assistance to Germany was unpopular, it did not foster discrimination in Canada as did the previous war. In 1944 the Empire Club in Toronto invited Per Wijkman, a former consul general sometimes called Canada's first Swedish ambassador, to speak about Sweden's relationship with the British Empire. His speech gave a

detailed account of the war from Sweden's point of view, as well as noting shared events throughout history, such as the epic poem *Beowulf*.[47]
The same year a high-profile article published in *Maclean's* magazine
told of a British air force officer shot down over the ocean and rescued
by Swedes, titled "The Swedes Are Our Friends."[48]

Sweden's major contributions during the war were helping approximately 8,000 Jews to escape from Denmark to Sweden, accepting 35,000
refugees from Estonia, and the arranging by Count Folke Bernadotte
for the release of 19,000 Norwegian and Danish prisoners from German concentration camps.[49] In contrast Canada put the *War Measures
Act* in force again, and German, Ukrainian, Italian, and Japanese civilians were interned without trial, along with a few Swedes and others.
The government's response to the fall of Denmark and Norway was to
intern 400 more "enemy aliens."[50]

In Port Arthur Swedes, Finland Swedes, and Finns put on a concert
early in 1940 to raise money for the Finnish Red Cross.[51] These activities
would be curtailed when Finland sided with Germany in the Continuation War.[52] In Alberta a central committee of Swedish, Norwegian, and
Danish lodges quickly created a foundation for Norwegian relief, the
result of a 1938 meeting of 1,600 members of their respective orders
at Sylvan Lake.[53] The newspaper *Scandinavian News*, first published in
London, Ontario, then in Toronto, kept readers up to date on the war
situation from 1941 to 1945. Under the banner headline were the words
"For a free and independent Scandinavia," and featured top right was
an oversized "V" for Victory and below it the Morse code symbol: dot
dot dot dash.

Although the central committee in Alberta was very successful in
providing relief to Norway, ethnic cooperation in British Columbia did
not produce significant results. The Scandinavian Central Committee
had been founded in Vancouver in 1936 as an umbrella group to coordi-
nate activities among fourteen clubs representing Swedes, Norwegians,
Danes, Icelanders, and Finns. The group donated to the Red Cross and
the Blood Donor drive, and also purchased a war bond, but there is
no indication that it supported Norway during its German occupation.
Instead, its energies seemed to focus on political wrangling.[54]

"The minister of everything," C.D. Howe, mobilized Canada for war.
Under his guiding hand industry expanded enormously to supply not
only guns and small arms, but also airplanes, military vehicles, and
ships, more than half of them ordered by Great Britain. For the first
time women were hired on a large scale to work in factories. Swedes

included Signe Parke,[55] a riveter at Boeing in Vancouver, and Christina Sundberg,[56] a welder at Canadian Car & Foundry in Fort William, which built Hurricanes and Helldivers.

Wartime brought restrictions. For example, the post office was not allowed to send postal money orders overseas; therefore, the Nordstjärnan club in Edmonton was unable to pay its annual dues to Sweden's Society for the Preservation of Swedish Culture in Foreign Lands. Locally, motorists were restricted to a limit of thirty-two kilometres (twenty miles) from the city. The club was all set to turn down Herman Selin's[57] invitation to a weekend at Hay Lakes, about forty-eight kilometres away, when Herman eliminated the problem by arranging to meet them halfway with his truck.[58]

Many items were rationed, including meat. When Gust Freeberg[59] decided to slaughter a bull in December 1943, he had to get a permit from the Wartime Prices and Trade Board, and then provide meat coupons to cover the chilled weight of the meat sold. For personal use he had to register with the Local Ration Board, and turn coupons over to them. But Freeberg lived in Graham, a small railway village west of Thunder Bay, and opportunities to sell the meat were limited. In February he reported that if the local retailer did not buy what remained, the frozen meat would spoil with the onset of warm weather.

Like rationing, censorship of mail affected everybody, not just Swedes. Daniel Anderson[60] of Norquay, Saskatchewan, corresponded with his brother Albert in Sweden from 1929 to 1967, an unbroken succession of letters except for the years 1941 to 1944, which are missing. Two envelopes dated 1945 are stamped "OPENED BY EXAMINER," and the letters are marked with thick vertical lines, making them difficult to read.[61] It seems as though Daniel's contact with Sweden was severed during the war years.

The United States entered the war in December 1941, after the Japanese bombed Pearl Harbor. Fear of a Japanese invasion of Alaska sparked construction in 1942–3 of the preliminary road that became the Alaska Highway. Completed in just eight months, it ran from Dawson Creek, British Columbia, to Big Delta, Alaska, a distance of 2,333 kilometres, and was extended to Fairbanks the following year. An estimated 27,000 soldiers and civilians were involved in the project, including contractor Emil Anderson[62] of Fort William, who moved his company to British Columbia on the strength of a sixteen-kilometre contract.

Einar Eng[63] was responsible for warehouses from Dawson Creek to Fort Nelson, and his wife, Myrtle, a cook, eventually became head chef in Fort St John. One day in 1944, shortly after the arrival of a new commanding officer, she noticed that the Canadian flag, at that time the Red Ensign, was not flying beside the United States flag as usual. Upon enquiring, the officer told her that the highway and right-of-way were American territory by treaty and therefore merited only one flag. Myrtle responded that there would be no food for American soldiers until the Canadian flag was reinstated. She won the day.

The war years were exciting times for pilots. In 1943 Albin Hagglund, editor of *Canada posten*, wrote an article titled "How the Swedish People Co-operate" for the *Winnipeg Tribune*'s Unity Within Variety series.[64] The article featured a photo of himself in uniform and another of the five Stahlbrand brothers of Montreal, all of whom enlisted in the Royal Canadian Air Force (RCAF).[65] Donald Carlson,[66] son of Baptist minister Gustav Carlson of Wetaskiwin, joined the RCAF as chaplain, despite, or perhaps because of, two older brothers having been wounded in the First World War.[67] A grandson, Alan Carlson, won the Distinguished Flying Cross. Clarence Lundeen[68] of Preeceville, Saskatchewan, won both the Distinguished Flying Cross and the Distinguished Flying Medal.

The British Commonwealth Air Training Plan had designated Canada to train fliers because it was located outside the war theatre. At its peak almost 1,500 aircrew graduated each month under the plan, but a gradual reduction began in 1943. One of the flight instructors in Fort William, Oscar Sideen, invented a device to demonstrate the physical intricacies of an aircraft caught in a tailspin. It should come as no surprise that some of the trainees were involved in crash landings.[69]

Nurse Ally Malmborg[70] joined the No. 5 Canadian General Medical Corps based in Taplow, England, at a military hospital built by the Canadian Red Cross. In 1943 she was sent to Algiers to care for patients in a British hospital of makeshift canvas, travelling by ship. The trip both ways was harrowing because of enemy aircraft flying overhead. Others who survived the war were Martin Sandberg,[71] whose marriage disintegrated during his absence, and Valfrid Lundgren,[72] who, after discharge, migrated back to Sweden, where he delighted in showing off his "battledress."

Those who did not return included Georg Nilsson,[73] killed at Juno Beach on D-Day, and his buddy Harvey Nystrom,[74] who survived Juno Beach to die four days later. The aforementioned O.G. Johnson[75] of Newfoundland lost two sons in the war. Ludvig De Geer,[76] a member of the Swedish nobility who was raised in pulp-mill towns across Canada, was killed in France. He was the only son of engineer Gerhard De Geer, who had come to Saint John, New Brunswick, in 1905.

The war in Europe ended on 7–8 May 1945, VE Day, and VJ Day followed before the end of summer. Out of a population of 11.5 million, more than a million Canadians had enlisted in the three armed forces. Of these, 42,042 lost their lives, compared with 60,661 in the earlier conflict. Men who had been conscripted towards the end of the war, conscientious objectors or so-called zombies,[77] were the last to be demobilized. A group from Camp Shilo, including at least one Swede, got their share of war-like conditions on 7 August, when a terminal grain elevator beside them exploded from internal combustion. They had been posted to Port Arthur to help unload grain cars, and were sitting on the grass beside Pool 4, waiting for the next set of cars to be brought forward.

Suddenly a deafening roar filled the air along with giant slabs of concrete falling on the empty cars, crushing them flat. The tops of three bins from a neighbouring elevator, Pool 5, had blown off and the walls of the workhouse, 54.9 metres above the ground, had blown out, sending tonnes of debris raining down from above. By the time firefighters and police arrived the conscripts had climbed to the top of Pool 4 and had thrown a rope to an injured worker on Pool 5. He managed to catch it, pull over a thicker rope, and anchor it to a large pipe, while one of the Swedish conscripts, Verner Loov, winched it tight. One after another they crossed the chasm hand over hand.

Then the men had to climb up a scorched rope to reach the dead and injured: "One body had a concrete post lying over it. As we lifted that post my foot broke through the debris a little and we could hear the pieces hitting down below. We were on top of an empty bin, which was about 90 feet to the bottom! One fellow we found was buried to his neck in wheat, which was on fire, smoldering, so he was being cooked alive. Another man was skewered with a reinforcing rod from the concrete so evidently he did not survive. I never knew which of the people we lowered over the side survived."[78]

The death toll numbered twenty-six. While police and others took the injured to hospital, the conscripts climbed down a long ladder set up by the firemen. This day had proven that they were not cowards; they just didn't like the idea of having to kill people.

For Canada's Swedes, the two world wars were quite different from each other. The 1914 to 1918 conflict was characterized by discrimination on the home front: the formation of two Scandinavian battalions, some pro-German and anti-British sentiment, harassment by officials, and a nativist riot on Logan Avenue. None of these impulses was present in the Second World War. Instead, Swedes cooperated with other Scandinavians to send aid to occupied Nordic countries, and with other Canadians to defend their world against fascism. Reasons for the change in attitude between the two conflicts are many-faceted, but somewhere along the line immigrants and their descendants had been transformed from Swedes living in Canada into Canadians of Swedish descent.[79] The levelling that took place during the Depression played a part in this acculturation, as well as the dearth of new immigrants during that decade. Nationalism also played a significant role. Canadians looked forward to the loosening of ties with Great Britain, especially since Canada had emerged from the war with the national pride and confidence that befitted an independent country.

Chapter Seven

The Swedish Press

Widespread literacy among immigrants suggests that Swedish-language newspapers played an important role in Canada. The press not only helped with language retention and kept readers informed about events here and in the Old Country, but also confirmed their ethnicity and sense of belonging to a group. Newspapers reflected both the areas and eras of major concerns: religion, temperance, politics, business, and social life. However, most of them, like *Canada-tidningen* in Winnipeg and *Svenska Pressen* in Vancouver, had to struggle for financial survival. The reality of a large country with a scattered and relatively small number of Swedes, plus competition from similar publications in the United States, prevented the development of an adequate subscriber base.

Winnipeg

Beginnings

Canada's first Swedish-language newspaper, *Den skandinaviske canadiensaren* (The Scandinavian Canadian), was established in September 1887 by Winnipeg's immigration agent, Emanuel Öhlén. It functioned both as a publication of the Mission Covenant Church and as the federal government's monthly "immigrant brochure," because Öhlén had arranged with the Department of Agriculture for its distribution in Scandinavia and the United States.[1] Official funding came to an end two years later, in September 1889.

In January 1891 Öhlén sold his paper to John E. Forslund of the Canadian Pacific Railway's immigration department, who continued to focus on attracting immigrants. The following May the federal government bought 10,000 copies for distribution in Scandinavia and the United States.[2] Photographs of Canadian scenes had been added, along with the familiar advertising, notices, letters to the editor, and society news. In 1892–3, C.O. Hofstrand continued the Mission Covenant focus as editor.[3]

Canada's second Swedish-language newspaper, *Sions väktare* (Guardian of Zion), was also a religious monthly, having been founded in 1892 by the new Lutheran pastor, Svante Uddén. Since Uddén represented the Augustana Lutheran Church the two papers were in direct competition to each other and, according to one observer, "were conducted with a genuine theological hatred."[4]

In 1894 Konstantin Flemming,[5] a typographer, took over Uddén's paper, renamed it *Väktaren* (The Guardian), and transformed it into a secular weekly. The two men became business partners and together bought Canada's first Swedish print shop.[6] The following year Flemming incorporated both papers, *Väktaren* and the faltering *Skandinaviske canadiensaren*, into a secular weekly called *Canada*, which functioned from 1895 to 1907.

Flemming was described as "a good journalist with a humorous pen."[7] His paper reflected the times by focussing not so much on attracting immigrants as familiarizing those already here with their new country and its institutions.[8] Included in the masthead in 1896 were the words "The only Swedish Weekly Newspaper in the Dominion of Canada." Under Flemming's management *Canada* became a Liberal newspaper, employing a succession of publishers and editors[9] until 1907, when he left and the name changed to *Svenska Canada-tidningen* (The Swedish Newspaper in Canada). It would become one of Canada's major Swedish newspapers.

Canada Posten

In 1904 the Mission Covenant pastor in Winnipeg, J.M. Florell, revived the congregation's religious paper by publishing *Canada posten* (The Canada Post) twice a month to give moral instruction to believers. The following year he became full-time editor of a new *Canada posten*,[10] a Christian weekly with paid subscriptions, backed by the Swedish-Canadian Publishing Company in its new building across from the church. After a year Florell returned to Minnesota, and Andrew Hallonquist, merchant and immigration officer, became president and business manager.[11] His grandson, Bill Hallonquist, described him as "a strict and religious man, a reformist Lutheran who encouraged dozens of other Scandinavians to emigrate ... [and tried] to convert them to his Church."[12] The paper had only two owners, Andrew Hallonquist and his son Ernest, who likely subsidized the paper because it ceased publication with the latter's death in 1952.[13] Editors of *Canada posten* included C.O. Hofstrand (ten years), Adolph Liljengren (from 1919 to 1922), and, lastly, Albin Hagglund.[14] Peter Ringwall from Red Deer Lake, Alberta, was a regular contributor, under the byline "Från Stugan och Sjöstranden" (From the Cottage and the Beach).[15]

Svenska Canada-tidningen before the First World War

In 1909 *Svenska Canada-tidningen* moved its office from Fountain Street to Logan Avenue. The number of advertisers was 241, double that of two years earlier, most of them from non-Swedish Winnipeg firms. The geographic spread of the rest mirrored Swedish immigration from northern Ontario to the Pacific Ocean.[16] At the same time the growing market, particularly for work clothing, encouraged firms to hire Swedish-speaking clerks and to add a Swedish translation to their advertising in mainline newspapers.[17]

Svenska Canada-tidningen promoted a sense of Swedishness by publishing historical articles and poems about Sweden's Age of Greatness, and about current events with news and editorial comments about political and cultural life in the Old Country, sometimes adding national rhetoric to the local news. The emphasis on Swedishness was especially evident under editors from the United States, such as C. Albin Jones, whereas the editor from 1910 to 1912, B. Enström from Sweden, stressed the current scene in Swedish culture. As a result historian Lars Ljungmark found the keen interest in author August Strindberg "stunning if compared to the literary lagging behind of the Swedish-American cultural environment of the same time period."[18]

Financial problems continued to plague a succession of publishers[19] until 1913, when P.M. Dahl, publisher of the Norwegian weekly *Norrøna*, took over. Dahl was described as "a Swedish-ized Norwegian, a resilient and cunning businessman with thick skin and a conniving personality."[20] His first editor was Nils F:son (Fredriksson) Brown,[21] a young journalist with three years' experience at *Svenska amerikanska posten* in Minneapolis. It was he who bore the brunt of censorship during the First World War.

Censorship

Brown's ordeal began with the appointment in 1915 of the zealous chief press censor Major Ernest J. Chambers, who devoted most of his attention to foreign-language newspapers. If he had his way they would all be shut down, but that power rested with his superior, the Secretary of State.[22] Nevertheless, Chambers gave the impression that he had sole authority, and an unsolicited letter from him struck terror into every editor's heart. Brown's first letter asked permission to reprint an official report already published in a Swedish-American newspaper, concerning a German U-boat's first trip. The request was curtly denied a week later as follows, "I received the translator's report ... on no consideration can I consent to publication."[23]

Publishing a pro-German article in the column "Farmare och filosof" (Farmer and Philosopher) earned Brown an official visit in April 1917 from the press censor for western Canada, Frederick Livesay, followed by a severe letter from Chambers. Rudolf Einhardt,[24] a Saskatchewan farmer with a university degree, wrote the column, but this did not free Brown from responsibility. Accordingly he and Dahl visited Livesay's Winnipeg office, apologized for the slip, and produced back issues in which Einhardt's earlier columns had been accompanied by editorial comment. They also turned over a translation of the most recent editorial, severing ties with Einhardt.[25]

Brown mistakenly thought Chambers was objecting to his strongly worded critique about Fritz Kilman, a recent immigrant imprisoned for pro-German sympathies: "Shortly after joining the 38th Battalion in 1914, a 'drunken' army doctor 'forcefully' injected him with an unnamed substance, which left Kilman partly paralyzed. Three weeks later, he was arrested without explanation, interned, and informed that he was under suspicion of being a German spy. He was only rescued from this 'barbaric treatment' after spending six months in internment and following intervention from the Swedish and Danish consulates."[26]

Nor did the chief press censor take issue with his racist attack against the English: "The English bullying and conceit, by which they act as if they were superior to the Swedish race, has a bad influence on the Swedes ...The English in Canada hate the Swedes, because the words 'I am a Swede' are passwords for employment, and the English do not, of course, enjoy being turned down when a Swede is hired."[27]

Instead, Chambers seems to have targeted *Svenska Canada-tidningen* for indications of anything less than wholehearted support for the allied war effort, which did not reflect the feelings of many readers. Brown had to walk a fine line in order to keep subscribers and advertisers happy. The very survival of the paper depended upon it. Already in 1915 he had pleaded for payment of subscriptions so that the paper could cover pressing debts.[28]

After a personal interview in August 1917, Chambers described Brown as "a morose type of an individual who listened to what I had to say but had very little to say for himself except to briefly claim that he had been doing his best to observe the censorship requirements." Their strained relationship may well have influenced Brown's fundamental change in political beliefs, from liberal to socialist, during his stay in Canada.[29] Chambers continued to take the paper to task for pro-German references even after the war was over, and, subsequent to the Russian Revolution in 1917, began objecting to Bolshevik articles as well.

Censors did not have serious objections to the Mission Covenant's *Canada posten* or the Norwegian paper *Norrøna*, even though the latter was a labour paper during the years 1910 to 1920 with Brown as editor from 1917 to 1919.[30] However, in August 1918 both *Svenska Canada-tidningen* and the temperance paper *Idog* (Industrious) fell afoul of Chambers's list of banned books, which included one published in England, titled *Victory and Defeat*. *Idog,* a short-lived publication sponsored by the Grand Lodge of the temperance group Independent Order of Good Templars (IOGT) in Winnipeg, with Alfred Egnell as editor and P.M. Dahl as manager,[31] was censured for reprinting a section taken from a pamphlet issued by the American Anti-Saloon League. The quote speculated on the benefits to society if prohibition had been enforced during the war.[32] The Grand Lodge did not publish again until 1923, when it published a traditional Christmas annual called *Nordisk jul* (Nordic Christmas), with Axel J. Carlson and G.H. Silver as editors. Unfortunately no copies have survived.

The chief press censor's dislike for IOGT probably stemmed from that group's opposition to the conscription law passed in July 1917. The following October he harassed Port Arthur's newspaper *Framåt* (Forward) out of existence. The IOGT Study Circle had launched the monthly tabloid in February 1916 with Oscar Johnson[33] as editor. When circulation grew to between 400 and 500 copies, it merited mention in *Svenska Canada-tidningen*, albeit as an upstart.[34] Contents included updates from the Grand Lodge in Winnipeg and IOGT lodges in Port

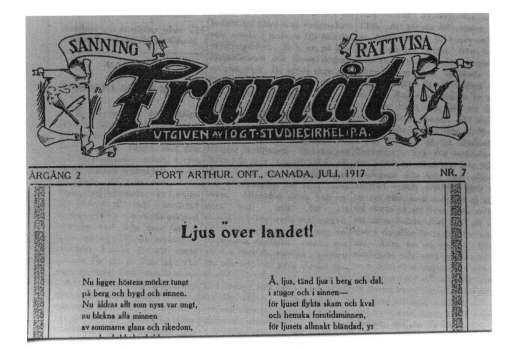

Masthead of the July 1917 issue of *Framåt* (Forward), published by IOGT Study Circle in Port Arthur, a Swedish temperance organization. The paper's mottoes were *Sanning* (truth) and *Rättvisa* (justice).

Arthur and Kenora, poetry, jokes, lessons in the widely proposed international language Esperanto, local news, commercial advertising, articles from other publications on the evils of alcohol, and notices of local meetings such as the Scandinavian Socialist Society Verdandi and both Vasa lodges.[35]

The chief press censor's translator, J.P.D. van Veen, wrote on 19 October 1917 that "*Framåt* contains harmless essays," but after Chambers and Livesay joined forces to investigate the paper, the study circle not only ceased publication, but also disbanded.[36] The minute book gives no indication that the November meeting would be its last, indicating a felt need for secrecy. At the same time the paper's typesetter, Len Enroth, was let go from his full-time job at the *Daily News-Chronicle*. He was reinstated after the demise of *Framåt*.[37]

Svenska Canada-tidningen after the First World War

By the time Dahl died in 1946 he had hired at least eleven more editors for *Svenska Canada-tidningen*,[38] each with their own strengths, but none of them were experienced journalists like Brown. In 1929 the recent immigrant Esse Ljungh[39] replaced Carl Rydberg as editor and guided the paper's destiny throughout the Depression years. A former student of law and economics who had mastered seven languages, Ljungh was described as a "talented and temperamental writer [who] performed his duties with great skill and precision."[40] One of his first moves was to change half the paper's language to English. After a disagreement in May 1931 he quit, and Rydberg took over until December, when Ljungh returned, shortened the paper's name to *Canada-tidningen*, and changed the format to a magazine, which lasted until 1934. In a 1933 editorial Ljungh argued for an updated view of modern Sweden to replace the old "proud history" approach. We are done for, he wrote, if we get more Gustav Adolf and Karl XII as sandwich food when what we need to promote Sweden is hard crispbread.

Most of Ljungh's "hard crispbread" came from the American Swedish News Exchange, established in 1921 with offices in Stockholm and New York. Its purpose was to provide reliable information in the form of articles and stories, interviews, and a weekly trade letter, all sent by cable.[41] These resources supplemented his pithy editorials praising the ideal of modern Swedish cooperation and tolerance, at the expense of Canadian society, which, he felt, lacked these qualities. He also criticized Canada's "British colonial policy" towards immigrants and their children, which made them feel like something less than full citizens who had the right to criticize government actions. Then in 1939, when Britain's royal couple visited Winnipeg, he encouraged a sense of national pride by exhorting readers, with the right bestowed upon them by citizenship, to pay tribute along with other Canadians.[42]

Canada-tidningen continued publishing until 1970. When Esse Ljungh left in 1941 Arthur A. Anderson became interim editor, then Konstantin Flemming came out of retirement to take over the paper he had started so long ago. Two events took place in 1952, Flemming's death and the demise of the Mission Covenant paper, *Canada posten*, so that its editor, Albin Hagglund, moved over to *Canada-tidningen*. Helge V. Pearson[43] had replaced P.M. Dahl as publisher of both *Canada-tidningen* and

Norrøna in 1946. It was he who edited the paper during its final days after Hagglund's death in 1965.

Helge V. Pearson had a distinguished career that included radio broadcasts for Canadian Broadcasting Corporation's International Service, election as president of the Canadian Press Club, and involvement in most of Winnipeg's Swedish societies. His editorial written for the paper's sixtieth anniversary in 1952 offers a glimpse of its male orientation and class attitudes: "So long as Swedes build and live in the west, so long as the Swedish language rings out loud and clear in the colourful but rough turn of tongue of the lumberjack, in the simple phrases of the farmer, in the daily speech among menfolk, then there may be room for a Swedish-language paper in Canada."[44]

Canada-tidningen published its final issue on 1 July 1970, before being absorbed by Chicago's *Svenska Amerikanaren-tribunen*. The same year *Norrøna* was sold to Gunnar Warolin of Vancouver.[45] These losses marked the end of an era for Winnipeg.

Vancouver

Beginnings

The only Swedish newspaper still in existence in Canada, *Swedish Press*, was established in Vancouver in 1929 as the Swedish-language *Svenska pressen*. British Columbia's first Swedish paper, the weekly *Svenska Vancouver posten* (The Swedish Vancouver Post) had been founded in 1910 by Oscar Sundborg, a snuff manufacturer from Chicago.[46] Although circulation hit 2,500 the following year,[47] both Sundborg and his newspaper disappeared in 1914.

Very little is known about other Vancouver newspapers.[48] *Svenska Canada kuriren* (The Swedish Canada Courier) was published for only one year, 1914. A predecessor, *Canada tribunen* (The Canada Tribune) had appeared in 1912–3, and then resurfaced in 1918 with James Leider as editor. The following year it was absorbed by the Norwegian newspaper *Canada skandinaven* (The Canada Scandinavian), and the name changed to *Norseman*.[49] For much of *Canada skandinaven*'s existence from 1911 to 1919, it alternated between Norwegian- and Swedish-language editions every other week, and the editor, Nels Westby, retained Leider as the Swedish-language editor. *Norseman* lasted until 1923, after two years of publishing in the English language.

Svenska pressen/Swedish Press

It was two Finland Swedes, Helge Ekengren[50] and Paul Johnson, who founded *Svenska pressen*. Ekengren provided space in the same building as his travel agency, and the first issue was dated 24 January 1929. The four-page weekly gave equal space for news from Sweden and Finland. When Ekengren left in 1933, Matt Lindfors[51] became editor, assisted by Rud Manson,[52] who had already worked there for three years. Nobody knew that Rud was married, or that he was never able to earn enough money to bring his wife to Canada as they both wanted. Their profoundly moving correspondence came to light only after his death.[53]

Financial difficulties dogged *Svenska pressen*, despite inventive appeals and refinancing schemes. In 1936 Lindfors sold the paper to Seattle's *Svenska posten*, which printed his weekly Vancouver page. Less than a year later he got it back and changed the name to *Nya svenska pressen* (The New Swedish Press). In 1943 it was reorganized as a private company under the name Central Press Limited, having purchased its own printing equipment. A board of directors was elected and shares sold to pay capital expenses.[54] At this time Lindfors was busy elsewhere and Einar Olson[55] took over as editor for five years, followed by Rud Månson until Lindfors returned in 1961. Maj Brundin[56] wrote articles under the pseudonym *Röksignaller* (Smoke Signals) and also served on the paper's board of directors.

Lindfors was a tireless promoter of Sweden and things Swedish,[57] especially among children. As *Farbror Olle* (Uncle Olle) he wrote a weekly column in Swedish, and in 1935 founded a club called *Vårblomman* (The Spring Flower). Members performed on his local CJOR radio program *Echoes from Sweden* just before Christmas, with prizes for those who signed up new members. The year before he had founded a young people's club, *Diamanten* (The Diamond), also based on a weekly column, which by 1938 had 600 members. Farbror Olle organized the first of many summer camps at Swedish Park,[58] which usually wound up with a public music program presented by *Diamanten* as well as races, vocal solos, and a public dance with live music.[59] Naturally these activities were duly reported in *Nya svenska pressen*.

The paper faced another crisis in 1984 when the editors, professional journalist Jan Fränberg[60] and his wife, Vicky, decided to return to Sweden. By this time the paper was publishing only ten issues a year. "The problem," lamented Jan, "was that the subscribers were dying." At this point *Nya svenska pressen* was one of only five surviving Swedish newspapers on the continent.[61]

While it was true that original subscribers were dying, it was also true that most of their children and grandchildren could not read Swedish and did not have strong feelings towards Sweden. Immigration had virtually halted during the years from 1930 to 1950 because of the Depression, the Second World War, and reconstruction in Canada. When North America became a favoured destination once again, many immigrants had already learned English at school as a compulsory subject. The loss of subscribers, coupled with escalating printing costs, sounded the death knell for hundreds of ethnic newspapers in North America.

Sture Wermee,[62] who had worked as typographer and sometime editor since 1952, was determined that *Nya svenska pressen* should survive. Along with Swedish consul Ulf Waldén and others, he scouted around for an editor and found Anders and Hamida Neumüller.[63] The couple agreed to try it for a year as a monthly, with the backing of the Swedish Press Society. They switched the name to *Swedish Press/Nya svenska pressen*, adopted a smart magazine format, and started producing the paper on a Macintosh computer. The Swedish Charitable Association, which raised money through bingos, funded purchase of the new equipment, and the first issue came out in January 1986. Continuing to contribute were journalist Ann-Charlotte Berglund, cartoonist Ernie Poignant,[64] and Sven Seaholm,[65] the paper's poet laureate. New contributors included Mats Thölin[66] with sports, Adele Heilborn with news from Sweden, and Roberta Larson with reports from the Swedish Canadian Rest Home.

Editor Anders Neumüller credited Canada's multicultural policy and Vancouver's Expo '86 with generating enough advertising revenue to see *Swedish Press* through its critical first year. He also came close to meeting his goal of doubling the number of subscribers.[67] Since then *Swedish Press* has become an international resource, keeping readers informed in an interesting way about happenings in Canada, Sweden, and the United States, very little of which is included in the mainstream media. As a communicator it also substitutes for a national Swedish organization in Canada, something that has never existed in a meaningful way. Only a few of its thirty-four pages are in Swedish, and translations are available online. In 1994 Neumüller began publishing the quarterly *Scandinavian Press* in a similar magazine format, but all in English. Associate editors provided copy from Denmark, Finland, Iceland, and Norway. Since then Anders and Hamida have sold both magazines and moved to Sweden. The new website for Swedish Press is swedishpress.com, and for Scandinavian Press is scandpress.com.

Canada-Svensken/The Swedish Canadian

The Finland Swede Thorwald Wiik launched Canada's third, secular, Swedish-language newspaper in Toronto in 1961. *Canada-Svensken* appeared with the parallel title *The Swedish Canadian*. It claimed to be "the leading Swedish language paper in Canada," bringing readers "Swedish and Finland-Swedish news from home and across Canada." It started as a semi-monthly, and then became a monthly, with the last issue dated 1978. A test version in English, *Swedish Canadian*, with the hopeful byline "The voice shared by all Swedes in Canada," appeared in 1970.[68]

All four newspapers attempted to introduce the English-language *Svenska Canada-tidningen* in 1931. The English page in *Canada posten* began in the late 1920s and was directed towards youth. In addition to *Canada posten,* an English-language Conference paper was launched in 1943, which became *The Covenant Messenger.*[69] Matt Lindfors experimented with an additional English-language paper in Vancouver in 1944, but it did not fly.

Religious Newspapers

Except for *Canada posten,* religious newspapers in the twentieth century were short-lived. *Canada härold* (Canada Herald), a monthly tabloid of eight pages published by the Augustana Lutheran Church, debuted in April 1914 with Pastor T.J. Tengwald as editor, and the last surviving issue is dated March 1915. An attempt to revive the paper in 1919 under the name *Canada nyheter* (Canada News), with Pastor J.W. Lindberg of Kenora as editor, was also short-lived.[70]

The only religious publication for youth, *The Young Canadian,*[71] was published in 1908 by Immanuel Lutheran Church, Port Arthur, to help organize a young people's club. Unfortunately no copies survive. Before the First World War *Canada posten* published several Christmas annuals with articles and illustrations, titled *Norrsken* (Northern lights).[72] *Canada posten* also published an almanac in 1913 and 1914.

Socialist Publications

The politics of Nils Fredriksson Brown changed during his sojourn in Canada, and in 1919 he resigned from *Svenska Canada-tidningen* to establish Canada's first Swedish socialist newspaper.[73] *Forum*, a twice-monthly publication, stands out as the only labour newspaper in North America to promote the preservation of Swedish culture.[74] It included literary reviews, poetry, short stories, a serialized novel, articles from Sweden, contributions from well-known socialists, and strong, perhaps too strong, editorials. The subtitle, "Frisinnad tidskrift för svenska farmare och arbetare" (Independent Magazine for Swedish Farmers and Workers), defined its socialist stance.

Brown "possessed a brilliant pen and a lucid intellect, [and] edited the editorials better than anyone before or since."[75] He and his partner Victor Lundberg supported the Saskatchewan Non-Partisan League and the One Big Union. However, they experienced increasing difficulty keeping the paper afloat and in order to pay pressing debts "borrowed" from Brown & Lundberg Company, which transmitted money orders from immigrants to relatives in Sweden. After the partners were arrested in March 1921, Dahl paid Brown's bail and allowed him to appeal for money through *Svenska Canada-tidningen* in order to pay the $2,000 that *Forum* owed Brown & Lundberg's creditors. Eventually enough money was raised and the pair received suspended sentences. Brown returned to the United States and Rudolf Einhardt took over as editor of *Forum*. The paper folded in 1924.[76]

The only other Swedish socialist newspaper was the monthly *Frihets-vännen* (The Friend of Freedom), a Christian paper published in Winnipeg from 1922 to 1924. The aim of editor and publisher Carl August Larson,[77] a Lutheran pastor who lived in Wadena, Saskatchewan, was to represent the Swedish Lutherans of Canada and to oppose "the money power." Larson came from Fairmont, Minnesota, where he had received a suspended sentence in 1918 on a trumped-up charge of disloyalty.

Another example of the Social Gospel in print was the 1923 socialist songbook published in the tradition of Joe Hill by a regular contributor to *Forum*, N.J.L. Bergen[78] of Wetaskiwin. *Nya sånger för folket*[79] (New Songs for the People) featured patriotic songs about Canada's western provinces, sung to the tune of well-known anthems, while "Bolshevikerna," for example, followed a Swedish melody. Some lyrics were written by others, such as H.P. Myers's satirical "Rocky Fellow" (Rockefeller), sung to "Yankee Doodle." Bergen was a Baptist missionary "richly endowed for the mission field as a speaker, singer and musician,"[80] who found it impossible to raise a growing family on a missionary's salary. In 1912 the family moved in with a relative in Ferintosh and five years later bought a farm in the Bulyea district of Wetaskiwin. The 1923 songbook seems to have been published for a summer gathering.

Communist Publications

Two Communist newspapers surfaced during the Depression. In 1932 the Vancouver club of Finland Swedes began putting out the short-lived *Klasskampen* (The Class Struggle), while the twice-monthly Winnipeg newspaper *Frihet* (Freedom) lasted from 1933 to 1937. The most substantial of the Canadian papers, it was published in Swedish, Norwegian, and Danish, with a children's feature in English. Although all the editors were Swedes – August Wallin,[81] Martin Palmgren,[82] and Helge V. Pearson – there was a genuine attempt to make *Frihet* a Scandinavian paper.[83]

The Winnipeg club also published two short-lived annuals in the mid-1930s. *Midvintertidskrift* (Midwinter Magazine) appeared as a pre-Christmas publication in 1936 and 1937, and *Röd maj* (Red May) celebrated International Workers' Day for the year 1935.[84] Sweden's traditionally joyous festival welcoming spring and the return of light, *Första maj* (First of May), which followed the giant bonfires of the previous evening, *Valborgsmässoafton* (Walpurgis Night), had been officially replaced in 1890 with International Workers' Day. As might be expected, the focus changed as workers' organizations marked the occasion with demonstrations of solidarity.

Other Publications

In 1969 Toronto's business community began publishing *The Scandinavian Canadian Businessman* in Willowdale as a quarterly magazine, with Erik Melander as editor. After his death his sons Steen and Lars carried on until 1985, when Eva Terp bought it and changed the name to *Scandinavian Forum*. It lasted until 1993.

Other organizations with significant publications were the Scandinavian Centre in Edmonton, which published a monthly newspaper in English for almost thirty years, from 1958 until 1987. The paper began as *Scandinavian Centre News*, and then, after the building was demolished in 1981, changed its name to *Scandinavian News*. In Winnipeg Rose Peterson began publishing a similar paper in 1973 with the same name, *Scandinavian News*. Printed in Steinbach, it had a circulation of 700.[85] These two examples do not presume to be a full list. Instead, they represent the flurry of regular newsletters that have been put out over the years by various organizations, both religious and secular.

Canada's only surviving newspaper, *Swedish Press/Nya svenska pressen*, received new impetus as the clean and compact computer replaced the dirty, noisy, and labour-intensive typesetting of yesteryear. It continues to keep readers informed about events here and in the Old Country and confirms their ethnicity and sense of belonging to a group, but from the home rather than from a downtown business establishment.

Swedes in Canada have produced a priceless heritage of secular, religious, political, and literary newspapers over the years. Although the first one began as a religious publication, when its usefulness as a government, and later CPR, propagandist ended, it amalgamated with a religious competitor to become a mainstream newspaper. The only religious newspaper to survive for a lengthy period, *Canada posten*, was subsidized by dedicated publishers, and the two mainstream papers survived only with great difficulty. Unfortunately neither *Canada posten* nor Vancouver's *(Nya) Svenska pressen* has inspired scholarly study, unlike their mainstream contemporary *(Svenska) Canada-tidningen*, despite their availability on microfilm.[86]

Chapter Eight

The Depression, Strikes, and Unions

The 1930s dawned with a depressed economy, which resulted in a continuation of strikes after the First World War and a great deal of union activity. International unions from the United States and from Russia wooed workers, especially in the logging industry. Those who chose Russia were labelled Communists. The government of Canada used force and the threat of deportation to restore the illusion of peace. The Depression lasted for a decade, until the declaration of the Second World War.

The Depression

The Depression of the 1930s was disastrous for many Canadians, but especially for immigrants. Property owners and those who were able to keep their jobs, even at reduced pay and hours, had money and were able to benefit from the lower cost of living. It was Canada's farmers, young people, small-business people, and the unemployed who bore the brunt of the hard times, and many Swedes fit into these categories. The four western provinces, notably Saskatchewan, were especially hard-hit. By 1933 one in five Canadians depended on government relief for survival.

The demand for minerals decreased as industries cut back on production. In Sudbury the nickel mine closed and former employees with families were given food vouchers. Without work people could not pay doctors or craftsmen, let alone rent or taxes. The Salvation Army provided food and beds, and soup kitchens served 500 meals a day. The situation abated somewhat in 1934 when Germany began placing orders for nickel,[1] but most of the rest of the country continued to suffer until the declaration of war in 1939.

Markets dried up for wheat. The railway to Churchill, on Hudson Bay, was finally completed in 1931, with its first shipment of wheat arriving from Weldon, Saskatchewan, the following year.[2] Wheat could now be shipped from all three of Canada's coasts, but the Depression, being worldwide, dictated very low prices. To make matters worse the Prairies suffered a succession of natural disasters. Drought, grasshoppers, and windstorms destroyed crops year after year.

Viola Anderson, who lived with her parents on a farm north of Shaunavon, described how these years affected her and her family:

When the crash came, the wheat prices went down to 18 cents a bushel. Papa was very downhearted but Mama said not to worry we would get by. The drought came too and it no longer rained ... There was dust everywhere choking and blinding you outside, and inside it made little drifts along the newly dusted window sills ... Nothing much grew, but we planted every year and never gave up hoping. Russian thistles and stinkweed managed to survive the drought and was all that the cattle had to eat. The weeds made the milk and butter rank and almost impossible to eat. We often had only potatoes, salt pork, and bread. We had no fruit or extras.

Another year passed and still the wind blew, more dust, and no rain. Papa was crying behind the barn because he had to shoot Barney, his faithful old horse who was too old to scrounge for himself, and all the feed was gone. Grasshoppers came in clouds and blotted out the sun, they ate what little of the crop that grew and cleaned up the garden. They even ate holes in our clothing. Then there were armyworms – they stripped even the leaves on the trees. We went barefoot from May to September to save shoe leather; we used shoes for church, to go to town, but not for school.

We were getting older and there was a lot of chores to do as Papa could no longer afford a hired man ... Papa at last was forced to go on relief, he had spent every dime of the money he had saved so frugally. Relief was 13 dollars a month, and since it was so hard to make ends meet, decided I would get a job. I worked 14 hours a day for 5 dollars a month, room and board, with a bonus of 25 dollars for staying 6 months, all of which the government paid. It was most demeaning, and my happy childhood days were over. I was now 14.[3]

At Ponteix, east of Shaunavon, Hans and Agda Magnuson planted a vegetable garden one morning, and then took their children on an outing. When they returned in the evening, strong winds had uncovered the peas, beans, and corn seeds, and blown some away. Hans remarked philosophically, "It isn't too bad when you can get the seed back,"[4] but it was almost impossible to remain optimistic under such conditions.

Small businesses suffered, too. Johan August Johansson,[5] an electrician, opened Kenora's first electrical shop. With the Depression his customers were unable to pay their accounts and the store went bankrupt. At least he still had his trade to fall back on, if there was work to be had. In the early 1920s Victor Anderson opened a grocery store in Lindale, Alberta, and ran it until 1955: "The worst time of all these years was in 1937, when we had fifty-four of our customers on relief. They got the big sum of from $5 to $14 a month."[6] Somehow, both Anderson and his customers survived.

Ernie Lind was single during the Depression, and, for unemployed single men, soup kitchens and begging were the chief sources of food. Relief was only for families. Ernie, short and slender and never tipping the scales at more than fifty-seven kilograms, was hungry many times.[7] These bachelors, particularly seasonal labourers and recent immigrants, owned neither homes nor farms. Most of them rode the rods, stealing transportation on freight trains, vainly seeking employment.

> The dangerous part of this kind of travelling was not the chance of getting caught, but rather the physical risks which threatened those who practised "free" train travel, that became the test of manhood for the jobless. The necessity of jumping off well before the station could mean that one stumbled or got stuck with clothing and was dragged by the train, possibly to be crushed on the rails. It was at least as dangerous to run along a train and pull oneself up. The riskiest moment was before one got a good grip on a railing or something else protruding from the train. Often the railcars were locked so the tramps had to climb up on top of the cars, maybe to lie down on top of the canvas around a load of wood. To end up there in wind and cold was particularly gruesome in the Rocky Mountains' tunnels [enveloped by smoke from the locomotive].[8]

They were called "tramps," "hoboes," and "bums." They lived without shelter; they begged meals along the railways between rides, and were always willing to work for food. Finding a warm place to sleep in the winter was a problem, and railway policemen were seldom understanding.

Per Ivar Tornblom[9] of Port Arthur, one of those who rode the rods during the Depression, became a military casualty during the Second

World War. His brother Rolf recalled one of his stories: "Rounded up with others on one occasion, herded into an unheated sand house and strip-searched by railroad police. Any money found was taken away. Then they were run off the railroad property, and out of town ... [he was] quite bitter and cynical about his country and its authorities."[10]

Per Ivar had emigrated from Hälsingland as an infant with his parents, who eventually ended up on a farm in Harstone, Ontario. His dad, coppersmith Ivar Tornblom, was not cut out for farming, but worked at the Port Arthur shipyards during both wars.

Strikes

The callous attitude of officials and governments stemmed from the First World War and the fear of a Bolshevik revolution. The cooperation of business and government in putting down the Winnipeg Strike in 1919 was based on this belief, and the massive display of sympathy strikes and marches in most industrial centres across the country only served to confirm these fears. Armoured cars, troops, and machine-gun units moved into Winnipeg, and the government quickly passed legislation to broaden the definition of sedition and to allow for deportation even of the British-born. Since most of the strike leaders fitted that description, they were arrested. The strike ended on "Bloody Saturday," when police violence broke up a peaceful parade of strikers and veterans. Disillusioned workers returned to worse conditions than before, and the labour movement languished. Neither the international unions nor the Trades and Labour Congress had supported their cause.[11]

An earlier strike stopped construction of the Canadian Northern Railway along 644 kilometres of track between Yellowhead Pass and Vancouver along the Fraser River. The strikers belonged to Local 327 of the Wobblies (Industrial Workers of the World), which got its message across through songs, many of them written by the Swedish-American Joe Hill.[12] Every year saw a new edition of the union's pocket-sized *Little Red Songbook*.

Hill came to Yale to assist with the strike, and one of the songs he composed was the still-popular "Where the Fraser River Flows," sung to the tune of "Where the Shannon River Flows." Soon all 4,200 strikers were singing this saucy and catchy tune as they walked the picket lines. The publicity surrounding Hill's 1915 execution for a crime he said he did not commit has made him a symbol for the unjustly convicted.

Immigrants were often blamed for strike action. The 1934 strike at Noranda mine in Quebec is known as the "foreigners' strike" because it resulted in a significant drop in the number of foreign-born employees in the workforce, from 50 to 25 per cent. Before the strike 354 foreign-born naturalized Canadians were employed, but afterwards that number had shrunk to 195. Of fifteen Swedish employees, only seven kept their jobs.[13]

Unions

Only a few Swedes in Canada assumed a leadership role in labour organizations. Emil Berg[14] chaired the committee that organized Edmonton's sympathy strike in 1919. His father had been blacklisted in Sweden for helping to found *Metallarbetareförbundet* (the metal workers' association), and the family became so poverty-stricken that two of his sisters died of starvation and cold. After his father's death from a work-related condition in 1894 Emil was farmed out to a relative.[15] He espoused the workers' cause for the rest of his life.

Berg was an important figure in the One Big Union (OBU), and after its collapse transferred his allegiance to more traditional labour circles. His job with Emil Skarin's Crown Paving Company freed him from want and allowed him to follow a fulfilling labour career. He was a member and officer of Local 92 of the Hod Carriers', Building and Common Laborers' Union of America, ending up as Canadian representative. Locally he served on the executive of the Edmonton Trades and Labour Council and the Alberta Federation of Labour, and nationally as vice-president of the Trades and Labour Congress of Canada for thirteen years. He represented the Canadian labour movement at international meetings in London, Geneva, and Stockholm. Emil Berg was appointed a Member of the Order of the British Empire in 1947.[16]

In Port Arthur the Scandinavian Home Society[17] provided a venue for planning union activities, but details are sparse. Since most of its members were Swedes they were wary of attracting official notice, an aftermath of events during the First World War. They were also overshadowed by the more numerous and more radical Finns, whose buildings lay just around the corner. However, it is known that many Swedes joined Port Arthur's Unemployed Workers' Association founded in 1924 by the One Big Union. The Finnish Labour Temple was headquarters for the OBU's Lumber Workers' Industrial Union. Those who split from the OBU formed the Lumber Workers' Industrial Union of Canada

(LWIUC), an affiliate of Red International of Labour Unions in Moscow.[18] Port Arthur's was the sole Scandinavian branch of the LWIUC to be organized in Canada.[19]

The only indication of the Communist political stance adopted by some Scandinavian Home Society members was a constitutional amendment in 1926 to allow a non-Scandinavian, Harry Bryan, to become a member. Bryan was president of the LWIUC, which had just concluded a successful strike,[20] indicating substantial support among the membership. The Scandinavian Home became a popular meeting place and mailing address for bush workers.

In the logging industry, workers in both British Columbia and northern Ontario belonged to the Communist-led LWIUC, which in 1936 merged with the Lumber and Sawmill Workers Union. This marriage lasted in Ontario, but the following year British Columbia decided to join the International Woodworkers of America instead. Employers had been dead set against unions since 1919, when the BC Loggers Association formed an employment agency in Vancouver, through which every logger had to be hired on an annual basis. Union activists and Communists were blacklisted, and could not get work. Employed loggers who complained to management about conditions, or who brought copies of *BC Lumberworker* into camp, were fired on the spot and blacklisted.

Al Parkin, a labour journalist, assisted by the Finland Swede John Eklow, a former logger, founded *BC Lumberworker* in 1934. The paper grew from a mimeographed sheet to an eight-page weekly, half of it loggers' reports from the camps. Copies were smuggled into camps by union organizers, who always found a safe refuge in the fallers' bunkhouse, which housed mostly Swedes. Only there could they sell copies of the paper and collect money and union dues without interference.[21] "In the struggle that won the minimum wage for the industry [in 1934], the Scandinavians played a large part in educating the loggers in the idea of union membership. Eric Hallbom, Karl Palmgren, Karl Eklund, Ted Gunrud and Andy Hogarth travelled as organizers with Jack Brown and Jack Gillbanks throughout the camps in 1931 and 1932. In addition there were the camp delegates, among them Hjalmar Bergren, Axel Oling, Eric Bjorklund, Ernie Dalskog and Eric Graff."[22] Although Swedes were not anxious to serve as leaders, the solid block of Scandinavian support in the camps made union activity possible. At the same time the majority of workers were reluctant to sign up with the union.[23]

In northern Ontario, Finns played a key role in union activities for bush workers because of their dominance in the industry. In Port Arthur the massive Finnish Labour Temple and the Communists' little Finn Hall stood side by side on Bay Street. Both became centres for the unemployed. In the spring of 1930 the bodies of two union organizers, Viljo Rosval and Janne Voutilainen, were found in a shallow stream deep in the bush. Many people believed that they had been murdered, and their funeral procession became a mass demonstration of 5,000 workers and the unemployed. Unlike other local demonstrations, police did not harass this one.

In 1934, when 3,500 loggers on Vancouver Island walked out and gathered in Vancouver, Scandinavians made up 24 per cent of the workforce.[24] The strike relief committee served 800 meals a day at *Hembygden*, a Swedish café on Carrall Street. Although union recognition eluded the strikers, they were able to win minimum-wage legislation and the right to collective bargaining. *Svenska pressen* supported the vote to end the strike, contrasting the rights of workers in British Columbia with those in the "more enlightened" homeland of Sweden.[25]

Hjalmar Bergren[26] and Ernie Dalskog[27] became full-time organizers for WLIUC. Dalskog was eventually elected president of the British Columbia District Council, and in 1945 was instrumental in organizing workers at sawmills across the interior. However, in 1948 the International Woodworkers of America expelled him and other Communists for life, victims of the Cold War in the United States.

Hjalmar Bergren and his wife, Myrtle, lived in Lake Cowichan on Vancouver Island, the backbone of British Columbia's logging industry. During the 1934 strike the women did all they could to help their husbands. For example Hildur Grip darkened the windows in her washhouse so that labour organizers could meet there undisturbed. During the 1946 strike Hildur worked within the International Woodworkers of America (IWA) Ladies Auxiliary and took part in the Trek to Victoria. The auxiliary, which included Gulli Olson, Lorrie Beline, and many non-Scandinavians, organized fundraising and provided a soup kitchen during the strike, but found that they were not welcome within the IWA after 1948. Accordingly the Scandinavians among them founded the Scandinavian Club, which, among other events, carried on the annual pre-Christmas tradition of Santa Lucia.

Results of Unemployment

The federal government refused to take responsibility for unemployment, except for the Department of National Defence's establishing unemployment relief camps for single men when provincial governments refused to do so. Elof Kellner described his living conditions in such a camp in British Columbia: "Young men were forced into work camps where they had to wear armbands and build roads for 20 cents a day. There were 200–250 men living in the bunkhouses, sleeping in bunk beds. We had to go to a barn and get hay for mattresses and we had to supply our own blankets. Worst of all, there were no sanitary facilities – there was a washbasin and a pail of water, that was it. I was there for three months. We felt so dirty, every Sunday, my brother and I took a large pail and we built a fire and cooked our underwear in order to kill the bugs."[28]

In April 1935 the men decided to strike, and 1,500 of them went to Vancouver, where they tried to resolve the problem through negotiations and demonstrations. Receiving no results, they decided to ride the rods to Canada's capital city and lay complaints before Parliament and Prime Minister R.B. Bennett. Thus, the On-to-Ottawa Trek began with a thousand men in Vancouver and ended in Regina with double that number.

Herb Eldstrom, a homesteader, happened to be hitchhiking from Calgary to Moose Jaw at this time:

When we got to Moose Jaw everyone was ordered off the train by the RCMP [Royal Canadian Mounted Police]. Moose Jaw was our destination, so we got off the train as it was slowing up before coming to the station. We walked beside the train and when we got to the station we couldn't believe our eyes as we watched the Mounties with black snake whips that could reach to the top of the boxcars. I watched one man coming down the ladder and a Mountie hit him across the face with his whip and cut him. There was blood running down his clothes but that wasn't enough and the Mountie hit him again. That's the day I decided never to vote Conservative as long as I live.[29]

There were three hundred men heading for Regina on this train, and "most of them were starving, tired and poorly clothed."

It was decided to send a committee of eight to Ottawa while the rest of the men waited in the Regina Exhibition Grounds. Negotiations were unsuccessful, and the committee returned to call off the trek. They held a rally on 1 July to ask for last-minute assistance from the townspeople. Kellner recalled that RCMP officers poured out of three vans and began lobbing tear gas into the crowd, touching off the Regina Riot. The result of this, the most violent episode during the 1930s, was one dead, dozens injured, and 130 rioters arrested.

During the Depression more than 30,000 immigrants were deported, primarily because of illness or unemployment. The "deportation weapon" was often used to relieve municipalities, employers, and the state of unproductive or troublesome immigrants.[30] The reason Erik Westman[31] was deported in 1927 was his claim with Ontario's Workmen's Compensation Board. The legislation allowing deportation of immigrants who had become "a public charge" was twisted to include not only those eligible for compensation for work-related injuries, but also those who applied for relief.

Communism

The red thread of Communism dominated the tangled web of union organizations in Canada during the 1930s. Workers were seldom Communist to begin with; they were radicalized through unemployment and its inevitable result: hunger. Historian Eva St Jean traced such a change in attitude through Martin Johansson's letters home from 1928 to 1934: "The letters indicate that Martin was not only optimistic but also politically naive and bound by tradition and the Lutheran faith ... [Already by 1931] Martin had moved from a proponent of Canada's west as a possible land of immigrant dreams, to someone who, struggling to secure work, began to appreciate the logic of a revolutionary critique of capitalism."[32]

Martin rationalized begging for food by removing the shame. He was not a beggar, a drifter, or a vagrant; he was a worker without work. He even participated in a demonstration in Nelson, British Columbia, over a municipal decision to cut down on the quantity and quality of meals provided to transients.[33]

Two party members lived in Fir Mountain, Saskatchewan. David Einar Holmberg[34] joined in 1935 after two and a half years in a relief camp in Alberta. He also belonged to the new political party Co-operative Commonwealth Federation (CCF), now New Democratic Party. In 1940 he was convicted under a section of the Defence of Canada Regulations and sentenced to two months in jail.

Oscar George Lindholm[35] became chair of the party in Willow Bunch, Saskatchewan. At the same time he was president of the Fir Mountain Lodge of the United Farmers of Canada, councillor of the rural municipality, and director of the Consumers' Co-op. A solid citizen, he did not experience government harassment. Similarly Neil Jacobson,[36] a locomotive engineer living in Saskatoon, attended the 1937 national convention in Toronto. The following year he became local chair of the party and a member of the provincial committee. He was also a member of the Saskatoon Trades and Labour Council, the Joint Committee of Railway Unions, and the CCF.

During the 1920s and early 1930s the greatest threat to the languishing Trades and Labour Congress was the nascent Communist Party of Canada, which wanted to bring the Canadian labour movement in line with the policies of Red International of Labour Unions and in this way overthrow the capitalist system. However, most members in Canada viewed the party as a window of hope to end the misery of the Depression in the face of an unresponsive and repressive government. In 1931 authorities raided the Toronto office and eight Communist leaders were jailed for sedition.[37] The following year two Swedes were deported: Emil Sandberg[38] from Port Arthur and Ivar Johnson[39] from Vancouver. Sandberg was chair of the Port Arthur branch of the newly founded Scandinavian Workers and Farmers League (*Skandinaviska arbetar- och lantbrukarförbundet i Canada*), a mass organization 1,200 strong controlled by the Communist Party.[40] The Winnipeg group was led by Fred Steele, also known as Fritz Stål,[41] who came from the sawmill district of Ådalen where the Swedish military had recently killed five people during a strike. Clubs also existed in Vancouver, Edmonton, Calgary, Flin Flon, and Pellatt, Ontario. The last congress was in 1936.

Two Swedish Communists stand out from the rest. Einar Nordstrom[42] immigrated from Närpes, Finland, in 1930 with no experience whatever in politics, unions, or temperance organizations. After a year on railway construction in British Columbia and a period of unemployment, he joined Port Arthur's Scandinavian Workers and Farmers League and became an active Communist. In addition to union activity, and jobs as a seasonal bush worker and later as a full-time milkman, he established a long-lived co-operative book and music store, arranged for public concerts with folk musicians such as Pete Seeger, and for many years coordinated a summer camp for the Youth Communist League. He was also the local representative for the Communist newspaper *The Worker*, which later became *The Clarion*.

Bruce Magnuson,[43] a farmer's son from Värmland, spent five years working on prairie farms before arriving in Port Arthur in 1933 to look for work in logging. His arrival coincided with the beginning of a bush workers' strike organized by the LWIUC, and he joined the union in the hopes of getting work when the strike was over. Strike duties gave him an opportunity to experience police brutality at first hand as a picketer, to take minutes at general strikers' meetings, and to read pro-Communist literature from the cooperative bookstore. After further reading during recuperation from a bush accident he decided to join the Communist Party.

In quick succession Magnuson became secretary of LWIUC (1935), a key player in the merger of LWIUC and the Lumber and Sawmill Workers Union (1936), and secretary of the Port Arthur Trades and Labour Council (1937). He claimed that Communists organized 292 strikes in Canada during the Depression, and that more than 80 per cent of them were successful.[44] Magnuson was interned for more than two years during the war[45] and remained active in the party for the rest of his life, running unsuccessfully in four elections: provincially in 1951 and 1975, representing Port Arthur and St Catharines, respectively; and federally in 1968 and 1984, representing Windsor-Walkerville and Sudbury. In 1988 he was living in Toronto as the last publisher of the party organ *The Canadian Tribune* (from 1940 to 1989).

Both Magnuson and Nordstrom joined the Scandinavian Home Society, which had managed to survive the Depression by taking a mortgage that was finally paid off in 1955. The membership elected Nordstrom to the executive for fifteen years, from 1947 to 1962, and Magnuson as treasurer in 1957–8.[46] During Magnuson's term the manager of the Scandinavian Home Society's restaurant feared a Communist takeover, but there is no evidence to suggest that either man ever contemplated such a move.

Karelia

During the 1930s Communist recruiters organized emigration to Soviet Karelia, east of Finland's easternmost province of Karelia, in order "to build the first democratic nation to be led by labourers." Some idealistic Swedes went from Canada, along with up to a thousand others from the United States, Sweden, and Finland.[47] The nightmare began when they became the target of Stalinist purges. Otto Johan Högberg,[48] Ilmari Kinnunen,[49] and Hjalmar Mattson[50] left from Canada, and Viktor Johan Lindberg,[51] David Larsson,[52] and Hans Verner Julius Krykortz,[53] who had remigrated to their homeland, left from Sweden. Of the above, two died and the rest returned to Sweden with memories they feared to discuss because of reprisals.

Canada's troubled economy, political unrest, and general misery ended in 1939 with declaration of the Second World War, when the hoboes of yesterday, many of them immigrants, were transformed into soldiers. The decade left many with an accumulation of debt that would take years to pay off, and memories that would last a lifetime. If there was a positive side, it was the willingness of Canadians, mostly on an individual basis, to help those in need, whether foreign-born or not.

Heavy casualties of future leaders during the First World War has been blamed for official ineptitude during the Depression, although established perceptions of the role of the state also played a part in making Canada one of the most severely affected countries in the world. One result was the formation of political reform movements, notably J.S. Woodsworth's Co-operative Commonwealth Federation. Ultimately the state assumed responsibility for the economy and for social welfare with establishment of the Bank of Canada (1934), the Canadian Wheat Board (1935), and national unemployment insurance (1940).

Chapter Nine

Earning a Living

All immigrants had to be able to support themselves in order to survive. Those who could not do so for health reasons were not allowed entry to Canada. During the first, second, and third waves of immigration, the men either homesteaded or took labouring jobs on the railways, in construction, or in extractive industries like mining and logging, whereas the women were hired as domestics, waitresses, or cooks. During the fourth wave many immigrants, both male and female, had a trade or profession. This chapter examines the contributions made in the extractive and construction industries, social services, agriculture, animal husbandry, the fur trade, inventions, design, the arts, and politics.

Women's Work

Unlike men, women seldom had trouble finding a steady job. Christina Swanson's Swedish maids ranged in age from sixteen to forty-two. Their marketable skills were household chores learned at home – tending fires, washing and ironing clothes, preparing and serving food, doing dishes, dusting, sweeping, polishing, scrubbing, making beds, running errands, caring for children and seniors, and the like. Domestics were in demand by the upwardly mobile and by widowers with children, but some women took lighter work as cooks or chambermaids. The girls who came in 1904 were placed in Christina's home area of Waterville, in Quebec City, and in Montreal, but a few went farther afield.[1]

Emma Lundström[2] chose Fort William because her sister Helena lived there and her sister-in-law, Annie Walberg, ran the boarding house where she would work. It housed the fourteen employees of Mount McKay Brick & Tile Company, a short-lived Scandinavian enterprise that had hired Annie's husband as foreman.[3]

When this job ended Emma worked at a downtown boarding house, but could not handle the sixteen-hour days so she hired on in a private home for $10 a month. She quit after the man of the house, a magistrate, chided her for coming home after ten o'clock on her afternoon off.[4] She then asked Marie Orstad to accompany her to a job interview. Mrs Orstad[5] supported domestics in many ways, opening her home for afternoons off and for periods between steady employment. And so Emma became housekeeper for a minister with seven children. Her wages climbed to $15 a month and for the first time she was allowed to eat with the family.

Her next job in the kitchen of the hospital, where her sister Matilda worked as a waitress, allowed Emma more time to socialize and to join the Swedish Baptist choir. But when Matilda told her of the superintendent's request that "he wanted the part of the chicken that was last to fly over the fence," Emma evidently thought that she was the "chicken" he wanted. She quit and began working in a private home, this time for a lawyer.[6] It would be her last paid position. After seven years with seven jobs she married Otto Walberg, her sister's brother-in-law. Emma and Otto founded a grocery store, which supported their seven children and enabled her to visit Sweden.

Working conditions for Swedish maids were seldom ideal. Elin Lindell's employer in Vancouver asked her to taste the supper mushrooms in case they were poisonous.[7] Karin Randin[8] immigrated on her own in 1910, and her first job was with a well-to-do Winnipeg family: "She slept in a pantry converted to a bedroom, which was furnished with a bed, a dresser and a chair. The room was without windows so she couldn't see outside. Eventually this cell turned into a prison; she couldn't associate with the family because she didn't know how to talk fluently in their gibberish – English; I guess this is why she had to eat her meals in her room. She soon hated the dingy wallpaper and the single light bulb, which hung from the ceiling ... Often she cried herself to sleep."[9] As if in answer to prayer, Karin received a letter about a Swede in Saskatchewan who needed a housekeeper. This job worked out much better.

That a woman's place was in the home, not in the public sphere, was a widespread opinion among both sexes. As a result job opportunities were limited until further training enabled women to become nurses, teachers, and office workers. Descendants of Swedish immigrants, like

Not all Swedish maids immigrated under this scheme. Ellen Berglund, left, came to Canada with her parents in 1907. In 1913 she was employed in one of Port Arthur's grand homes, along with another maid, a gardener, and a handyman. Courtesy of Elinor Barr, Broman Collection.

other women, were directed to service-sector employment by Canada's educational system, and some excelled at their chosen field.

Nursing

When Mary Berglund[10] retired in 1972 she had served the railway community of Ignace, Ontario, for thirty years, pioneering the role of nurse practitioner. The Canadian Pacific Railroad had done away with its company doctors in 1942 by arranging for a medical insurance plan called AMS. Ignace was lucky to have a resident registered nurse willing to take on the responsibility of ministering to the sick and injured without the benefits of an office, drug store, ambulance, or salary. Instead, the family kitchen served as a waiting room and the bathroom as a treatment room, where she kept drugs supplied by doctors in Dryden, 113 kilometres away. She delivered more than a hundred babies, often in the back seat of a provincial police car racing to Dryden hospital. In recognition of her contribution the Ontario Medical Association presented her with an honorary membership, the only nurse to be so honoured. When Ignace eventually got a health care facility, the name chosen was Mary Berglund Community Health Centre.

Nutrition

Olga Anderson and her sister Esther Williams[11] both worked as teachers, then as nutritionists. Esther became Alberta's first district home economist in 1943, a profession also followed by her daughter. Olga left the Prairies in 1951 to work as nutritional advisor with the Newfoundland Department of Health. She required several assistants to help her carry out the province's mandate, and for seventeen years was responsible for the weekly radio program *Kitchen Corner*, followed by a similar TV program.

Weaving

When immigration began again during the 1950s and 1960s domestics were no longer in demand, but similar employment as an au pair was the easiest way to get landed immigrant status.[12] The immigrants who came in the 1970s brought advanced skills, but still in the service sector. Gone were the women who used to weave colourful rag rugs (*trasmatta*) for neighbours and friends. Instead, Lilly Bohlin[13] established a School of Weaving in Victoria, and students from around the world gravitated to her studio, the Weaver's Loft. Christina Pokrupa[14] came to Winnipeg as a bride, also bringing with her skills learned in Sweden. She became active in the larger community, teaching and demonstrating weaving at the University of Manitoba and the Crafts Guild of Manitoba as well as at Folklorama's Swedish pavilion.

Physiotherapy

Gunnel Gavin[15] graduated in Stockholm as a physiotherapist and had practised in Göteborg before marrying and immigrating to Vancouver. Because her credentials were not valid in Canada, she worked in a hospital while finishing her Canadian exams at the University of British Columbia. She founded Gunnel Gavin Physiotherapy Associates in 1983.

Clothing Design

Linda Lundstrom[16] made a name for herself as a designer of women's clothing. She learned to sew on her mother's sewing machine, began making her own clothes at age eight, and, after training in Canada and Europe, established Linda Lundstrom Limited in Toronto. After a visit to Japan, where the ancient kimono was making a comeback as contemporary apparel, she used Inuit and Sami winter wear as models to design her famous Laparka coat ("lap" is for the Sami people and "parka" for the Inuit). She credits her Canadian and Nordic heritage with the basic ideas of layering and decoration that characterize the coat.

Filmmaker

Eva Wunderman[17] has won many awards for the 150-plus productions she has directed. They include the TV series *Weird Homes*, and the CBC documentary *Crystal Fear, Crystal Clear* about three families and their children's addiction to crystal methamphetamine. She lives in Hope, British Columbia, where she once worked as a travel agent and radio announcer on CKJO. It was her radio voice that led to a job as narrator and eventually to her film career.

Men's Work

The lives of many male immigrants, even those who homesteaded, were characterized by an unending search for steady employment in a wide variety of labouring jobs in the logging, mining, construction, and transportation industries. Most were seasonal or temporary jobs, so that single men became rootless and married men became part-time husbands and fathers. In 1911 Emil and Ellen Johnson started married life in Saskatchewan, where Emil worked on construction. The family moved to Daysland, Alberta, for a railway job, then homesteaded near Hinton. While Ellen took care of the homestead, Emil worked in a coal mine at Pocahontas, operated a taxi at Brule, and guided big-game hunting parties. He also hauled supplies from Hinton to Luscar Coal Mines by pack train and ran an automobile agency in Entrance, near Hinton. In 1920 the couple sold the homestead and moved to Edson for a job on railway construction. A similar job took them to Vernon, British Columbia. In 1926 the family settled in Edmonton, but Emil's job as superintendent took him to Saskatchewan. When railway expansion stopped in 1929 he was laid off.[18] In eighteen years he had held ten jobs entailing six major moves.

The occupations of sixty-nine men who married in Augustana Lutheran churches in Fort William and Port Arthur in Northwestern Ontario reveal the kinds of work, both rural and urban, available from 1906 to 1921. The records show twenty-four carpenters, twelve railway workers including a roadmaster, twelve labourers, five farmers, four tradesmen, two grocers, two cooks, and one each of schoolteacher, stationary engineer, boardinghouse keeper, restaurant owner, streetcar conductor, stone worker, cement worker, and watchman.[19]

Canada experienced hard times in 1923, and few jobs were available for the flood of new immigrants who arrived in response to the federal government's aggressive campaign.[20] In December 1923 Consul General Magnus Clarholm[21] informed the Foreign Affairs Department in Sweden of high unemployment.[22] The following March he wrote a sharp letter to the commissioner of immigration in Ottawa:

> On the 1st instant I had a personal interview with your Office in Ottawa and I then called attention to the fact that it often happens that Swedish immigrants ... are allowed to land here with very little money in their possession and that they after a short time apply to this Consulate General as destitute after having in vain tried to get employment.
>
> I further stated ... that it was my intention to refer Swedish immigrants of that category to your Immigration Agent here, as your Department and your agents are encouraging immigration from my country, and as it is an international rule that destitute aliens are taken care of by the authorities of the country where they are residing.[23]

The last sentence was wishful thinking. Although J.S. Woodsworth made a similar motion in Parliament in 1925[24] it was not until 1940 that Canada passed legislation to support the unemployed. Other consular correspondence recorded the experience of two immigrants who returned to Sweden in May 1924 because "even if wages are small there will not be starvation as here [in Canada]."[25]

During the fourth wave, some immigrants with a trade or profession were given false information before leaving Sweden. In 1958 Karl Larsson[26] was told that his electrician's ticket, or licence, would be accepted in Canada. "Those papers did not mean a thing to the inspector in Winnipeg. This was a written exam ... I wrote the exam using an English and a Swedish dictionary. It was a lot of work because it had to be done in a certain time. First you had to understand the question, solve it in Swedish in your mind, transfer it into English. That was a tough day. After being a journeyman I wrote another exam for the contractor's licence."[27] Larsson started his own business in 1970 after several years as an industrial electrician.

Railway Construction

The first Swedes to work on railway construction came from the United States in 1875 under contractor F.L. Erickson. They worked on the CPR west of Fort William, and Sweden is reflected in six of the original forty-five station names: Carlstad, Kalmar, Linkoping, Ostersund, Oxdrift, and Upsala.[28] The work could be dangerous. In 1909 six Swedes and a Norwegian were killed in a blasting accident on the Northern Transcontinental Railway.[29] The bodies were brought by sleigh to Nipigon, a distance of some 240 kilometres to the south, and buried, with Pastor S.R. Christensen of Port Arthur officiating. The same year a three-storey hotel had been built of cement blocks in Nipigon for workmen coming and going, called Skandia House. The landmark structure survives as Skandia House Bed and Breakfast, but minus the top storey and a half.[30]

Olof "Tie" Hanson[31] began taking contracts to supply railway ties as construction of Canada's third transcontinental railway, the Grand Trunk Pacific, moved westward from Edmonton. He walked 1,287 kilometres along the proposed route to survey the timber and won large contracts eastward from Prince Rupert, the Pacific terminus. By the time the railway was completed in 1914 Hanson was well established in the logging industry.

Prince Rupert was built on Kaien Island, at the mouth of the Skeena River. Since the island consisted of a heavily forested mountain, the ground had to be levelled for railway installations. Alfred Nilsson[32] was among the thousands of immigrant labourers who "moved the mountain" by drilling holes in the rock and filling them with dynamite. He also blasted tunnels along the line to Yellowhead Pass. During this time he witnessed the violent strike at Kelly's Cut and lived in construction camps of unspeakable squalor.

Railway Employees

In 1887 immigrant agent Öhlén reported that he had assisted 332 Scandinavians, and that almost a third of them went to railway jobs, thanks to two Winnipeg roadmasters (responsible for track maintenance). The Norwegian O. Johnson had charge of the southern route, and Charles Pansar,[33] a Swede, oversaw the line westward to Brandon. For many Swedes this would be their first job in Canada, allowing them to earn enough money to buy land or to send a ticket home. For others, like Peter Andrew Benson,[34] it became a career.

A number of Swedes became section foremen. They had to be physically fit to maintain the tracks by walking their section (six to nine kilometres each way) every day, shimming up ties to level the tracks, keeping the switches free of debris, breaking beaver dams, and supervising section men. Swedes also worked as carpenters on bridge-and-building gangs and as labourers on extra gangs building new trackage, constructing snowsheds in the mountains, replacing ties, and other heavy jobs.

Three Swedes were among the sixty workers killed in the Rogers Pass snow slide in 1910. They had been clearing the tracks from an earlier snow slide, with roadmaster Jon Anderson in charge. His daughter described the event: "My Dad, Roadmaster, was with a rotary plough crew armed with axes, saws and shovels about a mile above Glacier when they ran into a slide filled with trees. He trudged back to a snow shed where he phoned the dispatcher and asked for more men. While he was away a second slide [from the opposite direction] buried all the workers including his brother."[35]

The three Swedes were buried at Golden, their headstones enclosed by a white picket fence. A photograph dated 1911 shows a group of men wearing CPR mourning ribbons gathered at the graves.[36] Jon Anderson was so affected by the tragedy that, after testifying at the inquest, he moved his family to Victoria where there were no Rocky Mountains and very little snow.

Logging Industry

Another major employer was the logging industry, both in the bush and in sawmills. A visitor from Sweden, Ivar Vennerström, compared logging in both countries in 1925:[37]

> The destruction of forested land in Sweden is nothing compared to here [in British Columbia]. Here they cut down the Douglas firs and cedars ... at the height of a man, not at three inches above the ground as in Sweden. The remaining trees, often taller than the tallest in the Swedish forests, are not left for long. They are snapped like matchsticks when heavy machinery accelerates and pulls the felled timber whirling and skipping forward. A hundred foot high trees break into pieces and the area looks like a battlefield where heavy artillery has decimated everything ...
>
> British Columbia's forests are full of Scandinavians. They prefer being lumberjacks to being farmers. As workers they are liked, they put in more effort than others but they tend to waste their earnings. Money runs through their fingers ... Like a well-arranged community the [logging] camp lies in the midst of the big lonely forest. This one is one of the bigger and better in this part of B.C. 160 men live here. Nothing resembles how Swedish lumberjacks in Sweden live, all crowded into one single house located all by itself far in the snowy forest.[38]

However, Scandinavian loggers in British Columbia never made up more than 24 per cent of the workforce during the 1920s and 1930s,[39] and were always outnumbered by men of British origin.[40]

Although the food was usually tasty and plentiful, lice were a major nuisance in the bunkhouse: "You could get three kinds of lice: head lice, body lice and crab lice that settled in on your private parts and forced you to shave and use some kind of ointment to discourage new infestation."[41] Elimination of this problem began with Finnish saunas, or steam baths, which provided the facilities to allow personal cleanliness.

In 1906 P.B. Anderson,[42] a logging contractor, crossed the international boundary, but just barely, to build a sawmill near Cultus Lake, British Columbia. His forty-year career in Canada took him up the mainland coast, to Vancouver Island, and to Harrison Lake in the southern interior to cut what he estimated to be two and a quarter billion feet of

British Columbia logs. "I've always known how to make money," he recounted. "But I didn't know how to keep it. I've been broke several times."[43] Nevertheless, his estate amounted to a healthy $73,978.[44]

A far-sighted Port Arthur contractor who had been trained in forestry in Norway, Oscar Styffe,[45] was concerned about the depletion of North-western Ontario's forests. In 1937 he applied to the Ontario government for a timber limit on which to practise sustained-yield logging of ties and pulpwood. The limit, approximately 155 square kilometres, was located on the eastern shore of Lake Nipigon. "Our idea and intention is to estab-lish a community in a section of the area suited, and give each man a certain acreage to live on, where he can eventually build his own abode ... Under this arrangement, the whole area would be operated on at the same time and the cutting supervised so that only the mature timber be cut and strict attention paid to care in felling so that the younger growth is not damaged any more than is necessary, in the course of operations."[46] Unfortunately the timber limit went to another firm, and clear-cutting continued as usual. The Ontario Ministry of Natural Resources did not recognize sustained-yield logging as a worthwhile goal until 1994.

Mining Industry

Swedes who worked in the mining industry seemed to favour gold. The Klondike gold rush began in mid-July 1897, when a Seattle newspaper reported that new millionaires had arrived by steamship with "a ton of gold." That fall and winter 100,000 hopeful gold seekers followed the call to untold riches, some of them clutching a new Canadian map with the gold fields coloured an exuberant yellow.[47] They travelled by boat to Skagway, on the Alaska panhandle, and walked more than forty-three kilometres north over the Coast Mountains, either through White Pass or Chilkoot Pass, to the headwaters of the Yukon River.[48] The trip was cold and arduous, especially when a person was burdened with a heavy backpack and carrying a rifle.

Only 30,000 people made it over the mountains. White Pass became known as Dead Horse Trail. The enterprising Eric Hegg[49] beat the odds by using goats to pull his camera equipment, chemicals, and personal supplies. Before leaving Skagway he took the famous photograph of an unbroken line of men moving ant-like up Chilkoot Pass, their bod-ies dark against the snow. Accompanying him was the aforementioned P.B. Anderson, who whipsawed lumber at Lake Bennett to build a nine-metre boat, with a darkroom in the bow.[50]

Otto Nordenskjöld[51] and his party[52] entered the Klondike through Chilkoot Pass, their supplies and equipment loaded onto five horse-drawn wagons purchased in Skagway. Nordenskjöld, a geographer from Sweden, had been commissioned by A.V. Eck & Company of Stockholm to stake claims. His tent sat among a thousand others on the shore of Lake Lindemann, their occupants busy building boats and rafts while waiting for breakup. Then began the long (1,000 kilometres) journey to Dawson down the swollen river, through narrow mountain passes, churning rapids, and swirling whirlpools. Afterwards, he wrote that the river was full of wrecks.[53]

The group staked claims all summer, then Nordenskjöld left for Sweden with his field notes and photographs purchased from Eric Hegg.[54] One of them showed a donkey and her foal standing in a crowded street in Dawson, with sandwich boards hanging over their backs to advertise "Hegg's Gallery." Hegg's photographs no longer need to be advertised. They can be found in most accounts of the Klondike, including Charlie Chaplin's 1925 silent movie *The Gold Rush*.

In June 1898 the Canadian government hurriedly organized the Yukon as a territory, and sent the North-West Mounted Police to keep order. The new capital, Dawson, was already a supply centre because of its location where the Klondike and Yukon rivers meet. Earlier prospectors had bought their supplies at Forty Mile, downstream near the Alaska border. One of them was Charlie Anderson,[55] the "Lucky Swede."

Anderson was lucky to make two fortunes, but singularly unlucky to lose them both. He came to the Yukon from Tacoma, Washington, in 1893, and earned a small stake by working a claim. After getting wind of the fabulous strike on Bonanza Creek in August 1896, the one that set off the gold rush, he bought a claim from three Americans for $800: No. 29 on Eldorado Creek. By the end of the year he had found the motherlode.

His fortune was estimated at almost a million dollars in 1899, when he married Grace Drummond, a dance-hall girl. The couple moved to San Francisco where Grace proved to be a different kind of gold digger from her husband. After the divorce Anderson was broke. He made a second fortune from gold finds in Nome, Alaska, and invested it in San Francisco real estate just before the earthquake in 1906. Down but not out, the Lucky Swede spent his final years looking for copper and gold on mineral-rich Texada Island in British Columbia. He assured friends that he would not shave until becoming rich again. Charlie Anderson died in 1939 with a full beard.[56] His luck had run out.

The above sketch was drawn on birchbark. On the back, Alfred Geijer wrote, "I built this log cabin in the fall of 1897 beside Bonanza Creek, Yukon." The plants at the bottom are pressed flowers from the Yukon. *En Smålandssocken emigrerar* (1967), 207.

Alfred Geijer,[57] like many others from Långasjö, emigrated to earn money to buy a better life in Sweden. In Dawson he worked for an American company as supervisor of the machine extracting gold, earning a production bonus. He saved enough money to realize his dream, and more. His store and sawmill in Sweden expanded to become today's Geijer Timber Company, one of Småland's leading providers of wood products.[58] Carl Nilsson,[59] also from Småland, made good in the Klondike, too, but most gold seekers did not become rich, no matter how hard they worked.[60]

Another gold-mining mecca was Northwestern Ontario, with Kenora and its stamp mill as the hub, reaching out to Mine Centre east of Fort Frances and Gold Rock south of Wabigoon. Swedes could be found in all of them, as prospectors, miners, workmen, and entrepreneurs.[61] Kenora's major producers were the Sultana, Regina, and Mikado mines.

In 1901 there were 160 people living at Sultana mine, and 38 had been born in Sweden. The year before, three Swedes had been killed in explosions. The first was underground, where John Olson and Charles Thunstrom were thawing the volatile explosive nitroglycerine. The second was in the blacksmith shop, where Adolph Hedlund and August Anderson were cutting a nitroglycerine can in half for use as a spittoon.[62]

The copper and silver mines of the Kootenays in south-central British Columbia also attracted Swedes. Ola Lofstad[63] arrived in Greenwood in 1896 and became a long-time resident. Three years later a husky six-footer, John Eek,[64] arrived from Montrose, Iowa, to work in the furnaces of the newly opened smelter. At the same time he filed on a homestead in nearby Myncaster, built a cabin and outbuildings, registered his brand "JE," built up a herd of cattle, and later bred Percheron and Hackney horses.

Archivist John Richthammer has documented more than a hundred Swedes in the area of Red Lake, Ontario, site of a major gold rush in 1926. Red Lake is located above the 50th parallel, 170 kilometres from the nearest railway point at Hudson. That first summer more than a thousand prospectors detrained at Hudson and followed the Lac Seul waterways north, a twelve-day journey. Later the route was mechanized with tractor trains and steam-powered pulleys to drag heavy machinery over the portages between Ear Falls and Red Lake. There were twelve producing mines at the height of the boom, which continued into the 1940s.[65]

Ed Fahlgren[66] first came to Hudson in 1934 as credit manager for Starratt Airways, then moved to Red Lake as office manager for the Cochenour-Willans Syndicate, and through a series of promotions became president and general manager. After retirement in 1978 he was appointed to head the Royal Commission on the Northern Environment, which covered all of Ontario north of the 50th parallel, and paid special attention to the plight of the First Nations.

Zeballos, on the west coast of Vancouver Island, mushroomed as a community in 1938, the year that Privateer gold mine went into production.[67] One of the discoverers, Albert Blom,[68] had a disagreement with his partner Alfred Bird and was living in a tent. He later left for Vancouver: "[Upon his return] Bird mentioned that Blom had been in bad shape physically because he had been on a two-month drunk. On the third night alone in [Alex McDonald's] cabin he had gone over to Bird's cabin and borrowed Bird's 30.30 rifle ... [on 18 December 1937 he] dressed himself in his best clothes, laid down on the floor, put the muzzle of the gun to his heart and pulled the trigger, ending his life."[69]

Blom's estate, mostly option agreements for mineral claims, was valued at close to $19,000.[70]

Engineers also contributed to Canada's mining industry. Ernst Adolf Sjöstedt[71] worked in Bridgeville, Nova Scotia, then in Sault Ste Marie, Ontario, until his death on the *Titanic*. Erik Nyström[72] was employed at Victoria Mines, Ontario, then moved to the Geological Survey of Canada in 1903. The following year he was appointed to the four-man commission sent to Sweden to study the electric method of producing iron and steel. Jonas Einar Lindeman[73] worked for the federal Department of Mines from 1906 to 1915, and then returned to Sweden. A later mining engineer, Hans Lundberg,[74] developed the concept of using electricity to determine the location and size of an ore body. He came to Toronto in 1926 to found Hans Lundberg Limited, and twenty years later began using helicopters. By the late 1950s his company had discovered ore deposits in twenty-eight countries worth five billion dollars.[75]

Co-operative Movement

Settlers who grew wheat on the Prairies before the establishment of systems like bulk purchases and proper marketing were often unable to make a profit until the Saskatchewan Grain Growers Association adopted the co-operative system.[76] Frank Eliason[77] became a champion of the movement soon after arriving in Wynard, Saskatchewan, in 1910. During eight years in the United States he had become an active Socialist under Eugene Debs. After a Scot named McDaid told him he would be able to practise Socialism under the system of the Saskatchewan Grain Growers Association he transferred his support: "They bought their necessities at cost and sold their products in the best possible market and the excess earnings were turned back in the form of patronage dividends to the producer and consumer after handling charges had been met. Mr. McDaid referred to this system of merchandising as the Rochdale Plan."[78]

When a Grain Growers Association was formed in Wynard, Eliason became secretary of this and twelve other locals. The association had a trading department that made bulk purchases of commodities like binder twine, lumber, coal, flour, and fruit. His job was to take orders from the farmers, distribute the goods, and also to write insurance.

Not surprisingly, local merchants, agents, and professional people strongly opposed these activities. Bank interest on loans was 10 per cent, which many farmers considered to be usury. Eliason negotiated solutions to writs for collection of bills and threats of foreclosure, rather than the farmer's having to pay the added expense of a lawsuit. Reprisals soon followed. These included a town bylaw forbidding the sale of goods without a licence, and a notice from the railway against allowing delivery of goods from a boxcar. Eliason took the stand that he neither bought nor sold merchandise, but was paid for the service of assembling goods bought collectively by the farmers. Through the activities of Frank Eliason and others like him, virtually all wheat farmers became members of the Grain Growers Association.

Agriculture

Immigrants settled on the Prairies as homesteaders or owners of purchased land, and also farmed in Ontario and British Columbia. Charles Lindholm[79] moved his family to Wetaskiwin in 1922 after nine drought years of the twelve spent in Iddesleigh, Alberta. He took up land west of New Norway with the goal of raising the best crops in the area, and accomplished this through buying seeds from the renowned Swedish firm Svalöv. The result was "Lindholm Seed Farm, Producers, Processors & Retailers of Quality Pedigreed Seed – Wheat, Oats, Barley, Canola, Peas, Established 1922." The family took pride in its heritage, printing the company logo and business cards in the traditional yellow and blue of the Swedish flag. During the early 1960s when Iddesleigh was preparing its history, *Some Did – Some Didn't Win Their $10.00 Bet with the Government*, Charles Lindholm was a major contributor as one of the earliest residents.

The detailed letters of Edwin Thomeus,[80] a homesteader in Magnolia, Alberta, are a marvellous resource recounting the day-to-day activities of a homesteader, relationships with neighbours, and comments about current events. While away working at his first job he made arrangements to return to his land the following summer of 1906: "I have quite large poplar timber on it and plan to use some of same to build a house. I have given my partner [Joe Larson] instructions regarding how much timber I want to have ready so I can begin building my cabin as soon as I return to the homestead. Rostron [*sic*] and Jansson owe me 7¼ days work because I selected the homesteads for them."[81]

Thomeus was prepared to return and enlist if Sweden went to war with Norway, even though it would mean paying a fine for skipping out on his compulsory military duty.[82]

Of all the commercially important agricultural areas in North America, the Peace River valley is the northern-most. Its fertile prairie east of the Rocky Mountains extends from Fort St John in British Columbia to Valleyview in Alberta, northwest of Edmonton.[83] The area benefits from lower mountains that allow warm Pacific air masses (chinooks) to moderate the weather. With an average of 110 frost-free days, more rain than east-central Alberta, and seventeen hours of daylight at mid-summer, crops were comparable to, and sometimes better than, those further south. The Wembley farmer Herman Trelle[84] beat out the rest of the continent in 1926 to become "wheat king" at the Chicago Fair. He would duplicate this coup four more times during the 1930s.

Although hundreds of Swedes settled throughout the Peace River country,[85] the largest number chose Valleyview. David Halldin[86] arrived with his brother Joe in 1928:

From the top of the hill you could see two valleys, east and west. To the north the woodlands stretched for miles and miles. When the district later was christened Valleyview it was a fitting name indeed ...

About 80 or 90 per cent of the settlers were of Scandinavian descent; there were also a few Germans and Hungarians, half a dozen Scotchmen. The Swedes were definitely in the majority, to the regret of our first pioneer, Oscar Adolfson, who had hoped for a Norwegian community ... In 1930 we organized a Scandinavian Club. We were the majority of the newcomers. But there was some old diehard Swedes who organized a Swedish Club. It was not very successful. The Scandinavian Club was responsible for much worthwhile entertainment. We put on dances, plays in Scandinavian languages, and we even had a good choir ...

To begin with we danced in the schoolhouse on Saturday evenings. On Sundays the schoolhouse was used for church services ... The lay minister said the schoolhouse was used by the Devil on Saturday nights ... We had a few theater groups coming [to perform in our community hall] as soon as the roads permitted. I remember a group that came at least twice a year – "Ola the Swede." It was a comedy team. The program was a mixture of Swedish and English and quite funny. Bands were always welcome. Then there was dancing all night. We also had our own music – two excellent accordion players.[87]

David Halldin claimed that it was James Oliver Curwood's adventure novels that drew him irresistibly to the Canadian wilderness. Both brothers spent time at the nearby Cree reserve, sometimes trading oats and eggs for moccasins, moose meat, and tanned moosehides.

Andrew Anderson[88] developed Fogelvik Farm at Alsask, Saskatchewan, in 1910. That same year a nephew, Nels Benson,[89] came to help out as a mechanic. Crop yields fluctuated from eight bushels of wheat per acre to forty-five (from seven hectolitres per hectare to thirty-nine hectolitres per hectare), depending on rainfall; therefore, Andrew practised dry farming, which meant leaving half his fields fallow each year. He also left half the property forested to hold the water. His holdings grew to 1,736 hectares, and in 1931 the farm was run with tractors and sixty-two horses.[90] The following year he sold his showpiece and he and his wife, Hannah, retired, but not for long. In 1934 he started a second Fogelvik Farm at Innisfail, south of Red Deer, which he operated until his death in 1945.

His daughter and son-in-law, Helen and Knut Magnusson,[91] came from Sweden to settle the estate and ended up staying in Innisfail. Knut, a civil engineer and graduate in forestry and farm economics, ran the property on a scientific basis, and under his management Fogelvik Farm became one of the highest producing farms in Alberta. The Magnussons are credited with introducing Landrace pigs and Viking ponies to Canada and also with developing Merion Blue grass seed and Creeping Red Fescue as commercial crops. In the late 1950s Knut hired young men from the Nordic countries under Canada's Assisted Passage scheme.[92]

Paul Boving, a professor of agriculture at the University of British Columbia since it began and an avid promoter of things Swedish, developed several new strains of forage crops and grains.[93] Another graduate of Sweden's Alnarp Agricultural Institute, Sixten Högstedt,[94] specialized in animal husbandry, and spent the rest of his career breeding Jersey cows at the experimental station in Harrow, Ontario.

Horticulturist Gustaf Krook[95] came to Brandon in 1907 to work at the CPR's garden-and-plant school. The railway company encouraged employees to beautify stations and section houses with flowers and formal gardens. Eventually Krook became overseer for the western lines and in 1917 for the eastern lines as well from his base in Wolseley, Saskatchewan.

Nurseryman Sven Sherdahl[96] came from Kansas in 1890 as an older pioneer. He built the Dominion Hotel in Vancouver, later leasing it to return to his first career. Most of the holly hedges in the West End and Shaughnessy Heights originated from this, Vancouver's first nursery.

Dairying

Small dairies were common in Canada until 1963, when it became illegal to sell unpasteurized milk. John and Helga Taft[97] operated a dairy farm in Wabigoon, Ontario, to supply local needs. The milk was kept cold with ice until the arrival of electricity in 1950. John, a stonemason, built the stone fireplaces and cairns in provincial parks, including Aaron Park near Dryden. In Saskatchewan Alex Johnson[98] and his wife Grace bought Sunny Side Dairy west of Moose Jaw, and he delivered milk to city residents in a brightly painted, horse-drawn wagon. The family milked up to thirty cows twice a day, by hand. Wives and children contributed a great deal to these family dairies.

Fur Trade

When jobs were scarce, some homesteaders tried trapping for the winter. Not all were as successful as Dan Ericson,[99] whose partner was his father-in-law, Nils Holm.[100] After sixteen months in northern Saskatchewan they returned home to Minnedosa in 1919 with $2,200 gross profit.[101] A nice nest egg for Dan, who became a Mission Covenant pastor.

A tradition that endured throughout the immigration period was an appreciation of nature in its many forms. In some respects Sweden's right of common access to pick berries and mushrooms on private land was duplicated in Canada's hinterland. The Swedish author Albert Viksten maintained that Canadian trappers were nature lovers despite, or perhaps because of, their calling.[102] Peter Bergenham[103] spent most of his life as a trapper. "Peter trapped with deadfall traps," wrote his sister Caroline, "never the cruel leg hold trap."[104] The family was thrilled in 1935–6 when he was chosen to appear with two others as "Indian" paddlers in the Gaumont British film *The Silent Barrier*, which chronicled CPR construction through Rogers Pass. Peter was an expert canoeist, said to be the only person to navigate all the rapids on the Columbia River between Golden and Revelstoke.[105]

Ben Nelson[106] worked as a fur buyer in northern Ontario from 1918 to 1940. Except for eleven years with the Schnaufer Fur Company of Toronto he travelled the railways, buying furs from trappers along the line. Ben drowned on the Batchewana River in 1947, leaving his Ojibwa wife, Yvonne, and nine children. Ben Junior wrote about a sister's visit to Sweden in 2001: "She met hundreds of relatives who were so proud when they found out that her mother had been a Canadian Indian. It had been 95 years since Ben had left Sweden and yet even her third cousins knew about him."[107] Yvonne traced her fur-trade ancestry back to Charles Boyer, who was born at Michilimackinac about 1720 and in 1744 was trading at Lac la Pluie, now Fort Frances.

In 1921 Sven Klintberg[108] realized his dream of establishing a fox farm at Bird's Hill near Winnipeg, calling it Winnipeg Silver Fox Company. He had graduated from Stockholm's School of Economics in 1912, and spent time in Prince Edward Island, the cradle of Canada's fur-farming industry, before moving west to manage a large fur farm. After founding his own facility Sven and his brother took care of 700 to 800 silver foxes. He won national awards for male breeding animals, and in 1933 represented Manitoba in the Canadian National Silver Fox Breeders Association event.

Gus Ronnander[109] founded Ronnander's Mink Ranch in East Kildonan, Manitoba, in 1933, but moved 3,000 animals to Charleswood in 1941, where his brother Andy[110] owned another mink ranch. He served as president of the Manitoba Fur Breeders' Association at a time when there were approximately fifty mink ranches in the Charleswood area. One of his legacies is a street in Charleswood named Ronnander Cove.

A Swede named Lundihn had a fox and mink ranch at Tyrone, near Bowmanville, Ontario. Lundihn worked as fur buyer for Eaton's in Toronto, and hired Ben Swanson[111] to work for him. In 1949 Swanson bought a fox and mink ranch near Alliston, Ontario. The operation included a packing plant that provided food for the area's mink farms. One year he butchered eighty-four horses that had been displaced by tractors, and in 1951 bought his first load of whale meat – twenty-three tonnes. Swanson sold the ranch in 1987.

Fishing

Salmon fishing became a major industry on the west coast during the 1880s, after Ben Young[112] of Astoria, Oregon, built canneries in Canoe Pass at the mouth of the Fraser River, and on the Skeena River to the north. Ben and his wife, Christina, came from the fishing village of Lomma in southern Sweden, and by the time he sold his Canadian canneries in 1891 the exodus from Lomma had already begun.[113] Christina's brother, Paul Swenson,[114] and brother-in-law, Alfred Jenson,[115] became managers of canneries in Canada. The cannery at Canoe Pass produced

1,000 to 1,200 crates of tinned salmon every day. Each crate weighed twenty-two kilograms.[116]

Some of the Swedes lived on houseboats and others bought farm property. Nils Sandell[117] lived in Surrey when his father, grandfather, and younger siblings joined him in 1891, and ten years later bought a fruit farm in Burnaby. Sandell Road in Surrey, now 128th Street, and Sandell Street in Burnaby are named after the Sandell family.

These immigrants had gone to school and confirmation classes together during the 1860s, but there is no record of picnics, excursions, or even church events. However, Cecilia Erickson told of a party to celebrate the cannery's only holiday, the 24th of May, Queen Victoria's birthday: "We held it yesterday so that people would be able to rest today (Sunday). We decorated the loft above the Cannery so nicely that it reminded me of our wedding day. We had invited everybody [fishermen] from two nearby Canneries as well. We ate at five and then danced till midnight when food was served again. Afterwards dancing continued till two when the party broke up. We women had baked pies and cakes and other good things, all cold food, coffee and tea."[118]

In addition Swedes from Sweden operated important commercial fisheries on Lake of the Woods, and Swedes from Finland on Lake Superior near Thunder Bay.

Entrepreneur Eric Jurell[119] started the company Eric of Nanaimo in the 1980s to design fishing tools, including his Sillbiten fishing lure, which caught the world's official second-largest red snapper. In the late 1990s he began manufacturing crayfish cages so that Swedes, and others, could catch their own in British Columbia's lakes and rivers. The Swedish tradition of crayfish parties (*kräftskivor*) takes place in August.

Building Construction

The need for country elevators, terminal elevators, homes, and other structures was so great that Swedes often found work as carpenters, whether they had apprenticed or not. As early as 1902 farmers began banding together to build country elevators beside the railway to store their grain until it was shipped to market. Every community had at least one country elevator, until recently the most distinctive landmarks on the prairie horizon. Saskatchewan Co-operative Elevator Company was founded in 1911, but already by 1904 one of the engineers in charge of elevator construction was a Swede named Fredrick Bergström,[120] with headquarters in Regina. Many Swedes were hired to build country elevators.

Charlie Pearson and his crew of carpenters stopped working long enough to pose for a photo in the summer of 1951. They are building an elevator annex at Kronau, Saskatchewan, southeast of Regina. Courtesy of Lynne Collier.

Swedes were also responsible for two museum buildings in the Red Lake area. Nels Anderson[121] quit his job as a fur trader to haul freight up the Lac Seul waterway during the gold rush. When Highway 105 displaced the marine portages he built a tourist camp at Snake Falls, then constructed Ear Falls District Museum. All told, he built an estimated 300 log structures in Northwestern Ontario. John Gustafson[122] quit mining in 1944 to found the Red Lake Lumber Company, complete with sawmill. During the 1970s he restored the derelict, two-storey, log residence at Sam's Portage and moved it to Red Lake as a museum. Gustav Einar Erickson[123] had built the structure for the superintendent of the marine portage system.

As a carpenter Art Carlson[124] built head frames and other structures until his marriage in 1941. When the couple decided to go into the tourist business, Art built a lodge and cabins of logs. Viking Island Lodge, the area's first fly-in fishing camp, is located in Woodland Caribou Wilderness Park. Swedes are also credited with building Minaki Lodge north of Kenora in 1927, which the Canadian National Railway billed as the Jewel of the North. The structure was destroyed by fire in 2003 and has since been rebuilt.[125]

Swedes living in the original colony of Scandinavia were given an extraordinary opportunity to exercise their log-building skills in Riding Mountain National Park during the 1920s and 1930s. The original forest reserve was formally declared a national park in 1930. The federal parks branch not only imposed design controls on new buildings, but also encouraged early owners to upgrade their cabins. Buildings in the townsite of Wasagaming constructed from 1930 to 1932 would be in the Tudor Rustic style, as were all other new structures.[126]

One of the contractors hired to build cabins was carpenter A.J. Sjogren,[127] who had moved from Hilltop to what became Wasagaming around 1918. He furnished his own cottage with handmade tables, shelves, clocks, and fretwork, and outside carved a tall "totem pole" with seats around the base so that he and his wife could enjoy the outdoors while working at sedentary tasks.

John Anderson[128] was a major contractor for park buildings. Before starting that work he bought imported Swedish tools and materials in Winnipeg.[129] While staying at Norway House he hired a number of unemployed log craftsmen to supplement his existing crew.[130] The administration building, Danceland, and the saddle-notched log Park Theatre were the larger structures built under his direction.

Gotfrid Johnson[131] learned the art from a master log builder from Sweden, Harry Spenar. With his son Herbert and brother-in-law David

Carlson he built the first log cabin at the north end of Clear Lake, and several more later. Then he built the golf clubhouse, where he also used his skills as a stonemason, and the fire hall with its lofty hose-drying tower. Busy with other contracts, he hired George Bergman and Axel Nelson to build the twenty-six-room Wasagaming Lodge, which he took over as a family enterprise. He later added the Johnson cabins with his son-in-law Ernest Gusdal,[132] who had built the park's first restaurant, the Wigwam.

Gotfrid Johnson and his son Herbert also built a cabin on the south shore of Beaver Lake for the park's first naturalist, Grey Owl, his wife, Anahero, and their pet beavers, Rawhide and Jelly Roll. "Even though Grey Owl stayed in the park less than a year, his colourful and flamboyant personality left a lasting impression on the people of the area. My parents [Ernest and Lillian Gusdal] and grandparents often recalled his skill in telling tales, especially spine chilling ghost stories around the camp fires."[133]

Herbert Johnson had already developed a keen interest in the area's wildlife. He raised two moose calves after their mother died in a forest fire, and they were featured in a National Film Board film.

Some immigrants were skilled journeymen. A finishing carpenter named O.P. Olson[134] arrived in Saskatchewan with a handmade case holding a two-armed guitar with three extra bass strings. He built specialized furniture for his home and replaced his sod barn with a much larger one, using fieldstones for the footings and walls. It had Dutch double doors on the front and two distinctive cupolas on the roof, which could be seen from kilometres away. He also built an oven of stone and brick so that his wife could bake large circles of flatbread or hard tack (*tunnbröd or knäckebröd*) twice a year. Hard tack was dry and could be stored almost indefinitely.[135]

Shipbuilding

Ontario's shipbuilding industry attracted several Swedish naval architects. Arendt Ångström[136] moved to Toronto in 1893 as manager of Bertram Engine Works, partly purchased by the Canadian Shipbuilding Company in 1903. Ångström designed the steamers *Toronto* and *Kingston*, the passenger tender *Hiawatha*, and the lake steamer *Cayuga*.[137] His replacement at Bertram Engine Works was John W. Gerell.[138] Erik Tornroos[139] began his working career at the Canadian Shipbuilding Company, then moved to the Port Arthur Shipbuilding Company. There, he drew up plans for the steamships *Huronic* and *Noronic*, and also for the hockey time clocks that used to hang in Fort William Gardens and Maple Leaf Gardens.

Engineers

Chemical engineer Gottfrid Larsson[140] worked as head chemist for St Mary's Cement Company, founded by his brother-in-law, John Lind. The company manufactured Portland cement from local limestone. Larsson was an active member of St James Anglican Church, the Masonic Order, and Scottish Rite. He published a number of articles on cement production, and after his death his herbarium of more than two thousand pressed plants was donated to the Royal Ontario Museum.[141]

In 1952 Nils Adler,[142] a structural engineer, joined the Canadian firm Read Jones Christoffersen in Vancouver, and transferred to Toronto in 1968 to build the company's office there. The Swedish company Skanska controlled the Foundation Company of Canada, which built Toronto's CN Tower, the tallest free-standing structure in the world at 553 metres. Construction took place from 1973 to 1976, with the tower's tapering shape achieved with Skanska's slip form process of pouring concrete, and the restaurant revolving on SKF roller bearings.[143] The architect in charge during construction, Edward R. Baldwin, had Swedish roots through his mother.[144]

Inventors

Sweden's inventors paved the way for profitable industries through a series of inventions including the safety match (1844), spherical bearings (1907), and the refrigerator (1925). But perhaps the most famous invention was dynamite by Alfred Nobel, who, through his will, established the Nobel prizes that are awarded with great ceremony each December. In 1964 the eminent Canadian historian Donald Quayle Innis wrote an article titled "Sweden – An Example for Canada." He praised Sweden's worldwide markets for products completely manufactured at home: "Sweden's industries can be classed under four headings. They are based on natural resources, fashion, quality and inventions ... Swedes played a major part in developing the modern cream separator, three-wire electric wiring and the two-way conversion of high voltage direct to alternating electric current. Each successful Swedish invention gives rise to a Swedish owned industry."[145]

Immigrants continued the tradition in Canada with limited success. In the mid-1920s electrical contractor Knute Karlson[146] of Elmwood, Ontario, invented a splitter box, which came into general use in large service installations.

John Edlund[147] of Claresholm, Alberta, retired in 1929 so that he could devote more time to inventing. He had already devised a combination life preserver/suitcase soon after the sinking of the *Titanic*: "It is equipped with a pair of waterproof trousers which, together with the valise proper, forms a buoyant watertight suit ... Sufficient food for several days can be kept in the suitcase. The wearer of the suit may remain in the water from four to five days without danger of sinking or death from exposure."[148] Travellers embarking at New York could rent an "Ever-Warm Safety Suit" for $8 from the National Life Preserver Company, but wartime shortages stopped production. Like many others, Edlund did not become rich with his inventions. As a hobby he delighted in the Swedish sport of finger pulling. He practised every day by lifting a 136-kilogram-weight with each of his fingers.

Sometimes necessity was the mother of invention. In 1932 Carl Lilja,[149] who owned a farm in Alberta's North Hayter district, lost his right leg below the knee in a farm accident. He got around on crutches until he designed a wooden leg from a poplar branch. Hollowing out one end for the stump, he padded it well, then fastened light iron strips, with hinges at the knee, to the wood and to a twenty-five-centimetre-wide leather band around his upper leg. A narrow strip of leather over his opposite shoulder kept everything in place. He carved a foot, attaching it to the bottom of his prosthesis with light iron strips and springs. His rewards were twofold: to continue farming and to walk with scarcely a limp.

Allan Burman[150] of Vancouver was a fervent speaker for Technocracy, an organization that led him into the world of ideas. He took his invention of jet propulsion to the University of British Columbia in the 1930s. "Forget it," they said. "Impossible." This was the fate of most of his inventions. James Swanson of Kelwood, Manitoba, patented rust- and smut-resistant fertilizer and wheat, corn, and oats seed in 1934.[151] More recently, G.M. Lindberg was one of those at the National Research Council of Canada responsible for developing the Canadarm, the mechanical arm first used on the second space shuttle mission, STS-2, in 1981.[152]

Sven Johansson began his life in Canada as a reindeer specialist, then, with incorporation of his Discovery Dance at the age of sixty-five, he became a choreographer based in Victoria. His studio relies upon his invention, the ES Dance Instrument, which allows performers to flout gravity and dance in mid-air. With proper stage lighting none of the equipment is seen, only the dancer or dancers. The technique premiered in 1992 in Victoria, and since then has been used for his own artistic dance productions as well as theatrical productions such *Peter Pan, Fiddler on the Roof*, and *Aqua Ballet*, a 2001 pilot project in airborne water dance. Discovery Dance also pioneered dance for the disabled in 1994, the same year Johansson was invested as a Member of the Order of Canada. His choreography has won international awards, and has been aired on CBC TV and Canadian Bravo TV.[153]

Visual Artists

An artist has to be talented to be able to earn a living. Augustana Lutheran Church's altar painting and cherub sculpture in Erickson were the work of Nils P. Lithander,[154] who lived in the Scandinavia area from 1911 to 1923. His portraits and paintings of home scenes from the Old Country, using enlarged photographs, were popular, and his Biblical scenes hung as altar paintings in Lutheran churches in Scandinavia, Clanwilliam, and Danvers, a Norwegian settlement. On the side he made violins and taught music. In 1922 the family moved to Brandon for a couple of years, possibly with the hope of his being hired by Brandon College, then returned to Chicago.

Canada's Group of Seven may have found inspiration in the landscape paintings of Scandinavian contemporaries. Swedish artists who came to Canada include Malte Sterner,[155] whose etching of the Chateau Frontenac is owned by the Fine Arts Museum in San Francisco. On the east coast the William E. deGarthe gallery at Peggy's Cove is identified by his thirty-metre granite sculpture, *Fisherman's Monument*, honouring fishermen, their families, and the legendary Peggy. Born in Finland, deGarthe[156] immigrated to Halifax in 1926. In 1948 he exhibited eighty-three works in Chicago under the name Birger Degerstedt, and sold most of them. However, he is best known for his seascapes. In addition to his work in the gallery at Peggy's Cove, a representative collection is on permanent display at the Public Archives building in Halifax.

Olle Holmsten[157] immigrated in 1953 and spent his most productive years as a sculpture instructor at the Alberta College of Art from 1963 to 1980. The work he completed through commissions and his belief in the potential of his students became his strength and his purpose: "I am trying to make people aware of the constructive values of the human body. The endless surprises of natural form. Sculpture is sensual. It should be a 3-dimensional dance, not just a stuck-on piece of decoration." His Edmonton commissions included a sculpture of Princess Louise for the Legislative Building and five major works for the provincial museum and archives.

In Delia, Alberta, Jim Pearson[158] is pursuing his "Vanishing Sentinels" project. An accomplished graphic artist, since 2002 he has been mapping and recording the company history of the province's grain elevators, and preserving the remaining standing elevators and annexes on film. His website states that Alberta had 1,759 wooden grain elevators in 1938, but by 2006 there were only 237 left.

Clarence Tillenius[159] of Winnipeg was one of Canada's foremost wildlife artists for more than half a century. His paintings graced covers of the monthly magazine *The Country Guide* for twenty-five years, and calendars of Monarch Life Assurance, now Manulife, for thirty-six years. He fashioned eighteen dioramas for museums, three-dimensional exhibits of mounted wildlife in front of a curved background with painted scenery. One of the most spectacular is *Buffalo Hunt* in the Manitoba Museum, and in preparation he positioned himself within a stampeding herd. Others can be seen at the provincial museums in Victoria and Edmonton, the Cultural Heritage Centre in Baker Lake, and the Canadian Museum of Nature in Ottawa, which in 2007 dedicated his dioramas as National Treasures.

Tillenius's commercial art career began in 1935, when *The Country Guide* bought his painting of a grizzly bear and a skunk meeting on a narrow mountain path, titled *Ascent or Descent.* The following year he lost his right arm in an industrial accident and learned to draw again with his left arm. Among those influencing his work was Sweden's Bruno Liljefors (1860–1939), who pioneered the painting of wildlife in its natural habitat. In 1989 Tillenius was keynote speaker at the opening of the Bruno Liljefors exhibition in Göteborg. In Canada he was awarded the Order of Manitoba in 2003 and the Order of Canada in 2005. The same year Edmonton's Pirkko Karvonen[160] produced the film *Tillenius: The Art of Nature*, which premiered at the Winnipeg Art Gallery. A permanent collection of Tillenius's works is housed at the Pavilion Gallery in Winnipeg's Assiniboine Park.

Sound Mixer

Lars Ekstrom[161] is a freelance sound mixer who has forty-eight films and TV series to his credit. He told a reporter that his career "would have been impossible for me to do in Sweden." He immigrated to Alberta in 1975 and moved to Vancouver six years later.

Politicians

Olof Hanson, Liberal member for Skeena, British Columbia, from 1930 to 1945, was the first foreign-born, non-British subject to be elected to the federal parliament.[162] Lorne Nystrom, NDP member for

Yorkton-Melville, Saskatchewan, from 1968 to 1993 and from 1997 to 2004, was the youngest Canadian ever elected to the federal parliament. David L. Anderson, Conservative member for Cypress Hills-Grasslands, Saskatchewan, first elected in 2000, is the most recent.

Provincial politicians include C.H. Olin, Liberal member for Wetaskiwin, Alberta, in 1909, the first Swedish immigrant to be elected to a provincial legislature; Albert Hermanson, who during the early 1920s served two terms as Liberal member for Canora, Saskatchewan; Rolf Wallgren Bruhn, Conservative member for Salmon Arm, British Columbia, from 1924 to 1942; and Gordon Stromberg,[163] Conservative member for Camrose, Alberta, from 1971 to 1986. A third-generation farmer, Stromberg was an avid collector of heritage farm machinery and other artifacts. Harry Strom is the only Swedish descendant elected to lead a province. He served as Social Credit premier of Alberta from 1968 to 1971. However, most Swedes were content to fill less prestigious political roles on local boards and councils.

During the early waves most immigrants earned their living through hard physical labour, except for a handful of immigration agents, engineers, naval architects, and other educated men hired by government, industry, and institutions. After the Second World War employment became increasingly specialized and education-oriented, allowing unprecedented opportunities for both men and women.

Chapter Ten

A Woman's Place

As in most agricultural societies, a Swedish woman's role as homemaker was ordained before she was born. She was expected to marry and have children, and to run her home with skills learned from her mother. These included sewing, weaving, and needlework in addition to preparing food, cleaning, and washing clothes. Farm wives also milked the family cow, kept chickens, and grew a vegetable garden. Families lived in self-sustaining communities, so that women socialized with the same small circle of neighbours during the week as they did at church on Sunday.

This all changed with immigration to the Prairies. Homesteaders had to start from scratch by building a house, digging a well, and clearing the land, often helped by their wives, which was in addition to wives' other responsibilities. Homesteads were too far apart to visit neighbours, even on a weekly basis, so women not only missed the companionship they had known in the Old Country, but also had few opportunities to learn English until their children started school. The following pages reflect on the lives of immigrant women in Canada.

Gender Roles

The patriarchal system had been firmly established in Sweden's rural agricultural communities for centuries. Men were responsible for making major decisions for the family and for teaching their sons to do heavy outdoor work, while women tended the sick and elderly and taught their daughters homemaking skills. Immigrants before 1930 came from an industrializing country that was shifting from rural to urban and from farm to factory, but the patriarchal system remained pretty well intact during the process.

Carolina Berglund pours coffee from the traditional copper kettle for her husband, Carl, around 1910. Men often drank their coffee from a saucer through a sugar cube (*sockerbit*) clenched between their front teeth.
Courtesy of Elinor Barr.

After deciding to emigrate, some couples had to part until the husband could earn enough money to send a boat ticket. If he had bad luck finding a job the wife would remain in Sweden as a "Canada widow."[1] Others became Canada widows because they refused to accompany their spouse, or because their husband took the opportunity of emigration to shed marital ties.

A 1922 legacy from Halland offers an example of male supremacy in legal matters. The procedure was to send a bank draft in Swedish kronor, payable in dollars by the New York Bank. Augusta Peterson of Falun, Alberta, had sent a letter of authorization to the executor of her father's estate, signing it "Augusta Charlotta Peterson (*född* [nee] Carlson)." A month later she received a registered letter containing a bank draft made out to her as Mrs Aron Peterson.[2] Evidently none of her own names were legal; just those of her husband.

Daily Lives

During the early 1990s researcher Lesley Erickson carried out a study of the interplay between ethnicity and gender among Swedish women in southeastern Saskatchewan.[3] Along with the nearest town, Dubuc, Stockholm was home to a solid block of Swedes, with another cluster along the railway to the south at Whitewood, Percival, and Broadview. The author made observations based on personal experience and print material, including the history *Three Score and Ten* and the insightful novel *Wild Daisies* by Thelma Hofstrand Foster.

Erickson found that the women were competent homemakers and proud of that status. Young girls left home as early as fourteen to work at jobs that made use of household skills. For example, Lena Strandlund[4] worked at the Broadview Hotel until her marriage to Olaf Pearson, and Katie Anderson[5] worked at Percival's CPR dining hall until she wed Lena's brother. Women's brief fling at independence did not end at marriage. On the contrary, responsibility for decision making and farm work would fall on their shoulders whenever husbands worked away from home.

Jens and Karen Olson[6] filed on a homestead in Stockholm in 1889, and then moved to Whitewood, where Jens followed his trade as a tailor. A merchant provided the material and paid him five dollars for making a three-piece suit and twenty-five cents for a pair of overalls. Four years later Karen moved onto the homestead with her eleven children, while Jens continued working in Whitewood. With her children she ran the

Large, elegant hats were a sign of social status in 1910, when the Booth sisters of Minnedosa, fair-haired Frida and dark-haired Anna, posed for this portrait. For many years ladies wore hats for every special occasion, including going to church. Courtesy of Walter Syslak.

farm, entering the marketplace by selling butter for ten cents a pound (.45 kilograms), packed in thirty-five-pound (15.8 kilogram) tubs. Her capability complemented a bubbling personality.

> No one who knew Karen Olson will ever forget her. She dispensed hospitality with a lavish hand, her Swedish waffles with homemade jam and whipped cream appearing on her table as though by magic, while she kept up a lively flow of conversation as she prepared the food. Her son, Emanuel, farmed her land as well as his own and lived at home. Pink-cheeked, bright eyed, and smiling, Mrs. Olson kept this lovely home, which was always brightened with many house plants, in immaculate order until shortly before her death at the age of ninety-three.[7]

Later, Laura Isakson would earn between thirty-five and forty cents a pound (.45 kilograms) for the 1,200 pounds (544 kilograms) of butter she made each year.[8] Purchase of a cream separator freed women from the time-consuming task of skimming the cream by hand. Most chose the Swedish brand, de Laval.[9]

Women from northern Sweden – that is, from Lappland to northern Värmland – assumed milking duties.[10] They were knowledgeable about farming and accustomed to being away from their husbands, if only during the summer. In the spring they drove the farm animals to pastures in the hills, living together in chalets (*fäbodar*). They used a form of singing called *kulning* to call grazing animals home; these were high, clear melodies that carried for long distances.[11] Their tasks were to take care of cattle, horses, sheep, and goats; protect them from bears; cut hay in swamps and meadows; milk the cows morning and evening; and to make butter, cheese, and soft whey-cheese (*mesost*). In their spare time they knitted socks and mitts for the coming winter.

During the rest of the year visiting, especially on Sundays, was a treasured break from everyday routine. Kerstin Kvarnberg wrote about the loneliness she felt during her first year on an isolated homestead near Leduc, Alberta: "If father [her husband] had not insisted, I would never have left. Here there is nothing but a huge land full of willows and trees, and in summer when it rains it is impossible to go out without wading over your boot tops in water. I am so sad many times over such conditions that I lose all hope and will power. Oh, if it could be undone! I remember the fun when all the neighbourhood women could come to visit me [in Sweden], but now that is impossible.[12]

Companionship could be found in church, if one was nearby. Here, too, the New Stockholm women played a leading role, in delaying the founding of the Mission Covenant church until they were satisfied with its doctrines and tenets, and in the Lutheran Ladies' Sewing Circle's purchasing an organ[13] before the turn of the century. Erickson compared the two faiths: "Members of the Swedish Mission Church, unlike Swedish Lutherans, strongly bound their ethnicity to their religion. Swedish women of the Mission Church were therefore instrumental in establishing a church that would act as a safety valve against assimilation. The majority of Swedish women in southeastern Saskatchewan, however, belonged to the Lutheran faith, which provided them with a variety of outlets for their energies as well as access to information networks of education."[14]

Erickson pointed out that the women not only attended church more often than the men, but they also participated much more in ethnic-oriented activities, unlike French, Ukrainian, Polish, and Doukhobor immigrants. She made the general statement that Swedish men did not use the church as an instrument of social control over women to the extent that other ethnic groups did, because of their relatively casual attitude towards the church.[15]

Nevertheless, it was men who were elected to executive positions, while women, like their sisters in mainstream churches, were limited to providing refreshments, teaching Sunday school, and raising funds through the sale of baking and handwork, bazaars, draws, and similar events. The latter often exceeded other church income, so women offered no apologies for turning down official requests for dinners and other events.

Gender bias permeated the social fabric, so that in secular organizations and the workforce women also played a subordinate role providing domestic-related services to men.[16] Involvement in church activities such as choir and Sunday school gave the women access to informal networks that helped them deal with rural isolation. All the organists at Percival's Lutheran church were women. The Percival Church School established in 1911 was the first to give adults formal training in Swedish, English, math, history, Christianity, and music.[17]

The Immigration Experience

Erickson's conclusions about the capability and resilience of women were confirmed elsewhere. The women who crossed the ocean alone to join husbands faced many challenges. Anna Söderberg[18] left Sweden in

1909 with two small daughters, and Selma, who was only three at the time, tells her mother's story: "When we arrived in England she sat on her trunk with my sister on her knee, myself standing beside her, and the trunk and suitcases had to be checked. She did not understand a word of what they said or what they wanted. She said she sat there and cried. She was only 23 and pregnant with her third child. However, some way or other we were on our way over the ocean. She was seasick all the way, but not my sister or myself. She said we just crawled and mauled all over her."[19]

Their homestead in Malakwa, British Columbia, was near the CPR station and store, and it was there that nine more children were born. They called their mixed farm Horseshoe Ranch because of the shape of a nearby slough that provided many happy hours of rafting in summer and skating in winter.

In 1900 about sixty Swedish families from Jämtland moved to the logging community of Millertown in central Newfoundland. An English-speaking worker named Goodyear[20] commented that each man owned a smart, tailor-made suit of black *vadmal*, a kind of felt material, to wear on Sundays and special occasions. The women, who wore cotton dresses, kept both themselves and their homes scrupulously clean. Floors were scrubbed daily, and everyone removed their shoes and socks before entering a home. Women, children, and young girls went barefoot in summer, washing and drying their feet outside before crossing the threshold. Goodyear felt that the Swedes he met were far superior to other groups when it came to hygiene, food, and health, and more humane in their treatment of animals.[21] However, they "were more or less despised" because of their open attitudes towards sex.[22] Several people of both sexes, for example, thought nothing of sleeping in the same room. Later he admitted that "we, that is the Anglo-Saxon race, seem to be somewhat prudish."

Margareta Sillen[23] broke down and cried in 1895 when she saw the small, lonely cabin north of Scandinavia, Manitoba, that would be her new home. She and her husband, John, had lost their farm in Sweden after overextending to build a barn and granary. John left for Canada, filed on a homestead, and worked for three years to send boat tickets for her and the two children. The thought of living under such primitive conditions came as a shock. Where would she put her spinning wheel and carders, and her forms for making loafsugar? Her prized silver bowl would surely look out of place in such a rude building. But she also brought a piece of cheesecloth that had been soaked in *tätmjölk*,[24] a form of yogurt, then dried. She would use it as a starter to make John's favourite food, sprinkled with sugar and cinnamon from her special perforated spoon. It was good to be back together again.

Margareta never took up her father's offer of a ticket back to Sweden. Instead, she transformed the tiny cabin into a home that grew with add-ons as six more children came along. Life was not easy. Like other farm wives she did the milking, tended the chickens, and during the winter let the stove die down at bedtime in order to prevent a house fire. When she lit it the next morning, the water in the reservoir would be frozen solid.[25] In 1914 the family moved near Hilltop, where John had built a two-storey frame home with a large verandah. When he visited Sweden in 1926 Margareta decided not to accompany him. Her future and that of her children lay in Canada.

By the time the railway reached Eriksdale, Manitoba, in 1910, a number of families from northern Sweden had already taken up homesteads. With backgrounds in lumbering and mining they had little experience in farming. Nevertheless, they welcomed the chance to own land as an alternative to poorly paid manual labour in Winnipeg, in logging camps, and on railway construction.

John Lindell[26] was an exception, having worked in southern Sweden as a farm hand (*dräng*). During the 1960s his wife, Paulina, was interviewed by her English daughter-in-law, who wrote her account in broken English, the language she learned working as a domestic. Paulina called her husband "the old man," a common expression in both languages at that time. When speaking to him directly she would have used his surname rather than his Christian name:

> I vas crazy, I should never qvitt vorking in New York. Old Man vas in Canada, ve vas writing. I came te Vinnipeg te get married ...
>
> Old Man had vork in bush camps, den he vas vit building railroads. Ve vas living in rooms on Logan Avenue, but he vants te farm. Ve don't talk too good English, it vasn't much vork for us te get. Times vas pretty hard, I tell you. Den he start vorking nort' vit a survey gang.
>
> Von time he has been gone few mont's, he come home all excited.
>
> "Vi ben surveying land up nort'. Dere is mines and dey vants te haul rock out by rail. Dey are putting railroad t'rough nort', east of Lake Manitoba. For ten dollars ve can homestead a qvarter section up dere. Den ve have land of our own. Some places is bad for stones, but I got a good von picked out. Lotsa game; deer, rabbits, and plenty vild fruit." Seems like Old Man vas never going te stop talking det time.[27]

They left Winnipeg in March 1905 with baby Hilda and a few belongings, travelling by train to the end of the track at Oak Point, by livery
to Brandt's store at Lily Bay, then forty-eight kilometres by dog team.
Then, they lived in a tent until their log house was built, with Paulina
working alongside her husband. "Every minute after ve had plant det
oats, ve vork on de house. Pretty soon de valls is up. Den ve have te get
tarpaper for det roof. Ve had bring lumbers for det door, de vindow ve
has, and some nails vit from Vinnipeg ... Dey vas lotsa Indians, but dey
vas good neighbours I tell you. Many times dey has brought deer meat
or fish to our place, I tell you dey sure taste good ... Dem show me how
to snare rabbits, qvick."[28]

Paulina's positive experience with the First Nations was not at all
unusual.

Childbirth

Wherever they lived women were responsible for acting as midwives
until the 1920s because most births took place in the home, attended
by one or two female relatives or neighbours. The high rate of death
in childbirth meant that a woman risked her life every time she got
pregnant. Few midwives had formal training; proximity was the key
element. In New Stockholm Bill Pearson was one of the many babies
delivered by Svea Stenberg.[29] "I was born March 25, 1893, I have been
told, and the day weatherwise was far from nice. The midwife, Mrs.
Stenberg, had made the trip two and a half miles on a stone boat with
the old grey horse Grolle wading through the drifts ... A little joke of
Mrs. Stenberg's was that I looked so miserable that she hesitated to give
me the slap so necessary at birth to have you draw your first breath! The
Stenbergs became my Godparents."[30]

Author Victor Hugo Wickström wrote about visiting the Stenberg
farm, Sveaborg, in 1904. He enjoyed the meal Svea served him and
noted the menu in his book: *kalops*, a beef stew cooked with whole all-
spice and bay leaves.[31]

In the Kitchen

Immigrants had to make adjustments to traditional recipes for baking cakes
and cookies, not to mention pancakes, waffles, and yeast breads, because
Canadian wheat flour did not have as much gluten as Swedish flour. Barley flour being unavailable, wheat or rye flour had to be substituted for
the staple hard tack. Some food traditions, like *tätmjölk* and *långmjölk/tjock*

mjölk, disappeared when settlers began buying pasteurized milk because the starters worked well only with whole milk. Similarly the end of home butchering led to the disappearance of home-cured meats such as salted tongue, head cheese, jellied pig's feet, and salt pork, as well as sausages (*blodkorv*) and pancakes made from fresh beef blood.[32]

Mealtime customs included saying grace before meals:

I Jesu namn till bords vi gå, välsigna Gud den mat vi få
Och skydda med din milda hand, i nåd vårt hem och fosterland.

(We come to the table in Jesus' name, God bless the food we are getting,
    And protect us with your gentle hand, have mercy on our home and native land.)

Afterwards guests thanked the host and hostess in a ceremonial way: "At mealtime it was the proper thing to say to the hostess, '*Tack för mat*' [thank you for the food] at the conclusion of the meal. Mr. Ohlen, Dominion Immigration Agent, did this in a very stately manner. He stood up, turned to the hostess and said, '*Tack, Mrs. Johanson*,' then to the host with '*Tack Mr. Johanson*,' at the same time making to each a stately bow. They replied and bowed in return, saying '*Tack för tack*' [thank you for the thanks]."[33] Children did the same, except that they extended their hand instead of bowing.

Some food traditions continued past the second generation. After completing her family history Sharon Fitzsimmons of Edmonton thought of a delightful twist as a follow-up. Why not trace the family's heritage through their recipes? The result was *A Family Heritage Cookbook for Five Generations of the Peterson Family: One Hundred Years of Cooking in Western Canada*, published in 2003. A trained observer of patterns, Sharon described the changes in food preparation from the time when most of it was home grown to today's well-stocked stores. She also noted the changes in each generation as other food traditions came into the family. For her, as for her Swedish grandmother, cooking was a family affair, and the best times were to be had in the kitchen.[34]

Male Attitudes towards Marriage

According to historian Eva St Jean, Swedish men did not base their masculinity on being able to control women, but rather on the higher social standing that came with marriage. To them, women had a social worth far beyond sex, a worth that was magnified for immigrants.[35]

The dream of marriage to a Swedish woman became a symbol of the sense of security both with one's own ethnicity as well as with one's sexuality ... Femininity and masculinity are not concepts that can be seen in isolation, but rather in relation to one another. For heterosexual men, the need for interaction with the opposite sex was deep, and it represented a normalization of life and a contact with the homeland ... Without a woman, man lacked dignity, without a woman the dream of a world where each man's contribution was meaningful for himself and the society in which he lived, wilted.[36]

Many men never fulfilled their dream, the main reasons being gender imbalance and isolated workplaces. In 1911 there were 2.36 Swedish male immigrants for every Swedish female in Canada, with the ratio rising to 4.55 in British Columbia and to 10.1 in the northern part of the province.[37] For these men the chance of marrying a Swedish woman was very slim; indeed, of marrying at all. Working in isolated all-male mining, logging, and construction camps with no set address offered few chances to meet the opposite sex, let alone to offer them a settled life.

Bachelors often wrote home to Sweden, inquiring about single women who might be willing to emigrate, and ads for mail-order brides appeared in newspapers in Canada, the United States, and Sweden. Not all were serious. A fellow from Empress, Alberta, wrote that he had heard there were 200 female millionaires in Sweden and wondered if one of them might be interested in somebody who was still working on his first million.[38]

One might think that gender imbalance was the main reason that some men married non-Swedish wives, but Swedish women also chose mates from different ethnic backgrounds. Again, proximity was the key.

Unusual Women

For the most part women were satisfied with playing a subordinate, although significant, role in organizations, but sometimes grew impatient and took matters into their own hands. An example is the group of ladies, headed by Ida Stone, who in 1906 founded Immanuel Augustana Lutheran Church in Port Arthur. Because of their initiative they expected to be allowed to vote on church matters, but the men held out until 1917.[39] During the interim the women refused to raise money and the congregation barely survived.

Another example is Frida Engblom of Vancouver. After listening to the men dither about having to close the Lutheran church in 1913

Photo studios provided props such as cigars, playing cards, beer bottles, and hats for their male customers. The Nelson brothers, Carl wearing a wide brimmed hat, center, and Emil a derby, had this picture taken in Alberta in 1911. They mailed it as a photo postcard to keep in touch with their brother Olof, who lived in Ontario. Courtesy of Elinor Barr, Broman Collection.

because of a large debt, she turned the tide by declaring in no uncertain terms that the church would continue to function, even if she had to keep it open by herself. Mrs Engblom was an entrepreneur in one of the few fields open to women: operating a boarding house. A very capable lady, she cooked for as many as seventy boarders each day.[40] They had to follow two rules: no drinking and no fighting.

In exceptional circumstances women operated businesses founded by a male relative. Oscar Sundborg's daughter, Nita Sundborg, worked as editor of his *Vancouver posten* (1910 to 1914).[41] However, her editorials "steadfastly relegated women to the domestic and silent sphere" and she supported suffragettes not at all. Her article about a suffragette's speech ignored what was said, and, instead, focused on the stereotypical female attributes of frailty and obsession with motherhood.

Women were a tremendous asset to the building of Canada. Their massive free labour pool provided food and clothing for their families, a comfortable home, religious instruction for the children, and sometimes a little money from egg and butter sales. Most were content with their lot, and met life's challenges with determination and good humour. The patriarchal system began to break down only during the Second World War, when urbanization and an abundance of jobs for both men and women not only made life much easier, but also changed the way that genders interacted.

Chapter Eleven

Swedishness in Canada

The previous chapter looked at the patriarchal system of gender relations that immigrants brought with them from the Old Country, but their total cultural baggage included much more and changed over time. We have already seen how the political ideas of newcomers to Winnipeg before the First World War conflicted with the goals of earlier immigrants. Ongoing industrialization and urbanization since the late 1800s also resulted in the nationalization of folk arts and customs. Sweden's present image was only in the development stage when immigrants began populating the Prairies, and therefore the meaning of "Swedishness" has changed over the years.

"Swedishness" has been variously defined as "the feeling of affinity and kinship," "solidarity, support and uniformity," and "Swedish unity and the preservation of Swedish culture."[1] That the word first appeared as the early immigrants were dying off indicates a generational shift, that it targeted descendants who were born in Canada and who had little personal knowledge of the Old Country. The identities of the immigrants themselves had been shaped primarily by religion, but their descendants felt that ethnicity was more important.[2] The identities of succeeding generations of descendants were influenced by the "Swedish" customs practised by their immigrant parents and extended family, and by secular and religious organizations.

In Canada, social status and class were often directly related to ethnicity, so that immigrants were caught between the need to adapt to new ways and the comfort of familiar habits. Some overextended themselves to act like the Anglo-Saxon majority, but that group seldom accepted "foreigners" as equals. One of the results was that immigrants turned to each other for companionship and to achieve common goals, even though they might not have done so otherwise. Although their descendants often acted in a similar manner, the reason was to confirm their ethnicity. The following pages examine the development of customs and organizations in Canada, the appreciation of nature, and the activities of music, radio, sports, philanthropy, and education, as they shifted over time and space.

Customs

The popular Santa Lucia pageant is a good example of how customs can evolve over time. The tradition began in Sweden's distant past as a family event celebrated in the morning with songs like "Staffansvisan,"[3] but became public in 1928 when a Stockholm newspaper launched a Lucia contest in response to a similar pageant in New York. Matt Lindfors organized Canada's first public Lucia function in Vancouver in 1936, with fourteen-year-old Ruby Arnesson as Lucia.[4] This charming pageant takes place on 13 December, with Lucia symbolizing the return of light as winter days grow longer. She wears a long white gown with a red sash around her waist, and is crowned with a wreath of lit candles. Following her are younger children in long white gowns holding candles and singing Swedish words to the Italian song "Santa Lucia,"[5] with the "star boys" wearing high pointed hats. The coffee, saffron buns (*lussekatter*) and ginger snaps (*pepparkakor*) that Lucia serves afterwards hark back to the original family celebration.[6]

In Sweden the Christmas meal and gift exchange took place on Christmas Eve. Festivities began by dipping rye bread in the kettle the ham was cooked in, followed by dancing around a Christmas tree lit with wax candles. This was a slow dance, perhaps for safety's sake, with everybody joining hands and singing "Now it's Christmas Time Again."[7] Then, they sat down at a table loaded with, among other dishes, sliced ham, *lutfisk*, pickled herring, party herring, breads, cheeses, and boiled rice smothered in cinnamon and served with milk. After the meal one of the men left and soon the Christmas elf (*jultomte*) came to ask, "Are there any good children here?" (*Finns det några snälla barn här?*) before coming in to distribute the gifts. The women of the house had begun cleaning and cooking early in December in preparation for festivities and visiting, which lasted until the twelfth night in January, when the Christmas tree was ceremoniously tossed out the door.

A Christmas Eve custom in Waterville, Quebec, was to put lit candles

The Santa Lucia pageant is not a religious event, but sometimes it takes place
in a church. In 1984 Jennifer Boegh was chosen to be Lucia and, followed by
her younger attendants, performed the moving ceremony in Immanuel
Lutheran Church, Thunder Bay, Ontario. This was one of the last times
candles were lit. For safety reasons the Lucia headgear is now electric,
powered by batteries. Courtesy of Beth Boegh.

in each double-hung window, two in the upper part and two on the sill.
Children liked to press their noses against the frost-rimed glass to watch
the lights from neighbouring homes flickering across the snow. This night,
too, the animals received a special tidbit, and birds found a sheaf of grain
tied to an outside post. Early next morning families went to church for
julotta.

Just as Swedes danced around the Christmas tree to celebrate the
winter solstice, so for the summer solstice they joined hands around
a Midsummer pole decorated with fresh greenery and flowers. On the
Sunday before Midsummer in Scandinavia's Mission Covenant church,
poplar branches were placed around the entrance and window frames,
and the floor was strewn liberally with leaves. The custom in Sweden

was to use sweet-smelling birch, but the best substitute on the Prairies was poplar. For the first wedding in Scandinavia's Lutheran church, members made a garland of leaves to hold the bride's veil, a substitute for the traditional filigree bridal crown.[8]

Another custom was names days. Swedish almanacs listed a boy's name and a girl's name for almost every day of the year. Those whose name, or even a second name, was included in the list could expect visitors that day bringing baked goods, flowers, and perhaps a little present. Birthdays were not celebrated to the same extent, and only within the family circle.[9]

In Sweden each parish has its own distinctive folk costume (*folkdräkt*) for both men and women, to be worn at Midsummer, while folk dancing, and on other festive occasions. At first the colourful dress from Leksand, Dalarna, was thought of as a national costume, but ever since 1983, when Queen Silvia wore the summer-weight blue and yellow *Svenska dräkten*[10] for Flag Day on the 6th of June, the new daisy-decorated style for men, women, and children has become popular.

Immigrants in New Stockholm had already chosen the First of July for celebration in 1886, to mark the day they first arrived in the colony. Then, in 1909 Pete Larson's North Vancouver Hotel went all out to celebrate Canada's birthday with canoe races, bronco busting and a beauty contest, followed by a whole-steer barbecue and fireworks. An employee, Fred Burman,[11] described a tug-of-war between Captain Kidd's sailors and Pete Larson's Swedes; "Pete was all of two hundred fifty pounds then, if not more, and Captain Kidd about the same. I watched them both get a foothold, and kept my eyes on the blue and gold flag in the middle of the rope. For a few minutes the flag was pulled first to one side and then to the other. Then one after another of Pete's men let go with one hand so they could spit on it. Pete shouted, 'Pull, you devils!' but it didn't help. Captain Kidd began to draw in more and more rope. Pete made such a furrow with his feet that it finally became a bank."[12] After his defeat, Pete made the excuse that he had only tailors and shoemakers on his team.

Gradually Swedes began joining with other Canadians in celebrating the First of July. Christmas customs have been modified, so that lutfisk has become a symbol of former times and is eaten as a separate meal. Several organizations keep up with the Midsummer tradition and raise a pole, and also put on a Lucia pageant. A number of individuals own Swedish folk dress, particularly if they belong to a folk-dance group.

Anna Sideen sewed Leksand folk costumes for the 1907 baptism of her daughters, Mary and Emy, holding her hand, while Charlie sports a new hat.

Finger pulling was a gentlemanly art among Swedish men, along with
arm wrestling. Here, Helmer Staffanson and Olof Malquist try their luck at
Swedish Park in North Vancouver, during the 1930s. Note the vests, ties, and
armbands worn to the picnic! Courtesy of the Committee for the Swedes in
British Columbia Photo Exhibit, 2010, Ella Wickstrom collection.

Organizations

Immigrants formed secular groups for social, cultural, economic, and
political reasons. An organization was able to arrange celebrations and
other events, and also to raise money for projects such as building a meeting place or funding philanthropy. Dynamic individuals often played a
key role in these group activities. The following pages show how organizations waxed and waned over time in order to meet changing situations.

The moral issue of temperance played a major role until the 1920s.
Many immigrants belonged to temperance societies (*nykterhetsförening*)
in the Old Country, and their commitment to abstain from alcoholic
beverages was reinforced by the three major religious bodies. The largest groups were Sweden's Blue Ribbon (*Blåbandet*) and the Independent
Order of Good Templars or IOGT (*Godtemplarorden*), imported to Sweden from the United States in 1879.

In Winnipeg the IOGT Lodge Stridshjelten (The Struggle Hero),
backed by the Lutheran congregation, replaced in 1894 the short-lived

Scandinavian Temperance League, founded by Mission Covenant members in 1892. Both dominated non-religious social life during their short existence, and both foundered over religious issues.[13] In contrast, members of IOGT Lodge Framtidens Hopp (Hope of the Future), founded in 1902,[14] did not have strong religious ties. At first it affiliated with the English-speaking Grand Lodge, but in 1915 it initiated Canada's only Scandinavian Grand Lodge, responsible for twelve IOGT lodges in Saskatchewan, Manitoba, and Northwestern Ontario.[15]

In addition to meetings, Framtidens Hopp offered organized social activities including Midsummer picnics, begun in 1893, which have become an annual tradition.[16] The lodges themselves disappeared in the mid-1920s as a result of legislation passed by the four western provinces to control liquor sales through government outlets so that safe products were available in "wet" communities.

The three lodges in British Columbia – Vancouver, New Westminster, and Victoria – affiliated with British Columbia's Grand Lodge. Lodge Linnea in Vancouver, founded in 1908, imposed strict abstinence. In 1910 the lodge refused to celebrate King George V's coronation because the occasion lent itself to drunkenness. Members were stricken from the list for belonging to Svenska Klubben, a social group that made liquor available to members. Lodge Linnea is credited with starting the British Columbia Prohibition Association.

Members enjoyed an active social life with literary and musical afternoons, bazaars, picnics, and socials such as pickled herring suppers, which allowed members from logging camps to enjoy Swedish food after a winter of cookhouse fare. Although IOGT frowned on dancing the lodge allowed ring games (ringlekar) after meetings as part of its social activities. Lodge Linnea held out the longest, until 1937, disbanding in 1940.[17] The IOGT continues to function as the International Organization of Good Templars, a non-governmental agency with headquarters in Sweden.

The initial impetus to found the New Stockholm colony had come from the short-lived Scandinavian Society,[18] formed in Winnipeg in 1884 to provide a platform for Scandinavians to work and play together. Meetings were held at Hotel Svea, and members who had not signed the pledge felt free to drink there. It was the president, Emanuel Turner,[19] who called the September 1885 meeting that founded the anti-temperance Scandinavian Colonization Society of Manitoba, resulting in the Noreus debacle at Scandinavia (see chapter 4). The last straw for temperance supporters took place on New Year's Day 1886, when the donation of a flag was celebrated with loud singing and hurrahs from the hotel's rooftop.[20]

The following selection of rhyming couplets, written a few days later, illustrates the emotional intensity of temperance advocates in matters of liquor, cards, and tobacco:

Platform of the Ladies of Rich Hill
The man that chews the navy plug
Will in our parlor get no hug.
Who smokes or drinks or cuts a deck
Shall never never kiss my neck.
If you drink wine and other slop
You never shall hear my corset pop![21]

Another example is G.H. Silver,[22] a founding officer of IOGT's Grand Lodge, who in 1924 resigned as editor of *Svenska Canada-tidningen* over Dahl's insistence that he accept an ad for the alcohol-based tonic Kuriko.[23]

The school district of Freedhome, between New Stockholm and Dubuc, entered the ranks of IOGT in 1905 by founding Scandia Lodge. Regular meetings for adults, both male and female, gave members an opportunity to learn parliamentary procedure by leading the study circle. The lodge collected a library and readings were assigned so that each member could speak at meetings. Topics could include anything from modern business practices to what it meant to be rich.[24] The lodge also organized youth classes in reading and writing Swedish, and in choral singing and music theory, and sponsored performances of skits, musical selections, and songs from Sweden's IOGT songbook.[25] Otto England[26] played a pivotal role in the music program. He organized a choir in 1907 and, later, a six-piece orchestra that included three of his sons, with himself on cello.[27]

Because the new schoolhouse proved inadequate for meetings, members formed Freija Recreational Company as a joint stock company to fund construction of a hall. With 400 shares sold at $5 each, and money borrowed from the Ladies' Sewing Circle, the shell of the building was completed as 1908 drew to a close. Freja Hall became an activity centre, and continued as Freedhome Community Hall long after 1926, when Scandia Lodge began breaking up.

Pioneers in Eriksdale, Manitoba, brewed their own beer from a commercial malt extract, and made wine from dandelions, chokecherries, and even beets. Home brew was popular, mostly distilled from potato mash, also a potent concoction called "pumpkin rum." Against these odds Mrs Alice Forslund[28] founded IOGT Lodge Alprosen (Rhododendron) in 1912. At first Alprosen arranged Midsummer picnics on the lake at Mulvihill, and then during the 1920s sponsored dances in Nord and Nylund schools. According to the musicians very few adhered to the lodge's temperance requirement. In fact, Manitoba's prohibition law of 1917 led to a number of illegal stills, which endured well beyond its repeal in 1923.[29]

The Swedish Library Association (*Svenska nationalbiblioteket*) grew out of the 1917 annual meeting of IOGT's Grand Lodge at Round Lake, south of New Stockholm, with Winnipeg's vice-consul, Peter Bernhard Anderson, as president. The purpose was to preserve Swedishness by making books available in the Swedish language.[30] Seventeen local libraries were organized,[31] although some lodges had already begun collecting books on their own to support study-circle discussions.

Each branch would take turns hosting a summer annual meeting and collect a dollar from members, with half going to the Central Committee.[32] With high hopes Young, Saskatchewan, named its library Wennerberg[33] after Swedish educator and composer Gunnar Wennerberg. However, it was not long before the Open Shelf Library in Regina began servicing residents with English-language books by mail.[34] At first Winnipeg's public library housed Tegnér[35] library, but by 1934 the books sat in Fountain House on Logan Avenue.[36] Not surprisingly, the Mission Covenant church in Winnipeg formed its own library organization, Svenska folkbibliotek, in 1918.[37]

The Swedish Canadian League (*Svenska förbundet i Canada*) was founded in 1917 to forge closer links with Sweden through ocean commerce.[38] The initiative by Consul General Bergström in April 1917 was a political ploy after breakdown of wartime trade negotiations between Sweden and England.[39] The list of sixty members reads like a Who's Who of prominent Swedes,[40] and includes consular representatives, government employees, nobility, engineers, newspaper editors, and businessmen. The lone Prairie representative on the executive board was Vice-Consul Peter Bernhard Anderson of Winnipeg,[41] and the only member listed as a farmer was Chas. Peterson[42] of Wadena, formerly a railway contractor. The organization held its annual meeting in Quebec City and dropped out of sight the following year with Bergström's transfer to Tokyo.[43]

Winnipeg's IOGT records ceased in 1926,[44] the same year Grand Lodge revived the Swedish Canadian League with a new constitution in order to carry on the work of the Swedish Library Association. However, its larger purpose was to promote Swedishness. A committee was struck at the 1928 annual meeting to receive funds for an old folks' home in Winnipeg. The collected amount, $1,000, went towards the project when it finally materialized in 1965.[45]

For its 1931 annual meeting in Wadena the Swedish Canadian League published an impressive forty-four-page yearbook, to be sold for twenty-five cents.[46] Official greetings came from Canada and Sweden, and more than a hundred of Wadena's Swedish residents were named. Mayor Leonard Wreede[47] welcomed the delegates, following by meetings and entertainments. The high point was the raising of the Swedish flag donated by the Society for the Preservation of Swedish Culture in Foreign Lands. From Winnipeg, O.L. Holmgren[48] attended as the society's representative in Canada.

The league's much smaller publication in 1932 featured a homecoming in Jämtland's capital, Östersund, and included G.H. Silver's poem "Jämtland."[49] Meetings stopped in 1934, resuming briefly before finally closing the books in 1941.[50] The Depression, and fear that ethnic reprisals might be repeated during the Second World War, had claimed Canada's only national Swedish organization.

Before the rise of insurance companies, sick-benefit societies were formed to help with medical and funeral expenses. Winnipeg's Norden Society, founded at Hotel Svea in 1900, also functioned as a prestigious male social group. Money from initiation fees, weekly payments, and fundraisers was invested, and stipulated amounts were given to members on receipt of a doctor's certificate. This group survived almost eighty years, long after the financial benefits ceased to be relevant.

Finland Swedes swelled the ranks of Vancouver's Sällskapet Svea,[51] founded in 1908 by the snuff manufacturer Oscar Sundborg. The men became a close-knit group through fundraising activities such as festivals, picnics, and dances. For its first Midsummer Fest the group hired a boat to ferry participants across Burrard Inlet to the spacious grounds of Pete Larson's North Vancouver Hotel, complete with musicians in the bandstand and dancing in the pavilion.

In Port Arthur the Norrskenet Society founded by Finland Swedes in 1905 gradually began admitting other Swedes. Reorganized as a social club in 1992, it is Canada's oldest Swedish sick-benefit society still in existence.[52] The International Order of Runeberg, named for Finland's national poet, formed lodges in Ontario – notably Sault Ste Marie, Hamilton, and Blind River – and British Columbia. Vancouver's lodge was instituted in 1924. The Scandinavian Fraternity of America[53] also had several lodges in British Columbia.[54]

After the provincial group Västgöta gille was founded in Winnipeg by American migrants from Västergötland in 1907, immigrants from Sweden promptly created Masgille for those from Dalarna and Norrlands gubbar for men from the northern provinces.[55] A later provincial group, Härjedalsgillet, was founded in 1958 as an international organization with headquarters in Vancouver, admitting both male and female members. They kept in touch through annual conventions, and in 1965 donated a Memorial Stone to Gammelgården in Sveg, Härjedalen, to commemorate the province's emigrants. Another legacy is the hardcover book of members' autobiographies compiled by Carol Black and published in 1982.[56]

The Vasa Order of America, founded in Connecticut in 1896, began spreading into Canada in 1912. Membership offered sick and death benefits for both men and women within an ethnic social framework. For many it transcended differing religious and political views, but Augustana Lutherans felt a divided loyalty when it came to drinking, dancing, and the lodge funeral ritual.[57] Today, the Vasa Order is among Canada's oldest secular Swedish organizations.[58]

The first lodge was instituted in Vancouver as #229 Förgät mig ej (Forget me not), affiliating with Pacific Northwest District Lodge. By 1913 the movement had spread across the country to Waterville, Quebec, which affiliated with New England District Lodge. The following year Winnipeg's Strindberg Lodge joined with new lodges in Kenora, Port Arthur, and Fort William to form Canada's first district lodge, Central Canada District Lodge #16.[59] After censorship of the IOGT newspaper *Framåt* in 1917 the Fort William and Port Arthur lodges disbanded and it was not until 1929 that Port Arthur chartered another Vasa lodge.

In Winnipeg the women formed their own group within the lodge in 1918, calling themselves the Strindberg Sisters, probably as a result of perceived persecution during the First World War. With the onset of the Second World War they became concerned that the government might freeze their bank account,[60] and decided to spend the money. Accordingly in 1940 Strindberg Lodge bought five hectares on Roblin Boulevard in Charleswood for a Swedish park and meeting place. Shares were sold in order to construct a building and to incorporate the Sylvia Recreational Company Limited to manage the property, to be called Vasa Lund.

The grounds at Vasa Lund hosted Midsummer from the beginning, and in 1973 became the site for the annual Folklorama's Swedish pavilion. The hall, also called Vasa Lund, was the venue for meetings, waffle brunches, Christmas parties, and wedding receptions. In 1951 the Ladies' Auxiliary to the Swedish Male Choir organized the first Lucia pageant there. The Swedish Canadian Home for Senior Citizens was built on the property in 1964 and Vasa Lund Estates apartments in 1999. A new Vasa Lund building is planned.

There were 208 Swedes in Calgary in 1922, of whom 55 became charter members of Branting Vasa Lodge. The name came from the father of Swedish socialism, Hjalmar Branting, who had won the Nobel Peace Prize the year before. The lodge celebrated its first Lucia in 1959, and the same year organized the Young Vikings and set up the Young Viking Scholarship Fund.[61] In addition to suppers, bazaars, and sporting events, Branting has served lutfisk dinners since 1962, with members encouraged to attend in folk dress. The lodge became a shareholder in Calgary's Scandinavian Centre in 1962.[62]

The 1988 Winter Olympics saw Branting Lodge and the Swedish Society jointly hosting the Swedish Canadian Western Jamboree at the Scandinavian Centre. Guests included a delegation from Falun, the Swedish hockey team, and the president of the Swedish Olympic Committee, Prince Bertil, with his wife, Princess Lilian. Later, Ambassador Ola Ullsten and Consul Zoumer held a smörgåsbord reception at the Westin Hotel for 350 guests, including King Carl XVI Gustaf and Queen Silvia. In June a Midsummer pole was raised as a focus for festivities that included forty-four folk dancers and musicians from Sweden.[63]

Arvid and Minnie Nelson[64] moved to Edmonton in 1927, hoping to transfer their membership from Engelbrekt Lodge in Kenora. They finally did so two years later, when Skandia Lodge was founded in the Nelson home. The following year Arvid attended the Central Canada District #16 meeting in Winnipeg, which resulted in the founding of Alberta District #18 in 1931 with five lodges. Skandia Lodge's chair, Julius Hober from Jämtland, became the first district deputy, and before the decade was out eight more lodges had been added.[65]

In 1947 Skandia Lodge applied for a certificate of incorporation in order to buy six hectares on Pigeon Lake and develop them as a community village. Vasa Park[66] eventually became the site of eighty cottages, a clubhouse, a baseball diamond, tennis courts, a children's play area, and a boat launch. The lots for cottages were leased, and rules laid down. Vasa Park remains unsurpassed in Canada as a Swedish summer haven.

Skandia Lodge became the driving force behind Edmonton's Swedish events, so much so that the Pioneers Vasa Lodge was formed in

1980 as an activity club for those who preferred a more relaxed group. In 1993 the lodge participated in a three-week display of Scandinavian crafts and craftsmanship, in cooperation with the Alberta Craft Council and the Scandinavian Studies Association,[67] which supports the Scandinavian Studies program at the University of Alberta.[68] The lodge has published the newsletter *Skandia Page* since 1994, and in 2002 Grand Lodge chose Edmonton as the venue for its first convention in Canada.

The Vasa Order of America maintains an archive in Bishop Hill, Illinois, and six times a year publishes *The Vasa Star*, a magazine that keeps members informed about lodges in Canada, the United States, and Sweden. In 2000 Lennart Petersson[69] of Edmonton became the first Canadian president of the archives. Since joining Skandia Lodge in 1956 he served as chair, district deputy, and district master. At the Grand Lodge level he became the first Canadian vice-grand master, and then held the highest office of all, that of grand master.

Women began to be elected to the administrative level in organizations after the Second World War, partly because of their contributions to the war effort in uniform and in factories. Two women stand out as driving forces behind Swedish activities in Edmonton and Vancouver. A daughter of immigrants, Linnea Lodge[70] has been a member, often a founding member, of most Swedish organizations in Edmonton. As an accountant she was in demand as treasurer and auditor. Since joining Skandia Vasa Lodge in 1939 she was also active in the district lodge, attending Grand Lodge conventions every four years since 1958. Grand Lodge appointed her cultural director for Canada, then for both countries, the first Canadian to hold this office. In addition to many other awards, she was presented with Sweden's Order of the Polar Star in 1989 and in 1993 with Canada's 125th Anniversary Medal.

Irene Olljum[71] came originally from Estonia, where being a Swede meant being more Swedish than Swedes in Sweden. Because the existing social group in Vancouver was English-speaking, she helped found Svenska kulturföreningen/Swedish Cultural Society for new immigrants in 1951. Irene held every executive position, served as president of the Swedish Press Society and the Swedish Coordinating Committee, and in 1988 was appointed to British Columbia's Cultural Heritage Advisory Committee. The same year she received a certificate of appreciation from the Swedish National Committee of New Sweden '88 in the United States "for outstanding initiative, achievement and service in promoting Swedish-American friendship and trade." In 1991 she was presented with Sweden's Order of the Polar Star.

Neither of these women could have contributed in such a high-profile way fifty years earlier. Post-secondary education, fewer children, lighter household duties, and changing attitudes were eroding the patriarchal system of yesteryear and broadening opportunities in the workplace and in the political, religious, and social spheres.

The community hall in Silverhill celebrated its ninetieth anniversary in 2009, but with urbanization new buildings became necessary in the cities, many of them the result of cooperation among Nordic groups. The Scandinavian Cultural Centre on Erin Street in Winnipeg began with the selling of debentures in 1960. A similar movement in Edmonton founded the Scandinavian Centre Cooperative Association,[72] which celebrated the centre's official opening in 1964. The building was used for meetings, wedding receptions, dances, and *Scandapades*, a popular show put on by Scandinavians. However, the city expropriated the property for the Yellowhead Freeway Development, and the rebuilding fund suffered serious losses during the 1980s recession.

The Scandinavian Centre Cooperative Association remained active, organizing the Scandinavian Pavilion at Edmonton's Heritage Days festival, founded in 1976, every year until 1983, when a change in the law made it necessary to incorporate a non-profit group to run it. The result was the founding of the Scandinavian Heritage Society of Edmonton, which has been organizing the Scandinavian Pavilion and other showcases ever since.

When Edmonton's Klondike Days chose Scandinavia as its ethnic focus in 2003, the Scandinavian Trade and Cultural Society was incorporated to facilitate the ten-day event, calling it "Spirit of Scandinavia." Inside the gates was a replica Viking ship and a forest, home of the two-metre trolls Hodda and Gubben, who guided guests through the exhibits, events, and workshops. The trade show represented modern Scandinavia, with displays by IKEA, Husqvarna, and Volvo, to name but a few.

Enthused by discoveries made during research for the cultural displays, the society published a travel guide to relevant Alberta sites. Volunteers took photographs, carried out research, wrote feature pages, and provided information. The result released in 2007, *Scandinavian Connections: A Guide to Sites in Alberta: Denmark, Finland, Iceland, Norway, Sweden*, is in full colour, well designed, and a delight to read either for pleasure or to plan a sightseeing tour.

Many organizations have been formed through the years to support sports, business, and other interests, but most of them also had a social focus, and two became members of Sweden's Society for the Preservation of Swedish Culture in Foreign Lands. Founded in 1908, during the 1970s the society shortened its name to Riksförening Sverigekontakt.[73] Members pay an annual membership and receive the quarterly magazine *Sverigekontakt*.

Nordstjärnan[74] (North Star) was founded in 1929 in Edmonton as an exclusive society of no more than eighteen members, all male. In 1932 the group organized a Gustav II Adolf Fest to honour the 300th anniversary of the Battle of Lutzen. The entire program of music and speeches was broadcast by radio. Svenska kulturföreningen/Swedish Cultural Society was founded in Vancouver in 1951, also as a member of the Society for the Preservation of Swedish Culture in Foreign Lands. One of the benefits was funding for a school (from 1965 to 1969) where children learned songs and folk dances to perform in costume, a forerunner of the later Swedish schools supported by the Swedish government.[75] Founded by Matt Lindfors to accommodate immigrants after the Second World War, the organization has been an active force in Vancouver's Swedish events.

In Victoria three ladies founded the Swedish Canadian Social Group in 1956, and its musicians figured prominently in activities. In 1965 Diane Hornfeldt became the group's first Lucia. In 1997 her dad, Hans Hornfeldt,[76] reactivated the group as the Swedish Club of Victoria, and by 2000 the Swedish flag had been hoisted over their meeting place, the Sons of Norway Hall. Members host visiting Swedes, including sports teams, and catch enough crayfish to hold an annual *kräftskiva* feast. Nels Granewall has been baking *semlor* buns every Easter since 1989 for Swedish exchange students.[77]

Cities with a significant Scandinavian population usually formed a social group. Dan Harris founded the Canadian Nordic Society in Ottawa in 1963, with Swedish ambassadors automatically becoming honorary members. It is a local rather than a national group, sponsoring a lecture series as well as organizing family and adult social events such as Midsummer and the Lucia pageant, which is held at the embassy of Sweden. Members are kept informed through the society's website and the newsletter *Nordic News*.[78]

Montreal's Swedish organization, Svenska Klubben,[79] began in the 1930s, and then in 1952 the Swedish Women's Club was established to organize the Lucia pageant and other events. In 1982 a brand-new Svenska Klubben was formed with a new constitution to operate the Swedish School, to publish the newsletter *Gult och Blått* five times a year, and to arrange celebrations for Flag Day (6 June), Midsummer, and other events.

The Scandinavian Society of Nova Scotia was founded in Halifax in 1980, but had its beginnings in 1976. One of its goals is to promote interest in the culture, customs, and traditions of the five Scandinavian countries through school visits, participation in the Multicultural Festival, and other events. The group has an extensive library and informative website, and publishes a quarterly newsletter.

Women who came to North America during the 1970s were concerned that their children should learn the Swedish language and culture in an organized way. For this reason Agneta Nilsson of Los Angeles founded SWEA (Swedish Women's Educational Association) in 1979. It has become a worldwide non-profit organization of Swedish and Swedish-speaking women devoted to promoting Swedish culture and tradition, and to encouraging friendship and personal growth among members. There are two branches in Canada. The Vancouver branch, founded in 1989, arranges social events for members, supports other Swedish groups, and carries out international SWEA duties, such as the twenty-fifth-anniversary project of donating large wooden *Dala* horses, one of Sweden's national symbols, for public display. SWEA Vancouver's Dala horse, created by retired cabinetmaker Ulf Frisk,[80] was installed in front of the Scandinavian Community Centre. Members such as Yvonne Spence and Birgitta Dannberg are also active in the Swedish school.[81] In 2006 the group awarded its first undergraduate scholarship for Swedish language studies in Sweden.[82]

The SWEA Toronto was founded in 1982 by members of Solveig Westman-Olsson's Swedish Cultural Group, and has since grown to more than 200 members. General meetings are held in the Swedish church, but subgroups get together in each other's homes for meetings of book clubs, film evenings, and other activities, according to where they live. The group holds its two-day Christmas Fair (*julmarknad*) at Harbourfront, with a program that includes a Lucia pageant, folk dancing, and singing, as well as an impressive market with Swedish merchandise, arts and crafts, books, imported food items, and baked goods. Swedish lunches can be purchased at the café, children can participate in Christmas workshops, and visitors can browse through the booths and displays. Since 1987 the event has funded a one-year scholarship for a Canadian student to attend a Swedish university that participates in an exchange program. SWEA Toronto puts out the magazine *SWEA Bladet* to complement the twice-yearly international magazine *SWEA*. Members also receive the monthly newsletter *SWEA Toronto Kalendern*.[83]

Another recent contribution by women is schools where children can learn the Swedish language and culture. In 1988 there were 42 Swedish schools for children in various parts of the world, and by 2000 their number had grown to more than 150. Funded at first by Sweden's Society for the Preservation of Swedish Culture in Foreign Lands, the Swedish government soon took over responsibility through Skolverket (Swedish National Agency for Education) with other assistance from Svenska utlandsskolornas förening (Association for Swedish Schools in Other Lands). The "schools" consist of language classes for children and youth based on Swedish heritage and culture, and are held outside regular school hours. The Swedish school in Calgary was founded by Margaretha Malik in 1975, Vancouver's in 1978 with teacher Märta Lundquister, and Toronto's in 1983. Since then Swedish schools have been organized in Burlington, Ottawa, Montreal, and Victoria, usually starting in private homes and then moving to rented premises.

At Calgary's Swedish school the classes are divided into play school, kindergarten, elementary school, and preparatory Swedish, and meet Saturday mornings at the Scandinavian Community Centre. The children experience and practise Swedish traditions, song, and dance, and do Swedish handicrafts, participate at cultural events, and attend a "culture camp" each spring, all organized by the Swedish Society. Advanced Swedish is a two-level credit course for high school students, the first such program for the Swedish language in Canada. These classes meet one evening a week, and students wear the traditional student cap (*studentmössa*) upon graduation. They play a pivotal role in Swedish celebrations, and in 1988 competed with other schools throughout the world as part of the fiftieth anniversary celebrations of the Association for Swedish Schools in Other Lands.[84]

The Swedish school in Vancouver is sponsored by Svenska kulturföreningen/Swedish Cultural Society, and parents must be included among its 500 members. Classes for children aged three to thirteen are held at the Scandinavian Community Centre and include preschool, kindergarten, and supplementary Swedish education from grades one to six as well as

Sofia school grades seven to nine, according to the Swedish education system. These are especially valuable for children whose parents plan to return to Sweden.

SWEA initiated the Swedish School in Toronto for children and youth aged four to fourteen, and classes are held at the Agricola Church. In 1991–2 the Toronto District School Board's program for International Languages accepted the Swedish School. "The school's foremost goal is to maintain and strengthen the language in children who already know Swedish, but we also have children of Swedish descent who have an interest in learning Swedish and about Swedish culture ... The curriculum ties in tightly with Swedish traditions, everyday events, and subjects such as geography, history, and Swedish literature. A combination of group- and individual work in addition to song, theatre, and play is used to strengthen the knowledge of spoken as well as written Swedish."[85]

A major highlight for the children is participation in SWEA Toronto's Christmas Fair at Harbourfront, but picnics and other outdoor activities are also organized. In 2005 the Swedish School Association in Toronto began introducing satellite groups in Burlington, Etobicoke, and Barrie, which meet once or twice a month, with the schoolwork being completed at home with a parent as teacher. A training package, support, and materials are available for distance courses.[86]

The sequence and purposes of the above organizations mirror the social needs and attitudes of Canada's Swedes for more than a century, from the moral issue of temperance through the safety net of sick-benefit societies, to groups committed to various methods of preserving Swedishness. These include a large number of ethnic societies, the Vasa Order of America (since 1912), the Swedish Library Association (from 1917 to 1941), the development of ethnic properties (since 1960), Swedish schools (since 1975), and SWEA (since 1982). The great majority were initiated by individuals working as volunteers, supported by national and international groups.

Nature

The special feeling that Swedes have for nature has already been mentioned several times, but the contribution of Eric Ericson[87] stands out as unique. He created a summer wonderland in Fort Frances, Ontario, behind his Gardenview Café and grocery store. During the 1950s and early 1960s the bird sanctuary at Eric's Lund became a magnet for

Summer picnics were a favourite leisure pastime for families and for groups. Here, the Johanson family, from Luleå, Sweden, pose on the grass in Port Arthur in the early 1920s. The patriarchs, Alfred and John, lie in front, while Anna practises winking in the back row. Courtesy of Eric Johnson.

tourists, attracting 5,000 visitors a year. His daughter Vi Hautala told how it all began:

> [In 1940] he started to straighten Biddeson Creek and lined the banks with stones. Next was a dam to create a pond ... Peonies lined the steps to the creek; pear and cherry trees were planted and grapes grew over a trellised bench and arbour. A fence was lined with phlox beside our playhouse. He built a ferris wheel; each box carried differing blooms. This sat on the top of the hill and he built a Chinese water garden fed by a hose system ...

He would order swans – white trumpeters and black Australian, and they floated happily around the pond. My earliest memories of him are of peering out the bedroom window at 7 am and seeing him head down the steps to feed the quacking menage of ducks. Then head up the hill to feed the pheasants ...

A wishing well collected donations to "help feed the birds." This seemed to be in lieu of charging admission as we had many guests and a book for them to sign. Sundays were especially busy. Claire Wallace came from the CBC and Premier George Drew also toured ... I do believe we had Richard and Lynn Harrington visit as well.[88]

At its height Eric's Lund was home to fifty different varieties of wildlife in thirty-five displays, all identified. Ericson built little houses for them, including one with a revolving drum for a fox squirrel. After his death in 1964 Eric's Lund reverted to nature.

Music

Listening to adults singing as they worked, and watching them play and make instruments, encouraged children to follow their example with musical games, ring dances, and action songs as part of everyday life. They started as infants, riding back and forth on an adult's foot to the rhythmic "*Rida, rida ranka*" (Ride, ride a rocking horse). The school-teacher in Eriksdale, Manitoba, noted that Swedish children had a good ear for music and a fine sense of rhythm, and that all the boys were accomplished dancers.

The Swedish boys, she continued, often broke into song while dancing, a practice which the older English women considered highly indecorous, indeed a form of exhibitionism.

Like herself, however, not a few of their daughters chose Swedish husbands ... [The Swedes] brought with them and kept alive the musi-cal traditions of Jämtland and the northern provinces, lilting and lively dance music, and held in high esteem the fiddlers and accordionists who could play it by ear ... very few of them ever received formal instruction in music. Many of the English families, however, tried as soon as possible to have their children take piano lessons.[89]

Jöns Nord was one of the Olssons from Föllinge, Jämtland, a family that had for generations produced renowned *spelmän* – fiddlers who learned to play and compose tunes without formal training. His uncle,

Göran Olsson Föllinger, studied classical music and became a famous violinist and recording artist in Europe. Göran always liked to end his concerts with a traditional Jämtland tune (*jämtlåt*). He performed in Winnipeg in 1927 during a North American tour.[90]

Jöns Nord's three sons were also musical. Ole was a self-taught fiddler, but the other two had formal training and distinguished themselves in Winnipeg, Edvard as a pianist and organist, and Simon as a violinist. In Sweden the popularity of the accordion began to rival the fiddle during the 1800s. It was said that Eriksdale's dances were always a success if accordionists Erik Landin or his sons were playing.

Alf Carlson[91] of Vancouver was known as "Mr Accordion" for good reason. Since arriving in Vancouver in 1924 he played solo and with his own orchestra, ran a music school with more than sixty pupils, and bought and sold accordions. It was Alf Carlson and his student Walter Hendricson who played Swedish music on Matt Lindfors's program on CJOR Radio.

The singing cowboys Sleepy and Swede performed on radio and in rural dance halls from 1932 to 1947, also cutting several records for the CBC. They sang a Swedish-English mix of sentimental ballads, including "Livet i finnskogarna" (Life in the Finland woods), "Nikolina," "Min hemlängtan" (My longing for home), and Swede's own composition "Hobo from Sweden,"[92] accompanying themselves on harmonica and guitar. Eventually they formed their own rhythm section called The Tumbleweeds, which later became The Rhythm Pals.

Sleepy was Les Frost, an Irishman, and Swede was Nils Nilsson[93] from Åmål, Dalsland. For concerts they dressed in matching outfits, with white pants and glitzy black shirts, boots, and cowboy hats. When they decided in 1946 to cross Canada on horseback, giving concerts and radio interviews along the way, black pants became more practical. Their horses, Pojken (the boy) and Spook, had to be shod seven times during the trip. After Sleepy retired Swede continued performing with Pojken in the Casey Carnival shows.

Carl Friberg[94] made a name for himself as director of the Royal Canadian Air Force (RCAF) Band. His career began with the Second World War, and afterwards he directed the RCAF Training Command Band from 1947 to 1951, then again from 1955 to 1961. The band travelled extensively, performing at the Banff Winter Carnival and the Calgary Stampede. In 1951 a special concert was transmitted to Sweden by short-wave radio to mark the twenty-fifth anniversary of the Swedish air force.

The tradition of male voice choirs was followed for many years by Svenska sångarbröderna in Winnipeg, formed in 1913, and the Bellman

This thirty-voice Swedish male choir was founded in Winnipeg in 1913 with V. Anderson, centre, as director. Later, A.A. Anderson led the group. When numbers dwindled, Icelandic and Norwegian men were allowed to join, but eventually the Svenska sångerbröderna passed into history. Courtesy of Ted Simonson.

Male Chorus in Vancouver from 1946. Vancouver hosted conventions of the American Union of Swedish Singers in 1959 and 1967.[95] Sweden's Orphei Drängar, widely regarded as the best male choir in the world, performed in Vancouver, Edmonton, Winnipeg, and Toronto in 2008 as part of its North American tour. Based in Uppsala, Sweden, the eighty-four-voice choir dates from 1853 and has always been a torch bearer for the Swedish choral tradition.[96]

In 1994 the Wermland Vocal Ensemble visited Thunder Bay at the invitation of Glenn Mossop,[97] music director of the city's symphony orchestra. The ensemble's final performance, *Nordic Voices*, featured its choral director, Gunno Palmquist, as guest conductor. The program included the world première of the composition "Songs of the Mountain, the Moon, and Television," by Bengt Hambreus,[98] who had immigrated in 1972 to teach musicology at McGill University.

Violinist Eva Svensson of Montreal, and tenor Lary Benson and soprano Eva Bostrand of Edmonton, are among those who carry on the classical music tradition in Canada, and Bengt Jörgen's Ballet Jörgen performs new and creative works in Toronto and on tour. Ballerina Annette av Paul joined the Royal Winnipeg Ballet in 1964. She danced in the CBC's first colour spectacular, *Rose La Tulippe*, and for Swedish TV and BBC, retiring in 1984. Then she founded Ballet British Columbia as its artistic director, followed by directing the dance program at Banff Centre for the Arts.

Canada has succeeded in attracting a wide range of Swedish musicians, from folk to classical, from instrumental to voice, from dance to ballet. This tradition earned worldwide recognition with the popularity of the pop music group ABBA, founded in 1972.

Radio

The CBC Radio broadcast to Sweden on weekdays from 1946 to 1961. A team from Sweden came to Montreal, and by 1948 the program had fifty "listening clubs." The supervisor's wife, Karin Färnström, taught McGill University's first Swedish-language course in 1948,[99] and in 1954 a Stockholm publisher put out the couple's illustrated book *Framtidslandet Kanada* (Canada: The Land of the Future).[100] During the fifteen-year existence of CBC's international service Sweden had an unprecedented opportunity to learn about Canada on a daily basis.

In 1957 announcer Sture Persson asked Matt Lindfors to interview the Swedish industrial magnate, Axel Wenner-Gren,[101] best known for popularizing the Electrolux vacuum cleaner. He had made a deal with Premier W.A.C. Bennett to develop an integrated industrial empire in northern British Columbia that would include heated polar cities and a monorail connecting the province to the Yukon. For his part the premier had granted Wenner-Gren resource rights to one-tenth of the province. Afterwards, Lindfors was commended for his diplomacy in handling the controversy that led Wenner-Gren to abandon the project and Bennett to found BC Hydro in order to complete the massive Peace River dam.[102]

While Lindfors acted as a link in the CBC's network, his contemporary at *Canada-tidningen*, Esse Ljungh, made radio drama his career until retiring in 1969. Ljungh began working in drama in Sweden, and in Winnipeg turned to Little Theatre. In 1930 he directed the Swedish Amateur Players, who performed the third act of *The Vermlanders* at the Winnipeg Folk Arts Society's first annual festival.[103] He also produced shoestring productions for local radio stations. The CBC hired him as a freelance producer in 1938 and then full time in 1942, and in 1944 he moved to Toronto as national supervisor of Radio Drama. According to the *Canadian Theatre Encyclopedia*, "His effect on the national theatre, its writers and actors cannot be underestimated; theatre practitioners, who could rarely earn a living in theatre, could now count on radio drama for some income and some of Ljungh's shows, such as 'Author meets the critic,' encouraged an ongoing discussion of the nation's literature [including theatre]. Moreover, Ljungh supervised adaptations of theatre works, like Shakespeare's King Lear and Rolf Hochhuth's Soldiers."

Evidently W.O. Mitchell fashioned the character Jake, in his 1961 book *Jake and the Kid*, after a Swedish farmhand. Its adaptation for radio became one of Ljungh's best-known series. He also directed the soap opera series *Brave Voyage* and the musical *General Electric Hour*.[104] Esse Ljungh became a Member of the Order of Canada in 1981.

Drama had come a long way since dialect plays from the United States were performed before full houses in Winnipeg. Gus Heege's *A Yenuine Yentleman* in 1896 and *Yon Yonson* two years later were very popular. However, the company lost its audience in 1903 when Irish actors played most of the parts.[105] In the 1930s radical theatre of social protest against unemployment began, performed by local amateur groups.[106]

Sports and Exercise

To many of those raised in the land of the midnight sun, skiing in winter was as natural as walking in summer. Children learned to ski as soon as they could walk, using handmade skis and a single ski pole. The ninety-kilometre Vasaloppet, the oldest and biggest cross-country ski race in the world, attracts thousands of skiers every March to retrace the 1520 route of King-to-be Gustav Vasa. Individuals were skiing in Canada in the 1890s, and by 1910 had founded ski clubs in Montreal and Winnipeg (1904), Quebec and Toronto (1908), and Ottawa.

In Winnipeg the Swedish group On Skis introduced cross-country ski races in Elmwood in 1904 and added ski jumping the following winter. The Swedish Ski Club began welcoming non-Swedes in 1914 by changing its name to Winnipeg Ski Club.[107] When Adolph Palmquist[108] arrived in Montreal in 1903, skiing had become popular enough to form a ski club the following year. Palmquist eventually owned a factory that manufactured skis by machine, and in 1921 the Canadian Amateur Ski Association held its first ski competition, won by E. Sundberg.

Montreal's Viking Ski Club was founded in 1929 by Norwegian ski jumpers, but over the years has given way to cross-country skiing. Two events in the classic cross-country races, the twenty-kilometre Jack Wahlberg Loppet and ten-kilometre Jan Nordstrom Loppet, are named for Swedes. In 1950 Jack Wahlberg represented Canada in the world championships at Lake Placid, and Jan Nordstrom was the club's master trail-cutter.[109]

Hugo Holmberg won many skiing competitions in Sweden, and had more than thirty pins, medals, and silver cups to prove it. In the 1920s he and his family lived in Finmark, Ontario, where he built ski runs and jumps on Lindstrom's farm. The family swept the prizes at the Fort William Ski Club competition in the early 1930s. Hugo won the senior men's race; son Hilding, the junior men's race; daughter Elsa, the women's race; and son John, the ski jumping. John claimed a practice jump of 64.6 metres and a recorded jump of 59.7 metres.[110]

Rudolph Verne[111] is recognized as the promoter who brought skiing to Vancouver. In 1922 the potential inspired him to start a ski factory and to open a ski shop. After 1,500 spectators turned up to watch the first ski race around Stanley Park he founded the Hollyburn Pacific Ski Club and began to develop the 762-metre-level ski run on Cypress Mountain. In 1926 he established Hollyburn Lodge, moving to the 914-metre level beside First Lake. Here, three cousins from Dalarna and one of their wives[112] built a lodge, rental cabins, and a ski jump with a run out over the frozen lake. It took nineteen men to bring a piano over the rough trail. The lodge became a popular gathering place for skiers, and is still in use, although it is now part of Cypress Park and the Nordic ski area.[113]

Winnipeg's Logan Avenue was a rough-and-tumble place in 1909 when the popular wrestlers Charles Gustafsson and the Norwegian Knut Hoel founded the Scandinavian Athletic Club Odin. Competitors adhered to strict rules of fair play, and "no American or other 'thugs' were allowed to compete."[114] Competitions were characterized by lively betting and lots of noise, sometimes with the added attractions of boxing, teeth-power tests, and vaudeville songs, followed by a public dance.

The 1912 Summer Olympics in Stockholm was a source of great national pride for *Svenska Canada-tidningen* and its readers, not only because Swedish athletes won sixty-five medals, more than any other country, but because the event marked a number of firsts: electronic timing devices, women's events in swimming and diving, and competitors from all five continents symbolized by the Olympic rings. It was also the last time that medals of solid gold were awarded.[115]

At the 1932 Olympics hockey player Victor Lindquist[116] tipped in the winning goal to win the gold medal for Winnipeg. A second-generation Swede born in Gold Rock, Ontario, he played with the Winnipeg Monarchs in 1934–5 when they won the World Hockey Championship, and the following year he became coach of Sweden's national hockey team. Erik "Swede" Hornquist played for British Columbia's Kimberley Dynamiters in 1936 when the team won the Allan Cup,[117] and during the 1932–3 season[118] became the first Swedish-born player in the National Hockey League. He scored a total of thirteen points, four goals and nine assists, for the Ottawa Senators, who were in the National Hockey League for a short time during the 1930s.

Sixteen of the Sofia Girls (*Sofiaflickorna*), gymnasts from Sweden, toured North America in 1956. The Scandinavian Canadian Club of Toronto and the Swedish-Canadian Club in Vancouver sponsored their Canadian tour, with Matt Lindfors as tour manager. The girls had performed more than 600 times throughout Europe, under the guiding hand of Maja Carlquist, author of *Rhythmical Gymnastics*. She had improved upon the methods of Sweden's "father of gymnastics," Per Henrik Ling (1776–1839). The girls ranged in age from fourteen to twenty-one, spoke English, and wore smart blue tunics. Lindfors arranged a series of one-night stands that began with Victoria and ended with Massey Hall in Toronto.[119]

The instant success of ParticipACTION, a Canadian government program promoting healthy living and physical fitness, is credited to the 1973 public-service announcement on television that showed a sixty-year-old Swede jogging effortlessly beside a puffing thirty-year-old Canadian. The memorable clip caught the public imagination and led to a profitable fitness industry, not to mention a few good-humoured jokes. On his ninetieth birthday Bill Nordstrom of Armstrong, British Columbia, wore a T-shirt asking the question "30 year old Canadian?" on the front, and on the back answered "No, 90 year old Swede."[120]

The 1920s began with a well-publicized physical feat involving a Swede. In 1921 Charlie Burkman[121] got laid off from the shipyards in Halifax. He and a chum decided to walk westward along the railway lines (those were the days before highways) looking for work. They funded their journey by selling postcards with photos of themselves. As it turned out four more people joined in after a Halifax newspaper

SALE OF THESE CARDS IS MY ONLY
SUPPORT
PRICE: — WHATEVER YOU WISH TO GIVE

SOUVENIR OF
CHARLIE BURKMAN, GLOBE TROTTER
With 3 years to walk around the world for $20,000

After his marathon walk from Halifax to Vancouver, Charlie Burkman was offered $20,000 to walk around the world. Above is the photo postcard he sold to finance his trip, a journey that aborted in its early stages. Courtesy of Elinor Barr Collection.

publicized the event, and Charlie's "leisurely walk" became a race covered by media across the country. Pierre Berton told the story of "The Great Cross-Canada Hike" in his book *My Country*. This extraordinary event involved four men and one woman who walked from the Atlantic to the Pacific, a distance of 5,840 kilometres, from January to June 1921.[122]

Swedes made three major contributions to sports and healthy living. Skiing became a popular mainstream sport after being introduced to North America by Swedish and Norwegian immigrants. Swedish hockey players began making their mark during the 1930s, leading to the spectacular success of imported Swedes beginning in 1973 (see chapter 12). And it was the reputation of Swedes as being in good physical condition that contributed to the success of the Canadian government program ParticipACTION.

Philanthropy

Although Swedes disagreed on political, religious, and temperance issues, they sometimes agreed long enough to make significant contributions towards helping others if the need was great enough. A significant example is the hospital in Wetaskiwin. *An Act to Incorporate The Scandinavian Hospital in Wetaskiwin* was passed in 1908[123] in response to a petition signed by thirty-eight men with Scandinavian names, including alderman Charles H. Olin and the Baptist pastor Gustav Carlson.[124] The first of three hospital buildings opened in 1909 in a two-storey log home, financed in no small part by the Ladies' Aid. Pastor Carlson's wife, Matilda Carlson, served as president for many years. When the City of Wetaskiwin took over the hospital around 1932, the Ladies' Aid changed its focus to become the Scandinavian Welfare Society.

Another landmark example is the Scandinavian Home Society[125] in Port Arthur, founded in 1923 to offer an organizational framework to support the flood of newcomers arriving in response to the government's campaign for immigrants during a period of major unemployment. Without work, these young men became forerunners of today's "street people." The reading room started with the labour newspaper *Ny tid* from Chicago and books from the IOGT library, but soon added a donation of forty books from Sweden's King Oscar II's Travelling Library Association.[126] The long-time president was Vice-consul Oscar Johnson, former editor of *Framåt*.

The society erected its building in 1926, with a restaurant and kitchen on the main floor and clubrooms and library upstairs. Construction was financed entirely through the society's own efforts. No banking institution would lend money, and *Svenska Canada-tidningen* published neither an appeal for funds, as promised by a representative, nor the professional photo of the completed brick building.[127] Given the high rate of unemployment until 1927, and differing opinions on what to do about it, one cannot help but admire Oscar Johnson's leadership ability in carrying the Scandinavian Home Society's building project through to completion.

Official support for people with disabilities was limited, and Swedish organizations often helped countrymen in distress. Oscar Forssell[128] of Silverhill was blinded by dynamite, and in 1917 became one of the first people in British Columbia to receive a pension from the Workmen's Compensation Board, $27 a month for life. His daughter, Ella, told how he managed: "My father did all the work on our place, except when he needed a horse for haying or plowing newly cleared land. He dug all our gardens and cut all our wood, did our milking and cleaned the barn, picked our apples and cherries so we never thought of him as being blind. He built our house, barn and chicken house with a small bit of help ... he used the scythe as well as any sighted person. My parents worked together, blasting, burning and clearing land for gardens, hay and pasture."[129]

Another man, Walter Sorenson,[130] lost his sight at age seven in a farm accident, and his parents sent him to the Brantford School for the Blind in Ontario. He graduated in piano from the Toronto Conservatory of Music in 1935, and for thirty-five years worked at the Canadian National Institute for the Blind concession stand in Edmonton's government buildings. He called his customers by name, and his neighbours enjoyed the piano music that wafted through his windows on summer evenings.

The dream of a Swedish old folks' home came true in 1943 with the opening of the Good Shepherd Lutheran Home in Wetaskiwin. Although the home is open to all, it was the Canada Conference of the Augustana Lutheran Church that in 1916 established a fund for such a facility.[131] The fund swelled over the years, notably with a 1929 bequest of almost $15,000 from the estate of Lars Johan Malm.[132] Malm lived his final days in the home of Pastor Otto Eklund,[133] one of the few Augustana pastors to become a Canadian citizen. The Good Shepherd

Lutheran Home housed only nine residents at first, but has expanded steadily ever since.

Thora Johnson did something in 1945 that would change the lives of many Vancouverites: she invited twelve women to her home and together they founded the Swedish-Canadian Rest Home Association. They were inspired by a vision: to build a decent home for seniors so that they need not continue living on $20 a month in squalid, vermin-infested rooms. The ladies elected an executive, formed the Sunset Circle as an auxiliary, and set about raising money.

The following year the association bought twelve timbered lots and began clearing the land, first by hand and then with a bulldozer. Through a great deal of cooperative effort, cajoling, and fundraising the $120,000 building was finally completed in 1949, with fifty-five rooms. It had been designed by architect Paul Johansen and built under the supervision of president Harold Swanson, a retired mechanical engineer. Elin Rylander[134] was hired as matron and her husband, John, as maintenance man, with John Leander[135] as recreation director.[136]

After only six years the property was expropriated in order to build the Second Narrows Bridge, and the association was forced not only to find a new site, but also to erect a new building for its residents. The second rest home, on Duthie Avenue in North Burnaby, opened in 1957, adding Swedish-Canadian Manor in 1967, the Gustav Vasa Apartments in 1989, and the Valhalla condominiums in 1991.[137] By this time the number of Swedish residents had slipped below 20 per cent and the association was faced with the dilemma of whether to keep the property. As might be expected, many of the early volunteers had left their hearts at the original site.

The impetus for building the Swedish Canadian Home for Senior Citizens in Winnipeg came from a bequest of $20,000 from contractor Nels Pearson,[138] a dedicated Lutheran and one of the organizers of the Sylvia Recreational Company, which owned the Vasa Lund property. His nephew, Richard Josephson, took part in planning for the company to donate more than 1.6 hectares of land as well as money. His widow, Elvira Pearson, turned the first sod in 1965. Vasa Lund Estates runs the home as a separate entity and accepts applications from any senior citizen, whether or not of Swedish origin.[139]

Swedes were far more attentive to the need for building old folks' homes, a hospital, and a home-away-from home for single immigrants than for founding educational facilities. Working separately, volunteers in Port Arthur, Wetaskiwin, Vancouver, and Winnipeg conceived the idea and raised the money to construct and manage these institutions, all of which eventually became mainstream.

Education

The Baptist Church founded the only Swedish post-secondary institution in Canada, the Scandinavian Department in Brandon College, in 1907. It not only provided a broad post-secondary education, but also was able to grant degrees through affiliation with McMaster University in Hamilton.[140]

A graduate in theology, Emil Lundkvist, had been hired in Sweden to teach Swedish language and literature, and to tour the Prairies giving lectures, recruiting students, and soliciting donations. The Mission superintendent from the Minnesota Conference became deeply disturbed when he heard that Augustana congregations were providing both funds and students to a Baptist educational institution.[141] During the 1910–11 school year, twenty Scandinavian students were enrolled.[142]

In 1915 Carl H. Lager[143] replaced Lundkvist as head of the Scandinavian Department. Students from Canada, United States, and Sweden studied four years to earn a Bachelor of Arts degree. Courses included a broad spectrum of music, languages (English, French, German, and Swedish), history, classics, and philosophy, as well as mathematics, chemistry, physics, geology, biology, and political economy.

Despite its Baptist orientation Brandon College turned out a significant number of Swedish graduates who were not Baptists. With the onset of the Depression students could no longer afford the tuition, and the Scandinavian Department closed in 1932. This, the first post-secondary institution in Canada to offer courses in Swedish language and literature, existed for only twenty-five years.

Universities have also made contributions to Swedish culture. In 1934 Professor Paul Boving[144] talked the University of British Columbia into dedicating $35,000 of its Carnegie grant towards adult education courses in Scandinavian arts and crafts, Scandinavian literature, and Swedish literature.[145] He introduced Swedish culture to English-speaking Canadians by representing Vancouver's Swedish community on many occasions, and by translating Swedish poetry into English.

In 1950 a group of Montreal businessmen established the Canadian-Scandinavian Foundation to provide scholarships to Canadian university students studying in Sweden, Norway, Finland, Denmark, or Iceland. One of the founders, Gustaf Hellström, had immigrated from Södermanland in 1915. His job involved promoting trade with Canada among the Scandinavian countries.[146]

The Canadian Institute for Nordic Studies (CINS) was established in 1987 at the University of Alberta. CINS operates through an endowment, one-third of which came from the Swedish Institute in Stockholm and two-thirds from the Alberta government. This money funds an annual graduate scholarship, undergraduate travel bursaries, speakers, and conferences. Decisions are made by a twelve-member board, which includes the president of the Association for the Advancement of Scandinavian Studies in Canada (AASSC).[147]

AASSC was founded in Ottawa in 1982 with Christopher Hale (University of Alberta) as president, Gurli Aagaard Woods (Carleton University) as editor of *AASSC Newsbulletin*, and Edward W. Laine (Public Archives of Canada) as chair of the editorial board for *Scandinavian-Canadian Studies/Études Scandinaves au Canada*.[148] Nordic literature predominates in this annual scholarly publication, with an occasional article on other subjects. The organization holds its conferences and annual meetings at the Congress of the Humanities and Social Sciences.

The Royal Norwegian Embassy provides travel grants to Norway for AASSC members; SWEA International offers a scholarship of $6,000 to doctoral candidates in Swedish language, literature, and area studies; and the Brucebo Fine Arts Foundation in Gotland, Sweden, has, since 1971, awarded two annual scholarships to Canadian artists, preferably painters, in the early stage of their career. One is the Brucebo Summer Residency scholarship and the other is the W.B. Bruce European Fine Arts Travel Scholarship. Jan Lundgren[149] of McGill University's Geography Department has been handling the applications for thirty-five years, introducing young Canadian artists to Sweden through the scholarships.

Brucebo is the home that William Blair Bruce (1859–1906) of Hamilton, Ontario, and his wife, the wealthy Caroline Benedicks (1856–1935) of Stockholm, built on the Baltic island of Gotland. The pair had met in Paris as budding artists, he a painter and she a sculptor, and chose the fishing village of Skälsö as a permanent home because "they were so charmed by its colours and its light which blurred all the sharp edges."

Bruce was Canada's first impressionist painter, and after his death Caroline offered a major collection of his works to the Hamilton Art Gallery. This collection became the gallery's centrepiece at its opening in 1914. The rest of Bruce's works are housed at Gotland's Fornsal Museum. His correspondence and plates of his paintings were published in 1982 under the title *Letters Home*.[150]

Swedish organizations mirrored Canadian norms. The temperance movement involved both countries, and sick-benefit societies reflected the mutual aid offered by fraternal organizations throughout the world. The later groups were different in that they emphasized various interpretations of Swedishness: ethnic societies, provincial groups, Swedish libraries, the Vasa Order, Scandinavian meeting places, SWEA, and Swedish schools. This chapter has shown the integration process at work – that is, how traditional ideas were reinterpreted in light of the Canadian experience. The new environment changed the way Swedes identified themselves within their ethnic group and how they related to other individuals and groups. Although the definition of Swedishness has changed over the years, it is still a viable goal among those with a high ethnic consciousness.

Chapter Twelve

Links with Sweden

The world has changed since Sweden appointed its first official representative in Canada, and the two countries now enjoy exchanges undreamt of a century and a half ago. Improvements in transportation and communication have simplified official, business, and personal contacts for various purposes, including genealogy, employment, education, conferences, medicine, and sports. Newspapers and documentaries from the other country are as close as your personal computer. Migration is now a two-way street because Canada has become a sending nation. The following pages give an overview of links between the two countries.

Business Ties

In 1988 Sweden was Canada's ninth-largest source of direct foreign investment, with a hundred Swedish subsidiaries. Half of them had manufacturing facilities employing more than 8,000 Canadians. The major Swedish investors were Stora Kopparberg in Cape Breton, Volvo in Halifax, ASEA, Atlas Copco and Pharmacia in Montreal, Astra in Toronto, Tetrapak in Aurora,[1] Ontario, and IKEA's nine stores distributed across Canada.[2] Another 350 firms had distributors in Canada, or had arranged licensing agreements or joint ventures. They were very competitive: "The aggressiveness of Swedish multinationals in international business, particularly their success in cutting losses when necessary, led one experienced foreign observer to comment recently that 'inside every smiling, taciturn Swedish businessman beats a Viking heart.'"[3]

In contrast, only eighteen Canadian firms, mainly high-technology companies, had a presence in Sweden. By 1999 Swedish multinationals had increased their corporate presence in Canada to 150 Swedish subsidiaries and another 400 companies represented by agents, distributors, and representatives. Despite all this activity, Canada ranked only seventeenth among Sweden's export markets, or about 1 per cent of the total.[4]

Official Visits

Prime Minister Palme's cross-Canada tour in 1974 was returned in 1980 by Prime Minister Trudeau, followed by Governor General Schreyer's visit in 1981 as part of his Nordic tour. When King Carl XVI Gustaf and Queen Silvia visited 14–19 March 1988, it marked the first time Sweden's reigning monarch had set foot in Canada.[5]

The royal couple's state visit began in Ottawa, with stops in Toronto, Winnipeg, Victoria, and Vancouver, and included a trade and industry delegation. The itinerary included visits to the rest homes in Winnipeg and Vancouver. His Majesty unveiled a wooden sculpture by Elmar Schultes, a tribute to Swedish pioneers, and presented John Leander's widow with the Order of the Polar Star to honour her late husband. The king also received several mementoes. The visits ended with the distinguished guests joining in the singing of the popular "Hälsa dem därhemma" (Greet those at home),[6] a song of homesickness and longing.

The royal couple's second state visit took place 24–8 October 2006, at the invitation of Governor General Michaëlle Jean. They were accompanied to Ottawa, Montreal, and Toronto by an industry delegation, which focused on business opportunities in the energy and automotive sectors, research and development programs, and cooperation in the medical field.[7] The king looked forward to visiting Quebec City, and also said, "I will be learning more about the cooperation in Arctic research between Canada and Sweden. The Arctic region, to which both our countries belong, is ecologically vulnerable. It is most important to follow climate change and other environmental impact carefully."[8] Sweden is recognized as a world leader in solving environmental problems through innovative technology, specializing in waste management, renewable energy, and environmentally friendly urban planning.

Unofficial royal visits included attending the 1988 Olympic Games in Calgary, accompanying a delegation from the Royal Academy of Engineering Science, and representing the international scout movement.[9] In addition to his other royal honours, His Majesty King Carl XVI Gustaf is the High Protector of the Swedish Order of Freemasons, a tradition that began in 1753 with King Adolf Fredrik. The Masonic Order has always been accepted by Sweden's state church, unlike the Augustana Synod in North America. Many of its members, clergy, and bishops are Masons.[10]

Philanthropy

Canada bestowed its first ever honorary Canadian citizenship upon Raoul Wallenberg[11] in 1985, and in 2001 declared the date of his arrest, 17 January, as Raoul Wallenberg Commemorative Day. After the German invasion he had been sent to Budapest by United States authorities to lead a mission to rescue Hungary's Jews. In six months he and his colleagues saved thousands of Jews from certain death by issuing fake passes and establishing safe "ghettoes": "Wallenberg was well aware of how flashy papers printed in colour with signatures, seals and stamps impressed the Germans. The result was a document printed in yellow and blue with the Tre Kronor – three crowns from the Swedish state symbol – and the signature of the Minister. Once again, these documents had no legal support whatsoever."[12] Raoul Wallenberg's name has become an international symbol for humanitarianism. After Soviet troops arrived in Budapest to end the German occupation the Russians took him away, and his fate is unknown.[13]

Per Anger, Swedish ambassador to Canada from 1976 to 1979, was one of Wallenberg's colleagues. As head of the International Raoul Wallenberg Federation in Stockholm, he wrote the book *With Raoul Wallenberg in Budapest*,[14] narrated NBC's four-hour film *Wallenberg. A Hero's Story*, and travelled widely as part of the international effort to secure his release. In Edmonton he unveiled six paintings by Armand Frederick Vallee that documented Wallenberg's time in Budapest. In Vancouver a plaque in Wallenberg's honour was installed at Queen Elizabeth Park.[15]

Alfred Nobel (1833–1896), the inventor of dynamite, left a will stipulating that most of his estate was to be invested, with the income "distributed annually in the form of prizes to those who have during the preceding year conferred the greatest benefit on mankind." He identified five equal prizes in chemistry, physics, physiology/medicine, literature, and peace, the last to be awarded in Oslo, Norway. Today, the awarding of the Nobel Prizes has a high profile because the event is regularly featured in mainstream media abroad, unlike other newsworthy events. The Nobel Banquet is always held in Stockholm City Hall on 10 December. There, the royal family and more than a thousand guests pay tribute to the winners with champagne, a gourmet three-course dinner, speeches, and a dance. To give an idea of the organization required to stage the prestigious event, it takes thirty people six hours to lay the tables.[16]

Canada's ten official winners of the Nobel Prize are F.G. Banting and J.J.R. Macleod (1923 Medicine), Lester B. Pearson (1957 Peace), G. Herzberg (1971 Chemistry), J.C. Polanyi (1986 Chemistry), R.E. Taylor (1990 Physics), Michael Smith (1993 Chemistry), the Pugwash Conferences on Science and World Affairs (1995 Peace), Willard Boyle (2009 Physics), and Alice Munro (2013 Literature).[17]

In 1929 Stockholm's National Museum of Ethnography acquired a totem pole after asking Swedish officials in Canada to find one. Consul Olof Hanson of Prince Rupert was charged with the task. An international incident was averted in 1994 when the Swedish government agreed to return the museum's centrepiece to its creators, the Haisla First Nation in northwestern British Columbia. According to Gil Cardinal, director of the National Film Board film *Totem: The Return of the G'psgolox Pole*, the pole had been commissioned in the early 1870s by G'psgolox to commemorate his family, who had died of smallpox and been brought back to life.

At first the museum displayed the pole outdoors, but, because of deterioration, a new building was constructed for it in 1980. Only eleven years later, the Haisla laid claim to it and a unique repatriation process began. Haisla artists Henry Robertson and Barry Wilson carved a replica for the museum, and the original pole was returned in 2006, to be stored at British Columbia's Museum of Anthropology until a suitable home is built for it. The museum's director told reporters, "I think the common feeling among Swedes is that it was the right thing to do."[18]

Genealogy

Many Canadians have re-established contact with Swedish relatives by tracing their family tree. Nils William Olsson was the first to publish a handbook in 1963, and in 1981 founded the quarterly magazine *Swedish American Genealogist*. A comprehensive step-by-step handbook, *Your Swedish Roots*,[19] came out in 2004. Sweden's records are among the most extensive and complete in the world, and a growing number of them are available on CD or online as databases.

The world's largest charted family, Långarydssläkten, numbered 140,000 persons in 1988 when it was accepted into the *Guinness Book of Records*. All the descendants derived from a single couple living in Långaryd parish, Småland, fifteen generations ago, and over time they have spread throughout Sweden and the world. The authors of the monumental, four-volume work *Långarydssläkten* list descendants individually according to a precise numbering system.[20] The count from seventeen pages chosen at random yielded 268 Långarydssläkt who came to Canada. They settled from Ontario westward, including the Yukon and Northwest Territories. Carl Hjalmer Anderson, already mentioned as a victim of the Rogers Pass snow slide, and his brother Jon were members of this select group.[21]

Two documentaries aired on Swedish television featured immigrants to Northwestern Ontario. Gunnar Gustafson[22] immigrated in 1929 and worked as a section foreman at Armstrong, Ontario. He lost touch with his family in Sweden, who remembered him as a strong, adventurous young man. His children, on the other hand, thought of him as a strict disciplinarian. After his death in 1992 the Swedish family travelled to Armstrong to meet their new-found relatives. The 2005 film *En fjäder i garderoben* (A feather in the wardrobe) interviewed both families as they struggled to reconcile their differing memories of the enigmatic Gunnar.

The second documentary, *Sagan om en ring* (The story of a ring), told about Birgit Kostenius's search for her grandmother, Kristina, who had immigrated to Kenora in 1912, hoping to be able to send for her eight-year-old son Runo. She married farmer Erik Fandén and moved to nearby Laclu, where she died in 1948 without seeing her son again. When Runo's daughter Birgit Kostenius visited in 1979 one of the people who had known Kristina showed her the family photos Runo's wife had sent, and gave her Kristina's wedding ring. Birgit wore this prized possession on a chain around her neck until it was stolen in 1994. *Sagan om en ring* was filmed in Kenora and Laclu, and aired in 2003 as part of the series *Din släktsaga*.[23]

The documentary also told how Kristina and her four siblings were separated after their parents died. His mother's parents adopted Gustaf Westin, but the others grew up in poor circumstances. Gustaf vowed that one day he would bring the family together again, and as adults they all immigrated to Kenora. With this background, Kristina's separation from Runo must have been very difficult. She herself had suffered a hearing loss because of rough treatment in her foster home.[24]

Education and Emigration

Today Canadians have the option of sending their children to one of Sweden's international boarding schools. Marion and Stig Petersson[25] of Wetaskiwin sent each of their three children to Holsby Brunn Bible

School in Småland, which is associated with Torchbearers International, for a year. Some descendants of immigrants chose to move to Sweden. Daniel Fuglesang[26] of Thunder Bay graduated from Holsby Brunn, then attended Uppsala University and Lund University. The subject of his doctoral dissertation was the Etruscan site in San Giovenale, Italy, excavated by King Gustav VI Adolf, among others, during the 1950s and 1960s. Bob Lilja's eldest son also moved to Sweden, working as a teacher in Stockholm.[27]

Jennifer Saxell's music and art career has taken off since 1991, when she moved to Ystad on Sweden's south coast. She grew up on Vancouver Island, but during a holiday in Sweden fell in love with the town's fairytale streets.[28] Eleanor Sander of Kenora had already learned Swedish during an extended visit in 1984–5, and then married Ingemar Lavesson. The pair operates a bed-and-breakfast near Moose Park in Skåne. Eleanor is particularly interested in sharing her heritage: "Many visits are made by the relatives on both sides of the ocean and Swedes and Canadians now have a new opportunity to learn about life in the other country. Because so many of the early immigrants never got back to Sweden, there were many stories that went untold. The modern society and technology will not let that be repeated."[29]

Canadian expatriates can find a community forum as well as Swedish and Canadian links on the Internet. In 2004 the webmaster was Tracy Nilsson, who was born in Edmonton.

Canada Geese

Canada geese are not native to Sweden. Bengt Berg of Värnanäs imported them in the early 1930s. First he introduced the birds to Kalmar Sound on Sweden's east coast.[30] They did not do as well as expected, so in 1940 he placed more birds in central Sweden, where they made themselves right at home on Mälaren and Hjälmaren lakes. More than 50,000 Canada geese were counted at the beginning of the 1980s and they have become a problem, as in Canada.

Medicine

In the medical field, Henry Delichte of St Alphonse, Manitoba, donated bone marrow in 1998, the first donor under the new Canadian Blood Services. He was a perfect match for Håkan Larsson, of Sandviken, Gästrikland, who was undergoing chemotherapy for leukemia. A grateful Håkan described their special relationship by saying, "Henry gave me back my life."[31]

Literature

Heidi von Born[32] has been a major force in introducing Canadian literature to Sweden. Since 1980 she has produced radio programs, organized readings at the annual Göteborg Book Festival, and translated poetry and seen to its publication in newspapers, magazines, and an anthology. The reason is her fascination with Canada, which she finds mysterious, proud, and warm. In 1988 she taught creative writing at the University of Victoria, which conferred an honorary doctorate upon her.[33] When Dennis Browne was Canadian ambassador to Sweden he and his wife attended the Göteborg Book Festival several times. He wrote, "For us it was a great experience to meet so many talented and truly interesting Canadians, and to see their work held in such high regard."[34]

Canadian Studies

The Nordic Association for Canadian Studies/L'Association Nordique d'Études Canadiennes (NACS/ANEC) was founded at Denmark's University of Aarhus in 1984, after the Canadian government began working through the International Council for Canadian Studies. "The first few years were an uphill struggle, trying to convince academic environments in Denmark, Sweden, Norway, Finland and Iceland that Canada was worth studying in its own right – not merely as part of British, American or Post-colonial Studies. The increasingly independent international role that Canadian governments forged for Canada, however, helped to increase awareness of Canada as a truly unique society."[35]

NACS/ANEC built up an academic community through triennial conferences coupled with an ambitious publications series, and in 1991 the Canadian Studies Centre (CSC) was founded at the University of Aarhus. It was supported by the Canadian government to advise students and to recommend student-exchange programs between Nordic and Canadian universities. Aarhus University offers Canadian Studies courses at the bachelor's and master's levels, assisted by CSC's extensive lending library. NACS/ANEC offers student scholarships and arranges for annual seminars, guest lecturers, readings and workshops in cooperation with CSC.

In 2007 NACS/ANEC president Keith Batterbee justified Canadian studies as follows:

It is of course not at all surprising that Canada as such is of interest –
one of the major Western societies that has come about through the great
migration of the past half-millennium, but with a number of distinctive features: its two official languages, its regional variety, its northern
environment, its flourishing literatures and arts, its complex relationship
with its own indigenous peoples alongside its very high rates of ongoing immigration; its ongoing process of rethinking its constitution, and in
particular its engagement both at home and internationally with issues of
human rights. For all these reasons, Canada deserves serious international
attention.[36]

So far the emphasis has been on literary studies, but a new generation of
"Canadianists" from various disciplines has made the study of Canada
increasingly comprehensive.

Global Swedes

The Society for Swedes around the World, or SVIV (*Föreningen för svenskar i världen*), is a lobby group for the 400,000 Swedes who live abroad.
Two high-profile successes are dual citizenship and a system of voting in Sweden's elections. SVIV's website acts as a global contact point
and discussion forum, and each annual conference spotlights Swedes
from a different country. SVIV performs all its functions in the Swedish
language.

The popularity of IKEA furniture stores, the musical group ABBA,
Swedish hockey players, and more recently the best-selling novels of
Stieg Larsson are making contemporary Sweden better known among
Canadians. At the same time many Swedes know more about Canada
geese than they do about Canada, despite the efforts of Heidi von Born
and others. It is hoped that this book will help to edge Swedish minds
out of the giant American shadow that has obscured Canada for so long.

THE SWEDES IN CANADA'S NATIONAL GAME

They Changed the Face of Pro Hockey

*By Charles Wilkins**

It would have been unimaginable during the 1960s or seventies, but when representatives of the thirty National Hockey League (NHL) teams gathered in Montreal in late June of 2009 to conduct their annual draft of junior-aged players, it quickly became apparent that this would be "the year of the Swede," as the media called it. No less than seven Swedish-born junior stars, most of whom will eventually become household names in Canada, were chosen in the first round alone: Victor Hedman, Oliver Ekman-Larsson, Magnus Paajarvi-Svensson, David Rundblad, Jacob Josefson, Tim Erixon, and Marcus Johnsson.

Many more followed in subsequent rounds.

Only one Swedish-born player, Mats Sundin, has ever been chosen first overall in the NHL entry draft (by the Quebec Nordiques in 1989). Like so many Swedes who have come to Canada to play hockey Sundin, who has also played in Toronto and Vancouver, has become a well-known presence in this country. Indeed, during the past forty years many of the most recognizable Swedes in Canada have been the talented young men who have come to the country to play professional hockey and sometimes to live permanently. The list is long: Anders Hedberg, Ulf Nilsson, Lars Erik Sjoberg, Kent Nilsson, Peter Forsberg, Hakan Loob, Thomas Steen, Tommy Salo, Daniel Alfredson, Fredrick Modin, Niklas Sundstrom, Markus Naslund, and the Sedin twins Henrik and Daniel. Many more Swedish players – including NHL all-stars Niklas Lidstrom and Henrik Zetterberg of the Detroit Red Wings – have become well known in Canada while playing with American-based teams.

Several Swedish players – Juha Widing, Ulf Sterner, and Thommie Bergman among them – enjoyed modest success in the NHL prior to the

---

* Charles Wilkins is the author of *Breakaway* (1995) and co-author of *Hockey, the Illustrated History* (1985), *Forever Rivals* (1996), and *After the Applause* (1985), among other non-hockey titles. He lives in Thunder Bay.

early 1970s. The most prominent of the three, Juha Widing, played his junior hockey with the Brandon Wheat Kings and eventually farmed in central British Columbia. But it was the arrival of two young men from northern Sweden in 1973 that would change not only the profile of the Swedish hockey player in Canada, but also the very face of Canadian and North American hockey.

Until the early seventies European players had been considered too fragile, not aggressive enough, for the Canadian-style game. Apart from their presumed delicacy, the Swedes were considered unwelcome interlopers by lesser North American players who stood to lose jobs to the light-hitting but highly skilled foreigners.

However, by 1973 the need for talented players had increased dramatically in North America. The NHL had recently expanded from six to sixteen teams (there are now thirty) and the twelve teams of the newly founded World Hockey Association were poaching players from the NHL by the dozens.

Against that backdrop, the Toronto Maple Leafs dispatched scout Gerry McNamara to Sweden to assess the skills of a goaltender named Curt Larsson who, as it turned out, was injured when McNamara arrived. In order not to waste the trip McNamara acted on a tip concerning a pair of young players named Inge Hammarstrom and Borje Salming and attended a game between Gävle's Brynäs IF club and a touring Canadian senior team.

During the course of the game, McNamara took his eyes off the brilliant and durable Salming only long enough to glance around the rink to ensure he was the only scout in the building. "Salming not only stood up to this tough Canadian team," said McNamara, "he dished their dirt right back at them. He didn't back up an inch."

Years later Hammarstrom recalled the pair's signing with the Maple Leafs a few months hence: "I remember lots of guys in Sweden said we'd be back home before Christmas. But both Borje and I said, 'We've got news for you. It'll be over our dead bodies.'"

And it nearly was.

"In my second game in the NHL," Salming recalled in 2006, "I went into the corner with Dave Shultz [the most violent of the Philadelphia Flyers]. He ignored the puck and just hit me with his stick. I hit him back across the back of the legs. He hit me across the chest, so I hit him the same way. Then we dropped our gloves and had a fight."

No Swedish hockey player from the past would have dared.

Borje Salming of the Toronto Maple Leafs was among the first of many Swedish hockey stars to play for Canadian NHL teams during the late twentieth century. Courtesy of Dan Diamond.

Leaf owner Harold Ballard once said of the less aggressive Hammar-strom that he could "go into the corner of the rink with a dozen eggs in his pocket" and that not one egg would get broken. But Salming was different. For nearly two decades he was not only one of the best defencemen in the NHL, but his cold-blooded fearlessness permanently altered long-standing perceptions about Swedish players.

Meanwhile, in 1974 Anders Hedberg, Ulf Nilsson, and Lars-Erik Sjoberg entered the World Hockey Association (WHA) in Winnipeg, where they were credited with reviving the career of former NHL star Bobby Hull. The great left winger's vocal admiration both of his Swed-ish teammates and of Swedish pros generally added significantly to the Swedes' new lustre in pro hockey.

Throughout the 1980s, each new wave of Swedes in the NHL was as durable as, or more durable than, the last. When defenceman Ulf Samuelsson showed up in 1984, his aggressive, sometimes "dirty," play immediately earned him the nickname "Robocop" or *Tuffe Uffe*. Peter Forsberg, who entered the league with the Quebec Nordiques in 1994, is considered one of the toughest and most talented players ever to com-pete in pro hockey. When Alexander Steen, the son of Thomas Steen, joined the Maple Leafs in 2005 it marked the first time that a Swedish father and son had played in the NHL.

"With the acceptance of the early Swedes, the floodgates opened," Gerry McNamara once said. Next came the Finns, the Czechs, the Slo-vaks, and Russians – a group of Europeans that now comprises some 30 per cent of active NHL players.

"It's easy to forget that it began with the Swedes," former Leaf captain Mats Sundin said recently. In particular, with one legendary defence-man named Borje Salming, who with his courage and talent forever changed the face of Canadian and professional hockey.

Chapter Thirteen

Language, Discrimination, and Assimilation

Until fairly recently learning English was one of the most difficult challenges facing immigrants. In 1962 English became a compulsory subject in Sweden's elementary and secondary schools. As a result most Swedes are competent in the language, so that immigrants to Canada as well as English-speaking visitors to Sweden find little difficulty in understanding or in making themselves understood. This chapter will focus on the Swedish language and naming traditions, language learning, discrimination (both negative and positive), and the process of assimilation.

Language

Up to 1901 most people in Sweden followed the patrilineal system of naming;[1] that is, Erik's son Anders would be called Anders Eriksson, and his daughter Anna would be called Anna Eriksdotter. A wife did not change her patronymic upon marriage, and each generation had a different patronymic derived from the father. Sometimes the patronymics were shortened, as in Olofsson to Olsson and Jonasson to Jonsson. In North America, the first "s" was almost always dropped in names ending in "son," and the patronymic itself was anglicized so that Eriksson became Ericson or Erickson; for example, Svensson Swanson, Nilsson Nelson, and Bengtsson Benson. The letter "k" was almost always replaced by "c," and people with the patronymics Johansson, Jonasson, Jönsson, and Jansson often chose the surname Johnson, and sometimes Johnston or Johnstone. As a rule most Swedish patronymics end in "son," whereas Danish and Norwegian patronymics end in "sen."

In Sweden, particularly in the province of Dalarna, both men and women preceded their Christian name and patronymic with the name of the farm on which they lived. This helped distinguish them from others bearing the same name. The custom continued in Canada by using a man's trade as his identifier, as in Butcher Anderson and Blacksmith Johnson of Waterville, Quebec.[2] In Vancouver's early Swedish community there were Jeweller Peterson, Shoemaker Peterson, and Electrical Peterson. To distinguish himself from the others, Emil "Homer" Peterson took the name of the street he lived on, Homer Street.[3]

In Sweden name duplications became so confusing during compulsory military service that soldiers were assigned surnames during their tour of duty. These surnames were often of one syllable, and could be military terms like *Svärd* (sword), personal attributes like *Stark* (strong), objects from nature like *Falk* (falcon), or occupations like *Smed* (blacksmith). After discharge some dropped their patronymics in favour of their military surname, while others used both.

During the 1500s the clergy began Latinizing their Christian names, as in Petrus for Petter, and also taking a Latinized surname commemorating their birthplace or an object from nature, to be passed on to descendants. An example is the botanist Carolus Linnaeus, whose father chose his surname from the linden tree when he was ordained. After Carolus Linnaeus was elevated to the nobility, he changed his name to Carl von Linné. "Von," "de," or "af" often preceded noble surnames. The father of one of Linnaeus's students, Anders Dahl, was also a pastor but he chose a short surname. Dahl became a leading botanist, and the dahlia plant is named for him. Another method the clergy used to form surnames was to add the Greek word *ander* (man), as in Silander and Litander.

Surnames were first used by the nobility and wealthy landowners, then by the clergy, merchants, and townspeople, and eventually by the rural population. By 1901, when the government passed a law forcing everybody to adopt a surname to pass on to their descendants, some had already chosen names from nature, the most common surnames. They often compounded words like *berg* (mountain), *ström* (stream), *blom* (flower), *kvist* (twig), and *löv* (leaf), adding it to their patronymic. The receiving population in Canada found this seemingly cavalier attitude towards personal names confusing, especially when fathers, sons, and brothers chose completely different surnames.

The four Svensson brothers who immigrated during the 1880s each took a different surname: Lindwall, Lindgren, Palmquist, and Stromberg. The prefix *"strom"* was in honour of their birthplace, Ström in Jämtland. Four related brothers, sons of Erik Zakrison, chose Stromquist, Svedberg, Zakrison, and Erikson, the latter following the traditional patrilineal pattern. All filed on homesteads in New Stockholm, Saskatchewan.[4] Having different surnames in the same family was not at all unusual at this time.

Many immigrants could read, due to a church policy of home instruction that began in the 1690s, and men who had experienced military service were often able to write as well.[5] Compulsory education began in 1842, and writing ability among Swedish children in 1860 was 50 per cent, swelling to 90 per cent by 1880.[6] The lower classes also benefited from training as tradesmen and artisans.

In 1906 certain changes in spelling were decreed by royal circular (*Stavningsreformen*), drawn up on the advice of the education administration (*Läroverksöverstyrelsen*) and the Swedish Academy. The letters "t" or "tt" replaced "dt"; "v" replaced "f," "fv," and "hv"; and "upp" replaced "up." Before this time the spelling for the city and university in Uppsala was Upsala,[7] but languages are living entities that keep changing. When emigration started the word for girl was "*jänta*," then "*flicka*," and now "*tjej*."

The Swedish alphabet varies slightly from the English alphabet. Its three extra vowels – å, ä, and ö – are important because they can change the meaning of a word as well as its pronunciation. For example, "*man*" means "man," "*män*" means "men," and "*mån*" means "moon." Before "q" was added to the Swedish dictionary to accommodate the word "quisling," the letters "kv" answered this purpose. People wanting to anglicize a name like Blomkvist simply changed the "kv" to "qu." Those with the surname Ljung, however, might choose the spelling Young in North America because these names sound similar. The Swedish letter "j," even with another letter preceding it, is pronounced like our "y." The combination "sj" is an unknown sound in English, often rendered as "sh." Those with the surname Sjöholm might choose Seaholm instead, since "*sjö*" means "lake" or "sea." Similarly Berg, pronounced "berry," could become Barry, and Holm could become Holmes. The possibilities are endless.

Changes in pronunciation led to difficult choices, especially for those with surnames beginning with the extra vowels, or the letter "y." Ågren is pronounced Ogren, so people could choose between Agren and Ogren, or even Green. Ängblom is pronounced Engblom, which is less problematic. And vowels with a minimal change in pronunciation, like Österberg, could result in simply dropping the umlaut. Impossible to duplicate is the Swedish letter "y," with its closed "ee" pronunciation. Thus Ytterström and Nyman became Utterstrom and Nieman or Newman. And then there were those who adopted a completely different surname, some for the simple reason that their mail got mixed up with a namesake living nearby. The first generation seemed to accept these changes without difficulty; however, descendants researching the family tree can become frustrated when dealing with Swedish surnames that changed with each generation.

Every province in Sweden had its own dialect, so that a person's origin was apparent as soon as he or she spoke. Like other dialects, Jämtland's "*jämska*" varied slightly from community to community, and could differ from Stockholm Swedish in vocabulary, grammar, and word order. Both "*jämska*" and the Skåne dialect, "*skånska*," derived from Danish as it was spoken in the 1600s, when Jämtland and Skåne were among those provinces turned over to Sweden through peace treaties. However, the transportation route to Trondheim, Norway, kept Jämtlanders in touch and left its mark on *jämska*. Norway belonged to Denmark until 1814. The result is that Danish, Norwegian, and Swedish, and their dialects, are different but mutually understandable.

The pastor in New Stockholm, C.O. Hofstrand, preached in *skånska*, but his *jämska*-speaking flock could understand what he said by listening closely. Descendants of New Stockholm's pioneers continue to share a deep feeling of kinship with their forebears. A Swedish visitor claimed he heard *jämska* still being spoken there in the 1950s.[8]

Immigrants were expected to learn English, to obey Canadian laws, and to conform to the customs of the resident majority, but were given very little help to do so. The only official assistance was a Swedish-English dictionary provided by immigration agents. There were no organized classes teaching English as a second language until after 1905 and then only in Winnipeg. There were no brochures or other help to explain basics like the monetary system, banking, imperial weights and measures, or the Fahrenheit thermometer, all of which were different in Sweden. Until 1889, when the metric system was introduced, immigrants were accustomed to an older way of measuring. To complicate matters, the Swedish "mile" measures six and one-quarter English miles (ten kilometres).

John Olof Englund,[9] a staunch Baptist, learned English from bibles in both languages rather than from the dictionary. Eight years after immigration, his language skills earned him the right to name Kipling, Ontario, and to become its postmaster in 1900. Anyone who has tried to learn a second language can relate to the time and effort required to accomplish this goal, the frustrations along the way, and the disappointment at not getting the accent quite right.

The Swedes who came in 1900 to the lumbering town of Millertown, Newfoundland, found a willing teacher in Roland Goodyear, a young Newfoundlander who was hired as the blacksmith's helper.[10] "When I entered the shop for the first time, not one of these men understood a word of English and, once they learned that I could read and write, my standing improved rapidly. During slack periods my time was taken up in teaching them English. My smith [Lindahl] had with him his Swedish-English dictionary. He would pick certain words such as 'hammer' and 'bellows' or 'good day and how are you' and I would give him the pronunciation in English. In the process of teaching them I picked up a little Swedish myself."[11]

Naturally immigrants spoke Swedish in the home until learning English. In 1887, when John and Matilda Frejd[12] immigrated to Bruce Mines, Ontario, they were the only Swedes around. John worked for the Canadian Pacific Railway and Matilda followed her profession of midwifery, at the same time running their farm. After the teasing their eldest daughter endured at school because she couldn't speak English, the couple spoke only that language in their children's presence.

In Vancouver hotel owner Justus Swanson and his wife, Beata, also spoke English in the home. The daughters felt embarrassed when their parents spoke Swedish in front of their friends, prompting Beata to make a decision, "We are now in Canada, and the Swedish language must be forgotten."[13] On the other hand John and Helga Taft[14] of Wabigoon, Ontario, taught themselves to read and write English but spoke Swedish to their daughter because they did not want to transfer their accents to her. Instead, she learned English at school.[15]

In most cases each language filtered into the other. In Eriksdale, Manitoba, Swedes called *spisen* (the stove) "*stoven*," *bil* (car) "*kar*," and *tåg* (train) "*tren*,"[16] while their English neighbours began using the terms "long milk" (*lång mjölk*) or "thick milk" (*tjock mjölk*) for a Swedish dairy delicacy. In the case of the traditional Christmas Eve dish, *lutfisk*, the word was anglicized to lute fish so that the meaning of the curing agent, *lut* (lye), was lost to that of a musical instrument and ultimately confused with the Norwegian word for the same dish, *lutefisk*. Those Swedes who visited the homeland noticed a similar situation there and "commented, not without chagrin, on the prevalence of Americanisms in the spoken Swedish they encountered."[17] Correspondence with relatives in the Old Country usually continued only while the original immigrants, both adults and children, were alive. The second generation seldom learned to speak Swedish, let alone write it.[18]

A few parents made a point of teaching their children Swedish. O.P. Olson and his wife, Alma,[19] of Earl Grey, Saskatchewan, always spoke Swedish in the home, and Alma taught all six children to read and write the language. For their part Alma and O.P. learned to speak, read, and write English. The most prominent book in their home library was *Webster's Unabridged Dictionary*.

The school system offered the most effective means of teaching Anglo-conformity. Pupils who had been born in Sweden or raised in a Swedish milieu left teachers with the formidable task of introducing the language of instruction at the same time as they tackled the curriculum. The teacher at New Stockholm school in 1900, W.J. Sisler, wrote about his first day with twenty children from grades one to eight, and went on to describe his method of teaching them English. At that time schools opened in April and closed in October because of problems with winter transportation and heating.

> I knew that the Swedes were a musical people so I took a chance and asked the class if they could sing. They evidently had been accustomed to class singing. The oldest girl present just looked at two or three of the senior pupils, nodded to each, gave them the key note and they sang in four parts a lovely little song beginning "Over in the meadow runs a merry brooklet with its silver sheen." There were three or four of the older boys who carried the tenor and bass very well while the girls managed the first and second soprano. This gave me a start and within a few days I taught them two or three new part songs which they enjoyed very much. The children were all very quiet, polite and never talked back when spoken to, in anything but the most quiet and respectful manner.
>
> One of the first rules that I made was that only English was to be spoken at school or on the playground. Going home or on the way to school they could do as they pleased ... there was never any serious problem of discipline and neither rod nor strap, nor any form of severe punishment was ever used ...
>
> A good deal of time was spent in trying to correct pronunciation. There are certain sounds which are not used in Swedish, Norwegian or Danish – w, th, wh and qu. They sound "with" as "vit," "both" as "boot," "where" as "vere," "quick" as "kvick," "winter" as "vinter." I showed them exactly how to use the tongue, lips, teeth and breathing in order to make the sound. They learned quickly and I soon found that they were correcting each other outside the school as well as in.[20]

Sisler credited his experience in the New Stockholm school for his appointment as principal of Winnipeg's Strathcona School in 1905. This school taught English to immigrant children and, later, to adults. Teachers received instruction as well. His "direct method," as he called it, toppled the prevailing theory that teachers had to know both languages in order to be effective, and he wrote several how-to books on the subject.[21]

Not all teachers were as perceptive as Sisler. The Hall sisters, Brita, thirteen, and Emma, eleven,[22] immigrated in 1904 and the following summer attended Norland School in Scandinavia, Manitoba. The young teacher, a second generation Swede, taught three grades for three months.

> We were placed with Grade One and were called up to the front, and taught such words as "book," "desk," "chair" when the article was pointed out. We also struggled with "the." We tried ta, da, va and fa but the teacher didn't seem satisfied. We had no such sound in Swedish ...
>
> We were given Primary Readers. Imagine eleven and thirteen-year-olds learning three letter words! Bertha and I were soon able to read our lessons even if we didn't know what many of the words meant and were before long promoted to Grade 2 ...
>
> Swedish was the language of the playground the first while. But one Monday morning before first recess we were told only English was to be used. Anyone who disobeyed would be punished.[23]

This was to be their only formal schooling, and they learned English on their own in the workforce. Emma kept her Christian name, but at school Brita became Bertha and in later years she regretted this loss of personal identity.[24]

It has been suggested that immigrants generally achieved higher marks in school than the rest of the population,[25] but whether that was because they tried harder has not been determined. In any case, education was a high priority among Swedish immigrants.[26] In September 1916 the school in Silverhill, British Columbia, opened with twelve students whose first language was Swedish, replacing another school 5.6 kilometres away. All the teachers were English-speaking. One of them received the response "Håll käften" in unison so often that she asked her landlady what it meant. Upon hearing that it meant "shut your mouth" the teacher chastised the pranksters.[27] However, she could not chastise the school inspector, who asked her, within hearing of the children, "Have you no white children in your school, only Swedes?"[28]

Immigrants have told some funny stories about their experiences learning English. Those travelling across the country were confused by For Rent signs because in Swedish these words mean "too clean," and some thought that General Store was a very famous military man because the name appeared so often.[29] Mrs Gudmundson of Coleman, Alberta, went to the store to buy sugar, asking for "socker." She came home with sockeye salmon and got quite a surprise when she opened the tin.[30] Given the isolated nature of labouring work, Carl Nelson's sad story is not unusual. While employed on a section gang between Winnipeg and Souris he learned the language of the rest of the crew, thinking it was English. Alas, his new acquisition was Ukrainian![31] Similarly, nine-year-old Emil Shellborn and Wasey were best friends in school. "To me," Emil recalled, "Wasey was a good teacher ... he spoke Ukrainian to me and I talked back to him in Swedish. So we both made good progress."[32] Unfortunately both boys thought they were learning English.

Matt Lindfors[33] in Vancouver initiated a school for adult Scandinavians to learn English as a second language in 1927. He had immigrated four years earlier, learned English on the job, and attended the University of British Columbia for a year. His Scandinavian School of English offered private lessons and evening classes where three progressive courses were offered. Each course of twenty-five lectures cost $10, and after completion students received a diploma. For five or ten cents they could buy a copy of the school paper, *Gnistan* (The Spark), edited by Lindfors. He advertised the opening of each term in *Svenska pressen*, and in 1929 the paper published an article complete with photos. Unfortunately the Depression forced the school to close in 1931. That the Vancouver Board of School Trustees offered a night-school course in English as a second language in 1937 and hired Lindfors to teach it was a sign of changing times.[34]

That bastion of Swedish culture, the church, did its best to keep the Swedish language alive, but not all Swedes attended church, or followed the same religion. Children who did attend church learned hymns and prayers and took confirmation classes, but English soon began to infiltrate the various programs for young people.

Until recently the Swedish language has been almost totally neglected by Canadian universities, with the exception of Brandon College from 1907 to 1932. The University of Manitoba offered a course from 1911 to 1918,[35] Professor Thure Hedman[36] taught Swedish sporadically at the University of Toronto from 1920 to 1950, and the University of Guelph's attempt in 1968 failed after three years.[37] A change came in 1974 when the University of British Columbia started offering beginner and intermediate courses, taught by Canada's only lecturer from the Swedish

Institute in Stockholm. Since 1993 this has been Lena Karlström, who also teaches Scandinavian literature. Peter Stenberg headed the department for many years.

The University of Alberta added Swedish to its Scandinavian-language courses in 1985, thanks to sizeable and continuing donations from Anna Marian Campbell, who was of Swedish descent. The lecturer since 1994 has been Marianne Lindvall, working under department head Christopher Hale, who prepared the "Swedes" entry in the 1999 *Encyclopedia of Canada's Peoples*. In 2008 he was named Officer of the Royal Norwegian Order of Merit. Another University of Alberta professor who made a significant contribution was the geographer William Wonders,[38] whose studies included Scandinavians in central Alberta. Professor Wonders' ties with Sweden were significant, and he was the keynote speaker at the 1987 Conference of the Nordic Association for Canadian Studies at Lund University.

Because universities do not cover the cost of language lecturers, funding has posed a continuing problem. At the University of British Columbia the lecturer's salary has been paid in part by donations from Swedish concerns in Vancouver, including IKEA, the forestry company Sunds Defibrator, the Swedish community, and once by the Swedish embassy. At the University of Alberta the Scandinavian Professorship Endowment Fund and its predecessor have been fundraising since 1990, and in 2009 received a donation of $400,000 in memory of Henry Cabot and Linnea Lodge, which will cover an academic teaching position.[39] The University of Alberta is the only Canadian university to offer a Bachelor of Arts degree in Scandinavian, a Bachelor of Arts combined Honours degree in Scandinavian, and a Bachelor of Commerce degree/major in European Studies-Scandinavian.[40]

Positive and Negative Discrimination

The derogatory expression "big dumb Swede" was a widespread North American phenomenon, and probably stemmed from character traits learned in the Old Country. Outward signs of shyness and humility, and a penchant for speaking slowly and carefully, were not characteristics that North American Anglo-Saxons considered admirable, and may be another reason, in addition to language, why so many immigrants preferred to live in Swedish communities at first.

Although Swedes did not suffer official discrimination like some other immigrants did, they and their children were sometimes singled out for special attention. Ann Stolz, who was born in Canada, attended a rural school in northern Manitoba during the 1920s: "I could not understand why we were called the dirty Swedes because we certainly were not dirty; we were very clean. My mother was a very clean woman with a very clean home. We had regular meals on the table. That is what I could not understand. That hurt me. We were called that."[41]

Similarly, Frank Eliason's children suffered socially because of his job. As secretary for the local Grain Growers' Association, a cooperative, in Wynard, Saskatchewan, he had won the respect of the farmers but not the townspeople.[42] "[My children] were all excellent scholars and as a rule were leading in the classes but in all social activities they were discriminated against and held back. For instance, they were not asked to take part in plays, literary efforts and other social activities connected with school work. They often asked me if I knew why they were discriminated against and while I understood the situation I was unable to do very much about it. At times they were jeered at and called 'Progressives' and the poor kids did not know the meaning of the word."[43]

Martin Johansson was overwhelmed by the racism he experienced on the Prairies during the 1930s: "Scandinavians are not that well liked any more, just because Sweden was on Germany's side during the war, and the hatred grows beneath the smiling surface ... We Swedes are not counted as white in this country any more ... One is hated wherever one goes, at work and in town and everywhere. Crazy Swede or Goddamned black bastard or outsiders, those are the names you get now, from all."[44] At the same time he railed against Poles and Galicians, calling them "bohunks" and "goddamned blacks," reflecting the indignities that he had suffered himself.

John Murray Gibbon, public relations director for the CPR, did not agree with the prevailing exclusionist attitude towards immigrants and its accompanying Anglo-conformity. From the company's head office in Montreal he arranged New Canadian Folksong and Handicraft festivals across the country to celebrate what he called the "Canadian mosaic." The festival in Winnipeg took place at the Royal Alexandra Hotel in June 1928. The Swedish contingent consisted of performers in folk costumes. Two women demonstrated their spinning and weaving, backed by a display of woven textiles, including a landscape. A group of forty Swedish dancers and musicians playing accordions and violins presented folk dances, including *Oxdansen* (the ox dance), and "the Bellman Quartet sang with great charm a succession of songs by the Robert Burns of Sweden, C.W. Bellman."[45]

Gibbon's 1938 book, *Canadian Mosaic,* influenced the "cultural mosaic" concept later adopted in Canada's multiculturalism policies.

Printed references to Swedes by neighbours, journalists, teachers, co-workers, surveyors, and other ethnic groups were almost always positive. In 1897 Canon Wharton Gill, an Anglican, journeyed to Scandinavia, Manitoba, to officiate at a wedding. He made some sensitive observations during his ride to the church:

> Their log houses had an air of their own, entirely different to the log house of the Englishman or the Canadian. Here were wide-spreading eaves, quaint little windows in the roof, rustic porches with trailing vines, seats on the shady side of the house made from the spruce or the tamarac [*sic*]. The lake and wood land, that seemed too rough and broken for the Canadian who wanted to grow prosaic wheat, appealed to the memory and imagination of the impulsive Scandinavian, who loved to see, in the new land, the new home, a scenery that spoke to him of the old home of his people.[46]

Similarly James Dickson, carrying out an official survey of an adjoining rural township in 1900, commented in his field notes as follows: "Now all the east and south sides of the township are occupied, and a number in the interior also. A large proportion of them are Scandinavians mostly from Sweden. They are all doing well apparently, and were highly spoken of by all classes whom I met."[47]

Lars Ljungmark based his history of Winnipeg on newspaper accounts in *Svenska Canada-tidningen,* so his assessment of how Swedes saw themselves was from an urban viewpoint: "Swedes are law abiding (in contrast to Americans), hard working (many times mentioned in contrast to British immigrants). They cannot bluff or boast (sometimes as opposed to Norwegians). They are physically very strong and hardy."[48]

An English-language study in 1913 confirmed this view: "The Swedes in Canada ... are of robust constitution, industrious and frugal, cleanly and neat in their persons and homes; as a general thing, intellectual and mystical. Beggars and illiterates, they hate. The Swedes, man or woman, is ready to work at anything ... be it on the farm, in the workshop, in the lumber camp."[49]

In 1925 the Swede Ivar Vennerström toured Canada and wrote his impressions from a visitor's standpoint:

> [The immigrant] will find a rich country with ample possibilities for the future. However, Canada's economical development is still on a primitive

level. Canada is still a foreign [British] colony, where foreign people and capital act like robbers ...

He will find a country where the social safety net does not quite exist. A working day prescribed by law does not exist. Old age pensions have not yet been created ... Sweden is far ahead of Canada when it comes to protecting workers against illness, poverty, unemployment, old age living conditions ...

But what he does not find is a country full of lazy people, dreamers, [and] spongers. A good future is built through work. Nothing is easy ... One must put up with being a stranger and sometimes isolation until things become familiar. If he can take it, the outlook is good.[50]

Immigrants did not seem to have problems accepting other cultures, quite often turning to them for assistance and sometimes for companionship. In 1904, after more than thirty years in North America, Andrew Telning wrote home about his experience in Burnt Lake, near Red Deer, Alberta: "You wonder how we get on with people from foreign countries. That is going pretty good. Here lives Americans, Germans, Icelanders, Chinese, Japanese, Finnish, Russians, Norwegians, Danish and all of us are good friends. Isn't that strange?"[51]

The immigrant population of Eriksdale, Manitoba, was roughly half Swedish and half British. In his 1976 study[52] George Houser commented on their relationship with each other:

In all that pertained to the common good there were no barriers to cooperation between the Swedish and British pioneer settlers of Eriksdale ... there nevertheless persisted through two generations certain polarities ... The first polarity was one of aptitude. In most practical matters the Swedes were the mentors of their English speaking neighbours. Swedish carpenters taught them the snug log construction of Norway and the northern provinces of Sweden. Many a Swedish farmer had to teach his English neighbour the correct way to fell trees, while his wife passed on the Swedish methods of curing game, especially moose, which was unknown in England.

On the other hand there was a polarity of attitudes. Swedes resented the superior attitude of those Englishmen who tended to exclude themselves when referring to "foreigners" in Canada ... The Swedes came to Canada with fewer illusions than the English and took pride in hard work and achievements which many of the English considered drudgery. It is also generally agreed that most of the English housewives were more concerned with the appearance of their table than with the flavour of the meals. In their homes a white tablecloth and matched set of dishes were considered indispensable, even for every day use. In Swedish homes, on the other hand, except on special occasions the table was covered with a piece of oilcloth. The dishes did not necessarily match, but there was an abundance of good food, well prepared and appropriately seasoned.[53]

They got along despite differences in behaviour and expectations.

The situation was much different in urban centres where earlier immigrants from Great Britain and Ontario had established a strong Anglo-Saxon presence. In Winnipeg this group "neither believed in, nor subscribed to, a multicultural view ... British tradition was the order of the day."[54] By the 1920s ethnic groups in Winnipeg lived in ghettoes, with Swedes congregating along Logan Avenue. Under similar circumstances in Vancouver Richard and Signe Edenholm[55] joined Lodge Linnea for its social events, not for its stand on temperance: "We would have been lonely. The English didn't mix with us immigrants. We joined Linnea to make friends and have some fun."[56] Both rural and urban Swedes learned to adapt to the environment in which they found themselves.

Most immigrants, not just Swedes, had to put up with the superior attitude of Anglo-Saxon bosses in the workplace. The Englishman F.C. Cooper captured the mood in his memoir about working for the Canadian Northern Railway in Port Arthur, Ontario, in 1909: "The dagos were a very mixed lot, but they worked hard for the most part, and were paid by piecework. The majority of them were Swedes and Italians, with the inevitable concertina."[57]

Although immigrants from the middle class were few in number, they, too, were affected by the exclusive attitude of the receiving population. Sam Widenfelt found that Canadian firms "will not employ a Canadian or person who is not of Anglo-Saxon descent."[58] He left for the United States in 1921 after working at the Swedish consulate in Montreal for more than a year. His job was to write reports on Canadian industry for the Department of Foreign Affairs in Sweden, including reports on trade between the two countries, pulp and paper, and the Montreal harbour.

Assimilation

Some immigrants reacted to Anglo-conformity by rejecting Swedish culture and assimilating with the Anglo-Saxon majority. An early example is Charles Davis Anderson,[59] who arrived in present-day Winnipeg via the Red River in 1872, after almost twenty years in Chicago.

Although recognized as Winnipeg's first Swede he did not take part in Swedish events. Instead, the highlight of his life was becoming the first grand master of the local Independent Order of Odd Fellows.

Martha Crane[60] was thirteen in 1906 when she immigrated with her parents and siblings to Yorkton, Saskatchewan. When the family returned to Sweden three years later she stayed in Canada, eventually landing a job in the cosmetics department at Eaton's in Winnipeg. There is no record of her joining Swedish organizations, and she did not keep in touch with her immediate family even during trips to Europe and Sweden. After retirement she married Arleigh Crane, and outlived him by twenty-eight years.

None of the twenty-two Swedes listed in the 1957 *Who's Who in Alberta* were affiliated with Swedish organizations, even though sixteen had at least one parent born in Sweden. Religions named were Anglican, United, and Mormon. The nineteen men and three women were white-collar workers, with professions in business, education, and agriculture predominating. They belonged to a wide range of fraternal groups (Masons, Eastern Star, Elks, Rotary, Moose, and Kiwanis) and were active in legions, chambers of commerce, civic groups, sports clubs, and work-related organizations.[61] These individuals had achieved upward social mobility by assimilating into, and being accepted by, Canada's mainstream.

Although some immigrants were able to achieve assimilation, most had limited opportunities to observe Canadian customs through personal experience. City dwellers had access to transportation and shopping, but were not welcomed socially. The neighbours of those who lived in rural areas were usually immigrants, too, either Swedish or from other European backgrounds, as were the workers with whom the men associated. Swedish maids who worked in Anglo-Saxon households gained such experience, but from a middle-class viewpoint.

On the whole, first-generation immigrants experienced difficulty being accepted by Canadians of Anglo-Saxon descent. Among those who succeeded were logging contractor and Member of Parliament Olof Hanson, naturalist Louise de Kiriline Lawrence, and labour leader Emil Berg. The second generation fared much better. A Canadian education and being able to speak without an accent levelled the playing field, so they had fewer challenges to overcome. High-profile examples are Arthur Erickson,[62] the first Canadian architect to be widely known internationally; Tom Berger,[63] the fighting judge who brought the First

Nations into the Canadian constitution; and the gardening guru who became lieutenant governor of Alberta, Lois Hole.[64]

One of the attributes most commonly given to Swedish immigrants was their readiness to assimilate to Canadian ways. A 1913 Presbyterian study worded it this way: "The Swedes in Canada have broken entirely with the customs and observances in their own land, indeed the whole Swedish nature is essentially modern. They are thus not prevented from becoming true Canadians."[65]

Most first-generation Swedes who immigrated before the Depression wanted to assimilate, and indeed gave the impression of having succeeded, but only a few were accepted as equals by the Anglo-Saxon majority. The rest had to wait for the acceptance of their children and succeeding generations.

Chapter Fourteen

Literature

A relatively high level of literacy allowed Swedish immigrants not only to read, but also to compose articles and poems for newspapers, chapters in books, and even entire books. At first most were written in Swedish and published in the United States, such as Pastor Uddén's 1898 book about Canada; then in 1904 travelogues published in Sweden began appearing. Four years later, the establishment of the Swedish Canadian Publishing Company in Winnipeg resulted in publication of C.O. Hofstrand's fictional *Gudarnes flyttning till Canada* (The Flight of the Godly to Canada).[1] Later, the large market in Sweden for books about the New World attracted not only immigrant workers who had returned to their homeland, but also established authors. During the 1930s some of them ushered in a new literary genre.

Canadian Wilderness Adventures: A Literary Genre in Sweden

Until Adrian Molin,[2] Ivar Vetterström,[3] and others[4] began publishing factual material about Canada in the 1910s, immigrants had only a foggy idea about the New World. Their expectations had been shaped by immigrant brochures and by translations of fiction popular in the United States. These began with James Fenimore Cooper's romantic novel, *The Last of the Mohicans*, but by the turn of the century other authors had transformed his east-coast trappers into gun-toting cowboys and Indian fighters on the western plains. The Wild West became a dominant theme in books, comics, and later movies, and generations of Swedish boys, like their contemporaries in North America, grew up playing "cowboys and Indians."[5] The mystique lives on today in

Sweden, where the theme park High Chaparall offers, among other things, a street front where shootouts and bank robberies are staged by actors in period costume.[6]

The ideas put forward by a new genre, novels about wilderness adventures in the North, also targeted male readers, but from a different viewpoint. Here, man was pitted against nature, where survival depended upon wilderness skills. The genre began in the early 1900s with Jack London's *The Call of the Wild*, set in the Klondike during the days of the gold rush. Then came the delightful exaggerations of Robert Service's Yukon poetry and the adventure novels of environmentalist James Oliver Curwood. The new genre, published in Swedish, included all three themes: adventure, exaggeration, and the environment. Andrew Macfie (1846–1926) and Algot Sandberg (1865–1922) were early proponents, followed in the 1930s by the popular Karl Gunnarson, Harry Macfie, and Albert Viksten.[7]

Karl Gunnar Schulze chose "Karl Gunnarson"[8] as a pen name, replacing his German-sounding surname with the patrilineal version of his second name. He worked as an estate manager before immigrating to Canada in 1928, and then held a variety of jobs until driven back home, as he says, by hunger pangs. After publication of his first book, *Som emigrant i Kanada* (As an Immigrant in Canada), he switched careers and lived by the pen for the rest of his life. The four books he published in this genre from 1930 to 1945 were reprinted several times.

His first book was realistic, written in the first person and telling about people he met on the Prairies and in Winnipeg. He wrote a mixture of fiction and journalism, and "his image as a bohemian with a vague gentry background and his intellectual and racial prejudices suited his predominantly rural and male audience very well."[9] Karl Gunnarson, or at least his fictional image as a Canadian hero, is one of the main characters in Bertil Cullberg's 1955 novel, *Harnesk och sadel* (Harness and Saddle).[10]

Harry Macfie[11] was the great-grandson of William Thorburn, a Scot who emigrated to Uddevalla on Sweden's west coast to export oats to London, England. Harry's grandfather, William Macfie, had introduced curling to Sweden in the 1890s.[12] His father, the author Andrew Macfie, brought Harry to Winnipeg in 1898 at the height of the Lake of the Woods gold rush.[13] Harry moved to Kenora, became a mining engineer, and began a string of adventures that included working at the Sultana gold mine.[14] Along with partner Sam Kilburn[15] he spent several winters trapping on Star Lake, near Falcon Lake on the Manitoba border. Together, they visited Fort Frances, Norway House, The Pas, and Alaska, but parted in 1905 when Harry returned to Sweden. His dream of finding gold seemed further away than ever.

Harry returned to Canada in 1925 to visit his partner, who had been gassed in the First World War and was living as an invalid in a cabin in Muskoka, Ontario. Sam asked Harry to name the cabin and he chose Wasawasa, an Indian word meaning "far, far away." The two men reminisced each evening around a campfire, to the delight of visitors. Ten years later Harry wrote his first book about their time together, titling it *Wasa-Wasa*.[16] An English version, the only Swedish book of this genre to be published in English, was titled *Wasa-Wasa: A Tale of Trails and Treasure*.[17]

The stories are in the form of a memoir, with names of real places and, presumably, real people. Harry described the terrain and its inhabitants vividly, almost caressingly. But he found that the wilderness he knew two decades ago had disappeared in the interim: "The roaring waterfall [at Fort Frances] is dumb. A big power station has been built on the American side of the falls, and instead of glimmering campfires hundreds of lights shine from the great International Falls paper mills. The howls I hear are not those of Indians' dogs but of saw-blades and machines which are cutting and biting to death the magnificent forests which grew around Rainy Lake. I went sorrowfully up to the top, where the old fort used to lie. Everything was gone, levelled to the ground, but I knew the place."[18] These passages take on a nostalgic quality as Harry mourns not only the environmental changes, but also their effect upon First Nations people, with whom he had a close relationship, especially Mandamen of Falcon Lake.[19]

Altogether, Harry published eight books, four of them about Canada.[20] Among his prized possessions were a beautifully crafted deerskin jacket made by an Ojibwa girl named Amik, a Mountie hat from his time with the Royal Canadian Mounted Police, and Sciopticon slides, which illustrated his lecture tours in Lappland during the 1930s and 1940s.

Harry Macfie was famous not only for his books, which were reprinted and translated into several languages, but also for introducing the Canadian canoe to Sweden on a commercial basis. In 1932 he began building canoes in his workshop at Ljungskile, with the help of his children, using skills learned from the Ojibwa. He sold about a hundred of them to customers in Sweden, covering the frame with canvas instead of birchbark, and painting a star on the bow in memory of Star Lake. In 1938 he sold his blueprints and rights to a carpenter named Mårten Gedda, and by 1945 Gedda had sold more than 900 canoes. Today, the Swedish word for canoe is *kanadensare*, which means "Canadian."

The Harry Macfie Canoe Club was founded in 1985 by Kurt Rehnström and his son Mats. Two years later the club held its first annual Rendezvous, with members in period costume paddling and tenting along one of Sweden's many waterways. Preben Mortensen had two Montreal canoes built from original drawings provided by Fort William Historical Park in Thunder Bay. Several of its 100 or so members travelled to Canada to follow Harry's pathways on Lake of the Woods and Falcon Lake, among others.[21] Bertil Wockatz has come to Canada three times, noting that maps show a MacFie Lake and a Kilborn Lake in the area of Harry's trapping cabin. Further research was disappointing to him, however. These were coincidental names belonging to Manitoba war casualties.[22]

When Harry Macfie made his final trip to Canada in 1938 he found a highway cutting across his former hunting grounds, and on Falcon Lake Ojibwa were sitting in factory-made canoes with outboard motors on the stern.[23] His books had recorded people and events in the Canadian wilderness of yesteryear. No other individual has done as much as Harry Macfie to raise Canada's profile in Sweden as a place where wilderness canoe adventures are still possible.

Albert Viksten[24] might have continued cutting charcoal wood for the rest of his life had it not been for Ivar Vennerström, editor of *Nya Norrland* in Sollefteå. He noticed Albert's writing talent, helped him complete high school, then hired him as a journalist. After the First World War Albert signed up on a Norwegian sealing ship. This experience, and trips to Germany and Italy, provided enough material for several books and established his future career as an author.

In 1937 the magazine *Folket i Bild* (The People in Pictures) sent him to the United States on assignment.[25] Afterwards he went to Vancouver to reunite with his brothers Adolf,[26] Gus,[27] and Erik,[28] who had immigrated in 1928. Gus and Adolf were trappers on Horsefly Lake in the Kootenays, where Adolf had a gold claim. The brothers decided to buy a 1925 Studebaker and drive to Horsefly Lake to spend their treasured time together in the wilderness.

Albert called it "the most beautiful lake in the world," a sixty-four-kilometre stretch set in a cleft between mountains, the home of moose, bear, deer, mink, marten, beaver, coyote, and sometimes a cougar. "Already by dawn I was back seated by the creek to enjoy the coming of the day ... The squirrels began their peculiar bird warbles in the balsam spruces close by and a kingfisher's grating sound could be heard further up the creek. Far away in the narrow sound a wedge of white foam moved towards the shore. I saw through the binoculars that it was a deer, probably looking for fresh grass."[29]

The natural world played a pivotal role in Albert Viksten's life. In 1939 he was presented with the lakeshore cottage Ängratörn in Hälsingland, a nature paradise that soon became his favourite place to write. There, at what he called his "Horsefly Lake in Sweden," he planted Canadian pines and tried to introduce beavers. "Nature's power," he confided on his seventy-sixth birthday, "has been my religion ... [I] consider myself a God-fearing heathen."[30]

The reception for the book about his trip, *Vilda Vägar Västerut* (Wild Paths Westward), was overwhelming, and Albert published three more books about Canada.[31] In 1963 he visited his daughters, Märta Wilson and Karin Koerner,[32] who had immigrated to the west coast. It is thanks to Karin that some of his writings have been translated into English. In her book titled *Albert Viksten: A Portrait of My Father* she chose selections that showed his love of nature and close ties with his brothers.[33]

Albert Viksten was known as "Sweden's foremost storyteller" because of his lecture tours and broadcasts on Radio Sweden. More lasting are his literary legacy and the cottage at Ängratörn. The property, bequeathed for the use of Sweden's artists, is cared for by the Albert Viksten Society (*Albert Viksten sällskapet*), which organizes a two-day celebration every July in his honour.

Albert's brother, Adolf Viksten, also published a book in this genre, *Bland jägare och guldgrävare i Canada* (Among Sportsmen and Gold Seekers in Canada), in 1979. Adolf became something of a legend as a young man, when he out-boxed the Swedish champion, Rudolf Mångelin, during his North American tour. Adolf wrote in his steam bath (*bastu*), looking out at the trees, bushes, and flowers. Like Albert, he loved nature and drew strength from it.[34]

Of the above thirteen books only Harry Macfie's *Wasa-Wasa*, and excerpts from Albert Viksten's first book and his treatise on Vancouver from *Guds Eget Land* (God's Own Country) have been translated into English. The rest are accessible only to those who read Swedish. Yet, novels of this genre, quite aside from their literary value, encompass a wealth of information about Swedish perceptions of Canada that are unavailable elsewhere. That they differ from the image of the American Wild West is clear. First Nations people are treated with respect, those in authority uphold laws, and guns are used to kill animals, not people. When interest in Canada was at its height – that is, until the 1960s – there was even a Swedish comic strip that chronicled the adventures of a Mountie named "Canada" Olsson.[35]

The Canadian wilderness adventures genre was also popular in other Nordic countries and some books in that genre have been translated into English. Helge Ingstad, the Norwegian who later discovered the Viking settlement at L'Anse aux Meadows, wrote about travelling with the First Nations in the Northwest Territories. A translated version was published as *The Land of Feast and Famine* (Knopf, 1933). Erik Munsterhjelm, a Finland Swede, had his books published as *Fool's Gold* (1955) and *The Wind and the Caribou* (1974), both by Macmillan. The genre helped the Nordic countries to understand that Canada was different from the United States. During the early 1900s the boundaries were blurred because the word "Amerika" had been used for the entire North American continent. These well-read books helped to solidify the northern wilderness as the image of Canada, complete with canoes, snowshoes, and toboggans.

Books Awaiting Translation into English

Novels, memoirs, and poetry can impart insights that are difficult to discern in histories and other general works. The following pages list Swedish-language books that would interest English-speaking Canadians, and also some English-language books, including memoirs, which appear as a group for the first time.

A 1984 novel by the literary giant Sven Delblanc,[36] *Kanaans land* (Land of Canaan), is frankly autobiographical and tells the story of his family's struggle for survival in Minitonas, Manitoba, during the Depression.[37] Delblanc shared his feelings about his birthplace: "Canada is so utterly unlike its neighbor to the south, is proud of its unique character and seeks to preserve it at all costs. We know a tremendous amount about the United States through reporting and novels, through TV and films. The Swedes know next to nothing about Canada, and a writer who once tries to tell about human fates and to smuggle into the reader a crumb of knowledge about this unknown land faces great difficulties."[38]

Kanaans land is the third in a series of four novels.[39] McClelland and Stewart's 1990 plan to publish an English version failed and Canada still awaits a novelist of Steinbeck's stature,[40] like Sven Delblanc, to tell what the 1930s were like on the Canadian Prairies.

Delblanc has often been compared to Vilhelm Moberg, famous for the Emigrant series of four novels about the fictional Karl-Oskar and Kristina Nilsson from Småland, who settled in Minnesota. Moberg's books provided the basis for a film starring Liv Ullman and Max von Sydow and for the folk opera *Kristina from Duvemåla*. His research notes formed the nucleus of the international archives in Växjö, which opened in 1968.[41] According to author Anders Sandberg, both Moberg and Delblanc combined "the clarity of science and fact with the completeness of art and fiction."[42]

Delblanc tells the story from his mother's point of view. She had been terribly homesick, not for people, but for the familiar geography she had grown up with: "The long summer days, the short winter days, and the very distinct and rapid change from the darkness of winter to the light of summer ... [where] moderate changes in temperature are matched by moderate rainfalls, snowfalls and winds ... [across a landscape of] thin soils, rocky outcrops, lakes and coniferous forests."[43] Manitoba's endless horizon, merciless sun, and violent thunderstorms frightened her, and she never became accustomed to the prairie environment. To her, even the moon was larger than the one she had known in Sweden.

Although Delblanc was bilingual only a few of his writings have been published in English. Correspondence with his half-sister in Winnipeg, Alice Boychuk, was published posthumously in both languages as *Kära Alice/Dear Alice*. His letters reflect two themes: love for Alice, and sadness at the misery their father brought to both families. He once wrote that "Sweden was a pale but benevolent mother, Canada a distant lover, whom I would sometimes visit for passionate embraces."[44]

The second book deserving of publication in English is *De sista svenska rösterna* (The Last Swedish Voices) by Gunnar Nilsson. He toured Canada for three consecutive years in the mid-1970s in order to interview survivors of a disappearing group, Swedish immigrants before the Depression. The book was not published until 1995 because his position at Swedish Television did not allow enough time to write it and to choose the photographs.[45]

One of his stories is about Manfred Johnson,[46] the prospector who discovered the ore body that spawned Elliot Lake, the "Uranium Capital of the World." In 1953 Johnson coaxed his employer, R.C. Hart, to fly him to Quirke Lake because he had seen something interesting on an old map. His Geiger counter went crazy, and he followed the vein for a kilometre or more. Rio Algom took over development of the mine, but Johnson was never officially recognized as its discoverer.

A third book that cries for availability in English is Lars Ljungmark's detailed history of Swedes in Winnipeg, *Svenskarna i Winnipeg*, published in 1994. It seems a shame that Canadians cannot access books about their own country written by leaders in their fields – a prairie novel, pioneer reminiscences, and an urban ethnic history. Other books worthy of translation are the 1923 history of Swedes in British

Columbia[47] researched and written by Hans Bergman,[48] and Carina Rönnqvist's recent study,[49] which looks at Swedish identity in Canada.

Immigrant Authors

John Utterström[50] based his 1962 novel *Straws in the Wind* on experiences at Yellowhead Pass during construction of the Grand Trunk Pacific Railway (later Canadian National Railway) in 1910–11. The title refers to immigrants having to drift from job to job in order to earn a living, a fact of life with which he was quite familiar.

In 1930 John travelled up the Skeena River to Telegraph Creek by dogsled, snapping photos along the way. Two years later his book *Pälsjägarliv med kamera och bössa* (Trapper's Life with Camera and Gun) was published in Stockholm. Harry F:son[51] Fabbe accompanied him to Telegraph Creek and in 1932 published the book *I slagbjörnens spår med bröderna Utterström: Bland indianer och storvilt* (On the Trail of the Grizzly with the Utterström Brothers: Among Indians and Wild Game). At the same time John produced and directed a feature-length film, *On the Trail of the Grizzly*, which played in Stockholm and in Hollywood.[52] Utterström and Fabbe were early contributors to the Canadian wilderness adventures literary genre.

Frederick Philip Grove[53] was born and raised in Germany but posed as a Swede after coming to Manitoba in 1912. He cemented the fabrication in his 1946 autobiography, *In Search of Myself*, which won a Governor General's Award, and the deception was discovered only after his death. In his first novel, published in 1925, *Settlers of the Marsh*, he tells the story of his alter ego and his struggles to learn English so that he could become integrated into Canadian society. According to Professor Jane Mattisson, "The experiences of Frederick Philip Grove are incorporated into and lived out in the character of [the Swede] Niels Lindstedt, who develops from a naive and insecure young man into a harmonious, mature character with a clear idea of his place in the country of his adoption."[54] While the story itself is interesting, it also offers an insight into changes in an immigrant's self-image as he acquires the linguistic and social skills that confirm his identity and sense of belonging.

Louise de Kiriline Lawrence[55] is best known as a naturalist. For her, birds were much more than a hobby; they were an obsession. From her log cabin overlooking Pimisi Bay, east of Lake Nipissing, she wrote four bird books,[56] seventeen scientific papers, and more than forty popular articles for *Audubon* and other journals. She had come from much different circumstances, growing up in a stately manor house beside the Baltic Sea. Her father, Sixten Flach, a university-trained naturalist who helped establish the bird sanctuary on Stora Karlsö, Gotland, introduced her to birds as a child. To them she devoted the final half-century of her long and fruitful life.

Her autobiography, *Another Winter, Another Spring: A Love Remembered*, tells about her debut at the court of King Gustav V on New Year's Eve 1914, spending the winter "in extravagant opulence" with her Danish godmother, then joining the Red Cross and becoming a nurse. While working in a prisoner-of-war camp in Denmark she fell in love with a wounded White Russian lieutenant, Gleb Nikolayevich Kirilin, and married him in 1918. He and Louise returned to Russia, but one day he disappeared. She stayed, hoping to find him, until 1924, when she heard rumours of a mass execution of White Russian officers.

She immigrated to Canada in 1927, upgrading her nursing credentials in Toronto before joining the outpost service of the Canadian Red Cross, which sent her to Bonfield, east of North Bay. A colleague, Georgina Rawn, described her redheaded friend: "She was a very striking person. She often wore trousers, with high leather boots and long gloves and a big muskrat coat. She was very tall and very strong ... When she undertook something, she put her whole self into it She knew every family in her whole district, and she never refused a call."[57]

When the Dionne quintuplets were born in May 1934, Dr Dafoe hired Louise to care for them. The following year the Ontario government took custody of the babies away from their parents and gave it to Dr Dafoe, with the result that Quintland became a bigger tourist attraction than Niagara Falls. At this point Louise left her job and wrote *The Quintuplets' First Year*, published in 1936, hoping that her first-hand account would help people to understand what was happening with the quintuplets.

In 1939 Louise married carpenter Len Lawrence, and he helped to launch her career as a naturalist by identifying the Canadian birds on their property. Louise joined the American Ornithologists' Union in 1946, becoming the first Canadian woman to be voted an elective member. She won many awards and honours, and made lasting friendships with eminent bird watchers. She once commented that "studying nature is a worthwhile way to spend your life."[58] The fact that it gave her profound pleasure was an added bonus.

Hälle Flygare[59] came to Canada in 1962 as a forestry professional and for many years worked as park warden in Banff National Park. He wrote two books published in Sweden, *Storvilt i Canada* (Big Game in Canada) in 1970 and *Buffelmarker* (Buffalo Tracks) in 1975, and provided the photographic images for Banff National Park's classic field guide *Wildflowers of the Canadian Rockies*.

Fascinated by Alexander Mackenzie, the first person to cross the continent from Atlantic to Pacific, he published three, successively expanded, trail guides so that others could experience his journey first-hand. The Sir Alexander Mackenzie "Canada Sea-to-Sea" Bicentennial Expeditions took place from 1989 to 1993.[60] One of the participants was Jim Smithers of Lakehead University, whose Outdoor Recreation course students covered the route from Lachine to Bella Coola, a distance of 8,500 kilometres, over a period of several years. Canoes came from the reconstructed fur-trade post at Fort William, headquarters for Macken-zie's employer, the North West Company.

One of the goals of the Alexander Mackenzie Voyageur Route Asso-ciation is "to encourage the preservation, enhancement and interpreta-tion of the natural, archaeological and scenic heritage of the Route." This is long overdue. Mackenzie accomplished his feat in 1793, twelve years before the Lewis and Clark expedition, yet the Lewis and Clark National Historic Trail is well established as part of the National Trails System in the United States.

Britt Holmstrom[61] lives in Regina but returns to Sweden for visits as often as possible. Four of her novels have been published in Canada: *The Man Next Door*, *The Wrong Madonna*, *After we Crossed the River*, and *Claudia*. In *Claudia*, the action takes place in four different countries and tells how the protagonist deals with murder, mayhem, and mothers.

Irina Hedman[62] of Toronto wrote Sweden's first factual travel hand-book, published in Swedish in 1976 with the title *Canada*. "I was particu-larly keen on pointing out how much Canada differs from the USA," she confided. "There was a lot of ignorance about Canada in Sweden."

Eva St Jean chose to write about Swedes in British Columbia for her 2004 doctoral dissertation at the University of Victoria. The work, titled "Swedes on the Move," looks at politics, culture, and work from 1909 to 1950. She has also written a number of articles for scholarly journals.

Signe Olson,[63] a domestic in Port Arthur, dealt with daily frustra-tions and loneliness by writing. She chose wide-ranging subjects, all spiced with deep Christian faith. About 300 poems and essays, all signed "Signe," were published in Swedish Baptist newspapers dur-ing her lifetime.[64] More than eighty of them were written in Canada, before her move to St Paul.[65]

The translated poetry of five Swedes was featured in the 1935 anthology *Canadian Overtones*.[66] Three of them stand out. Arthur A. Anderson,[67] a Winnipeg businessman and Swedish consul from 1955 to 1963, was lauded for his technical competence. He published *Dust*, a 126-page volume of verse, in 1934, and also translated Robert Service's poems into Swedish. A book published by the Society for the Preservation of Swedish Culture in Foreign Lands included his chapter on Canada.[68]

Gerhard Hilarius Silver[69] wrote the poem "My Son," which had already been published in his chapbook *I vargatider: En näve kampdikter* (In Wolfish Times: A Handful of Battle Poems) in 1918,[70] a protest about social injustices during the First World War.

The third poet, Sten Wiktor Goerwell,[71] mirrored the feelings of many immigrants:

> Let Canada take us
> As men; not remake us.
> We're more than crude brawn; we've a brain and a heart.
> In the glorious frame
> Of Canadian fame
> Let the children of Sweden contribute their part![72]

Goerwell published the chapbook *A Time of Breaking* in 1922, and in 1931, after graduating from Manitoba Law School, a treatise on politics entitled *Liberalism and the Future*.

Continuing the Tradition

First-generation immigrants have contributed generously to Canada's literary pool, and descendants have followed in their footsteps. The following published authors of the second and third generation wrote in a number of genres, from novels and poetry to scholarly works and histories.

There are four novelists of note. Thelma Hofstrand Foster, probably a descendant of C.O. Hofstrand of New Stockholm, authored *Wild Daisies*. The setting is a Swedish colony in eastern Saskatchewan during the 1920s and 1930s. Lloyd Person's concern about the way prairie towns were vanishing resulted in his 1974 novel, *Growing up in Minby*, which is written in the style of W.O. Mitchell. *Minby* means "my village" in Swedish, and the main characters are the narrator and his Swedish family.

Because Byrna Barclay[73] was raised by her widowed mother and Swedish grandmother, almost all her novels and short stories have a

Swedish twist. Her dad, whose heritage was English and Cree, died before she can remember. The search for roots led to her first three novels, written from 1982 to 1985, *Summer of the Hungry Pup*, *The Last Echo*, and *Winter of the White Wolf*.

Julie Lawson has published more than twenty novels for young people, but was inspired to write *Goldstone* by her family's involvement in the Rogers Pass snow slide. The heroine is a young girl who inherits her mother's goldstone pendant, only to suspect that it can foretell the future.

Poetry is well represented. Among published poets Margaret Avison,[74] who won two Governor General's Awards, is said to have had a "streak of yellow and blue," and educational opportunities in Quebec made it possible for Ralph Gustafson to pursue a literary career that included co-founding the League of Canadian Poets and winning the 1974 Governor General's Award for *Fire on Stone*. Fred Wah's mother emigrated from Sweden to Swift Current as a child. Although his book *Waiting for Saskatchewan*, which won the 1985 Governor General's Award for poetry, features his mixed heritage, it focuses on the Chinese side. A prolific writer of poetry, fiction, and criticism, Wah has also edited literary journals, including the world's first online literary magazine, *SwiftCurrent*.

Bernice Lever[75] has given readings on five continents, and from coast to coast in Canada. A prolific author, her poem "Woman" in *Yet Woman I am* (1979) focuses on her grandmother, Anna Brita Strid, who immigrated from Hälsingland to Alberta in 1906:

> Grandma content
> in her bedroom rocking chair
> – store teeth set aside –
> sucking on the curved stem
> of her black pipe,
> smoking and rocking
> while she darned socks
> – still under the urge to be practical –
> telling us heirloom stories
> of how she hid
> small Swede potatoes and
> other seeds in her apron pockets
> all that long trip
> – by boat, train and foot –
> to the new land to grow the food
> they'd always known.

A teacher of English as a second language, Bernice developed a colour-coding system to help students recognize patterns basic to understanding sentence structure. Her English grammar textbook, *The Colour of Words* (1990), was perfected through in-class use and student feedback at the Ontario college level.

Since 1996 T. Anders Carson[76] has published four books of poetry, a CD, and an anthology. He grew up near Ottawa, but spent 1982–3 with his grandmother in Oskarström, Halland.

Swedish descendants are also responsible for major scholarly works, both religious and secular. As his seminary thesis, E. Earl Anderson chose an intimate study of the Swedish Evangelical Lutheran Bethesda church in his hometown of Kenora, and Ferdy Baglo's thesis, which was published in 1962 as *The Story of Augustana Lutherans in Canada*, is recognized as a classic.

Elinor Barr compiled the bibliography *The Swedish Experience in Canada* and wrote the first history of a secular Swedish institution, *The Scandinavian Home Society*, before embarking on the Swedes in Canada project. Gerald F. Holm,[77] provincial toponymist for Manitoba, authored the monumental *Geographic Names of Manitoba* and co-authored its counterpart, *A Place of Honour: Manitoba's War Dead Commemorated in its Geography*.

Two dedicated women chose significant themes from Canada's history, one in pictures and the other in prose. Ethel Anderson Becker collected and preserved Eric Hegg's glass-plate images of the Klondike gold rush and published some of them in her 1949 book *Klondike '98*. Myrtle Bergren immortalized the union struggles on Vancouver Island in two books, *Bough of Needles: Eleven Canadian Short Stories*, said to be fictional, and *Tough Timber: The Loggers of British Columbia – Their Story*, based on interviews with labour activists, including her husband, Hjalmar.

Histories come in many disguises. John Pearson published three histories of his chosen home, Surrey, British Columbia, titled *Land of the Peace Arch* (1958), *Land of the Royal Kwantlen* (1961), and *The Valley of the Fraser*, completed by his son Lorne Pearson and published in 2005. John also wrote his memoirs in the form of a daybook, and they have been translated but not published.

Irene Howard authored the first history of an urban Swedish community, *Vancouver's Svenskar*, and then featured her own Swedish-Norwegian family in *Gold Dust on His Shirt*. Christopher Oslund, curator of Haileybury Heritage Museum, recorded the history of a little-known Swedish community in *One Hundred Years of Swedish Settlement in*

Timiskaming. Emma Ringstrom, a former owner of Wasagaming Lodge, was well acquainted with the log buildings constructed by Swedes in Riding Mountain National Park. Nevertheless her book, *Riding Mountain Yesterday and Today*, does not neglect the contributions of other nationalities.

Memoirs

Some of those immigrants who had their memoirs published in Sweden chose provocative titles that translate as "Scorched Wings"[78] and "With Good Humour in My Suitcase."[79] Others felt that "Fifteen Years in Canada"[80] and "The Emigrant's Memories"[81] best described their books. Most of these authors had high hopes of building a new life in North America, but all returned to Sweden. Looking for work, R.E. Carlsson[82] came at least twice. His journeys resulted in two books with the translated titles "Men of the Old School: Stories from British Columbia" and "Young Man Went West: A Report on the Prairies." Albin Plym lived in Canada from 1909 to 1921. His memoirs about the degradation and danger of working as a labourer are recounted in detail in two books with the translated titles of "Life as a Labourer in Canada" and "Labourers and Gold Seekers."[83] His article "Twelve Years in Canada's Wilderness" is included in a book that published interviews with almost a thousand emigrants who had returned to Sweden.[84]

Svante Uddén, Canada's first resident Swedish Lutheran pastor, published the first Swedish-language book about Canada in 1898, in the United States. It was a memoir and travelogue titled *Från Canada* (From Canada).

Edwin Alm, self-appointed cultural ambassador between Vancouver and his hometown of Östersund, Sweden, published an account of his successful career in real estate, *I Never Wondered,* in 1971. Contractor Swan Swanson's memoirs were edited and published posthumously by his grandson, Roy Swanson, in 1992. In addition to editing *Swan Swanson – Immigrant* and *The Forgotten Army,* Roy wrote and published *Swanee's Cabins* and *The Divine Spark.* Electrician Knute Karlson of Elmwood, Ontario, near London, wrote *A Swedish Immigrant in Canada 1911–1971,* crediting a higher power for directing him on a successful life's journey.

Henry Bengston spent two years in Port Arthur, Ontario, before moving to Chicago in 1909 to follow a career in the American labour movement. The early chapters of his memoir *On the Left in America,* and an autobiography published in *Bryggan/The Bridge,* include his Canadian experiences. Bruce Magnuson arrived in 1928 to become a Communist and major player in union activities during the 1930s. His book, *The Untold Story of Ontario's Bushworkers: A Political Memoir*, was published in 1990.

After settling in Alberta William Loov wrote his memoirs, *Twenty-Five Years Away from Home*, which were translated and published by his children in 1995. The account is sprinkled with Swedish humour. Some of Edwin Thomeus's correspondence was translated and published in 1983 as *Letters of a Swedish Homesteader: Life in Magnolia 1905–1912.* Additional translations by his son Tom Thomeus remain unpublished. Mildred Rasmussen's *A Swedish Girl: En Svenska Flicka* is also about life on the Prairies. She was seven at the start of the Depression, and makes some interesting observations about those years.

Emma Hall Carlson originally wrote *We Come to Canada and Our First Ten Years* for her family, but after it was published a copy was presented to King Carl XVI Gustaf during the royal couple's visit to Winnipeg in 1988. Karl Olafson's *A Sentimental Journey*, published in 2006, documents the daily lives of the family of a section foreman living beside the railway tracks in Northwestern Ontario. In 2003 Linda and Bertha Sjoback of Thunder Bay published a book about their dad, a Finland Swede, under the title *Emil.*

Ivah Anderson's memoir, *Other Days Around Me: My Life in the Rainy River District*, was published in 1992. The first half is about growing up with an English pioneer background and the second tells about her marriage to Axel Anderson, who taught her to appreciate Swedish culture. Lucy Lindell, one of Eriksdale's English daughters, who married a Swede, compiled the history *Memory Opens the Door* and an autobiography, *Rites of Passage*, "In loving memory of Art, my husband, my partner, my friend."

The above offers a fair sampling of published books about Canada written by or about Swedes. Many more writings were either published in small quantities for a specific purpose, such as memoirs, family histories, and collections of correspondence, or not published at all. Swedes have left a continuous stream of print information that has made its way into Canada's nooks and crannies over the years. Up to now much of this treasure trove has remained hidden in personal collections or forbidden by language, and the existence of a significant body of literature was a well-kept secret.

Chapter Fifteen

Emerging Visibility

The preceding chapters have set out in detail many aspects of the Swedish presence in Canada, and now it is time to return to the question of low ethnic identity, already put forward by Carina Rönnqvist, that "Swedishness in Canada was more a matter of private feelings and liaisons than of an organized unity,"[1] and to discuss how identities developed differently for the four waves of immigrants.

Every immigrant before the Second World War, with the exception of those from Britain, experienced Anglo-conformity and the receiving society's exclusive attitude towards foreigners, policies supported by all three levels of government. The events that shaped the private feelings and liaisons of Swedish immigrants who arrived during the first and second waves came as a consequence of the First World War – increased discrimination from all quarters because Swedes were thought to be pro-German and therefore disloyal, rude treatment at the polls during the 1917 federal election, and harassment by the chief press censor of Canada's only secular Swedish weekly and other publications, followed by the nativist riot in the Swedish heartland of Logan Avenue in Winnipeg in January 1919, with no police protection for people or property. Although the incidents themselves involved only a few people they became common knowledge within the Swedish community. All Swedish immigrants and their children experienced wartime discrimination, which extended into the 1920s and 1930s. Those in positions of authority were blamed, with the result that many immigrants acquired a lifelong distrust of officialdom.

While it is difficult to gauge internal factors, the learned behaviour of humility seems to have played an important role. Sweden's degrading class system had demanded outward submissiveness to the upper class and political and religious leaders. Over the centuries individuals and families had devised ways to deal with perceived injustices from those in positions of authority. Undoubtedly immigrants transferred to the New World their customary methods of handling resentment, either in the privacy of their own homes or in the company of other Swedes. With the overpowering emphasis on Anglo-conformity, their outward behaviour would appear as having low ethnic consciousness. There are very few, if any, records of Swedish immigrants openly defying authority.

The third wave of immigrants during the 1920s, many of them bachelors, shared experiences that affected all immigrants: unemployment, relief camps, riding the rods, strikes, and the ever-present threat of deportation. The discrimination they experienced during the Depression was not based on ethnicity but on class, which bonded together immigrants from different countries. This group had neither the time nor the inclination to be overly concerned with ethnicity.

Canada's ethnic organizations and churches offered an extension of the home, where the Swedish language and customs, including food, could be enjoyed and celebrated openly. The arrival of Swedish newspapers in the mail was eagerly awaited, as were letters from home. For many in Winnipeg, Logan Avenue provided their first experience in the new country. It continued to be a Swedish mecca for immigrants as well as a church home for Winnipeg families for fifty years. But these outlets diminished one by one as English became the working language, as immigrants died and contact with Sweden was lost, and as children born in Canada grew up without the strong feelings towards Sweden that were held by their parents. And finally, immigration halted with the Depression and the Second World War.

In the meantime Sweden had moved from a peasant economy to become one of the most industrialized nations in the world. The fourth wave of immigrants, which arrived in Canada after the Second World War, had experienced the weakening of the class system and the success of the Middle Way. Many, including those representing Swedish companies, did not feel a need to hide their ethnicity, unlike those who had arrived during the first and second waves. Soon the Swedish language prevailed again in a secular organization in Vancouver and in Toronto's Lutheran congregation. Later, the Swedish Women's Educational Association's (SWEA) two-day Swedish Christmas Fair at Harbourfront brought Swedish culture to the general public in a high-profile way.

The world had changed, and would change even more with ocean transportation being replaced by air travel, and instant communication via computer and the free telephone Skype. Because of technological advances, postwar immigrants were able to keep up with developments in Sweden, preserve family ties through personal visits, and maintain their first language through SWEA and SVIV and that of their children through Swedish schools.

Intermarriage continued, but not all such marriages weakened Swedish ties. Non-Swedish spouses who embraced their partner's Swedishness include German-born Rudolf Zoumer, who became Calgary's Swedish consul in 1970, Rose Wozniak Peterson, who published *Scandinavian News* in Winnipeg during the 1970s, and Lucy Lindell and Zetta Persson, both with British backgrounds, who interviewed residents and published important histories of Swedish communities in Eriksdale (1970) and Stockholm (1959).

The general perception seemed to be that the Swedish experience is negligible because of the immigrants' seemingly effortless assimilation into the Canadian mainstream. The preceding pages have demonstrated that assimilation and acceptance were goals seldom achieved by immigrants from the first, second, and third waves, and have given logical explanations for this misconception.

However, the activities and accomplishments of the fourth wave of immigrants, and descendants from previous waves, reflect a relatively high ethnic consciousness. It will take time to overcome the public expectation of low ethnic consciousness among Swedes and their descendants. Meanwhile, a good percentage of them want to know more about their collective past, and have contributed to this book in many ways to make their dream come true. Such a book, and spinoffs from it, has the potential to raise the profile of Swedes in Canada, not only among those of Swedish descent but among others as well. Although some Swedes have made light of their heritage in the past, a number of contemporary Swedes, both immigrants and descendants, are no longer content to remain invisible. Swedish hockey players, for example, enjoy a very high profile.

Immigrants from all four waves have contributed to Canada's development by their willingness to participate in the political, economic, and social life of the country. They fought beside other Canadians in two world wars and survived the Depression. They published national newspapers continuously since 1887, three of them during the Depression, as well as writing a steady stream of other works in many genres. A number of individuals have made contributions that resulted in their being honoured with local, provincial, and national awards. The introduction of cross-country skiing can also be attributed to Swedes.

In addition, Swedish organizations have left a legacy of built structures: old folks' homes, country elevators, cemeteries, churches, and meeting places. Swedish individuals and companies have built the CN Tower, ships on the Great Lakes, and the log structures in Riding Mountain National Park and elsewhere.

Swedes in Canada today, both immigrants and descendants, are living in an era in which they can be openly proud of their heritage. There is no need to be invisible any longer.

APPENDICES

Place Names

By the time Canada opened the Prairies to European immigrants, six stations along the new transcontinental railway and several geographic features along her seacoast already bore Swedish names. During the 1880s ethnic place names began appearing to supplement those reflecting the earlier Aboriginal, French, and British presence. The year 1885 saw the founding of two Swedish colonies, New Stockholm and Scandinavia, and many more Swedish place names would follow. Some commemorated places or events in Sweden or the United States, while others were chosen to honour the immigrant postmasters, pioneers, homesteaders, prospectors, and trappers who helped build Canada as we know it today. Some of the more recent names commemorate Canadian soldiers who died in the line of duty.

Swedish settlement and activities in Canada are commemorated by names stretching westward from New Brunswick to British Columbia, and northward to the Arctic Ocean. With only one exception the names in the Northwest Territories and Nunavut are coastal features named by polar explorers. The list includes communities, school districts, railway stations and sidings, lakes and seas, passages, islands, bays and beaches, points and peninsulas, rivers and creeks, glaciers, passes and valleys, ridges and hills, and mountains and peaks. In all, 130 are official place names.

Postal authorities regularly anglicized ethnic names, but railways placed restrictions on station names only when there were duplications. With the passage of time some geographical names were duplicated many times (there are eleven *Swede Creek*s), transferred to nearby geographic features, or disappeared altogether, while others were accepted as official. Still others, such as those named after churches, were in common local usage but never achieved official status. The English translation of Otto Robert Landelius's landmark book, *Swedish Place-Names in North America*,[1] has been an invaluable resource. Nevertheless the following do not represent an exhaustive list.

Note that an asterisk (*) denotes official status according to the Canadian Geographical Names website www.rncan.gc.ca/search-place-names/search?lang=en. The number of asterisks (* to ****) denotes the number of features carrying the official name.

* Alsike, AB, a village southwest of Edmonton, was founded in 1908. The name derives from Alsike clover, which in turn was named by Linnaeus, who first cultivated it in Alsike parish, Uppland.[2] Commercial demand for this forage crop during the 1920s may be the reason for naming the post office Alsike in 1933.
* Andrew River, NW, which flows into Anderson River, was named for Andy Ronnander, a trapper who lived along its banks for several years until 1936.[3]
Asker, AB, was a school district in Mecca Glen named for Asker parish in the province of Närke.
Asplund, AB, was a post office[4] from 1940 to 1946 near Valleyview in the Peace River valley, with Mission Covenant pastor B.A. Werklund as postmaster. The name means "poplar grove." The main Valleyview post office had opened in Williamson's store in 1929.[5]
Avesta, MB (see Erickson)
* Bergland, ON, is a Swedish and Norwegian farming community in the Rainy River valley. Bergland, which means "rocky or mountainous country," was named in 1907 by the first postmaster, Peter L. Tofte, because of a large, high rock near his place called Tofte Rock.[6]
* Berglund Lake, ON, a speckled trout lake north of Ignace, was named for Tony Berglund,[7] who helped provincial authorities stock area lakes after the Second World War.
* Bjorkdale, SK, a former railway village northeast of Saskatoon, and nearby Bjork Lake, were named in 1911 for Charles Björk, who had settled there seven years earlier.[8]
* Boquist Lake, BC, northwest of Prince George, was named for the resident trapper and rancher John Boquist, who had immigrated from northern Sweden as a boy.[9]
** Bruhn Creek and Bruhn Ridge, BC, forty kilometres northwest of Salmon Arm, were named for Rolf Wallgren Bruhn, Conservative MLA for Salmon Arm from 1924 to 1942.[10]
* Calmar, AB, a town southwest of Edmonton, was named in 1900 by postmaster Carl John Blomquist to commemorate the city of Kalmar.[11] He and P.E. Dalquist were sent by their neighbours in North Dakota in 1894 to find a good place to settle in Canada.
Calumet, AB, was a school district named by Gust Bergquist who came from Calumet, Michigan.[12]
* Candy Hill, ON, a rounded knob that rises above the fertile Slate River Valley near Thunder Bay, was named by the teenagers who gathered

at Swedes Corners on Saturday nights for fellowship and to eat Lena Fugelsang's delicious homemade candy. The farms of four families adjoined at the foot of Candy Hill, at Swedes Corners, along what is now called McCluskey Drive. After Lena left home her younger sister Lily took over as candymaker, so that the name Candy Hill was well established as a destination by the 1920s.[13] In 1978 authorities changed the official name to Candy Mountain at the request of a private ski resort. Complaints from surprised local residents were dismissed, and road signs changed from Candy Hill Road to Candy Mountain Road. In so doing a charming legacy from a more innocent past has been recast into something quite different.

* Cape Nathorst, NU, the southernmost cape on Ellef Ringnes Island, was named by the second Norwegian polar expedition to arctic Canada (1898–1902), under Otto Sverdrup. It honours the Swedish professor and arctic explorer Alfred Gabriel Nathorst (1850–1921).[14]

* Carlson Bay, MB, on Kustra Lake, was named in 1984 for the Second World War casualty Gordon L. Carlson of Erickson.[15]

*** Carlson Creek, Carlson Lake, and Carlson Point, BC, northwest of Vancouver, commemorate Herman and Olivia Carlson, who in 1909 purchased land at the mouth of the creek later named for them. Carlson Point is located on the Sechelt Peninsula.[16]

* Carlstad, ON, a former railway station near Upsala west of Thunder Bay, was named in 1876 by Sir Sandford Fleming, engineer-in-chief of the government railway that became the Canadian Pacific Railway (CPR). It commemorates Karlstad, the capital city of the province of Värmland. Although the station no longer exists, the official name Carlstead Bay survives on nearby Lac des Mille Lacs.[17]

** Dahl Creek, BC, drains into Bigelow Lake, south of Smithers. It was named for railway contractor Martin Dahl,[18] who in 1911 settled on 129.5 hectares near that community. Another Dahl Creek forty kilometres south of Terrace commemorates a Finland Swedish trapper.

* Dahlia, ON, a railway station in Algonquin Provincial Park, was named by A.J Hills, who admired the park's beautiful scenery. Since dahlias do not grow wild in the park, it probably commemorates the Swedish botanist Anders Dahl (1751–1789), who lent his name to the flower.[19]

* Edberg, AB, a village southwest of Wetaskiwin, was named in 1902 by the first postmaster, John Edstrom.[20] He chose "Ed" as part of his surname and "berg" for the hill on which his home, store, and post office were located. When the railway built its Edberg station a few kilometres to the east in 1910, the year John died, his son Oscar moved the store and post office to the station. There, a small community developed with a grain elevator, lumberyard, school, and church. Edberg Lake lies nearby.

*** Egnell, BC, now called Sheslay, is a town northwest of Telegraph Creek. It was originally named for Albert Egnell,[21] manager of Lower Post

(Liard Post) from 1881 to 1892 and from 1897 to 1900, when he died from a gunshot wound. Egnell's name survives officially in nearby Egnell Creek, Mount Egnell, and Egnell Lakes.

** Ekblaw Glacier and Ekblaw Lake, NU, on the east shore of Ellesmere Island at Baird Inlet, were named for the Swedish-American scientist Walter Elmer Ekblaw.[22]

** Emil Lake and Emil Creek, BC, in the Coast Lake District, were named for Emil Widen, an early resident.[23] He and two other men arrived in April 1911 with just one pair of snowshoes for the three of them, towing a sleigh loaded with groceries.

* Englund Lake, SK, southeast of Bjorkdale, was named in 1951 for the Canadian soldier Sigvard Daniel Englund,[24] who was killed in action in Ortuna, Italy, in 1942.

**** Erickson, BC, a railway station near Creston, was named for Eric Gustaf Erickson,[25] who in 1882 was hired in Calgary as a CPR section foreman and who became a superintendent. Erickson post office opened in 1908. The nearby landmarks of Erickson Ridge, Mount Erickson, and Erickson Creek are likely named for him as well.

* Erickson, MB, a town south of Minnedosa, was named for Albert Erickson[26] in 1905, when the Canadian National Railway (CNR) bypassed Scandinavia to locate its station on his homestead. Erickson became postmaster in 1908 and requested the name Avesta after his home city in Dalarna, but later that year decided to name the post office after the station. He had applied for his homestead in 1899 and received title five years later.

* Eriksdale, MB, a community 96.5 kilometres northwest of Winnipeg, was named in 1911 for Jonas Erik Erikson,[27] whose homestead became the site for a CNR station. The name Eriksdale was chosen because a station named Erickson already existed, and Eriksdale post office opened the same year. Erikson was the area's first settler, having squatted there before filing on his homestead in March 1906.

** Falun, AB, a community west of Wetaskiwin, was named by Charles Strom[28] in honour of his birthplace. The post office opened in 1904, with G.G. Forssell as postmaster. Falun Creek, which drains into Bigstone Creek, rises nearby. The Augustana church was named Dalby after a parish in Dalarna. Falun is the capital city of the province of Dalarna, the original site of Stora Kopparberg (now Stora Enso), the world's oldest existing limited liability company, with the first share dating back to 1288. The Great Copper Mountain is a mammoth pit these days, the mine having closed in 1992, and has been declared a UNESCO World Heritage Site. Over the years slag from the mine has provided a key ingredient for the popular falu-red paint,[29] and the deep red cottage of the Swedish countryside has become a national symbol.

* Finland, ON, a community forty-five kilometres northwest of Fort Frances, named its post office in 1913 for the large number of Finland Swedes who had settled there.[30]

* Forslund, SK, a former railway station on the CPR between Colonsay
and Young, was named in 1910 for J.E. Forslund[31] of the railway's
immigration department.
Forslund, BC, a locality on the west shore of the Arrow Lakes, was named
for Albert Forslund,[32] who established a residence there about 1907,
originally called Forslund's Landing. He operated riverboats between
Arrowhead and Revelstoke until retiring in 1926.
Fredrickson Creek, Frederickson Lake, and Frederickson Peak, BC, in the Cassiar
district north of Hazelton, were named in 1932 for a hunter and prospector
who lived in a log cabin on the Ingenika River.[33]
Freedhome, SK, between Stockholm and Dubuc, began as a school district but
the name came to represent the community. It was named for the Freed
brothers, Oscar and Eric, who built the school in 1905.[34]
* Frolander Bay, BC, on the mainland opposite Texada Island, was named for
Peter Frolander, who owned land there. Annie Bay, part of Frolander
Bay, is named for his wife. She inherited his property and leased part of
it to the government for a school named Annie Bay School.[35]
* Gunnar, SK, an abandoned mining camp on Crackingstone Peninsula in
Lake Athabasca, was named for Gunnar Mining Limited, which in turn
was named for prospector Gunnar Berg.[36] From 1952 until 1964 the mine
produced five million tonnes of uranium ore.
* Hagglund Creek, BC, east of Fife railway station, was named for Per Levi
Hagglund.[37] In 1911 he and six other Swedes founded the so-called
Hilltop Settlement through which the creek flowed.
* Hallonquist, SK, a former railway station southeast of Swift Current, was
named by the CPR in 1924 to recognize Joseph Eskil Hallonquist.
Formerly a chief clerk in the Moose Jaw office, he won the
Distinguished Flying Cross and the Italian Medal for Valor during the
First World War. The first settlers had arrived from the United States
in 1910, but there was no post office until the railway went through
fourteen years later.[38]
Hanall, BC, was a flag stop on the CNR between Smithers and Prince Rupert
where Olof "Tie" Hanson[39] founded a sawmill community in 1921. The
post office functioned as Hanall until 1926 except for 1921–2, when it
was called Royal Mills. The first part of the name comes from Hanson's
surname, but the rest is unclear.
Hansen's Landing, BC (see Wasa)
* Hanson Lake, BC, east of the town of Burns Lake, was named for Olof "Tie"
Hanson (see Hanall).[40]
* Hedman Lake, SK, is located west of Reindeer Lake in the northeastern part
of the province. It honours a Canadian soldier of Swedish descent, Ira H.
Hedman, who was killed in France during the Second World War.[41]
Highland Park, AB, was a community located southeast of Wetaskiwin. The
name came from Willie Nordgren, because the rolling hills reminded him
of his former home in Highland Park, MI.[42]

* Hillgren Lakes, BC, a chain of small lakes between the Liard and Coal rivers just south of the Yukon border, were named for Knut Lambert Hillgren, a local trapper, lumberjack, and prospector.[43]
* Hilltop, MB, was named by Frank Hillstrand, postmaster from 1900 to 1952 except for the seven years he lived in Winnipeg. This job paid $12.50 a year.[44]
* Hokanson Point, MB, a geographic feature on Hecla Island in Lake Winnipeg, was named for Captain John C. Hokanson, whose passenger ship ran aground on a nearby reef in 1935.[45]
* Holst Point near Minaki, ON, was named for Leonard Holst,[46] who had built a hotel there just before 1910, when the CNR decided that its line should cross the Winnipeg River nearby. In 1927 the company built the upscale Minaki Lodge of logs, dubbing it the Jewel of the North. Swedes are credited with its construction. Minaki Lodge burned to the ground in 2003 and has since been rebuilt.
* Jenny Lind Island, NU, located southeast of Victoria Island at the southern entrance to Victoria Strait, was named in 1851 by Scottish polar explorer John Rae to honour singer Jenny Lind. Originally called Lind Island, the name was officially changed in 1946 to be more specific. The island is uninhabited, but was once part of the North American defence system.[47]

Johnson Beach, AB (see Sandholm Beach)

* Johnsons Landing, BC, a village on the eastern shore of Kootenay Lake, was named for Algot Johnson, who emigrated in 1901 and planted an apple orchard there.[48]
* Jonsson Island, MB, lies in Nueltin Lake, which straddles the Manitoba-Nunavut border. It was named for the area's sole permanent resident, trapper Ragnar Jonsson.[49] The naming in 1972 broke two of the guiding principles set forth by the Geographical Names Board of Canada: to use personal names only in exceptional circumstances and then not during that person's lifetime. Manitoba's Director of Surveys Allen Roberts, who had met the gregarious Jonsson in 1959 while surveying the 60th parallel, took the opportunity to deliver a commemorative scroll in person. To his surprise he found Jonsson living on the island named for him.[50]
** Josephine Bay and Josephine River, NU, are located on the southwest coast of the Boothia Peninsula. They were discovered in 1831 by the English polar explorer John Ross, who named them in honour of Josephine, who in 1823 married the future King Oscar I of Sweden and Norway.[51] She was the daughter of Napoleon I's adopted son.
* Kalmar, ON, a former railway station named in 1876 by Sir Sandford Fleming, commemorates the capital city of the province of Småland. It was located west of Thunder Bay, between Savanne and Upsala. The name was officially transferred to nearby Kalmar Lake.[52]

* Kipling, ON, midway between Sudbury and North Bay, was named in 1899
   by John Olof Englund, the second postmaster. It honoured his favourite
   author, Rudyard Kipling, who would win the Nobel Prize for Literature
   in 1907.[53] Because most residents were Swedish or Norwegian, the
   community was known as Little Scandinavia.[54]
** Krusenstern Lake and Krusenstern Point, NU, located in the southeastern
   part of the Boothia Peninsula, were discovered and named in 1831 by the
   English polar explorer John Ross. The name commemorates Admiral Adam
   Johan von Krusenstern (1770–1846), a Swedish explorer, geographer, and
   admiral in the Russian navy.[55]
* Lars Lake, BC, between the railway stations of Houston and Forestdale in
   the Bulkley Valley, was named for labourer Lars Anderson,[56] who later
   settled near Smithers as a farmer.
Larson Bay, BC, in West Vancouver, Larson Station on the Pacific Great Eastern
   Railway, and Larson Elementary School on Larson Road were named
   after the Vancouver hotel man, Pete Larson.[57]
* Lindale, AB, was named in 1914 by the first postmaster, Charlie Lindell.[58]
   He had requested Lindell Valley, but postal authorities dropped "valley"
   and anglicized the rest. A post office named Lindell already existed in
   British Columbia.
* Lindbergh, AB, a village on the North Saskatchewan River east of
   Edmonton, was named in 1927 for the Swedish-American aviator
   Charles A. Lindbergh, who made his historic flight across the Atlantic
   that year. The community began as Tyrol, but had changed its name to
   Mooswa in 1912.[59]
Lindbergh Island, BC, an island of ten hectares in the Strait of Georgia, was
   named in 1927 for the Swedish-American aviator Charles A. Lindbergh
   at the request of the property's owner, Paul Lambert of Detroit, MI.[60]
** Lindell, BC, a village southwest of Cultus Lake in the lower Fraser Valley,
   was named for Andrew Lindell, who settled there in the early 1890s. The
   post office opened in 1906 with Sigfrid Edstrom as postmaster. On the
   south shore of Cultus Lake is a summer resort called Lindell Beach.[61]
* Lindgren Lake, AB, located in the northeastern part of the province, was
   named in 1958 to honour the Swedish-American geologist Waldemar
   Lindgren.[62]
*** Lindquist Lake, Lindquist Pass, and Lindquist Peak, located in central BC,
   were named in 1921 by a land surveyor to honour Charlie Lindquist, a
   trapper who had lived in Canada for fifty years.[63]
* Linkoping, ON, a former railway station named in 1876 by Sir Sandford
   Fleming, commemorates Linköping, the capital city of Östergötland. The
   name survived for many years on both the CPR and adjacent CNR as
   Linko Siding, west of Thunder Bay between Savanne and Upsala, and
   still exists officially as Linko.[64]

Little Scandinavia, ON (see Kipling)

* Lofquist Lake, ON, near Nipigon was named for Maurice Gottfred Lofquist,[65] local reeve and an advocate of game conservation. The lake has a public beach.

* Lund, BC, a town on the western shore of the Malaspina Peninsula, was named by the Thulin brothers, Fred and Charlie, who had settled there in 1889. When the post office opened in 1892 they called it Lund for no other reason than that it was Swedish and easy to pronounce.[66] Lund is a city in southern Sweden, home of Lund University, founded in 1668.

Lundberg Island, NL, is the former name of an island off the coast of Labrador between Nain and Cape Mugford. It commemorated the Moravian missionary Johannes Lundberg, who worked in the area from 1811 to 1850. The name was dropped in favour of the original First Nations name, Kikkertarjote Island.[67]

** Lundbreck, AB, a railway village west of Lethbridge, derived from the Breckenridge and Lund Company, a firm with local mining interests and a sawmill. Only Mr Lund was Swedish.[68] Lundbreck Falls is nearby.

Lundemo, AB, northeast of Wetaskiwin near Hay Lakes, was named for Inga Lunde,[69] whose enthusiastic letters home persuaded many families to emigrate from Lake Malgomaj in Vilhelmina, Lappland.[70] The suffix "mo" means "sandy soil." By 1908 there were enough Swedes to found the Swedish Evangelical Lutheran Wilhelmina congregation. When the railway came through in 1912, nearby Hay Lakes became the station, and after the post office closed in 1949, Lundemo came to be called Wilhelmina after the church.

Malin Glacier, NL, a small feature on Brave Mountain on the coast of northern Labrador, was discovered by Carl-Gösta Wenner and named by the Finland Swedish geologist V. Tanner, leader of the 1939 Nordic-American scientific expedition to Labrador. The feature commemorates Wenner's fiancée, Malin af Geijerstam.[71]

* Malmgren, SK, a former CPR station 96.5 kilometres southwest of Saskatoon built ca. 1928, commemorates the Swedish meteorologist and explorer Finn Malmgren. In 1926 he landed on the north coast of Alaska after a flight over the North Pole with Roald Amundsen in the airship *Norge*. He died two years later on the polar ice north of Spitzbergen after the disastrous Nobile expedition.[72]

* Malmo, AB, a community on Red Deer Lake southeast of Wetaskiwin and east of the Battle River, was named in 1911 by the first postmaster, G.W. Bradenburg, who hailed from Malmo, Nebraska. The name commemorates Malmö, Sweden's third largest city. In 1944 Elim Mission Covenant Church changed its name to Malmo Mission Covenant Church.[73] (See New Sweden.)

* Matson Creek, YU, which flows into Sixtymile Creek, was named for John
   Matson, a Swede who discovered gold there in 1898 and worked the
   claim for fifty years. In 1933 he married "Klondike Kate" Rockwell, a
   former dance-hall entertainer in Dawson.[74]
* Mattson Lake, MB, northwest of Knee Lake, was named for a well-known
   Swedish mine owner at Oxford Lake at the suggestion of Dr Stone of the
   Department of Indian Affairs in Ottawa. It replaced the original name,
   Black Duck Lake, which was considered too common.[75]
* Monitor, AB, east of Red Deer, replaced the post office Sounding Lake
   in 1913. This year marked the fiftieth anniversary of the American
   Civil War battle between John Ericsson's famous ship *Monitor* and the
   Merrimac.
* Mount Sandin, BC, lies west of the Liard River and between mileposts 570
   and 575 on the Alaska Highway. It was named in 1942 for "Swede"
   Sandin, a foreman during construction.[76]
New Stockholm, SK (see Stockholm)
New Sweden, AB, located southeast of Wetaskiwin and west of the Battle
   River, was served by Emanuel Mission Covenant Church, which in 1904
   adopted the name New Sweden Mission Church. This church spawned
   two sister congregations, Malmo and Wetaskiwin.[77]
New Sweden, MB (see Scandinavia)
Nicholson, BC, located south of Golden, was named in honour of the
   Niklasson family, who immigrated from 1889 to 1893 to farm in the
   area.[78]
* Nobel, ON, an industrial community on Georgian Bay, was named in 1912
   when Canadian Industries Limited established an explosives factory
   there. The name honoured Alfred Nobel (1833–1896), the Swedish
   inventor of dynamite. The post office was established as Ambo in 1910
   and changed to Nobel in 1913.[79]
* Nordenskiold River, YU, which drains into the Yukon River near Carmacs,
   was named in 1883 by the American polar explorer Lieutenant Fredrick
   Schwarka. It commemorates the Swedish professor, Count Nils Adolf
   Erik Nordenskiöld (1832–1901).[80]
*** Nordenskiold Islands, NU, a small archipelago lying in Queen Maud Gulf,
   was named in 1905 by Roald Amundsen during his first polar expedition
   (1903–6), which successfully navigated the Northwest Passage. This name
   commemorates Count Nordenskiöld, above. Nunavut's Nordenskiold River
   and Nordenskiold Cape are likely named for him too.[81]
* Nordin, NB, a community near the mouth of the Miramichi River, was
   initially called Rosebank but was renamed for Oscar William Nordin,[82]
   who managed the sawmill there. Nordin post office operated from 1905
   to 1968. The firm also ran sawmills at Rexton and Richibucto, but closed
   down its Nordin operation around 1913 when O.W. is said to have

moved to Montreal. Another Swede, blacksmith John August Peterson,[83] was sent to Nordin in 1906 by his company in Alsen, Jämtland. When the mill closed he and his family moved westward, eventually ending up in Riverland, Manitoba.

* Nordstrom Lake, SK, was named in 1956 for Frank Nordstrom[84] to commemorate his winter transportation of fish from northern Saskatchewan to Prince Albert. He designed and built a half-dozen fishing boats suited for the north, and also constructed the first motor-driven snowplough to clear a winter road to and from Cree Lake.

* Nyberg Lakes, SK, two small lakes in the northwestern part of the province, were previously called Twin Lakes. They are named for John Nyberg, a trapper whose cabin was located on the isthmus between them.[85]

Nygren, SK, a small village near Estevan, was named for Gus Nygren, who had settled in the area ca. 1904. He moved to Squamish, Washington, around 1924.[86]

Offerdal, AB, north of Wetaskiwin, was a school district named by immigrants for Offerdal parish in the province of Jämtland.[87]

Ogren Lake, MB, southeast of Nejanilini Lake, was named in 1974 in memory of Sergeant Carl Ogren, whose plane went missing in the Bermuda Triangle during the Second World War. His body was never recovered.[88]

Ohlen, SK (see Stockholm)

Ohrnsville, AB, located near Warburg, was named in 1906 by the first postmaster, homesteader Erick Öhrn.[89] The post office closed in 1914.

* Olin, AB, a former CNR station west of Wetaskiwin, was named for Charles Olin,[90] who in 1909 became the first Swedish immigrant to be elected as a legislator.

* Olson, BC, a railway siding used for transporting logs at Crowsnest Pass from 1910 to 1917, was named for Einar C. "Stoney" Olson, an employee of the Elk Lumber Company in Fernie, which operated two logging camps at the siding.[91]

* Oscar Bay, NU, on the southwest coast of the Boothia Peninsula and Ross Strait, was discovered by English explorer John Ross during his 1829–33 expedition. He named it for the crown prince of Sweden and Norway, later King Oscar I.[92]

* Oscar Peak, BC, a mountain between the Skeena River and Portland Inlet, was named for Oscar Olander, who in 1900 settled on the Kitsumkalum River to the southeast. The name represents the gratitude of government surveyors for the lodging and other help that he gave them.[93]

Ostersund, ON, a former railway station near Kenora named in 1876 by Sir Sandford Fleming, commemorates Östersund, the capital city of the province of Jämtland. Originally located on the south shore of Laclu, the station was relocated further east in 1936 and renamed Laclu to correspond to the settlement of the same name on the north shore, a popular summer retreat for Winnipeggers. The road linking the two is still called Ostersund Road.[94]

* Oxdrift, ON, a former railway station named in 1880 by Sir Sandford Fleming, derives from an old Swedish word meaning the use of oxen as dray animals.[95] It lies directly north of a fourteen-kilometre portage over which oxen pulled heavy wagons of supplies from one lake to another during construction of the railway. Oxdrift, a farming community near Dryden, is the only place in the world so named.[96]

* Palmquist, ON, a former CNR village west of Hearst, was named for roadmaster Charlie Palmquist.[97]

* Poignant Creek, BC, near Sumas Mountain southeast of Vancouver, was named for Carl Poignant,[98] who homesteaded at the corner of Harris and Turner roads. An enterprising man, Poignant brought running water to his own home and two others through ten-centimetre wooden pipes by damming a spring on the mountain.[99]

* Prince Gustaf Adolf Sea, NU, and NW, an inland sea ringed by the islands Ellef Ringnes, Lougheed, Mackenzie, King, and Borden, was named by Otto Sverdrup during the second Norwegian polar expedition of 1898 to 1902. It commemorates Crown Prince Gustaf Adolf, who reigned from 1950 to 1973 as King Gustaf VI Adolf of Sweden.[100]

Ringwall, AB, the future site of Ferintosh, functioned as a post office from 1908 to 1914 with Peter Ringwall[101] as postmaster. Because the Ringwall homestead overlooked a beach on Red Deer Lake, the grounds were often used for picnics and community gatherings. Peter Ringwall called his home Stugan vid Sjöstranden (House beside the Beach) and his byline in *Canada posten* was "Från stugan och sjöstranden" (From the House and the Beach).

* Rosen Lake (1), BC, southwest of Fernie, was named for Andrew Johan Rosen.[102] Postmaster and justice of the peace in nearby Jaffray, he had bought lakeshore land from the CPR during the 1920s and sold the subdivided lots for summer cottages.

* Rosen Lake (2), BC, a small lake on Read Island, is named for Charles Rosen.[103] He bought sixty-five wooded hectares on the island, including the lake, and for forty-five years cultivated a six-hectare farm there while manufacturing wood products such as shingles and lumber. He never married.

*** Sandell Bay, Sandell Lake, and Sandell River, BC, lie on the eastern shore of Rivers Inlet. They commemorate Olof Sandell,[104] a foreman in the salmon canneries. Olof and his First Nations wife lived on a houseboat on the Skeena River. Some time after his wife's death he drowned in Darby Channel, leaving to mourn a parrot that could speak Swedish, English, and a First Nations dialect.

Sandholm Beach, AB, is a summer resort on Pigeon Lake, west of Wetaskiwin. In 1931 Fjalar Johnson bought a large tract of land on

Big Point and subdivided it into cottage lots. Eventually the cottage owners changed the name to Sandholm Beach because they preferred a Swedish-sounding name. Neighbouring Johnson Beach honours Fjalar Johnson.[105]

* Sandin Brook and Mount Sandin, BC, are located in the northern part of the province, but the origin of the name is obscure. Sandin Brook crosses the Alaska Highway.[106]

* Scandia, AB, located south of Brooks, was founded in 1914 when the Augustana Colonization Association began selling CPR land to be improved by irrigation. Pastor L.P. Bergström had named the community Uppland, but in 1924 the settlers voted to name the post office Scandia because the first farmers came from Scandia, Minnesota.[107]

* Scandinavia, MB, was established in July 1885. After a rocky beginning James Hemmingson,[108] a Dane, bought the existing sawmill and opened a post office in 1886, changing the colony's name from New Sweden to Scandinavia.

* Simmons Peninsula, NU, on the southwest shore of Ellesmere Island, was named by the polar explorer Otto Sverdrup for Herman Georg Simmons, who took part in his 1898–1902 expedition. Simmons was a professor of zoology and botany at the Ultuna Agricultural College in Uppland, Sweden.[109]

Smoland, MB, south of Minnedosa, was founded in 1907 by land agent and Mission Covenant pastor Victor J. Wallin. He called the settlement Småland because the original settlers of long-standing came from that province,[110] and the church founded the following year became known as Smoland Mission Covenant Church.

Snoose Valley, BC, was the original name given to Gillies Bay on Texada Island because so many Swedes settled there as farmers to supply the mines and the community of Van Anda.[111]

* Soeder Bay and Soeder Island, SK, are located in Table Lake in the east-central part of the province. They were named in 1952 to commemorate Paul and Glen Soeder, brothers from Saskatoon who were killed during the Second World War.[112]

** Solander Island and Solander Point, BC, were named by Captain James Cook on his third voyage (1776 to 1780), which took him along British Columbia's coast. They commemorate Swedish botanist Daniel Solander,[113] who had taken part in Cook's first circumnavigation of the globe. Solander was a student of Carl Linnaeus.

* Stockholm, SK, located in the Qu'Appelle Valley, was established in September 1885 when Immigration Agent Emanuel Öhlén chose the site and named it New Stockholm in honour of his home city. Ohlen post office opened in 1887. Settler Alex Stenberg[114] is credited with the CPR's assigning the name Stockholm[115] to the new railway station in 1904. Stockholm post office opened nearby, and Ohlen post office, nineteen

kilometres away, closed in 1910. Businesses like Stenberg's general store began relocating to Railway Avenue, renamed Stenberg Avenue in 2000.

* Stolz Lake, MB, northwest of Wekusko Lake, was named in 1973 for prospector Carl Stolz,[116] who worked in the gold mines at Herb Lake. He had moved his family from The Pas to Herb Lake in 1924.

Svea, AB, by Battle Lake, took its name from the Lutheran church founded in 1898, which was named for Svea, MN, home of the presiding pastor, Olof Lindgren. Svea is a girl's name and also the personification of Sweden, as in Mother Svea.

* Swanson, SK, sixty kilometres southwest of Saskatoon, was named in 1907 for the first postmaster, Abraham Daniel Swanson,[117] who had arrived from North Dakota two years earlier. One of the first mechanized farmers in Saskatchewan, he eventually owned 2,630 hectares, which were cultivated with an eighteen-share plough.

* Sweaburg, ON, a small town eight kilometres south of Woodstock, was named during the Crimean War for the former Swedish fortress Sveaborg near Helsinki, Finland. In 1855 a joint French-English naval fleet attacked the fortress, calling widespread attention to its name. Sweaburg post office functioned from 1857 to 1915.[118]

* Swedberg Creek, BC, west of Rossland, is named for John P. Swedberg, who earned his living in abandoned mines where he found rich deposits of gold. Swedberg was worth $200,000 in 1914, but lost all his real estate when the mining industry collapsed with the onset of the First World War. He and his two partners committed suicide in 1915.[119]

* Swede Creek, BC, which empties into the Kootenay River in Kootenay National Park, was so heavily used by Swedes going into the Kootenays and taking up homesteads that it became known as Swede Creek. Similar official names in British Columbia alone are Sweden Creek and Sweden Lake near Prince George; Swede Point on Pitt Island near Prince Rupert; Swedish Creek, eighty kilometres southeast of Revelstoke;[120] and Swede Saw Mountain along the coast. The Canadian Geographical Names database lists thirty-seven official names beginning with the letters "swed."

Swede Creek (1), YU, which flows into the Upper Liard River, commemorates a trapper known only as "The Swede," who lived there between 1900 and 1930. His trademark was a narrow, nine-metre, dugout canoe that handled remarkably well, especially in treacherous water.[121]

* Swede Creek (2), YU, which flows into the Yukon River a few miles above Dawson, was named by the mining recorder in 1898, when a group of Swedes staked the Discovery and other claims. The news spread like wildfire in the saloons, dance halls, and gaming parlours made famous by the poet Robert Service. Elle Andra-Warner, author of his biography, whispered in my ear that his inspiration to write "The Cremation of Sam McGee" came from witnessing a Swede's last rites.[122]

* Swede Johnson Creek, YU, which flows into the Kluane River, was named
    for Ernest "Swede" Johnson, who discovered the first gold found on
    Tatamagouche Creek.[123]
Swedes Corners, ON (see Candy Hill)
Swedetown, ON, was located in North Cobalt, along King Edward and Cobalt
    streets. According to the 1901 census, 3.7 per cent of the population in
    the Timiskaming area spoke Swedish as a first language, more than those
    who spoke French.[124]
Swedeville, QC, a suburb of Waterville, grew up around John Knutson's
    sawmill around 1900.[125] Today only the road sign "Chemin Swede" hints
    that it was once the site of a thriving Swedish community.[126]
Swedish Town, AB, was the name for the east side of Wetaskiwin in the early
    1900s.[127]
* Telford, MB, a former railway station named in 1876 by Sir Sandford
    Fleming, commemorates Thomas Telford, the Scottish engineer who in
    the early 1800s designed the Göta Canal through central Sweden. For
    this deed he received the Order of Vasa from the King of Sweden.[128]
    Many emigrants would travel through this 87.4-kilometre waterway
    with fifty-eight locks, on their way from the Baltic Sea to the port of
    Göteborg on the North Sea.
* Thorsby, AB, a town southwest of Edmonton, was named by the first
    postmaster, August Sahlstrom,[129] to honour the city where his family's
    grand manorial estate was located. He had settled in Thorsby with
    nephews Charlie and Walter, and later Gustav, but by 1923 all had
    moved away. Six years later, when the CPR extended its line from
    Lacombe to Leduc, the community took on new life and in 1949
    became a village. During the 1990s Thorsby was twinned with Torsby,
    Sweden, and Thorsby, Alabama.[130] The Sahlström family's manorial
    estate in Torsby, Värmland, has recently been converted into a period
    museum and art gallery. Formerly called Torsby herrgård and renamed
    Sahlströmsgården, it features works of the talented Anna Sahlström
    (1856–1956), her siblings Bror and Ida, and other artists who spent time
    there.[131]
*** Thulin Creek, Thulin Lake, and Thulin Passage, BC, were named for
    the Thulin brothers, Fred and Charlie, who founded both Lund and
    Campbell River.[132] (See Lund.)
* Tungsten, NW, a small mining community, was founded in 1961 and a post
    office established in 1968. Tungsten was mined there, which derives from
    two Swedish words meaning "heavy stone." Also called "scheelite," it
    was discovered and named in 1781 by Swedish chemist Carl Wilhelm
    Scheele (1742–1786).[133]
Twopete Creek, YU, which flows into the Tay River, commemorates a pair of
    prospectors named Pete, one of them with the surname Nelson.[134]

Uppland, AB (see Scandia)

*** Upsala, ON, a former railway station named in 1876 by Sir Sandford
Fleming, commemorates Uppsala, the capital city of Uppland. In the
early 1900s the spelling changed from Upsala to Uppsala because of
changes in the written language instituted by the Swedish government.
Upsala survives as a community west of Thunder Bay.[135] Upsala Creek
and Upsala Lake lie nearby.

* Vega, AB, an agricultural community northeast of Fort Assiniboine, was named
for the Swedish cream separator Vega. The Vega brand appeared in Eaton's
catalogue during the 1930s. Postmaster Christina Erickson established Vega
post office in 1930.[136]

Wallinberg, SK, was a parcel of land in the Hyas-Norquay area named and
sold by Victor J. Wallin and his brother, Elmer, a real-estate agent, who
established the Swedish Canadian Colonization Company based in
Winnipeg from 1904 to 1910. (See Smoland.)

* Warburg, AB, a small town southwest of Edmonton, was founded in 1906
by settlers from Frillesås parish, Halland. It commemorates Varberg, a
coastal city in Halland, the name requested in 1912. After considerable
delay, postal authorities imposed Warburg, a rather inappropriate
anglicization during wartime, and the post office opened in 1916.[137]

*** Wasa, BC, is a community located in the Kootenay River valley north of
Cranbrook. It was named by postmaster Nils Hanson in 1902 to honour
the Swedish royal house of Vasa.[138] Originally called Hansen's Landing,
he changed the name to Wasa before the spelling of his surname could
be corrected. Wasa Creek and Wasa Lake, BC, are named for the nearby
community.

* Westerose, AB, a town beside Pigeon Lake, is an anglicized version of
Västerås, capital city of the province of Västmanland. Johan Norström,
the oldest settler, came from an adjoining parish. "Well," he reasoned,
"The Dalecarlians [people from Dalarna] called their post office Falun, so
I suppose we'll call ours Västerås." The post office opened in 1907.[139]

* Wickstrom Lake, MB, south of Island Lake, was named in 1973 for Second
World War casualty Fred E. Wickstrom of Erickson.[140]

Wilhelmina, AB (see Lundemo)

* Yarbo, SK, east of Regina, is pronounced the same as Järbo in Gästrikland,
but the origin of the name has been lost.

Appendix 2

Firsts for Swedes in Canada

1749	Swedish visitor – Pehr Kalm visits Montreal
1767	Swedish immigrant – The Reverend Paul Bryzelius, Lunenberg, Nova Scotia
ca. 1798	Swedish descendant born in Ontario – Catherine Wood[1]
ca. 1809	Swedish descendant born in Quebec – Thomas Johnsen[2]
1811	Swedish immigrant to Manitoba – Jacob Fahlstrom via Hudson Bay
1811	Swedish immigrant to Labrador – Moravian missionary Johannes Lundberg
ca. 1818	Swedish descendant born in New Brunswick – Susanna Smith[3]
1850	Swedish consulate – Quebec City
1855	Swedish consul – Count Alfred Falkenberg, Quebec City
1871	Swedish immigrant to Manitoba – Charles Johnson, Minnedosa
1872	Swedish immigrant to Winnipeg via Red River – Charles Davis Anderson from Chicago
1872	Swedish immigrant to British Columbia – Eric Anderson, Surrey
1873	Immigration agent in Sweden – William McDougall
1875	Swedish labourers arrive in Fort William, Ontario, to build the railway westward
1876	Swedish place names appear on official map as railway stations in Ontario
1876	Swedish consul in the West – Henry Rhodes, Victoria, British Columbia
1879	Swedish-owned hotel – Andrew Johnson, Manitoba House, Port Arthur, Ontario
1881	Swedish vice-consul in the West – Thomas Howard, Winnipeg, Manitoba
1884	Swedish Dominion immigration agent – Emanuel Öhlén, Winnipeg

1884	Scandinavian organization, the Scandinavian Society – Emanuel Öhlén, Winnipeg
1885	Swedish congregation – Mission Covenant, Winnipeg
1885	Scandinavian colony – Scandinavia, Manitoba
1885	Swede to fight in the Northwest Rebellion – Andy Johnson from Halland[4]
1886	Swedish homesteader in Saskatchewan – Nils Johanson, New Stockholm
1886	Swedish homesteader in Alberta – John Hallgren, Springvale district, near Red Deer
1886	Ukrainian Swede to immigrate – Hindrik Utas from Gammalsvenskby, Ukraine
1887	Swedish newspaper, *Den skandinaviske canadiensaren* – Emanuel Öhlén, Winnipeg
1887	Swedish Mormon to migrate from Salt Lake City – Johannes Anderson from Sweden
1887	Resident Mission Covenant pastor – Andrew Johnson, Winnipeg
1889	Augustana Lutheran congregation – New Stockholm, Saskatchewan
1892	Resident Augustana Lutheran pastor – Svante Uddén, Winnipeg
1892	Swedish temperance society – Mission Covenant congregation, Winnipeg
1892	Swedish Dominion immigration agent for USA – C.O. Swanson, Waterville, Quebec
1892	Swedish Baptist congregation – Waterville, Quebec
1894	Swedish domestics to emigrate under government scheme – C.O. Swanson, Waterville
1894	Swedish secular newspaper, *Väktaren* – Konstantin Flemming, Winnipeg
1894	Swedish print shop – Winnipeg
1898	Book about Canada published in Swedish – Svante Uddén, *Från Canada*
1900	Swedish sick- and death-benefit society – Norden, Winnipeg
1902	Swedish Good Templar Lodge (IOGT) – Winnipeg
1906	Anglican Swedish Mission – St Ansgarius, Port Arthur, Ontario
1907	Swedish institution to grant university degrees – Brandon College, Manitoba
1908	Hospital incorporated by Scandinavians – Wetaskiwin, Alberta
1908	Swedish champion of cooperative movement – Frank Eliason, Wynard, Saskatchewan
1909	Elected provincial MLA – Charles H. Olin, Wetaskiwin, Alberta

1912	Vasa Lodge – #229, Förgät mig ej (Forget me not), Vancouver
1915	Scandinavian Grand Lodge IOGT – Winnipeg
1915	Swedish consul general – David Bergström, Montreal
1917	Swedish national organization – Svenska förbundet, Consul General David Bergström
1917	Swedish library association – founded at IOGT meeting, Round Lake, Saskatchewan
1919	Swedish labour leader – Emil Berg, Edmonton
1919	Swedish socialist newspaper – *Forum*, Nils F:son (Fredrickson) Brown, Winnipeg
1926	Scandinavian society-owned clubrooms and restaurant – Scandinavian Home, Port Arthur
1927	Scandinavian school to teach English to adults – Matthew Lindfors, Vancouver
1930	Swedish member of parliament – Olof Hanson, Skeena, British Columbia
1930	Wilderness adventures Swedish literary genre – Karl Gunnarson, *Som emigrant i Kanada*
1932	Swedish grower of alfalfa – O.P. Anderberg, south of Brooks, Alberta[5]
1932	Swedish-born hockey player in NHL – Gus Forslund, Ottawa Senators[6]
1936	Santa Lucia – arranged by Matthew Lindfors, Vancouver, with Ruby Arnesson as Lucia[7]
1943	Swedish old folks' home – Good Shepherd Lutheran Home, Wetaskiwin
1956	Swedish ambassador – Oscar Uno Konrad Thorsing, Ottawa
1968	Provincial premier of Swedish descent – Harry Strom, Alberta[8]
1975	Swedish school teaching Swedish language to children – Calgary
1982	Branch of Swedish Women's Education Association (SWEA) – Toronto
1988	Official visit by Sweden's reigning monarch – King Carl XVI Gustaf and Queen Silvia

Vasa Order of America

Lodge #	Name	Location	Instituted
229	Förgät mig ej	Vancouver, BC	1912 06 24
242	Midnattssolen	Hamilton, ON	1912 12 07
244	Flora	Victoria, BC	1913 02 05
259	Strindberg	Winnipeg, MB	1913 07 13
261	Nordstjärnan	Port Arthur, ON	1913 08 09
262	Klippan	Fort William, ON	1913
264	Välgöraren	Waterville, QC	1913 09 06
293	Engelbrekt	Kenora, ON	1914 04 14
346	Vårblomman	Annieheld,* SK	1916 07 13
372	Bernadotte	Haglof,* SK	1918 03 11
374	Majblomman	Toronto, ON	1918 05 20
375	Idog	Eriksdale, MB	1918 07 08
385	Viking	Lac du Bonnet, MB	1920 09 05
413	Nornan	Vancouver, BC	1922 02 11
417	Branting	Calgary, AB	1922 03 25
436	Vänskapslandet	Fort Frances, ON	1924 01 20
440	Skansen	Vancouver, BC	1924 02 25
489	Stjärna	Wabigoon, ON	1926
499	Valhalla	Montreal, QC	1927 08 21
500	Enighet	Aldergrove, BC	1927 08 21
509	Liljan	Canwood, SK	1928 04 08
513	Norden	Meeting Creek, AB	1928 04 29
524	Berglands *väl*	Bergland, ON	1928 11 25

(*Continued*)

(Continued)

Lodge #	Name	Location	Instituted
535	Majblomman	Nelson, BC	1929 05 04
539	Sleeping Giant	Port Arthur, ON	1929 07 12
540	Örnen	Vancouver, BC	1929 09 21
542	Stjernan	Port Alberni, BC	1929 09 28
543	Fraser	Port Hammond,* BC	1929 10 27
549	Skandia	Edmonton, AB	1929 11 24
560	Klippan	Flin Flon, MB	1930 04 16
564	André	Hay Lake, AB	1930 11 09
565	Tegner	Staveley, AB	1930 11 16
569	Norrland	The Pas, MB	1931 07 01
573	Hoppets ankare	Eagle River, ON	1931 12 19
574	Offerdal	Wetaskiwin, AB	1932 01 31
575	Nordstjärnan	Falun, AB	1932 01 31
577	Buford	Buford, AB	1932 03 13
578	Svea	Cherhill, AB	1932 04 15
579	Lethbridge	Lethbridge, AB	1932 04 16
582	Foothills	Calgary, AB	1933 04 01
583	Nordens blomma	Polling,* BC	1933 08 12
591	Polarstjernan	Perow,* BC	1934 08 09
592	Framtid	Southbank,* BC	1934 08 11
593	Nordstjärnan	Vallerund,* SK	1934 10 28
596	Nordic	Vancouver, BC	1935 04 07
597	Viking	Chauvin, AB	1935 06 09
607	Sunshine	Coaldale, AB	1938 01 30
610	Enighet	Finmark, ON	1938 12 04
612	Valhalla	New Westminster, BC	1943 05 09
613	The Star of the North	Flin Flon, MB	1946 01 13
670	Lindholmen	Medicine Hat, AB	1963 02 23
690	Cariboo	Quesnel, BC	1970 05 24
733	Red Deer	Red Deer, AB	1984 11 19
744	Valley Vasa	Mission-Abbotsford, BC	1989 06 17

* Not listed in current provincial directory

Source: Thanks to Vasa Archives, Bishop Hill, IL.

Ambassadors

1943–51	Per Gustaf Adolf Wijkman, Envoy
1951–6	Klas Erik Böök, Envoy
1956	Oscar Uno Konrad Thorsin, Envoy
1956–62	Oscar Uno Konrad Thorsing, Ambassador
1963–5	Ragnvald Bagge, Ambassador
1965–9	Per Lind, Ambassador
1969–76	Åke Malmaeus, Ambassador
1976–9	Per Anger, Ambassador
1980–4	Kaj Björk, Ambassador
1984–9	Ola Ullsten, Ambassador
1989–95	Håkan Berggren, Ambassador
1995–2000	Jan Ståhl, Ambassador
2000–5	Lennart Alvin, Ambassador
2005–10	Ingrid Iremark, Ambassador
2010–14	Teppo Tauriainen, Ambassador
2014–	Per Sjögren, Ambassador

Source: Foreign Affairs Archives, Stockholm; *Kungl. Utrikesdepartementets kalender 1870–2001*; see also "Swedish Consulates" on Embassy of Sweden website.

Consuls General

Montreal

1916–18	David Christian Bergstrom, Consul General
1918–21	Carl Otto von Dardel, Consul General (Acting)
1921–36	Magnus Clarholm, Consul General
1936–9	Oscar Costans Görgodt Lundquist, Consul General
1939–41	Gustaf Lowenhard, Consul General
1941–3	Per Gustaf Adolf Wijkman, Consul General
1953–6	August Herman von Hartmansdorff, Consul General
1960–5	Ingvar Anders Harald Grauers, Consul General
1966–9	Stig Engfeldt, Consul General
1969–72	Gösta Brunnström, Consul General
1972–4	Sten Aminoff, Consul General
1975–80	Olof Bjurström, Consul General
1980–5	Claes-Erik Winberg, Consul General
1985–9	Bengt Rösiö, Consul General
1991–3	Karin Ahrland, Consul General

Quebec City

1993–4	Robert Normand, Consul General
1994–	Paule Gauthier, Consul General

Toronto

1974–90	Ingmar Gustaf Söderström, Consul General
1991–3	Mats Marling, Consul General
1993–2001	Robert J. Stocks, Consul General

Vancouver

1969–84	Karl-Axel Ståhl, Consul General
1988–91	Karl Bertil Eriksson, Consul General
1991–2005	Per Eric Magnus Ericson, Consul General

Source: Foreign Affairs Archives, Stockholm; *Kungl. Utrikesdepartementets kalender 1870–2001*; see also "Swedish Consulates" on Embassy of Sweden website.

Consuls

Calgary

Office opened 1894
Rudolph H. Zoumer, appointed 1970
Armilda "Anne" Zoumer, appointed 1983
Gunilla Mungan, appointed 1993
Patrick B. Carlson, appointed 200?
Joseph Lougheed

Edmonton

Office opened 1921
Emil Richard Ture Skarin, appointed 1945
Olof Sigurd Franzén, appointed 1969
Lars Göran Fahlstrom, appointed 1978
Donald George Bishop, appointed 1994
Kristina Williams, appointed 2007

Fredericton

Office opened 1993
Rhona Beverlee Levine Ruben, appointed 1992
Allen Melvin Ruben, appointed 1996
Earl Brewer, appointed 2005

Halifax

Office opened 1861
Sven Magnusson Lagerberg, appointed 1918
James MacGregor Davison, appointed 1946
Walter Otis Barnstead, appointed 1952
Frank Gordon Hatcher, appointed 1959
Harold Wilfred Wesley Hyson, appointed 1964
Gunnar Knut Gustaf Jennegren, appointed 1974
Kaj Holger Gerhard Nielsen, appointed 1991
George T.H. Cooper, appointed 1999
Cheryl Hodder

Montreal

Office opened 1856, in 1906 moved from Quebec City to Montreal
Gustaf Erik Gylling, appointed 1906
Hamilton A. Gault, appointed 1909
Einar Henrik Lindquist, appointed 1911 (Attaché)
Carl Gothard Gylfe Anderberg, appointed 1913
Carl Axel Adolf Wollert, appointed 1913 (Attaché)
Hans Fredrik Johansson Widenfelt, appointed 1916
Bertil Arne Renberg, appointed 1927
Louis Carl DeGeer, appointed 1938 (Attaché)
Olof Ripa, appointed 1957
Bo Wernström, appointed 1976
Erik Häggström, appointed 1979
Inger Johannesson, appointed 1990
Anne-Marie Dunn, appointed 1992
Marie Giguére, appointed 1993
Lionel Paul Hurtubise, appointed 1997
Daniel Johnson, appointed 2005

Prince Rupert

Office opened 1910
Olof Hanson, appointed 1924
Philip M. Ray, appointed 1953

Quebec City

Office opened 1850
George Pemberton, appointed 1852 (Acting)
Baron Alfred Falkenberg, appointed 1855
M.C. Johnson, appointed 1872 (Acting)
Wilhelm Anthony Schwartz, appointed 1873
Folke Cronholm, appointed 1905
Timothy Hibbard Dunn, appointed 1954
Georges de Léry Demers, appointed 1967
Robert Normand, appointed 1990
Paule Gauthier

Regina

Office opened 1974
Larry Alvan Kyle, appointed 1973
Ronald Earl Shirkey, appointed 1991

Regina and Saskatoon

Office opened 1981
Larry Alvan Kyle, appointed 1981
Dale Robert Doan, appointed 1990

Saint John

Office opened 1857
Vernon Stewart Northrop, appointed 1969
Gerard Andrew McGillivray, appointed 1970
Office closed 1993

St John's

Office opened 1867
John Osborne Williams, appointed 1918
Arthur Williams, appointed 1923 (Acting)

Joseph Pierce Cary, appointed 1926
Olaf Christian Olsen, appointed 1936
Joseph William Allan, appointed 1945
John Ernest Hickey, appointed 1954
Maurice Gregory Devine, appointed 1963
Edward Patrick Quigley, appointed 1973
Peter Norman Outerbridge, appointed 1975
Albert E.P. Hickman, appointed 1994

Toronto

Office opened 1881
Andrew Dyas MacLean, appointed 1930
Josef Emanuel Ander, appointed 1939
Nils Fredrik Anders Peder Kallin, appointed 1957
Leif Holmvall, appointed 1979
Lars H. Henriksson, appointed 2001

Vancouver

Office opened 1887
Emil Axel Johan Ståhl, appointed 1930
Charles Barneby Stahlschmidt, appointed 1937 (Acting)
Karl-Axel Ståhl, appointed 1948
Ulf Waldén, appointed 1984
Anders Neumüller, appointed 2005
Thomas Gradin

Victoria

Office opened 1876
Henry Rhodes, appointed 1876
Robert Ward, appointed 1879
Thomas Robert Smith, appointed 1900
Aaron Gonnason, appointed 1911
Olof Hanson, appointed 1920

Winnipeg

Office opened 1881
Harold John Smith, appointed 1917
Gustaf Schroder, appointed 1928
Herman Peter Albert Hermanson, appointed 1928
Arthur Antonius Anderson, appointed 1955
Edwin Otto Carlson, appointed 1963
Neil Edwin Carlson, appointed 1980

Source: Foreign Affairs Archives, Stockholm; "Förteckning å svenska och norrska consuler, utfärdad af Kongl. Maj:ts och Rikets Commerce-Collegium ..." (1850–69); see also Kungl, "Utrikesdepartementets kalender 1870–2001"; see also "Swedish Consulates" on Embassy of Sweden website. Records are missing for the following years: 1939–45, 1947–50, 1952–4, 1956, 1958, 1960, 1962–3, 1965, 1967–8, 1970–1, and 1977.

Vice-Consuls

Baie Verte and Tidnish, NB

Office opened 1878
Joseph Read, appointed 1886

Bathurst, NB

Office opened 1870
John Ferguson Jr, appointed 1870
John Sievewright, appointed 1880
John Ferguson, appointed 1886
George Gilbert, appointed 1897

Bersimis, QC

Office opened 1876
Theophile Girouard, appointed 1875
Charles Sheriff, appointed 1888
Robert Hudson Montgomery, appointed 1890

Bridgewater, NS

Office opened 1870
Fletcher Bath Wade, appointed 1882

Buctouche, NB (see Richibucto)

Office opened 1857
John Bowser, appointed 1861
John Clare Rap, appointed 1878
John Clark Ross, appointed 1878

Burrard Inlet, BC (see Vancouver)

Office opened 1887
Benjamin Springer, appointed 1886

Calgary

Office opened 1894
Charles Waldemar Christian Peterson, appointed 1893
John August Nolan, appointed 1901
John Engelbert Forslund, appointed 1920
John William Hugill, appointed 1925
Thomas Leo O'Keefe, appointed 1938
Gunnar Johan Viktor Swalander, appointed 1960
Eva Henderson, appointed 2002

Campbellton, NB

Office opened 1870
John MacAlister, appointed 1882
William Albert Mott, appointed 1888

Caraquet, NB

Office opened 1878
Joseph Lane Bishop, appointed 1879
John James Vibert, appointed 1883
Philip Rive, appointed 1884

Cascumpec, PEI

Office opened 1875
George William Howland, appointed 1874

Chatham and Newcastle, NB

Office opened 1890
Ernest Hutchison, appointed 1889
Robert Murray, appointed 1910
John Adams Creaghan, appointed 1919
Donald Sutherland Creaghan, appointed 1925

Chicoutimi, QC

Office opened 1884
James George Scott, appointed 1883
Benjamin Alexander Scott, appointed 1885
Jean Alfred Gagné, appointed 1889
Louis de Gonzague Belay, appointed 1890

Dalhousie, NB

Office opened 1861
Arthur Ritchie, appointed 1860
George Haddon, appointed 1863

Dawson, YU

Office opened 1900
Thomas Dufferin Patullo, appointed 1900
William David Radford, appointed 1910
Thomas Andrew Firth, appointed 1920

Edmonton, AB

Office opened 1921
Emil Richard Ture Skarin, appointed 1920
Olof Sigurd Franzén, appointed 1951

Escouminac, QC

Office opened 1863
John Edmund Barry, appointed 1862
David Ouellet, appointed 1879

Edward Vachon, appointed 1882
John Topping, appointed 1886

Gaspé, QC

Office opened 1870
James John Lowndes, appointed 1869
Francis George Egan, appointed 1883

Halifax, NS

Office opened 1861
James Black Oxley, appointed 1860
Edmund Duckett Tucke, appointed 1875
Isaac Henry Mathers, appointed 1882
James MacGregor Davison, appointed 1906
C.E. Bryant, appointed 1951 (Acting)

Hamilton, ON

Office opened 1873
Silas Edward Gregory, appointed 1873

Kenora, ON (formerly Rat Portage)

Office opened 1896
Axel Christian Helenus Helander, appointed 1896
Gustaf Severin Larsson, appointed 1898
Berndt Olai Berg, appointed 1902

Liscomb, NS

Office opened 1882
Samuel Creighton, appointed 1882

Little Glace Bay, NS

Office opened 1886
Edward Douglas Rigby, appointed 1886

Magdalena River

Office opened 1876
Edward Vachon, appointed 1876

Matane, QC

Office opened 1874
Alexander Fraser, appointed 1874

Métis, QC

Office opened 1879
David Blair, appointed 1880
William Dudley Fischer, appointed 1888
William Seals, appointed 1895

Minnedosa, MB

Office opened 1896
Robert Hill Myers, appointed 1896

Miramichi, NB

Office opened 1858
Robinson Crocker, appointed 1858
Richard Hutchinson, appointed 1865

Montreal, QC

Office opened 1856
Henry Chapman, appointed 1856
Johan Fredrik Wulff, appointed 1872
Daniel Connelly, appointed 1882
Gustaf Erik Gylling, appointed 1897
Carl Otto David von Dardel, appointed 1918
Nils Leon Jaenson, appointed 1921
Gustaf Hilding Lundh, appointed 1950
O.H. Erlandsson, appointed 1955
C.E. Westberg, appointed 1957

H.H. Hesselgren, appointed 1959
M.E.K. Elgqvist, appointed 1966
Björn-Gösta Sporrong, ppointed 1974
Karin Sjöberg, appointed 1989
Anne-Marie Dunn, appointed 1991
Gunnel Yates, appointed 200?

New Stockholm, SK

1893–1913
Christian Olsson Hofstrand, appointed 1893

Northport, NS

Office opened 1877
John Moore Burns, appointed 1885
David Patterson Ferguson, appointed 1886

Ottawa, ON

Office opened 1881
Roderick Edward O'Connor, appointed 1881
Robert Charles Wilkins MacCuaig, appointed 1882

Parrsboro, NS

Office opened 1870
Alexander Stewart Townshend, appointed 1882
Niels Carl Nielsen Nordby, appointed 1886

Pictou, NS

Office opened 1873
John Russell Noonan, appointed 1873
John Richardson Davies, appointed 1874

Port Arthur and Fort William, ON (now Thunder Bay)

Office opened 1921
Johan Oscar Johnson, appointed 1921

Joel Koreen, appointed 1946
Bernard Koreen, appointed 1957

Portage la Prairie, MB

Office opened 1894
Frans Alfred Leonard Harlin, appointed 1893

Prince Rupert, BC

Office opened 1910
Olof Hanson, appointed 1910
Arthur Brooksbank, appointed 1948

Pugwash, NS

Office opened 1860
Henry Gesner Pineo, Jr, appointed 1859
Abraham Akerley Stevens, appointed 1874
Hibbert Crane Black, appointed 1892

Quebec City, QC

Office opened 1850
Baron Fredrik Andreas Falkenberg, appointed 1874
Edward Hans Jörgen Schwartz, appointed 1882
Ernest Frederick Würtele, appointed 1899
Richard Bagge, appointed 1902

Consulate moved to Montreal, no longer represented Norway
Harold Kennedy, appointed 1909
Francis Mary Duggan, appointed 1910
Charles Gwyllym Dunn, appointed 1927

Regina, SK

Office opened 1917
Albert Olson, appointed 1916
Charley Emanuel Johnson, appointed 1920
Reginald James Balfour, appointed 1960

Richibucto and Buctouche, NB

Office opened 1857
George McLeod, appointed 1857

Richibucto, NB (see Buctouche)

R. Hutchinson, appointed 1861
George Alfred Hutchinson, appointed 1911

Rimouski, QC

Office opened 1869
George Silvain, appointed 1868

Rivière Ouelle, QC

Office opened 1888
George MacNaughton, appointed 1887

Saguenay, QC

Office opened 1870
David Edward Price, appointed 1856

St Étienne, QC

Office opened 1866
Edwin Hilier, appointed 1866
Jacob Murray, appointed 1892
Edwin Hilier, appointed 1897

St George, NB

Office opened 1976
Hugh Ludgate, appointed 1875

Saint John, NB

Office opened 1857
John W. Cudlip, appointed 1857

William Thomson, appointed 1874
John Henderson Thomson, appointed 1885
John Royden Thomson, appointed 1904
Robert Thomas Leavitt, appointed 1906
Mathew Boyd Edwards, appointed 1912
John Osborn Williams, appointed 1918
David Willett Ledingham, appointed 1930
Leslie Lonsdale Harrison, appointed 1950
Vernon Stewart Northrop, appointed 1960

St John's, NF

Office opened 1867
Robert Henry Prouse, appointed 1866
Kenneth R. Prouse, appointed 1905 (Acting)
Arthur Williams, appointed 1923

St Margaret's Bay, NS

Office opened 1883
James Henry Burnes, appointed 1883
Charles Reed Hill, appointed 1884

St Stephen, NB

Office opened 1870
James Mitchell, appointed 1882

St Thomas de Montmagny, QC

Office opened 1898
Paul Geoffrey Owen, appointed 1898

Ste Anne des Monts, QC

Office opened 1875
Téodore Jean Lamontagne, appointed 1874

Sault au Cochon, QC

Office opened 1875
Grant William Forrest, appointed 1874

Shediac, NB

Office opened 1859
Richard C. Scovil, appointed 1859
William John Millner Hannington, appointed 1873
James Inglis, appointed 1884

Sheet Harbour, NS

Office opened 1870
Finlay MacMillan, appointed 1882

Sherbrooke, NS

Office opened 1878
Donald MacLean, appointed 1885

Ship Harbour, NS

Office opened 1878
Lewis Fiske Hill, appointed 1885

Sydney and North Sydney, NS

Office opened 1872
W.H. Archibald (North Sydney only), appointed 1872
Arthur Harry Bourinet, appointed 1877
John Edward Burchell, appointed 1881
Joseph Gill Angwin, appointed 1906
Joseph Gill Angwin, appointed 1906
Obed Nelson Mann, appointed 1927

Tadoussac, NS

Office opened 1884
Joseph Radford, appointed 1883

Three Rivers, QC

Office opened 1875
George Balcer, appointed 1874

Toronto, ON

Office opened 1881
James Sarin MacMurray, appointed 1880
Anton Lund Hertzberg, appointed 1895
George Kerr, appointed 1910
William James Beaton, appointed 1924
Andrew Dvas MacLean, appointed 1930
Dana Harris Porter, appointed 1932
Richard Atkinson Lambertson Biggs, appointed 1935
Tage Arthur Wilhelm Löndén, appointed 1977
Lisbet Margareta Jakobsen Fabricius, appointed 1991
Agnetha Nilsson Edwards, appointed 200?

Trois Pistoles, QC

Office opened 1869
Nazaire Têtu, appointed 1868

Vancouver, BC (see Burrard Inlet)

Office opened 1887
John Charles Maclure, appointed 1896
John Martin Whitehead, appointed 1901
John Charles Maclure, appointed 1901
Richard Vance Winch, appointed 1906
Karl-Axel Ståhl, appointed 1937
Karl Rudolf Kurt Domellöf, appointed 1956
Eva Karin Henderson, appointed 1988

Victoria, BC

Office opened 1893
William Arthur Ward, appointed 1893

Wetaskiwin, AB

Office opened 1920
Jonas Peter Johnson, appointed 1921

Winnipeg, MB

Office opened 1881
Thomas Howard, appointed 1882
James Arthur Green, appointed 1882
Harold John Smith, appointed 1904
Peter Bernhard Anderson, appointed 1917

Yarmouth, NS

Office opened 1867
John Wentworth Moody, appointed 1866
Bowman Brown Law, appointed 1895

Source: Foreign Affairs Archives, Stockholm; "Förteckning å svenska och norrska consuler, utfärdad af Kongl. Maj:ts och Rikets Commerce-Collegium ..." (1850–69); see also
Kungl, "Utrikesdepartementets kalender 1870–2001"; see also "Swedish Consulates"
on Embassy of Sweden website. Records are missing for the following years: 1939–45,
1947–50, 1952–4, 1956, 1958, 1960, 1962–3, 1965, 1967–8, 1970–1, and 1977.

Honour the Pioneers

Donor	Pioneer/s	Origin	Year to Canada	Settlement	Commemorating
Angus, Patricia, and Dr Lynn Sargeant	Johan Ulrich and Anna Mathilda (Jonasson) Frejd	Undenäs, Västergötland	1887	Bruce Mines, ON	
Anonymous	Oscar and Svea Anderson	Rönnäs, Lappland	1909 1913	Kathyrn, AB	
Axelson, Vivian (Lawson), Gene Edward Axelson, Ellen (Axelson) Smith	Axel Eugene Johansson Axelson	Överklinten, Västerbotten	1928	Geraldton, ON	Wife Vivian Frances Lawson Axelson
Baker, Barbro Nilsson	Brita Nilsson Baker	Torsby, Värmland	1959	Vancouver, BC	
Barber, H. Douglas	Olaf Peter Olson	Dorotea, Lappland	1904	Earl Grey, SK	Olaf and Alma Olson
Barr, Peter and Elinor	Carl and Carolina Berglund	Mäland, Skog, Ångermanland	1907	Finmark, ON	Audrey Broman (1922–2001)
Barr, Peter and Elinor	Neil and Anna Sideen	Bodsjö, Jämtland, and Gräfsåsen, Jämtland	1900	Stanley, ON	Marion Muldoon (1926–2001)
Bissett, Alice (Johnson)	Ingrid (Lofstrom) Johnson	Ballnor, Hälsingland	1912	Chatfield, MB	
Bjorklund, Donna and Sharon	Elis Manfrid and Edit Maria Viktoria (Vikstrom) Björklund	Boden, Norrbotten	1923 1924	Port Arthur, ON	

Name	Relatives	Place of origin	Year	Location	Notes
Bjorkquist, Constance June	Ida Margareta Blomquist	Hede, Härjedalen	1911	Maidstone, SK	
Blaine, Jean	John Peter and Brita (Gärdwall Andersdotter) Bergenham	Hälsingland and Offerdal, Jämtland	1892 1893	Moberly, BC	
Brown, Aina (Bjork) and Gloria (Brown) Roberton	Oskar Emil and Alvina (Lundmark) Bjork	Piteå, Norrbotten	1912 1924	Timmins, ON	Parents and grandparents
Carlson, Evar Yngve	Evert and Hulda (Olson) Carlson	Västergötland and Bohuslän	1912 1908	Simmie District, SK	
Carlson, J. R.	Kristina Persson Carlson	Gagnef, Dalarna	1929	Sudbury, ON	
Carlson, Lynn and Neil	Edwin Otto and Beda Linea (Rosenquist) Carlson	Dalarna and Värmland	1929 1930	Winnipeg, MB	
Carlson, Nancy and family	Gustaf Carlson	Vetlycke, Torsås, Småland	1928	Port Arthur, ON	Grandparents Gus and Vera Carlson
Cousineau, Delsie	Olaf Bernard Olson	Hede, Härjedalen	1911	Sprague, MB	Elin Irene Jarf
Danard, Lillian (Sjodin) and Ann-Mari (Sjodin) Westerback	Erik and Agnes Margareta (Viklund) Sjodin	Bjärtrå, Ångermanland, and Ullånger, Ångermanland	1923 1924	Fort William, ON	
Domier, Elaine	Karl Sundberg family	Söderhamn, Hälsingland	1903	Stockholm, SK	Harald Sundberg
Edwards, Enid A.	Alexander and Svea (Hess) Stenberg	Stockholm	1887	Stockholm, SK	
Enarson, Amy	Gust and Elizabeth Backstrom	Skövde, Västergötland, and Karlstad, Värmland	1898	Highland Park near New Norway, AB	

(Continued)

(Continued)

Donor	Pioneer/s	Origin	Year to Canada	Settlement	Commemorating
Engdahl, Allan and Aina Baron	Emil Ernest and Hannah Engdahl	Färila, Hälsingland, and Hamra, Dalarna	1908 1911	Kenora, ON	Emil and Hannah Engdahl
Epp, A. Ernest	Ingvar Gösta Lundin	Stora Tuna, Dalarna	1927	Winnipeg, MB	
Ersson, Per and Rayhni	Arvid Jonsson	Bodsjö, Jämtland	1922	BC	Wife Ester Jonsson
Ersson, Per and Rayhni	Per and Martha Jonsson	Bodsjö, Jämtland	1926	BC	Amy Danared
Fitzsimmons, Sharon (Peterson)	Andrew Peterson	Livsdal, near Norberg, Västmanland	1908	Rich Valley, AB	
Hamilton, Janet	Anna Dahlin	Jämtland	1893	Ferintosh, AB	Flora Watson and Lois Fraser
Harri, Diane Lynn (Walberg)	Helena Augustina Lundström	Bjursträsk, Norrbotten	1904	Slate River, ON	Renus Alfred Walberg
Harri, Diane Lynn (Walberg)	Nils Alfred Walberg	Vännfors, Vännäs, Västerbotten	1902	Slate River, ON	Renus Alfred Walberg
Harri, Diane Lynn (Walberg)	Olaf Konrad Lindberg	Kasa, Grundsunda, Ångermanland	1902	Slate River, ON	Edith Anna Margaret Lindberg
Harri, Diane Lynn (Walberg)	Olga Carolina Sellin	Själevad, Ångermanland	1902	Slate River, ON	Edith Anna Margaret Lindberg
Havel, Dr J. E.	Anne Marie (Luhr) Havel	Vaxholm, Stockholm archipelago	1959	Montreal, QC, and Sudbury, ON	
Hewitt, Margaret (Ronnander)	Gus and Margaret Delin (Oder) Ronnander	Bjuråker, Hälsingland, and Järvsö, Hälsingland	c1902 1916	Winnipeg, MB	
Hicks, Fay	Sven Svensson	Jämtland	1867	SK	
Hirsch, Ellen (Larson)	Gustaf Adolf Natanael Larsson	Kinneved parish, Västergötland	1927	Edmonton, AB	

Name	People	Place in Sweden	Year	Place in Canada	Notes
Holmes, Janet A. and siblings	Sven Otto Norman	Bjärtrå, Ångermanland	1916	Wabigoon, ON	
Holmgren Family	Jonas "Helmer" and Selma (Westman) Holmgren	Malmberget, Lappland	1908 1910	New Hill, AB	
Johnson, Becky	Johan August Johansson and Anna Britta Börjesdotter	Istorp, Västergötland	1892	Kenora, ON	Ken Johnson (1921–2007)
Johnson, Dr Leavert	Per and Karna (Jönsdotter) Johnson	Östraby, Skåne, and Vollsjö, Skåne	c1893	Malmo District, AB	
Johnson, Elvira "Vera" and Mavis Hyde	Johan Amos and Gustafva Carolina (Haraldson) Johnson	Höreda, Vetlanda, Småland, and Karlstorp parish, Småland	1898 1898	Scandinavia, MB	Carl Amos Victor Johnson
Johnson, John, Kenneth, and Jean	Erik Ruben Norman	Bjärtrå, Ångermanland	1915	Wabigoon, ON	
Johnson, Ken and Isabel	Hans Bernhard and Agda Teolina (Carlson) Magnuson	Tanumshede, Bohuslän	1908 1924	Notre Dame, now Ponteix, SK	
Johnson, Kenneth, Ruth, Ross (dec.), and Sharon	John Helmer and Anna Erika (Norman) Johnson	Strinne, Bjärtrå, Ångermanland, and Pitholmen, Piteå, Norrbotten	1912 1916	Wabigoon, ON	Parents Anna and John
Johnson, W.R. and Gayle	Signe (Berglund) Johnson	Nora, Ångermanland	1907	Finmark, ON, and Hendersonville, NC	

(Continued)

(Continued)

Donor	Pioneer/s	Origin	Year to Canada	Settlement	Commemorating
Johnstone, Irene M.	Marcus August Sylvester and Elizabet Katerina (Eriksson) Blomquist	Åsele, Lappland	1912	Hayter, AB	Grandparents and uncles Fred and Eric who died 1914 on the Empress of Ireland
Jones, Keith and Carol	Mary (Karlsson) and Charlie Johnson born Knut Håkansson	Gräfsåsen, Jämtland, and southern Sweden	1909 before 1911	Port Arthur, ON	
Kletke, Herb and Helen	Johan Hornfeldt and Eva Amalia (Eriksdotter) Holmstrom	Bursjöholmen, Arnäs, Ångermanland, and Åsele, Lappland	1910 1911	Inwood, MB	
Knisley, Roberta (Jones)	Neil and Anna Sideen	Bodsjö, Jämtland, and Gräfsåsen, Jämtland	1900	Stanley, ON	Ellen (Sideen) Jones (1907–1992)
Knutson, James	Hanna Wahlgren Knutson	Hjorted, Småland	1889	Waterville, QC	
Knutson, Marilyn	Ann Anderson	Hallaryd parish, Småland	1900	Stratton, ON	
Knutson, Marilyn	Anna Andersson	Sweden	1920	Stratton, ON	
Landine, Maureen	John and Karin Persson	Torsby, Värmland	1892	Stockholm, SK	
Landine, Maureen	Kristoffer and Inga Landin	Åsele, Lappland	1903	Stockholm, SK	
Lilja, Adolph, and Selma (Lilja) Reid	Carl Johan Lilja	Dalskog, Dalsland	1916	Hayter, AB	Emma Lilja
Lilja, Bob and Elsie	Karl Johan Lilja	Dalskog, Dalsland	1916	Hayter, AB	
Lind, Luella	Ernst Valdemar Lind	Kålhög, Lilla Ryland, Tanumshede, Bohuslän	1927	Calgary, AB	Father, grandfather and great-grandfather

Name	Person	Place (Sweden)	Year	Place (Canada)	Relationship
Lind, Luella	Karl Vincent Lind	Raftötången, Bohuslän	1920	Cochrane, AB	Uncle
Lindholm, family of Ernest	Charles and Anna Christina (Ohman) Lindholm	Lovsberg, Småland, and Delsbo, Hälsingland	1902 1897	New Norway, AB	
Linneborg, Henry's children	Nils (Gullickson) and Frida Maria Augusta (Holmgren) Linneborg	Malmberget, Lappland	1907	New Hill, AB	
Lockhart, Elsie	Gustav Julius (Hellberg) Hill	Södertälje, Södermanland	1910	Vancouver, BC	Father
Lockhart, Elsie	Judith Sofia (Solberg) Hill	Stockholm	1912	Vancouver, BC	Mother
Loov, Verner Bertil	Edwin Anders William and Augusta Carlotta (Carlson Loov	Älmhult, Småland	1927 1928	AB	Parents William and Asta Loov, and sister Solveig (Loov) Penner
Lundgren, Margaret	Carl Fritiof (Israelson) Melin	Sandås, Lappland	1902	Meeting Creek, AB	
Maertens-Poole, Beverly J.	Sven Emil Folke (Nilsson) Nelson	Mörlunda, Småland	1928	Hughenden, AB	
Matson, Harold E.	Gustaf Eugene and Tea Viktoria (Salomonsson) Mattson	Norrbyskär, Västerbotten	1913	Fort William, ON, area	
McDonald, Helen E.	Beata (Johansson) Swanson	Kinnared, Halland	1887	Vancouver, BC	Hilma Anna Justina (Swanson)
McGlade, Meliny	Staffin and Anna (Forsberg) Melin	Strädalen, Härjedalen	1912	Weldon, SK	

(Continued)

(Continued)

Donor	Pioneer/s	Origin	Year to Canada	Settlement	Commemorating
Monkman, Lois (Enborg)	Swan Enborg	Burseryd, Småland	1887	Port Arthur, ON	Parents Swan and Rose Enborg
Moslenko, Dorothy, and Muriel Macdonald	Peter and Bertha (Bjorklund) Berglund	Nora, Ångermanland, and Värmland	1907 1907	Finmark, ON, and Fort William, ON	
Ness, Jason	Gustav Edvard Åkerström and Brita Selina Linde	Bergsjö and Hassela, Hälsingland	1902 1904	Lake De May, AB	Esther Catherine (Akerstrom) Ness
Nordstrom, Carol John	Carl and Hilda Nordstrom	Gaddaröd, Skåne, and Löddeköpinge, Skåne	1909	Canwood, SK	
Nordstrom, Sylvia	Elis R. Malby	Gävle, Gästrikland	1956	Port Arthur, ON	
Nordstrom, Sylvia	John Erland Göte Nordstrom	Järbo, Gästrikland	1964	Port Arthur, ON	
Norlander, Ivan	E. Manfred Norlander	Nora, Ångermanland	1929	Norquay, SK	Parents E. Manfred and Mable Grace (Haglund) Norlander
Nystrom, Karen	Nils Viktor Nystrom	Piteå, Norrbotten	1914	Wabigoon, ON	Bert E. Nystrom
Nystrom, Karen	Olga Katrina Nystrom	Strinne, Bjärträ Ångermanland	1916	Kenora, ON	
Ohrn, Ralph	Erik Gotthard and Matilda (Eliason) Öhrn	Hamrånge parish, Gästrikland, and Morrum, Blekinge	1900	Warburg, AB	
Olafson, Karl and Ruth	Fridolf Svante and Hilma (Palmgren) Olofson	Norraryd, Skåne, and Vermanshult, Skåne	1923 1928	Sioux Lookout, ON, and Port Arthur, ON	
Olson Family	Olaf Bernard Olson	Hede, Härjedalen	1911	Sprague, MB	Elin Irene Jarf

Olson, Norman D.	Erick and Sofia (Swenson) Paulson	Laxsjö, Jämtland	1909	Bawlf, AB	
Oslund, Stone E.	Axel Sigurd Åslund	Jämtland	1924	Sioux Lookout, ON	
Pearson, Ida (Johnson)	Carl J. and Olga (Carlson) Johnson	Småland and Västmanland	1894 1895	Scandinavia and Erickson, MB	
Peterson, Sharon	Andrew Peterson	Livsdal, near Norberg, Västmanland	1908	Rich Valley, AB	
Petersson, Marion (Ringwall)	Peter (Ericksson) and Gölin (Skanse) Ringwall	Överhogdal, Hälsingland	1900	Ferintosh, AB	
Petersson, Sandra	Hilda Johansson Hansson	Knarrebo Åby, Småland	1928	Edmonton, AB	
Petersson, Sandra	Oskar Eskil Hansson	Stockholm	1927	Edmonton, AB	
Roberton, Gloria and Lorne and family	Aina Marie (Bjork) Brown	Piteå, Norrbotten	1924	Timmins, ON	Mother
Rydman, Harold and Perry	Gustav and Hulda Rydman	Tingsås, Småland	1908	Edmonton, AB	
Ryland, Ida	Sven Arthur Justinus Carlson	Fyrunga, Västergötland	1910	Swift Current, SK	
Sahlstrom, Robert and Gregory	Karl Johan Sahlström II	Utterbyn, Torsby, Värmland	1905	Thorsby, AB, and Castlegar, BC	Gwen Killough Sahlstrom
Sargent, Margo E.	Justus (Svensson) Swanson	Älmehult, Småland	1891	Vancouver, BC	Johan Ragnvald (John R.) Swanson
Shellborn, Lula	Anders and Beda Jansson	Smedjebacken, Dalarna, and Kramfors, Ångermanland	1894	Scandinavia (Erickson), MB	

(Continued)

(Continued)

Donor	Pioneer/s	Origin	Year to Canada	Settlement	Commemorating
Shellborn, Lula	John August and Kristina Skoglund	Kramfors, Ångermanland	1893	Hilltop District (Erickson), MB	
Sideen, Wesley and Carol Ann, and Neil and Carol Sideen	Anna Regina (Karlsson) Sideen	Gräfsåsen, Jämtland	1900	Stanley, ON	Marion Muldoon (1926–2001)
Simonson, Ted	Edwin Otto Carlson	Dalarna	1929	Winnipeg, MB	
Simonson, Ted	Märta Ingeborg (Hallquist) Simonson	Larv, Västergötland	1928	Winnipeg, MB	Doug Simonson
Simonson, Ted	Nils Valfrid and Märta Ingeborg (Hallquist) Bengtsson	Larv, Västergötland	1928	Winnipeg, MB	Ed Carlson
Sjoberg, Edna	Lars and Emelie (Persson) Oman	Kärråkra, Västergötland	1886	Clanwilliam, MB	
Sjoberg, grandsons Lawrence and Donald	Johan and Margareta Sillen	Sihl, Ångermanland	1892 1895	Scandinavia, MB	
Sjoberg, grandsons Lawrence and Donald	Johan and Clara Sjöberg	Vindeln, Västerbotten	1904 1905	Clanwilliam, MB	
Skandia Lodge #549	Edvin Emanuel Bergqvist	Skellefteå, Västerbotten	1928	Edmonton, AB	
Skandia Lodge #549	Julius Carlson	Spekeröd, Bonhuslän		Edmonton, AB	
Skandia Lodge #549	Einar Erickson	Östrafors, Malung, Dalarna		Edmonton, AB	
Skandia Lodge #549	Carl Johan Gottfrid Friedholm	Madesjö, Kalmar, Småland		Edmonton, AB	
Skandia Lodge #549	Julius Hober	Jämtland		Edmonton, AB	

Skandia Lodge #549	Minnie (Larsson) Nelson	Vingåker, Södermanland		Edmonton, AB	
Skandia Lodge #549	David Ernst Norén	Östmark, Värmland		Edmonton, AB	
Skandia Lodge #549	Aksel Pearson			Edmonton, AB	
Skandia Lodge #549	Bror Wilhelm Persson	Lund, Skåne	1928	Edmonton, AB	
Skandia Lodge #549	Eric Pierre	Hällesjö, Jämtland	1927	Edmonton, AB	
Skandia Lodge #549	Karl Bruno Ramstedt	Mörsil, Jämtland		Edmonton, AB	Wife Elsie Ramstedt
Skandia Lodge #549	Albin Samuelson	Lattefors		Edmonton, AB	
Skandia Lodge #549	Anna Skoog	Berg, Jämtland		Edmonton, AB	
Skandia Lodge #549	Hans Skoog	Kyrkås, Jämtland		Edmonton, AB	
Skandia Lodge #549	Abraham Wahlgren	Vålänger, Ångermanland		Edmonton, AB	
Smith, Ellen (Axelson)	Axel Eugene Axelson	Överklinten, Västerbotten	1928	Geraldton, ON	Axel Eugene Axelson and Gene Edward Axelson
Smith, W. Robert and Helen Elizabeth Smith Conrad	Charles John and Martha Agnes (Granlund) Erickson	Stockholm and Stöde, Medelpad	1907 1907	Clyde, AB, and Metiskow, AB	
Sund, Sonja (Winquist)	Albert Hjalmar Winquist	Hökon, Loshult, Skåne	1915	Edmonton, AB	
Sundmark, Vernon, Cecil, Carol, and Maitland	John and Johanna Sundmark	Kramfors, Ångermanland, and Söderköping, Östergötland	1893 1895	Erickson, MB	John and Johanna Sundmark
Syslak, Walter	Carl and Anna C. Booth	Gunnilbo, Västmanland, and Ånglefors	1893	Hilltop, MB	
Tennis, Leonard	Johan (Kristiansen) and Anna Tennis	Gammalsvenskby, Ukraine	1890	Ferintosh, AB	

(Continued)

(Continued)

Donor	Pioneer/s	Origin	Year to Canada	Settlement	Commemorating
Tornblom, Erik	Hildur and Ivar Tornblom	Söderhamn, Hälsingland	1912	Harstone, ON	
Trepanier, Kathy	John Birger Sjoberg	Vindeln, Västerbotten	1905	Clanwilliam, MB	
Vasa Pioneers #12 and Skandia Lodge #549	Arvid Jonas Nelson	Umeå, Västerbotten	1909	Edmonton, AB	Arvid Jonas Nelson and his wife, Minnie Evelyn Larson, founders of Skandia Lodge #549, Edmonton
Wicklund children, Linnea, George, and Alma	Nils and Signe (Gustafson) Wicklund	Björne, Ångermanland and Hässle, Småland	Before 1920 1920	Edmonton, AB	
Wickman, Sharon	Frans Oscar Teodor and Anna Augusta Wickman,	Piteå, Norrbotten	c1909	Pellatt Township, ON	
Wickstrom, family of Stan and Betty	Peter Adolph and Eugenia Maria Amelia (Johnson) Wickstrom	Enanegar, Hälsingland and Sundsvall, Medelpad	1918	Calgary, AB	
Williams, Esther	Oscar and Svea Anderson	Hajom, Västergötland, and Småland	1910 1913	Keoma, AB	
Williams, Richard and Karen	Johan Sigfrid Anderson	Kinnared, Halland	1889	Revelstoke and Victoria, BC	Lillian Williams
Williams, Richard and Karen	Lydia Ericsson	Forshaga, Värmland	1899	Revelstoke and Victoria, BC	Lillian Williams

Notes

1. Under an Invisibility Cloak

1 H. Arnold Barton, "Why Don't We Know More about the Swedes in Canada?," *Swedish Pioneer Historical Quarterly* 28, no. 2 (1977): 79–81.

2 H. Arnold Barton, "Editor's Introduction," *Swedish-American Historical Quarterly* 33, no. 1 (1982): 3. With this issue the *Swedish Pioneer Historical Quarterly* changed its name to *Swedish-American Historical Quarterly*.

3 Harald Runblom, "The Swedes in Canada: A Study in Low Ethnic Consciousness," *Swedish-American Historical Quarterly* 33, no. 1 (1982): 4–20, translated by Raymond Jarvi from "Svenskarna i Canada. En studie i låg etnisk medvetenhet," in *Historieforskning på nya vägar: Studier tillägnade Sten Carlsson*, ed. Lars-Göran Tedebrand (Lund: Studentlitt, 1977), 213–28. For a similar article on Scandinavians as a group, see Jörgen Dahlie, "Scandinavian Immigration, Assimilation and Settlement Patterns in Canada: Large Landscape Limited Impact?" in *Finns in North America: Proceedings*, ed. Edward W. Laine, Olavi Koivukangas, and Michael G. Karni (Turku, Finland: Siirtolaisuusinstituutti, 1988), 9–12.

4 Lars Ljungmark, "Swedes in Winnipeg up to the 1940s: Inter-ethnic Relations" in *Swedish Life in American Cities*, ed. Dag Blanck and Harald Runblom (Uppsala: Centre for Multiethnic Research, 1991), 64–6. The book *Sweden: The Middle Way*, written by the American Marquis Childs and published in 1936, chronicled his research on the reform policies of the Swedish Social Democratic Party. It became an international bestseller.

5 The Danish Federation is actively collecting research material, and publishes documents, articles, and memoirs in an impressive hardcover book presented at its annual Heritage Seminars. This umbrella

organization plans to open the Danish Canadian National Museum and Gardens in Spruce View, Alberta, in 2010.

6 Carina Rönnqvist, *Svea folk i Babels land: Svensk identitet i Kanada under 1900-talets första hälft* (Umeå: Kulturgräns norr, 2004), with an English summary on pages 319–25.

7 Gerald Friesen, *The Canadian Prairies: A History* (Toronto: University of Toronto Press, 1984), 244.

8 Rönnqvist, *Svea folk i Babels land*, 322, 328.

9 Dag Blanck, *Becoming Swedish-American: The Construction of an Ethnic Identity in the Augustana Synod, 1869–1917* (Uppsala: Uppsala University, 1997). Reprinted with an added index as *The Creation of an Ethnic Identity: Being Swedish American in the Augustana Synod, 1860–1917* (Carbondale: Southern Illinois University Press, 2006).

10 Ibid., 23.

11 Carina Rönnqvist, "Scattered Swedes and Single Settlers: On Ethnic Identity Reflected in Nationalistic Sentiments, Gender and Class in 20th-Century Canada," in *Swedishness Reconsidered: Three Centuries of Swedish-American Identities*, ed. Daniel Lindmark (Umeå: Kulturgräns norr, 1999), 94, states that "Swedishness in Canada was more a matter of private feelings and liaisons than of an organized unity."

12 As paraphrased in William C. Wonders, "Scandinavian Homesteaders in Central Alberta," in *The New Provinces: Alberta and Saskatchewan 1905–1980*, ed. H.B. Palmer and D.B. Smith (Vancouver: Tantalus Research, 1980), 164.

13 Ibid., 187–99.

14 Allan Kastrup, *The Swedish Heritage in America: The Swedish Element in America and American-Swedish Relations in Their Historical Perspective* (Minneapolis: Swedish Council of America, 1975), 703–6.

15 University of British Columbia Library, Special Collections (henceforth UBCL SC), Matthew Lindfors Fonds, A IV B; M.M. Lindfors, Vancouver, to Esse W. Ljungh, Winnipeg, 14 March 1938; see also Frank Torell, Associate Director, Swedish American Tercentenary Association Incorporated, Chicago, to M.M. Lindfors, Vancouver, 17 May 1938.

16 Scandinavian Heritage Project, Oscar Johnson Collection; *Souvenir Programme, Tercentenary 1638–1938 All Swedes' Day, Port Arthur and Fort William, Sunday, July 17*th; see also "Lakehead Swedes Mark Settlers' Day," *Port Arthur News-Chronicle*, 18 July 1938; see also "Swedish Picnic Committee," *Fort William Daily Times-Journal*, 18 July 1938; see also *Souvenir Programme, Second Annual All Swedes' Day, Port Arthur – Fort William, Queen's Park, Port Arthur, Sunday, July 16, 1939*; see also "District

Swedes Unite at Second Annual Picnic," *Port Arthur News-Chronicle*, 17 July 1939.

17 Emigrant Institute, Växjö, Sweden: "Stories of Swedish Pioneers in North America: A Selection of Essays submitted in a Contest in 1948 sponsored by the Swedish American Line to commemorate the Swedish Pioneer Centennial, presented to Emigrantinstitutet utvandrarnas hus, Växjö, by G. Hilmer Lundbeck."

18 Eva St Jean, "Swedes on the Move: Politics, Culture, and Work among Swedish Immigrants in British Columbia, 1900–1950," PhD diss., University of Victoria, 2004, 282.

19 Per Anders Rudling, "Scandinavians in Canada: A Community in the Shadow of the United States," *Swedish-American Historical Quarterly* 57, no. 3 (July 2006): 151–94.

20 Lars Ljungmark, *Swedish Exodus*, trans. Kermit Westerberg (Carbondale: Southern Illinois University Press, 1979), 11. Revised translation of *Den stora utvandringen*, 1965.

21 Gulbrand Loken, *From Fjord to Frontier: A History of the Norwegians in Canada* (Toronto: McClelland and Stewart, 1980), 13, which states that "Norwegian statistics report that of 49,600 emigrants in the period from 1854 to 1865, all but 2,800 came to America via the Quebec route."

22 Jesus Lopez-Pacheco, "'America': It Goes with Everything, Like it or Not," *The Globe and Mail*, 1 August 1995.

23 During a visit to Scotland in 1984 a tourism worker wrote "American" beside my name in his record book. When I explained that I was Canadian he stated that it was the same thing. He did not understand the difference until being asked if he would like to be called an Englishman.

24 R. Zoumer, "Ett brev från Kanada," *Bryggan/The Bridge* 3, no. 3 (1971): 68–9.

25 Åke Daun, *The Swedish Mentality*, trans. Jan Teeland, foreword by David Cooperman (Pennsylvania State University Press, 1996), 52, 207. Thanks to Joanna Daxell for bringing the Jante Law to my attention. For an irreverent discussion on the Swedish character, see Colin Moon, *Sweden the Secret Files: What They'd Rather Keep to Themselves* (Sweden: Today Press, 2008); see also Gillis Herlitz, *Swedes: What We Are Like and Why We Are as We Are* (Uppsala: Konsultförlaget, 1995).

26 Formerly the Manitoba Museum of Man and Nature.

27 Carl Gustav Boberg (1859–1940) composed the lyrics as a poem, "O större Gud," in 1885 after being awed by the majesty of a thunderstorm. After its publication in a Småland newspaper the following year he turned the rights over to the Covenant Church (*Svenska missionsförbundet*). In 1888

he listened to his lyrics being sung to an old Swedish folk melody in a church in the neighbouring province of Värmland. The original hymn was translated into English by Stuart K. Hine as "How Great Thou Art," and popularized in North America by George Beverly Shea on Billy Graham crusades beginning in Toronto in 1954, and by Elvis Presley in his album of the same name in 1967. Boberg served as editor of the Christian weekly *Sanningsvittnet* (Witness to the Truth) from 1890 to 1916 and was elected to the Swedish parliament, where he served from 1912 to 1931.

28 Carl Jularbo (1893–1966) was born Karl Karlsson in Jularbo, Dalarna. He had a very distinctive musical style that played a significant role in forming the Swedish accordion tradition. Although he could not read music his repertoire included more than 1,500 tunes. His son Ebbe Jularbo (1915–1991) carried on the tradition, and Jularbo clubs exist in both Sweden and Norway.

29 Other Swedish words in Canadian dictionaries are "ombudsman" and "orienteering."

30 Irene Larson, "The Bergstrom-Erickson Family," in *Caviar and Venison: Memories of Lettonia and Newcombe,* ed. Vivian Nespor and Ray (Sonny) Burnside (Winnipeg, 1991), 61.

31 David G. Delafenêtre, "The Scandinavian Presence in Canada: Emerging Perspectives," *Canadian Ethnic Studies* 27, no. 2 (1995): 46.

32 "Hört och hänt: Arthur A. Anderson: Svensk konsul, skald, SAL-chef, kördirigent m.m.," *Svenska Pressen,* 21 March 1956.

33 Lilly Setterdahl, comp., *Swedish-American Newspapers: A Guide to the Microfilms held by Swenson Swedish Immigration Research Center, Augustana College, Rock Island, Illinois* (Sioux Falls: Augustana College Library, 1981), 34–5.

34 UBCL SC, A VII B, Seaholm Collection; Erik Kjellberg, Stockholm, Sweden, to Olof Seaholm, Vancouver, 21 August 1973.

35 Correspondence with Erik Kjellberg, Stockholm, 9 February 2003.

36 Matthew Lindfors (1899–1971), long-time editor of *Nya svenska pressen,* was deeply involved with Swedish activities in Vancouver, bringing Swedish films and radio programs to British Columbia and the Prairies. His fonds include correspondence, speeches, manuscripts, publicity material, and photographs.

37 Olof Seaholm (1897–198?) was born Olof Sjöbom in Östberget, Linsell, Härjedalen, and immigrated in 1928. He married Minnie Davidson in 1951 and retired from Willock Industries Limited in 1965. He belonged to most of Vancouver's Swedish organizations. His collection includes photographs and negatives, newspaper clippings, magazines, books,

the published poems of Sven Seaholm (no relation), and organizational records for Härjedalsgillet, IOGT, Scandinavian Central Committee, and Swedish Canadian Rest Home. See Carol Black, *Härjedalsgillet* (North Vancouver, 1983), 253–4; see also UBCL SC, Olof Seaholm Collection, A VII B, Box 1, handwritten autobiography, 3 pages.

38 These include the organizational records of IOGT Lodge Linnea #76. UBCL SC also houses the Peter B. Anderson Fonds, Paul Boving Fonds, and the Swedish Cultural Society records for 1949 to 1970.

39 Elinor Berglund Barr, *The Swedish Experience in Canada: An Annotated Bibliography* (Växjö: Emigrant Institute, 1991).

40 Ibid., 5.

41 Pamela Wallin (1953–) grew up in Wadena, Saskatchewan, the daughter of William and Leone Wallin. She became Canada's consul general in New York.

42 Ralph Gustafson (1909–1995) was born in Lime Ridge, QC, the son of Carl Otto Gustafson, who immigrated in 1896 from Växjö, Småland. He wrote more than twenty-nine books of poetry and edited several anthologies of Canadian poetry. See Ralph Gustafson, "A Preface and some Poems: Canada's Kinship with Scandinavia," *Northward Journal: A Quarterly of Northern Arts, The Nordic Issue* 18–19 (1980): 75.

43 Emigrant Institute, Växjö, "Stories of Swedish Pioneers in North America," #500, James B. Thompson, "Swedish Settlers in Canada and Their Influence," 8–9.

44 Irene Howard, *Vancouver's Svenskar: A History of the Swedish Community in Vancouver* (Vancouver: Vancouver Historical Society, 1970), 75.

2. Emigration from Sweden, Immigration to Canada

1 Emory Lindquist, "Appraisals of Sweden and America by Swedish Emigrants: The Testimony of Letters in *Emigrationsutredningen* (1907)," *Swedish Pioneer Historical Quarterly* 17, no. 2 (April 1966): 78–95.

2 Translations are *"Att skära guld med täljkniv," "Lätt fånget – lätt förgånget," "Det är inte guld allt som glimmar,"* and *"Stundom finner även en blind höna ett korn."* Thanks to Stenåke Petersson, Släktforskarnas hus, Leksand, for suggesting these homilies.

3 The Swedes in Canada Immigrant Database consists of twenty-five fields, including name, sex, parents' names, birthplace in Sweden, birthplace if not in Sweden, year of birth, year of emigration, year and destination of immigration to USA, USA information, year and destination of immigration to Canada, age of immigrant, reason for

emigration, year and place of marriage, name of spouse, number of children born in Sweden, number of children born in North America, place and province of residence, whether permanent resident or not, occupation, religion, year and place of death, notes, and source/s of information. The entries are taken from published and unpublished materials. Principal publications are twelve histories from Alberta, seven from Saskatchewan, and three each from British Columbia, Manitoba, and Ontario, as well as eight from Sweden (Arnoldsson's *Amerika-emigranterna från Örkened*, Wickström's "Bland svenskar i Canada" in *Genom sju kungariken*, Nilsson's *De sista svenska rösterna, En Smålandssocken emigrerar*, Österberg's *Från Calmare Nyckel till Leif Viking*, Andersson's *Långarydssläkten*, Hedman's *Svenskbysläkter*, and the Landelius Biography Collection), assisted by *CD Emigranten* (2001). Unpublished items include family histories, individual profiles, memoirs, correspondence, oral histories, Attestation Papers from the First World War, the Census of Canada, the membership list for Strindberg Vasa Lodge in Winnipeg, and the research material for my Scandinavian Heritage Project. The provinces (*landskap*) rather than the counties (administrative districts, or *län*) represent geographical boundaries.

4 A total of 1,740 persons came from Norrland: Jämtland 441, Lappland 329, Ångermanland 231, Hälsingland 218, Härjedalen 146, Västerbotten 134, Medelpad 130, and Norrbotten 111.

5 A total of 1,425 persons came from Göteland: Småland 573, Skåne 363, Västergötland 155, Östergötland 67, Halland 63, Bohuslän 52, Göteborg 38, Dalsland 32, Blekinge 29, Malmö 25, Öland 18, and Gotland 10.

6 A total of 733 persons came from Svealand: Dalarna 286, Värmland 172, Stockholm 119, Västmanland 50, Gästrikland 40, Södermanland 24, Uppland 24, and Närke 18.

7 Franklin D. Scott, "Sweden's Constructive Opposition to Emigration," *The Journal of Modern History* (September 1965): 335.

8 Franklin D. Scott, *Sweden: The Nation's History* (Minneapolis: University of Minnesota Press, 1977), 373.

9 Gösta Bagge and E.H. Thornberg, *Emigrationsutredningen*, vol. 7, part 1: *Manliga utvandrare under år 1907*; and Kerstin Hesselgren, part 2: *Kvinnliga utvandrare under år 1907*.

10 *Emigrationsutredningen*, vol. 7, part 3, "N:r 200, H.M., Canada. Emigrerade 1883. Från Kristianstads län," 174.

11 Ibid., "N:r 216, C.W.H., Canada. Emigrerade 1893. Från Uppsala län," 189.

12 Lars Ljungmark, "On Emigration, Social Mobility, and the Transfer of Capital," *Swedish-American Historical Quarterly* 41, no. 3 (1990): 161, citing

Emigrationsutredningen 29 (1910): 74. Dollar amounts are based on the 1899 exchange rate according to Riksbank Sverige: 1 krona = US$.26.

13 Scott, "Sweden's Constructive Opposition to Emigration," 316.

14 Adrian Molin, *Några drag af kolonisationen i Canada* (Some Features of the Colonization in Canada), (Stockholm: Geber, 1913). Another book, *Hur svenskamerikanerna bo* (How Swedish-Americans Live), dealt in a similar way with housing and neighbourhoods in North American cities, complete with floor plans and city maps.

15 Molin, *Några drag af kolonisationen i Canada*, 50–1.

16 Sten Carlsson, "Why Did They Leave?" in *Perspectives on Swedish Immigration: Proceedings of the International Conference on the Swedish Heritage in the Upper Midwest, April 1–3, 1976, University of Minnesota, Duluth*, ed. Nils Hasselmo (Chicago: Swedish Pioneer Historical Society, 1978), 25–35. See also Lars Ljungmark, "Push and Pull Factors Behind the Swedish Emigration to America, Canada, and Australia," in *European Expansion and Migration: Essays on the Intercontinental Migration from Africa, Asia, and Europe*, ed. P.C. Emmer and M. Mörner (New York: Berg, 1992), 79–103.

17 For an explanation of the agricultural crisis, see Lars Ljungmark and Sune Åkerman, "The Unknown Emigration – Swedes in Canada 1870–1970," in *Migration i ett norrländskt perspektiv* (Arkiv i Norrland 16, 1998), 82–7.

18 Only two small pockets of Swedish immigrants were found, one in Dunnville, Ontario, and the other in Sherbrooke, Quebec. Three occupations suggest prior arrangements for employment: furriers in Montreal, a dyer in Sherbrooke, and watchmakers in St John's, Newfoundland.

19 I am grateful to Elisabeth Thorsell, Järfälla, for providing a diskette of this database. Sten Aminoff left Canada to become Swedish ambassador in New Zealand from 1974 to 1979, and his book *Svenskarna i Nya Zeeland* (The Swedes in New Zealand) was published in Sweden in 1988. Had he remained in Canada, he might have written a similar history here.

20 In 1861 Thomas Johnsen and three younger brothers lived with their wives in South Malbaie, Gaspé, where they worked at fishing and farming, and Catherine Wood and her husband were farming in Oxford County, Ontario.

21 Some of the individuals in Aminoff's database have not been included because of obvious error or insufficient information.

22 A. Ernest Epp, *Nordic People in Canada: A Study in Demography 1861–2001*, research report for the Lakehead Social History Institute, Thunder Bay, 2004, table 1.

23 Scott, *Sweden*, 413.

24 Ibid., 417.

25 Henry Bengston, "Autobiography," 1, original manuscript for "Upplevelser Östanhavs och Västanhavs," in *Bryggan/The Bridge* (1970–2), translated by his daughter Margit Fredrickson, Northfield, Minnesota.

26 Lars-Göran Tedebrand, "Strikes and Political Radicalism in Sweden and Emigration to the United States," *Swedish-American Historical Quarterly* 34, no. 3 (July 1983): 198–200, 205–7; see also Nils-Gustav Hildeman, "Swedish Strikes and Emigration," *Swedish Pioneer Historical Quarterly* 8, no. 3 (1957): 87–9.

27 Lars Ljungmark, *Svenskarna i Winnipeg: Porten till prärien 1872–1940* (Växjö: Emigrantinstitutets vänner, 1994), 120–4. One of those undoubtedly involved was Helmer Johnson (ca. 1879–1953), a building contractor who lived in Winnipeg from 1909 to 1953. He was an avid Social Democrat and not at all shy about expressing his political opinions. See Landelius Biography Collection, volume 2, #142.

28 Tedebrand, "Strikes and Political Radicalism in Sweden," 203.

29 Lars Johan Jansson (1868–1922) was born in Västgöthöjden Ullehytte, Gustav Adolf, Värmland, and in 1891 married Anna Kristina Olsson (1868–19?), from Skog, Gästrikland; they had five children from 1891 to 1903. Lars-Janne, as he became known, also had a liaison with Amanda Ulrika Johansson (1872–1954) from Kimstad, Östergötland, widow of his brother, August Johansson. Lars-Janne and his first wife divorced in 1911, and that year she immigrated to Camrose, Alberta, with her three youngest children to join the two eldest. Life was not easy for the families of labour activists, especially of those with a roving eye. Jansson died in Siggängen, Sala, Västmanland, at the age of fifty-seven. Thanks to Stig Söderberg, Askim, Sweden, for family information. See also *Magnolia: The First Hundred Years* (Entwhistle, AB: Magnolia Press, 2000), 156–7.

30 Roland Svensson, "Lars-Janne: Den störste av Gustavas folkrörelsepionjärer," *Gustavabygden 2005*, nr. 47, 14–16; nr. 48, 4–7; *Gustavabygden 2006*, nr. 49, 7–8.

31 The seven Swedes who filed on homesteads in Magnolia in 1905 were Olaf Brandt, Nils Anton Gylander, Lars-Janne Jansson, Joe Larson, A. Lunnell, Oscar Rostrum, and Edwin Thomeus. See Edwin Thomeus, *Letters of a Swedish Homesteader: Life in Magnolia 1905–1912*, trans. Harold Anderson (Stony Plain, AB: Library and Archives Committee, Multicultural Heritage Centre, 1983), 5.

32 *Magnolia*, 258. The sale price was $3,000.

33 Agnes Johansson (19?–1918) married Otto Anderson (18?–1935) in 1907,
    and the couple filed on a homestead where seven children were born.
    Otto had grown up in Västergötland and immigrated to Alberta in 1906
    via the United States.

34 Thomeus, "Mrs. Amanda Jonsson," *Magnolia*, 256–9.

35 Ella Forssell Wickstrom, Karin Edberg-Lee, and Linda Eide Kask,
    Recollections of Silverhill: An Informal History of an Immigrant Settlement
    (Vancouver, 1990). The blacklisted men who sailed from England on the
    CPR steamship *Lake Manitoba* in 1909 were Jonas Gidlöf, Oscar Forssell,
    Henry Green, Ivar Johnson, Oskar Johanson, and Syver Lowe.

36 Carina Rönnqvist, "Från ett framtidsland till ett annat:
    1900-talsutvandringen från Norrbotten till Kanada," *Oknytt 3–4* (2002):
    50–72. The first group consisted mainly of families, and the second of
    single men.

37 Albin Plym, "Tolv år i Canadas vildmarker," in *Från Calmare Nyckel till
    Leif Viking: Ett samlingsverk för in- och utvandrare, svenskar ute och hemma*,
    ed. C. Österberg (Stockholm: Riksinstitutet för släkt- och bygdeforskning,
    1959), 65. Albin Plym was born near Jönköping, Småland, and in 1909
    immigrated to Canada. He was working in Rossland, British Columbia,
    before returning to Sweden in 1921.

38 Johan Gabrielsson Ståhl (18?–1960) was born in Jämtland. Both he and his
    brother Hermann had participated in the labour demonstration with Per
    Nilsson-Tannér, who contacted them ca. 1968 because he planned to write
    a history of Jämtland's labour movement. As the family was leaving for
    Canada, a man approached Johan to confess his guilt and that Johan had
    been wrongfully accused. See Dolores Welsh, "Familjen Ståhl i Canada,"
    Bodsjöboken (1999): 13–14, trans.Lennart Brunfelt. Thanks to Norman
    Olsson, St Albert, Alberta, for donating a copy of a letter he sent to Mrs
    Olof Johnson, Fosston, Saskatchewan, 25 May 1980.

39 Axel Wallgren (1838–1911) was born in Ejstad socken, Gotland, the son
    of a pastor. In 1863 he married Henrique Beata Klingstedt (1846–1926)
    from Torp, Orust, Bohuslän, and they had ten children. Axel emigrated in
    1890, when the youngest child was ten, and returned to Sweden in 1909.
    His wife would have nothing to do with him, and he died in Stockholm,
    where his son Åke lived. See Folke Elfving, "Minnen från Resteröd,"
    Minnesbilder från Ljungskilebygden (Ljungskileortens hembygdsföreningen,
    1995), 9–21.

40 Erik Adrian Giöbel (1899–1977) was born in Närke, the second son in
    a middle-class family. His father was descended from Paulus Giöbel, a
    glassblower from Bohemia, who migrated to Sweden via Norway in the

1700s. His mother, Anna Bolling, came from a military family in Västerås. In 1906 his father, whose father before him was a forester, became head of the Board of Crown Forests and Lands in Stockholm, and bought a large property at Tullinge, where he built the family home. He died in 1925.

41 Ingrid Giöbel-Lilja, *Erik for till Canada* (Stockholm, 1985), 7. Her first book, an autobiography, was titled *Att gå i gräsen*. Ingrid travelled to Canada in 1980 to piece together the story of Erik's struggle for existence, freedom, and dignity. She tells of his being cheated out of $100 for a non-existent course in Toronto, then in 1936 writing a letter to *Svenska Canada-tidningen* from a Salvation Army hostel. Erik was a loner, which is not surprising, given his background, and turned to music and the Swedenborgian religion for consolation.

42 Bror Nils Ivar Granevall (1911–1966) was born in Mörrum, Blekinge, and signed up with the Swedish Merchant Marine until breaking his leg in 1932. The following year he married his nurse, Asta Märta Botilda Håkansson (1910–1966) from Karlshamn, Blekinge, and changed his surname from Gummesson to Granevall. He worked as editor of a weekly newsmagazine in Göteborg until 1940, then, for health reasons, went back to farming in Lindholmen. Thanks to son Nels Granewall, Victoria, British Columbia, for family information.

43 Harald Fegræus (1862–1940) was born in Stenkumla, Gotland, the son of land surveyor Ludwig Fegræus. He studied English and engineering, and applied to the CPR on the advice of his uncle, Gustav Falk. He worked for the CPR until 1886, and then went to the United States. See Gunnar Werner, *Från Gotland till Nordamerika: Några drag ur en gotländsk emigranthistorik 1884–ca1900* (Linköping, 1979), 5–18.

44 Emigrant Institute, Växjö; Harald Fegræus Collection, 22:15. About 600 of his letters have been preserved. The four from Canada were sent from "Camp at Qu'Appelle" and "Camp at Moose Jaw."

45 Don W. Thompson, *Men and Meridians: The History of Surveying and Mapping in Canada, 1867 to 1917* (Ottawa: Department of Energy, Mines and Resources, 1967), 2:36.

46 Library and Archives Canada (henceforth LAC); *Canadiska Pacific Jernvägen: Upplysninger om Manitoba och det Canadiska Nordwesten* (ca. 1886), the CPR's recruiting brochure, which includes a section on Scandinavia, Manitoba, titled "Beskrifning öfver kolonien 'Nya Skandinavia'."

47 LAC; W.J. Wills, Ottawa, correspondence from Mr Dyke recommending employment of E. Ohlen, 30 May 1884. Emanuel Öhlén (1861–1931) was born in Övergran, Uppland, worked in the grocery business in

Stockholm before emigrating, and affiliated with the Mission Covenant Church. In 1886 he donated meteoric stones found in Sweden to the Manitoba Historical Society, evidently his sole attempt to promote both his homeland and himself among Winnipeg's Anglo-Saxon majority. Very little is known about his personal life except that he had a wife and son. He resigned around 1890, and made strenuous efforts to get another government post. The parade began with letters of recommendation that Canada appoint him as emigration agent for Scandinavia. See LAC, RG 17, I-1, Box 687, file 78654; Box 694, file 79475; Box 713, file 81867. In 1894 Premier Thomas Greenway of Manitoba sent a letter to the consul general in Quebec City, in support of other petitions, recommending that the government of Sweden give Ohlen a suitable government post. See Manitoba Archives, LB A/358, Thomas Greenway Letterbook. Öhlén also lobbied to become vice-consul in Montreal in 1897, with letters of support from the Scandinavian National Society of Montreal and the Scandinavian Evangelical Mission of Montreal strongly protesting the appointment of G.E. Gylling, who "has taken neither interest or part in Scandinavian colonization in Canada and that he has done nothing to promote commercial relations between Canada and Sweden and Norway." See Riksarkivet, Stockholm, Utrikesdepartmentet, Grupp.14, I. See also LAC, MG 26-J1, William Lyon Mackenzie King Correspondence, 1 March 1928, in which Öhlén is corresponding from his position as Canada's consul general, Stockholm, Sweden. According to http://consuladoperumontreal.com, from 1899 to 1902 Öhlén served as Peruvian consul in Montreal.

48 *Civil Service List of 1890*, 130.

49 LAC; *Skandinaviska National Föreningens Höge Beskyddare Hans Exc. Premier Ministern af Dominion af Canada Sir John A. McDonald, K.C.B., etc., tillegnas denna bok vördsamligen af Skandinaviska National Föreningen i Winnipeg* (Winnipeg, 1886).

50 Måns P. Peterson (1849–1937) was born in Ingelstorp, Skåne. In 1874 he left Sweden bound for Negaunee, Michigan, and reached Winnipeg in June after six weeks of travelling overland with P.P. "Läsare" Johnson. Known as the second Swedish pioneer to come to Winnipeg, he sold water door-to-door, then wood and coal. An avid supporter of the Mission Covenant faith, he became a justice of the peace and executive member of the Liberal Party. See Landelius Biography Collection, volume 3, #120; see also Gunnar Nilsson, *De sista svenska rösterna: Resa bland emigranter i Kanada* (Stockholm: Carlsson, 1995), 100–1; see also Axel

J. Carlson, "The Swedes in Canada," *Scandinavia: A Monthly Magazine Devoted to the Interests of Scandinavians Everywhere* 1, no. 5 (May 1924): 30.

51 The agents were Alfred Åkerlind, Ottawa; W. Anderson, Quebec; O. Grönlund, Halifax; and A.J. Freder, Göteborg. Alfred Åkerlind (ca. 1862–19?) immigrated in 1883 from Stockholm to Quebec. His mother and younger brother joined him the following year in Ottawa, where he worked for the Department of the Interior as Scandinavian interpreter, at one point helping C.O. Swanson in the West. For his interest in the Olympic games, which were held in Stockholm in 1912, he was decorated with the Olympic Medal in 1920. Among others he is credited with introducing skiing to Canada. See Carlson, "The Swedes in Canada," 30. Much of the information about individual emigrants comes from the 2001 CD-ROM database *CD Emigranten*, a joint project of the Emigrant Institute in Växjö, the Emigrant Register in Karlstad, and the Gothenburg Emigrant (Regional Archives, Department of History at the University of Gothenburg, *Riksföreningen Sverigekontakt*, and the City of Gothenburg).

52 Lars Ljungmark, "Canada's Campaign for Scandinavian Immigrants 1880–1895," in *Canada and the Nordic Countries. Proceedings from the Second International Conference of the Nordic Association for Canadian Studies, University of Lund, 1987,* ed. Jørn Carlsen and Bengt Streijffert (Lund: University of Lund, 1988), 220.

53 LAC; *Nya Stockholm, nybildad skandinavisk nybygge i Nord-Amerikanska Western, 160 acres land fritt till hvarje person, fyld 18 år* (Enköping, 1886), which translates as "New Stockholm, the newly formed Scandinavian colony in North America's west, 160 acres of free land to every person 18 years of age and over."

54 Nils Johanson (1841–1909) was born in Öhn, Ström, Jämtland, trained as a shoemaker, married Karin Zakrisdotter (1839–1920) in Sweden, and had five children from 1863 to 1882. In 1883 the family immigrated, moving to New Stockholm, where Johanson became postmaster and land guide in 1886. "Nils, though small in stature, was an energetic man of sound judgement and strong convictions and was well liked and respected in the colony," wrote Lucille Lindwall Szumutku in "Nils and Karin Johanson," 3, typescript included in a collection gathered by the Swedish Historical Society, Stockholm, Saskatchewan, for the Ohlen '86 celebration, henceforth Stockholm Binder. See also Gladys M. Halliwell and M. Zetta Persson, *Three Score and Ten 1886–1956: A Story of the Swedish Settlement of Stockholm and District* (Yorkton: Redeemers' Voice Press, 1959), 8–14.

55 The New Stockholm colony consisted of four townships, 28 and 29 in Ranges 2 and 3.

56 Landsarkivet i Östersund, Gunilla Hansson Collection; "Jämtar grundade ett Stockholm i Kanada," 160. Return men are credited with bringing the following immigrants to New Stockholm: from northern Sweden the families of J.N. Berglund, A. Janson, E. Kristofferson, P.A. Norlin, O. Nilson, I.P. Sjödin, O. Teng, and J. Teng, and single men E. Hammarström, J.P. Nordin, and J.A. Westin; from Skåne the C.O. Hofstrand family, M.A. Lindblom and Kalle Mårtenson; from Denmark the Bang and Axel von Holstein-Rathlow families; and from Minnesota the A.G. Sahlmark family. See Manitoba Archives, MG 14, C 28, Box 1, File 1, W.J. Sisler Collection, C.O. Hofstrand, "Stockholm," *Canada posten*, 16 May 1951, second of five parts.

57 The 1886 founding of New Stockholm and Scandinavia were separated by only a few months.

58 C. O. Swanson (1844–1906) was born Carl Olof Svensson. He immigrated in 1871 and married Ella C. Draper in 1872. Their two children were raised in Waterville, in an imposing two-storey home with a cupola. He worked as a carpenter in a furniture factory, which he later owned. See *History of Compton County: And Sketches of the Eastern Townships, District of St. Francis and Sherbrooke County* (Belleville: Mika, 1975), 191.

59 When his father died in 1880 C.O. Swanson returned to Grinstad, Dalsland, to bring his stepmother and siblings to Waterville. Kajsa Swanson (1826–1905) came with stepchildren Christina, Peter, John, Herman, and Mary. Olof Swanson had immigrated in 1870 and married the daughter of Waterville's first mayor. Olof and Herman served as postmasters from 1902 to 1914. See "Swanson Family," in Gary Caldwell, *Waterville 1876–2001* (Sherbrooke: Éditions Louis Bilodeau, 2000), 108. Others from Grinstad include C.O. Peterson and Anders Magnus Ohlsson.

60 LAC, RG 76, volume 7, file 67. The *McKinley Tariff Act* passed in 1890 forced farmers to buy high-priced protected American products, but sell their produce in unprotected world markets.

61 Philip Taylor, *The Distant Magnet: European Emigration to the U.S.A.* (New York: Harper & Row, 1971), 82.

62 Information about C.O. Swanson's career comes from Kenneth O. Bjork, "Scandinavian Migration to the Canadian Prairie Provinces, 1893–1914," *Norwegian-American Studies* 26 (1974): 10–17.

63 Swanson's house was located on 32-45-26-W4. See *Pioneer Pathways: Rural Wetaskiwin*, 2 vols. (Wetaskiwin Circle 8 Historical Society, 1981),

2000. Thanks to Jim Knutson, Waterville QC, for sending "Waterville" photocopies from *Sherbrooke Daily Record*, 6 April 1900, 13, 16, and other information.

64 Landelius Biography Collection, volume 3, #206, *Svenska folkets tidning*, Minneapolis/St Paul, 29 June 1904; see also *Medbörgaren*, Lindstrom, Minnesota, 16 March 1905.

65 *Pioneer Pathways*, 1200.

66 For a study of Swedish maids in Chicago see Stina Hirsch, "The Swedish Maid, 1900–1915," Master's thesis, De Paul University, 1985.

67 LAC, RG 76, volume 167, file 49149, part 2. In a handwritten letter to W.D. Scott, Superintendent of Immigration, Department of the Interior, dated 11 March 1909, Christina Swanson summed up her feelings about the program being discontinued: "I must say I regret very much to give it up, it has been very interesting and I have certainly enjoyed it very much, although it has been a little difficult at times especially since my dear brother C.O. Swanson died."

68 *Canada* (Winnipeg), 20 January 1898. Thanks to Joanna Daxell, Coaticook, Quebec, for sending a photocopy of this clipping. The girls' names are Ester Ågren, Anna Anderson, Helga Anderson, Christina Berg, Elisabeth Bergman, Maria Byström, Lisa Eriksson, Lisen Erikson, Jenny Gustafson, Hulda Hanson, Elin Hedman, Anna Höglen, Carin Höglen, Katharina Isackson, Mina Janson, Elisabeth Larson, Anna Larsson, Frida Lindberg, Anna M. Lofgren, Selma Mässen, Hulda Österberg, Ellen Sandelin, and Elin Westin. In 1898 one Swedish crown was worth US$.26, according to Sveriges Riksbank, Stockholm. The numbers seem to have decreased by 1907, when she was credited with thirty-one girls and received a cheque for $124.

69 LAC, RG 76, volume 167, file 49149, part 2. An unsigned letter of complaint dated 26 March 1909 hints at ulterior motives on Christina's part. "Last Sunday no less than nine girls, from 15 to 22 years of age, left [from Sundsvall to Canada, via Trondheim]. They were in charge of a woman, who it seems now made the trip to America for the third time. This movement seems somewhat peculiar. Only young girls are given free tickets – no older women and no men. Are our authorities acquainted with the nature of this traffic?"

70 Mary Spafford, "Swede Girls for Canadian Homes," *The Canadian Magazine* (April 1907): 545–9. The bias of employers is clearly expressed on page 546: "There is naturally a prejudice on the part of Canadian housekeepers against unskilled labour, but the exigencies of the modern servant problem have driven many a one, in sheer desperation, to this

extremity, when, contrary to expectation, the venture has not proved so altogether deplorable."

71 Signe Olson (1890–1963) was born in Övre Ullerud parish, Värmland, and in 1911 paid 140 crowns ($36) for a steerage ticket on the *Empress of Ireland* from Göteborg to Quebec. Thanks to grandson G. William Carlson, St Paul, for family information.

72 The Clavet home at 350 Arthur Street (now Red River Road) was designed by architect Thomas Hanley, built in 1906 by Burleigh & Gilker, and demolished in 1975 to make way for a seniors' complex. The remaining grand homes in the area have been designated as a Heritage District. Thanks to John S. Hannam, Assistant City Clerk, Thunder Bay, for this information.

73 G. William Carlson, "The Pietist Poetry of Signe Olson Peterson: 'The Letter Started On' Understanding the Immigrant Experience," *The Baptist Pietist Clarion* 6, no. 1 (June 2007): 13.

74 Ibid., 14, from "The Letter Started On" (*Det påbegynta brefvet*), as published in *Svenska standaret* 9, no. 51 (December 1915): 3, and translated by Tom Coleman. The poem is about a young woman who died alone in hospital before being able to finish a letter to her mother in Sweden. Printed with the permission of grandson G. William Carlson, St Paul.

75 *En Smålandssocken emigrerar: En bok om emigrationen till Amerika från Långasjö socken i Kronobergs län*, (Växjö: Långasjö emigrantcirkel, 1967), 808. This hardcover book of 928 pages profiles 1,423 emigrants. More than a quarter of them came to Canada. For a detailed analysis, see St Jean, "Swedes on the Move," 49–135.

76 *En Smålandssocken emigrerar*, 797. The dollar amounts are based on the 1899 exchange rate according to Riksbank Sverige; that is, US$1 = SEK3.78.

77 Roadmasters in British Columbia from Långasjö and year of emigration: Helmer Carlson (1925), Fritz Fransson (1926), Karl Fransson (1911), Ernst "Snow King" Johansson (1908), Frank Lind (1902), Harry Strand (1928), Hugo Strand (1928), and John Strand (1924). On being promoted to roadmaster, Karl Johansson (1907) and Oskar Johansson (1913) were transferred to Saskatchewan.

78 Ljungmark, "On Emigration, Social Mobility, and the Transfer of Capital," 160–1, citing *En Smålandssocken emigrerar*, 817. The dollar amounts are based on the above exchange rate.

79 About 1,200 people emigrated from Långasjö parish; however, *CD Emigranten* lists 1,303 emigrants from Örkened. In addition, Kjell Arnoldsson, *Amerika-emgranterna från Örkened 1861–1961* (Lönsboda,

1961): 3, 25–6, states under the heading "Many travelled illegally," that 286 persons are listed as non-existent in the church records in addition to the 1,600 who emigrated legally.

80 *Stenindustrins historia i Örkened åren 1890-1980* (Hässleholm: Nord-Skåne, 1981), 92–102.

81 Arnoldsson, *Amerika-emigranterna från Örkened*, 14–23.

82 Karl Bengtsson (1898–1959) was born in Rågeboda, Örkened, Skåne, and married Ester Bengtsson (1897–1971) from nearby Gylsboda. Son Eric Bengtsson became a railway engineer and married Margaret Broadfoot. Thanks to Eric Bengtsson and his daughter Lisa Bengtsson, Thunder Bay, for family information.

83 Section men and section foremen include Karl Anderson (later roadmaster at Port Arthur), Gust Anderson, Charlie Bengtsson, Olof Bergquist, Anton Clarin, Edvin Clarin, Sture Frosteson, John Johnson, Nels Johnsson, Oskar Karlson, Oskar Severin Karlson, Pelle Kulberg, Gust Lodin, Oskar Lövquist, Bror Martinson, Charlie Martinson, John Martinson, Manfred Nelson, Sture Nelson, Ernst Olson, Valdemar Olsen, Olle Olson, Charlie Palmquist, Gust Swanson, Henry Swanson, Karl Swanson, and Gust Witzell. Thanks to Eric Bengtsson, Thunder Bay, for providing this list of twenty-seven names.

84 Roadmasters from this area include Karl Bengtsson, Sandfried Bengtsson, August Erickson, Charlie Olson, the brothers Andy and Joe Peterson, and Vic Swanson. Thanks to Eric Bengtsson, Thunder Bay, for providing these names.

85 Olof Persson (1866–19?) came to Canada in 1890, returning in 1899 to buy a farm in Loshult parish. He came back in 1910 to earn money to build a barn. During the 1920s four of Olof's sons followed his example. One who remained in Canada, Ivar Albert Person (19?–1981), became roadmaster for the Northern Alberta Railway, now CNR. Thanks to daughter Carin Routledge, Edmonton, for family information.

86 Nils Palmgren (1866–19?) came to Canada for the third time in 1923, with his eldest son, Olof Palmgren (1900–19?). Nils returned to Sweden but Olof stayed, married, worked for the Algoma Central Railway all his life, and died in Sault Ste Marie, Ontario. Thanks to Kenneth Palmgren, Hästveda, Sweden, for family information, notably "Palmgren and Olofsson families in North America," *Norra Skåne*, 29 November 2005.

87 LAC, RG 2, A2A, volume 5616; "Prosecution by the Swedish authorities of Mr. Carrick, British Vice Consul at Gefle, Sweden," Governor General's Office, Ottawa, 6 June 1906, referred to the Privy Council; see also RG 6, A1, volume 126, file 242, "No. 42384/Confidential/Foreign Office/

December 1906." Despite political pressure, the Davison Lumber Company did not reimburse Mr Carrick for his legal fees. *CD Emigranten* reveals that fifty-two young men left Gästrikland in November and December 1905, and two in January 1906, bound for Halifax.

88 Information about Millertown relies heavily on Roland C. Goodyear, "Lewis Miller and Harry J. Crowe" (1968), unpublished memoir donated by John Munro, Halifax, with the permission of Clarice Goodyear, Gander, Newfoundland. John Munro believes that the memoir was part of, or developed from, a Forest History Appendix that Roland C. Goodyear wrote for the 1955 Report of the Newfoundland Royal Commission on Forestry. According to *Daily News*, St John's, Newfoundland, 11 September 1900, "Thirty-three Swedes arrived by the Siberian [Allan Line] and will settle down in the interior of the Island." For early photos from the Lewis Miller Museum in Millertown see http://www.communityofmillertown.ca.

89 It is believed that the epithet "red Indian" derived from the now-extinct native people of Newfoundland, the Beothuk, who painted their bodies with red ochre. Red Indian Lake was the site of the encampment where the young Beothuk Demasduwit, or Mary March, was captured and her husband killed. Their baby son died soon afterwards. Lady Hamilton painted her portrait, the only known original likeness of a Beothuk, in St John's in 1819.

90 The destinations of only a few are known. Neil and Anna Sideen moved to Stanley, Ontario, in 1902. Bachelor Mauritz Anderson ended up in Riverland, Manitoba, in 1906, according to *Logs and Lines from the Winnipeg River: A History of the Lac du Bonnet Area* (Lac du Bonnet: Senior Citizens Historical Society, The Lac du Bonnet Pioneers Club, 1980), 375–6. Thanks to granddaughter Bertha Risbey, Winnipeg, for the information that the brothers Wilhelm and Edward Nilsson and their families filed on homesteads in Lillesve, Manitoba, in 1908. Because the land for Lillesve cemetery was donated by Wilhelm and Olina Nilsson, their grandchildren have placed a commemorative plaque inside the gates; see *Wilderness to Wildlife: Chatfield, Fishlake, Narcisse, Sandridge, Clematis, Willowview, Neveton, Markland, Wheathill,* (Selkirk: Chatfield Oldtimers Club, 1981), 184–5.

91 Olof Gustav Johnson (1875–1964) was born in Sandviken, Jämtland, and married Marian Woodman (1880–1948). His sisters Amanda and Märta immigrated, also nephews Erik Nilsson and Ludvig Andersson. Thanks to granddaughter Amanda Gellman, Windsor, Ontario, for family information.

92 John Hägglund (1885–1976) was born in Arnäs, near Örnsköldsvik,
    Ångermanland, and in 1909 married Amanda Johnson (18?–1939) from
    Växjö, Småland. The business closed in 1982. See Ruth E. Hagglund,
    "Building a Home in Fort William: The Origins and Development of
    the John Hagglund Lumber and Fuel Company," HBA diss., Lakehead
    University, 1984; see also "Well-Known City Resident Celebrates His 90th
    Birthday," newspaper clipping dated July 1975; see also John Hagglund,
    "Starting out in the Lakehead: A Personal Tale of Arriving," *Lakehead
    Living*, 29 March 1978.

93 Ljungmark and Åkerman, "The Unknown Emigration," 92.

94 Märta Jansson (1887–19?) was born in Sandviken, Jämtland, and ca. 1907
    immigrated to her brother, O.G. Johnson, in Millertown, Newfoundland.
    Both her letters on birchbark are dated 2 February 1907 and addressed to
    relatives in Sandviken. She moved to Winnipeg and in 1909 married Jack
    Bogseth (1880–19?), who had immigrated from Häggenäs, Jämtland ca.
    1906. Thanks to grandson Rocklee Bogseth, Peterborough, Ontario, for
    sending copies of these letters.

95 Adolf Gottfrid Larsson (1874–1956) was born in Tydje parish, Dalsland,
    and in 1898 graduated as a chemical engineer in Copenhagen. He worked
    in Sweden and Germany before emigrating to the United States. By
    1905 he was employed by the Grey & Bruce Portland Cement Company,
    Durham, Ontario, where he met John Lind. Lind married Gay Heming
    and in 1908 Gottfrid married her sister Laura. In 1952 he retired from St
    Mary's Cement Company, which was owned by his brother-in-law John
    Lind. Thanks to grandson Richard Gottfrid Larsson Holt, St Mary's,
    Ontario, for sending family information and copies of correspondence
    that had been donated to St Mary's Museum.

96 Letter from Gottfrid Larsson, St Mary's, Ontario, to Oskar Larsson,
    Sweden, 24 September 1916. None of the surviving letters dated during
    the First World War show signs of being censored.

97 Jacob Fahlstrom (ca. 1794–1859) was immersed in the English language
    during five years with the Hudson's Bay Company, and then became
    fluent in Ojibwa and probably French. He married Margaret Bonga,
    daughter of an Ojibwa woman and Pierre Bonga, a Black man who
    worked for the North West Company ca. 1804–14 and then for the
    American Fur Company. Pierre's dad, a West Indian slave, was
    manumitted at Mackinac ca. 1790, according to the journal of Alexander
    Henry the younger, page 24. In Minnesota Fahlstrom converted to
    Methodism, and in 1840 received certain ministerial powers, becoming
    known as Father Jacob. His descendants and others have adopted

different spellings of his surname. Emeroy Johnson, in his article "Was Oza Windib a Swede," *Swedish-American Historical Quarterly* 35, no. 3 (1984): 207–20, suggests that native people called him Oza Windib (Yellow Head) because of his flaxen hair. A free Iroquois contemporary in the fur trade, Pierre Hatsinaton, was also called Yellow Head (*tête jaune*), according to *Colin Robertson's Correspondence Book September 1817 to September 1822* (Toronto: Champlain Society, 1939), 261. See Elinor Barr, "Jacob Fahlstrom Challenge," *Swedish American Genealogist* 4 (2005): 5–8; see also Alf Brorson, "On the Stage of History," *Bryggan/The Bridge* 3 (2008): 12–13.

98 Manitoba Archives, mfm C.1/294, 2M-21; "Ships' Logs, Eddystone, June 15, 1811 to Dec. 4, 1811, Thomas Ramsay, Master." I am grateful to Ted Simonson, Winnipeg, for tracking down information, particularly from the records of the Hudson's Bay Company Archives. Dates and other details relating to the Hudson's Bay Company and the Red River settlement can be found in Herbert J. Mays, "Macdonell, Miles," *Dictionary of Canadian Biography Online.*

99 Ibid., mfm 5H9, North West Company Ledgers 1811–21.

100 Allan Kastrup, *The Swedish Heritage in America*, 198. In 1964 the Minnesota Methodist Historical Society dedicated a granite marker at the family burial ground in memory of "Father Jacob" and his wife, Margaret Bonga.

101 Eric Anderson (1852–1911) was born in Halland, Sweden, and went to sea at the age of eleven. In British Columbia he married Sara Morrison McClintock, who died in 1902, then Sigvoon "Runney" Sigurdson (1870–1922). Anderson sold his property to the BC Electric Railway in 1909 on condition that a stopping place called Anderson Station be located there. See John Pearson and Lorne Pearson, *The Valley of the Fraser: A True Historic Narrative from Surrey's Formative Years* (City of Surrey, 2005), 93–4; see also UBCL SC, Seaholm Collection, "Eric Anderson" and "The Eric Anderson Cabin."

102 Their son Clarence began practising medicine in Winnipeg in 1906.

103 Paul W. Gates, "Official Encouragement to Immigration by the Province of Canada," *The Canadian Historical Review* 15, no. 1 (March 1934): 26. The "Province of Canada" refers to earlier names for Ontario and Quebec, which are Upper Canada and Lower Canada, respectively.

104 Lars Ljungmark, "Canada's Campaign for Scandinavian Immigration, 1873–1876," *Swedish-American Historical Quarterly* 33, no. 1 (January 1982): 23–34. William McDougall (1822–1905) was an Ontario lawyer and politician who attended all three Confederation conferences. His political career took a downturn after Louis Riel's men refused him entry into the

territory he had come to govern, now Manitoba, as its first lieutenant-governor.

105 Hans Mattson was a Swedish-born American who distinguished himself in the Civil War and also as a propagandist for the immigration of Swedes to Minnesota from 1869 to 1873. For an account of his work in Sweden in 1871, with the goal of annexing Canada to the United States, see Mauri I. Jalava, "The Scandinavians as a Source of Settlers for the Dominion of Canada: The First Generation, 1867–1897," *Scandinavian-Canadian Studies* 1 (1983): 6.

106 The hotels were the Prospect and the Clifton, site of today's Oakes Garden Theatre. See Joan Magee, *A Scandinavian Heritage: 200 Years of Scandinavian Presence in the Windsor-Detroit Border Region* (Toronto: Dundurn, 1985), 43; see also correspondence from George Bailey, Niagara Falls, Ontario, November 2004.

107 *Swedish Press*, August 1993, 17. Jenny Lind gave three concerts in Toronto.

108 Lars Ljungmark, "Canada: An Alternative for Swedish Emigration to the New World, 1873–1875," *Swedish-American Historical Quarterly* 35, no. 3 (July 1984): 253–66. For Hans Mattson's comments on the Canadian venture, see Lars Ljungmark, "Hans Mattson's Minnen: A Swedish-American Monument," *Swedish Pioneer Historical Quarterly* 29, no. 1 (1978): 63. The acting consul who replaced Baron Falkenberg forwarded the complaints of the Norwegian immigrants in Moisie to the Foreign Office in Stockholm. Nevertheless, some of those who went to Montreal were imprisoned for breach of contract, and the agent in Oslo was fined for recruiting contract labour in violation of Norwegian law. For another unsuccessful importation of Norwegian workers in 1873 to Silver Islet mine see Elinor Barr, *Silver Islet: Striking it Rich in Lake Superior* (Toronto: Natural Heritage, 1988), 75–6. For a list of these men see her *The Scandinavian Home Society 1923–1993: A Place to Meet, A Place to Eat* (Thunder Bay: The Society, 1996), 117.

109 John Dyke had lived in Liverpool since his appointment in 1869 as Ontario's immigration agent, and since 1876 as Canada's immigration agent.

110 Ljungmark, "Canada's Campaign for Scandinavian Immigrants 1880–1895," 215.

111 Ibid., 216.

112 Ibid., 216–17, 219. The ad's headline, published in fifty Swedish newspapers, is given as "Manitoba Situated Close to Minnesota and Dakota in America." See University of Minnesota, Immigration History Research Center, henceforth UM IHRC, *En kort beskrifning öfver Manitoba,*

ett af Norvesterns bördigaste hveteland (Göteborg, 1883), which translates as "A short description of Manitoba – one of the best wheat-lands in the North West."

113 In 1926 Axel R. Mellander worked in Calgary as Canada's agent for Nordsvenska Kredit of Stockholm, Sweden.

114 Glenbow Archives, CPR Fonds, M2269, file 1004; Superintendent of Colonization, CPR, Winnipeg, to Calgary, Memorandum for Mr MacAlister, 2 November 1925; see also Memoranda for Mr Colley dated 15 April, 5 and 21 May 1926. Board members were from Calgary and area: president John Hugill, a lawyer; vice-president Rev Anton Nelson; secretary Axel R. Mellander; members Anton Persson, Erik Johnson, H.B. Hornstrom, Walfrid Hornstrom, and John Erickson.

115 Ibid., file 1827; Superintendent of Colonization, CPR, Winnipeg, to Calgary, Memorandum for Mr Colley, 13 July 1927.

116 Herman Peter Albert Hermanson (1881–1956) was born in Håsjö, Jämtland, the son of Herman and Ann Hermanson. The family immigrated in 1901 and homesteaded in Buchanan, Saskatchewan, in 1903. Albert married schoolteacher Ruby M.I. Harmer of Kingston, Ontario, served as secretary-treasurer of the rural municipality of Buchanan and the village of Buchanan from 1910 to 1919, and was elected MLA in 1917 and 1921. He lived in Winnipeg from 1925 to 1936 as agent for the Swedish American Line and served as Swedish consul from 1928 to 1955. A member of Strindberg Vasa Lodge, the Masonic Order, and the Saskatchewan Grain Growers' Association, he moved to Niagara Falls, Ontario, in 1955.

117 H. Arnold Barton, *A Folk Divided: Homeland Swedes and Swedish Americans, 1840–1940* (Carbondale: Southern Illinois University Press, 1994), 251–3, 344; see also his "Swedish Reactions to the Emigration Question Around the Turn of the Century," *Swedish-American Historical Quarterly* 44, no. 2 (April 1993): 98. One of the reasons immigrants turned to Canada was because their passports were accepted instead of the visa required by the United States.

118 Calculated from immigration figures published in *The Canada Year Book*, 1921 to 1931. According to Epp, *Nordic People in Canada*, table 11 and table 12, the population of Swedish ethnic origin increased by 20,073 – that is, from 61,503 to 81,576 – leaving only 1,575 persons to cover natural increase and immigration from the United States.

119 Ivar Teodor Vennerström (1881–1945) was a newspaperman and Social Democratic politician, serving as a member of the Swedish Parliament from 1915 to 1936.

120 Ivar Vennerström, *Kanada och Kanadasvenskarna: Studier och reseintryck* (Stockholm: Tidens förlag, 1926), 123.

121 LAC, RG 76, volume 245, file 165833; Albert Hermanson, Manager, Swedish Canadian Information Bureau of the Swedish American Line, Winnipeg, to W.J. Egan, Deputy Minister of Immigration, Ottawa, 23 January 1926.

122 UM IHRC: *Canada* (Göteborg: Canadian National Railways, 1926). The office address was Fredsgatan 1, Göteborg. A similar publication came out in 1928, adding information about three areas in Saskatchewan already settled by Swedes: Shellbrook, Melfort-Birch Hills, and the Maidstone-Lashburn-Waseca area.

123 LAC: *Arbetstillfällen och jordförvärv i Canada* (Job Openings and Acquisition of Land in Canada).

124 Loken, *From Fjord to Frontier*, 13–14; see also Orm Øverland, ed., transl., and intro., *Johan Schrøder's Travels in Canada, 1863* (Montreal: McGill-Queen's University Press, 1989), 6–8.

125 Magee, *A Scandinavian Heritage*, 17. For an account of the perils of early railway travel, see pages 18–25.

126 Handwritten notes from "Konsulsstaten," *Förteckning å svenska och norska consuler, utfärdad af Kongl. Maj:ts och rikets Commerce-Collegium, 1850–69,* provided by Göran Rydeberg, Foreign Affairs Archives, Stockholm, May 2004.

127 Gerard Knut Alfred Falkenberg (1819–1873) was born in Träslöv, Halland, the son of Ulrik Falkenberg of the noble family Falkenberg af Trystorp. In 1841 he immigrated to Quebec City, where he became a merchant and shipbroker, married Elisabeth Kimball in New York, and had seven children. I am grateful to Rolf Brodin, Edane, Sweden, for providing official information about the Falkenberg family and for explaining the three classes of Swedish nobility: count, baron, and knight. Details about Alfred Falkenberg's period as consul come from the Foreign Affairs Archives, Stockholm; *Kungliga Utrikesdepartementets kalender 1870–1880.*

128 "The Dinner at Quebec," *Saint John Morning Telegraph,* 24 October 1864, 2.

129 Alfred Falkenberg was awarded Sweden's Royal Order of the North Star and Royal Order of Vasa, also Norway's Order of St Olaf.

130 Riksarkivet, Stockholm: General Konsul, Montreal, Grupp 14/3-7/1902-22, Circular N:o 1, To the Consuls of Sweden, "Disposition of the Archives 1906," Stockholm, 27 April 1906. Under this arrangement Canada's archives were to be taken over by the Swedish consulate, and the United States archives by the Norwegian consulate.

131 The seven were Halifax, Parrsboro, Sheet Harbour, and Sydney and North Sydney in Nova Scotia; and Saint John, Chatham and Newcastle, and Richibucto and Buctouche in New Brunswick.

132 Riksarkivet, Stockholm: 1902 års dossiersystem, 869, grupp:14, Avd: Montreal, Mål:3, Nordisk Familjebok forts. Se A140.

133 Information about shipping lines came from the website http://www.norwayheritage.com.

134 James Åkerström (ca. 1857–1931) was born an only child in Sweden. Just before leaving, his mother died and his father remarried. James married Elizabeth Betts (ca. 1873–1961) in Montreal in 1889, and later moved to Winnipeg. Thanks to grandson Ernie Melville, Thunder Bay, for family information.

135 Viveka Janssen, "Swedish Settlement in Alberta, 1890–1930," *Swedish-American Historical Quarterly* 33, no. 2 (April 1982): 115. The dollar amount is based on the 1899 exchange rate according to Riksbank Sverige; that is, US$1 = SEK3.78.

136 Ibid., 114–15; see also Kristian Hvidt, "Emigration Agents: The Development of a Business and its Methods," *Scandinavian Journal of History* 3, no. 2 (1978): 200–2; see also Arthur Grenke, *The German Community in Winnipeg: 1872–1919* (New York: AMS Press, 1991), 9–10. Janssen credits Molin, *Några drag af kolonizationen i Canada*, 59 ff, for her information, while Grenke cites government correspondence from 1901 to 1908 from Library and Archives Canada.

137 "The Swedish America Line: The Shipping Company with the World's Most Exclusive Cruise Liners – The White Viking Ships," *Swedish Press*, May 2001, 17, and August 2003, 23.

138 Erick Carlson, "History of my Life in Canada," typescript, 1. Erick Carlson (ca. 1908–19?) was born in Torbjörntorp, Västergötland, as was his buddy Gunnar Johanson (ca. 1904–19?), who travelled with him. Thanks to Kerstin Guillemaud, Fort St John, British Columbia, for donating this memoir.

139 Thanks to Carrie-Ann Smith, who kindly provided me with what little information there was about Swedes in Pier 21's Library/Resource Centre.

3. Immigrants

1 Birgitta Wallace, "Viking Farewell," *The Beaver* (December 2006–January 2007): 19–24. See also her *Westward Vikings: The Saga of L'Anse aux Meadows* (St John's: Historic Sites Association of Newfoundland and Labrador,

2006). The Vinland Sagas, *Greenlanders' Saga* and *Erik the Red's Saga*, recount oral traditions written down in the 1200s and 1300s. Danish antiquarian Carl Christian Rafn published English and Latin translations in 1837 and 1838. Provinces on Sweden's western seacoast that were part of the Danish hegemony during Viking times are Skåne, Halland, and Bohuslän.

2 A.H. Guernsey, "Folk-Life in Sweden 1871," *Swedish American Genealogist* 23, no. 2 (June 2003): 65–84. Reprinted from *Harper's New Monthly Magazine* (January 1871).

3 Trades noted in the 1851, 1861, and 1871 censuses are baker, blacksmith, brass finisher, cabinetmaker, carpenter, crafts finisher, dyer, furrier, jeweller, machinist, maltster, mariner, miller, plumber, saddler, shipwright, shoemaker, silversmith, tailor, tanner, tinsmith, upholsterer, and watchmaker.

4 Ljungmark, *Svenskarna i Winnipeg*, 15, 29.

5 Jon Setterlund (ca. 1868–1910) and his wife, Anna Maria (18?–1943), immigrated in 1910 with six children under the age of seventeen. Jon died shortly afterwards and the eldest, Ingeborg, went to work as a domestic. Thirteen-year-old Axel became the man of the house, and Greta lived in New Norway to go to school. "Things were very hard for us, and many a meal consisted of salt pork and potatoes," wrote Marta (Setterlund) Kelley in her typescript, "Anna Maria (Persson) Setterlund." Thanks to granddaughter Kay Lindholm, New Norway, Alberta, for donating this document; see also *Prairie Echoes: Precious Memories of the Former Hillcrest Municipality: Metiskow, Cadogan, Cairns* (Cadogan: Hillcrest Heritage Society, 1976), 426–7.

6 Correspondence from Anna Nilsson, Menisino and Lee River, Manitoba, to her cousin Märta Vilhelmson, Jämtland, 27 October 1929 and 1 March 1933. Thanks to Diane Neal, Lac du Bonnet, Manitoba, for sharing these documents.

7 Correspondence from Jon Persson, Ohlen Post Office, Saskatchewan, to Florentine, 17 June 1899, in "Translation of letters from Nils Dahl and Jon Persson to their younger sister Maria Setterlund, 1886–1910." Thanks to Maureen Landine, Stockholm, Saskatchewan, for donating this binder of correspondence translated by Doris Paulson and typed by Mona Jacob.

8 Epp, *Nordic People in Canada*, table 9.

9 Ibid., 50.

10 Ibid., 52.

11 The term "Finland Swedes" has been chosen because it more closely identifies them as Swedes living in Finland. Other terms such as "Finn

Swedes" or "Swede Finns" could be mistaken for the considerable number of Finns living in Sweden.

12 Mika Roinila, *Finland-Swedes in Canada: Migration, Settlement and Ethnic Relations* (Turku, Finland: Institute of Migration, 2000), 54, table 3.1; see also Susanne Österlund-Pötzsch, *American plus: Etnisk identitet hos finlandssvenska ättlingar i Nordamerika* (Helsinki: Svenska litteratursällskapet i Finland, 2003), which includes a summary in English; see also Anders Myhrman, "The Finland-Swedes in America," *Swedish Pioneer Historical Quarterly* 31, no. 1, (1980): 16–33.

13 Roinila, *Finland-Swedes in Canada*, 74–5.

14 Roinila, *Finland-Swedes in Canada*, 104–7. See also Oscar Johnson Papers, "History of Port Arthur and Fort William," 2, concerning A.J. Johnson (ca. 1864–1951), who immigrated to Port Arthur in 1883, worked as a contractor for the city, and in 1907 built a grocery store: "Johnson is from Dalarna. His wife is from Finland, and maybe because of this he hasn't been active in the Swedish community, either religious or political." In 1905 the high school register listed their daughter's religion as Presbyterian.

15 Roinila, *Finland-Swedes in Canada*, Table 5.2, "Swedish Mother Tongue and Finnish Racial Origin by Province, 1921–1941," 81. It is not known whether this number includes descendants.

16 These unsubstantiated numbers come from the Swedish Finn Historical Society's flyer encouraging membership. The society, founded in 1991 in a worldwide effort to collect and preserve historical and genealogical information and to share it with others, has an archives, library, genealogy office, and a website, and produces a publication called *The Quarterly*.

17 Pehr Kalm (1716–1779) was born of Finnish parents in Ångermanland, Sweden, but spent most of his life in Finland. After completing his studies under Linnaeus at Uppsala University, he began a lifelong teaching career at Åbo Academy, Finland. In 1757 he fulfilled his dream of being ordained as a Lutheran pastor. His Christian name, Pehr, is variously spelled.

18 Martti Kerkkonen, *Peter Kalm's North American Journey: Its ideological Background and Results* (Helsinki: Finnish Historical Society, 1959), 115. For a published version of his letter to Benjamin Franklin, see John Bartram, *Observations on the inhabitants, climate, soil, rivers, productions, animals, and other matters worthy of notice, made by Mr. John Bartram, in his travels from Pensilvania [sic] to Onondago, Oswego and the Lake Ontario, in Canada, to which is annex'd, a curious account of the cataracts at Niagara, by Mr. Peter Kalm, a Swedish gentleman who travelled there* (London: J. Whiston and B.

White, 1751), 79–94. This account was reprinted as *Travels in Pensilvania* [*sic*] *and Canada* (Ann Arbor, 1966).

19 Kerkkonen, *Peter Kalm's North American Journey*, 99–118; see also Nils William Olsson, "Pehr Kalm and the Image of North America," James Ford Bell Lecture #7 (1970), 3–15; see also W.R. Mead, "A Northern Naturalist: Per Kalm, Disciple of Carl Linnaeus," *The Norseman* 12 (1954): 98–106, 182–8; see also Carl Raymond Cronmiller, *A History of the Lutheran Church in Canada* (Kitchener: Evangelical Lutheran Synod of Canada, 1961), 1:27–30. Kalm's diaries were republished with additional material in *The America of 1750; Peter Kalm's Travels in North America*, ed. A.B. Benson, 2 vols. (New York, [1937] 1966). Linnaeus credited him with finding sixty new plants in North America, and used his name for two of them: *Kalmia Latifolia* for mountain laurel and *Kalmia Augustifolia* for sheep laurel. Mountain laurel is the state flower for both Pennsylvania and Connecticut.

20 LAC, RG 76, volume 668, file C19279; Valcmas Report, Halifax, Nova Scotia, 15 December 1948.

21 LAC, RG 76, volume 914, file 581-3-10; "Organizations – Swedish," typescript.

22 Anne Zoumer (1926–) was born Armilda Pallas in Pallasmaa, Muhu, Estonia. In 1948 in Sweden she married Rudolf H. Zoumer (1914–1996), who was born in Bonn, Germany. See Ann-Charlotte Berglund, "Treats," *Swedish Press*, January 2004, 27; see also "Calgary Notes," *Swedish Press*, March 1996.

23 After 1975 the Order of the Polar Star was awarded only to foreigners and members of the royal family.

24 Christian von Rosenbach (1928–1987) was born in Estonia, and spent time in Upper Silesia, Austria, Vienna, and Sweden before immigrating to Canada in 1951. The following year he married his fiancée, Ingrid Kristoferson (1927–), who was born in Lindau, Germany. His father, Nicolai von Rosenbach (1901–1977), was born in St Petersburg, Russia, as a member of Swedish nobility whose family had been named to *Riddarhuset* in 1642. In 1924 he married Irene Harms (1901–1959) in Tallinn, Estonia. After Irene's death in Canada Nicolai married Nora Huene (1910–1974). He died during a visit to Springe, Germany. Thanks to Ingrid von Rosenbach, Burlington, Ontario, for family information.

25 Unless otherwise cited, information comes from Jörgen Hedman, *Svenskbysläkter: Släktförteckningar över familjerna från Gammalsvenskby i Ukraina* (Visby: Ödin, 1994), and Jörgen Hedman and Lars Åhlander, *Historien om Gammalsvenskby och svenskarna i Ukraina* (Stockholm:

Dialogos, 2003), appendix titled "Svenskbyborna i Canada: De första emigranterna (1885–1926)," 449–64. Thanks to Jörgen Hedman for donating these and several other books.

26 Hindrik Kristiansson Utas (1854–1935) married Beata Kristoffersdotter Kling (1852–?) in Gammalsvenskby, where their children were born. See Victor Hugo Wickström, *Genom sju konungariken: Reseminnen* (Östersund, 1904), 200.

27 Andreas Hindrickson Sigalet (1844–1913) married Walba Kristiansdotter Annas (1848–1915) in Gammalsvenskby, where their children were born.

28 Johan Andreasson Utas (1880–1953) immigrated in 1902 as a widower, and then married Ragnhild Augustsdotter Fredriksson (1889–19?) from Sweden. The other families included Andreas Sigalet's brother Johan Hindrickson Sigalet (1847–?), his wife, Katarina Götzdotter Schilling (1836–?), and grown daughters Barbara and Maria, who came in 1900.

29 Wickström, *Genom sju konungariken*, 198–200.

30 *Calvary Lutheran Church, 1898–1973, 75th Anniversary* (Wetaskiwin, 1973), 3, 14–16, and *Calvary Lutheran Church, Wetaskiwin, Alberta, 1898–1998, 100th Anniversary* (Wetaskiwin, 1998), 4 (previously Svea Lutheran Church).

31 Johannes "John" Andreasson Malmas (1863–1945) married Katarina Kristiana Knutas (1867–1952) in Gammalsvenskby, and immigrated in 1888. Six children were born in Alberta. See "Malmas Memories," 5, typescript donated by Roxann Buskas, Wetaskiwin, Alberta.

32 *Mecca Glen Memories*, 1st ed. (Ponoka, AB, 1968), 86.

33 Wickström, *Genom sju konungariken*, 200–1.

34 Per Anders Rudling, "Ukrainian Swedes in Canada: Gammalsvenskby in the Swedish-Canadian Press, 1929–1931," *Scandinavian-Canadian Studies* 25 (2004–5): 68, states that "no fewer than 170 lived in Alberta, the remainder living in British Columbia." The quote from Helge Nelson, *Swedes and the Swedish Settlements in North America*, 2 vols. (Lund: Gleerup, 1943), 359, that "20 per cent of the Swedish stock [in Alberta in 1931] are immigrants from Gammalsvenskby," is wrong. According to Epp, *Nordic People in Canada*, table 12, the census figures for Alberta in 1931 were 19,828 Swedes, so that 20 per cent would be 4,000 persons rather than the 200 Gammalsvenskbyborna reported by Rudling and others.

35 Jörgen Hedman, *Gammalsvenskby – The True Story of the Swedish Settlement in the Ukraine* (Stockholm, 2005), 31.

36 LAC, RG 95, volume 1957, Swedish Lutheran Immigration Aid Society of Canada. Three of the executive members were pastors (Anton Arvid

Nelson of Saskatoon, Otto Eklund of Ferintosh, and Nils Johnson Lundahl of Dubuc), and two were merchants (Charles Aldo Johnson of Water Glen and Peter Nelson of Winnipeg). Ferdinand Eugene Baglo, *The Story of Augustana Lutherans in Canada* (Saskatoon: Canada Conference of the Augustana Lutheran Church, 1962), 48, knew very little about it. The society stopped filing with the Department of the Secretary of State, as required, in 1951.

37 The committee consisted of four men: Pastor Hoas, Johan Buskas, Wilhelm Knutas, and Andreas Malmas.

38 Rudling, "Ukrainian Swedes in Canada," 80; see also Hedman, *Gammalsvenskby.*

39 LAC, RG 30, volume 5635, Devlin Papers; Emil Hallonquist, Winnipeg, Inter-Departmental Correspondence to T.P. Devlin, Canadian National Railways, 26 April 1930, 2–3. The Bolsheviks were radicals who seized power in Russia in 1917, and the following year founded the Communist Party.

40 Ibid., 3.

41 Ibid., 3–4.

42 Andreas Andreasson Malmas (1880–1944) married Julia Mickelsdotter Norberg in Gammalsvenskby, and migrated to Sweden in 1929, then to Canada to lead the settlement in Meadows.

43 Rudling, "Ukrainian Swedes in Canada," 82.

44 Nilsson, *De sista svenska rösterna*, "Svenskbybor," 123–4.

45 LAC, RG 30, volume 5635, Devlin Papers; Emil Hallonquist, Winnipeg, Inter-Departmental Correspondence to T.P. Devlin, 1 December 1930.

46 The families, as written on Meadows's 1996 cairn, were Andrew and Julianna Malmas, Fredrick and Margareta Malmas, John and Emma Malmas, Peter and Alvina Malmas, Julius and Maria Norberg, John and Maria Norberg, Andrew and Elfreda Norberg, Ted and Meta Norberg, Peter and Katarina Hoas, John and Kristina Hoas, and Leo and Maria Lally (Knutas).

47 Petter Andreasson Hoas (1892–19?) married Katarina Pettersdotter Norberg (1891–19?) in Gammalsvenskby. The family migrated to Sweden in 1929 and to Canada in 1930, coming to Meadows the following year.

48 Rudling, "Ukrainian Swedes in Canada," 83; see also Folke Hedblom, "The Gammalsvenskby People: Swedish-Canadian Immigrants from South Russia," *Swedish-American Historical Quarterly* 34, no. 1 (1983): 32–48; see also *Edmonton Journal*, 1 September 1930, "300 Swedish Repatriates May Seek Alberta Farms. CPR Ready to Provide Financial Assistance

for Group"; see also "Gammal-svensk – The Swedish Community," in *Meadows: Centennial 1970* (Meadows: Meadows W.A. Community Club, 1970), 36–44.

49 Hedblom, "The Gammalsvenskby People," 46.

50 John Hoas (1913–2008) was born in Gammalsvenskby and married Kristina Malmas (1912–2003), also from Gammalsvenskby, in 1937 in Winnipeg. They joined Winnipeg's Strindberg Vasa Lodge in 1961. For personal interviews, see Nilsson, *De sista svenska rösterna*, 122–6, and *Swedish Press*, November 2005. Thanks to John Hoas for information about Svenskbyborna in Canada and in Ukraine.

51 Mikael Håkanson, "The Svenskbybo-people in Canada – A Dying Culture?," *Bryggan/The Bridge* 15, no. 4 (1983): 104–9.

52 Andrew Erickson Bloomquist (1856–1910) was born in Borlänge, Dalarna, and emigrated to Willmar, Minnesota. His marriage to Christine (18?–1893), also from Borlänge, ended when a makeshift henhouse roof fell and killed her. In 1895 he married Anna Norberg (1876–19?) from Gagnef, Dalarna. The family moved to Bowbells, North Dakota, in 1903. In 1910 Andrew died of a ruptured appendix, and two years later Anna married John Westberg, from Minnesota, ending up with fourteen children. The family continued farming, moved to Brooks, Alberta, in 1919, and two years later returned to North Dakota to help Anna's aging parents. Today, descendants live in both countries. Thanks to Leif Bloomquist, Toronto, for family information.

53 Nelson, *Swedes and the Swedish Settlements in North America*, 354. This book is based on a 1933 visit to study the prairie provinces and British Columbia.

54 William C. Wonders, "Mot Kanadas Nordväst: Pioneer Settlement by Scandinavians in Central Alberta," in *Geografiska annaler, 65B* (1983), figure 1, 132. He based his study on homestead records centred on Camrose, from Bearhills Lake to Bawlf and from Hay Lakes to Donalda. It did not include purchased lands.

55 Ibid., figure 9, 143. The vast majority of settlers who emigrated directly from Sweden originated in the northern and central provinces, specifically Vilhelmina, Lycksele, Östersund, Härnösand, Sundsvall, Söderhamn, Långåset, Uppsala, Stockholm, Hårby, Karlstad, Norrköping, Gålstad, Jönköping, Vårgårda, Göteborg, and Karlskrona.

56 Ibid., table 4, 141. Of the 48.5 per cent who came from the United States, 12.4 per cent were from Minnesota, 8.2 per cent from South Dakota, 5.4 per cent from North Dakota, and 22.5 per cent from other states. See also his "Scandinavian Homesteaders," *Alberta History* 24, no. 3

(Summer 1976): 3; see also his "Scandinavian Homesteaders in Central Alberta," 151.

57　Of the 569 who designated a state, 43.1 per cent came from Minnesota, 23.7 per cent from New York, 9.5 per cent from Illinois, 2.8 per cent from both South Dakota and Washington, 2.6 per cent from Nebraska, 2.5 per cent from North Dakota, 2.1 per cent from Pennsylvania, and the remaining 10.9 per cent from seventeen other states.

58　Wonders, "Scandinavian Homesteaders in Central Alberta," 154.

59　Jöns Andersson (1866–1940) was born in Ullstorp, Skåne. He immigrated in 1893 and married Mathilda "Tillie" Jarvis (1873–1966). Anderson died in Saskatoon. Thanks to Leif Mörkfors, Sweden, for donating photocopies of John Anderson's correspondence from 1911 to 1914, for family information, and for the article by Earl McGill, Battleford, Saskatchewan, "John Anderson: A Tribute" (1940), typescript.

60　John Anderson, Hill Side Farm, Minot, North Dakota, to Sven Månsson and wife, Tomelilla, Skåne, 26 November 1911.

61　John Anderson, Triple Lake Farm, Paynton, Saskatchewan, to Sven Månsson and wife, Tomelilla, Skåne, 2 January 1914.

62　Helmer Domier, "Norquay and District in the Early Years," in *Norquay Nostalgia: 1912–1982* (Norquay: Norquay Nostalgia Book Committee, 1982), 44.

63　"Swedes Do Well: Scandinavian Settlers Are Acquisition to Golden West," *Weekly Columbian*, New Westminster, 10 April 1906, reprinted from the *Winnipeg Telegram*. Thanks to Lorne Pearson, Surrey, British Columbia, for sending a photocopy of this article.

64　*Minnedosa Valley Views: Minnedosa's 100th Anniversary* (Winnipeg: Centennial Committee, 1982), 446–9. Charles Johnson emigrated from Långemåla, Småland, and became the first mail carrier between Portage la Prairie and Minnedosa. His brothers Fred and August came in 1879 and 1881, and farmed south of Minnedosa. Charles later moved to Mozart, Saskatchewan.

65　LAC; *Småland: Victor J. Wallin's svensk-amerikanska koloni vid Minnedosa, Man.* (Winnipeg: The Swedish Canadian Publishing Co., 1907). Thanks to archivist Art Grenke for bringing this brochure to my attention.

66　John W. Berg (1855–1922) was born in Viskafors, Västergötland, and migrated ca. 1885 via Minnesota, working as section foreman at Plum Coulee, Manitoba. In 1887 he married Mary Skoglund (18?–1900) from Värmland, who was working for M.P. Peterson in Winnipeg. After her death he married Hilda Hallgren (18?–1905). The family farmed in Scandinavia and Clanwilliam before moving to Minnedosa in 1906. See *Minnedosa Valley Views*, 233–4.

67 *Minnedosa Valley Views*, 62–5; see also Keith C. Fullerton, *One Hundred Years: The Evangelical Covenant Church in Canada* (Winnipeg: Evangelical Covenant Church of Canada, 2004), "Minnedosa Evangelical Covenant Church," 93–6.

68 Fullerton, "Valley Evangelical Covenant Church (Alpine-Durban)," in *One Hundred Years*, 97–100.

69 John Bengtson (1869–ca. 1964) was born in Galesburg, Illinois, and in 1901 married Gerda Person (1877–ca. 1956) from Wilcox, Pennsylvania. They had accompanied their parents to Nebraska while they were quite young, and farmed near Hordville. The couple brought their five children to Scandia in 1919. See *Scandia Since Seventeen* (Scandia Historical Committee, 1978), 209–10.

70 Glenbow Archives, CPR Fonds, M2269, file 1827; John Bengtson, Scandia, to J.W. Hugill, Calgary, 19 January 1927.

71 Charles John Anderson (18?–1954) was born in Värmland and emigrated to Ohio, then to Omaha, where he was active in Salem Church. Pastor Elving told him about irrigated land in Alberta, and he and his son Carl came to Scandia in 1918. His wife, Bertha (18?–1940), followed in 1919 with five children. See *Scandia Since Seventeen*, 185–6, 194–5.

72 *Salem Lutheran Church, Scandia, Alberta: 75th Anniversary Celebrations* (1994), 5–6. The first deacons were J.A. Hawkinson, John Bengtson, and Chas. J. Anderson. See also *Scandia Since Seventeen*, 95, 228, 249, 294; see also Emigrant Institute, Växjö, Mrs A.M. Peterson, "Scandia, Alberta," #377, in "Stories of Swedish Pioneers in North America," 1–9.

73 Glenbow Archives, CPR Fonds, MG 2269, file 1022; James Colley, Assistant Superintendent of Colonization, CPR, Calgary, to W. Fischer, Invermere, British Columbia, 4 March 1929.

74 Birthplaces of the Scandia congregation of 202 persons were: United States, eighty-two; Sweden, sixty; Canada, forty; and unknown, twenty. See Harald Runblom, "*Svenskarna i Canada*," figure 6 (Place of birth of members of two Alberta congregations, 1900–1934), 219.

4. Settlement Patterns

1 William C. Wonders, "Norden and Canada – A Geographer's Perspective," A Theme Paper presented at Canada and the Nordic Countries, the Triennial Conference of the Nordic Association for Canadian Studies, Lund University, Sweden, 11–14 August, 1987, 5, 8, 11, 18.

2 Nelson, *Swedes and the Swedish Settlements*, 352–3.

3 Of 6,164 immigrants, 439 did not specify their place of settlement. The
other numbers were: 1,295 Alberta, 1,272 Ontario, 1,010 British Columbia,
963 Saskatchewan, 830 Manitoba, 179 Quebec, 42 Yukon, 32 New
Brunswick, 32 Nova Scotia, 10 Newfoundland, 9 Northwest Territories.

4 Helge Nelson (1882–1966) was principal of a *folkhögskola* in the Swedish
countryside until 1916, when he was appointed professor of geography at
Lund University until 1947. He based his books and articles on extended
trips to Canada in 1921, 1925, and 1933. Nelson named Carl Sundbeck
and P.P. Waldenström as authors of helpful travel information.

5 Census of Canada, 1871.

6 Thanks to Elaine Hogg, Port Hawkesbury, Nova Scotia, for bringing
this company to my attention, and to Lars Anderson for personal
information.

7 Nelson, *Swedes and the Swedish Settlements*, 341.

8 Riksarkivet, Gen. Kons. i Montreal, Grupp 14, 13–17, 1902–23 (46, 9E);
Lammers, secretary, *Svenska förbundet i Canada* to David Bergström,
Montreal, 28 June 1917.

9 Consul General of Sweden Bengt Rösiö, "Letter from Montreal," *The
Swedish-Canadian Chamber of Commerce Newsletter* 13 (December 1988): 6.

10 Nelson, *Swedes and the Swedish Settlements*, 341.

11 Landelius Biography Collection, volume 2, #356. In 1929, under the
proprietorship of Gotfred Löwengren, Kausman's Café offered a
smörgåsbord for lunch and dinner with beer from his own brewery.

12 Sigrun Bulow-Hube (1913–1994) was born in Linköping, Östergötland,
and graduated in 1935 from the Royal Danish Academy of Art, School
of Architecture. She became senior consultant for the office of Design
Canada and a partner in Montreal's AKA Furniture Company, and was
the first female to join the Association of Canadian Industrial Designers.

13 Lars Forssell, "Flickan i Montréal," in Lars Forssell, *Upptåg* (Stockholm:
Bonnier, 1967).

14 Nelson, *Swedes and the Swedish Settlements*, 342.

15 *Thunder Bay Sentinel*, 17 April 1879, includes a list of hotels receiving a
liquor licence. Andrew Johnson (1850–1905) emigrated to the United
States in 1876, and two years later in Port Arthur married Katrina "Katie"
Gretta Nilsson Laurin (ca. 1846–1937), a Finland Swede. In addition to
Manitoba House, they owned a later hotel called Norway House. Thanks
to Brent Scollie, Ottawa, for information about Andrew Johnson. For his
wife, see Marc Metsaranta, ed., *Project Bay Street: Activities of Finnish-
Canadians in Thunder Bay before 1915* (Thunder Bay Finnish-Canadian
Historical Society, 1989), 32–3.

16 Andrew Wadson (ca. 1864–1919) was born in Närpes, Finland, and in 1887
     married in Port Arthur Mary Rosina Mickelson (ca. 1865–19?). His Port
     Arthur hotels were, successively, Bay View, Tracey House, Albion, and
     Kimberley. He also sold liquor wholesale and retail from 1894 to 1898.
17 Swedish families included the Andersons, Bengtsons, Carl Berglunds,
     Herman Berglunds (not related), Bostroms, Bromans, Carlsons,
     Cassmans, Englemarks, Ericsons, Gustafsons, Haglunds, Lindstroms,
     Lofgrens, Nelsons, Nordquists, Paulsons, Selanders, Sjolins, Skogs,
     Stroms, Sundbergs, Svensons, and Tillbergs.
18 These include Bratland's near Vermilion Bay, and Berglund's and
     Gummeson's near Ignace.
19 Lennard Olson, Conmee Township, Ontario, whose dad, Oscar Olson,
     worked for Shevlin-Clark in Fort Frances, identified the Swedes.
20 Bertil A. Forsberg (ca. 1903–1960s) was born in Sweden and immigrated
     to Port Arthur in the early 1920s. He was active in the Scandinavian
     Home Society until 1926, when he moved to Fort Frances. He
     married Alfie Dahlin and the couple adopted a daughter, Florence. A
     coloratura soprano, she was murdered in New York while performing
     in the Broadway hit *Wonderful Town* with Rosalind Russell. See Barr,
     Scandinavian Home Society, 174; see also *Winnipeg Tribune*, 16–22 July 1953.
21 Sigurd Lindberg (1896–19?) was born in Nordmaling, Ångermanland, the
     son of John Lindberg and Klara Backlund. The family immigrated to Port
     Arthur from 1923 to 1927. Sigurd married late in life and had no children.
     He died in Fort Frances. See Barr, *Scandinavian Home Society*, 179.
22 This section relies heavily on the history by Christopher Oslund, *One
     Hundred Years of Swedish Settlement in Timiskaming* (Haileybury: Rosanne
     Fisher, 1996).
23 C.C. Farr, owner of a local limestone quarry, wrote the pamphlet in 1893
     and revised it in 1896. See ibid., 3.
24 Erik Persson (ca. 1858–19?), his wife, Karin (ca. 1863–19?), and three
     children were neighbours of the Oslunds in Järna parish, Dalarna, and the
     families travelled to Haileybury together.
25 Johan Oslund (1846–1923) was born Johan Jansson in Axsjöberg, Tynsjö
     parish, Värmland, and changed his patrilineal surname to Åslund
     during military service, married Maria Nilsdotter, and in 1870 moved
     to Mjölbergsåsen, Dalarna. His children were Stina, John, Neil, Alex,
     Caroline "Lena," and Nathaniel. In 1889 Maria died in childbirth, and
     in 1894 Johan, or T.J., as he was called after his parish and Christian
     name, married widow Christina Fernholm and became stepfather to
     her six children. His eldest daughter Stina married and remained in

Sweden when the rest immigrated in 1896. Lena worked as a domestic in Compton on arrival in Canada.

26 Stina Lisa "Christina" Kristoffersdotter (1851–1930) married Anders Andersson Fernholm and lived in Nås, Dalarna. Her children were Andrew, John, Mary, Mathilda, Anna, and Emma. Andrew brought his wife, Emma Myhr, and baby to Canada. Mary worked as a domestic in Compton and Mathilda in Montreal on arrival in Canada. John remained in Sweden for one year to finish his apprenticeship as a shoemaker, arriving in 1897.

27 Oslund, *One Hundred Years of Swedish Settlement in Timiskaming*, 11. In 1906 two of the sons, Andrew Fernholm and John Oslund, went to the Prairies, but returned after ten years in Meacham, Saskatchewan. See also Artur Strid, "Från Södra Hulta till Lake Temiskaming: Några emigrantöden," in *Särtryck ur Osby Hembygdsförenings årsbok 1989*, 49, which states that Olof, Sven, and August Nilsson were brothers, sons of Nils and Bengta Johannesson, who lived on a little torp on Björnön, Loshult, Skåne. They married three Fernholm sisters: Sven married Mathilda and August married Anna in 1905; Olof married Emma in 1907. Two other Nilsson siblings, Karl and Ingrid, returned to Sweden. See also Oslund, *One Hundred Years of Swedish Settlement*, 5–8.

28 Johan Gottfrid Hammarström (ca. 1880–19?) was born in Ljusne, Hälsingland, and married Anna Maria Gräs (ca. 1879–19?). In 1906 he immigrated to Haileybury via North Bay, Ontario, with daughter Elsa, his parents, sisters Johanna and Selma (with her husband, Hugo Högberg, and two children), brother Bill, and Anna Maria's sister Elin and her brother Edward Grace with his wife Hilda and newborn daughter.

29 Nils Gustaf Ljungberg (ca. 1877–19?) immigrated in 1906, and the following year his wife, Anna Kristina, came with their son.

30 Axel Herbert Hedman (ca. 1881–19?) immigrated via North Bay in 1906, and his wife, Ida Kristina, followed in 1907 with two sons.

31 Ernst Ferdinand Mannerström and Hugo Julius Mannerström immigrated via North Bay in 1906 with their wives, Johanna Wilhelmina and Elisabeth and children.

32 Oslund, *One Hundred Years of Swedish Settlement*, 8–14.

33 Riksarkivet, Gen. Kons. i Montreal, Grupp 14, 13–17, 1902–23 (46, 9E); Lammers, secretary, *Svenska förbundet i Canada* to David Bergström, Montreal, 28 June 1917. Harald A. Leverin worked for the Department of Mines, H. Claughton Wallin for the forestry section of the Department of the Interior, and Dr O. Malte Malte was in charge of experimental farms.

34 Martin L. Friedland, *The University of Toronto: A History* (Toronto: University of Toronto Press, 2002), 332. Emil Wallberg had immigrated from Värmland at an early age and received his training in Illinois, moving to Canada in 1892. See Landelius Biography Collection, volume 3, #254.

35 Joseph Ander (ca. 1882–1963) was born Josef Emanuel Ander in Norrköping, Östergötland. He visited Sweden in 1938, the year he founded Atlas Polar Company, and in 1963 his son Ralph Ander took over as president. See Landelius Biography Collection, volume 1, #011.

36 Björn Leyner (ca. 1924–2004) was born in Stockholm and joined Astra in 1946.

37 Nils Fredrik Anders Peder Kallin served as consul in Toronto from 1957 to 1974. He arrived in the mid-1950s, after serving in China and Japan.

38 "Company File: Scandinavian Centre," *Swedish Press*, May 1988, 17; see also "Toronto Notes," *Swedish Press*, July 1996, which reported that Westin's new company, Plan for Success Inc., offered "a broad range of services geared towards helping small and medium-sized European companies develop and support markets for their products in Canada and throughout the NAFTA region."

39 Nelson, *Swedes and the Swedish Settlements*, 354–6.

40 *Forest to Field: Centennial History of Rural Municipality of Clanwilliam and Village of Erickson, Manitoba, Canada, 1884–1984* (Erickson, 1984), 9; see also John Langton Tyman, *By Section, Township and Range: Studies in Prairie Settlement* (Brandon: Assiniboine Historical Society, 1972), 119; see also LAC, RG 17, volume 450, file 49112, Ennis to W.C.B. Grahame, 5 August 1885, and Grahame to John Lowe, Department of Agriculture, Ottawa, 10 August 1885. The four adjoining townships were granted by Sir David Macpherson, in one of his last acts as minister of the Department of the Interior.

41 Tyman, *By Section, Township and Range*, 121, states that the total area cultivated by 1890–1 was less than one section.

42 LAC, RG 17, volume 461, file 50366, Ennis to the Minister of Agriculture, 17 November 1885; see also "A Visit to New Sweden, December 4, 1885, To the Editor of the Tribune," in *Forest to Field*, 11.

43 The colony, now part of the Rural Municipality of Clanwilliam, centred on Otter Lake, townships 17 and 18 in ranges 17 and 18, with a corner of present-day Riding Mountain National Park in the northeast.

44 Ibid., Ennis to Minister of Agriculture, 17 November 1885: "Owing to a feeling generated by a few Swedes in Winnipeg headed by Mr. Ohlin [*sic*], Assistant Immigration Agent to Capt. Graham [*sic*], it was decided

only to locate Swedes in this new colony who joined a temperance or Blue Ribbon Society of which only eighteen Swedes formed the main body. This action on the part of Mr. Ohlin caused a rupture ... I do not hesitate to say that had the Assistant Immigration Agent in Winnipeg [Mr Ohlin] fulfilled his appointment and assisted instead of opposing the settlement of Scandinavians in the Province the number of settlers would have been larger."

45 The Winnipeg directors included D.H. Harrison, Minnedosa's MLA, and Rufus Stephenson, Inspector of Colonization Companies. Since both were leading Conservatives, it is not surprising that Premier Norquay himself addressed the meeting. The Scandinavian Colonization Society of Manitoba letterhead lists vice-president Anton Smith, secretary Emanuel Turner, treasurer John Anderson, and directors D.H. Harrison, Rufus Stephenson, and Joseph Mulholland of Winnipeg, also the mayors of Minnedosa and Birtle. For a blow-by-blow account of the meeting 1 September 1885, see LAC, RG 15, D-11-1, volume 397, file 12751, "The Scandinavians: They Organize a National Society on Saturday Night," *The Daily Manitoban.*

46 The *1884 City Directory* for Eau Claire, Wisconsin, lists John H. Noreus, "Dealer in all kinds of Sewing Machines and Organs; All kinds of Machines Repaired by an Expert 2 Bridge west end Kelsey street bridge, res 403 S Barstow."

47 LAC, RG 17, volume 472, file 51699, Ennis to John Lowe, Department of Agriculture, Ottawa, 22 February 1886. See also Tyman, *By Section, Township and Range,* 121, who quotes from the Immigration Report for 1886, 76, that "One of their number [was] spreading untruthful reports, [so that newcomers] expected on their arrival to find comfortable houses, stock, farm implements ... as well as steamboat facilities for navigating Otter Lake."

48 LAC, RG 17, volume 480, file 52638, Ennis to J.A. Green, Winnipeg, 22 April 1886. See also "Fire at New Sweden, Dec. 11, 1885, News Item," in *Forest to Field,* 12. When the immigrant house burned down on 5 December, its twenty-six occupants, including Ennis, barely escaped with their lives. Noreus, more interested in the loss of his personal belongings, valued the building and its contents at the inflated sum of $12,000. When he finally returned to the colony in the New Year he assured Ennis that the overdue accounts and wages would be paid as soon as the immigrant house was rebuilt.

49 LAC, RG 17, volume 480, file 52638, Ennis to J.A. Green, Winnipeg, 22 April 1886. The streets were named after directors Stephenson

and Mulholland, Land Commissioner A.F. Eden of the Manitoba & Northwestern Railway, and Vice-Consul Green, among others. See also "A Visit to New Sweden, December 4, 1885, To the Editor of the Tribune," in *Forest to Field*, 10.

50 "New Sweden, April 23, 1886," credited to the *Manitoba Sun*, in *Forest to Field*, 12. Only two members of the deputation of ten are named: Anderson and Engman. They left satisfied after Land Commissioner A.F. Eden assured them that "any style, title or authority he [Noreus] had taken upon himself was entirely self-assumed."

51 Jens "James" Hemmingson (1858–1931) was born in Själland, Denmark, immigrated to Canada in the early 1880s, and worked on Great Lakes tugboats before settling in Winnipeg, where he managed the hotel Woodstock House and married Clara Munson (1863–1930) from Sweden. A nephew was left in charge of the hotel when they moved to Scandinavia. Hemmingson resigned as postmaster in 1892, having earlier applied for a homestead where the couple lived out their lives. See *Forest to Field*, 412.

52 See *Forest to Field*, 13, for the 1886 townsite plan, titled "Scandinavia, subdivision of part of SW¼ Sec 7: Tp 18: Rge 17, and part of SE¼ Sec 12: Tp 18: Rge 18." The original plan was not registered in the Land Titles Office and therefore has no legal status. The first patent for these properties went to James Hemmingson. Thanks to Ted Simonson, Winnipeg, for sorting out this confusing issue.

53 Unless otherwise cited, information about post offices and postmasters comes from data posted on ArchiviaNet by Library and Archives Canada.

54 Cited by Tyman, *By Section, Township and Range*, 121, from Report of March 21st, 1889, RG 15, 201549. The Dominion government provided $1,200 in compensation for fire losses, the province paid $500 in 1885 and a further $850 in 1886 towards building a road north from Minnedosa, and the Manitoba & Northwestern Railway paid $682 to needy settlers.

55 The Hemmingson Lakes southwest of McCreary are named for James Hemmingson. See Gerald F. Holm, *Geographical Names of Manitoba* (Winnipeg: Manitoba Geographical Names Program, 2001), 110.

56 Johan Fremling (1842–1917) was born in Fremmestad, Värmland, and in 1870 emigrated to the United States, was ordained in 1871, and served in Minnesota and Wisconsin, also as secretary and president of Minnesota Conference boards. See Conrad John Emanuel Bergendoff, *The Augustana Ministerium: A Study of the Careers of the 2,504 pastors of the Augustana Evangelical Lutheran Synod/Church, 1850–1962* (Rock Island: Augustana Historical Society, 1980).

57 Baglo, *Augustana Lutherans in Canada*, 13.

58 Nelson, *Swedes and the Swedish Settlements*, 58.

59 Norris Lake, originally Morris Lake, was named for John Morris, Dominion land surveyor, who worked in the area from 1872 to 1873. The painter of the sign at the stopping place mistakenly put an "N" instead of an "M" as the first letter, and the name stuck. See Manitoba Archives, MG 14, C 28, Box 1, File 1, W.J. Sisler Collection, "Swedish Colony in Rockwood" by W.J. Sisler, from the compilation of Gustav Gullikson (1951); see also Otto Helander and Judith Johnson, "Swedish Colony of Norris Lake," in R.A. Quickfall, ed., *Rockwood Echoes: 90 Years of Progress 1870–1960: A History of the Men and Women Who Pioneered the Rockwood Municipality* (Stonewall: Rockwood-Woodlands Historical Society, 1960), 252.

60 Ibid., 249–51. The original thirteen men included Axel Anderson, Peter Berglund, Martin Halvarson, Fred Johnson, John Johnson, Severin Johnson, Olaf Lofving, Fred Nelson, A. Nordquist, John Nordstrom, Hans Olson, and Rikard Olsen. The name of the thirteenth man is not listed. For the names of other Swedish settlers, see Sisler, "Swedish Colony in Rockwood," 2–3; see also *The Interlake Beckoned: A History of Inwood and Surrounding Districts* (Inwood: Inwood History Book Committee, 1980).

61 Per Olof Nordin (ca. 1869–1942) was born in Norrbäcken, Medelpad, and cut short his civil engineering studies to immigrate to Winnipeg in 1893. He married Maria Wall (1872–1943) from Löberöd, Skåne, in Winnipeg's Baptist church in 1897. Nordin used his civil engineering skills in the construction of the Norman dam in Kenora in 1921, and in installing mining machinery at God's Lake gold mine in 1933. See *100 Years of History: Rockwood Municipality* (Stonewall, 1982), 312–14.

62 See *Swedish Press*, December 2002, for a photo of the ribbon-cutting ceremony with Carol Langston, 100-year-old Charlie Bjork, and his sister, Selma. The property, which includes Nordin's massive stone-and-frame barn painted red, the milk house, and a blacksmith shop of Swedish design, was sold in 2006.

63 Ibid, 95–6, 118.

64 Adam Clayton, "Marking History: Restored Pioneer Cemetery Unveiled," *Stonewall Argus*, 25 July 2004. Helen Kletke, Brian Korotash, and Wayne Enberg had refurbished the cemetery with municipal and provincial funding and a grant from the Interlake Community Foundation.

65 Ljungmark, *Svenskarna i Winnipeg*, 30. In comparison, there were 2,193 Icelanders, 100 Danes, 88 Norwegians, and 3 Finns.

66 Ibid., 104.

67 Logan Avenue was named for Robert Logan (1773–1866), councillor of Assiniboia from 1823 to 1839 and owner of the property on which Fort Douglas stood. His son, Alexander Logan, served as mayor of Winnipeg from 1879 to 1880, and in 1882 and 1884.

68 The federal government built immigrant houses as temporary housing for immigrants, commonly called "immigrant halls" or "immigrant sheds" in cities. Brandon and Emerson each got one in 1882, and Port Arthur in 1883. See LAC, mfm C4669-70, H. H. Smith, Commissioner of Dominion Lands, Winnipeg, to Department of the Interior, Ottawa, 11 July 1892.

69 The Scandinavian Hotel was run by a Swede named Simonson, and Hotel Svea by the Norwegian M.A. Meyer, but both catered to all Scandinavians.

70 Lars Ljungmark, "Snusboulevarder och snusandet i Svensk-Amerika," in *Göteborgs-Emigranten 5*, ed. Per Clemensson, Lennart Limberg, and Lars Ljungmark (Göteborg: Projektet Göteborgs-Emigranten, 1996), 115–17, names other Snoose boulevards as Chicago Street in Chicago, Payne Avenue in St Paul, and Cedar Avenue in Minneapolis, as well as Snoose Corner and Snoose Junction in Seattle.

71 Ibid., 123. From the 1820s to the 1930s, Sweden consumed more snuff per capita than any other country, followed closely by Norway and Iceland.

72 Ibid., 118, 120. This comment is credited to a 1994 interview with members of Strindberg Vasa Lodge.

73 Oskar L. Sundborg (ca. 1867–19?) emigrated from Stockholm in 1887 with the destination of Boston, later becoming associated with Chicago.

74 Ljungmark, "Snusboulevarder," 119–20.

75 Saskatchewan Archives, Accession No. R83-17, Collection No. R-E1430, Carl Ian Walker, "Sven Erikson Svedberg, A Swedish Pioneer," 4. Kuriko tasted like Coca Cola without the fizz, according to Ellen Dahl.

76 Ljungmark, *Svenskarna i Winnipeg*, 79–80.

77 John Albert Gustafson (1871–1948) was born in Högstena, Västergötland, and immigrated to Canada in 1891. He worked for the CPR until 1909, when he opened a grocery store, then a tobacco shop. Treasurer and trustee of Zion Lutheran Church, he was also a member of Strindberg Vasa Lodge, the Norden Society, and founder and long-time president of the Old Timers Association (1913 to 1993). He did not marry. When he died his nephew, Nils Hammarstrand, took over. See Landelius Biography Collection, volume 1, #330; see also Manitoba Archives, Swedish Community Oral History Collection, C553-554, Karin Graydon.

78 Walter Syslak, "Swede Town," *Swedish Press*, November 2001, 34; see also "The Hammarstrand family" by Karin Graydon, typescript donated

by Walter Syslak; for a photo of the store see Ljungmark, *Svenskarna i Winnipeg*, 228.

79 Philip Eckman (1879–1938), a dentist born in Granite Falls, Minnesota, opened a practice in Winnipeg in 1910. See Landelius Biography Collection, volume 1, #196.

80 Edwin Otto Carlson (1910–2006) was born in Djupdalen, Stora Skedva, Dalarna, and emigrated without his mother's permission in 1929, landing in Winnipeg. In 1934 he married Beda Linnea Rosenquist (ca. 1911–1985), who, in 1929, emigrated from Gunnarskog, Värmland. The couple had one son, Neil. In 1939 Ed and his wife founded Carlson Decorating, which expanded to include sandblasting. Ed was Swedish consul from 1962 to 1980, and belonged to many Swedish clubs as well as Kiwanis, the Masonic Order, the Shrine, and the Winnipeg Executive Association. After Beda's death, he married Esther Eriksrud Rylander Landro (1893–1992) from Toten, Norway. Thanks to Ed Carlson for family information; see also *Swedish Press*, February 2000, 27; see also *Winnipeg Free Press*, "Sandblasting Company Has Left Its Mark on City: Carlson Family Celebrating 60 Years in Business," n.d.

81 Ed Carlson, "Some memories from Logan Ave. in the dirty thirties," typescript, 3 pages.

82 Ljungmark, "Swedes in Winnipeg up to the 1940s," 67.

83 C.H. Nilson (1885–1937) was born in Hönby, Skåne. He belonged to Zion Lutheran Church and the Norden Society, and represented the Vasa Order at Grand Lodge. His son was named Halley because he was born at the time of Halley's comet in 1910. See Landelius Biography Collection, volume 3, #016; see also Syslak, "Swede Town," 34.

84 *Water under the Bridge: History of the Little Grassy River, McCrosson-Tovell, 1891–1993* (Sleeman, ON, 1994), 360, mentions Kuriko and Oleoyd. Anna Sideen sold Oleoyd, Pirico, and Magvigori in Stanley, Ontario, during the 1920s and 1930s.

85 Nilsson, *De sista svenska rösterna*, 136. Thorin came from Värmland.

86 Syslak, "Swede Town," 34; see also J.C. Royle, "What Have the Swedes Brought to Us?," *Winnipeg Tribune*, 25 April 1942; see also *Winnipeg Tribune*, "Winnipeg Loses Role As Centre For All Swedes," 21 March 1956; see also Nilsson, *De sista svenska rösterna*, 108–9.

87 Epp, *Nordic People in Canada*, table 7 and table 8. Saskatchewan's total population in 1901 was 91,279 and in 1911 had risen to 492,432.

88 Ibid., table 12. See also Nelson, *Swedes and the Swedish Settlements*, 356–8.

89 Alan B. Anderson, "Assimilation in the Bloc Settlements of North-central Saskatchewan: A Comparative Study of Identity Change among

Seven Ethno-religious Groups in a Canadian Prairie Region," PhD diss., University of Saskatchewan, 1972, 98.

90 Stockholm Binder, "Memories from the First Days," fiftieth anniversary speech given by Karolina Johanson Lindwall, 1936.

91 Ibid., "Nils and Karin Johanson," 2–3, and "Zakarias Erikson Lindwall," 4, both written by Lucille Lindwall Szumutku. The two-storey dwelling rested on a foundation of large stones and measured 4.5 by 6 metres.

92 Ibid., "Nils and Karin Johanson," 3, and "Zakarias Erikson Lindwall," 4. A government grant of $500 in 1892 allowed them to build a road and a wooden bridge with a yoke of oxen, two teams of horses, a plough, two road scrapers, and broad axes, with Zakarias Lindwall as foreman. According to Öhlén's Immigration Report of 1887 the society's directors were honorary president Emanuel Ohlen, president Charles Sahlmark, vice-president Nils Johanson, secretary Alex Stenberg, treasurer Wilhelm Soderberg, and two honorary members: J.H. McTavish of the CPR and W.B. Scarth, MP, of the Canada North-West Land Company. According to ibid., C.O. Hofstrand, "New Stockholm History," 12, the society was joined by another local group, the Farmers' Union, in 1901.

93 Nelson, *Swedes and the Swedish Settlements*, 357, crediting Carl Sundbeck, *Svensk-amerikanerna, deras materiella och andliga sträfvanden: Anteckningar från en resa i Amerika* (Rock Island: Augustana Book Concern, 1904), 468.

94 Alfred Nordström (1879–1980) was born in Gaddaröd, Skåne, and emigrated to North Dakota in 1900. He married Ellen Persson (1876–1951) in 1903. See *Chronicles of Canwood and Districts: Moose Valley, Sugar Hill, Moonbeam, Boro Green, Sandy Lake, Stump Lake, Balsamdale, Silver Cliff, Dry Creek, Silent Call, Nestledown, Summit Prairie, Blue Heron, Canwood* (Canwood, SK, 1981), 226–7. Thanks to Bev Haug, Saskatoon, and Carol John Nordstrom, Abbotsford, British Columbia, for family information, including Gary Nordstrom's "A Brief History of Peter and Inga Nordstrom and Their Family."

95 Erik Anderson (1857–1936) was born in Dalarna and emigrated to the United States in 1876. In 1889 he married Johanna Sommarstrom (1863–1958) from the Åland Islands. See *Quarter Stake Echoes* (Shaunavon, SK: South Shaunavon History Club, 1981), 20–3.

96 Anders Gustav Anderson (1855–1928) was born in Dalarna and emigrated to the United States. In 1897 he married Amelia Sofia Englund (1850–1942) from the Åland Islands in St Hilaire, Minnesota. They adopted a daughter. See ibid., 14–15.

97 "The Gift: Memoirs of Viola Anderson," 2. Thanks to Margaret Anderson, Shaunavon, for donating this seven-page typescript.

98 August Dahlman (ca. 1871–ca. 1970) emigrated from Undenäs, Västergötland, in 1904, but grew up in Ekshärad, Värmland. A Winnipeg immigration official had mailed homestead information to him three years earlier. He married a sister of P.B. Holmgren from Pennock, Minnesota, who homesteaded north of Estevan. He left his wife with her brother in Estevan for three successive winters while he fulfilled the requirement of living for six months each year on his isolated homestead near Meyronne. When he gained title in 1911 his wife and children joined him. See Saskatchewan Archives, RE 2946, August Dahlman, "Estevan, Assiniboia, N.W.T., Canada," typescript.

99 Thanks to Lila Martinson, Assiniboia, Saskatchewan, for sending a copy of the article "The Iron Cross" by Laura Dahlman, which included a photo.

100 Adolf Nordin is the son of Emil Nordin, who came to Buchanan in 1907 via Isanti, Minnesota. Emil had emigrated in 1903 from Kyrkbyn, Hassela, Hälsingland, and in 1911 married Erika Forsman, from Mekinock, North Dakota. Thanks to Adolf Nordin and his granddaughter Arlie Nordin for a tour of the cemetery and for family information.

101 Pete and Mabel Russell, *The Parks and Recreation Facilities of Saskatoon* (Saskatoon, 1981), 69–70. The park is located along Pinehouse Drive and between Warman Road and Primrose Drive.

102 Epp, *Nordic People in Canada*, table 7, table 8, and table 12. Alberta's total population in 1901 was 73,022 and in 1911 had risen to 373,943.

103 Nelson, *Swedes and the Swedish Settlements*, 359–63.

104 John Johnson Hallgren (1841–1934) was born in Stockholm, Sweden, and in 1866 migrated to New York, then to Winnipeg, where he married Mary Ann McDonald (d 1932), daughter of a policeman who had been shot near Fort Garry. John changed his surname from Johnson to Hallgren because of mix-ups with mail. See *Mingling Memories* (Red Deer: Red Deer Historical Society, 1979), 667–8.

105 Janssen, "Swedish Settlement in Alberta," 117, citing Molin, *Några drag af kolonisationen i Canada*, 51–2.

106 Nelson, *Swedes and the Swedish Settlements*, 360.

107 Emil Rikard Thure Skarin (1882–1970) was born in Bjurträsk, Lycksele, Lappland. He immigrated to Canada in 1902 and in 1914 married Amanda "Ada" Fryk from Sunne, Värmland. See Ada Skarin, "Emil Rikard Thure Skarin, 1882–1970," in Ossian Egerbladh, *Bjurträsk och Söderby byar i Lycksele socken* (1976), 70–4; see also Carl Wrick, "*Födelsedagar 28 april*," Landelius Biography Collection, volume 3, #169.

108 Lars Fahlstrom, "Emil Skarin (1882–1970)," typescript dated 2003.

109 Jonas Peter Johnson (1882–19?) was born in Sweden, the eldest son of John and Bertha Johnson. The family immigrated to Winnipeg about 1885. Johnson worked for a Swedish newspaper there for twelve years, then established a real-estate office in Wetaskiwin. In 1907 he married Martha Olstad, who had come from Minnesota with her parents at the turn of the century. Johnson was Liberal in politics and Methodist in religion. See John Blue, *Alberta, Past and Present, Historical and Biographical* (Chicago: Pioneer Historical Publishing, 1924), 3:311–12.

110 Landelius Biography Collection, volume 2, #156, newspaper clipping datelined New York and headlined "Känd svensk i Kanada förskingrar, Vice-konsuln J.P. Johnson häktad, Misslyckade fastighetsspekulationer orsaken," 11 January 1929.

111 Thanks to Ken Domier, Edmonton, for sending information from the 1906 Census of Canada and the *1914 Henderson's Directory.*

112 Gus Rydman (1884–1951) was born Gustaf Herman Fransson in Gräflingeryd, Tingsås, Småland, and emigrated to Minneapolis in 1902. In 1910 he married Hulda Theresia Gustafsdotter (1884–1981) from Kampingemåla, Gertonsgård, Södra Sandsjö, Småland, who had emigrated to St Paul in 1907. Thanks to daughter-in-law Perry Rydman, Edmonton, for family information.

113 Andrew Kvarnberg (18?–1934) was born in Rista, near Gagnef, Dalarna. He emigrated to Minnesota in 1902, the following year homesteading near Calmar. Despite gnarled and painful hands from arthritis, he handcrafted several violins and zithers, furniture, and skis so the children could get to school in wintertime. See Elsie Kvarnberg Simmons, "Andrew and Kerstin Kvarnberg and Family" (1989), typescript. Thanks to granddaughter Verna Larson, Edmonton, for family information.

114 Carl Herbert Ohrn (1887–1974) was born in Youngstown, Ohio, the son of Erik Gotthard Öhrn and Matilda Eliason. In 1922 he married Alma Sandstrom (1893–1965), the daughter of Olaf and Christine Sandström from Dalarna. The couple came to Canada in 1899 from Rutland, North Dakota, and homesteaded northwest of Calmar. Thanks to Ralph Ohrn, Edmonton, for family information and the brochure produced for the grand opening.

115 Albin Benson ended up as sole owner, servicing the area for twenty years. See *Golden Memories: Warburg and District*, n.d., 192.

116 Emanuel Petterson Cronquist (1854–1924) was born in southern Sweden, and married Hilda Carlsdotter (1852–1943) in Värmland. The couple immigrated to Burnt Lake in 1894. Emanuel adopted the surname Cronquist to avoid confusion with mail delivery. He belonged to the

Red Deer Board of Trade. See Red Deer and District Archives, Emanuel Cronquist Fonds, MG 133, "The Cronquist Family"; see also *Along the Burnt Lake Trail: A History of Shady Nook, Burnt Lake, Centerville, Pine Hill, Marianne, Kuusamo and Evarts* (Red Deer: Burnt Lake History Society, 1977), 184; see also "Cronquist House: Rescued Old House Becomes Centre of Activity," in *News and Views: Alberta Historical Resources Foundation*, 1983; see also Lynne Van Luven, "The Cronquist House: 61 Years of History Overlooking City," *Red Deer Advocate*, 1968.

117 William Loov (1895–1955) was born Edvin Anders Vilhelm Lööv in Ronneby, Blekinge. In 1920 he married Asta (1893–1957), born Augusta Charlotta Carlson in Väckelsång, Småland. Thanks to Verner Loov, Edmonton, for family information. See also Edvin Anders William Loov, *Twenty-Five Years Away From Home: Experiences of a Swedish Immigrant in Canada 1927–1952* (Calgary, 1995).

118 Per Anger (1913–2002) served as Swedish ambassador to Canada from 1976 to 1979. A colleague of Raoul Wallenberg in Hungary, Anger visited Canada in 1986 to mark the forty-first anniversary of his disappearance.

119 Gordon Stromberg, son of Enock Stromberg, served as MLA for Camrose from 1971 to 1986.

120 Nelson, *Swedes and the Swedish Settlements*, 361–6, which duplicates his "British Columbia and the Swedish Element in the Population," in *Geografiska annaler* (1935), 634–9.

121 Epp, *Nordic People in Canada*, 60.

122 Carl August "Charlie" Petersson Thulin (1863–1932) was born in Tryserum, Småland, and in 1886 emigrated to a relative, Karl Johan Thulin, in Burlington, Iowa. After a brief stay he travelled to British Columbia, reaching Port Moody in time to help build the railway to Vancouver and become a contractor. In 1892 he married Beata Swanson's sister, Mary Johanson (ca. 1866–19?) from Kinnared, Halland. See Howard, *Vancouver's Svenskar*, 20–1.

123 Fredrick Gottfrid "Fred" Peterson Thulin (1873–1935) immigrated in 1889. He married Ida Emelia Vainio.

124 For the Thulin brothers' business activities, see Helen A. Mitchell, *Diamond in the Rough: A History of Campbell River* (Campbell River: Upper Islander Print, 1966), 96–105, 158, which includes a translation of Eric Herner's "Svenska innebyggare," 1 November 1947, 99–100; see also Fred Thulin's obituary in Landelius Biography Collection, volume 3, #236; see also "Lund B.C.," *Swedish Press*, July 2003, 15.

125 Rolf Wallgren Bruhn (1878–1942) was born in Resteröd, Bohuslän, and immigrated to Canada ca. 1896, marrying in 1902. The couple had

three children: Ted, Frederick, and Alvera. See George M. Abbott, "Rolf Wallgren Bruhn, Pioneer and Politician," *Okanagan History* 59 (1995): 87–95.

126 Folke Elfving, *Sagan om Nörve: En nittioåring skriver om en hundraåring* (Göteborg, 1993). In 1993 *Nörve* was in private hands and still sailing.

127 For details of his business career, see Denis Marshall, *Sawdust Caesars and Family Ties in the Southern Interior Forests* (Salmon Arm: Salmon Arm Branch, Okanagan Historical Society, 2003). In 1924 Bruhn equipped one of his towboats, named *Alvera* after his daughter, with a two-cylinder diesel engine of Swedish manufacture, "which came to Sicamous with a technical representative to teach the owners how to operate it."

128 "Millionaire and Minister in Canada Is Career for School Weary Rolf," translation of a 1987 article by Hans Brattberg published in a Stockholm newspaper, provided by Denis Marshall, Salmon Arm, British Columbia. Both Bruhn and Macfie came from the Uddevalla area in Bohuslän, and the reporter worked for *Bohuslänningen.*

129 He held the riding until his death in 1942, serving as minister of Public Works when the Conservatives were in power from1928 to 1933 and again in 1941 under a coalition government.

130 Abbott, "Rolf Wallgren Bruhn," 93. For a biography by a Swedish immigrant, see St Jean, "Swedes on the Move," 184–98.

131 UBCL SC, Matthew Lindfors Fonds; typewritten letter on "City of Revelstoke, Office of the Mayor" letterhead from Arvid Lundell to Matthew M. Lindfors, Vancouver, 7 December 1966, in response to his request to W.J. Blomquist, Malakwa, for information about Swedes in Malakwa. Arvid Lundell was an alderman for fourteen years and mayor for five years. He seems to have been publisher of the weekly newspaper as well.

132 Ljungmark, "Snusboulevarder," 118.

133 Frank William Hart (1857–1935) was born of Swedish parents in Knoxville, Illinois, attended a Swedish school as a child, and was twenty-nine years old upon his arrival at Port Moody. He left Vancouver in 1895, and is said to have made two fortunes in the Klondike. He died in Prince Rupert.

134 Irene Howard, "Vancouver Swedes and the Loggers," *Swedish Pioneer Historical Quarterly* 21, no. 3 (1970): 163–5; also her research notes from Frank Hart's typescript "Reminiscences" (1929), housed at the British Columbia Archives, Victoria. The City of Vancouver Archives has a photograph of Hart's welcome arch.

135 UBCL SC, Seaholm Collection, A VII B, typescript "Hart's Opera House, Carrall Street in Chinatown" by J.S. Matthews, archivist, City of Vancouver Archives, April 1963.

136 Irene Howard, "Pete Larson, North Vancouver Hotelman," *North Shore Historical Society Newsletter* 1, no. 7 (October 1976): 3–5.

137 Her sister Alma and husband, Axel Peterson, who had a jeweller's shop on Cordova Street, were first to come in 1887. The same year her brother Frank opened a shoemaker's shop on Abbott Street. Her sisters Hilda and Sigrid came and married unrelated men named Nelson.

138 Howard, "Vancouver Swedes and the Loggers," 166–7. Emil Peterson (1870–1937) arrived in Vancouver in 1888, and then sent home for his fiancée, Marie-Louise Winqvist. She in turn sent for her sister, Johanna, who married a workmate of Emil's, Louie Anderson.

139 Anne-Charlotte Harvey, a professional singer and actress from Stockholm, was the featured performer at the Snoose Boulevard Festival in Minneapolis, held in April 1972 to celebrate the neighbourhood's Scandinavian heritage. Some of her repertoire of immigrant songs were recorded that year under the title *Memories of Snoose Boulevard*. See Ann-Charlotte Harvey and Richard H. Hulan, "Teater, visafton och bal: The Swedish-American Road Show in its Heyday," *Swedish-American Historical Quarterly* 37, no. 3 (1986): 135–6.

140 *Swedish Press*, May, June, and July 1987.

141 *Swedish Press*, January 1986. There are more than 3,000 rune stones in Sweden, with some along the Volga River and in northern Europe, dating from the Swedish Vikings, 800–1050 A.D.

142 Those who worked towards the incorporation were Solveig Carlgren, Gun Holms, Matti Klaar, Anders Neumüller, Brita Norman, Irene Olljum, and Lennart Osterlind.

143 Lennart Osterlind (1937–) was born in Sweden and grew up in South Africa. When he returned to Sweden he was educated in fine arts, printing and typesetting, and graphic design. He worked as a graphic designer in Sweden, Switzerland, and Beirut until 1968, when he and his wife, Margareta, came to Vancouver. He has been in the insurance business ever since, with art as a sideline. Lennart helped found Sweden House Society, helped negotiate the purchase with the Norwegian consul, and is still serving on the board. See www.lennart.artsites.ca.

144 Consul Tor Virding, "The History of Roald Amundsen Centre" (February 1997), typescript, 8 pages; see also Lennart Osterlind, "President's Report for the AGM, Scandinavian Community Centre Society, 5 March 1996," both documents donated by Greta Nelson, Burnaby, past secretary of SCCS.

145 *Viking Ship News*, Burnaby and Vancouver (Spring 2003). Thanks to volunteer Tina Reid, Abbotsford, for sending information and print material.

146 Otto Nordling (1907–1978) was born in Luleå, Norrbotten, and in 1914
    immigrated with his parents and brothers Oscar and Tory to Dawson,
    Yukon, where Axel and a sister were born. After graduating from high
    school he worked in Dawson's Bank of Montreal. He served seventeen
    years in the Canadian army, retiring as a sergeant in 1957. During the
    Second World War he edited *The Canadian News* at the army camp in
    Manila, and afterwards was posted to Ottawa from 1947 to 1952. In
    1945 he married Captain Margery Langley of Revelstoke, the daughter
    of mining engineer A.G. Langley. Library and Archives Canada, City of
    Vancouver Archives and Yukon Archives hold the Otto Nordling Fonds.
    See also Linda E.T. MacDonald and Lynette R. Bleiler, comps., *Gold &*
    Galena: A History of the Mayo District (Mayo: Mayo Historical Society,
    1999), 433.

147 City of Vancouver Archives, Otto Nordling Fonds; Otto Nordling,
    Vancouver, to Prime Minister Diefenbaker, Ottawa, 12 July 1957.

148 Barbro Nilsson Baker was born in Torsby, Värmland, and emigrated to
    Minneapolis in 1958. While visiting her sister Brita and husband, Peter
    Baker, in Winnipeg, she met Peter's brother, Stephen, and the couple
    married in 1961. Stephen's job took them to Oregon, California, Langley,
    Whitehorse, and Winnipeg, where Barbro was very active in the Swedish
    community. The Bakers retired to Victoria, British Columbia. See *Swedish*
    Press, May 1989 for Barbro, and July 1998 for Brita.

149 Ulf Beijbom, *Guldfeber: En bok om guldrusherna till Kalifornien och Klondike*
    (Stockholm: Natur och kultur, 1979). For ten articles about his trip see
    Smålandsposten, September and October 1979.

150 Yukon Archives; "Laths guldgrävarmapp överlämnad till borgmästaren i
    Dawson," *Svenska pressen*, 11 June 1979.

151 Anne Tempelman-Kluit, "Detective Traces Gold Rush Immigrants,"
    undated newspaper clipping; see also Willy Läth, "Hos familjen Dahlgren
    i Whitehorse," *Smålandsposten*, 14 February 1981. Thanks to Barbro Baker,
    Victoria, British Columbia, for forwarding these articles.

152 Emil Dahlgren (ca. 1899–19?) and his wife, Lilly (ca. 1895–19?),
    immigrated to Canada from Stora Tuna, Ragunda, Jämtland, in 1928. Emil
    was a carpenter who could play the mouth organ, and Lilly worked as a
    cook.

153 Sven Börje Johansson (1924–) was born at Säffle, Värmland, and grew
    up near Göteborg on Sweden's west coast. Overwhelmed in his teens by
    the horror of the Second World War, he moved to northern Sweden to
    live close to nature and contemplate life's mysteries. Instead, the Sami
    taught him about reindeer husbandry over a period of a dozen years.

He decided to immigrate to Canada's unspoiled North when a massive hydroelectric project flooded the upper Luleå River basin, where he and the reindeer lived.

154 Northwest Territories Archives, Sven Johansson Fonds, N90-002; Sven Johansson, "The Canadian Reindeer Herd" (typescript, 1965), 9. The collection includes his 1967 film *Canadian Reindeer Project* on videocassette.

155 "N.W.T.'s Only Reindeer Herd Is Missing," CBC News, 8 January 2008. The herd owner was Sami descendant Lloyd Binder of Kunnek Resource Development Corporation. The wildlife biologist was Rick Farnell.

156 Staffan Svedberg, *Expedition Canada: Kanotexpedition över canadansiska tundran* (Kiruna, 1972), monograph translated by Anne-Marie Axelsson and Rolf Esko as *A Report of the Swedish Canoe Expedition Across the Canadian Barrens*. The six men were Rolf Esko, Arne Lindgren, Erik Svedberg, Staffan Svedberg, Bengt Windelhed, and Kjell Windelhed, ages twenty-one to thirty-two.

5. Religion

1 Mark A. Granquist, "Smaller Religious Groups in the Swedish-American Community," *Swedish-American Historical Quarterly* 44, no. 4 (October 1992): 217, credits Conrad Bergendoff, "Augustana in America and Sweden," *Swedish Pioneer Historical Quarterly* 24, no. 4 (1973): 238, for this estimate.

2 Information to be found in a *flyttningsbetyg* includes the applicant's full name, occupation, place of residence, birth date and place, destination, and Christian knowledge, followed by the date and place of certification, the official stamp and signature of the pastor, and the page of entry in the church register. For men who had undergone compulsory military service, the regimental number was also noted.

3 For a fascinating look at personal information that can be gleaned from church records in Sweden, see Irene Howard, *Gold Dust on His Shirt: The True Story of an Immigrant Mining Family* (Toronto: Between the Lines, 2008), 25–35, 230.

4 There are many such references, one of them printed in *Evangelical Covenant Church of Minnedosa, Manitoba, (Smoland Mission Covenant Church), 50th Anniversary 1908–1958*, as "Swedish, 'The language spoken in Heaven!'"

5 Daun, *The Swedish Mentality*, 140–1, 151, 166–7.

6 For a study of Congregationalists, Episcopalians, Seventh Day Adventists, Pentecostals, Salvation Army, Mormons, and Pentecostals in the United States, see Mark A. Granquist, "Smaller Religious Groups in the Swedish-American Community," 217–29.

7 Paul Petter Waldenström (1838–1917) was ordained in the Church of Sweden in 1863, after graduating with a doctorate from Uppsala University, to become editor of the original *Pietisten* from 1868 to 1917, and pastor, author, reformer, teacher, and Member of Parliament from 1885 to 1905. He had a profound influence in defining the Covenant Church on both sides of the Atlantic.

8 Augustana is the Latin name for Augsburg, as in the Augsburg Confession of 1530.

9 The Augustana Evangelical Lutheran Church was organized in Chicago in 1860, moved to Paxton, Illinois, in 1863, and finally to Rock Island in 1875.

10 Mark A. Granquist, "The Augustana Synod and the Episcopal Church," *Lutheran Quarterly* 14 (2000): 173–4; see also Rev Thomas Burgess, *Swedish Folk Within Our Church: The Rise, Normal Decline and Glorious Results of Half a Century's Work* (New York: Church Missions House, Foreign-Born Americans Division, 1929), 3–16; see also Carl Henrik Lyttkens, *The Growth of Swedish-Anglican Intercommunion between 1833 and 1922* (Lund: Gleerup, 1970).

11 Knute Selisu Totterman (1873–19?) was born in Ingå parish, Nylands län, Finland, and emigrated to the United States, where he was ordained to the diaconate in 1899 and to the priesthood in 1901. Totterman was not heard from again even though he had a sister, Olga Lindström, living in Port Arthur. Her grandchildren were unaware of their great-uncle's existence.

12 Diocese of Algoma Archives, Sault Ste. Marie, Ontario: "Extract of Boyce Report, St Ansgarius, P.A., December 11, 1912." Boyce described Totterman as "a man of singleminded devotion but a somewhat medieval spirit." The Swedish Lutheran pastor L.L. Laestadius (1800–1861) inspired the Laestadian revival. Finnish Laestadians who emigrated to the United States in 1866 founded the Apostolic Lutheran Church of America. Their doctrine favoured simplicity, and included the laying on of hands for absolution after the confession of felt sins.

13 Ibid.

14 Elinor Barr, "Swedes at the Lakehead 1900–1930," *Papers & Records* (Thunder Bay Historical Museum Society) 20 (1992): 52–3.

15 Ida Kristina Danielsson Stone (1877–1960) was born in Bamböle, Finnström parish, Åland Islands, and emigrated to Minnesota, where her brother Johan worked in Mesabi iron mines. In 1898 she married Anton Olofsson Stone (1862–1930) from Bua, Forshälla parish, Bohuslän, who had immigrated to Minneapolis in 1882. His brother, Augustana Pastor Emanuel Stone, officiated at the wedding. The couple lived in Two Harbors, Minnesota, until moving to Port Arthur in 1903. Thanks to grandson Ted Stone, Thunder Bay, for family information.

16 Beth Boegh, *Immanuel Evangelical Lutheran Church, 1906–2006: 100 Years of Faith and Fellowship* (Thunder Bay, 2006): 2–6. Immanuel shared its pastor with Zion Church in Fort William, also founded in 1906.

17 For examples of the importance of women's contributions to Alberta's Augustana churches, see Carina Rönnqvist, *Svea folk i Babels land*, 215–22.

18 Barr, "Swedes at the Lakehead," 52.

19 G. Everett Arden, *Augustana Heritage: A History of the Augustana Lutheran Church* (Rock Island: Augustana Press, 1963), 186. From 1877 to 1879 "the publications of the Mission Friends, *Sions Baner*, *Chicago-Bladet*, and *Missionsvännen* were filled with articles highly critical of the Augustana Synod and its religious leaders, while such Augustana journals as *Hemlandet*, *Augustana*, and *Skaffaren* attacked the Mission Friends personally, as well as their theology and practice, charging them with gross heresy, error and waywardness." Although these newspapers were very different from each other, all participated in pointing the finger against the other denomination.

20 New Stockholm had been founded three years earlier by immigration agent Emanuel Öhlén and M.P. Peterson of Winnipeg. Members elected C.O. Hofstrand as pastor even though he had not been ordained. A former high school teacher in Sweden, Hofstrand soon learned English with the help of Dr Hugh MacKay of nearby Round Lake Indian Mission. Afterwards the Canadian government granted him authority to perform religious rites and sent a book for recording marriages, baptisms, funerals, and other church matters. A log church was built and dedicated in 1895, with everything handcrafted except for the pulpit Bible, donated by Öhlén.

21 Anders Gustaf Sahlmark emigrated as a child from Västergötland to the United States.

22 Saskatchewan Archives, Saskatoon, A 23, Kasper Persson Landine, "A Story of New Stockholm's First Church Activities."

23 With itinerant pastor J.S. Ryding presiding, the synod's constitution was

adopted and a petition drafted for membership in Minnesota Conference. The charter roll had ninety-eight names – men, women, and children. See Baglo, *Augustana Lutherans in Canada,* 9; see also *New Stockholm Lutheran Church 1889–1989: A Century of Faith.* Johan Sven Ryding (1858–1912) was born in Larfs, Västergötland, and in 1861 emigrated to the United States, was ordained in 1881, and served mostly in Minnesota. See Bergendoff, *The Augustana Ministerium.*

24 Christer Olsson Hofstrand (ca. 1854–1924) immigrated in 1888 from Löderup, Skåne, with wife, Maria, and five children. Two more were born in New Stockholm. Hofstrand served as Mission Covenant pastor in New Stockholm and Winnipeg, as vice-consul from 1893 to 1913, and as editor of *Canada posten.* He retired in 1921 and died in Negaunee, Michigan. He is described by Svante Uddén as "a 'Waldenström' believer and almost a reformed as far as sacraments go." See Swenson Swedish Immigration Research Center (henceforth SSIRC), The Erik Norelius Papers 1851–1916, Svante Uddén, Winnipeg, to Erik Norelius, 20 July 1894.

25 Augustus G. Olson (1860–1931) had an off-and-on career with the Augustana Synod because of his divorce. He was born in Tampico, Illinois, ordained in 1887, and served as pastor in the United States until coming to Canada in 1889. Two years later he accepted a call to Winnipeg, where Hofstrand presided at his second marriage. When he accepted the call to the Augustana Church in New Stockholm, it was as a lay preacher. After transferring to the Church of Sweden in 1900 and being readmitted to Augustana in 1902, he served as pastor of Bethesda Church in Kenora from 1903 to 1907, then in the United States until 1913, when he left Augustana for good. Both A.G. and his wife are buried in the Covenant cemetery in New Stockholm where he had served the congregation for many years. See Bergendoff, *The Augustana Ministerium;* see also Halliwell, *Three Score and Ten,* 51; see also Baglo, *Augustana Lutherans in Canada,* 10–11, 15–16. In a letter to Norelius, 12 January 1894, Uddén described Olson as "a somewhat gifted preacher."

26 Stockholm Binder, C.O. Hofstrand, "New Stockholm, July 6, 1894," a translation of his letter published in *Den skandinaviske canadiensaren.*

27 Stockholm Binder, S.E. Swedberg, "New Stockholm, July 11, 1894," a translation of his response published in *Den skandinaviske canadiensaren.* "For my part I consider them to be just about as good, so I will not hold either one or the other church as the only right one. I believe there can be faithful people within both congregations, and even unfaithful ones, so that if it were possible to agree about one church and congregation,

I would gladly join it regardless of whether it is called Mission or Augustana."

28 Erik Norelius (1833–1916) was born in Hassela, Hälsingland. In 1850 he emigrated to the United States and was ordained in 1856. In 1865 he founded Vasa Children's Home. He was editor of several church publications including *Korsbaneret*, president of Minnesota Conference from 1874 to 1881 and from 1899 to 1911, and author of a massive two-volume history of Swedes and Swedish churches in the United States. See Bergendoff, *The Augustana Ministerium.*

29 Manitoba Archives, MG 14, C28, Box 1, File 1, W.J. Sisler, "The Swedish Colony – New Stockholm, written in 1940 from Notes and Observations made while residing in the Colony 1899–1901," 7.

30 Ibid., 7–8.

31 Kate Sahlmark came from Värmland. In the fall of 1887 she and her husband left Minnesota for New Stockholm to join A.G.'s brother, Charles, and brought along a carload of effects, which included four horses and the colony's first binder. Charles Sahlmark had arrived in the spring of 1887 with his wife, Hannah Maria, and six children. Their son Alexander is said to be the first white child born in the colony. Charles Sahlmark became a justice of the peace. See Halliwell, *Three Score and Ten*, 19–24.

32 Arden, *Augustana Heritage*, 4–12.

33 *Hilltop Baptist Church, 100th Anniversary, 1896–1996*, 34.

34 Alex G. Davidson, "The Swedish Constitution, Nordic Esotericism in Baroque Splendour," Pietre-Stones Review of Freemasonry, www. freemasonry.com/swedish_constitution.html (2005). The tradition of Sweden's reigning monarch being named High Protector of the Swedish Order of Freemasons began in 1753 with King Adolf Fredrik. The order has always been accepted by Sweden's state church, and many of its members, clergy, and bishops are Masons.

35 Correspondence from Donald Sjoberg, 27 September 2007.

36 "Vårt missionsarbete i de britiska provinserna Manitoba, Assiniboia och Alberta i N. Amerika," in *Korsbaneret: Kristlig kalender för 1894*, ed. Erik Norelius, 47–70; see also J.G. Dahlberg, "Canada-missionen" in *Korsbaneret: Kristlig kalender för året 1914*, ed. O.V. Holmgrain (Rock Island: Augustana Book Concern, 1914), 59–105; see also "Canadamissionen dess uppkomst och bedrivande inom provinserna Ontario, Manitoba, Saskatchewan och Alberta till år 1913, då Canada-konferensen bildades," in Emil Lund, *Minnesota-Konferensens av Augustana-Synoden och dess församlingars historia* (Rock Island: Augustana Book Concern, 1920), 91–101.

37 Baglo, *Augustana Lutherans in Canada*, 5; see also G.H. Lager,
    "Svenskarna i Canada," in *Svenskarna i Amerika: Populär Historisk
    Skildring i ord och bild av svenskarnas liv och underbara öden i Förenta
    Staterna och Canada*, ed. Karl Hildebrand and Axel Fredenholm
    (Stockholm: Historiska förlaget, 1925), 2:334. Lager wrote, "Many fear
    that western Canada is a wasteland, a wild gigantic prairie, covered
    almost all year with ice and snow."
38 Lars A. Hocanzon (1837–1919) was born in Nysund, Närke, and in
    1869 emigrated to the United States, was ordained in 1871, and served
    mostly in Minnesota churches and in mission work. See Bergendoff, *The
    Augustana Ministerium*.
39 Baglo, *Augustana Lutherans in Canada*, 6–7.
40 Lars Gustaf Almén (1846–1912) was born in Tösse, Dalsland, in 1870
    emigrated to the United States, was ordained in 1876, and served in
    Illinois, Minnesota, and South Dakota. See Bergendoff, *The Augustana
    Ministerium*; see also J. Fremling, "L.G. Almén," *Korsbaneret: Kristlig
    kalender för året 1914*, 167–77.
41 "Congregational History" in the program for the anniversary service,
    Bethlehem Lutheran Church, Erickson-Scandinavia, Manitoba, 1891–1941.
42 To follow the career of an itinerant Augustana pastor from Hallock,
    Minnesota, see Bruce William Anderson's excellent account of his
    grandparents, *Pioneer Missionary: Lars Petter Lundgren and Wife Alma:
    The True Life Story of a Pioneer Ministry in Minnesota's Last Frontier, North
    Dakota, and Canada 1892–1923* (Niles, MI: The author, 2004).
43 Svante Uddén (1853–1937) was born in Lekåsa, Västergötland, and in
    1861 emigrated to the United States, was ordained in 1884, and served
    in Minnesota until coming to Canada (1892 to 1898). He was the author
    of *Från Canada*, and founder and editor of *Sions Väktare*. See Bergendoff,
    The Augustana Ministerium. Uddén is described as "a decent and helpful
    man, but not very productive or brilliant as a religious speaker," in Ivar
    Vennerström, "Den skandinaviska Canadapressen: Stipendieberättelse,"
    in *Publicistklubbens årsberättelse 1929*, 2.
44 Baglo, *Augustana Lutherans in Canada*, 10.
45 Ibid., 18. The ten congregations were located at Battle Creek (Water
    Glen), Alberta; New Stockholm, Percival, and Fleming, Saskatchewan;
    Winnipeg, Scandinavia, Hazelwood, Tyndall, and Whitemouth,
    Manitoba; and Rat Portage (Kenora) in Northwestern Ontario. Only
    half of these congregations survived: Water Glen, New Stockholm,
    Scandinavia, Winnipeg, and Kenora. A congregation not mentioned was
    Wetaskiwin, founded the same year as Battle Creek.

46 W.B. Anderson, *The Covenant Church in Canada 1904–1994: A Time to Remember* (Prince Albert: Evangelical Covenant Church of Canada, 1995), 165–72. The four congregations were located in Winnipeg, Manitoba; New Stockholm, Saskatchewan; and in New Sweden and Malmo, Alberta. Malmo built a church in 1902.

47 SSIRC, The Erik Norelius Papers, Uddén to Norelius, 12 January, 5 May, 20 July 1894; 5 March 1895; 25 March 1896. Ida Hallin, an exchange student from Sweden attending Augustana College, extracted letters from Canada from this collection in 2004. See also Ljungmark, *Svenskarna i Winnipeg*, 42.

48 Erik Norelius Papers, 19 October 1894: "When I read in the papers that the committee is working in other areas and that another congregation which was granted a similar loan has received the whole amount ... then I hardly know what conclusion to draw." See also 5 March 1895: "If I do not get help on the field I will not for much longer speak for the church in Canada."

49 In 1888 Uddén found Swedes all the way from Rat Portage (Kenora), Ontario, to Dunsmere near Medicine Hat, Alberta. The largest number lived in New Stockholm, Scandinavia, and Winnipeg, but there were also some living in Fleming, Selkirk, Dufrost, and Plum Coulée, Manitoba. Swedes working for the railway at Oak Lake and Portage la Prairie were dismissed as itinerants.

50 The name Rat Portage refers to muskrats trapped for the fur trade, but this name stamped on bags of flour produced by the flour mill suggested another kind of rat. The name Kenora, adopted in 1905, derives from the first two letters of the adjacent communities of Keewatin, Norman, and Rat Portage.

51 Baglo, *Augustana Lutherans in Canada*, 8, 13, 15. For a history of the church see E. Earl Anderson, "*Si Gud's Lam*/Behold the Lamb of God: The Story of the Swedish Evangelical Lutheran Bethesda Congregation, Kenora, Ontario, 1894-1994," PhD thesis, Lutheran Theological Seminary, Gettysburg, Pennsylvania, 1999. See also *Bethesda Lutheran Church, Kenora, Ontario, 50th Anniversary, 1894–1944*.

52 At this time there were seven sawmills in Kenora.

53 Axel Christian Helenus Helander (1871–1950) was born in Glimåkra, Skåne, and in 1891 emigrated to the United States. He was ordained in 1895, married Ellen Johansson, and moved to Rat Portage, where he lived from 1895 to 1898. He spent the rest of his career at various points on the eastern seaboard, serving immigrants and seamen. See Bergendoff, *The Augustana Ministerium*; see also SSIRC, The Erik Norelius Papers, Uddén to Norelius, 26 March, 5 April, 13 April 1896.

54 SSIRC, The Erik Norelius Papers, Uddén to Norelius, 5 May 1894.

55 Johan Fremling (1842–1917) was born in Fremmestad, Värmland, and in 1870 emigrated to the United States. He was ordained in 1871, and served in Minnesota and Wisconsin, also as secretary and president of Minnesota Conference board. See Bergendoff, *The Augustana Ministerium*.

56 *Bethlehem Lutheran Church, Wetaskiwin, Alberta, Seventy-Fifth Anniversary, 1898–1973*, 3.

57 Ibid., 4.

58 The name Svea remained with the old church and cemetery when a new church was built in 1953. Twelve years later the name of the congregation changed to Calvary Lutheran Church, Wetaskiwin. The old Svea church closed in 1970. See *Calvary Lutheran Church, 1898–1973*, 4, and *Calvary Lutheran Church, 1898–1998*, 6.

59 Olof Lindgren (1861–1927) was born in Mockfjärd, Dalarna, and emigrated to Svea, Minnesota, in 1880, working as a lay preacher until being ordained in 1906, when he accepted calls to Camrose and Czar, Alberta. He was president of Canada Conference from 1924 to 1927. See L.J. Fihn, "Canada Missionen," in *Minnesskrift 1858–1908 tillegnad Minnesota-Konferensens af Ev. Luterska Augustana-Synoden 50-års Jubileum*, ed. F.M. Eckman, 214; see also Baglo, *Augustana Lutherans in Canada*, 22–3, 44, 91.

60 Olof L. Save (18?–1931) married Frida Tornberg in Sweden and the couple had four children in Canada. The description of Olof L. Save as a Member of Parliament in Stockholm is unconfirmed. See *Lewisville Pioneers*, (Malmo: Malmo Women's Institute History Committee, 1963), 90.

61 Per Almgren (1863–1906) was born in Bingsta, Berg, Jämtland, and in 1890 emigrated to Rock Island, Illinois, where he graduated from Augustana College and was ordained in 1893. He served in the United States until accepting the call to Wetaskiwin in 1902. See Fihn, *"Canada Missionen,"* 216–17.

62 Both Dalby and Fridhem are places in Sweden.

63 Alf Brorson, *Något om Fryksande och Lekvatten i ett nordamerikanskt perspektiv* (Torsby: Fryksände församling, 2004), 9, 57–9. See also his "Fryksande, Minnesota," *Bryggan/The Bridge* 38, no. 2 (2006): 8–10, and "Fryksende i Kanada," *Siriklockan: Fryksände pastorats kyrkoblad* 16, no. 3 (2005): 10–11. Although Archive no longer exists and the Fryksende church closed in 1956, the congregation's former existence has aroused interest in Sweden, perhaps because there was also a Fryksande church near Evansville, Minnesota. Unlike the one in Saskatchewan, it is commemorated by a plaque.

64 Fihn, "Canada Missionen," 216–17; see also Baglo, *Augustana Lutherans in Canada*, 22.

65 Anna Margreta Almgren (1862–19?) was born Anna Margreta Grunden in
Hafre, Färila, Hälsingland. In 1894 she married Per Almgren in Sweden
and travelled with him to the United States. See *Bethlehem Lutheran
Church, Wetaskiwin, Alberta, 1898–1973*, 5–6.

66 "First Swedish Lutheran Church, Vancouver, British Columbia," in *Fifty
Years of the Columbia Conference 1893–1943: Historical Glimpses of Lutheran
Mission Work in the Pacific Northwest under the Auspices of the Columbia
Conference of the Lutheran Augustana Synod*, ed. Carl H. Sandgren (Rock
Island: Augustana Book Concern, 1943), 118–21.

67 Frida Oström Engblom (1870–1961) was born in Gideå, Ångermanland,
and immigrated with three small daughters in 1888 to join her husband
in Wetaskiwin. In 1907 she moved to Vancouver and built a house with
thirty bedrooms, an apartment downstairs, and a restaurant and kitchen.
See Irene Howard's research notes for a letter from her daughter, Mrs
Arthur A. Levine, Lewiston, New York, dated 1969; see also Howard,
Vancouver's Svenskar, 41.

68 Clifford Reinhardt, "Augustana Lutheran in Vancouver: A Swedish
Church on the Other Side of the Globe Celebrates a Hundred Years,"
Swedish Press, September 2003, 16.

69 *Wilhelmina Lutheran Church, Hay Lakes, Alberta: Living in God's Grace:
1908–2008*, 5.

70 *Wilhelmina Evangelical Lutheran Church: Fifty Years of Grace, 1908–1958*, 5;
see also ibid., 6.

71 Anna Greta Näslund Löfgren was the daughter of Johan and Lisa
Näslund of Nästansjö, Vilhelmina. She married Jonas August Löfgren,
from Siksjönäs, Vilhelmina, who had immigrated in 1912.

72 Per-Uno Ågren, "Från Vilhelmina to Wilhelmina," in *Västerbotten 1987*,
34; see also "To Catch a Vanishing History" from the poster for the 1984
exhibition "Vilhelmina to Wilhelmina." Vilhelmina is unique in having
a well-documented account of its settlers since colonizing began in the
1700s. Mr O.P. Pettersson (1859–1944) devoted the last twenty years of his
life to collecting oral traditions, compiling a dictionary of the Vilhelmina
dialect, and writing a detailed history published in three volumes, *Gamla
byar i Vilhelmina* (Old villages in Vilhelmina).

73 John P. Ocklin (ca. 1852–19?), Jonas Pearson, and Erik Landin were
brothers, all born in Jämtland, who immigrated to Eriksdale. Landin was
well known for the excellence of his accordion playing and his moonshine
whiskey, probably an embarrassment to Ocklin. Eriksdale pioneers did
not attend the existing Anglican and Presbyterian churches, either. See

George J. Houser, *The Swedish Community at Eriksdale, Manitoba* (Ottawa: National Museum of Man, 1976), 33–6.

74 Lois Knudson Munholland, *Pulpits of the Past: A Record of Closed Lutheran Churches in Saskatchewan up to 2003* (Strasbourg, SK: Three West Two South Books, 2004) offers a more complete list.

75 Baglo, *Augustana Lutherans in Canada*, 89–90.

76 Ibid., 54–6.

77 *St. Mark's Lutheran Church, Winnipeg, 100th Anniversary* (1990), 6–7; see also www.stmarkslutheran.ca/history.php.

78 Baglo, *Augustana Lutherans in Canada*, 30.

79 Ibid., 26–37; see also Emeroy Johnson, *God Gave the Growth: The Story of the Lutheran Minnesota Conference 1876–1958* (Minneapolis: Denison, 1958), 30–4.

80 Baglo, *Augustana Lutherans in Canada*, 46, 48.

81 Ibid., 45. For a first-hand account of the Canadian situation see Anton A. Nelson, "Treasured Reflections: An Autobiography" (1984), typescript donated by Donald Sjoberg. Nelson came to Calgary in 1924 as pastor of First Lutheran Church, and was president of Canada Conference from 1928 to 1939, then regional director. See also Bergendoff, *The Augustana Ministerium*.

82 Baglo, *Augustana Lutherans in Canada*, 44–5, 59; see also Donald W. Sjoberg, "Augustana in Canada – People and Places," speech delivered at the Augustana Heritage Association Gathering, St Peter, Minnesota, 26 June 2004, 6.

83 Nils Willison (1880–1964) was born Nils Olsson in Södra Rörum, Skåne, and immigrated to Torrance, Ontario, near Gravenhurst, with his parents in 1881. In 1904 he married Margaret White of Muskoka Falls, was ordained in 1914, and became a professor at Waterloo College, later serving Trinity Lutheran Church in Hamilton. See Cronmiller, *A History of the Lutheran Church in Canada*, 216–17.

84 Alfred Bertil Sander (1925–2005) was born near Stratton, Ontario, the son of immigrants from Dalarna and Västergötland. In 1946 he married Marie Johanna Van't Hull (1918–1977) and after her death married Ruth Hertha Kaisler. Thanks to daughter Eleanor Sander, Västra Torup, Skåne, for family information.

85 Donald Wilfred Sjoberg (1930–) was born near Hilltop, Manitoba, the son of immigrants from Dalarna and Ångermanland. In 1953 he married Trudy Woldrich from Regina. See Donald W. Sjoberg, "The Sillen Family in Sweden and Canada" (2002) and "The Sjoberg Family in Sweden and Canada" (2005).

86 Ferdinand Eugene Baglo served in Stockholm, Dubuc, and Broadview in Saskatchewan, and Tanganyika, Africa. He also edited *Faithfully Yours: Otto A. Olson (1920–1976): A Devotional Biography of the First President of the Central Canada Synod, Lutheran Church in America (1963–1976)*, published in 1978.

87 Sven Söderlund was born in Estonia, leaving for Sweden with his parents at the age of two and settling in Stuvsta, near Stockholm. Sven married Rose in England, where their three daughters were born. See *Swedish Press*, July 2004, 27.

88 Margit Sandberg married a man named Paulson from Blekinge. Thanks to Ruth Wahlgren Rinaldo, Toronto, for family information and also details about the early church. An early parishioner, she immigrated from Jönköping, Småland, in 1926.

89 Denationalization of the Swedish Church began in 1995.

90 Anna Runesson, "Svenska kyrkan i Toronto: en historik" (2006), typescript, 1–3. See also "SKUT – The Swedish Church Abroad," *Swedish Press*, July 1998, 18–20.

91 The original name was God's Scandinavian Congregation, later First Scandinavian Christian Mission Congregation. The word *Scandinavian* was in deference to the countries Denmark, Norway, and Sweden. See *Minnesskrift: Första skandinaviska kristna missionsförsamlingen, Winnipeg, Canada: Femtio år1885–1935, Femtioårs-jubileet den 25 januari 1935*, 10.

92 Erik Dahlhielm, ed., *Covenant Memories: Swedish Evangelical Mission Covenant 1885–1935: Golden Jubilee*, (Chicago: Covenant Book Concern, 1935), 296.

93 Ibid., 301–3. Congregations were organized at New Stockholm, Saskatchewan (1888); at New Sweden (1894), Malmo (1898), Highland Park (1901), and Meeting Creek (1905) in Alberta; at Smoland, Manitoba; and Hyas, Saskatchewan (1908), Brockington, and Norquay, Saskatchewan (1910); and Calgary, Alberta (1911). See also *Brockington Mission Covenant Church: Fiftieth Anniversary, 1913–1963*.

94 *Norquay Nostalgia*, 167–8; see also Fullerton, *One Hundred Years*, 92, 102–4; see also "Norquay Covenant Church members have Served Smorgs for More than 50 Years," *Norquay North Star*, 14 November 2007, 3. Thanks to Ken Domier, Edmonton, for sending information about Norquay Covenant Women's smörgåsbord.

95 For an account of a typical congregation, see "Swedish, The Language Spoken in Heaven!," in *Evangelical Covenant Church of Minnedosa, Manitoba, 1908–1958*, n.p.

96 "Canadian Covenant Heights Bible Camp," *Evangelical Covenant Church, Minnedosa, Manitoba, 1908–1983*, 33–4; see also *Days of Our Years: Golden Jubilee of the Evangelical Mission Covenant of Canada: A History in Commemoration of Fifty Years, 1904–1954* (Prince Albert: Evangelical Mission Covenant of Canada, 1954), 39–42.

97 *Days of Our Years*, 38–9.

98 Gustaf Aaron Quarnström (1875–1953) was born in Svarttorp, Småland. After apprenticing as a coppersmith, he emigrated in 1898 to New York, and the following year moved to Chicago to attend Risberg's *missionskola* and become a Mission Covenant pastor. He was ordained in 1902, and visited Sweden until 1904. In 1921 he left the United States to come to Canada, posted to Malmo, New Sweden, and Winnipeg. He served as superintendent in Canada from 1927 to 1946, and then retired to Sweden. Pastor Quarnström married three times, first in 1910 to Orlinda Lawrence (ca. 1884–1921), and they had children Leonard, Roland, and Ruth; then in 1923 to Othelia Berg (died 1946) of Minnedosa, and had daughter Harriett Orlinda. In 1952 he married Edit Furu, daughter of the coppersmith under whom he trained. The daughters moved to the United States while the sons remained in Canada. Roland became a teacher and school principal; Leonard became a pastor and served as Canada Conference superintendent for nineteen years. See Leonard Quarnstrom and Harriett Quarnstrom Swanson, "Gustaf Aaron Quarnstrom, 1875–1953," copy provided by Walter Syslak, Calgary; see also Landelius Biography Collection, volume 3, #831.

99 For details of the short-term Bible Institute operation in Norquay, see Ottilia Carolina Ericson, *Tillie's Triumphs*, (1967), unpublished typescript donated by Helen Moseson, Westaskiwin, 27–8.

100 *Norquay Nostalgia*, 169.

101 Thanks to Phil Anderson, Chicago, for this information.

102 W.B. Anderson, *The Covenant Church in* Canada, 298–300; see also *Days of Our Years*, 63–4.

103 Syslak, "Swede Town," 34.

104 Alison Mayes, "Worshipping the Past," *Winnipeg Free Press*, 26 March 2005, F3.

105 Adolf Olson, *A Centenary History: As Related to the Baptist General Conference of America* (Chicago: Baptist Conference Press, 1952), 479; see also E. Brandt, "Swedish Baptists," in *Pioneering in Western Canada: A Story of the Baptists*, ed. Colin C. McLaurin (Calgary, 1939), 357–80.

106 Brandt, "Swedish Baptists."

107 Grant Memorial Baptist Church, "*Medlemsbok för skandinaviska Baptistförsamlingen, Winnipeg, Man.,*" lists early members as Kristoffer and Kristina Hansson from Denmark, M.A. and Emma C. Meyer from Norway, and three couples from Sweden.

108 Margaret E. Thompson, *The Baptist Story in Western Canada* (Calgary: Baptist Union of Western Canada, 1975): 324–5.

109 Ibid., 333.

110 *Grant Memorial Baptist Church: Historical Highlights 1894–1994* (Winnipeg, 1994), 4–5. In 1950 Grant Memorial Baptist Church moved to Colony Street. The current structure on Wilkes Avenue was built in 1982.

111 *A History of Grant Memorial Baptist Church: Vision Unlimited: Prepared on the Occasion of Our 90th Anniversary Year 1895–1984,* 2.

112 Grant Memorial Baptist Church, "Medlemsbok för skandinaviska Baptistförsamlingen," lists early Swedish members J. and J. Vikberg, L. and Anna Nilsson, and T.O. and Mrs Nordin, who migrated from Jättendal, Hälsingland, in 1894 and left for Teulon, Manitoba, in 1907. See also Helander, "Swedish Colony of Norris Lake," 249–56.

113 *Forest to Field,* 111.

114 *Hilltop Baptist Church, 100th Anniversary, 1896–1996,* 35.

115 *Kipling 100, 1893–1993* (Kipling, 1993), 6–7; see also "Missionär Fred Palmborgs årsrapport," in *Årsbok för svenska baptistförsamlingarna inom America, 1908–1909* (Chicago: Svenska Baptisternas i Amerika allmänna konferens, 1909), 36–7.

116 Thompson, *Baptist Story in Western Canada,* 326.

117 J.P. Sundström, *Missionär,* "Rapport," in *Årsbok för svenska Baptistförsamlingarna inom Amerika: Innehållande Protokoll och Rapporter för Verksamhetsåret 1913–1914,* 50.

118 Thompson, *Baptist Story in Western Canada,* 328–31.

119 *Swedish Baptist Churches of America for 1942–1943,* Part II, *Statistics and Addresses* (Chicago: Swedish Baptist General Conference of America, 1943), 29–31.

120 Paulus Daniel Brytzelius, later Bryzelius (1713–1773), took his surname from his birthplace, Brytsbo, Jönsberg, Östergötland. He graduated from Uppsala University, preached in England and Ireland from 1734 to 1740, then joined the Moravian Brethren in Hessen, Germany. In 1742 he emigrated to Philadelphia with a large group. The following year he was ordained as a Moravian. He translated the Moravian catechism from German to Swedish, then was called to Pennsylvania and New Jersey, and then to Europe, including Ireland, from 1745 to 1754. He returned to the United States and ministered in Pennsylvania until 1760, when he left the Moravian Brethren and was ordained as a German Lutheran.

He preached in New Jersey until leaving for England in 1766. Nova Scotia's German Lutheran congregation had asked for a minister who could speak both German and English, but what they really wanted was a German Lutheran pastor. Bryzelius remained in Lunenburg with his wife, Mary Brown (1727–1817), and their children, as rector of St John's Anglican Church, later proclaimed a national historic site. See "The First Swede in Canada," *Swedish American Genealogist* (December, 2012): 31. I am grateful to Donald Sjoberg, Winnipeg, for bringing this significant pioneer to my attention.

121 Brian Cuthbertson, "A Historical and Architectural Survey," *The Diocesan Times*, December 2001.

122 Cronmiller, *A History of the Lutheran Church in Canada*, 47; see also Robert Murray, ed., *The Church of Sweden, Past and Present*, trans. Nils G. Sahlin (Malmö: Swedish Bishops' Conference, 1960), 282; see also E.A. Louhi, *The Delaware Finns: Or the First Permanent Settlements in Pennsylvania, Delaware, West New Jersey and Eastern Part of Maryland 1925* (New York: Humanity Press, ca. 1925); see also John H. Munnich, *225 Years: A History of Zion Evangelical Lutheran Church, Oldwick, New Jersey* (1939).

123 Thanks to Howard Blaxland, Montague, Prince Edward Island, and to Jean Tavanee, Kingston, Nova Scotia, for providing family information.

124 Johannes Lundberg (1786–1856) was born on the island of St Thomas in the West Indies, the son of Thomas Lundberg (1753–1794), who had joined the Moravian Church in Sweden and moved to Saxony, Germany, in 1779. He went to the West Indies as a missionary in 1785. At the age of six Johannes was sent to Germany, to the children's home of the Moravian Church, where he was raised, apprenticed as a carpenter, and became a teacher in the home. His first language was German, and he never saw his parents again. Johannes married in 1819 and returned to Germany in 1850 because of illness. See Otto Robert Landelius, *Swedish Place-Names in North America* (Chicago: Swedish-American Historical Society, 1985), 287–8.

125 The groom, Erik Gustaf Erikson (1873–19?), was born in Filipstad, Värmland, and immigrated in 1882 with his father and older brother, married Amanda Thoren (1875–?) of Minnedosa, Manitoba, and homesteaded in Scandinavia. Around 1912 Erik married Sarah Dorothy Ostrom (1891–1968) from Torsåker, Ångermanland, and moved to British Columbia during the 1920s. Thanks to grandson George Sward, Mission, British Columbia, for family information. See also Canon E.A.Wharton Gill, "A Norse Wedding in Manitoba," in *Forest to Field*, 34–6.

126 Bruce W. Taylor, *A Pioneer Ministry: St. Andrew's Presbyterian Church, New Liskeard, Ontario: Centennial History 1895-1995* (New Liskeard,

1995), 21 (photo), 31, 38; see also United Church Archives, Toronto, "Cobalt-Haileybury Scandinavian Presbyterian Mission, Marriage register 1915–1921"; see also Oslund, *One Hundred Years of Swedish Settlement*, 11–15.

127 Caldwell, *Waterville 1876–2001*, 93–4.

128 "Anton Andreason," *Malmo Mission Covenant Church: Seventy-five Years 1898–1973* (Malmo, 1973), n.p. Anton Andreason (18?–1947) did not marry. As a homesteader he was an active member of the New Sweden congregation until moving to Ohaton, Alberta, where he became secretary-treasurer for the Municipal District of Bawlf.

129 Members known to have come from Worcester are Karl and Emelia Bjorkgren, Victor and Amanda Johnson, and John and Ida Kristina Johnson Sald.

130 *New Sweden Mission Church 1894–1994: How Great Thou Art, O Store Gud* (1994). These payments continued until 1915.

131 Ibid.; see also "Waterville United Church," in Caldwell, *History of Waterville*, 93; see also *Our Scandinavian Missions, Alberta, N.W.T.* (Sherbrooke, QC: Canada Congregational Missionary Society, 1904).

132 C.W. Gillen, *Minnen från mina resor genom Norra Amerikas Förenta Stater och Canada* (Örebro, 1897), 261–2.

133 *Our Scandinavian Missions*, 6–7; see also *Highland Park Evangelical Free Church: 60th Anniversary* (1961), 4–5; see also Amy Enarson, "Highland Park," in *Memory Opens the Door: New Norway and District* (Edmonton: New Norway Community Club, 1978), 103–4.

134 Andrew Edgar "Ed" Hallgren (19?–1961) was born in Red Deer and in 1916 married a recent immigrant from Nice, France, named Marie Louise "Augustine" LeRoy (19?–1969). The couple farmed in Delburne, Alberta, before moving to Sylvan Lake. See Red Deer and District Archives, "Andrew Edgar Hallgren," typescript, 2 pages.

135 C.O. "Carl" Nordin was born in Sweden and his wife, Agnes Kivelton, was born in Norway. See *Who's Who in Alberta: A Biographical Directory* (Saskatoon: Lyone Publications, 1957), 321; see also Warren L. Heckman, *History of the Fellowship of Christian Assemblies* (Kankakee, IL: Olivet Nazarene University, 1994), 25.

136 Ljungmark, *Svenskarna i Winnipeg*, 135. For a view from the United States see Edward O. Nelson, "Recollections of the Salvation Army's Scandinavian Corps," *Swedish Pioneer Historical Quarterly* 29, no. 4 (October 1978): 257–76.

137 Einar Walberg (ca. 1898–1966) was born in Färila, Hälsingland, and ca. 1906 immigrated with his parents to Wainwright, Alberta. His

wife, Brikken "Bertha" Wallberg (1903–19?), also born in Färila, had immigrated with her parents to Garson, Manitoba, in 1904. Thanks to Alma Pippy, Winnipeg, for family information.

138 Correspondence with Sherry Lloyd, The Salvation Army Family Tracing Service for Southern Alberta, Calgary, 6 April 2006.

139 Johannes Anderson (1829–1920) was born in Oljann (Oljonsbyn, Dalarna?) and in 1865 emigrated to Utah, where he married Hannah from Lund, Skåne. See Blue, *Alberta*, 3:206–7.

140 Hjaldermar Ostlund (1878–19?), whose parents emigrated from Sweden in 1860, was born in Elsinore, Utah. He practised in Lethbridge during his entire career. See ibid., 2:264, 2:267.

141 *Pioneers and Progress: Calmar and District* (Calmar, AB, 1980), 748–9.

142 M. Andrew Anderson (1859–1938) was born Myr-Anders Andersson in Dalby, Värmland. He emigrated to Minnesota, where he married Kristina Halvorson (18?–1928) in Warren, Minnesota. The couple had three children before arriving in Bergland. See *Water Under the Bridge*, 128–9; see also Landelius Biography Collection, volume 1, #070.

143 Caroline Bergenham (1888–1992) was born in Offerdal, Jämtland, and her brother John Bergenham (1895–1999) in Golden, British Columbia, offspring of John Peter Persson Bergenham (ca. 1860–1931) and Brita Gardwall Andersdotter (1861–1965). The Bergenhams immigrated in 1892–3. Thanks to granddaughter Jean Blaine, Burnaby, British Columbia, for family information and correspondence.

144 Moira Farrow, "Animals 'Given' $500,000 home," *Vancouver Sun*, 16 August 1973, 21; see also Ann-Charlotte Berglund, "The Bergenham Sanctuary Svenskättlinggåve till B.C.," *Nya svenska pressen*, 18 October 1977; see also correspondence from Department of Recreation and Conservation, Fish and Wildlife Branch, Victoria, to Mr John Bergenham and Miss Caroline Bergenham, Moberly Station, British Columbia, 28 September 1971.

145 Emanuel Svedberg Swedenborg (1688–1772) was born in Stockholm, the son of Jesper Svedberg, professor of theology at Uppsala University and bishop of Skara. He graduated from Uppsala University, changing his surname to Swedenborg upon being elevated to the nobility.

146 Lennart Limberg, "Almost a Century's Work: Preserving Swedishness Outside of Sweden," in *Scandinavians in Old and New Lands: Essays in Honor of H. Arnold Barton*, ed. Philip J. Anderson, Dag Blanck, and Byron J. Nordstrom (Chicago: Swedish-American Historical Society, 2004), 141, 153.

6. World Wars

1 Figures from the 1911 Census of Canada show that for every Swedish-born female, there were 2.36 males, including children. Even taking intermarriage with other ethnic groups into account, the preponderance of bachelors is clear. See LAC, RG 76, volume 568, file 812779; Superintendent of Immigration, Ottawa, to C.G.G. Anderberg, Royal Swedish Consul, Montreal, 27 July 1914, which confirms that the high ratio of adult males continued in 1912 and 1913. From total immigration figures of 2,330 and 2,671 for those years, 1,441 and 1,869 were adult males. Adult females numbered 494 and 495, respectively, with children at 395 and 307.

2 *En smålandssocken emigrerar*, 866: "Many Swedes came down to Spokane from Canada. Some who were naturalized Canadians burned their papers and went over the boundary to the United States." See also Eva St Jean, "From Defiance to Defence: Swedish-Canadian Ethnic Awareness during the Two World Wars," *American Studies in Scandinavia* 34 (2002): 70.

3 Ljungmark, *Svenskarna i Winnipeg*, 168, records an 18 per cent decrease in Swedes from 1911 to 1916 and 13 per cent among other Nordic people.

4 Ljungmark, *Swedish Exodus* (Southern Illinois University Press, 1979), 145–7, records that 14,600 Swedes remigrated from the United States to Sweden from 1914 to 1918, 4,647 in 1914, dropping to 1,565 in 1918. Average remigration for the decade before 1914 was 4,735, and for the decade after 1918, it was 2,527. Examination of C. Österberg, ed., *Från Calmare Nyckel till Leif Viking: En samlingsverk för in- och utvandrare svenskar ute och hemma* (Stockholm: Riksinstitutet för släkt- och bygdeforskning, 1959) revealed that none of the informants who had lived in Canada had remigrated from Canada.

5 Thanks to Richard Gottfrid Larsson Holt, St Mary's, Ontario, for sending a nominal roll of 1,679 men born in Sweden who served in the Canadian Expeditionary Force between 1914 and 1918, also a list of 122 fatalities, compiled from the LAC and CWGC websites, as part of his dissertation on manpower in the Great War at the University of Western Ontario. His figures include 144 men in the 197th Battalion and 69 in the 223rd Battalion. Unfortunately compiling such a list for second-generation Swedes is impossible; military documents record only birthplace, not ethnic origin.

6 Ljungmark, *Svenskarna i Winnipeg*, 169–70.

7 The lone Canadian casualty, Gustav Adolph Nyblom, was travelling first class. See Elisabeth Thorsell, "Swedes on the Lusitania?," *Swedish American Genealogist* 29, no.1 (March 2009): 23.

8 Hans Norman, Harald Runblom, Ann-Sofie Kälvemark, and Lars-Göran Tedebrand, *Amerika-emigrationen*, (Uddevalla: Cikada, 1980), 222. *Tabell 24:1* shows 39 people left Sweden for Canada in 1915, 153 in 1916, 76 in 1917, and 57 in 1918, compared to more than 600 every year from 1910 to 1913.

9 For the relationship between Swedes and Norwegians in Canada, see Carina Rönnqvist, "Bröder och rivaler: Svenskarna, norrmännen och den skandinaviska identiteten i Canada, 1905–1945" in *Hembygden och världen*, ed. Lars Olsson et al. (Växjö, 2002), 329–45.

10 Thanks to Anette Rosberg Arnäs, Malmö, Sweden, for forwarding photocopies of clippings from both of Winnipeg's Swedish newspapers and the *Manitoba Free Press*, 19 January 1916 to 1 March 1916. Surnames of the three Norwegians were Berge, Cleven, and Haddeland.

11 Charles Avery Nord (1880–19?) was born Carl Arvid Nord in Trångsviken, Jämtland, and in 1892 immigrated to Dubuc, Saskatchewan, with his parents. His next of kin was Mrs Emmey Nord, Portage la Prairie. Nord was a member of the 90th Winnipeg Rifles when he joined the 223rd Battalion. After advancing to regimental sergeant major by the end of the war, he joined the police force in Kenora, where he served in the militia until 1929, thus completing thirty years of military service. Thanks to Richard Gottfrid Larsson Holt, St Mary's, Ontario, for enlistment details. See also Landelius Biography Collection, volume 2, #038.

12 Lars Gyllenhaal and Lennart Westberg, *Svenskar i krig, 1914–1945* (Lund: Historiska Media, 2004), 74.

13 LAC, RG 9, volume II, file B9; Canadian Expeditionary Force, 197th Battalion, Nominal Roll of Officers, Non-Commissioned Officers and Men; also 223rd Scandinavian Battalion. Thanks to Anette Rosberg Arnäs, Malmö, Sweden, for sending photocopies of these documents.

14 John Herd Thompson, *Ethnic Minorities during Two World Wars* (Ottawa: Canadian Historical Association, 1991), 9.

15 Thanks to Anette Rosberg Arnäs, Malmö, Sweden, for sending information about the graves of casualties.

16 Thanks to nephew Stuart Stevenson, Stockholm, Saskatchewan, for providing photocopies of the telegram, Fritz Stenberg's diary, and photos of his headstone at Canadian Battlefield Memorial Park, Bourlon Wood, France.

17 Ivor Thord-Gray (1878–1964) was born Thord Ivar Hallström in Stockholm. He joined the Merchant Marine at age fifteen, ending up in South Africa two years later. His military career began here, then worked its way through Asia, Mexico, Britain, and Russia. After retiring

he travelled in Europe and North America for treatment of his wounds, and became a citizen of the United States. See Gyllenhaal, *Svenskar i krig*, 75–6.

18 Grenke, *The German Community in Winnipeg*, 151–80.

19 Claes Sahlin, *Från Canada till Mexico: Reseskildring* (Chicago: Skandinaviska Socialistförbundet i America, 1916), 48–9.

20 Grenke, *The German Community in Winnipeg*, 159–63; see also Donald Avery, "Ethnic and Class Relations in Western Canada during the First World War: A Case Study of European Immigrants and Anglo-Canadian Nativism," in *Canada and the First World War: Essays in Honour of Robert Craig Brown*, ed. David MacKenzie (Toronto: University of Toronto Press, 2004), 272–99.

21 Thompson, *Ethnic Minorities during Two World Wars*, 5.

22 Ljungmark, *Svenskarna i Winnipeg*, 185–6.

23 St. Jean, "From Defiance to Defence," 61, citing Lars-Arne Norborg, *Sveriges historia under 1800- och 1900-talen: Svensk samhällsutveckling 1809–1992* (Stockholm: Almqvist and Wiksell, 1993), 251–9.

24 "Queen Is No Neutral: Victoria of Sweden Quoted as a German Sympathizer," *The New York Times*, 29 June 1915.

25 Scott, *Sweden*, 473, states, "The British watched the situation in Sweden closely. They no longer feared as much as they had previously that Sweden might join Germany in the war, and they tended to take a stiffer stance against Sweden's commercial demands ... They were not interested in resuming trade negotiations and gradually developed a policy to bring down the Swedish government in the hope that a succeeding liberal regime would be more friendly to them. The means they used was the notorious Luxburg affair."

26 St Jean, "From Defiance to Defence," 70–1, singles out Arne Lind (pseud.) as an example of a staunch pacifist who was also a member of IOGT. He emigrated to Two Harbors, Minnesota, in 1913, but in 1917 returned to Sweden to avoid the draft in the United States. When Sweden insisted that he carry out his compulsory military training, he migrated again, this time to Kimberley, British Columbia. Later he had a bitter argument with his son who, despite his father's wishes, enlisted in the Second World War.

27 Severt and Thomas Swanson were bachelors who came to Canada in 1914 from Ray, North Dakota. They were being investigated because of statements from neighbours.

28 LAC, RG 18, volume 1784, file 611, reports and correspondence from Royal North West Mounted Police, Regina District, 18 December 1915 to 16 March 1918.

29 LAC, RG 6, volume 596, file 269-120; correspondence from John McDougald, Commissioner of Customs, to Chief Press Censor, 8 November 1918.

30 British Columbia Archives, GR-57, "James Olson (Swede) Tanglefoot BC 1918."

31 LAC, RG 18, volume 1792, file 918; Inspector C.C. Raven, Weyburn Sub-district, to Constable Goude, Tribune, Saskatchewan, 25 May 1916.

32 Ljungmark, *Svenskarna i Winnipeg*, 171.

33 Handwritten on letterhead, "This is to certify that according to official documents this day produced before me Jonas Henry Erikson was born on the 7th day of December 1900 in the parish of Jockmock [*sic*] in the province of Lapland [*sic*] Sweden. His father resides in Sweden and is a Swedish subject. The Royal Swedish Consulate at Winnipeg Man. May 31st 1918, Peter Bernhard Anderson, Royal Swedish vice-consul." Henry was raised by Johan and Eva Holmström and used Holmstrom as his surname. His birth mother, Eva's sister, remained in Sweden. The Holmstroms immigrated in 1910–11, and in 1918 moved from Winnipeg to a farm in Inwood, Manitoba. See *The Interlake Beckoned*, 87–8. Thanks to daughter Helen Kletke, Teulon, Manitoba, for providing a copy of this letter with explanation.

34 Typewritten on letterhead, "This is to certify, on request, that Oskar Emil Björk, who was born on the 25th of April, 1892, in the parish of Piteå, Province of Norrbotten, Sweden, and now resides at Timmins, Ontario, Canada, is a Swedish subject, and that he is entered under No. 307 in the Register of Nationality kept here. This certificate is valid for one year. The Royal Swedish Consulate General at Montreal, this 5th day of June, 1918, No. 459, Fee: $0.50, C.A. Wollert, Acting Consul General for Sweden." Emil Bjork (1892–1954) immigrated to Canada in 1912. By 1914 he had settled in Timmins, where he worked for Hollinger mines for forty years as a machinist. His wife and daughter joined him in 1924. Thanks to granddaughter Gloria Roberton, Trenton, Ontario, for family information.

35 Ljungmark, *Svenskarna i Winnipeg*, 171–2; see also "Patriotism," *Framåt*, September 1917, 2.

36 LAC, RG 6, E, volume 577, file 247-3, part 1; Brown to Chambers, 25 February 1918.

37 Ljungmark, *Svenskarna i Winnipeg*, 165, 177–8.

38 Thompson, *Ethnic Minorities During Two World Wars*, 9.

39 Among the Swedes who died in British Columbia was Gunnar Klasson, twenty-nine, a CPR employee in Kamloops; see *En Smålandssocken emigrerar*, 438. See also British Columbia Archives, GR 57, box 28,

file 24-26, Correspondence between Royal Swedish Consul General and Provincial Police, Victoria, for Erik Gustaf Gunnar Andersson of Cranbrook, Nils Andersson of Phoenix, Anders Erikson of Nelson, and Fred Olson of Chilliwack. Thanks to Jason Ness, Edmonton, for family information about Betsy Åkerstrom, thirty-nine, of Camrose, who left six children aged seven to sixteen.

40 Andrew Westlund (1859–1939) was born in Västjärna, Dalarna, and emigrated to the United States in 1880. In 1898, after seven years of drought, the family moved to Calmar, where Elvina was born. See *Pioneers and Progress*, 203–5. Thanks to granddaughter Verna Larson, Edmonton, for family information.

41 Minnie Lundstrom was born Wilhelmina Blomqvist in Hede, Härjedalen, in 1881, the daughter of Ida Blomqvist (1860–1952). In 1902 she emigrated to Minnesota; in 1905 she married Herman Björkqvist from Gotland and had two sons. After his death from tuberculosis she applied for a homestead in the Milleton area, and in 1912 married Erik Lundström, who was born in Däla-Järna, Dalarna. Thanks to Connie Bjorkquist, Jasper, Alberta, for donating a hardcover copy of her book, *The Birch Branch: Bjorkquist Family History*, published in 2005, to supplement earlier versions.

42 Magnus Alfred Lindgren and his wife, Johanna, were born in Vilhelmina, Lappland. The family immigrated to Mulvihill, Manitoba, around 1904. Thanks to Ingalena Marthin, Vilhelmina, for family information about her father's cousins.

43 Michael Petrou, *Renegades: Canadians in the Spanish Civil War* (Vancouver: University of British Columbia Press, 2008); see also Howard, *Vancouver's Svenskar*, 83–4, 92–3.

44 Those who died included Karl Joseph Carlson (ca. 1886–1938), who worked as a stonemason in Delhi, Ontario, and at fifty-three died on the battlefield at Teruel. Isak Mattsson (1898–1938) was born in Sala, Västmanland, immigrating to Winnipeg in 1926, later working as a lumberjack and miner in British Columbia. He died of cancer in the notorious Burgos prison camp. Those whose fates are unknown include Nels Berg of Bloomfield, Nova Scotia; and Karl Holmberg, Axel Käck, and Gustav Adolf Westlund of Vancouver. Elis Mathias Frånberg (ca. 1905–19?) came from northern Sweden and immigrated to Canada in 1930. Thanks to archivist Myron Momryk, LAC, for personal information. See also Petrou, *Renegades*, 89, for Matheson, and 115 for Frånberg.

45 Harry Anderson (1902–19?) was born of Swedish parents in Capelton, Quebec. He took part in the On-to-Ottawa Trek and volunteered to fight

in the Spanish Civil War. Thanks to archivist Myron Momryk, LAC, for personal information.

46 Petrou, *Renegades*, 102–3.

47 The Honourable Per Wijkman, "Sweden's Relationship with the British Empire and with Canada in Particular," *The Empire Club of Canada Speeches 1944–1945* (Toronto: The Empire Club of Canada, 1945), 98–111. At this time Wijkman's official title was Envoy.

48 P.O. George Williams, DFM, as told to Geoffrey Hewelcke, "The Swedes Are Our Friends," *Maclean's* (15 September 1944): 13, 26, 28, 30.

49 Scott, *Sweden*, 503–9.

50 Thompson, *Ethnic Minorities During Two World Wars*, 11–12.

51 Program, "Concert in aid of Finnish Red Cross, Labor [*sic*] Temple, 314 Bay Street, Port Arthur, Friday, Feb. 23, 1940."

52 Lennard Sillanpää, "Participating in Canada's victory: The Finnish Community in Canada during World War II," *Siirtolaisuus-Migration* 2 (2004): 5–7.

53 Rönnqvist, "Bröder och rivaler," 339–40. The orders were Sons of Norway, the Vasa Order, and Dansk-kanadensisk Samfund.

54 Member groups came from both ends of the political spectrum, from the labour-oriented Scandinavian Workers' Club to the Swedish Club, founded in 1931 by Consul Axel Ståhl to organize banquets for visiting Swedish dignitaries. In 1944, when a motion was defeated to discuss purely Scandinavian issues at meetings and not to involve politics, four groups walked out in protest: the Swedish Club, the Icelandic society Isafold, the Danish Brotherhood, and the Norwegian Male Chorus. Most problems seemed to involve Sid Seaholm, chairman of both the Scandinavian Workers' Club and the Central Committee. The committee disbanded in 1947. See St Jean, "From Defiance to Defence," 72–6.

55 Signe Parke (1908–1998) was born in Sweden and in 1910 she and her mother immigrated to Silverhill, British Columbia, to join her dad, Ivar Ericson. Signe grew up in Silverhill, then in 1928 married Hugh Parke and moved to Vancouver. She belonged to the Vasa Lodge in New Westminster until it disbanded, then became a charter member of the lodge in Abbotsford. See Ella Wickstrom, "Mission, BC," *Swedish Press*, July 1998, 16.

56 Christina Matyczuk (1920–) was born Elin Christina Sundberg in Norberg, Västmanland, the eldest daughter of Karl Gottfrid Sundberg, a cross-country skiing racer, and Adela Södersten. The family immigrated to Fort William in 1923, later moving to a farm in nearby Ellis. Christina went to Fort William to work in Canada Car, and in 1941 joined the

Vasa Lodge. She married Peter Matyczuk in 1945. Thanks to Christina Matyczuk, Thunder Bay, for family information.

57 Herman Selin (ca. 1903–19?) was born Herman Sellin near Vilhelmina, Västerbotten, the son of Alex Kristoffer and Agata Sellin, who immigrated to Lundemo, Alberta, the year Herman was born.

58 LAC, Carl E. Soderquist Fonds; Soderquist, "En återblick" (1969).

59 Gust Freeberg was the son of Oscar Freeberg (1882–19?), who was born in Sweden. In 1910 Oscar married A.M. Larsson in Fort William, and the couple ran the Scandinavian Boarding House in Port Arthur from 1911 to 1914. Thanks to Nick Pappas, Thunder Bay, for donating copies of documents pertaining to the Freeberg family. The register of the Scandinavian Boarding House is in the care of TBHMS, B20/1/1.

60 Bror Daniel Anderson (1882–1971) was born in Gullnäs, Dalarna, and in 1905 married Anna Matilda Olson (1883–1947). Daniel emigrated to the United States in 1906, to be joined by his wife the following year. In 1912 the family moved to Norquay, where Daniel became its first blacksmith, later farming from 1918 to 1968. See Carol Shanner, comp., "Anderson Family History 1844–1985" (1985).

61 "Bror Daniel Andersson's letters: *Brev från Amerika 1906–1971*, CD copied by Släktforskarnas hus, Leksand, and donated by Sylvia and Gunnar Gullnäs, Grycksbo, Sweden.

62 Emil Anderson (1876–1959) was born in Växjö, Småland, and in 1898 emigrated to Minnesota, where he worked as assistant to O.W. Swenson, general superintendent of Foley Bros., railway contractors. In 1905 Anderson went to Fort William from Sudbury, became involved in various business enterprises, and was elected councillor in Fort William from 1924 to 1928 and in Neebing from 1922 to 1926. In 1942 Emil Anderson Construction Company opened a head office in Vancouver and a general office at Hope. Emil married Irene Mondoux (1881–1930) of Sudbury. See Brent Scollie, *Thunder Bay Mayors and Councillors*, 155–6.

63 Einar Elon Eng (1900–1959) was born in Färila, Hälsingland, and immigrated to Winnipeg, where in 1923 he married Hannah Antoinette Hagglund (1902–1927) from Kramfors, Ångermanland. After her death from cancer he married Myrtle Lillian Lofstrom (1905–1998), originally from Kroknäset, Täsjö, Ångermanland, and Renålandet, Jämtland. Einar played in the Regina symphony orchestra and on the radio in a trio. His instruments were cello, violin, and tuba. He became a grain buyer in Beatty, Saskatchewan, and was active in the CCF. Thanks to Allen Eng, Millet, Alberta, for family information.

64 LAC, RG 76, volume 245, file 165833.

65 Gust Wilhelm Stålbrand (ca. 1876–19?) was born in Örkelljunga, Skåne, and became a missionary. After working in the Congo he married Ingrid Henrietta Olsson (ca.1885–19?). The couple immigrated in 1912, and their five sons were born in Canada. Gust had died in an accident before the article was written. See Landelius Biography Collection, volume 3, #193.

66 Donald Gilbert Carlson (1906–1990) was born in Wetaskiwin. His parents emigrated from Lindesberg, Västmanland, to the United States in 1890 and moved to Wetaskiwin in 1904–5. Donald attended Brandon College and entered the Baptist ministry. Later he returned to the Air Force, serving in British Columbia and Alberta. After retirement he taught high school at Red Deer, and translated and published several of his father's works. Thanks to Katherine Peebles, Cupertino, California, for family information.

67 Werner John Carlson (1896–1978) was in the 31st Battalion when he was wounded by shellfire. Herbert Carlson (1899–1981), 187th Battalion, was gassed. Thanks to Katherine Peebles, Cupertino, California, for family information.

68 Clarence Lundeen (1915–1983) was born in Preeceville, Saskatchewan, the son of Nels Lundeen and Augusta Ryberg, who emigrated separately from Sweden and married in the United States before moving to Saskatchewan. Clarence married in 1945. Thanks to Linda Michaud, Regina, for family information.

69 Oscar Sideen (1911–1987) was born in Stanley, Ontario, the son of Neil and Anna Sideen from Jämtland. See Jim Lyzun, *Aviation in Thunder Bay* (Thunder Bay: Thunder Bay Historical Museum Society, 2006), 35–6.

70 Ally Viola Aurora Malmborg (1909–1999) was born in Malmö, Skåne, the daughter of Alfred Otto Ripa, who changed his surname to Malmborg during military training. Alfred's ancestors came from Normandy, and the Per Ripa House in Malmö, built in 1836, is a historic site. Alfred immigrated to Kenora in 1910 and the family followed. Ally trained at McKellar General Hospital School of Nursing, graduating in 1932. She worked as head nurse at McKellar during her entire career except for military service from 1942 to 1945. Thanks to Ally Malmborg, Thunder Bay, for family information. See also Laura Boast, "A Day to Remember: Nurse Recalls War Service," *Chronicle-Journal* (Port Arthur), 11 November 1991.

71 Martin Victor Sandberg (1912–1994) was born in Coronation, Alberta, the son of Per Victor Sandberg (1877–1950) from Filipstad, Värmland, who homesteaded in Federal, Alberta, in 1909. Martin married Anne Stephens in Peace River country and the couple had two sons. Thanks to Tim

Sandberg, Calgary, for family information including Victor's letters to his sister Verna (1941–2).

72 Valfrid Lundgren came from Piteå, Norrbotten, and enlisted in Red Deer in 1943. See Gyllenhaal, *Svenskar i krig*, 203–4.

73 See ibid., 202–4. Georg Nilsson (ca. 1906–1944) came from Gällared, Halland, and settled in Alberta.

74 Harvey Nystrom (1922–1944) was born in Buford, Alberta, the son of Karl Nystrom from Mala, Västerbotten. He and his friend Georg Nilsson joined the Canadian Scottish Regiment (Princess Mary's) and spent a year in England before going to France. He is buried in the Brettville sur l'Aize Canadian War Cemetery near Caen, France. Thanks to Verna Nystrom Nichols, Red Deer, Alberta, for family information. See also Gyllenhaal, *Svenskar i krig*, 203.

75 Raymond Johnson was born in 1915 and Otto Johnson in 1925. Thanks to Amanda Gellman, Windsor, Ontario, for family information.

76 Carl Gerhard Ludvig De Geer (1917–1944) was born in Bathurst, New Brunswick, the son of Carl Axel Gerhard De Geer (1877–1931), born in Skönberga, Östergötland, and Katie May Trueman (1884–1968) of Saint John. Thanks to niece Mary McIntosh, Annapolis Royal, Nova Scotia, for family information.

77 The number of conscientious objectors of Swedish origin is not known.

78 Verner Loov, Edmonton, correspondence dated 6 November 2005. Verner Loov (1926–2010) was born in Lund, Skåne, and emigrated with his mother and sister in 1928.

79 For a discussion of this phenomenon, see St Jean, "From Defiance to Defence," 81–4.

7. The Swedish Press

1 Ljungmark, *Svenskarna i Winnipeg*, 47–8, states that 2,000 copies were sent to Scandinavia and the same number to Canada and the United States. According to Vennerström, *"Den skandinaviske Canadapressen,"* 5, these figures derived from an article in the *Winnipeg Free Press* announcing the new paper, dated 15 October 1887. In Öhlén's correspondence with the federal government, housed at LAC, he has requested payment for 1,000 copies of *Den skandinaviske canadiensaren* every month from October 1887 to September 1889.

2 Lars Ljungmark, "The Northern Neighbor: Winnipeg, the Swedish Service Station in the 'Last Best West', 1890–1950, " in *Swedes in the Twin Cities: Immigrant Life and Minnesota's Urban Frontier*, ed. Philip J.

Anderson and Dag Blanck (Minneapolis: Minnesota Historical Society Press, 2001), 96.

3 Stockholm Binder, Reimar Remidav, "The Founding of the Stockholm Colony," *Svenska Canada-tidningen*, 1923, 7, trans. Mabel Fredlund. Hofstrand's wife remained in New Stockholm with the children, and pastor A.G. Olson took over his preaching post on a part-time basis.

4 Vennerström, *"Den Skandinaviska Canadapressen,"* 7. In 1892 "Den" was dropped from the title, resulting in a change to *Skandinaviske Canadiensaren*.

5 Konstantin Flemming (1873–1952) was born in Stockholm, and trained for three years as a typographer at the Norrtälje newspaper's print shop before leaving for Winnipeg in 1893. Until 1907 he worked as a typographer but also at times as editor or publisher, sometimes both, of Winnipeg's Swedish newspapers. He married in 1901, and from 1908 to 1938 was employed by Canada Customs. After retirement he edited *Canada-tidningen* from 1943 to 1952.

6 Vennerström, *"Den Skandinaviska Canadapressen,"* 3. For a while Flemming's print shop printed Russian, Hungarian, English, Rumanian, and Polish newspapers in addition to *Canada*.

7 Ibid., 2.

8 Ljungmark, *Svenskarna i Winnipeg*, 82–4. A list of Canadian newspapers, with names, dates of publication, and whether weekly or monthly, appears in Alfred Söderström, *Blixtar på tidnings-horisonten* (Minneapolis, 1910), 52.

9 Editors named are M. Zilliachus, C.A. Hemborg, and Augustus Ohlson. John E. Lidholm was publisher from 1906 to 1908. John E. Forslund was involved in both capacities for varying periods.

10 *Minnesskrift: första skandinaviska kristna missionsförsamlingen, 1885–1935*, 16–17. The masthead read *"Kristlig tidning för Skandinaverna i Canada,"* which translates as "Christian newspaper for Scandinavians in Canada." Surprisingly, the church's history book devotes only one sentence to its official organ; see Anderson, *The Covenant Church in Canada*, 7.

11 Andrew Hallonqvist (1862–1937) was born in Maås, Kinnared, Halland, in ca. 1882 immigrated to Winnipeg and worked for the CPR, and in 1889 moved to Winnipeg and became owner of a grocery store, an employee of Manitoba's Immigration Department, and owner of A. Hallonquist Steamship Agency, claiming to have sold his first steamboat ticket in 1887. He married Albertina (ca. 1868–19?) from Sweden, and they had three sons and two daughters. The eldest son, Emil, took over the shipping business. See Landelius Biography Collection, volume 2, #014; see also

Days of Our Years; see also Manitoba Archives, Swedish Community Oral History Collection (Manitoba Multicultural Museums Committee, 1986), Vera Hallonquist, C556-557.

12 Bonnie Bridge, "Historical Window Opened: Wrecker Reveals Century-old Main Street Signs," *Winnipeg Free Press*, ca. 1993.

13 Nilsson, *De sista svenska rösterna*, 338, claims that Andrew Hallonquist took over *Canada posten* in 1912. Hallonquist Drive in Winnipeg is named for Ernest's wife, Lillian, who served as city councillor. Ernest Hallonquist and his son Bill were also elected as city councillors.

14 Albin Hagglund (ca. 1893–1965) was born near Kramfors, Ångermanland, and immigrated to Canada with his parents in 1904. He worked as editor of *Canada posten* from 1927 to 1952, and of *Canada-tidningen* from 1952 to 1965. He was a member of Strindberg Vasa Lodge, Norden, Swedish Oldtimers, and Canada Press Club. See obituary, *Nya svenska pressen*, 15 January 1965. See also Vennerström, "*Den skandinaviske Canadapressen*," 4: "The southerly swarthy and gunpowder-spattered J.A. Hägglund, born in the capital of the unstable Ådalen, Kramfors, was a typographer for *Canada posten*, signed up voluntarily in the [first] world war, fought like a madman, later became the editor of *Svenska Canada-tidningen*, now [1929] director of the office of Canadian Pacific Railway in Göteborg, utterly energetic but perhaps somewhat wobbly in his opinions."

15 Peter Eriksson Ringwall (1861–1933) was born in Överhogdal, Hälsingland, and in 1883 immigrated to Cooperstown, North Dakota. Six children were born there, and four more in Canada. Thanks to Marion Petersson, Wetaskiwin, for family information.

16 Ljungmark, *Svenskarna i Winnipeg*, 136, 141.

17 See "Hamilton's Great Alteration Sale," which includes a box titled "*Stor utsäljning*," *Daily Times-Journal*, Fort William, 14 October 1907.

18 Ljungmark, *Svenskarna i Winnipeg*, 113–15.

19 UM IHRC, Tell Dahllöf Collection, Esse W. Ljungh, "*Några uppgifter om Canada-tidningen genom tiderna: Namn, utgivningsår, utgivare, redaktörer, sidoantal, spaltantal, format.*" The several publishers – John E. Lidholm (1906–8), C. Albin Jones (1908–10), and J.A. Hamberg (1910–13) – were outnumbered by the editors – C.A. Hemborg (1907), Augustus Ohlson (1907), Alf. Carlstrom (1908), C. Albin Jones (1908), John E. Lidholm (1909), John Dahlstrom (1909), B. Enstrom (1909–12), and Arvid Queber (1912–13).

20 Vennerström, "*Den Skandinaviska Canadapressen*," 2.

21 Nils F:son Brown was born Nils Fredrik Olof Åhlén (1886–1960) in Bro

parish, Uppland, and grew up in Uppsala where his father, Fredrik Åhlén, was a *kronofogde* (government official similar to a sheriff). He studied law at Uppsala University but did not complete his degree. Instead, he emigrated in 1910 to Minneapolis, where Swan J. Turnblad hired him to work on that city's largest Swedish-language newspaper, *Svenska Amerikanska posten*. There, he became a seasoned newspaperman under the tutelage of Emil Meurling and Johan Person. He married in 1913, and when Turnblad refused to give him a raise he quit to become editor of *Svenska Canada-tidningen*. He remained in Winnipeg until 1921, taking an active part in community affairs and joining both Norden Society and Strindberg Vasa Lodge. He returned to Sweden in 1953, and died there. See Ulf Jonas Björk, "A Swedish-American View of Sweden: The Journalism of Nils F. Brown, 1910–1953," *Swedish-American Historical Quarterly* 44, no. 1 (January 1993): 22, 30; see also his "Nils F:son Brown and the Decline of the Swedish-American Press, 1910–1940," *Swedish American Genealogist* 19, nos. 2–3 (June/September 1999): 221–5.

22 Gregory S. Kealey, "State Repression of Labour and the Left in Canada, 1914–1920: The Impact of the First World War," in *A Nation of Immigrants: Women, Workers, and Communities in Canadian History,* ed. Franca Iacovetta and Robert Ventresca (Toronto: University of Toronto Press, 1998), 388–9.

23 LAC, RG6, volume 599, file 273-11; Brown to Chambers, 15 November 1916, and Chambers to Brown, 22 November 1916.

24 Rudolf Einhardt (1874–19?) was born in Glemminge, Skåne, and graduated from Lund University in 1896 with a degree in history. He immigrated to Canada in 1906, and settled on a farm in Forgan, Saskatchewan. His column in *Svenska Canada-tidningen* expressed his socialistic and pro-German views. Already in the 26 April 1916 issue Brown had refused to publish Einhardt's "more dangerous" articles about the war. See St Jean, "From Defiance to Defense," 59n24. Einhardt replaced Brown as editor of *Forum* 1 May 1921.

25 LAC, RG 6, E, volume 577, file 247-3, part 1; Livesay to Chambers, 16 April 1917 and 20 April 1917. For an anti-German letter to the editor, see "Ett ord till tyskvännerna" (A word to friends of Germany), *Svenska Canada-tidningen*, 3 January 1917, by Mrs Olga Auleen, Paswegin, Saskatchewan.

26 St Jean, "From Defiance to Defence," 60.

27 Ibid., 67, as quoted from *Svenska Canada-tidningen,* 28 March 1917, and translated by the author.

28 Ibid., 56.

29 Björk, "A Swedish-American View of Sweden," 25–6.

30 Michael Brook, "Scandinavians," in *The Immigrant Labor Press in North America, 1840s–1970s: An Annotated Bibliography*, ed. Dirk Hoerder (New York: Greenwood Press, 1987), 99. Editors are listed as Carl Ingvar Olsen 1910–11, 1913–17, 1920–4; L.J. Siljan 1911–12; O.T. Tønder 1912–13; and the Swedes Nils F. Brown 1917–19 and Rudolf Einhardt 1919–?. The paper existed from 1910 to 1970.

31 "Godtemplarnas femte årsmöte: V.R. återvalt – Axel J. Carlson och G.H. Silver: Återvalda till redaktörer för Idog," *Svenska Canada-tidningen*, 19 February 1920. According to Ruth Bogusis, *Checklist of Canadian Ethnic Serials* (Ottawa, 1981), 276, *Idog* was published monthly "1918?–Apr. 1919?."

32 LAC, mfm T73, part 2, *Idog* to Chambers, 3 September 1918. See also Chambers to Nils Fredriksson Brown, 22 August 1918. According to a confidential letter from Chambers to van Veen, 22 August 1918, the book *Victory and Defeat* told "the inside story of what drunkeness has cost England. Evidently the anti-saloon league is distributing copies in America; it outlines the benefits that could have accrued if prohibition had been enforced during the war." Lloyd George had suppressed the book in England.

33 Oscar Johnson was born Johan Oskar Johansson (1883–1940) in Lilla Röd, Krokstad parish, Bohuslän. He fulfilled his military duty as sergeant in the medical corps and attended the University of Berlin before emigrating in 1909. After becoming naturalized in 1913, he returned to Sweden to court his future wife, Linnea Skog (1893–1969), born in Neferstad parish, Västmanland. She waited until after the war to immigrate, and in 1919 the couple married in Port Arthur and raised three children. Oscar Johnson, as he was called, owned and operated Central Manufacturing Company Limited, which made canvas products such as tents, awnings, CMC overalls, and even an experimental canvas boat that folded up for easy transportation. Johnson won a government contract during the war to manufacture hatch covers. He ran for municipal office as a Socialist in 1914, but most of his later activities outside of work centred on ethnic organizations: IOGT, the Scandinavian Home Society, Swedish Baptist Church, Immanuel Lutheran Church, Swedish sick- and death-benefit fund, and the Vasa Lodge. In 1921 he was appointed vice-consul. Thanks to daughter Millie Scollie, Thunder Bay, for family information.

34 "Framåt försvaras," *Svenska Canada-tidningen*, 3 January 1917.

35 Only three issues of *Framåt* have survived: February 1916, July 1917, and September 1917.

36 LAC, RG6, E 1, volume 578, file 247-6; O.F. Young, *Daily News-Chronicle*, Port Arthur, to Livesay, 16 October 1917, see also Herman W. Niinimäki, General Agent, Port Arthur, to Chambers, 18 October 1917, see also J.P.D. van Veen to E. Boag, Press Censor, 19 October 1917; see also Barr, "Swedes at the Lakehead," 55–6; see also Oscar Johnson Collection, Minute Book, IOGT Study Circle, Port Arthur, January 1915–November 1917.

37 Scandinavian Heritage Project, Oscar Johnson Collection, typed obituary of Len Enroth, who died 2 February 1925, by Oscar Johnson, probably a submission to *Svenska Canada-tidningen*. Lennart Enroth (1895–1925) immigrated from Järpen, Jämtland, in 1905 with his parents, John Enroth and Anna Backen, and siblings. The family settled in Port Arthur.

38 Their names, in roughly chronological order, are C.T. Martin, Erik Sjostrand, Reimar Remidav, Artur Engberg, G.H. Silver, J.A. Hagglund, Carl E. Rydberg, Paul Magnusson, Esse Ljungh, Arthur A. Anderson, and Konstantin Flemming.

39 Esse Willem Ljungh (1904–1991) was born in Malmö, Skåne, was raised in Linköping, and attended Uppsala University, where he studied law, economics, and philosophy. He also studied at the Royal Dramatic Theatre in Stockholm before immigrating in 1927 with his wife, Lola Gustafson (ca. 1904–1989), to a half-section in Radville, Saskatchewan, given to Lola as a wedding present by her grandfather. The couple had a son, Bert, in 1928, then in 1929 Esse left for Winnipeg while Lola went to Harrison Hot Springs, British Columbia, to work as a masseuse. In 1931 Esse and a lawyer friend walked to Vancouver, sponsored by the Hudson's Bay Company, and their exploits were written up in both Winnipeg daily newspapers. He talked Lola into bringing Bert to Winnipeg and they lived there from 1931 to 1943, and then moved to Vancouver. In 1951 Esse married actress Elizabeth Viola Lockerbie (1915–1968), best known for her voiceover on the TV series *Maggie Muggins*. See Landelius Biography Collection, volume 2, #336; see also "Swedes," in *Notes on the Canadian Family Tree* (Ottawa: Canadian Citizenship Branch, 1960), 124; see also UM IHRC, Tell Dahllöf Collection, Ljungh, "*Några uppgifter.*"

40 Helge V. Pearson, "*Canada-Tidningen*: Swedish Canada News," in *The Multilingual Press in Manitoba*, ed. Joyce Bowling and M.H. Hykawy (Winnipeg: Canada Press Club, 1974), 87.

41 Oscar Sidenius, "Making Sweden Known in America," *Scandinavia: A monthly magazine* 2, no. 5 (May 1924), 55–6; see also UM IHRC, Tell Dalhöf Collection, correspondence with Esse Ljungh, *Canada-tidningen*, 28 May 1940.

42 Ljungmark, *Svenskarna i Winnipeg*, 203–6.

43 Helge Valdemar Pearson (1910–1990) was born in Simrishamn, Skåne, and immigrated to Canada in 1927. He was publisher of *Canada-tidningen* and *Norrøna* from 1946 to 1970, later becoming president of Dahl Co. Ltd. He belonged to the Viking Club, Strindberg Vasa Lodge, and Norden Sick Benefit Society. See *Swedish Press*, June 1990, 19.

44 "Sextio år: För C.-T:s jubileumsnummer av Helge Pearson," *Canada-tidningen*, 19 June 1952; see also "The Third Dimension: He Helps Retain Swedish Language," *Winnipeg Tribune*, 18 January 1958; see also Roger Newman, "You and Your Neighbors: Scandinavians Stay Home," *Winnipeg Free Press*, 27 January 1962.

45 Pearson, "*Canada-Tidningen*," 88, and "*Norrona*," 141. Gunnar Warolin died in 1996, but the paper was discontinued earlier.

46 Oskar L. Sundborg (ca. 1867–19?) emigrated from Stockholm in 1887 with the destination of Boston, later becoming associated with Chicago.

47 Minute Book, IOGT Lodge Linnea, 9 December 1911, from Irene Howard's research notes.

48 Bogusis, *Checklist of Canadian Ethnic Serials*, 277. See also Jørgen Dahlie, "The Ethnic Press as a Cultural Resource: *Canada Skandinaven* and the Norwegian-Swedish Community in B.C., 1910–1930," *Scandinavian-Canadian Studies* 1 (1983): 15–26.

49 Einar Finsand started the Norwegian newspaper *Canada skandinaven* in Vancouver in 1911, and transferred it to Nels N. Westby in 1919. Westby edited and published it as *The Norseman*. See Martin Ulvestad, "Nordmændene i Amerika" (1905), 4, as translated by Olaf Kringhaug, Vernon, British Columbia, http://freepages.misc.rootsweb.ancestry.com/~maggiebakke/Ulvestad_New.pdf.

50 Helge Ekengren was born in Finland and immigrated in 1924 to Vancouver, where he started writing for *Canada skandinaven*. He eventually became Finnish consul for British Columbia and the Yukon, and during the Second World War campaigned to raise money for the people of Finland who were being hard-pressed by Russia. See *Swedish Press*, June 1989, 14, and June 1999, 7.

51 Matthew Matson Lindfors (1899–1971) was born Mattias Mattiasson in Offerdal, Jämtland, and emigrated in 1922 after a year at Brunnsvikens folkhögskola. He married Edla, who was born in Östergötland, and the couple had one son, Bill. See *Swedish Press*, June 1999, 7–8; see also UBCL SC, Matthew Lindfors Fonds, AIVB, Box 3; Per Nilsson-Tannér, "Offerdalspojke kulturambassadör i Canada," *Östersunds-Posten*, 20 September 1951.

52 Rudolf Månsson (ca. 1880–1958) came from Karlshamn, Blekinge, where his wife, Gerda (18?–1949), continued to live until her death. Their only child, Rut, had died young, and they raised a girl from Austria, Adele, from the age of nine. They were strict Methodists and belonged to the Salvation Army. Rudolf immigrated to Winnipeg in 1927, at age forty-seven, and ended up working for *Svenska pressen* in Vancouver from 1930 to 1954.

53 Ann-Charlotte Berglund, "Box of Letters," *Swedish Press*, June–July 2002, 26–9, reprinted from *Blekinge läns tidning*.

54 UBCL SC, Olaf Seaholm Collection, A VII B; Notice to the shareholders of Central Press Limited on letterhead, and the minutes of the first meeting of the Directors, 25 May 1943. The chair, Charles Brundin, had "long experience in the printing business."

55 Einar Olson was described as "an Ontario mechanic and blacksmith-cum-writer." See *Swedish Press*, June 1989, 14.

56 Laura Maria "Maj" Stålhandske Brundin (1905–1994) was born in Visby, Gotland, and immigrated to Canada in 1927. Two years later she married Charles Brundin in Vancouver. See "Vancouver Notes," *Swedish Press*, November 1994.

57 Irene Howard, "Svenskhet and the *Swedish Press*," in *Vancouver's Svenskar*, 95–9.

58 Swedish Park, at the mouth of Seymour Creek, was acquired in 1926, and became a popular place for summer outdoor events and picnics with its octagonal dance pavilion. Indoor activities began with the winterizing of the pavilion and addition of a kitchen and restaurant. The park was expropriated in the early 1970s. See *Swedish Press*, June 1989, 10.

59 UBCL SC, Matthew Lindfors Fonds, A IV B, Box 3; newspaper clipping, "The Greatest Swedish Festival of the Season: The Diamond Festival, Sunday, July 31, [1938] 2 p.m., Seymour Park ..."

60 Jan Fränberg (ca. 1953–2004), Vicky, and their son Mattias returned to Åkersberga outside Stockholm in 1986, and there, a daughter, Anna, was born.

61 *Swedish Press*, January 1986, 3, and January 1996, 3.

62 Sture Wermee sold his printing business in Stockholm and immigrated to Vancouver in 1952 with his wife, Vanja. He served as editor of *Nya svenska pressen* from 1971 to 1983, continuing to typeset and print the paper as well as commercial orders. Sture retired to Victoria. See Ann-Charlotte Berglund, "Sture Wermee," typescript, 2 pages; see also Gunnar Nilsson, "En entusiast i den mindre tidningsvärlden," *Swedish Press*, March 1996, 42, excerpted from his book *De sista svenska rösterna*.

63 Anders Neumüller was born in Sweden and his wife, Hamida, in Uganda. They met at Uppsala University, and continued on to England and the Isle of Capri before returning to Sweden. Anders became art director at Scandecor in Uppsala, and is the author of ten books published in Sweden on subjects ranging from posters to Christmas cards, from antiques to etiquette. Hamida worked as information officer for SIDA, which coordinated Swedish subsidies to agricultural co-ops throughout the world. In 1982 the couple brought their daughters to Vancouver. There, Anders worked in freelance advertising and Hamida opened a restaurant with her sister. In 1995 Anders was appointed consul for British Columbia and Yukon. See Ann-Charlotte Berglund, "At Home with the Editors, or Who Is Crazy Enough to Take over a Small Swedish Paper that Should Have Been Dead a Long Time Ago?," *Swedish Press*, June 1989, 20–1.

64 Ernie Poignant grew up in Matsqui, British Columbia, the son of Albin Poignant and Hedvig Maria Danielson (1891–1990), both from Sweden. He worked at *Nya svenska pressen* from 1947 to 1949 to learn the newspaper trade, and then went to the *Cariboo Observer* and then to the *Maple Ridge Gazette* in Haney. See *Swedish Press*, June 1989, 22.

65 Sven Seaholm (1913–2001) was born in Matfors, Medelpad, and immigrated to Vancouver in 1929. There, he became a hardwood floor installer. He married Helen from Stavanger, Norway, and the pair, who loved to dance, led the Lekstugan folk-dancing group. He was also a singer. See *Swedish Press*, April 2001 and November 2002.

66 Mats Thölin was an anaesthetist and sports enthusiast who came to Vancouver in 1981. His wife, Harriet, was a nurse. See *Swedish Press*, January 1987.

67 Anders Neumüller, *Swedish Press*, June 1999, 12–13.

68 Mika Roinila, "Finland-Swedes in Canada: Discovering Some Unknown Finnish Facts," in *Siirtolaisuus – Migration*, 1:1997; see also LAC, Amicus bibliographical information.

69 *Days of Our Years*, 45–8.

70 Ibid., 26–37; see also Johnson, *God Gave the Growth*, 30–4. See Scandinavian Heritage Project, Oscar Johnson Collection, for photocopies from the 8 July 1920 issue of *Canada nyheter*. Thanks to Jeannette Brandelle, ELCIC Archives, Saskatoon, for information and for allowing photocopying of original issues of *Canada härald*.

71 *The Young Swedish Canadian,* mimeographed on six to eight sheets of typewriter paper, put out several numbers in 1908 and possibly 1909. See Bengston, "Upplevelser Östanhavs och Västanhavs," 27.

72 Of the three surviving issues, one was edited by J. Sällström and two by C.O. Hofstrand.

73 An earlier socialist newspaper directed towards Scandinavians, *Skorpionen* (Scorpion), had been published in Winnipeg in 1914, with perhaps a single issue. The group that published *Skorpionen* represented either Skandinaviska förbundet av socialist partiet (Scandinavian Federation of the Socialist Party) or the more left-leaning Skandinaviska socialdemokratiska förbundet (Scandinavian Federation of the Social Democratic Party). See Brook, "Scandinavians," 107.

74 Brook, "Swedes," in *The Immigrant Labor Press in North America, 1840s–1970s: An Annotated Bibliography*, ed. Dirk Hoerder (New York: Greenwood Press, 1987), 155.

75 Vennerström, *"Den skandinaviska Canadapressen,"* 2.

76 Ulf Jonas Björk, "Swedish Ethnicity and Labor Socialism in the Work of Nils F:son Brown, 1919–1928," *The Historian* 56, no. 4 (summer 1997): 763–6.

77 Carl August Larson (1868–1925) was born in Vårdsberg, Östergötland, emigrated to the United States in 1891, and was ordained 1903 in Paxton, Illinois. In 1918 he migrated to Goodwater, Saskatchewan, then to Wadena from 1921 to 1925. In 1906 he married Selma Malmgren of Parkers Prairie, Minnesota. See Bergendoff, *The Augustana Ministerium*. See Brook, "Swedes," 137; for details about the charge of disloyalty, see Nels T.A. Larson (son of Carl August Larson), "Life in Saskatchewan, 1918–1925: A Story of a Pioneering Missionary Family," ed. Samuel Chell, *Swedish-American Historical Quarterly* 36, no. 1 (1985): 39–55; for an autobiography of pastor Nels T.A. Larson, see Anderson, *"Si Gud's Lam/ Behold, The Lamb of God,"* 172–6.

78 Nels James Laurentius Bergen (1873–1949) was born in Norhassel, near Sundsvall, Medelpad, the son of the Baptist pastor, Lars Hendrickson. He followed three older brothers to the United States in 1888, and through the generosity of an employer had private tutors in English and two years in medical school. But he decided to follow in his father's footsteps as a Baptist pastor, and without being ordained took over the church in Karlstad, Minnesota. Just before the turn of the century he was sent as a missionary to Grant Memorial in Winnipeg, and from there to Red Deer and then Wetaskiwin, where he married Emma. The couple had ten children between 1902 and 1924. The eldest daughter, Elinore, graduated from Brandon College, her board and tuition paid by her uncle, Henry Larson. See *Pioneer Pathways*, 451–8.

79 N.J.L. Bergen, *Nya sånger för folket* (Wetaskiwin, 1923).

80 *Årsbok för svenska baptistförsamlingarna inom Amerika* (1908), 47. Bergen's reports were published in the 1908, 1909, and 1910 yearbooks.

81 August Sigfrid Wallin (ca. 1897–19?) was a dairyman who immigrated from Husaby, Västergötland, to Winnipeg in 1924. He was leader of Vancouver's SALF and a member of the Communist Party.

82 E. Martin Palmgren (ca. 1904–19?) immigrated from Nederluleå, Norrbotten, to Vancouver in 1923. He was a labour organizer and a member of the Communist Party.

83 Brook, "Scandinavians," 95, 97.

84 Bogusis, *Checklist of Canadian Ethnic Serials*, 276.

85 Oscar Peterson (1907–19?) was born in Piteå, Norrbotten, the son of Johan Peterson and Emma Bergman. The family immigrated in 1910. In 1937 Oscar married Rose Wozniak, and the couple opened the Amazon Motel in 1952. See Manitoba Archives C570, Swedish Community Oral History Collection, Rose Peterson, 3–4.

86 A complete press run of *(Nya) Svenska pressen* is available on microfilm from the Legislative Library, Victoria, British Columbia, and of *Canada posten* and *(Svenska) Canada-tidningen* from the Legislative Library, Winnipeg, Manitoba. For the location of Canada's other Swedish newspapers on microfilm, see Lilly Setterdahl, comp., *Swedish-American Newspapers: A Guide to the Microfilms held by Swenson Swedish Immigration Research Center, Augustana College, Rock Island, Illinois* (1981).

8. The Depression, Strikes, and Unions

1 Nilsson, *De sista svenska rösterna*, 61.

2 *Leaves Green and Gold: Weldon, Shannonville, Windermere* (Weldon, SK: Weldon and District Historical Society, 1980), 11.

3 "The Gift: Memoirs of Viola Anderson," typescript donated by sister-in-law Margaret Anderson, Shaunavon, Saskatchewan. Viola married Max Etches and the couple raised four children in British Columbia. See also *Quarter Stake Echoes*, 26–7.

4 Hans Magnuson (1887–1975) was born in Glemen, Norway, and his parents returned to Sweden soon afterward. He immigrated to Saskatchewan via the United States, and in 1908 filed on a homestead southwest of Notre Dame. While breaking his land he also freighted with oxen between Swift Current and Notre Dame. In 1923 he travelled to Sweden and returned with a bride, Agda Karlsson (1892–1978). They visited Sweden in 1928 with two children and returned to have a third. Thanks to Isabel Johnson, Shaunavon, for family information. See also *Yesterday and Today* (Ponteix, SK, 1991): 2:1107.

5 Johan August Johansson (1879–1968) was born in Rödmossa,
Västmanland. He immigrated in 1908 to Kenora, where he married
Hulda Sjöström (1885–1977), who had migrated from Köpmanholmen,
Ångermanland, in 1911. Thanks to grandson Ahlan Johanson, Fort
Frances, Ontario, for family information.

6 Isobel Martin, ed., *Forests to Grainfields* (Berrymoor, AB: Berrymoor/
Canwood Historical Society, 1977), 249.

7 Ernst Valdemar Lind (1909–1997) was born in Kålhög, Lilla Ryland,
Tanumshede, Bohuslän, and immigrated in 1927 to Calgary, where he
worked as a carpenter and farmer. He married Mae Davis (1906–2000).
See "Memoirs of Ernest (Ernie) Waldemar Lind," 19. Thanks to Luella
Lind, Calgary, for donating this and other documents.

8 Ulf Beijbom, *Uppbrott från stenriket: Utvandring från Kronoberg och
kronobergare bortom haven* (Växjö: Emigrantinstitutets vänner, 2000), 244.

9 Per Ivar Törnblom (1912–1944) was born in Söderhamn, Hälsingland, the
son of Ivar Alexius Törnblom (1879–1974), who was born in Enköping,
Uppland, and seamstress Hildur Maria Blad (1888–1973), who was
born in Söderhamn. Both were Baptists. Ivar had his own coppersmith
shop in Söderhamn when he got a job offer from the Booth Coulter
Company in Toronto, so the family immigrated in 1912 to Toronto. In
1917 they moved to Port Arthur, where Ivar worked at the Port Arthur
shipyards. In 1920 he bought a farm at Harstone, although he did very
little farming but found work elsewhere. In 1940 the family moved to
Fort William. Included among Ivar Törnblom's papers are drawings for
a heated bathtub his company built in Söderhamn. Per Ivar Törnblom
left a wife, Kathleen Gray, whom he married in 1942. Thanks to Erik
Törnblom, Longlac, Ontario, and Rolf Törnblom, Thunder Bay, for family
information.

10 Rolf Törnblom, "Coming Home," *Green Mantle*, 27 November 1996, 5–7.

11 Irving Abella, *The Canadian Labour Movement, 1902–1960*, Booklet No. 28
(Ottawa: The Canadian Historical Association, 1975), 12–14.

12 Joel Hägglund (1879–1915) was born in Gävle, Gästrikland. Music
played a big part in his home and in the Free Church to which the family
belonged, and Joel learned to play the piano and the violin. In 1887 his
father died in an industrial accident and his mother died in 1902, at which
time Joel and his brother Paul emigrated to New York. Joel changed his
name first to Joseph Hillstrom, then to Joe Hill. His story has been the
subject of several articles and books, a play by Barrie Hill, Bo Widerberg's
movie (the official Swedish entry at the 1971 Cannes Film Festival), and
Alfred Hayes's song "I Dreamed I Saw Joe Hill Last Night." See Gunlög
Fur, "The Making of a Legend: Joe Hill and the I.W.W.," *Swedish-American*

Historical Quarterly 40, no. 3 (1989): 101–13; see also Nels Hokanson, "Swedes and the I.W.W.," *Swedish Pioneer Historical Quarterly* 23, no. 1 (1972): 25–35; see also Gibbs M. Smith, *Labor Martyr Joe Hill* (New York: Grosset and Dunlap, 1969), 24; for the song "Where the Fraser River Flows," see Barrie Stavis and Frank Harmon, eds., *The Songs of Joe Hill* (New York: Oak Publications, ca. 1960), 12–13.

13 Jean R. Burnet with Howard Palmer, *Coming Canadians: An Introduction to a History of Canada's Peoples* (Toronto: McClelland and Stewart, 1988), 68.

14 Carl Emil Berg (1888–1958) was born in Stockholm, Sweden, and immigrated in 1904. He worked as a miner and on railway construction on both sides of the border, becoming active in the Industrial Workers of the World (IWW) and its affiliate, the Western Federation of Miners. He moved to Edmonton around 1910, married, and had a daughter.

15 LAC, MG30, A127, volume 5, file 5-5, Carl Emil Berg Fonds; in his diary dated 10 January 1956 Berg wrote about his father who got pneumonia on the picket line, and who walked the streets for two years before finding work as a grinder at Bolinders. The dust affected his lungs and he died in February 1894. The daughters' names were Anna and Ester.

16 LAC, Carl Emil Berg Fonds; see also Verna Larson, poster "Emil Berg – Labour Leader."

17 The chief sources of information for this section are Barr, *The Scandinavian Home Society*, and her "Swedish Immigration to Canada, 1923–29: The Case of Port Arthur, Ontario," *Swedish-American Historical Quarterly* 51, no. 2 (April 2000): 150–61.

18 Ahti Tolvanen, *Finntown, A Perspective on Urban Integration: Port Arthur Finns in the Inter-War Period 1918–1939* (Helsinki: Yliopistopaino, 1985), 53, 55.

19 "Interview with Einar Nordström, Thunder Bay, Ontario, Canada, 18 September 1971," 2, typescript donated by Michael Brook, Nottingham, England.

20 John Pearson, the society's co-founder and board secretary, presided over the LWIUC's Scandinavian section. Representatives on the strike committee called in mid-September 1926 were society members Herman Grundström and A. Nilsson.

21 Howard, *Vancouver's Svenskar*, 74–5. Subsequent assistants were Eric Graff, Fred Lundstrom, and Henry Lundgren.

22 Ibid., 75.

23 St Jean, "On the Move," 86n.

24 Eva St Jean, "The Myth of the Big Swede Logger," *Swedish Press*, October 1999, 34.

25 *Svenska pressen*, 3 May 1934, 2, as recorded in Howard, *Vancouver's Svenskar*, 80–1.
26 Hjalmar "Bergie" Bergren (1905–198?) was born in Ransjö, Linsell, Härjedalen, the son of Karl Richard Olsson and Carolina Louisa Bergren. The family immigrated to Canada ca. 1912. He married Myrtle (1919–1979), who immigrated from England in 1926. The couple settled in Lake Cowichan on Vancouver Island. See Black, *Härjedalsgillet*, 35.
27 Carl Einar "Ernie" Dalskog (19?–1992) was born in Sweden and immigrated in 1923. See Daniel Francis, ed., *Encyclopedia of British Columbia* (Madeira Park: Harbour Publishing, 2000).
28 Elof Kellner was born in Rogsta, Hälsingland, and immigrated to Winnipeg in 1927. His older brother Erik Kellner came the following year. Elof shared his memories at the 1996 convention of the Canadian Labour Congress, held in Vancouver. See "Vancouver Notes," *Swedish Press*, October 1996, 20.
29 Herb Eldstrom, *Reflections and Recollections: A Collection of Memories* (Saskatchewan: The Author, ca. 1995), 28–9. Herbert Leonard Eldström (1912–2006) was born in Saskatchewan, the son of Nels Eldstrom and Mathilda Björk, who emigrated from Malmö, Skåne. His father rented land at Archive, Saskatchewan, and then homesteaded in the Hawley district. Herb married Bertha Jones in 1933 and had three children. Thanks to daughter Sheila Callen, Langley, British Columbia, for family information.
30 Valerie Knowles, *Strangers at Our Gates: Canadian Immigration and Immigration Policy, 1540–1990* (Toronto: Dundurn Press, 1992), 109.
31 Erik W. Westman (ca. 1892–19?) was born in Nordmaling, Ångermanland. See Barr, *The Scandinavian Home Society*, 36. His Workmen's Compensation Board file is protected by the *Freedom of Information Act*.
32 Eva St Jean, "'Letters from the Promised Land': The Ambiguous Radicalization of a Swedish Immigrant, 1928–1934," *Labour/Le Travail* (Spring 2004): 203, 219.
33 Ibid., 217.
34 David Einar Holmberg (1897–19?) was born in Vimmerby, Småland, and immigrated to Gravelbourg, Saskatchewan, in 1916. He worked on farms and ranches and in mines on both sides of the border, and suffered a mild nervous breakdown in 1925. Back in Saskatchewan, he had no steady employment from 1929 to 1935. In 1935 he married and settled on a farm, joining the Communist Party in Fir Mountain, Saskatchewan. Thanks to LAC archivist Myron Momryk for the above information.

35 Oscar George Lindholm (1888–19?) was born in Sweden, and in 1912 came to Canada via the United States. He homesteaded, and in 1916 married and was naturalized, moving to Fir Mountain, Saskatchewan, in 1932. Thanks to archivist Myron Momryk for the above information from LAC, MG10, K2, The Mackenzie-Papineau Battalion Fonds.

36 Nils Albert Jakobsson (ca. 1885–19?) was born in Östra Vemmerlöv, Skåne, and immigrated to Canada with his family in 1891, via the United States. He was conscripted into the Canadian army in 1918. Thanks to LAC archivist Myron Momryk for the above information.

37 Thunder Bay Historical Museum Society, A17/1/4; A.T. Hill, "Highlights of Labor History – Lakehead, Canada and World" (n.d.), 2.

38 Emil Sandberg immigrated to Canada in 1929. He was arrested during a public demonstration in Port Arthur and subsequently hospitalized with appendicitis. Thanks to LAC archivist Myron Momryk for the above information from Ivar (Einar) Nordstrom as told to Satu Repo, "Lakehead in the Thirties: A Labour Militant Remembers," *This Magazine* 13, no. 3 (July–August 1979); see also Tolvanen, *Finntown*, 65. Einar Edlund of Port Arthur was deported in 1934, according to "Interview with Einar Nordström," 2, typescript from Michael Brook, Nottingham, England.

39 Ivar Johnson was born in Sweden. Thanks to LAC archivist Myron Momryk for the above information from *Canadian Labor Defender* 3 no. 4 (November 1932).

40 Howard, *Vancouver's Svenskar*, 90.

41 Fritz Stål was an active socialist from Sandö, Ångermanland, an island in the Ångermanälven River below Kramfors. A raging national debate followed the Ådalen shootings in 1931. Bo Widerberg told the story in his film *Ådalen 31*. See Ljungmark, *Svenskarna i Winnipeg*, 211.

42 Ivar (Einar) Nordström (1909–1980) immigrated to Canada from Finland in 1930. He worked on railway construction in British Columbia, then in 1931 went to Port Arthur. He spent 1932 in a relief camp building the TransCanada Highway, and from 1937 to 1942 cut pulpwood when there was work. Later he worked for Co-op Dairy, then Palm Dairy. He married Rose Dahlin, who had three children from a previous marriage, and the couple had a daughter, Lori. For his views on the early years see "Einar: Part and Parcel of Canada" in Gloria Montero, *The Immigrants* (Toronto: James Lorimer, 1977), 213–17; see also Thunder Bay Historical Museum Society, A 19, Einar Nordstrom Fonds; see also Lakehead University Library Archives, MG2, Einar Nordstrom Collection.

43 Bror Adolf Hilding Magnusson (1909–19?) was born in Eda, Värmland. In 1928 he immigrated to Winnipeg and began working on a farm in

Wynard, Saskatchewan. His brother Martin G. Magnusson (ca. 1911–19?) arrived in 1930 and joined him on a Wynard farm. Bruce followed Martin to Port Arthur in 1933, after being naturalized as a Canadian citizen. In 1937 he married Kate Fountain from England, also a party member. They split up after his internment. His marriage to Eleanor Barrett lasted from 1946 to 1959 and resulted in three daughters. He spent the rest of his life with Marion, whom he met in 1962. For his career as a Communist see Bruce Magnuson, *The Untold Story of Ontario's Bushworkers: A Political Memoir* (Toronto: Progress Books, 1990); see also Scandinavian Heritage Project, Oral Interview, Bruce Magnuson, 20 October 1990.

44 Magnuson, *The Untold Story of Ontario's Bushworkers*, 6. See pages 143–6 for Magnuson's comments about Ian Radforth's book, *Bush Workers and Bosses: Logging in Northern Ontario 1900–1980* (Toronto: University of Toronto Press, 1987).

45 Martin Magnuson, a miner in northeastern Ontario, had difficulty enlisting while his brother Bruce was interned, but finally succeeded. See Archives of Ontario, Multicultural History Society of Ontario, Oral interview, Martin Magnuson, 27 April 1979.

46 Barr, *The Scandinavian Home Society*, 154–5.

47 Kaa Eneberg, "Recruitment of Swedish Immigrants to Soviet Karelia," in *Karelian Exodus: Finnish Communities in North America and Soviet Karelie during the Depression Era*, ed. Ronald Harpelle, Varpu Lindström, and Alexis E. Pogorelskin, special issue of the *Journal of Finnish Studies* 8, no. 1 (August 2004): 195.

48 Otto Johan Högberg (1911–?) was born in Karungi, Norrbotten, and in 1928 went to Sioux Lookout on an immigration scheme for bush workers. Two years later he was living with a wife and son Rudolph in St Catharines, Ontario, where he joined the Communist Party. Two years later in Petrozavodsk, his wife became involved with a Finnish Red Army officer and Otto smuggled Rudolph to northern Sweden, where he gave lectures for two months as arranged. Instead of returning to Soviet Karelia he hid in Stockholm, working in construction, then remarried and raised his son, who became an engineer. Thanks to Kaa Eneberg, Stockholm, Sweden, for the above information.

49 Ilmari Kinnunen (1911–19?) worked as a miner in Kiruna, Lappland, until immigrating to Canada in 1920. In 1931 he went to Kondopoga with his father and brother. In 1938 he was sentenced to be shot but somehow escaped death and was repatriated to Sweden in 1957. His father and brother disappeared without a trace. Thanks to Kaa Eneberg, Stockholm, Sweden, for the above information.

50 Hjalmar Mattson (1882–1937) was born in Bäckesta, Norrbotten, and in 1920 immigrated to Canada. He was recruited to Karelia in 1931 and died in Matrosji from unknown causes. Thanks to Kaa Eneberg, Stockholm, Sweden, for the above information.

51 Viktor Johan Lindberg (1901–19?) was born in Kiruna, Lappland, and immigrated in 1924 to Niagara Falls, Ontario. His wife and infant daughter followed, and subsequently two sons were born. The family went back to Sweden in 1930 and Viktor was recruited to two years in the Cola Peninsula, where he worked in the mining industry along with twenty others from Kiruna. Upon their return in 1933 the family was harassed by the Communist-dominated community for telling about the hardships suffered by their co-workers in Karelia. Thanks to Kaa Eneberg, Stockholm, Sweden, for the above information.

52 David Johan Larsson (1901–19?) was born in Älvsby, Norrbotten, and immigrated to Canada in 1918, returning to Sweden in 1926. In 1937 he and his wife came back from Kondopoga, where their little son died. He never spoke about the difficult years in Karelia, but his wife had no such inhibitions. Thanks to Kaa Eneberg, Stockholm, Sweden, for the above information.

53 Hans Verner Julius Krykortz (1912–1938) was born in Falköping, Västergötland, and adopted by a doctor's family. His surname is a version of the upper-class family name of his natural father, Strokirch. A construction engineer, he immigrated to Winnipeg in 1925, leaving a wife and daughter in Sweden. In 1932, shortly after his return, he left for Karelia with a Finnish woman and child. When arrested at a ski factory in 1938 he was living with a Swedish emigrant named Svea Holmström. The same year he was sentenced and shot near Petrozavodsk. Thanks to Kaa Eneberg, Stockholm, Sweden, for the above information.

9. Earning a Living

1 LAC, RG 76, volume 167, File 49149, Part 2, outlines Christina Swanson's activities from 1904 to 1909. In 1904 the girls went to Ontario (Toronto, Port Arthur, Fort William, Kenora, Vermilion Bay), Manitoba (Winnipeg, Swan River), Alberta (Wetaskiwin, Red Deer, McLeod, Innisfail, Calgary, Olds), and British Columbia (Vancouver, Cranbrook), probably because they had friends or relatives in those places.

2 Emma Elisabät Lundström (1883–1959) was born in Bjurträsk, Norrbotten, and her husband, Gustav Otto "G.O." Walberg (1880–1951), was born in Vännfors, Västerbotten. After marriage Emma moved to Fort

William and became an active member of the Zion Augustana Lutheran Church, Greenstone Rebecca Lodge, and the Children's Aid Society.

3 *Weekly Times-News*, 16 January 1904. The prime mover was K.O. Brune, and the company's property was located on Montreal Street, along the Neebing River, where the clay was thought to be suitable for the manufacture of bricks. Thanks to Brent Scollie, Ottawa, for bringing this clipping to my attention. See also LAC, mfm C-216, Correspondence Governor-General, for a 1906 letter addressed to the Norwegian Consul General, describing how the company had been defrauded of land and wages to the extent of $8,000 to $9,000.

4 The move cost Emma three weeks' pay. See *Daily Times-Journal*, 23 November 1907, for the English school conducted by the Lutheran Pastor Sjögren and his sister Helen Sjögren: "Matrons having Swedish or Norwegian girls in their employ would do themselves and the girls a great service by allowing them to go to school on Friday evenings at 7:30." Thanks to Brent Scollie, Ottawa, for bringing this clipping to my attention.

5 Marie Andersdotter Orstad (ca. 1865–1941) was born in Opdal, Norway, near Trondheim. She came to Port Arthur in 1891 and married Ingebrigt Orstad (1845–1924), moving from Port Arthur to Fort William after her husband's death. Thanks to the late Ellen Broman, Thunder Bay, for telling me about her experiences with Mrs Orstad.

6 Girls of today would not be so easily offended. Thanks to Mildred Walberg Main, Thunder Bay, for providing information about her mother's career as a domestic, and to Diane Harri, Thunder Bay, and Anna-Greta Edlund, Sweden, for family information.

7 Elin Forssell (1889–1980) was born Elin Maria Lexberg in Lilla Edet, Bohuslän, and emigrated in 1911. She married Karl Oskar Forssell (1888–1947) from Jämtland. See Wickstrom, *Recollections of Silverhill*, 31.

8 Karin Margareta Randin (1893–1963) was born in Linsell, Härjedalen, immigrated in 1910, moved from Winnipeg to Fairy Glen, Saskatchewan, to work for Robert Freed, met and married Oscar Bowman (1883–1928) from Östmark, Värmland, and had five children. Thanks to great-granddaughter Karmen Blackwood, Vancouver, for family information.

9 Edward L. Bowman, "Family Tree for Karin Margareta Randin" (1987), 1, typescript donated by Karmen Blackwood, Vancouver.

10 Mary Berglund (1902–1995) was born in Stanley, Ontario, the eldest daughter of Neil and Anna Sideen from Jämtland. She graduated from McKellar General Hospital School of Nursing in 1923, and in 1932 married Tony Berglund (1898–1966) from Ångermanland. See Dolores

Kivi, "The Florence Nightingale of the North," *Swedish Press*, October 1989, 19, translated by Per Ersson as "Mary Berglund – sjuksköterska i norr" and published in *Bodsjöboken* (1987), 20–32; see also Ingrid Bergstrom, "Mary Berglund: Not Your Average Backwoods Nurse," *The Canadian Nurse* 72, no. 9 (September 1976): 44–9; see also Karen Trollope Kumar, MD, "Mrs. B's Place," *Canadian Medical Association Journal* 143, no. 11 (1990): 1226–7.

11 Olga and Esther were born in Keoma, Alberta, the daughters of farmer Oscar Anderson (1881–1955) and his wife, Svea (18?–1964), from Hajom, Västergötland. Esther graduated from the University of Alberta and Olga from the University of Manitoba, later earning a Master's degree in Public Health from the University of North Carolina. See Olga Anderson, "Olga's Essay about our Family" (1974); see also correspondence from Esther Williams and Olga Anderson, Camrose, Alberta, dated January 2005.

12 "Everything You Want to Know about Au Pairs," *Swedish Press*, April 1997; see also "So You Want to Be an Au-pair," *Swedish Press*, April 2006.

13 Lilly Bohlin (19?–1991) was born in Broby, Sweden. She began studying textile and fine arts in Stockholm, and then taught weaving in Sweden, Scotland, Ireland, the United States, and Canada, including at the Banff School of Fine Arts. See *Swedish Press*, July 1991.

14 Christina Ulla Larsson Pokrupa (1938–2003) was born in Mönsterås, Småland, the daughter of Nils Theodore Herbert Larsson, an MP and senator. Christina apprenticed as a weaver in Stockholm, then earned teacher's diplomas in both weaving and sewing. In 1972 the Swedish International Development Authority hired her to teach spinning, weaving, and sewing in Lesotho, Africa. There, she met architect Jerry Pokrupa and returned with him to Winnipeg. The couple retired to Red Lake in 1999. She was an avid member of the Manitoba Orchid Society, and her *Phalaenopsis Philippinense* orchid exhibit in 2000 won the American Orchid Society's Award of Merit, which included being permanently named "Christina's Delight." Thanks to Jerry and Nils Pokrupa, Cochenour, Ontario, for the brochure "Tribute to Christina," which documents her life.

15 "Company File: Gunnel Gavin Physiotherapy Associates," *Swedish Press*, August 2003, 23.

16 Linda Lundstrom grew up in Cochenour, Ontario, one of six mining communities spawned by the Red Lake gold rush. Her father, Rickard Lundstrom, was born in Jokkmokk, Lappland, and immigrated with his parents in 1914 to a small, stony farm near Eriksdale. In 1930 the family moved to the northern end of Lake Manitoba and settled at Elm Point,

where they lived off the land, commercial fishing during the winter. Her Icelandic mother, Olive Johnson, was born at Lonely Lake, Manitoba. Thanks to Edith Shiells, Winnipeg, for donating "Lundstrom Family History: Sweden to Canada: Their Family Remembers" (2005) and other family information. See also "Company File: Linda Lundström Ltd.," *Swedish Press*, January 1992, 27.

17 Eva Wunderman was born in Sweden, where in 1973 she bought and ran the Stockholm restaurant Oss Emellan for three years. She was widely travelled in Australia and England before finally coming to Canada. See *Swedish Press*, February 1999 and April 2006

18 Emil Bernard Johnson (1888–1971) was born in Getinge, Halland, and in 1890 immigrated with his parents to Teulon, Manitoba. In 1911 he married Ellen Sophia Lindberg (1889–1969) from Stromsburg, Nebraska, who had migrated with her parents to Saskatchewan. See Verna Larson, comp., "Family Life Lines." For the job experiences of a single man from 1911 to 1915 in the Calgary-Edmonton area, see John A. Isaacson, "American-Swedish History of Many Illustrated by Experience," *Swedish Pioneer Historical Quarterly* 26, no. 4 (October 1975): 247–59.

19 Elinor Barr, "Swedish Language Retention," *Polyphony: Thunder Bay's People* 9, no. 2 (1987): 84–6, includes marriage records from Immanuel Augustana Lutheran Church and Zion Augustana Lutheran Church, Thunder Bay, which served a large hinterland.

20 See the following articles in *The Labour Gazette:* "Construction and Maintenance" (1924): 47; "Immigration to Canada during the Two Fiscal Years Ending March 31, 1925" (1925): 529–33; "Annual Review of Employment in Canada, 1924" (1925): 621; and "Convention of Association of Canadian Building and Construction Industries" (1925): 159.

21 Magnus Clarholm (ca. 1871–1946) was born in Värmland and educated in Uppsala. He served as consul general in the United States from 1906 to 1919, then in Calcutta, and from 1921 to 1936 in Canada.

22 E. Ericson, *Tänker du emigrera? Råd och upplysningar för utvandrare* (Karlskoga, Värmland: J.E. Ericsons förlåg, 1924), 105.

23 LAC, RG 76, volume 568, file 812779; Magnus Clarholm, Royal Swedish Consul-General, Montreal, to A.S. Fraser, Esq., Commissioner of Immigration, Ottawa, 19 March 1924.

24 *The Labour Gazette* (1925): 667.

25 LAC, RG 76, volume 245, file 165833; unsigned copy of a letter dated Toronto, 13 May 1924, addressed to Acting Swedish Consul-General, Montreal.

26 Karl Larsson (1927–) was born in Karlsberg, Västergötland, and in 1947 married Gunvor Boström (1923–) from Östersund, Jämtland, and had a son when they came to Canada. See Manitoba Archives, C565-566, Swedish Community Oral History Collection, Gunvor Larsson, 1, 4–6; Karl Larsson, 1, 5.

27 Ibid., 5.

28 Elinor Barr, "Station Names along the Canadian Pacific Railway: Fort William to Selkirk," *Canoma* (Geographical Names Board of Canada) 26, no. 2 (December 2000): 1–16. Only four other ethnic names were given, three Norwegian and one Hungarian.

29 The Swedes who died were Magnus Anderson from Värmland; Anton Wilhelm Gustafson from Västergötland; Oscar Emanuel Lundgren from Tynderö, Småland; Knud Lundquist from Källerhult, Småland; foreman Nils Sten Månson from Vinslöv, Skåne; Oscar Emanuel Sjöblom from Stockholm; and the Norwegian Knute Bjørneset. See Jordfaestede, Official Acts, Our Saviour's Lutheran Church, Thunder Bay; see also "Gruesome Journey over 150 Miles of Ice and Snow with 7 Dead Men," *Daily Times-Journal*, 22 February 1909.

30 The hotel was built of cement blocks made on-site, and the three-metre ceilings were covered with tongue-and-groove hardwood. Thanks to curator Betty Brill, Nipigon Museum, for sending information about Skandia House, including Bonnie Satten's booklet, *A Historical Walk Through Nipigon* (2003).

31 Olof Hanson (1882–1952) was born in Tännäs, Härjedalen, in 1900 migrated to the United States, spent three years going to night school in Spokane in order to learn English, in 1905 migrated to Canada, and took a homestead at Manville, east of Edmonton. In 1909 he became a Canadian citizen, and in 1910 married Martha Johnson, who in 1907 had immigrated with her parents to Gunn, near Edmonton. Their children were Linnea (1911–19?) and Sonny (1914–1950). He formed the Royal Lumber Company and built a sawmill at Hanall. In 1924 he contracted with his partner Shockley to build a bridge over the Skeena River at Terrace, in 1925 built the provincial government building in Smithers, became involved in the Lake Kathlyn ice harvest, and built a summer camp west of Smithers. In 1926 he built his company's headquarters in Smithers and became president of the Board of Trade in Prince Rupert. In 1930 he was elected Liberal MP for Skeena, and was re-elected in 1935 and 1940. In 1939 he built a house in Vancouver, and in 1948 was appointed to the Fisheries Commission. His companies were Hanson Lumber & Timber Co., Dybhavn & Hanson Ltd (real estate, insurance,

and brokerage), Royal Fish Co. with John Dybhavn, and Massett
Canneries Co. Ltd. A Lutheran and Mason, he was Swedish vice-consul
from 1916 to 1920 and from 1924 to 1946, and consul from 1947 to 1952.
In his will he left $373,000 to assist the poor in Tännäs. A Tribute in
Parliament, 1952, described him in the following way: "Clear thinker,
honest and faithful in his service and a credit to the country from which
he came." For a biography from a Swedish standpoint, see St Jean,
"Swedes on the Move," 198–209.

32 Nils Alfred Nilsson (1876–1948) was born in Yttersel, Resele,
Ångermanland. After working as a miner in Kiruna and Norway,
he immigrated to Canada in 1905 and acquired a farm near Kenora,
abandoning it in 1908 to go to Prince Rupert. There and along the line
he worked as a dynamite man. In 1913 he married Ingeborg Aarvik
Viggen (18?–1935). The family moved to various mining camps in British
Columbia and Idaho until 1935, when silicosis forced Nils Alfred to
retire. Thanks to Irene Howard, Vancouver, for family information. See
also Irene Howard, *Gold Dust on His Shirt: The True Story of an Immigrant
Mining Family* (Toronto: Between the Lines, 2008).

33 Charles Pansar (1846–1910) was born Carl Johan in Brobacken, Borgunda,
Västergötland, the son of Corporal Per Maëstoso. He married Christina
Jonsdotter (1850–?) and the couple came to Winnipeg in 1871 with
their infant son, Bernt Oskar. Thanks to Annelie Jönsson, Falköping,
Sweden, for the above information. See also Lars Ljungmark, *Svenskarna i
Winnipeg*, 40, 72, 87.

34 Peter Andrew Benson (1869–19?) was born in Kinnared, Halland, and in
1887 immigrated to Winnipeg, where his forty-seven years with the CPR
began. By 1903 he was roadmaster at Moose Jaw, later transferring to
Mission and Revelstoke, retiring to Vancouver in 1934. In 1898 he married
Amanda Johnson from Slättåkra, Halland. See Landelius Biography
Collection, volume 1, #081.

35 Letter from Lillian Williams, Courtenay, British Columbia, to Mr Carlson,
5 October 1989. Thanks to Richard Williams, Delta, British Columbia, for
this and other family information. Johan Sigfrid "Jon" Anderson (1871–
1964) was born in Kinnared, Halland, immigrated in 1899 to Winnipeg,
and in 1903 married Lydia Eriksson (1878–1977) from Forshaga,
Värmland. Another brother, Bengt Victor Anderson (1868–1915), died
later in a railway snowplough accident in Tuxford, Saskatchewan.

36 The three men were Carl Hjalmar Anderson (1879–1910), who had
immigrated with his brother Jon Anderson, Axel Johnson, (1878–1910)
from Långasjö, and Fritz Welander (1883–1910) from Ljuder, both in

Småland. Thanks to Richard Williams, Delta, British Columbia, for "List of men known to have died in the Rogers Pass slide of March 4, 1910." For the 1911 photo of the graves see *En Smålandssocken emigrerar*, 377.

37 For a later comparison see Jonny Hjelm, "Forest Work and Mechanization – Changes in Sweden and Canada during the Post-War Period," *Polhem: Tidskrift för teknikhistoria* (1994/3), 260–88.

38 Vennerström, *Kanada och Kanadasvenskarna*, 53, 60, 64.

39 St Jean, "The Myth of the Big Swede Logger," *Swedish Press*, October 1999, 34.

40 St Jean, "On the Move," 136–81, based on her 1999 MA thesis at the University of Victoria, "The Myth of the Big Swede Logger: An *Arbetskarl* in the Vancouver Island Forests, 1920–1948," 178.

41 Magnuson, *The Untold Story of Ontario's Bushworkers*, 11–12.

42 Peter B. Anderson (1866–1959) was born in Onsjö, Larv, Västergötland, in 1885 emigrated to St Paul, and in 1906 came to Canada to begin another career in British Columbia's logging industry. See UBCL SC, Peter B. Anderson Fonds, box 1, BC1960/1-4; P.B. Anderson, "My Life Story as I can Remember," typescript, 13 pages.

43 UBCL SC, Matthew Lindfors Fonds, A IV B 2/3, "Community Portrait, P.B. Anderson, lumberman," *Chilliwack Progress*, 18 April 1951.

44 Irene Howard's research notes, "P.B. Anderson Codicil."

45 Oscar Ragnvald Styffe (1885–1943) was born in Bossekop, Alta, Norway, the son of Johan Erik Styff, a sea captain born in Sweden, and Ragnhild Romstal. He graduated from Tromsö military academy in 1906, where he studied mathematics, forest mensuration, cartography, forest surveying, and accounting. In 1907 he married his childhood sweetheart, Ragna Magdalena Iversen (1887–1937), in Calumet, Michigan. The couple moved to Port Arthur in 1911 and had six children. Oscar learned the Finnish language while working in a local hotel, and in 1922 became accountant for Charles W. Cox Ltd., Timber Contractors. In 1927 he formed his own company, Oscar Styffe Ltd., incorporated in 1931, and in 1933 formed Gravel & Lake Services Ltd. His companies employed forty-five to fifty office workers and 350 to 500 seasonal bush workers. A Liberal in politics, Oscar Styffe served as a city councillor from 1935 to 1937, and in 1941 was appointed honorary vice-consul for Norway. Thanks to daughter Ingrid Blanchet, Thunder Bay, for family information. See also John Styffe, *Oscar R. Styffe, 1885–1943: The Man and His Companies* (Thunder Bay: Lakehead University Library, 1985); see also Lakehead University Library Archives, MG7, Oscar Styffe Collection.

46 LULA, MG 7, B, 17, 3, I50, Oscar Styffe Collection; Oscar Styffe, Port Arthur, to P.P. Schnorback, Filer City, Michigan, 31 March 1939. For the original application, see MG 7, B, 12, 26, I3. For a study of his companies, see Andrew J. Hacquoil, "'Let us all be optimistic from now on.' Oscar Styffe Limited 1927–1945: The Middleman of Northwestern Ontario and the Pulp and Paper Trade," Master's thesis, Lakehead University, 1994.

47 *The Beaver* (October/November 2004): 7. Province Publishing Company of Victoria and Vancouver produced the map in 1897.

48 For a description of preparations for the journey and the journey itself, see Johan Otto Olin, "We Went to the Klondike in 1898," *Swedish Pioneer Historical Quarterly* 10, no. 3 (July 1959): 91–104.

49 Erik A. Hägg (1868–1947) was born in Bollnäs, Hälsingland, and his parents emigrated to Wisconsin with six children in 1881. Eric, a self-taught photographer, opened a shop in Bellingham, Washington, in 1888, and it was from there that he set out for the Klondike. The Eric Hegg Collection is housed at the University of Washington in Seattle. See Ulf Beijbom, *Amerikabilder: Från utställningen Drömmen om Amerika och andra samlingar* (Växjö: Emigrantinstitutets vänner, 2002), 105–6; see also Murray Morgan, *One Man's Gold Rush: A Klondike Album, with Photographs by E.A. Hegg* (Seattle, WA: University of Washington Press, 1972); see http://content.lib.washington.edu/heggweb/.

50 Ethel Anderson Becker, P.B. Anderson's daughter, wrote the book *Klondike '98: Hegg's Album of the 1898 Alaska Gold Rush* (Portland, OR: Binfords and Mort, ca. 1949). She also collected and preserved Hegg's photographic glass plates, which had been scattered after his death.

51 Nils Otto Gustaf Nordenskjöld (1869–1928) was born in Hesselby, Småland, of Finland Swedish parents. His uncle, Adolf Erik Nordenskiöld, was a noted polar explorer. Otto Nordenskjöld earned his doctorate in geology at Uppsala University in 1894 and headed a mineralogical expedition to Patagonia before going to the Yukon in 1898. From 1901 to 1904 he led the Swedish Antarctic Expedition. This and later expeditions to Greenland and South America resulted in seven geographical features being named after him, none of them in Canada. See Emigrant Institute, Växjö, 22:3:7:A; newspaper clipping "Swedish Expedition for Klondyke [*sic*]. Scientific Exploration of the Yukon Country Financed from Stockholm."

52 They included Sweden geologist Frithiof Andersson from Uppsala; engineer C.E. Larsson from Göteborg; agriculturist Johan Åkerström from Luleå; builder and farmer J. Ahlgren from Eksjö, Jämtland; Gottfrid Sundeen from Gotland; and possibly Edw. Erikson Melander; and from

the United States Sven Lundblad from Motala, who had prospected in southern California; and E. Eriksson, who had worked as a miner in western Australia. See Emigrant Institute, Växjö, 22:3:7:A.28.

53 Sigvard Malmberg, "Första riktiga skildringen av guldrushen i Klondike, och vilka bilder!," *Svenska dagbladet*, 13 April 1979, from Otto Nordenskjöld's articles published by the same newspaper in issues dated 4 September 1898 and 13 November 1898. His articles took two months to arrive in Sweden by mail.

54 Ibid. These Hegg photographs were donated to the Emigrant Institute, Växjö.

55 Carl Johan Andersson (1859–1939) was born in Myckelby, Tingstad, Östergötland, near Norrköping, and migrated to the United States in 1887. In 1890 he was living in Tacoma, Washington. One of the earliest gold seekers in the Yukon, he became known as the Lucky Swede because he was one of the few to strike it rich.

56 "Statarsonen från Norrköping som blev Klondikes mest legendariske guldgrävare," *Norrköpingstidning*, n.d., written by George F. Pringle, Van Anda, Texada Island, British Columbia, and translated into Swedish by Sigvard Malmberg; see also Svenska Emigrantinstitutet, "Carl Johan Anderson – Lucky Swede," www.island-bound.com/Charlie-The-Lucky-Swede-Anderson.html; see also Sam Holloway, "The Two Stories of Charley Anderson," *The Yukon Reader*, n.d., 13–18; see also Bill Thompson, *Texada Island* (Powell River: Powell River Heritage Research Association, 1997), 77, 427, 453.

57 Alfred Geijer (1870–19?) was born in Långasjö, Småland, and in 1889 emigrated to Colhill, near Spokane, where his sister, Matilda Peterson, lived. See *En Smålandssocken emigrerar*, 201.

58 Ulf Beijbom, *Uppbrott från stenriket*, 155–6. Alfred Geijer brought home 30,000 kronor (US$7,800, based on the 1899 exchange rate) after working for Lawson Fuller and Nowgord in the Klondike. According to the diary of Emil Granfeld, a Smålander who worked under him at Magnet Hill Number 18, Geijer was a slave driver. See also Herbert Geijer, "Långasjö – Klondyke, [sic] tur och retur," in *En Smålandsocken emigrerar*, 203–9.

59 Carl Nilsson (1866–19?) was born in Virestad, Småland, and emigrated in 1888 to his older brother, Magnus, in Silver City, Idaho. They were nephews of the famous opera singer, Christina Nilsson. See Beijbom, *Uppbrott från stenriket*, 156–8.

60 Adolph Jensen, "Migration Statistics of Denmark, Norway and Sweden," in *International Migrations*, ed. Walter F. Willcox (New York: National Bureau of Economic Research, 1931), 2:298, states that "Emigration from

Scandinavia to Canada was particularly large in 1902–03 (gold discovered at Klondike)."

61 Work began at the Sweden mine in 1896 and the Swede Boys' Prospecting Company of Rainy River Limited was incorporated in 1899, but neither became producers. The incorporators were John Berg, George Asplund, and the Franson brothers John, August, and Erik.

62 Ontario Bureau of Mines, *Annual Report 1901*, 10:5, 42–3. One of the fragments severed Hedlund's jugular vein and he quickly bled to death.

63 Ola Lofstad (1863–19?) was born in Glimmingegård, Simrishamn, Skåne, and in 1896 migrated directly to Greenwood. He served on city council from 1927 to 1947, retiring because of poor health. See UBCL SC, Matthew Lindfors Fonds, A IV B, Box 2, "Ola Lofstad Honored By Greenwood City Council." See also Roger McKnight, "Anders Olsson in British Columbia: Six Letters, 1906–1908," *Swedish Pioneer Historical Quarterly* 30, no. 2 (1979): 94–102.

64 John Charles Eek (1862–1912) was born near Falköping, Västergötland, and in 1869 emigrated to Montrose, Iowa, with his mother and brother, to join his dad, who had gone the year before. He married Pauline Brandenberger (1872–19?), who was born in Donnellson, Iowa, and moved to the homestead in 1906. Descendants still live in the Rock Creek area in south-central British Columbia. See British Columbia Archives, "The Eek Story."

65 John E. Richthammer, *The End of the Road: A History of the Red Lake District* (Red Lake, ON: Red Lake District Festival Days Association, 1985), 43.

66 John Edwin Johnson "Ed" Fahlgren (1913–2001) was born in Kenora, the son of lumber contractor and commercial fisherman John Johnson Fahlgren and Theresia Ann Forsstrom, both from northern Sweden. In 1941 Ed Fahlgren married Helen Amethyst Woodside (ca. 1912–1986). See John Richthammer, "The Extraordinary Life of Red Lake District Pioneer Ed Fahlgren: From Accounting Clerk to Mine Manager and Northern Environment Commissioner," *District Life* (Red Lake), 24 January 2001.

67 "Zeballos – The Wonder Gold Field" and "Zeballos to Become Real Town," *Vancouver Sun*, 20 December 1937, 20–1; see also Ragnar Carlsson, "Guldlandetsgullgossar," *Levande Livet* (1938): 44.

68 Erik Albert Blom (1889–1937) was born in Resele, Ångermanland, and emigrated in 1911 to Portland. From there he volunteered to join the Canadian army (210th Battalion) in 1918. He is listed as a bush worker, but it was fishing that brought him to Zeballos. The six men who staked the claim in 1933 were Andy Donaldson, Mike Francis, Charlie Smith,

Joe Doyle, Alfred Bird, and Albert Blom. Thanks to great-niece Harriet
Boman, Sweden, for family information.

69 Jack Crosson, *Jack's Shack: Memories from the West Coast of Vancouver Island*
(Victoria: Currie's Forestgraphics, ca. 1990), 137–8.

70 British Columbia Archives, GR-2213, microfilm #B09668, file #02/O1938;
documents relating to the probate of Albert Blom's estate. A good portion
having to do with Privateer mine was disputed, and unfortunately the
will was not included among the documents. His brother in Sweden, Nils
Magnus Blom, always believed that he was murdered.

71 Ernst Adolf Sjöstedt (1852–1912) was born in Hjo, Västergötland,. In 1877
he graduated from Bergshögskolan in Uppsala as a mining engineer,
and in 1882 married Jessie Kathleen Winslow. A brother, Maths Sjöstedt
(1860–1924), also a mining engineer, joined him in Bridgeville at the
Pictou Charcoal Iron Company, later returning to Sweden to work for
another brother, Gustaf Sjöstedt, in Göteborg. See Landelius Biography
Collection, volume 3, #167 and #168.

72 Erik Nyström (1877–19?) was born in Stockholm and educated at
Tekniska högskolan and Bergskolan. In 1901 he immigrated to Victoria
Mines, Ontario, remaining with the Department of the Interior until 1908.
See Landelius Biography Collection, volume 1, #59.

73 Jonas Einar Lindeman (1877–19?) was born in Säbrå, Ångermanland, and
after graduation worked for LKAB at Kiruna. In 1905 he embarked on a
research trip to North America, and in 1908 married Kirsten Ericksen. See
Landelius Biography Collection, volume 2, #317.

74 Hans Lundberg (1893–1971) was born in Malmö and trained as a mining
engineer at Stockholm's Institute of Technology. In 1923 he emigrated
to New York with his wife, where he worked as field manager for
the Swedish-American Prospecting Corporation, testing his electrical
prospecting technique. He found the massive lead-zinc ore body at
Buchans, Newfoundland, in 1926. See Knud Graah Bolander, *Det nya
Canada: Ett möjligheternas land*, (Stockholm: Ljus, 1947), 76–9; see also
Landelius Biography Collection, volume 2, #339.

75 Kastrup, *The Swedish Heritage in America*, 575.

76 For an overview, see Helge Nelson, "The Interior Colonization in Canada
at the Present Day, and its Natural Conditions," *Geografiska annaler* (1923):
244–308.

77 Frank Eliasson (1883–1956) was born in Högen, Ör socken, Dalsland, and
emigrated to Pennsylvania in 1902. He married in 1904, but his wife died
in 1921, leaving him with nine young children.

78 Saskatchewan Archives; Frank Eliason, "Biography of a Swedish Emigrant," 29. The Rochdale Plan was a system of consumer cooperatives developed in Rochdale, England.

79 Charles Lindholm (1882–1969) was born Carl Oscar Englehard Lindholm in Småland, and emigrated to the United States in 1902 and to Alberta in 1910. In 1914 in Calgary he married Anna Kristina Ohman (1886–1983) from Hälsingland, who immigrated with her family in 1897. Thanks to son Ernest Lindholm, New Norway, Alberta, for family information.

80 Algot Edwin Gotthold Thomeus (ca. 1880–1955) was born in Gällberg, Västergötland, the son of Lutheran pastor Ragnar Thomeus. Because he did not feel called to the clergy, in 1903 he emigrated to Chicago and two years later to Magnolia, Alberta. In 1912 he travelled to Sweden and two years later returned with a bride, Gerda Sophia Anderson (ca. 1878–ca. 1964), who was a nurse. Their first two children died young, but Tom (1920–) survived to marry Doreen Smith in 1946.

81 Thomeus, *Letters of a Swedish Homesteader*, 11, letter dated 7 January 1906.

82 Ibid., 1, letter from Strathcona, Alberta, 16 July 1905.

83 Henry M. Leppard, "The Settlement of the Peace River Country," *The Geographical Review* 25 (1935): 62–78. See also C.M. Tracie, "Land of Plenty or Poor Man's Land: Environmental Perception and Appraisal Respecting Agricultural Settlement in the Peace River Country, Canada," in *Images of the Plains: The Role of Human Nature in Settlement*, ed. Brian W. Blouet and Martin P. Lawson (Lincoln: University of Nebraska Press, 1975), 115–22.

84 Herman Trelle (ca. 1894–18?) was born in Idaho of Swedish parents and came to Canada with them at the age of four. Wheat grown on his 283-hectare farm won first prize in 1926, from 1930 through to 1932, and in 1936. That year he was also named "oats king." See Landelius Biography Collection, volume 3, #241.

85 Nelson, *Swedes and the Swedish Settlements*, 353. See also Sune Åkerman, "The Story of the Bergsten Brothers in Canada: Ethnic Barriers, Unfavorable Sex Ratios, and the Creation of Male Households," in *Interpreting the Promise of America: Essays in Honor of Odd Sverre Lovoll*, ed. Todd W. Nichol (Northfield, MN: Norwegian-American Historical Association, 2002), 137–48.

86 David Halldin (1903–1981) was born in Ingarp, near Eksjö, Småland. In 1924 he immigrated to Malmo, Alberta, where he worked on farms for four years. His brother Joseph (1901–1970) joined him in 1927, and together they homesteaded at Valleyview. See *Where the Red Willows Grew* (Valleyview, AB, 1980), 97–8.

87 David Halldin, "Pioneering in Alberta's Peace River Country," *Swedish Pioneer Historical Quarterly* 33, no. 1 (1982): 54–6, 59.

88 Andrew Anderson (1871–1945) was born Anders Andersson in Odarslöv, Skåne, and emigrated to New York in 1894. There, he worked in a large department store during the day and at night attended a business course at the YMCA. He volunteered for the Spanish-American War, recovered from typhoid fever, became a mechanic, and married Hannah (18?–1973) before coming to Canada in 1910. The couple had a daughter, Helen. In 1888 Helen's daughter, Elna Magnusson Scheinfeld, published her grandmother's memoirs, *Fogelvik Farm: Hannah Anderson Remembers the Early Days.* See Glenbow Archives, Magnuson/Anderson Family Fonds, M 802, file 68, handwritten memoir; see also Landelius Biography Collection, volume 1, #038.

89 Nels Benson (1873–1951) was born Nils Bengtsson in Odarslöv, Skåne, and migrated in 1910. He filed on a homestead, but executed abandonment proceedings after only a couple of months. He worked for both Fogelvik Farms until his death. See Glenbow Archives, Magnuson/Anderson Family Fonds, M 802, box 5, file 88.

90 Nelson, *Swedes and the Swedish Settlements*, 366.

91 Knut Magnusson (1909–1970) was born in Sweden and educated in Stockholm. He met Helen Anderson on a family trip to Sweden, where they married. After a distinguished career in various land consolidation projects he came to Canada with his family after Andrew Anderson's death. The Magnussons decided to stay in Canada and make a home for his widow by taking over Fogelvik Farm. See Glenbow Archives, Magnuson/Anderson Family Fonds, M 802, box 5, file 74.

92 Ibid., Marius, Canadian Pacific Railway Company, Copenhagen, to Knut Magnusson, Innisfail, Alberta, 24 January 1958.

93 UBCL SC, Matthew Lindfors Fonds, A IV B, Box 1; 1949, announcement of the unveiling of a portrait of Dr Paul A. Boving in the Agriculture Building, University of British Columbia.

94 Sixten Högstedt (ca. 1895–1954) was born in Södermanland and graduated from Alnarp Agricultural Institute with a Master's degree in 1919. He worked at Sofielund in Ludgo, Södermanland, which is famous for animal husbandry, before migrating to Harrow in 1926. See Landelius Biography Collection, volume 1, #097.

95 Gustaf Adolf Krook (1878–1929) was born in Stockholm, the son of Herman Salomon Krook and Anna Lovisa Johansson. He immigrated in 1904 to Ottawa after studying horticulture and working in this field in Germany and France. He married Ida Beatrice Marineau (1882–1935)

in Ottawa and the couple had two daughters. See Landelius Biography Collection, volume 1, #108. Thanks to Delores Bolin, Alberta, for family information.

96 Sven Sjödahl (1841–192?) was born in Skåne, and learned the nursery trade in Denmark and Sweden. In 1865 he emigrated to Illinois, in 1866 homesteaded near Scandia, Kansas, and in 1870 married Marie C. Ericson. He imported prize tulips and daffodils from Holland. The couple retired to Long Beach, California. See City of Vancouver Archives, "Sven Sherdahl's Pioneer Days in Kansas," typescript by Ingvar Grimsvaard, n.d.

97 Johan Taft (1884–1972) was born in Bohuslän, and trained as a stonemason. He emigrated to Washington state in 1913, then moved to British Columbia, and finally, around 1920, to Northwestern Ontario to work at the Butler quarry, Gold Rock mines, and bush camps. In 1927 he married Helga Augusta Wickman (1895–19?), who immigrated from Ångermanland in 1923, and settled in Wabigoon. Thanks to daughter Lillian Rodke, Thunder Bay, for family information.

98 Alex Johnson (1895–1979) was born in Virestad, Småland. He immigrated in 1913 directly to Ingolf, Ontario, for employment on the CPR, changed his name when the CPR made out his first paycheque to Alex Edward Johnson instead of Axel Edvard Johansson, and worked his way up to conductor. In 1920 he married Mabel Grace Kridler (1903–1998) from Barnum, Minnesota, the daughter of Rhesa Kridler and Regina Hoberg. Thanks to daughter Fay Hicks, Abbotsford, British Columbia, for family information.

99 Daniel Nils Ericson was born in Kansas, the son of Carl Ferdinand Ericson and Clara Matilda Jonsson from Södermanland. In 1904 his parents moved to Smoland and he joined them to help with the farm. He was ordained as a Mission Covenant pastor, and in 1915 married Ottilia "Tillie" Karolina Holm (1892–19?) who was born in Laxsjö, Jämtland, and immigrated in 1904 to Scandinavia. Thanks to grandson Pastor Dan Pearson, Minnedosa, for family information; see also Ottilia Carolina Ericson, "Tillie's Triumphs" (1967).

100 Nils Erickson Holm (1864–19?) was born in Laxsjö, Jämtland, where he worked as a shoemaker. In 1891 he married Martha Lucia Gronlund (1868–19?) from Norderåsen, Jämtland, and the couple had two children when they immigrated to Scandinavia (1903 to 1905). Edith Marie was born in 1910. In 1934 Nils returned to Jämtland for a visit. See *Forest to Field*, 421–2; see also Landelius Biography Collection, volume 2, #079.

101 "Diary of Dan Ericson, 29 March 1918–19 June 1919," 42-page typescript transcribed by Leslie Daniel Ericson and donated by Pastor Dan Pearson, Minnedosa.

102 Albert Viksten, "Hermits of the Wilderness," in Karin Viksten-Koerner, *Albert Viksten: A Portrait of my Father*, trans. Anne-Charlotte Berglund (Victoria: Trafford, 2005), 86–93.

103 Peter Bergenham (1886–1965) was born in Offerdal, Jämtland, the son of John Peter Persson Bergenham (ca. 1860–1931) and Brita Gardwal Andersdotter (1861–1965). He immigrated in 1893 with his mother and siblings to Moberly, British Columbia, where he married Anne. Thanks to niece Jean Blaine, Burnaby, British Columbia, for family information.

104 Caroline Bergenham, "The 'Good Old Times' as I Remember Them," in *Golden Memories of the Town Where the Turbulent Kicking Horse Meets the Mighty Columbia* (Golden: Golden Historical Branch of the Centennial Committee, 1958). Thanks to niece Jean Blaine, Burnaby, for family information.

105 Andrew Kauffman and William Putnam, *The Guiding Spirit* (Revelstoke: Footprint Press, ca. 1986). Thanks to niece Jean Blaine, Burnaby, for family information.

106 Anders Bernhard Nilsson (1886–1947) was born in Osby, Skåne. In 1906 he emigrated to the United States and in 1908 moved to Mine Centre, Ontario. In 1918 he lived in Sault Ste Marie, and the following year married Marie Emelie Elize "Yvonne" Boyer (1898–1986), the daughter of Isidore Boyer, an Ojibwa, and Georgiane Lavoie. The couple had nine children. They lived near Yvonne's parents in Pangis, Ontario, then with the Schnaufer Fur Company at Circle Lake north of Lake Abitibi, and finally at Sault Ste Marie, Ontario. Thanks to son Ben Nelson Jr, Jellicoe, Ontario, for family information.

107 Correspondence with Ben Nelson Jr, Jellicoe, Ontario, 13 November 2001.

108 Sven I.J. Klintberg (ca. 1890–19?) was born in Sweden and came to Canada in 1912 to learn about fur farming. His brother, Gunnar Klintberg (ca. 1896–19?), married Elizabeth (ca. 1896–19?). The brothers returned to Sweden for a visit in 1927. See Landelius Biography Collection, volume 2, #179-181, 183; see also Vennerström, *Kanada och Kanadasvenskarna*, 25.

109 Gustav Per "Gus" Ronnander (1895–1980) was born in Bjuråker, Hälsingland, and was sent to his grandmother in Minnesota at age fourteen. He took English classes and trained as a barber, then in 1916 migrated to Winnipeg, where he worked as a barber at the McLaren Hotel. From 1919 to 1942 he operated Gus' Barber Shop on Logan

Avenue. In 1922 he married Margaret Delin Gunberg Oder (ca. 1901–1988) from Järvsö, Hälsingland. Gus retired in 1962. Thanks to daughter Margaret Hewitt, Winnipeg, for family information.

110 Anders Hilding "Andy" Ronnander (ca. 1905–2003) was born in Bjuråker, Hälsingland. His father insisted that Andy train as a doctor or lawyer, neither of which appealed to him, so in 1924 he immigrated to his brother Gus in Winnipeg. In 1955 Andy married Grace in Winnipeg. Thanks to niece Margaret Hewitt, Winnipeg, for family information.

111 Bernhard Sefanius "Ben" Swanson (1916–?) was born near Mörsil, Jämtland, son of Karl and Karolina Svensson. The family emigrated in 1925 and settled in Kelliher, Saskatchewan. Ben moved to Ontario in search of work after three years with no harvest. There, he married Lois Pringle. See Ben Swanson, "A little Bit of Sweden Comes to Canada," typescript (ca. 1995), 12, 22–31. Thanks to Ben's cousin, S.G. Pearson, Winnipeg, for donating this memoir.

112 Ben Young (1843–1911) was born Bengt Ljung in Lomma, Skåne. He came to the west coast on the *Australian* in 1868, jumped ship, in 1873 married Kerstin "Christina" Svensson (1850–1902), also from Lomma, and started a home cannery in 1874 in Astoria, Oregon. By 1882 Ben owned the British American Packing Company, which built both the British Columbia Packing House in Canoe Pass and the Phoenix Cannery on the Skeena River. In 1883 Christina welcomed her brother, Paul Swenson, eighteen, and sister, Hanna, fifteen. Both moved to British Columbia. See Birgitta Nilsson, *Från Lomma till Norra Amerika* (Bjärred, Skåne: 2005), 10–12; see also Howard, *Vancouver's Svenskar*, 28–31.

113 Ben Young, also known as the Salmon King, sold his Canadian canneries to the Anglo-British Columbia Packing Company in 1891. He started the Astoria Savings Bank and owned several buildings and businesses. The Benjamin Young House and Carriage House in Astoria are preserved historic properties. The input from his brother Anders Young (1850–1929) is unclear, but it seems that he was part owner of the Canoe Pass cannery and helped to establish it.

114 Paul Swenson (1864–1918) was born Pål Svensson in Lomma, and emigrated to Astoria, Oregon, in 1883. He returned to Sweden to marry Anna Mathilda Jenson (1868–1947), then came to Canada. See Nilsson, *Från Lomma till Norra Amerika*, 13–16.

115 Alfred Jenson (1870–1944) was born Alfred Jönsson in Lomma, and in 1893 married Hanna Swenson (1867–1947), who had immigrated in 1883, in New Westminster. See ibid., 13–16.

116 Ibid., 11.

117 Nils Sandell (1855–1926) was born in Lomma, and married Clara Bradona Olsson (1870–1960) from Holmsbu, Norway. After Nils's father, Nils Peter, changed his surname from Anderson to Sandell, the grandfather, Anders (1828–1912), followed suit. See UBCL SC, Seaholm Collection, AVIIB; "Nels Peter Sandell (Anderson)"; see also ibid., 24–6.

118 Nilsson, *Från Lomma till Norra Amerika.*, 9. Evidently the cannery's owner was English, to have Queen Victoria's birthday as the only holiday rather than Canada's birthday, the 1st of July.

119 Eric Jurell was born in Sweden and immigrated in 1951 to work as a forest ranger in Nelson, British Columbia. After a few years he began fishing instead. See *Swedish Press*, August 1999, 27.

120 Fredrik Bergström was born in Hönsinge, Skåne, and trained as an engineer. He emigrated to the United States in 1892, and in 1904 came to Canada as superintendent of construction for what became Saskatchewan Wheat Pool, Regina. See Landelius Biography Collection, volume 1, #095.

121 Nels Anderson (1895–1979) was born in Osby, Skåne, and immigrated in 1913 to work for the CPR at White River, Ontario, and for the CNR at Sioux Lookout. In 1919 he and a friend visited Red Lake as prospectors, then he moved to Hudson as a storekeeper and fur trader. In 1926 he joined the Hudson's Bay Company as post manager at Woman Lake. He married Margaret "Joy" Sapay from Lac Seul, and the couple raised five sons at Snake Falls. After her death he married Mary Agnes Bumstead McEvoy. Thanks to Joyce Appel, curator of Ear Falls District Museum, for providing biographical information.

122 John Gotfrid Gustafson (1908–1987) was born in the Åland Islands, and immigrated in 1926 to work in logging operations on the Anticosti Islands in the Gulf of St Lawrence, a job that ended soon after 1929. He arrived in Red Lake in 1932, and in 1935 married Astrid Olga Olivia Enquist (1912–19?) from Chatfield, Manitoba. Her brother Enar Albin Enquist worked in the mines as hoist man and stationary engineer. See John Richthammer, obituary, *The District News* (Red Lake), April 1987; see also *Wilderness to Wildlife*, 160.

123 Gustav Einar Erickson (1895–1984) was born in Sweden. See Richthammer, *The End of the Road*, 129.

124 Artur Hjalmar Ludvig Nilsson Carlson (1907–1996) was born in By parish south of Säffle, Värmland, and immigrated to Canada in 1929. In 1941 he married Florence Eleanor Bond (1914–) of Woodstock, Ontario. Thanks to Florence Carlson, Red Lake, for family information; see also "Viking Outpost Treats," *Swedish Press*, May 2003, 27.

125 *Chronicle-Journal* (Thunder Bay), 14, 15, and 29 October 2003.

126 C. James Taylor, Edward Mills, and Pat Buchik, *Riding Mountain National Park of Canada: Built Heritage Resource Description and Analysis* (Calgary: Parks Canada, Western Service Centre, 2001).

127 Alfred Johan Sjögren (1864–1951) was born in Färila, Hälsingland. He married Margit "Margaret" F. Larsdotter (1861–1940), and the couple had five children when they immigrated to Winnipeg in 1895. He worked as a carpenter until the family moved to a homestead in Hilltop, Manitoba, in 1897. Four more children were born in Canada. When he first came to Winnipeg his co-workers called him "strong arm" because of his unusual strength, so his sons adopted the surname Armstrong. Thanks to granddaughter Doris Cartwright, Sault Ste Marie, Ontario, for family information. See also *Forest to Field*, 630; see also Emma Ringstrom, *Riding Mountain: Yesterday and Today* (Winnipeg: Prairie Publishing, 1981), 59–61.

128 John Anderson (1883–1937) was born in Vindeln, Västerbotten, and emigrated in 1903 to his sister, Maria Peterson, in Minnedosa. He worked at various jobs, also acquiring and selling property, and became a builder and contractor. He married Bertha Hall in 1912. See *Forest to Field*, 266; see also Ringstrom, *Riding Mountain*, 61–3.

129 He bought the tools from John A. Gustafson's Swedish Canadian Sales on Logan Avenue.

130 His own crew was Edward Johnson, and Helge and Elis Holmberg. The others included George Bergman, Arvid and Karl Bo, Ole Molin, Axel Nelson, and Ole Nelson. Local workmen from the early days, mentioned in Ringstrom, *Riding Mountain*, were the Alguire brothers, Cecil Bow, Bill Clyde, Alex Erickson, Charlie Erickson, Eric Hall, Ted Neilson, Olov Olson, Ed Poole, Ole Ramstad, Mr Sadler, and Frank Thaczuk.

131 Gotfrid Johnson (1890–1973) was born in Minneapolis, the son of Amos Johnson and Gustava Carolina Haralson from Höreda, Småland. The family migrated to Minnedosa in 1898. In 1912 he married Olga Carlson (ca. 1891–1979), the daughter of Olof and Emma Carlson, who had emigrated from Stockholm, Sweden, with her family in 1903. Thanks to Vera Johnson, Niton Junction, Alberta, for family information and for forwarding Patricia Gusdal's typescript, "The Johnson-Gusdal Family and Riding Mountain National Park," dated 1983. See also *Forest to Field*, 446–8; see also Ringstrom, *Riding Mountain*, 63.

132 Ernest Gusdal (1905–1983) was born in De Graffe, Minnesota, the son of Mathias and Petra Gusdal from Norway, and accompanied his parents to Erickson, Manitoba, in 1911. After working at the Royal Bank from 1921 to 1928 he bought an existing store, which he operated until 1946. In 1932

he married Lillian Johnson (1913–1971), the daughter of Gotfrid and Olga Johnson. See *Forest to Field*, 385–6.

133 Patricia Gusdal, "The Johnson-Gusdal Family," 2–3.

134 Olaf Petter Olsson (1867–1951) was born in Berg, Ångermanland, close to the border with Lappland. In 1902, after completing his full military training of fifteen years, he married Alma Margretta Wiberg (1879–1962), from Rensjönäset near Dorotea, Lappland, and they immigrated in 1904.

135 Elof Olson, "And So it Happened: The Olson History" (1987), 53-page typescript donated by Doug Barber, Dundas, Ontario. See also *Between Long Lake and Last Mountain: Bulyea, Duval, Strasbourg* (Strasbourg, SK: 1982), 2:878–80.

136 Arendt Ångström (1858-19?) was born in Nordmark, Värmland, the son of the famous Carl Arendt Ångström. He emigrated to the United States as chief engineer of the Cleveland Ship Building Company, then moved to Toronto in 1893, married, and had three children. Ångström remained with the Canadian Ship Building Company until at least 1920. See "The Niagara River Line – What Might Have Been," *The Scanner, Monthly News Bulletin of the Toronto Marine Historical Society* 8, no. 5 (February 1976).

137 Mike Filey, *Toronto Sketches 4* (Toronto: Dundurn Press, ca. 1995), 147; see also Michael Moir, "Shipbuilding and the Waterfront Plan of 1912," 6.

138 John W. Gerell (ca. 1867–19?) was connected to Lundby, Bohuslän, and married Anna (ca. 1871–19?), who was born in the United States.

139 Lars Erik Tornroos (1878–1957) was born in Helsinki, Finland, and in 1903 graduated from Chalmers Tekniska Institute, Göteborg. By 1906 he was working at the Canadian Shipbuilding Company in Toronto. See *Port Arthur News-Chronicle*, 18 March 1957; see also "The Niagara River Line – What Might Have Been," *The Scanner* (February 1976).

140 Adolf Gottfrid Larsson (1874–1956) was born in Tydje parish, Dalsland. In 1898 he graduated as a chemical engineer in Copenhagen, then worked in Sweden, Russia, and Germany before emigrating to the United States. By 1905 he was employed by the Grey & Bruce Portland Cement Company in Durham, Ontario, where he met John Lind. Lind married Gay Heming and in 1908 Gottfrid married her sister, Laura Heming, in Owen Sound. Thanks to grandson Richard Holt, St Mary's, Ontario, for family information. See also Landelius Biography Collection, volume 2, #203.

141 St Mary's Museum, St Mary's, Ontario, "Description Gottfrid Larsson Sous-Fonds."

142 Nils Samuel Adler (1924–2003) was born in Sweden and trained as a structural engineer. See obituary, *Toronto Globe and Mail*, 19 December 2003.

143 "Swedish in Toronto," *Swedish Press*, August 1993, 17.

144 Henry R. Baldwin is the son of Professor Henry Baldwin and Birgit Sverdrup, daughter of Fritiof Sverdrup and Fanny Tegnér of Sweden. See correspondence with his sister, Harriet B. Bryan, Princeton, New Jersey, 21 August 2003; see also J.E. Havel, typescript, "Anne Marie Havel born Luhr," a first cousin.

145 Donald Quayle Innis, "Sweden – An Example for Canada," *Queen's Quarterly* 71, no. 1 (Spring 1964): 97, 100–11. Other Swedish inventions include the Celsius thermometer (early 1700s), potato vodka (1748), safety match (1844), blowtorch (1881), telephone handset (1885), Primus stove (1891), adjustable wrench (1892), precision measuring system (1906), spherical bearings (1907), automatic lighthouse (1909), refrigerator (1925), copier machine (1938), colour TV, local anaesthetic Xylocaine and Hasselblad camera (1948), ultrasound and electrocardiography (1950), Tetra Pak (1951), pacemaker (1958), Thorsman wall plug (1959), retractable seat belt (1961), three-point seat belt (1969), banknote dispenser (1976), Losec ulcer drug (1988), robot vacuum cleaner (1997), and the computer mouse and computer colour graphics invented by Håkan Lans. See *Swedish Press*, April 1995, 12; and April 2005, 17–21; see also www.swedensite.com; see also www. eng.si.se. Another suggestion for comparison is H.K. Larsen, "Swedish Planning: A Lesson for Canada," *Queen's Quarterly* 82, no. 1 (Spring 1975): 98–106.

146 Knute E. Karlson (1891–19?) was born in Sala, Västmanland, and immigrated in 1911 to Elmwood, Ontario, thinking it was Elmwood, Manitoba. In 1920 he married Frances and the family took their three-year-old daughter, Loreen, to Sweden for a year in 1931. Son Ross was born in 1935. Knute brought four brothers and two sisters to Canada. See Knute E. Karlson, *A Swedish Immigrant in Canada 1911–1971* (New York: Vantage, 1977), 57.

147 John Ludvig Edlund (1873–1957) was born in Botne, Norway, of Swedish parents. He went to sea as a lad, but after being shipwrecked three times he stayed in Denmark, where he worked in a creamery, became a photographer, and married Karen Andersen (1877–1973) of Fjelsted, Denmark. The couple had three children when they immigrated to Claresholm, Alberta, to join John's parents. His other inventions included anti-glare lenses for headlights, a portable lawn table, an adjustable fly screen, the Robo faucet, a sparrow trap, and markers built into an airplane's seat cushions to set out if the plane went down. He also invented a number of military devices. See *Where the Wheatlands Meet the*

Range (Claresholm, AB, 1974), 226–7; see also Glenbow Archives, John L. Edlund Fonds.

148 Isobel Moser, "Why Is This Man Wearing His Suitcase? Hint: He's Not Making a Fashion Statement," *Western Producer*, 1 April 1993, quoting an article in *Scientific American.*

149 Carl Johan Lilja (1887–1974) was born in Dalskog, Dalsland, and emigrated to the United States in 1907. After successive jobs in three states, and recuperation from a badly broken left leg, he took out a homestead near North Hayter, Alberta, in 1916. In 1922 he married Emma Floa, who had come to Saskatchewan from Minnesota with her parents, who were born in Norway. The couple had four children. Thanks to daughter Selma Reid, Cold Lake, Alberta, and son Bob Lilja, Calgary, for family information.

150 John Allan Clarence Gordon Overholt Burman (1919–1989) was born in North Vancouver. See Alfhild Green, "Allan Burman Passes," *Swedish Press*, April 1989.

151 Landelius Biography Collection, volume 3, #217.

152 Red Deer and District Archives; correspondence G.M. Lindberg, Director, National Research Council, Ottawa, to Morris Flewwelling, Red Deer and District Museum and Archives, Red Deer, 21 March 1983.

153 Ann-Charlotte Berglund, "A Most Unusual Sven Johansson," *Swedish Press*, April 1991, 17; see also her "Freedom From Gravity: A Reindeer Herder's Vision," *Swedish Press*, July 2007, 18–20.

154 Nils Peter Lithander (18?–1936) was born in Lit, Jämtland, emigrated in 1893 to attend the Chicago World's Fair, and went to art school before coming to Winnipeg in 1907. He married Augusta Wallquist (18?–1954) in Chicago and the couple had six children. During a stay in sanatorium he arranged for his family to stay in Scandinavia with his sister, Elisabet Hall. See *Forest to Field*, 394–6, 501, 634; see also Emma Hall Carlson, *We Come to Canada and the First Ten Years* (1954), 40–1. Thanks to Harriet Lee Carlson for donating a copy of this booklet via Barbro Baker, Victoria. Thanks also to Martha Neilson, Erickson, for showing me Lithander's original painting of his mother, her great-grandmother.

155 Malte Sterner (ca. 1900–1952) was born in Karlsborg, Västergötland, and studied at Konsthögskolan in Stockholm. In 1928 he emigrated to the United States but ended up in Vancouver. He married a Canadian. See Landelius Biography Collection, volume 3, #185.

156 William Edgar deGarthe (1907-1983) was born Birger Edward Degerstedt in Kasko, Finland. In 1935 he married Phoebe Agnes Payne, who encouraged him to become a full-time artist. See Alfreda Witbrow, "William Edgar deGarthe, 1907–1983: Ashes Interred in the William

deGarthe Monument, Peggy's Cove," in *The Haligonians: 100 Fascinating Lives from the Halifax Region*, ed. Roma Senn (Halifax: Formac Publishers, 2005), 36–7; see also Landelius Biography Collection, volume 1, #192.

157 Olle Holmsten (1915–1987) was born in Sweden and immigrated to Canada in 1953. From Edmonton he went to Vancouver, where he married Grethe. See "Olle Holmsten, 1915–1987," undated typeset page on Southern Alberta Institute of Technology, Calgary, letterhead, probably put out by SAIT at his death in 1987, photocopy donated by Linnea Lodge, Edmonton, Alberta.

158 Jim Pearson's great grandfather emigrated from Sweden to England, so that his grandfather, Ernest Pearson, was born in Birmingham in 1889. Ernest came to Calgary in 1906. Thanks to Jim Pearson, Delia, Alberta, for family information.

159 Clarence Tillenius (1913–2012) was born on a homestead near Sandridge, Manitoba, the son of Carl Ludvig Tillenius, who had immigrated from Västerås to Manitoba in 1902, and Inga Christina Smestad, who was born near Leonard, North Dakota, of Norwegian parents. The Tillenius family had achieved social status through a relative with the original surname Tillén, who was lady-in-waiting to the Queen of Sweden. In 1942 Clarence Tillenius married Ethel Anna Sankey of Waskada, Manitoba. Thanks to Clarence Tillenius, Winnipeg, for family information. See also Dane Lanken, "Scene Setter," *Canadian Geographic* (July–August 2003): 56–64; see also Gunvor Larsson, "Clarence Tillenius: The Nature Painter," *Swedish Press*, September 1992, 15.

160 Pirkko Karvonen was one of the Finnish children who spent the Second World War years in Sweden. Her Swedish foster mother introduced her to handcrafts, and her Finnish stepmother taught her to weave. After the family immigrated to Edmonton in 1951, she became a well-known textile artist. She and her husband Albert founded Karvonen Films in 1976. See Gunvor Larsson, "Tillenius: The Art of Nature in Winnipeg," *Swedish Press*, March 2005.

161 *Swedish Press*, August 1987.

162 St Jean, "Swedes on the Move," 204.

163 Gordon Stromberg's father, Enoch Stromberg, died in 1952. See *The Cornerstone* (Fall 1992): 15.

10. A Woman's Place

1 In Swedish, *Amerikaänka*.

2 Thanks to Inga Olsson, Sweden, for donating copies of the signed authorization stamped "Swedish Vice Consulate, Wetaskiwin" and the draft drawn on Göteborgs bank, dated 22 March 1922.

3 Lesley Erickson, "Interplay of Ethnicity and Gender: Swedish Women in Southeastern Saskatchewan," in *Other Voices: Historical Essays on Saskatchewan Women* (Regina: University of Regina, Canadian Plains Research Centre, 1995), 27–40.

4 Lena Strandlund (died 1979) was born in Percival, the daughter of Mikael Olafsson Strandlund and Karin Hansdotter from Offerdal, Jämtland, who emigrated in 1893. In 1909 she married Olaf Sigurd Pearson (1887–1975) from Föllinge, Jämtland, who had emigrated with his parents in 1907. See ibid., 39; see also *Centennial Tribute*, 382, 418.

5 Katie Anderson was born Brita Katarina Anderson Linn in Aspås, Jämtland, the daughter of stonemason Petrus Anderson Linn (1867–1915) and his wife, Amalia Bengston. The family immigrated to Percival in 1902. In 1918 she married Charlie Strandlund (1893–1978), who was born in New Stockholm. See Erickson, "Interplay of Ethnicity and Gender," 39; see also *Centennial Tribute*, 365, 416.

6 Karen Svenson Olson (1856–1949) was born in Renålandet, Jämtland, the daughter of Eric Svensson (1814–1872) and his wife, Anna Brita. Karen married Jens Olson and immigrated to New Stockholm with him, their children, and her mother in 1889. See Erickson, "Interplay of Ethnicity and Gender," 27; see also Stockholm Binder, "Anna Brita Svensson Westerlund."

7 Halliwell, *Three Score and Ten*, 50–1.

8 Ibid., 75. Isak Wilhelm Isakson (1872–19?) was born in Sweden with the surname Liminka and became a carpenter. He married in Gällivare, Lappland, to Laura Maria (1878–1964), who was born in Keskie, Finland. The couple had two children when they immigrated in 1902 and homesteaded near New Stockholm. Thanks to Della (Adeline) Dixon Brunskill, Stockholm, for family information.

9 Gustaf de Laval (1845–1913) invented his cream separator in 1878, and it became Sweden's first successful industrial export product. Along with others he founded AB Separator, later Alfa Laval, in 1883. Another of his inventions, a turbine, became the most widely used source of steam power in the world.

10 St Jean, "Swedes on the Move," 84, in discussing farm work in Långasjö in southern Sweden, states, "Milking by hand had sexual connotations. The teat was associated with the penis, and jargon associated with hand milking borrowed from expressions denoting male masturbation. Men who tackled female tasks risked being seen as feminized at the best of times – add the extra barrier of strong homosexual connotations and milking became unthinkable."

11 Erika M. Clark, "Swedish Immigrant Women" (Edmonton: University of Alberta, 1994),12, typescript.

12 Kerstin Pros Mattsson (1867–1961) married Andrew Kvarnberg (18?–1934) in Gagnef parish, Dalarna. Andrew homesteaded in Alberta in 1903 after a brief stay in Minnesota. His wife and children joined him in 1905. Thanks to granddaughter Verna Larson, Edmonton, for donating the 1989 typescript by Elsie Kvarnberg Simmons, "Andrew and Kerstin Kvarnberg and Family," and for other family information.

13 The organ can be seen at the museum in Yorkton, Saskatchewan. Karen Olson's mother, Anna Brita Svensson, made the presentation as the newly elected president of the Ladies Sewing Circle.

14 Erickson, "Interplay of Ethnicity and Gender," 36.

15 Ibid., 35.

16 Eva St Jean, "En karlakarl bland karlar: Brev av ensamhet och trånad från svenska immigranter i Kanada, 1900–1930," in Hembygden och världen: Festskrift till Ulf Beijbom, ed. Lars Olsson and Sune Åkerman (Växjö: Emigrant Institute, 2002), 246–62; see also her chapter 7, "The Frontier Thesis on Sexuality and Power and Swedish Women in British Columbia," in St Jean, "Swedes on the Move," 223–74.

17 Ibid., 36–7. In 1971 the Swedish Evangelical Lutheran Church erected an impressive plaque at Percival and District Cemetery to honour the first Swedish immigrants who built the church in 1900. "Truly they had the imagination and courage to dream dreams and, with God's help, make those dreams come true." Thanks to Sonja Boyce, Edmonton, for sending photos of this plaque and its location.

18 Halver Söderberg (1876–19?) was born in Tynderö, Medelpad, and in 1905 married Anna Åström (1886–1926) from Vemdalen, Härjedalen. See Black, Härjedalsgillet, 242–51.

19 Ibid., 244.

20 Roland C. Goodyear, "Lewis Miller and Harry J. Crowe" (1968), 11–12.

21 Ibid., 13. His example refers to the use of leghold traps in Canada, a device long outlawed in Sweden.

22 Scott, Sweden, 364–5, states, "According to a knowledgeable Swedish sociologist it was true for centuries that the majority of Swedish marriages came only after conception of a child ... Statistics have become more complete in recent years, but they do not indicate any fundamental change: in 30 to 35% of all Swedish marriages a child is already on the way (born within seven months)."

23 Margareta Johanna Eriksdotter (1867–1956) was born in Silsjönäs, Ångermanland, and in 1888 she married Johan Olof Sillen (1865–1930),

born in Sihl, Ångermanland. See *Forest to Field*, 621–4; see also "The Sillen Family in Sweden and Canada: A Family History Compiled by Donald W. Sjoberg" (Winnipeg, 2002), 1–10.

24 This was a food tradition carried on since the Viking age.

25 A reference to this common occurrence can be found in Martha Larson Lundman, "Beginnings" (1984), 2, typescript donated by daughter Eleanor Gardiner, Thunder Bay. Martha (1899–19?) was the daughter of Frank and Emma Larson of Hilltop, Manitoba.

26 John Tegelberg Lindell (18?–1955) came from Halland and adopted the surname Lindell upon landing in Canada. His wife, Paulina, came from Sandhem, Västergötland. See Lucy Lindell, comp., *Memory Opens the Door: History as told by Pioneers of the Central West-Interlake Area* (Eriksdale, 1970), 69–74.

27 Ibid., 69.

28 Ibid., 70.

29 Erickson, "Interplay," 34; see also Halliwell, *Three Score and Ten*, 16–17.

30 William S. Persson, "Memoir," typescript dated 1971, prepared in 1991 and donated by daughter Maureen Landine, Stockholm, Saskatchewan. Persson served as mayor for many years, and in 1991 the Village of Stockholm honoured him by renaming Dubuc Street as Persson Street.

31 Wickström, *Genom sju kungariken*, 193.

32 Houser, *The Swedish Community at Eriksdale*, 17–24.

33 Manitoba Archives, MG14, C28, Box 1, File 1, W.J. Sisler Collection: W.J. Sisler, "The Swedish Colony – New Stockholm," 9.

34 Sharon Fitzsimmons (1947–2008) was born in Rich Valley, northwest of Edmonton, the granddaughter of Andrew Peterson (1862–19?) and Ida Nelson, who immigrated from Livsdal, Västmanland, and from Småland. They married in 1894 and moved to Alberta in 1908. See Sharon Fitzsimmons, "The Peterson Family Story: Homesteading in Western Canada" (Edmonton, 1988)

35 Supporting this statement is the fact that Swedish swear words are mostly religious rather than sexual.

36 St Jean, "En karlakarl bland karlar," 315, 325–6.

37 Epp, *Nordic People in Canada*, table 10.

38 P. Koral, "Visa tryckt i går," *Svenska dagbladet*, 30 December 1931.

39 Boegh, *Immanuel Evangelical Lutheran Church, 1906–2006*, 6.

40 Howard, *Vancouver's Svenskar*, 39–41; see also St Jean, "Swedes on the Move," 243–5.

41 Ibid., 245–6.

11 Swedishness in Canada

1　Carina Rönnqvist, "Scattered Swedes and Single Settlers," 100.

2　Blanck, *Becoming Swedish-American,* 220.

3　The Lucia tradition began in Västergötland and had spread to Dalsland and Värmland before being adopted by the upper classes in other parts of the country.

4　Landelius Biography Collection, volume 1, #076.

5　The Swedish lyrics were written in 1924 by Arvid Rosen.

6　The Nobel Prize winner Selma Lagerlöf wrote the Swedish legend about Santa Lucia, illuminated by light, coming in a boat at night to distribute food in famine-stricken Värmland. For an English-language book with recipes and a pattern for Lucia's gown., see Ewa Rydåker, *Lucia Morning in Sweden,* illus. Carina Ståhlberg (Uppsala: E. Rydåker, 2002).

7　The custom of dipping in the kettle (*doppa i grytan*) was so widespread that Christmas Eve was called "*dopparedagen*," or dipping day. The traditional song to sing while dancing around the Christmas tree was "Nu är det jul igen" (Now it's Christmas time again).

8　The marriage in Scandinavia was John Daniel Sundmark (1872–1945) from Boteå parish, Ångermanland, and Hanna Sophia Andersdotter (1867–1961) from Söderköping, Östergötland. Thanks to Pat Sundmark, East St Paul, Manitoba, for sending family information, including her article, "Clanwilliam Settlers, John and Hanna Sundmark," published in *Generations: Journal of the Manitoba Genealogical Society* 29, no. 3 (2004): 24–5.

9　*Kipling 100,* 32, 28; Ingrid Carlson, "From Earth to Glory: Mom Carlson's Life Story 1906–1986" (ca. 1986), 19, re names days, reprinted in *Kipling 100,* 11.

10　Märta Jörgensen developed the Swedish national costume in 1902, modelled after a folk dress that Crown Princess Victoria had introduced at the Royal Castle of Tullgarn.

11　Fred Burman (1888–1984) was born in Skarpinge, Blekinge, and immigrated to Canada in 1909 to join his father. Both cleared land for Larson's fourth hotel, Canyon View, and helped build it. Fred worked in British Columbia for small lumber companies and married Tilde. See LAC, Fred Burman Fonds, "Memories" (Rock Bay, BC, 1963), typescript, 432 pages.

12　Howard, "Pete Larson, North Vancouver Hotelman," 4, quoting from "Fred Burman berättar," *Nya svenska pressen,* 20 July and 3 August 1976.

13 Ljungmark, *Svenskarna i Winnipeg*, 68–70, 146–7. Although Pastor Uddén helped found the Scandinavian Temperance League, he soon distanced himself from it, saying that Christianity should not be the main reason for their work. In 1910 all the temperance societies joined under the same banner, the Scandinavian Anti-Saloon League. The first six months were rife with conflicts, particularly between the IOGT and the Mission Covenant pastor, J. Sällström, who resigned from the league during a particularly stormy meeting. The will for temperance was strong, but religious intolerance was stronger.

14 The founders are recognized as Alfred Egnell (1864–1945) from Norrköping, Östergötland, and his wife, Ottilia (1880–1946), from Husum, Ångermanland. Chicago's *Kämpen* (The champion), was a twice-monthly magazine with the byline "for Swedish temperance societies in the United States and Canada." Founded in 1888, the byline suggests an earlier Swedish temperance society in Canada but perhaps that was wishful thinking.

15 Lodges belonging to Canadas skandinaviska storloge av I.O.G.T. were located at Canwood (Canwood), Freedhome/Dubuc (Scandia), Kelliher (Sveas borg), Percival (Hoppets ankar), Wadena (Folkets val), and Young (Youngs hopp) in Saskatchewan; at Elmwood (Elvdrottningen), Mulvihill (Alprosen), and Winnipeg (Framtidens Hopp) in Manitoba: and at Bergland (Linea), Kenora (Goda avsigten), and Port Arthur (I räddningsbåten) in Northwestern Ontario. See J.A. Hägglund, "Skandinaviska Godtemplarrörelsens i Canada Historia," *Svenska Canada-tidningen*, 14 May 1925.

16 Ljungmark, *Svenskarna i Winnipeg*, 69.

17 Howard, "Temperance and Good Times," in *Vancouver's Svenskar*, 51–4.

18 The Scandinavian Society created a fund to help sick members and new arrivals, among other initiatives. The group also decided to set up a voluntary Scandinavian company to defend Winnipeg during the North-West Rebellion, but it proved unnecessary.

19 Emanuel Turner, whose Swedish surname was Törner, came from Uppsala, Sweden, and had helped found agricultural communities in the United States. By 1889 he lived on a homestead in Scandinavia with his wife and children. See Tyman, *By Section, Township and Range*, 238.

20 Ljungmark, *Svenskarna i Winnipeg*, 45–6.

21 Manitoba Archives, MG 8B 64: Louise Ostlin Collection. Thanks to Barbro Baker, Victoria, for bringing this poem, which is credited to Louise Ostlin, to my attention. Although the poem itself is handwritten in English, the

Swedish words *"Carman, Den 10 januari 1886"* (Carman, 10 January 1886) appear between the title and the text.

22 In 1916 Gerhard Hilarius Silver (1889–1959) married Ellen Naemie Larson (1898–1949) from Malung, Minnesota, whose parents came from Dalarna. They lived on a farm in Bergland, Ontario, and the family moved to Fort Frances in 1943. See Vernon Silver, comp., "Gerhard Hilarius Silver (Thord Bjorke, pseud) and his Family, Bergland, Ontario." See also *Water Under the Bridge*, 307–10.

23 Correspondence with Vernon Silver, Atikokan, Ontario, 14 September 2006.

24 Details of meeting procedures were taken from Minute Book 1914-1917, IOGT #17, I räddningsbåten Study Circle, Port Arthur. Thanks to Milly Scollie, Thunder Bay, for donating the original minute book to the Scandinavian Heritage Project after restoration in 1992. See also Scott, *Sweden*, 354–5.

25 *Sånger för nykterhetsmöten utgifna af Sveriges Storloge af I.O.G.T.* (Stockholm: Oskar Eklunds boktryckeri, 1904), donated by John Freed, Freedhome. Another, published in 1924 by the same publisher, is titled *Goodtemplarordens sångbok utgiven av Sveriges storloge av I.O.G.T.*

26 Otto J. England (1871–1922) was born in Undersvik, Hälsingland, became a master stonemason, and immigrated to Winnipeg in 1902 with his wife and children, moving the next year to Freedhome. See George Closson, *Freedhome: 70 years* (Stockholm, SK, 1978), 118–19. Thanks to Stuart Stevenson, Stockholm, for family information.

27 Admittedly not cut out for the hard life of a homesteader, or perhaps because of it, he designed and built a one-horsepower log splitter. See Magee, *A Scandinavian Heritage*, 48.

28 Alice Forslund was born in Jämtland, and was the wife of John Forslund. She died in the early 1930s.

29 Houser, *The Swedish Community at Eriksdale*, 24–5, 31, 89.

30 Kermit B. Westerberg, "In Private and Public: The Dialogue of Libraries, Immigrants, and Society," in *Scandinavian Immigrants and Education in North America*, ed. Philip J. Anderson et al. (Chicago: Swedish-American Historical Society, 1995), 197–8, details the Swedish Library Association's unsatisfactory working relationship with Riksföreningen för Svenskhetens Bevarande i Utlandet (National Society for the Preservation of Swedish Culture Abroad). Publishers named were Albert Bonnier Publishing House and Carl Dahlén in New York, and Augustana Book Concern in Rock Island, Illinois.

31 Riksarkivet, Sweden, General Konsul i Montreal, Grupp 14/3-7/1902-23; typescript "Svenska nationalbiblioteket," signed by president Peter Bernhard Anderson and secretary Nils F:son Brown, 3 April 1918; see also "Biblioteksrörelsen," *Svenska Canada-tidningen*, 30 June 1917. Two libraries were founded in Ontario (at Kenora and McDougall's Mills), four in Manitoba (Heidenstam in Durban, Bellman in Inwood, Geijer in Mulvihill, and Tegnér in Winnipeg), ten in Saskatchewan (Svedenborg in Annieheld near Assiniboia, Ellen Key in Canwood, Linné in Dubuc, Strindberg in Fairy Glen, Wicksell in Fusilier, Viktor Rydberg in Hume, Oscar II in Percival, Fröding in Shaunavon, Oscar Fredrik in Wadena, and Wennerberg in Young), and one in British Columbia (Starbäck in Prince Rupert).

32 "Till svenskarna i Canada," *Svenska Canada-tidningen*, 6 May 1926, 3, which includes the constitution.

33 Annie Larson, "The Influence of Swedish Settlers in the District of Young," *Nya svenska pressen*, 15 January 1965, 6.

34 *Footsteps to Follow: A History of Young, Zelma and Districts* (Young: Young Celebration Committee, 1981), 363.

35 Esias Tegnér is recognized as one of Sweden's foremost poets.

36 Owner Ida Carlson McLaren (ca. 1868–19?) was born in Halland and immigrated to Winnipeg in 1890 as a domestic. She tried working on a farm in Starbuck, Manitoba, later returning to Winnipeg as a cook at Brunswick Hotel until buying Fountain House. Her marriage to A. McLaren (1915 to 1919) ended with his death and her return to Fountain House. See Landelius Biography Collection, volume 2, #358; see also Ljungmark, *Svenskarna i Winnipeg*, 224.

37 Riksarkivet, General Konsul i Montreal, Grupp 14/3-7/1902-23; C.J. Engvall, "Tillkännagifvande," *Canada posten*, 2 April 1918.

38 Ibid. (46-9E). "Canadian Swedes Form Association: Work for Closer Swedish-Canadian Relations, Consul-General Bergstrom President," *The Gazette*, Montreal, 9 April 1917. The constitution allowed for two subcommittees, one for trade and industry and the other for maritime affairs. Bergström was a former minister of defence.

39 Scott, *Sweden*, 472–3.

40 Almost half of the members lived in Quebec, with eight from Ontario, seven from Manitoba, six from British Columbia, three from Alberta, three from Saskatchewan, two from New Brunswick, and three from New York. Those from the East included five engineers from Montreal, thirteen employees of pulp and paper companies, seven representatives

of companies, three who worked for the federal government in Ottawa, and three from the Swedish Consulate in Montreal.

41 Bergström was elected president, with H. Helin of the Wayasagamack Pulp & Paper Company in Three Rivers as vice-president, W. Lammers of Swedish Steel & Importing Company in Montreal as secretary-treasurer, and E. Alsson of the Brompton Pulp & Paper Company in East Angus, Quebec, as a director.

42 Charlie Peterson (ca. 1863–1956) immigrated from Sweden in 1889, and was involved in railway construction from Ontario to Alberta. He hired mostly Swedes, once pre-paying 127 fares in order to meet a deadline. He homesteaded in Wadena in 1909, and also had a real-estate business. See Landelius Biography Collection, volume 3, #108.

43 Riksarkivet, General Konsul i Montreal, Grupp 14/3-7/1902-23 [46-9E], "The Swedish Association of Canada" with by-laws and list of members, W. Lammers, secretary, to David Bergström, Montreal, enclosing the minutes of the annual meeting, 28 June 1917. Thanks to Carl Widstrand, Ottawa, for translations, summaries, and comments about *Svenska förbundet i Canada* and *Svenska nationalbiblioteket*.

44 In 1926 the members of the executive council were Axel J. Carlson, O.L. Holmgren, Arthur Anderson, and Helmer Johnson of Winnipeg; Alice Forslund of Eriksdale; and Hjalmar Erickson, Alb. Noreus, and Hans Westin of Kenora.

45 UM IHRC; "Svenska förbundets ålderdomshem/Swedish old people's home: En vädjan till envar svensk i Canada att hjälpa oss skaffa våra gamla en fristad," in *Årsbok 1931, Svenska förbundet i Canada/Swedish Canadian League, Utgiven till Midsommartinget: Wadena, Sask. den 26, 27 och 28 juni, 1931*, ed. Percy Ekberg, 13. The proposal was made by J.W. Lundeen, and N.E. Johnson, Emil Näström, and Frank Pearson of Lac du Bonnet made up the committee.

46 Ibid.

47 Leonard Wreede (1874–1951) was born Anders Leonard Johansson in Västra Näset, Borgsjö, Medelpad, and took the surname Wreede upon his marriage in 1904 to Anny Pettersson (1884–1964) from nearby Ånge. The family immigrated in 1906 to Moosehorn, Manitoba, and moved to Alberta, after a short stay in the United States. In 1915 they moved to Wadena, where Wreede became a real-estate and travel agent. His wife was a staunch Baptist, and both their sons graduated from Brandon College and Regina Normal School. Wreede was Lutheran, and an active member of IOGT, the Agricultural Society, and the Union Hospital. Mayor

for eight years, he ran as a Conservative for the provincial legislature.
See *Remembering Times: Wadena and Area Dating Back to 1882* (Wadena:
Wadena History Book Committee, 1992), 2:1007–10; see also *Pages from the
Past: A History of Paswegin and School Districts Harrow, North Quill, Quill
City, Tiger Lily and Wooler* (Wadena: Paswegin History Committee, 1982),
362–3.

48 O.L. Holmgren (1867–19?) was born in Föllinge, Jämtland, and
immigrated in 1904 with his wife. After a year on a homestead the family
moved to Winnipeg, where O.L. worked as a carpenter. He was founding
chair of the IOGT Grand Lodge, and helped re-establish *Svenska förbundet
i Canada* in 1926. See Arthur A. Anderson, "O.L. Holmgren," Landelius
Biography Collection, volume 2, #081.

49 SSIRC; *Hälsning till hembygden Jämtland från jämtar i Canada och Förenta
staterna* (1932). Named were 212 families from Canada and 55 from the
United States, giving their address, birthplace in Jämtland, and year of
emigration.

50 Manitoba Archives, Box P5951, file 6; Protokollsbok för lokalavdelning
"Winnipeg" av *Svenska förbundet i Canada* (Minute Book for the Winnipeg
branch of the Swedish Canadian League), *1926–1941.* It was found in 1970
among other books donated to the Swedish Canadian Home for Senior
Citizens, and donated to the Manitoba Archives in 2001 by Ted Simonson,
Winnipeg.

51 Howard, "Poverty, Illness and Death," in *Vancouver's Svenskar*, 44–9.
In 1979 Micael Setterdahl microfilmed the Ritual Book, Register Book,
Dues Book, and Minute Books 1908–1965 for *Svenska sällskapet Svea*. For
an account of women's contributions to the organization, see St Jean,
"Swedes on the Move," 254–8.

52 Elinor Barr, *A Capsule History, Norrskenet, [Northern Lights], Swedish Sick
Benefit Society Est. 1905, Thunder Bay, Canada: 90*th *Anniversary, 2 April 1995.*

53 Balch Institute for Ethnic Studies, Philadelphia, Pennsylvania, MSS 123,
Scandinavian Fraternity of America, 1909–1992. Most of the collection
consists of records from Lyran Lodge #109, Syracuse, New York, and
Fram Lodge #282, Philadelphia, chartered in 1928.

54 UBCL SC, A IV B, Box 1, Matthew Lindfors Fonds; undated letter from
R. Hendrickson, Secretary Treasurer, Scandinavian Brotherhood of East
Kootenay, to Matt Lindfors, Vancouver; see also Bill Symes, historian,
"Chronicles of the Swedish Canadian Social Group," Victoria, where the
Annual Scandinavian Brotherhood Dance is mentioned in 1962.

55 Ljungmark, *Svenskarna i Winnipeg*, 152.

56 Black, *Härjedalsgillet*, 10–11.

57 Don Sjoberg, "Augustana in Canada – People and Places," speech, 26 June 2004.

58 *Vasa Order of America: A Swedish-American Fraternal Organization: Centennial 1896–1996*, (Vasa Order of America, 1996), 128, 141–9; see also Henry Hanson, "The Vasa Order of America: Its Role in the Swedish-American Community: 1896–1996," *Swedish-American Historical Quarterly* 47, no. 4 (1996): 236–44; see also Ruth Peterson, "Vasa Children's Clubs Keep Swedish Traditions and Heritage Alive," *Bryggan/The Bridge* 18, no. 3 (1986): 86–7.

59 Linnea Lodge, "The Vasa Order in Canada," *Vasa Star* (1971): 10; see also Barr, "Swedes at the Lakehead," 57.

60 Manitoba Archives C556-557, Swedish Community Oral History Collection, Vera Hallonquist, 11.

61 Their opening song, composed by Gertrude Dickau, and closing song, by Alice Jean Smistad, were copyrighted by Grand Lodge in 1981. Gertrude Dahlberg Dickau (1925–) was born in Flärke, Ångermanland, and in 1926 immigrated with her parents to the Falun district. She joined Wetaskiwin's Vasa Lodge in 1941, later transferring to Calgary. See "Gertrude Dickau's Biography" (1997), typescript donated by Donna Englund, Calgary.

62 Alice Jean Smistad, "History of Branting Lodge," speech at the 75th anniversary celebration, 19 April 1997, typescript donated by Donna Englund, Calgary.

63 Carin Pihl, "Calgary Notes," *Swedish Press*, February, March, April, August 1988.

64 Arvid Nelson (1887–1947) was born in Umeå, Västerbotten, and immigrated to Canada in 1909. He married Minnie Larson (1895–1970), who was born in Clarkfield, Minnesota, and migrated with her family to Warwick, Alberta. Arvid worked as a CNR carpenter in the Edson, Hinton, and Jasper areas, then in 1920 returned to Kenora. Thanks to Linnea Lodge, Edmonton, for sending a copy of her interview with their daughter Vera Fox.

65 Rae Biggs, "Vasa Lodges of Alberta," *Heritage* (Alberta Culture) 4, no. 6 (November–December 1976): 5.

66 Linnea Lodge, "Skandia: 60 Years in Review," 15–16. Linnea credits Evelyn Modin, "History of Vasa Park" (1987), for details about Vasa Park. Those who made the initial arrangements were charter members Albin Samuelson and Eric Pierre, and chair Herbert Hokanson.

67 The Scandinavian Studies Association was founded and incorporated in 1990 to raise funds for a second professorship in Scandinavian Studies at the University of Alberta. See Linnea Lodge, "A Profile of the Scandinavian Communities in Edmonton" (1992), 21.

68 Poster and acknowledgments donated by Linnea Lodge, Edmonton, coordinator of the event.

69 Lennart Petersson was born in Söderköping, Östergötland, and immigrated to Canada in 1956. He earned the Certified Management Accountant designation in 1965 and two years later married Joan. He has been actively involved in most of Edmonton's Swedish and Scandinavian organizations. Thanks to Lennart Petersson, Edmonton, for family information. See also *Swedish Press*, November 1998, 35.

70 Linnea Lodge (1923–) was born Anna Ragnhild Linnea Wicklund in Kamloops, British Columbia, the daughter of Nils Wicklund (1894–1973) from Aspsele, Björna, Ångermanland, and Signe Gustafsson (1902–1978) from Hässle, Småland. Nils returned to Sweden after his retirement, and both are buried in Vindeln, Västerbotten. In 1949 Linnea married Henry Cabot Lodge (1920–1994) from Newfoundland. She was employed by the Swift Canadian Company (later Gainer's) from 1943 to 1983 in accounting. Thanks to Linnea Lodge, Edmonton, for family information.

71 Irene Gunild Olljum (1926–) was born in Bergsby, Riguldi, Estonia, and went to Sweden during the legal expatriation of Swedes from Estonia in 1944. Her future husband, Rudolf Olljum, who was Estonian but not Swedish, set out in a dinghy with eleven others and was rescued by the Swedish coast guard. Irene and Rudolf met and married in Sweden, then in 1951 immigrated to Vancouver. See *Swedish Press*, November 1986, 34, and March 1991, 19–21; see also "The Swedish Cultural Society," speech delivered at the fiftieth anniversary banquet of the Swedish Cultural Society, Vancouver, 6 June 2001, published in *Swedish Press*, July 2001.

72 Lodge, "A Profile of the Scandinavian Communities in Edmonton," 17–18; see also University of Alberta, Special Collections; "Scandinavian Centre Is for All: Unity a Major Problem," *Edmonton Journal: Roots*, 1976.

73 Limberg, "Almost a Century's Work," 125–57. Riksförening Sverigekontakt is in the process of cataloguing and disposing of its rich emigration archives.

74 LAC, MG 31, H 92, Carl E. Soderquist Fonds; Carl E. Soderquist, "En återblick 1929–1969, tillägnad svenska klubben Nordstjärnen, Edmonton, Alberta" (1969). It was catechist Carl Wrick from Lund, Sweden, who suggested the idea of founding Nordstjärnan and affiliating with the Society for the Preservation of Swedish Culture in Foreign Lands

(*Riksförening för svenskhetens bevarande i utlandet*). Carl E. Soderquist (ca. 1895–19?) was born in Gunnarsnäs, Dalsland, and immigrated in 1924 to Camrose, moving to Edmonton in 1931.

75 Olljum, "The Swedish Cultural Society," speech delivered 6 June 2001. See also "Vancouver Notes: Irene Olljum Honored," *Swedish Press*, March 1991, 19–21.

76 Hans Hörnfeldt (1932–2009) grew up in Örnsköldsvik, Ångermanland, and married Gun-Britt Jonsson from Bureå, Västerbotten. The couple immigrated to Victoria in 1964. Hans had worked as a compositor at *Örnsköldviks Allehanda* for sixteen years, and in Victoria was employed by the *Times Colonist* until retiring. See *Swedish Press,* January 1992, 33; see also Bill Symes, "Chronicles of the Swedish Canadian Social Group."

77 *Swedish Press*, April 1989, August 1997, June and November 2000, May 2002. Granewall increased his recipe to include enough of the cream-filled delicacies for the Swedish Club as well.

78 Interview with Leena Sillanpaa, Ottawa, former president, 6 March 2005; see also Lars Öhman, "A Few Words about Dan Harris," *Nordic News*, November 2007.

79 Jan Lundgren, "Svenska Klubben i Montreals Historia," see http://www.svenskaklubben.ca/historien.asp.

80 Ulf Frisk was born in Kolmården, Östergötland, and moved with his family to Lidingö during the 1930s. There, he married Margareta in 1938 and the couple followed Ulf's brother to Vancouver. Ulf made Mora grandfather clocks and chests decorated with three-dimensional carvings instead of painted flat on the wood. He also made miniature Dala horses and Viking ships. See *Swedish Press*, September 2004, 27.

81 *Swedish Press*, November 1991 and September 1996.

82 *Swedish Press*, July 2004 and June 2006; see also http://swea.org/.

83 For a history, see Louise Enhörning, "SWEA History," *SWEA bladet, Commemorative Issue Celebrating the Official Visit to Toronto of Their Majesties King Carl XVI Gustaf and Queen Silvia of Sweden* (1988), 3–4.

84 Carin Pihl, "Calgary Notes," *Swedish Press*, May 1988.

85 The website for Calgary's Swedish school is http://swedishschool.com/english.

86 "Swedish Schools in North America," *Swedish Press*, June 1995; see also "Back to Swedish School," *Swedish Press*, October 2000; see also "*Svenska Skolan – Calgary – 1975–1995*," donated by Margaretha Malik; see also "Svenska Skolan Vancouver 1978–1988," *Swedish Press*, April 1988, 26–7; see also undated brochure, "*Svensk Skolan Toronto*."

87 Erik Gunnar Eriksson (1904–1964) was born in Rinkaby, Skåne, and in 1927 immigrated to Winnipeg. After bad experiences as a farmhand he decided to return to Sweden to learn a trade. He came back in 1933 as a butcher and opened a meat store in Fort Frances. In 1934 he married his clerk, whose parents came from Trondheim, Norway. Thanks to daughter Vi Hautala, Thunder Bay, for family information. See also Vi Hautala, "The Man From Skåne," *Swedish Press*, January 1996; see also *Fort Frances Times*, "Eric's Newest Pet, Fox Squirrel, Spins Cage at Dizzy Speed," 24 February 1960; "Eric's Lund, Open for the Season Presents 50 Varieties of Wildlife, in 35 Displays, All Identified," 2 May 1964; and an undated clipping with the headline "Eric's Lund Is Great Place to Monkey About."

88 Vi Hautala, "Eric Ericson, My Father," presentation to Norrskenet Swedish Society, Thunder Bay, 10 May 1999, typescript.

89 Houser, *The Swedish Community at Eriksdale*, 93–5.

90 Ibid., 52, 64–5. Nord school and Nord cemetery were named for Jöns Nord.

91 Alf Carlson (ca. 1905–1990) was born in Harplinge, Halland, and immigrated to Vancouver in 1924 as a blacksmith. See *Swedish Press*, October 1988, 15, and February 1991.

92 Saskatchewan Archives, Saskatoon, X 132; Nils Nilsson, *Swedish Ballads Sung by Sleepy and Swede* (sixteen songs).

93 Nils "Swede" Nilsson (ca. 1911–1993) became an orphan during the flu epidemic and was raised in foster homes. He immigrated to Montreal in 1930 and got his nickname from his first boss, an Ontario farmer. He rode the rods and played his guitar as a street busker, and met Frost in a northeastern Ontario mining camp. In 1939 Nilsson married Alma Bender. See Ann-Charlotte Berglund, "Swede Nilsson: The Swedish Radio Personality that Rode in to Everybody's Heart," *Swedish Press*, January 1994, 22–3; see also Hal G. Duncan, "Sleepy and Swede," *Western People*, 13 September 1984.

94 Carl Friberg (1910–19?) was born in New Zealand, son of Salvation Army brigadier Ernst Friberg from Oskarshamn, Småland. The parents and four sons spent 1924 and 1925 in Oskarshamn, in order to learn Swedish. See Ingvar Thorne, "Flygvapnets i Canada musikkår dirigeras av svenskättling," *Svenska Amerikanaren-Tribunen*, 28 February 1952, in Landelius Biography Collection, volume 1, #306; see also www.worldmilitarybands.com/RCAFbds.html.

95 "*Swedish Press* Visits the Bellman Boys: Singers Wanted," *Swedish Press*, November 1987, and Sven Seaholm, "Bellman Kören 1946–1991," sung

to the tune "Clementine," *Swedish Press*, July 1991. Sven and his brother Sid Seaholm were long-time members, Sid having served as the first president.

96 *Swedish Press*, July 1988, October 1989, and October 2008.

97 Glenn Mossop comes from a musical family. His grandfather conducted Summerland Singers and Players in Gilbert and Sullivan musicals, and his father worked as music director for Calgary schools. See *Swedish Press*, July 1990, 27.

98 Bengt Hambraeus (1927–2000) was born in Stockholm and received his doctorate in musicology from the University of Uppsala in 1956. He achieved international stature as a composer, organist, scholar, lecturer, and administrator, and in 1996 was awarded the Swedish Tribute for promoting Swedish-Canadian relations within the field of music. He died at his Hambraehill Farm in Glen Roy Apple-Hill, Ontario, near Montreal.

99 UBCL SC, Matthew Lindfors Fonds, A IV B, Box 1; "Canadas internationella radio talar svenska," *Canada-tidningen*, 23 December 1948; see also Landelius Biography Collection, volume 2, #194. Gunnar Rygheimer came from Stockholm; Sture Persson from Eslöv, Skåne; Gunnar Kristiansson from Malmö, Skåne; and Karin Farnström from Lidingö near Stockholm.

100 Gunnar Kristiansson and Karin Färnström, *Framtidslandet Kanada* (Stockholm: Natur och kultur, 1954).

101 Dr Axel Lennart Wenner-Gren's company, Alweg, which was based in Germany, developed the original Disneyland monorail, which opened in 1959, and the Seattle Center Monorail, which opened for the 1961 Century 21 Exposition.

102 UBCL SC, Matthew Lindfors Fonds, A IV B, Box 1; Sture Persson, Canadian Broadcasting Corporation, International Service, Montreal, to Matthew Lindfors, Vancouver, 25 February 1957.

103 Program, "Winnipeg Folk Arts Society, First Annual Festival, Playhouse Theatre, Friday and Saturday, Dec. 5th–6th, 1930," provided by Coray Schroeder, Bracebridge, Ontario, whose father, Axel J. Carlson, translated the third act into English for this performance.

104 LAC, Esse W. Ljungh Fonds, includes sound recordings of the radio dramas he produced.

105 Ljungmark, *Svenskarna i Winnipeg*, 75, 153.

106 Lars Ljungmark, "The Northern Neighbor: Winnipeg, the Swedish Service Station," 98.

107 Ljungmark, *Svenskarna i Winnipeg*, 147.

108 Adolf Johannes Palmqvist (ca. 1887–19?) was born in Avesta, Dalarna, and in 1903 immigrated to Montreal with his family. See Landelius Biography Collection, volume 3, #97.

109 "Swedish in Quebec," *Swedish Press*, September 1995, 21–3.

110 Hugo Holmberg (1880–19?) was born in Lycksele, Lappland, and in 1905 married Anna Stenlund (1882–194?) from Arvidsjaur. The couple emigrated with four children to Finmark in 1923–4. After homesteading in Chatfield, Manitoba, from 1925 to 1927 they returned to Finmark. Thanks to Ken Holmberg, Didsbury, Alberta, for family information.

111 Rudolf J. Verne (18?–1948) immigrated from Sweden, where he worked for a newspaper, to a job with an Alberta bank, then to Vancouver as a sports instructor. His enthusiasm for skiing was infectious, and he was a leading member of the Western Canada Amateur Ski Association, a contributor of articles to *Hiker and Skier*, and publisher of a short-lived newspaper called *Vancouver Skandinaven*. See Howard, *Vancouver's Svenskar*, 59–60.

112 Klockar Oskar Persson (1891–19?) was born in Hälla, Dalarna, and immigrated to Simpson, Saskatchewan, in 1923; Djäken Olof Andersson (1895–1977) was born in Ullvi, Dalarna, and immigrated to Nelson, British Columbia, in 1922; Israels Anders Andersson (1894–1976), also born in Ullvi, immigrated in 1921 to Boulder, British Columbia, where he changed his name to Anders Irving; and Brusk Stina Ersdotter (1903–1995), who married Anders Irving on the way to Vancouver in 1931. All came from the Leksand area of Dalarna, and all returned to Sweden in 1947, after selling their share of the development. See "Vancouver Notes," *Swedish Press*, January 1997 and January 2006; see also *Dalfolk* (Leksand, Dalarna), n:r 1, 2010, volume 23, 8.

113 "Vancouver Notes," *Swedish Press*, January 1997 and January 2006.

114 Ljungmark, *Svenskarna i Winnipeg*, 148–9.

115 Ibid., 147–50.

116 Victor Lindquist (1908–1983) was the son of Gus Lindquist. Retiring as a player after almost twenty years, he became a respected referee. Victor Lindquist was inducted into the Northwestern Ontario Sports Hall of Fame in 1994. See "Lilly Paulsen (nee Lindquist)" in *Rock, Fur, Forest, Lakes: A History* (Wabigoon: Wabigoon and District Historical Society, 1988), 392–3; see also "Victor Lindquist won Olympic Gold," *Thunder Bay Post*, 30 August 1994.

117 Landelius Biography Collection, volume 2, #089, "'Swede' Hornquist utsatt för olycka och fick stanna i Canada," *Nya svenska pressen*, 25 March 1937.

118 Gustaf "Gus" Ossian Forslund (1906–1962) was born in Umeå, Västerbotten, and in 1907 immigrated with his family to Fort William, later moving to Port Arthur.

119 UBCL SC, Matthew Lindfors Fonds, A IV B, box 2; program "First Canadian Tour of the Sofia Girls, Massey Hall, Toronto, 2 November 1956"; open letter from Otto Nordling, secretary, The Swedish Canadian Club, Vancouver, 29 May 1956; "Swedish Dedication to Health Pays Off on One-Night Stands," *Kenora Daily Miner and News*, 27 October 1956.

120 Charlotte Ericson, "Okanagan Notes," *Swedish Press*, March 1988; see also "Swedish Picks," *Swedish Press*, October 2006.

121 Charlie Burkman (1900–1968) was born in Port Arthur, the son of blacksmith John Burkman (1866–1954) and Anna Myllymaki (1880–1916). John immigrated from Nederkalix, Norrbotten, settling in Whitewood, Saskatchewan, before moving to Port Arthur around 1894. See obituary, John Burkman, *Port Arthur News-Chronicle*, 13 December 1954.

122 See also Shirley Jean Roll Tucker, *The Amazing Foot Race of 1921: Halifax to Vancouver in 134 Days* (Victoria, Vancouver, Calgary: Heritage House Publishing, 2011).

123 City of Wetaskiwin Archives; *Statutes of Alberta 1908*, Chapter 38, Section 1. Named are Aaron Anderson, Andrew W. Anderson, John Anderson, Nils Anderson, Olaf H. Anderson, John Asp, John Bakstrom, Gustav Carlson, Thomas Dahl, Ole Diedrickson, Hans B. Erickson, Ole Evenson, Gustaf Forsell, Knute A. Gullickson, John Hagstrom, Carl F. Hanson, Anton O. Hongestole, John Edward Johanson, Gustaf Johnson, O.H. Johnson, Andrew W. Lee, Charles Lundstrom, Martin Marker, O. Mattson, Charles H. Olin, Ole Olson, Even O. Olstad, Ludwig O. Olstad, Ludvig Peterson, Ole H. Ronnie, G.E. Sanden, Martin Sherbeck, Nils Schmidt, Daniel Sundval, Charles H. Swanson, Louis B. Wedin, John Wick, and Swan J. Youngberg, See also Archives of Alberta, Donald Carlson, "The Scandinavian Hospital in Wetaskiwin" (1976), typescript, 5 pages.

124 Gustav Carlson (1855–1919) was born in Lindes parish, Örebro, Närke, and worked as a miner and carpenter. He came in contact with Baptists at the age of twenty-one in Hudiksvall, Hälsingland, and ten years later attended Bethel Seminary in Stockholm, graduating in 1889. He married Johanna Matilda Delbom (1862–1951), who was born in Sala, Västmanland, and in 1890 they emigrated to the United States, where he served several congregations until 1904, when he accepted a call to Wetaskiwin. When his health failed in 1907, he took a homestead forty-eight kilometres to the west, and taught school at Lonesome Pine. Rev Carlson was appointed justice of the peace in 1914, and Matilda was

active in the Women's Christian Temperance Union. Thanks to Katherine Peebles, Cupertino, California, for family information. See also City of Wetaskiwin Archives, Gustav Carlson Family Fonds.

125 The chief sources of information for this section are Barr, *The Scandinavian Home Society*, and "Swedish Immigration to Canada, 1923–29," 150–61.

126 *Föreningen Oscar II:s Vandringsbibliotek* was founded in Stockholm in 1906 for the express purpose of providing good and useful literature to Swedish sailors and diaspora Swedes around the world. Swedish organizations, businesses, and private individuals financed it. See Westerberg, "In Private and Public," 197.

127 This lack of support from *Svenska Canada-tidningen* undoubtedly stemmed from P.M. Dahl's blaming the society for the damning article published in *Svenska Dagbladet* in August 1924, and linking it to the discontinuance of government funding for his newspaper.

128 Karl Oscar Forssell (1888–1947) was born in Jämtland and married Elin Maria Lexberg (1889–1980) from Lilla Edet, Bohuslän. Their daughter Ella married Holger Wickström (ca. 1918–2003) from Sjulsmark, Norrbotten, near Piteå. See Wickstrom, *Recollections of Silverhill*, 29–40.

129 Ibid., 32.

130 Walter Sorenson (1913–2004) was born at Wizard Lake, Alberta, the son of Oscar Christian Sorenson, born in Denmark, and Annie Erickson, who migrated with her parents to the Glen Park, Alberta, area from Gagnef, Dalarna, via the United States. He married Helena (19?–1987). Thanks to daughter Susanne Martin, Edmonton, for family information.

131 Baglo, *Augustana Lutherans in Canada*, 58–9. Money for the purchase of the home and property, $2,750, came from the merging of two funds, one for an old folks' home and the other for a children's home.

132 Landelius Biography Collection, volume 2, #366.

133 Otto Theodore Eklund (1884–1979) was born in Malexander, Östergötland, and in 1904 emigrated to Iowa, where he had siblings. Three years later he enrolled at Augustana College and after further education was finally ordained in 1916. He spent the rest of his life pastoring in the Meeting Creek area of Alberta, except for 1922 to 1927 in Vancouver, and retired in 1951 to his farm in Ferintosh. Pastor Eklund is buried in the Camrose cemetery. Thanks to Don Sjoberg, Winnipeg, for bringing his citizenship to my attention. See Landelius Biography Collection, volume 1, #216-217.

134 Elin Rylander (19?–1988) was born in Sweden. After her husband, John Rylander, died she married a man named Hollstedt. See Roberta Larson, "Duthie Doings, Spreading its Wings," *Swedish Press*, August 1988, 14.

135 John Leander (1901–1987) was born in Tvååker, Varberg, Halland, and immigrated to Canada in 1928. He worked for a Danish painter, and also found gold in the Cariboo, then began building houses. He married Evelyn (19?–1993), who immigrated from Sweden in 1926. The couple had a daughter, Jane Den Boer. See Niclas Erlandsson, "John Leander 85+," *Swedish Press*, July 1987, 20–1; see also Eric Matson, "John Leander in Memoriam," *Swedish Press*, November 1987; see also Eric Matson, "Vancouver," *Swedish Press*, May 1993.

136 Howard, *Vancouver's Svenskar*, 102–4; see also "Forty Years Young," *Swedish Press*, July 1987, 13.

137 Karin Trygg, "History of the Swedish-Canadian Rest home," typescript.

138 Nels Pearson (1887–1963) was born in Löberöd, Högseröd, Skåne, and emigrated to the United States in 1907. The following year found him in Winnipeg, where he and his brother Axel founded Pearson Brothers Construction, which specialized in building grain elevators. Axel returned to Sweden during the 1930s. Nels joined most Swedish organizations as well as the Odd Fellows and the Masonic Lodge, and served as treasurer for Canada Conference from 1927 to 1937. See Landelius Biography Collection, volume 3, #100.

139 Brochure, "The Swedish Canadian Home for Senior Citizens, 5419 Roblin Boulevard, Winnipeg, Manitoba." Serving on the original board of directors in 1965 were president Richard Josephson, vice-president E.O. Carlson, secretary Mrs E.M. Hallonquist, treasurer Hartwig Carlson, and E.A.L. Hammarstrand, Miss Elvera Olson, Mrs Nels Pearson, Henry Pehrson, and A.W. Swanson.

140 C.G. Stone and F. Joan Garnett, *Brandon College: A History, 1899–1967* (Brandon: Brandon University, 1969), 35. Thanks to archivist Tom Mitchell, McKee Archives/Library, Brandon University, for providing documents and references pertaining to the Scandinavian Department.

141 Baglo, *Augustana Lutherans in Canada*, 31–2.

142 Stone, *Brandon College*, 36.

143 Carl H. Lager (18?–19?) graduated from Bethel College, Stockholm, in 1905, then emigrated to the United States for post-graduate studies. After a stint at Marburg University in Germany, he carried out archaeological excavations in Jerusalem until 1912, then taught Semitic Languages and Literatures at the University of Chicago until being hired by Brandon College as a professor of Hebrew, Old Testament, and Swedish. Lager authored the chapter about Swedes in Canada published in Sweden's monumental 1924 history *Svenskarna i Amerika* (The Swedes in America) by Hildebrand. For Lager's chapter, see "Svenskarna i Canada," 334–50.

144 Paul Axel Böving (1871–1947) was born in Stora Månstorp, Skåne. In 1899 he graduated from Alnarp Aricultural Institute and worked as a manager of large farms in Sweden, Denmark, and Germany, as a teacher at Ronneby folkhögskola, and culture engineer for Fraenkel and Co. in Göteborg. In 1910 he immigrated to Canada, joining his brother Georg Böving at the government experimental farm near Ottawa. In 1911 he began teaching at the Macdonald Campus of McGill University in Montreal, then around 1915 accepted a position as professor of agriculture at the University of British Columbia in Vancouver. Böving was head of the department from 1919 to 1929, and married Miss Wren from England. See Landelius Biography Collection, volume 1, #114, 117; see also Howard, *Vancouver's Svenskar*, 61–6.

145 Landelius Biography Collection, volume 1, #114.

146 Ibid., volume 2, #065.

147 *Canadian Institute for Nordic Studies Newsletter* 1, no. 2 (November 1988); see also CINS website.

148 Edward W. Laine, "Editor's Introduction," in *Scandinavian-Canadian Studies/Études Scandinaves au Canada: a selection from the papers presented at the first annual meeting held at Ottawa, 1982* (Association for the Advancement of Scandinavian Studies in Canada, 1983), vii–ix.

149 Jan Lundgren was born in Växjö, Småland, and studied in Stockholm before beginning his long tenure at McGill. Married to Margareta, he is also a visiting lecturer in the United States and Sweden.

150 Joan Murray, ed. and intro., *Letters Home: 1859–1906: The Letters of William Blair Bruce* (Moonbeam, Ontario: Penumbra Press, 1982), 23; see also "William Blair Bruce, The Canadian Painter Who Made Sweden His Home," *Swedish Press*, January 2002, 18–19.

12. Links with Sweden

1 In 1976 Aurora twinned with Leksand, Dalarna.

2 IKEA has three stores in British Columbia, two in Alberta, three in Ontario, one in Quebec, and one inWinnipeg.

3 "Swedish Economy," *Visit to Canada of Their Majesties King Carl XVI Gustaf and Queen Silvia of Sweden* (Ottawa: Parliamentary Relations Secretariat, 1988), 2; see also "Canada/Sweden Bilateral Relations," 3.

4 "CompanyFile: Swedish Canadian Chamber of Commerce and Canadian Swedish Business Association," *Swedish Press*, September 1999, 25.

5 The king's grandfather, Gustaf Adolf, had entered Canada briefly as crown prince in 1926. The royal party crossed into Ontario at Niagara

Falls, met with dignitaries, and lunched at the Hotel Clifton, and their train left Canada at Windsor. The occasion was the 150th anniversary of independence in the United States. See Fritz Henriksson, *Med Sveriges kronprinspar genom Amerika* (Stockholm: P.A. Norstedt, 1926), 177–9.

6 *Visit to Canada of Their Majesties King Carl XVI Gustaf and Queen Silvia of Sweden;* for Winnipeg activities see "The King and Queen of Sweden First State Visit to Canada," *Scandinavian Press,* April 1988, 1, 4; for Vancouver see "Duthie Doings: The Royal Visit," *Swedish Press,* May 1988, 15, and "Vancouver," October 1988.

7 "Royal attendance Boosted Visibility for Swedish Companies," *Marketplace USA/Canada: A newsletter from the Swedish Trade Council in the U.S. and Canada* 4 (2006).

8 The Royal Court of Sweden, "Speech Given by The King at the State Banquet in Ottawa on 24 October 2006."

9 Ibid.

10 Alex G. Davidson, "The Swedish Constitution, Nordic Esotericism in Baroque Splendour," *Pietre-Stones Review of Freemasonry* (2005).

11 Raoul Wallenberg (1912–19?) was born into one of Sweden's most prominent banking families, the son of naval officer Raoul Oscar and Maj Wallenberg. His father died before he was born and his mother's father shortly afterwards, but he had a good relationship with his paternal grandfather, diplomat Gustaf Wallenberg, who died in 1937. In 1918 Maj married Fredrik von Dardel and the couple had two children, Nina and Guy, who spearheaded the international effort to get the Russians to release information about their brother. See "Interview: Nina Lagergren," *Swedish Press,* December 2001, 24–5.

12 *Jewish Virtual Library,* "Per Anger (1913–2002)."

13 It is probable that his connection with the United States led Stalin to believe that he was a spy.

14 Norstedt published the Swedish version, *Med Raoul Wallenberg i Budapest,* in Stockholm in 1979, followed in 1981 by *With Raoul Wallenberg in Budapest,* published in New York by Holocaust.

15 Correspondence from David Kilgour, MP Edmonton Strathcona, Chairman, Parliamentary Group for Soviet Jewry, Ottawa, to Linnea Lodge, Grand Lodge Cultural Director United States and Canada, Vasa Order of America Grand Lodge, Edmonton, 10 January 1986; see also *Swedish Press,* January 2006.

16 "StadshusKällaren Nobel," *Swedish Press,* December 2001, 34–5.

17 Lars-Åke Skagegård, *The Remarkable story of Alfred Nobel and the Nobel Prize,* trans. George Varcoe (Uppsala: Konsultförlaget, 1994): 98–107.

Other Nobel laureates who were born in Canada but worked in the United States include Charles B. Huggins (1966 Medicine), David H. Hubel (1981 Medicine), Henry Taube (1983 Chemistry), Sidney Altman (1989 Chemistry), Rudolph Marcus (1992 Chemistry), Bertram N. Brockhouse (1994 Physics), William Vickrey (1996 Economics), and Robert Mundell (1999 Economics).

18 The Canadian Press, "B.C. Natives Celebrate Return of Totem Pole from Sweden," *The Chronicle-Journal* (Thunder Bay), 27 April 2006; see also "Travelling Totem," *The Beaver* (August–September 2006); see also *Swedish Press*, "Interview: Gil Cardinal," January 2004, 20–1; "Interview: Per Kåks," March 2004, 20–1; "First of All," August 2000; "Vancouver Notes," February 2006. The pole was made of red cedar and stood nine metres high.

19 Per Clemensson and Kjell Andersson, *Your Swedish Roots: A Step by Step Handbook* (Provo, UT: MyFamily.com, Inc. and Genline AB, 2004).

20 Per Andersson and Johan Lindhardt, *Långarydssläkten: Länsman Anders Jönssons i Långaryd ättlingar under tre sekel*, 4 volumes (Stockholm: Draking, 2006). For an introduction in English, see the Långarydssläkt website, http://www.langarydsslakten.se/english.htm.

21 Thanks to grandson Richard Williams, Delta, British Columbia, for bringing to my attention that Jon Anderson belonged to Långarydssläkten, for letting me know about Andersson and Lindhardt's landmark work, and for forwarding information from it.

22 Gunnar Gerhard Gustavsson (1908–1992) grew up in Torsås, Småland, emigrated in 1929, and in 1935 married Josephine Wabasons in Ferland. Since she was Catholic, he was baptized before the ceremony. Thanks to Margareta Berg, Kalmar, and Gunnel Nyström, Halmstad, for sending the clipping "Bilden av en svenska i Kanada," *Göteborgs-posten*, 16 January 2005, and other information. Thanks also to Father Maurice, S.J., Thunder Bay, for sharing marriage details from his First Nations records.

23 Thanks to Birgit Kostenius, Luleå, Sweden, for bringing this documentary to my attention and sending information. Thanks also to Alfred Adamson, Keewatin, who knew Kristina, for sharing information about her ring.

24 Gustaf Westin (1878–1972) was born in Nätra, Ångermanland, the son of Nils Hansson Westin (1840–1881) and Chatarina Christina Widenström (1845–1883). His siblings were Hans (1874–1929), Kristina (1876–1948), Margareta (1878–19?), and Carolina (1880–19?). Gustaf immigrated to Kenora in 1903, returning in 1912 for Kristina so that she could work in his restaurant. He married Ida Margareta Norman (1884–1948). Thanks to Birgit Kostenius, Luleå, Sweden, for family information.

25 Stig Petersson was born in Torup, Halland, and lived in Havrida, Småland, before immigrating to Wetaskiwin in 1956. Marion is the daughter of Clarence "Kelly" Ringwall and Edna Backstrom, and granddaughter of Peter and Gölin Ringwall.

26 Daniel Todd Walberg Fuglesang (1967–2008) was born in Thunder Bay, the son of Diane Walberg Harri and Albert Fugelsang. His grandparents were Edith and Renus Walberg and Muriel and Axel Fugelsang. See Julio Gomes, "Student Follows Road to Ruins!" *Chronicle-Journal*, Thunder Bay, 10 September 2003.

27 Letter from Bob Lilja, Provost, Alberta, son of Carl and Emma Lilja, 22 February 2002.

28 Thanks to Heather Walker, North Vancouver, for information about Jennifer Saxell.

29 Correspondence Eleanor Sander, Västra Torup, Sweden, to Elinor Barr, Thunder Bay, 14 June 2005.

30 Thanks to Lasse Berg, Kalmar, Sweden, for bringing this introduction of Canada geese to my attention.

31 Patti Hacault, "Henry's Gift of Hope," *The Times* (Treherne, MB), 28 August 2000; see also her "The Delichtes Welcome a Special Visitor," 1 October 2001; see also Marica Ericson, "Håkan lever tack vare Henry," undated newspaper clipping.

32 Heidi von Born, "Promoting Canadian Literature in Sweden," in *Canada and the Nordic Countries*, ed. Jørn Carlsen and Bengt Streijffert (Århus: Nordic Association for Canadian Studies, 1988), 65–73; see also Ann-Charlotte Berglund, "Interview: Author Heidi von Born," *Swedish Press*, January 1993, 22–3; see also Nels Granewall, "Victoria Notes," *Swedish Press*, November 1992; see also Kerstin Connor, "På bokmässan i Göteborg: Michael Ondaatje, Margaret Atwood och jag," *Swedish Press*, December 1994.

33 Canadian authors whom Heidi von Born has translated into Swedish include Margaret Atwood, Barry Callaghan, Diane Keating, Gwendolyn MacEwan, Daphne Marlatt, Susan Musgrave, Michael Ondaatje, and Robin Skelton.

34 See Dennis Browne, Ottawa, "Canada as seen through the Eyes of Foreigners," Dialogue Canada, http://www.uni.ca/livreouvert/browne_e.html.

35 Mai Klaerke Mikkelsen, Robert Christian Thomsen, and Peter Bakker, eds., *NACS/ANEC Chronicle of Activities and Publications, 1997–2007* (Århus, Denmark: Nordic Association for Canadian Studies, 2007), 12.

36 Ibid., 123.

13. Language, Discrimination, and Assimilation

1 See Nils William Olsson, "Naming Patterns Among Swedish-Americans," *Swedish American Genealogist* 14, no. 2 (June 1994): 83–100; see also Henry A. Person, "The Swedes and Their Family Names," *Scandinavian Studies* 39, no. 3 (August 1967): 209–48.

2 Eastern Townships Research Centre, Sherbrooke, Quebec; Rev. Carl Gustafson, "Swedeville Integral Part of Waterville Story," in James Knutson, comp., "Scandinavian Settlers – Waterville" (1999).

3 The jeweller and shoemaker were the brothers Axel and Frank, who in 1887 came to Vancouver from Karlskrona, Skåne. The following year Emil Peterson (1870–1937) came from Kristinastad, Finland, sent for his fiancée, and established a home on Homer Street. Charles Hjalmar Peterson (18?–1949) jumped ship at the age of twelve, and in 1921 founded Peterson Electrical & Construction, which became a major firm erecting transmission lines throughout the province. See Howard, *Vancouver's Svenskar*, 36–8.

4 Stockholm Binder, "Anna Brita Svensson Westerlund," 1; see also Saskatchewan Archives, Regina, Carl Ian Walker, "Sven Erikson Svedberg, A Swedish Pioneer," 3. The parents of the first four brothers were Eric Svensson (1814–1872) and Anna Brita Zakrisdotter Svensson Westerlund (1831–1919). Erik Zakrison was Anna Brita's brother so the eight sons with different surnames were first cousins.

5 Ljungmark and Åkerman, "The Unknown Emigration – Swedes in Canada," 86; see also Britt Liljewall, "Migration, Literacy, and Networks or Letters from the Lost Land," *Swedish-American Historical Quarterly* 56, nos. 2–3 (April–July 2005): 147–8.

6 Liljewall, "Migration, Literacy, and Networks," 146.

7 Gösta Bergman, *Kortfattad svensk språkhistoria* (Stockholm: Prisma, 1984).

8 Landsarkivet i Östersund, Gunilla Hansson Collection; "Jämtar grundade ett Stockholm i Kanada," 160.

9 John Olof Englund immigrated in 1892 to Ottawa, where he worked as a carpenter. The family moved to the Kipling, Ontario, area in 1894 and he served as postmaster from 1900 to 1905. See Carlson, "From Earth to Glory," 31.

10 Blacksmith Lindahl was a brother-in-law to mill manager Hanson. His wife, Selma (1864–19?), was born in Burträsk, Västerbotten, as was their daughter Svea (1893–196?). Their son, Seth (1904–19?), was born in Glenwood, Nova Scotia. Thanks to John Munro, Halifax, for sending

relevant names from the 1921 Census for Bishop's Falls, Newfoundland, which lists Selma Lindahl as a widow.

11 Goodyear, "Lewis Miller and Harry J. Crowe," 11.

12 Johan Ulrik Frejd (1851–1914) was born in Ekby, Västergötland, and in 1879 married Matilda Gustafsdotter (1859–1928), who was born in Lilla Fallet, Ullervad parish, Västergötland. The couple were active members of the Methodist Church, often giving testimonials to their Lord. Through hard work and perseverance two of their children became teachers, one became a doctor, one became a nurse, and one was a graduate of the Agricultural College in Guelph. Thanks to granddaughter Pat Angus, Orillia, for providing "The Frejd Family Tree" by Arthur Cook as well as a copy of Matilda's graduation certificate from midwifery school, Barnmorske-läroanstalten in Göteborg, dated 16 June 1882.

13 Justus Swanson (1872–1935) was born in Brokhult, Älmhult, Småland, and in 1891 immigrated to Vancouver. In 1896 he married Beata Johansson (1868–1951) from Bohult, Kinnared, Halland. See Margo E. (Swanson) Sargent, "All the Way from Sweden" (1979), unpublished typescript, 29.

14 Johan Taft (1884–1972) was born in Bohuslän, and migrated to Northwestern Ontario ca. 1920 via the United States. In 1927 he married Helga Augusta Wickman (1895–19?), who migrated from Ångermanland in 1923, and settled in Wabigoon. Thanks to daughter Lillian Rodke, Thunder Bay, for family information.

15 Alan B. Anderson, "Scandinavian Settlements in Saskatchewan: Migration History and Changing Ethnocultural Identity," *Scandinavian-Canadian Studies* 2 (1986): 99, states, "Scandinavian Canadians have tended to feel that it is possible to maintain a general interest in the 'Scandinavian connection' without maintaining an ability to speak a Scandinavian language."

16 For other examples of "Swenglish" see Emil Berglund, "The First Years," *Bryggan/The Bridge* 7, nos. 2–3 (1975): 71.

17 For other examples see Roger Källström, "It's Not Your Father's Swedish Anymore," *Sweden and America* (Spring 1995): 17–19.

18 Houser, *The Swedish Community at Eriksdale*, 9–11, 14.

19 Olaf Petter Olsson (1867–1951) was born in Berg, Ångermanland, close to the Lappland border. In 1902, after completing his full military training of fifteen years, he married Alma Margretta Wiberg (1879–1962), born in Rensjönäset near Dorotea, Lappland. They immigrated in 1904–5. See Olson, "And so it happened."

20 Manitoba Archives, MG 14, C 28, Box 1, File 1, W.J. Sisler Collection, "The Swedish Colony – New Stockholm," 5–7.

21 William J. Sisler, *Spelling and Language Lessons for Foreign Classes Learning English* (Toronto: Macmillan, 1917) and *Peaceful Invasion* (Winnipeg: Ketchen, 1944).

22 Bertha (1892–1968) and Emma Hall (1893–19?) were born in Lit, Jämtland, the daughters of Erik Hall (1871–1938) and his wife, Elisabet Lithander (1871–1947). The family immigrated in 1903–4. See *Forest to Field*, 394–6.

23 Carlson, *We Come to Canada and the First Ten Years*, 19, 26.

24 Ibid., 26.

25 J. Donald Wilson and Jørgen Dahlie, "Introduction," *Canadian Ethnic Studies, Special Issue: Ethnic Radicals* 10, no. 2 (1978): 2.

26 Jorgen Dahlie, "No Fixed Boundaries: Scandinavian Responses to Schooling in Western Canada," in *Frontières Ethniques en Devenir/Emerging Boundaries*, ed. Danielle Juteau Lee (Ottawa: Canadian Ethnic Studies Association, 1979), 7:117–29.

27 Wickstrom, *Recollections of Silverhill*, 45.

28 Ibid., 5, quoting from Bergman, *British Columbia och dess svenska innebyggare*, 164.

29 Wickstrom, *Recollections of Silverhill*, 2.

30 "Eric Gudmundson by their [grand] daughter, Siv. W.," in *Crowsnest and Its People* (Coleman, AB: Crowsnest Pass Historical Society, 1979), 563. Eric Gudmundson and his wife immigrated from Sweden in 1923 with sons Uno, eight, and Arne, four. Helen was born in Coleman.

31 Carl G. Nelson, *Memoarer och reseskildringar* (San Diego, 1971), 28–9. Karl Gust Nilsson (ca. 1893–19?) emigrated from Vassända-Naglum parish near Vänersborg, Västergötland, in April 1913 and came directly to Winnipeg. After a year and a half in Canada he left for the United States.

32 Viola Burkett, "Shellborn, Magnus and Amanda," in *Forest to Field*, 615.

33 *Swedish Press*, Commemorative Issue, June 1999, 7–8; see also UBCL SC, Matthew Lindfors Fonds, A IV B, Box 3; Per Nilsson-Tannér, "Offerdalspojke kulturambassadör i Canada," *Östersunds-Posten*, 20 September 1951.

34 Ibid., English-language newspaper clipping and ad dated 30 September 1937.

35 Peter Stenberg, "Nordic Languages and Programmes at Canadian Universities in Comparison with US Universities," in Gudrun Björk Gudsteins and John Erik Fossum, *Rediscoveriong Canada: Culture and Politics* (Nordic Association for Canadian Studies #19, 2002), 202. See also Stone, *Brandon College*, 35, which states that in 1909 the University of

Manitoba made Swedish an optional subject at the request of the board of directors of Brandon College.

36 Thure Hedman (1886–1971) was born in Sweden, and studied in Switzerland, Germany, and the United States before arriving at Queen's University in 1915. Five years later he became associate professor of German at University College, University of Toronto, where he taught courses on Scandinavian theatre and the Danish, Norwegian, and Swedish languages, retiring in 1950. See Stenberg, "Nordic Languages," 201.

37 Ibid., Stenberg, "Nordic Languages," 202.

38 William Clare Wonders (1924–?) was born in Toronto. He founded the Department of Geography at the University of Alberta, and co-founded the Boreal Institute for Northern Studies, now called the Canadian Circumpolar Institute. In 1962–3 he was guest professor at Uppsala University, Sweden, which presented him with an honorary doctorate. In 1983 he was the keynote speaker at the annual meeting of Swedish geographers at Umeå University. His papers and library are housed at the University of Alberta Archives. Thanks to Carin Routledge, Edmonton, for checking the collection for relevant items and taking notes.

39 "Edmonton Notes," *Swedish Press*, March 2010.

40 Stenberg, "Nordic Languages and Programmes at Canadian Universities," 202, 204–5; see also K.W. Domier, "History of the Scandinavian Studies Association" (Edmonton, 2006), typescript, 2 pages; see also the university website.

41 Manitoba Archives C551-552, Swedish Community Oral History Collection, Ann Richter. Ann's dad, Carl Stolz (1883–19?), was born in Överkalix, Norrbotten, and immigrated to Prince Albert in 1912. Her mother, Johanna Näsman (1881–19?), who came from Orrmo near Lillhärdal, Härjedalen, followed in 1914 with their three sons. Ann was born in Valbrand, Saskatchewan, in 1919.

42 Saskatchewan Archives; Eliason, "Biography of a Swedish Immigrant," 29–31.

43 Ibid., 32. Frank Eliason (1883–1956) was born in Högen, Örs socken, Dalsland, and emigrated to Minneapolis, where he concluded that the producers of wealth, the labourers and the farmers, should unite to build a cooperative society. In 1910 he moved to Wynard and put his ideas into practice. In 1932 his draft document was accepted as the basis for the program adopted by the CCF political party, now NDP.

44 Eva St Jean, "Letters from the Promised Land," 212, 214–15.

45 John Murray Gibbon, *Canadian Mosaic: The Making of the Canadian Nation*, (Toronto: McClelland and Stewart, 1938), 226–9. Gibbon immigrated

from Scotland to Montreal in 1913 to begin his employment with the CPR, and in 1921 became founding president of the Canadian Authors Association. His book *Scots in Canada* was published in 1911, followed by *French Canadian Folk Songs* in 1928, and *Steel of Empire: The Romantic History of the Canadian Pacific* in 1935.

46 Canon E.A. Wharton Gill, "A Norse Wedding in Manitoba," in *Forest to Field*, 34.

47 Manitoba Archives, Surveyor Field Book, James Dickson, Dominion Land Surveyor, survey of Township 17, Range 18, west of Principal Meridian in Manitoba. Thanks to Ted Simonson, Winnipeg, for bringing this comment to my attention.

48 Ljungmark, *Svenskarna i Winnipeg*, 180, credits *Svenska Canada-tidningen* issues dated 8 April 1908, 27 January 1915, and 24 January 1917.

49 William McCloy, *Scandinavians in Europe and in Canada* (Presbyterian Church in Canada, Board of Home Missions, 1913), 27.

50 Vennerström, *Kanada och Kanadasvenskarna*, 123, 144, 148, 150–1; see also Gösta Bagge, "Kanada som immigrationsland: Några anteckningar från en studieresa," in *Sociala meddelanden 1925*, n:r 8 (Stockholm: Norstedt, 1925).

51 Red Deer and District Archives: Biography file, Telning Family; Andrew Telning's letter to his brother-in-law in Sweden, 18 October 1904. Andrew Telning (1852–1938) was born in Fågelvik, Sweden, the son of John Telning (1819–1912). Together they emigrated to Red Wing, Minnesota, in 1873, where Andrew married. The couple moved to Burnt Lake, Alberta, in 1902; in 1911 to Rocky Mountain House, Alberta; in 1917 to Victoria, British Columbia, then to New Westminster, and Essondale, and died in Nanaimo. See also newspaper clipping, "Pioneers of Central Alberta: Telning Family History Covers Span of 148 Years" (ca. 1967).

52 Houser, *The Swedish Community at Eriksdale*, is based upon interviews with thirty-eight principal informants. It is a study of Swedish ethno-cultural traditions in Ranges 5 and 6 west of Township 22 in what later became the Rural Municipality of Eriksdale.

53 Ibid., 93–4.

54 Ljungmark, "Swedes in Winnipeg up to the 1940s," 44.

55 Richard Edenholm was born in Kalmar län, Småland, and immigrated in 1907–8 to Vancouver. Signe (1900–19?) was Norwegian. In 1912 she came to Vancouver with her family, and in 1917 started as dining-room girl at Mrs Engblom's boarding house, where she met Richard.

56 Howard, *Vancouver's Svenskar*, 54.

57 F.C. Cooper, *In the Canadian Bush* (London, UK: Heath, Stanton & Ouseley, 1914), 41.

58 Landsarkivet i Göteborg; Sam Widenfelt's family archive: "Trip to Montreal 1920–1922." Sam E. Widenfelt (ca. 1897–19?) immigrated in May 1920. Preceding him at the Swedish Consulate from 1916 to 1918 was Hans Fredrik Johansson Widenfelt, probably a relative.

59 Charles Davis Anderson (1829–1914) emigrated from Sweden to Chicago in 1853, and in 1888 married Caroline S. Johnstone in Winnipeg. They had no children. See *Pioneers and Early Citizens of Manitoba: A Dictionary of Manitoba Biography from the Earliest Times to 1920* (Winnipeg: Peguis, 1971), 4; see also "Manitoba's First Grand Master Dead," *Manitoba Morning Free Press*, 27 July 1914; see also Jill Seaholm, "Swedish-American Lodges and Other Organizations," *Swedish American Genealogist* 26, no. 3 (September 2006): 12, which states that "The Odd Fellows started a Chicago Swedish lodge in 1872."

60 Märta Karolina Larsson (1892–1995) was born in Ragunda, Jämtland, the daughter of Karl E. and Sara Larsson. Thanks to Johnny Linden, Göteborg, for family information.

61 *Who's Who in Alberta: A Biographical Directory* (Saskatoon: Lyone Publications, 1957). Of the twenty-two, fifteen had been born in Alberta, two in Manitoba, four in the United States, and one in Sweden.

62 Arthur Erickson (1924–2009) was born in Vancouver, the son of Oscar Ludwig Erickson, whose parents immigrated from Skåne in the 1880s. Thanks to Don Erickson, Bowen Island, British Columbia, for family information. See "Interview: Arthur Erickson," *Swedish Press*, June 1993, 20–1.

63 Thomas Rodney Berger (1933–20?) was born in Victoria, practised law in Vancouver from 1957 to 1972, and in the 1960s was elected as MLA and as MP for the NDP. His father immigrated from Göteborg in 1912. See "Interview: Tom Berger," *Swedish Press*, June 1993, 24–5.

64 Lois Elsa Hole (1929–2005) was born in Buchanan, Saskatchewan, with a Swedish mother, Elsa Nordström from Småland. Hole wrote a number of books about gardening, appearing regularly on CBC TV's *Canadian Gardener*. See "Alberta Notes," *Swedish Press*, March 2005; see also "Alberta's Beloved First Lady: A Farmer, Businesswoman, School Trustee, University Chancellor and Lieutenant-Governor, Alberta's 'Queen of Hugs' Produced a Bountiful Harvest from a Lifetime of Good Works," *Edmonton Journal*, 8 January 2005.

65 McCloy, *Scandinavians in Europe and in Canada*, 22.

14. Literature

1 The National Library in Sweden holds a copy of Hofstrand's book.
2 Adrian Molin wrote several books and brochures published by the National Association Against the Emigration, including *Några drag af kolonisationen i Canada* (1913).
3 Ivar Vetterström, *Kanada och Kanadasvenskarna* (Canada and the Swedish Canadians), published in 1926.
4 Paul Waldenström, *Genom Canada* (Through Canada), published in 1905, is an early example, followed in 1924 by E. Ericson, *Tänker du emigrera?* (Are You Thinking of Emigrating?).
5 Ulf Jonas Björk, "The Dangerous Prairies of Texas: The Western Dime Novel in Sweden, 1900–1908," *Swedish-American Historical Quarterly* 55, no. 3 (July 2004): 165–78. For a study of the impact of these novels on immigrants to the Rocky Mountain region, based on their letters from 1880 to 1917, see Jennifer Eastman Attebery, "Swedish Immigrants and the Myth of the West," ibid., 179–91.
6 Gunlög Fur, "Romantic Relations. Swedish Attitudes towards Indians during the Twentieth Century," ibid., 155.
7 Bengt Streijffert, "Karl Gunnarson's Canada," in *Canada and the Nordic Countries in Times of Reorientation: Literature and Criticixm*, ed. Jørn Carlsen, (Nordic Association for Canadian Studies #12, 1998), 203.
8 Karl Gunnarson (1885–1954) was born Karl Gunnar Schulze in Vreta Kloster, Östergötland. His other titles about Canada are *Kamratliv och äventyr på Kanadas prärier* (Comrades and Adventures on the Canadian Prairies) in 1931, *Åter i Kanada som cowboy och pälsjägare* (Back in Canada as Trapper and Cowboy) in 1941, and *Som ranchägare bland indianer* (As a Ranchowner among Indians) in 1945. Thanks to grandson Lasse Schulze, Sweden, for family information. See also www.lysator.liu.se/runeberg/authors/schulgun.html.
9 Streijffert, "Karl Gunnarson's Canada," 204.
10 Ibid.
11 Harry Macfie (1879–1956) was born Andrew Harry Thorburn Macfie in Lysekil, Bohuslän, and in 1907 married Anna Maria Roland. The family lived in a house called Skottorp in Ljungskile. Thanks to granddaughter Eva Loader, Ljungskile, for family information. See also Dougald Macfie, "Så minns jag Harry!" *Minnesbilder från Ljungskilebygden* (Ljungskileortens Hembygdsförening, 1995), 36–41; see also ibid., Inger Dejke, "Guldgrävare – kanotkonstruktör – författare," 42–51.
12 Correspondence from Eva Loader, Ljungskile, Sweden, 4 June 2004.

13 For two decades, from 1891 to 1911, no other part of the province would match Northwestern Ontario in gold production.

14 Harry is named in the 1901 census as Henry McFee, a boarder in Kenora. At the same time there was a steamboat named *The Jenny Lind* plying Lake of the Woods.

15 Sam Kilburn (1877–1926) was born in Manchester, England. His mother was a highlander named Cameron, and related to the Macfies.

16 Harry Macfie and Hans G. Westerlund, *Wasa-Wasa: Äventyr som trapper och guldgrävare i Canada och Alaska*, (Stockholm: Bonnier, 1935), ch. 1. In the preface Westerlund states that Harry Macfie wrote the book himself but insisted that Westerlund's name appear on the title page. Westerlund admitted lightly editing the work.

17 Harry Macfie and Hans G. Westerlund, *Wasa-Wasa: A Tale of Trails and Treasure*, trans. from Swedish by F.H. Lyon (London: Allen and Unwin, 1951). Norton in New York published the translation simultaneously.

18 Ibid., 115–16.

19 Elisabeth Mårald, "A Postmodern Geographical Analysis of the Canadian Wilderness as Documented in Harry Macfie's Texts," typescript of a paper delivered at a 2004 conference in Riga.

20 In addition to *Wasa-Wasa* in 1935, there was *Lägereldar längesen* (Campfires of Long Ago) in 1936, *Norrskenets män* (Men of the Northern Lights) in 1938 about the RCMP, and *Farväl Falcon Lake* (Goodbye, Falcon Lake) in 1943. He followed up with two books about Alaska, *Drivved* in 1949, illustrated by his son Gordon Macfie, and *Alaskakust* (1951).

21 Thanks to Sven Eriksson, Mats Rehnström, and Bertil Wockatz for information about the Harry Macfie Canoe Club.

22 Reg Clayton, "Swedish Historian Follows the Trail of Turn-of-the-Century Adventurer," *Lake of the Woods Enterprise*, 9 July 2005; see also Bertil Wockatz, "I Harry Macfies fotspår," *Släktkrönikan; Tidning för medlemmar av Släktföreningen Thorburn-Macfie*, Nr 62 (December 1998): 24–5; see also Gerald F. Holm and Anthony P. Buchner, *A Place of Honour – Manitoba's War Dead Commemorated in its Geography* (Winnipeg: Geographical Names Program, 2002), 218, 252. Kilborn Lake is named after Sergeant Allison Frank Kilborn of Virden, and MacFie Lake after Private John G. MacFie of Selkirk.

23 "The Story about Harry Macfie," http://hem3.passagen.se/mare2504/hmcc/harry_eng.htm.

24 Isak Albert Viksten (1889–1969) was born in Graninge, Ångermanland, the eldest son of Fredrik Viksten and Fredrika Åberg. As a teenager he wrote the newsletter *Handposten* for workers in a single copy, and

submitted cartoons and articles to *Nya Norrland*. In 1924 he married Elisabet Brolin (1894–1970), and had the children Sven, Hans, Karin, and Märta.

25 The communist Member of Parliament, Karl Kilbom, founded *Folket i Bild* in 1934 as an alternative to the "yellow press."

26 Johan Adolf Viksten (1902–1986) married Mabel Kalmakoff (1910–19?) in 1939. They ended up on a fur farm in Surrey, British Columbia.

27 Gustav Algot Viksten (1904–1963) married Elsie Bessie Baker in 1952. The family lived in Whitehorse, where Gus trapped for a living. For one of Albert's stories about Gus, see "LastWord/SistaOrdet," *Swedish Press*, October 2005, 34.

28 Erik Ludvig Viksten (1905–1985) built a cabin on Horsefly Lake, and remained a bachelor all his life.

29 Albert Viksten, *Vilda vägar västerut* (1938), as translated by Ann-Charlotte Berglund in Viksten-Koerner, *Albert Viksten: A Portrait of My Father*, 53.

30 Albert Viksten, "Mitt Liv, Ett Äventyr" (1971) in ibid., 191.

31 *Guds eget land* (God's own country) in 1938, *I guldjägares spår: resan till Yukon och Alaska* (In Goldseekers' Footsteps: The Trip to Yukon and Alaska) in 1951, and *Pälsjägarnas paradis* (The Trappers' Paradise) in 1959.

32 Karin Elisabet Viksten-Koerner (1928–2005) immigrated first to Vancouver, then went to San Francisco, and finally to Victoria. In 1949 she married Nicholas Thomas Koerner (1925–2001). Karin was an artist, and her paintings have been displayed at, among other places, the Art Gallery of Greater Victoria.

33 In addition to Albert Viksten's own writings they include Karin's childhood memories and her journalist brother Sven's account of a trip to Canada in 1989. The book's translator, Ann-Charlotte Berglund, is a freelance journalist fluent in both languages. She also translated the poetry of Karin's other brother, Hans, which was published in 1999 along with his watercolours under the title *Life Is a Balancing Act*.

34 Geo. Johansson-Alvo, "Adolf Viksten: En kulturpersonlighet och original urtiden," *Swedish Press*, April 1987, 14–15, which includes one of his articles, "En liten stund," published in *Nya svenska pressen* in 1963; see also "Kändisen Adolf Viksten 80 år," *Nya svenska pressen*, 23 March 1983, 3.

35 Streijffert, "Karl Gunnarson's Canada," 206. The comic strip was published until about 1960 by the magazine *Rekordmagasinet*.

36 Sven Herman Axel Delblanc (1931–1992) was born in the Swan River Hospital in Manitoba, and lived with his parents, Siegfrid Axel Herman Delblanc and Anna Nordfält, and older sisters Elsa and Gudrun, in

Minitonas. Siegfrid immigrated in July 1927 and Anna and the girls followed in October. The family returned to Hedeby, Södermanland, in 1935, but after his divorce Siegfrid returned to Canada and raised another family. Sven studied at the University of Uppsala, receiving his PhD in 1965. By that time he had already published five of his thirty-nine books. Sven visited Minitonas in 1947 and again in 1983. See "Literary Giant Sven Delblanc: Interview," *Swedish Press*, March 1988, 34–6.

37 Photos of the family and their farm were published in Helge Nelson's "Kolonisation och befolkningsförskjutning inom Kanadas prärieprovinser," *Ymer* (1934): 176, and *Swedes and the Swedish Settlements in North America*, 356.

38 Alf Brorson, "Ett Piece of Canada in Sven Delblanc's Authorship," *Bryggan/The Bridge* 4 (2008): 8.

39 The four books in the series are *Samuels bok* (1981), *Samuels döttrar* (1983), *Kanaans land* (1984), and *Maria ensam* (1985), all published in Stockholm by Bonniers.

40 John Steinbeck won the Pulitzer Prize for his 1939 novel, *The Grapes of Wrath*, which told about a poor family of sharecroppers driven from their home in Oklahoma during the Depression. Steinbeck won the 1962 Nobel Prize for Literature.

41 Emigrantinstitutet has survived recent political bickering and continues to serve the public, but by appointment only. Family research service has been moved to the House of Emigrants in Göteborg.

42 L. Anders Sandberg, "Literature as Social History: A Swedish Novelist in Manitoba," *Prairie Forum* 13, no. 1 (Spring 1988): 84, quoting Y.F. Tuan, "Literature and Geography" in *Humanistic Geography*, ed. D. Ley and M. Samuels (Chicago: Maaroufa, 1978), 197. For a comparative study see Rochelle Wright, "Delblanc's *Kanaans land* and Moberg's Emigrant Tetralogy: Intertextuality and Transformation," *Scandinavian-Canadian Studies* 5 (1992): 81–93. See also Christopher S. Hale, "Ethnic Minorities on the Canadian Prairies in the Writings of Aksel Sandemose and Sven Delblanc," *Scandinavian-Canadian Studies* 8 (1985): 37–55.

43 Sandberg, "Literature as Social History," 93. Sandberg, a professor in environmental studies at York University, came to Canada in the mid-1970s to study at Simon Fraser University on an athletic scholarship. His honours essay explored the MacKenzie Valley Pipeline inquiry; his master's thesis, the British Columbia salmon canning industry; and his doctoral dissertation, the rise and fall of the steel industry in Nova Scotia. Most of his other publications deal with forestry in Ontario, Quebec, and the Maritimes.

44 Sven Delblanc, "A Storyteller's Story," *Saturday Night* 102, no. 12 (December 1987): 71.

45 Of his research material, ten oral interviews are housed at Glenbow Museum in Calgary. Everything else, including photographs and videotapes, was donated to the Emigrant Institute in Växjö, Sweden. See correspondence from Gunnar Nilsson, Farsta, 23 December 2004.

46 Manfred Johnson (1908–?) was born in Grundtjärn, Ångermanland, and immigrated in 1928 to Blind River, Ontario, where he heard there was bush work. See Nilsson, *De sista svenska rösterna*, 52–8.

47 Hans Bergman, *British Columbia och dess svenska innebyggare. Historia, topografi, klimat, resurser, biografi, med 5 fargtrycksplanscher och 150 illustrationer darav 68 portratt* (Victoria, BC, 1923).

48 Hans Bergman (187?–1926) was born in Tännäs, Härjedalen, and in 1893 emigrated to the United States but lived in Vancouver for a while, the home of his brothers Solomon and John Bergman. After completing the history of British Columbia in Swedish, Hans compiled a history in English of Scandinavians in Tacoma and Pierce County in the United States. See City of Vancouver Archives; Olof Seaholm, "Sweden's Contributions to Canada," typescript compiled in 1977; see also UBCL SC, A VII B, Seaholm Collection., "Hans Bergman"; see also Ivar Vennerström, *Kanada och Kanadasvenskarna*, 57–8.

49 Rönnqvist, *Svea folk i Babels land*.

50 John Utterström (ca. 1891–19?) was born in Överluleå parish, Norrbotten, and emigrated in 1909 to Chicago. In 1910 his older brother Otto Johansson (ca. 1888–19?) joined him in Seattle. When another brother, Edvin Utterström (ca. 1899–19?), emigrated in 1927, his destination was Vancouver. Thanks to John's daughter-in-law Rena Utterström, Bellingham, Washington, for family information. See also dust cover for John Utterström, *Straws in the Wind* (New York: Vanity Press, 1962).

51 F:son is the shortened form for Fredriksson.

52 According to correspondence with daughter-in-law Rena Utterstrom, 19 October 2006, "John and Sven [also] made a movie in Canada called *Itchy Scratchy* that was sold to the Swedish film industry."

53 Frederick Philip Grove (1879–1948) was born in Germany as Felix Paul Berthold Friedrich Greve. A translator, he spent a brief period in debtors' prison, then in 1909 emigrated to the United States, landing in Manitoba in 1912 under his new name. In his autobiography, *In Search of Myself*, he invented a childhood in Sweden and stressed his gift for languages.

54 Jane Mattisson, "Outside of Things: Swedish Emigrants, the English Language and the Canadian Prairie Dream," paper delivered at the

8th Nordic Conference for English Studies, Göteborg University, 24–6 May 2001.

55 Louise Vendela Augusta Jona Flach (1894–1992) was born in Svensksund, Vikbolandet, Östergötland, the daughter of Sixten Flach and Hillevid Neegaard from Denmark. Her parents were close friends of Prince Carl of Sweden, and her godmother was Princess Louise of Denmark. She spoke Swedish, Danish, German, French, and English. See Merilyn Mohr, "To Whom the Wilderness Speaks: The Remarkable Life of Louise de Kiriline Lawrence," *Harrowsmith* 83 (January–February 1989): 72–81; see also Marianne Gosztonyi Ainley, "In Memoriam: Louise de Kiriline Lawrence, 1894–1992," *The Auk* 109, no. 4 (1992), 909–10; see also LAC, Louise de Kiriline Lawrence Fonds, 5.13 metres.

56 *The Loghouse Nest* in 1945, *The Lovely and the Wild* in 1968, *MAR: A Glimpse into the Natural Life of a Bird* in 1976, and *To Whom the Wilderness Speaks* in 1980, all reprinted during the 1980s by Natural Heritage, Toronto.

57 Mohr, "To Whom the Wilderness Speaks," 76.

58 Ibid., 74.

59 Hälle Flygare (1936–) grew up in Hörby, Skåne. These days he conducts nature and wildlife photographic tours in Canada, Sweden, Norway, and Finland from his home base in Canmore, Alberta.

60 *The Sir Alexander Mackenzie "Canada Sea-to-Sea" Bicentennial Expeditions 1989–1993*, information folder published by Lakehead University, One Step Beyond Adventure Group, and the Alexander Mackenzie Trail Association, 1993.

61 Britt Holmström (1946–) was born in Malmö, Skåne, and before immigrating to Canada in the 1970s had already published the novel *Pepparmint-Gin* in Sweden. She earned a visual arts degree in Ontario, and bachelor's and master's degrees in microbiology in Saskatchewan.

62 Irina Hedman (1935–) was born in Viborg, Finland, now Vyborg, Russia. She was sent to neutral Sweden in 1944, learned Swedish, and graduated from Uppsala University. She married Rolf Hedman from Torsång, Dalarna, and in 1970 they immigrated to Toronto, where she worked at the Metropolitan Toronto Reference Library as a Nordic specialist. See *Canada* (Stockholm: Generalstabens litografiska.anstalts förlag, 1976). Thanks to Irina Hedman, Toronto, for family information.

63 Signe Olson Peterson (1890–1963) was born in Övre Ullerud parish, Värmland, and in 1911 immigrated to Port Arthur, where friends from the same area had founded a Baptist church. Thanks to Eva-Lena Nilsson, Emigrant Register, Karlstad, Sweden, for bringing this group to my attention. Canada's Apostle, Rev Fred Palmborg, organized the

congregation 24 September 1905, and the church was built in 1909. See Per Hedvall, "History of the Scandinavian Baptist Church in Port Arthur, 25th Anniversary" (1930), translated by Myrtle Koreen, which finishes with Signe's four-page poem in honour of the occasion. See also G. William Carlson, *"God Knows What is Best": Poems by Signe Olson Peterson*, Swedish poems edited and read by Jean Hanslin, Bethel College Library, 7 October 2000.

64 G. William Carlson, "The Pietist Poetry of Signe Olson Peterson," *The Baptist Pietist Clarion* 5, no. 1 (September 2006): 6. The Swedish Baptist papers *Svenska Standaret, Midvinter, Sondagskolan och Hemmet,* and *Sanningens Vän* published many of Signe's poems.

65 G. William Carlson, "The Pietist Poetry of Signe Olson Peterson: 'The Letter Started on' Understanding the Immigrant Experience," *The Baptist Pietist Clarion* 6, no. 1 (June 2007): 13.

66 Watson Kirkconnell, *Canadian Overtones: An Anthology of Canadian Poetry Written Originally in Icelandic, Swedish, Norwegian, Hungarian, Italian, Greek, and Ukrainian, and Now Translated and Edited with Biographical, Historical, Critical and Bibliographical Notes* (Winnipeg, 1935).

67 Arthur Antonius Anderson (1894–1969) was born in Malmberget, Lappland, and trained as a forester. He became manager of a sawmill and in 1919 married Maria Elizabeth Roos. In 1924 the family immigrated to Winnipeg, where Arthur became a prominent member of the Swedish community as a partner in the Hermanson-Anderson Steamship Agencies. See Kirkconnell, *Canadian Overtones*, 50, 54–7. In 2013 a granddaughter, Laurel Anderson-McCallum of Winnipeg, published his book of poetry in its entirety under the title *Stoft/Dust of Our Being*, with English translation by Ellen Boryen.

68 Arthur A. Anderson, "Svenskar och svenska insatser i Kanada," in Axel Boethius et al., *Vår svenska stam på utländsk mark: Svenska öden och insatser i främmande land* (Stockholm: Lindqvist, 1952), 235–57.

69 Gerhard Hilarius Silver (1889–1959) was born in Järpen, Jämtland, and in 1910 "Hille," as he was called, immigrated to Bergland, Ontario, where family members had settled on homesteads. See Kirkconnell, *Canadian Overtones*, 50, 52–4.

70 G.H. Silver (pseud. Thord Bjorke), *I vargatider: En näve kampdikter* (Bergland, ON: Författarens förlag, 1918), 39 pages, reprinted in 1986 by the Silver family, North Bay, who also published an English version in 1994 titled *In Wolfish Times (In Times of Strife): A Handful of Battle Poems*, translated by Irina Hedman. The English version includes biographies of author and translator. See also G.H. Silver, "Jämtland," in *Hälsning till*

hembygden i Jämtland från jämtar i Canada och Förenta staterna (Winnipeg: Svenska förbundet i Canada, 1932), 2–3. Silver also composed lyrics and music for at least one song.

71 Sten Wiktor Goerwell (1898–19?) was born in Eskilstuna, Södermanland, a relative of the celebrated poet Carl Jonas Ludwig Almqvist. He emigrated in 1920 and married Nance Margaret Sundin in 1926. See Kirkconnell, *Canadian Overtones*, 50, 58–60.

72 Kirkconnell, *Canadian Overtones*, 60, from "Salutation to the Swedish Students at Brandon College, November 12, 1921."

73 Byrna Barclay was born in Saskatoon. See *Livelong Legacies* (Livelong: Livelong Historical Society, 1981), 192–7; see also "Interview: Byrna Barclay," *Swedish Press*, April 1986, 18.

74 Margaret Kirkland Avison (1918–2007) was born in Galt and grew up in Regina and Calgary. Her Governor General's awards were for *Winter Sun* (1960) and *No Time* (1990). In 1984 she was made an Officer of the Order of Canada.

75 Bernice Lever (1936–) was born in Smithers, British Columbia, the granddaughter of Lars Erick Strid and his wife, Anna Brita Fors, who had immigrated to Camrose. Her paternal heritage is Swiss. Thanks to Bernice Lever for family information. See her website, www.colourofwords.com.

76 T. Anders Carson (1970–) lives in Portland, Ontario, with his wife and family. His books include *Objects in Mirror Are Closer than They Appear, Salt Pork and Sunsets, Folding the Crane, A Different Shred of Skin,* and *Unlocking the Muse: An Anthology of Contemporary Canadian Verse.* In 2004 the youth team he coached, Ontario's Portland Football Club, competed for the Gothia Cup in Göteborg. Through his perseverance the team managed to qualify, even though it included two girls. See Jonas Jakobsson, "Anders Carson kan konsten att hitta nya vägar," *Hallandsposten*, 2004.

77 Gerald F. Holm is a grandson of O.N.E. Holm, who emigrated from Jämtland to the Minnedosa area.

78 Axel V. Nilsson, *Brända vingar* (Ystad: Tryckeri-A.-B. Aurora, 1947). Nilsson immigrated to Montreal in 1923, and then worked at a power station at Lake St John, where he played in an orchestra. The following year he moved to New York, returning to Sweden in 1938.

79 David Flood, *Med gott humör i bagaget* (Uppsala: J.A. Lindblad, 1941). Flood probably migrated in the early 1920s. He opens his book by telling about labour problems in Värmland, and then tells about his many jobs before returning to Sweden. Five of the book's fifteen chapters are about

Canada, namely Red Lake, Great Bear Lake, Nelson River, Berens River, and Churchill.

80 Axel Linus Johnsson (ca. 1887–1945) was born in Rakåsa, Fölene, Västergötland, and died of tuberculosis in Bolltorp, Östergötland. He lived in Canada from 1906 to 1921. See Landelius binder, volume 2, #133. His book, *Femton år i Kanada*, is not listed by Sweden's national library.

81 Axel Törnblom, *Emigrantens minnen* (Vikmanshyttan: Eget förlag, 1982). Törnblom wrote the text for Alex Karlsson (born Axel Carlson), (ca. 1896–ca. 1986), who came to Winnipeg in late 1923 from Dalom, Ångermanland. He had trained as a goldsmith and worked for five years as a printer, but could find only labouring jobs as a bush-, sawmill, or railway worker in Northwestern Ontario – Kenora, Keewatin, Osaquan, Upsala, Fort William, Port Arthur, and Nipigon. Because of the quota in the United States Karlsson had to wait until ca. 1926 before leaving for Detroit where he had relatives. He returned to Sweden and died there.

82 Ragnar Emmanuel Carlsson (1899–1963) was listed as a sailor when he immigrated from Västervik, Småland, to Winnipeg in 1928. By this time he had published three books about the sea. He returned to Canada in 1935 as a mineworker, bound for Kamloops. His books about Canada are *Män av gamla stammen: Historier från Brittiska Columbia* (Stockholm: Seelig, 1942), and *Ung man gick west: Ett präriereportage* (Västervik: Rese Förlag, 1962). He published eight books in all.

83 Albin Plym, *Rallarliv i Canada* (1950) and *Rallare och guldgrävare* (1952), both published in Stockholm by Arbetarkultur.

84 Österberg, ed., *Från Calmare Nyckel till Leif Viking* (1959).

15. Emerging Visibility

1 Rönnqvist, "Scattered Swedes and Single Settlers," 94.

Appendix 1: Place Names

1 Otto Robert Landelius, *Swedish Place-Names in North America*, trans. Karin Franzén, ed. Raymond Jarvi (Carbondale: Southern Illinois University Press, 1985), 261–311.

2 Landelius, *Swedish Place-Names*, 261; see also Walter F. Wedin, "Seeds and Swedes: Emigrant Clover from Alsike," *Swedish-American Historical Quarterly* 57, no. 1 (January 2006): 33–59.

3 Anders Hilding "Andy" Ronnander (ca. 1905–2003) was born in Bjuråker, Hälsingland, and in 1924 immigrated to Winnipeg, where his brother Gus lived. Thanks to niece Margaret Hewitt, Winnipeg, for family information.

4 Unless otherwise cited, information about post offices and postmasters comes from data posted on ArchiviaNet by Library and Archives Canada.

5 *Where the Red Willow Grew*, 278–81.

6 Landelius, *Swedish Place-Names*, 296; see also *Water Under the Bridge*, 322.

7 Tony Berglund (1898–1966) was born Anton Berglund in Mäland, Skog, Ångermanland, and immigrated with his parents in 1907.

8 Landelius, *Swedish Place-Names*, 300.

9 Ibid., 269.

10 Ibid.

11 Ibid., 261. Carl John Blomquist (1866–1942) was born in Misterhult parish, Kalmar län, Småland, and emigrated to North Dakota in 1888. See also *Pioneers and Progress*, 176; see also Fihn, "Canadamissionen," 217; see also "Blomquists Broke Trails," in Clarence Howard Stout, *From Frontier Days in Leduc and District: 65 Years of Progress, 1891–1956* (Leduc Historical Society and the 75th Anniversary Committee, [1956] 1980), 129; see also *Scandinavian Connections*, 56–7; see also Harry Max Sanders, *The Story Behind Alberta Names: How Cities, Towns, Villages and Hamlets got their Names* (Calgary: Red Deer Press, 2003).

12 A.G. Bergquist, his wife, Anna, and two children came from Sweden in 1896 and in 1901 moved to land east of Ponoka, Alberta. See *Mecca Glen Memories*, 2nd ed. (2001), 229–30.

13 The Swedish families were the Fred Walbergs, Charles Lindbergs, and John Sandstroms; Fugelsangs were Norwegian. See Jen Thompson, "What's in a Name?", *Green Mantle*, 30 January 1995, 7; see also Scandinavian Heritage Project, Oral Interview 01-87 with Lily Fugelsang Green, Edith Lindberg Walberg, Esther Sandstrom Stokes, and Ed Walberg, 6 November 1987. The Walberg property is now known as Gammondale Farm.

14 Landelius, *Swedish Place-Names*, 290.

15 Rifleman Gordon L. Carlson (1918–1944) was the son of Henry and Emma Carlson. See *Forest to Field*, 314–35; see also Holm and Buchner, *A Place of Honour*, 61.

16 Landelius, *Swedish Place-Names*, 269.

17 Elinor Barr, "Station Names along the Canadian Pacific Railway: Fort William to Selkirk," 1–16, which includes Sandford Fleming's 1880 location map.

18 Martin Dahl (1867–19?) was born in Torp, Rölanda parish, Dalsland, and emigrated to the United States in 1884. He came to the Bulkley Valley in 1905. See Landelius, *Swedish Place-Names*, 269–70.

19 Ibid., 296.

20 Johan Anton Edström (1850–1910) was born in Lycksele, Lappland. In 1890 he and his wife, Eva Marie Joneson, emigrated to Kulm, ND. See ibid., 261–2; see also Sylvia Edstrom and Florence Lundstrom, *Memoirs of the Edberg Pioneers* (Edmonton, 1955), 6–10; see also Sanders, *The Story behind Alberta Names.*

21 Albert Egnell (1833–1900) was born in Vreta Kloster parish, Östergötland, went to sea at an early age, took part in the California gold rush, and became an innkeeper and justice of the peace in Montana before engaging in the fur trade in northern British Columbia. He married a First Nations woman, and it was their son who shot him accidentally. He was buried at Lower Post. See Landelius, *Swedish Place-Names*, 270–1.

22 Walter Elmer Ekblaw (1882–1949) was born in Rantoul, Illinois, the son of Swedish-born farmer Andrew Ekblaw. See ibid., 291.

23 Emil Eric Widén (1889–1965) was born in Haparanda, Norrbotten, and migrated in 1908. He was wounded in the First World War, and in 1921 married Ellen Hankin. Thanks to Leah Tourond, Houston, British Columbia, for this information.

24 Sigvard Daniel Englund (1922–1942) was born in Västbyn, Offerdal parish, Jämtland. He immigrated to Kelliher, SK, with his parents, Olof and Signe Englund, in 1927. See Landelius, *Swedish Place-Names,* 300.

25 Eric Gustaf Erickson (1857–1927) was born in Sweden. See ibid., 271.

26 E. Albert Erickson (18?–19?) was born in Avesta, Dalarna, and immigrated with his family to the Scandinavia district ca. 1896. In 1913 the family moved to Texas. See ibid., 284; see also *Forest to Field*, 352; see also *Geographical Names of Manitoba*, 76.

27 Jonas Erik Erikson (18?–1920) was born in Sandarne, Hälsingland. His son, Emanuel "Manny" Erikson, had already built a log cabin adjacent to his father's quarter by 18 March 1906, when incoming settlers John and Paulina Lindell spent the night there. Jonas applied for his homestead two days later. See Landelius, *Swedish Place-Names*, 284; see also *Geographical Names of Manitoba*, 76; see also Nilsson, *De sista svenska rösterna*, 316–18; see also Lindell, *Memory Opens the Door*, 72, 99, 111, 139, 148.

28 Linnea Lodge, Edmonton, interviewed John Holmlund in 1969, when he became district master for No. 18, Vasa Order of America. He stated that in 1906 his parents settled on land previously owned by Charles Strom, who was born in Falun, Dalarna, and who gave Falun, Alberta, its name. See Landelius, *Swedish Place-Names*, 262; see also *Scandinavian Connections*, 68–9; see also Sanders, *The Story behind Alberta Names.*

29 The little red cottage (*den lilla röd stugan*) reaped several benefits from falu-red paint – it protects the wood against humidity and rot, discourages insects, and minimizes fire hazard. Therefore it was used on barns and outbuildings as well, and always with white trim. See *Swedish Press*, September 2000, 15, for do-it-yourself recipes.

30 Landelius, *Swedish Place-Names*, 296.

31 John Engelbert Forslund (1863–1933) was born in Gävle, Gästrikland. He worked as the CPR's immigration agent from 1891 to 1928, first in Winnipeg and then in Calgary. See Landelius, *Swedish Place-Names*, 300–1; see also Landelius Biography Collection, volume 1, #294, #298; see also Ljungmark, *Svenskarna i Winnipeg*, 39, 246; see also Nilsson, *De sista svenska rösterna*, 338; see also Lager, "Svenskarna i Canada," 337.

32 Albert Forslund (1864–1938) was born in Sweden and immigrated to British Columbia before 1897. After his death his son Oscar took over the acreage, which was planted in fruit trees. See Landelius, *Swedish Place-Names*, 261; see also Landelius Biography Collection, volume 1, #290.

33 Landelius, *Swedish Place-Names*, 271.

34 Oscar Freed (1876-1938) was born in Gnarp, Hälsingland, and immigrated to Winnipeg in 1902 before joining his brother Eric in Freedhome. Oscar Freed was a correspondent for *Canada-tidningen* and an active member of the temperance group IOGT and Freja Hall. See Landelius Biography Collection, volume 1, #302; see also Closson, *Freedhome*, 2.

35 Landelius, *Swedish Place-Names*, 271–2; see also Golden Stanley, "Origins of Local Place Names," in Harry Taylor, comp., *Powell River's First Fifty Years: 1910–1960* (Powell River: A.H. Alsgard, 1960), n.p.

36 Gunnar Berg (1890–19?) was born Gunnar Sjöberg in Själevad parish, Ångermanland, and immigrated to Canada in 1909. In 1933 he and a younger brother sold a rich gold claim on Beresford Lake, Manitoba, to G.A. Labine, who named the resulting company Gunnar Gold Mines Limited. Labine retained the name Gunnar for his company's new uranium find. See Landelius, *Swedish Place-Names*, 301–3.

37 Per Levi Hägglund (1871–19?) was born in Trehörningsjö parish, Ångermanland, and immigrated to Canada in 1910. See ibid., 272.

38 Ibid., 303; see also *People Places: Saskatchewan and its Names* (Regina: Canadian Plains Research Centre, University of Regina, 1997), 130.

39 Olof Hanson (1882–1952) was born in Tännäs, Härjedalen. He made a fortune cutting ties for railway construction, later serving as Swedish vice-consul and consul from 1916 to 1955 and as Liberal Member of Parliament representing Skeena for almost fifteen years, beginning in 1930. See Landelius, *Swedish Place-Names*, 272–3; see also Howard,

Vancouver's Svenskar, 21; see also R. Lynn Shervill, "Olof 'Tie' Hanson," *Whistle Punk* (Spring 1986) 17–21.

40 Landelius, *Swedish Place-Names,* 272–3.

41 Ira H. Hedman (1918–1943) was born in Mazenod, Saskatchewan. His parents had moved from North Dakota in 1898, finally settling in Kennedy, Saskatchewan. See ibid., 303.

42 *Memory Opens the Door: New Norway,* 101. Willie was the son of Erick Nordgren. When he settled on his own land, he built his house at the edge of a large slough. Willie's Slough, as it was called, became the community skating rink during the winter.

43 Knut Lambert Hillgren was born in Helgum parish, Ångermanland, and came to British Columbia in 1926. See Landelius, *Swedish Place-Names,* 273.

44 Frank Alfred Hillstrand (1872–1962) was born in Solberga, Småland, and immigrated to Scandinavia with his parents in 1887. See *Forest to Field,* 417, 559.

45 John C. Hokanson was born in Duluth, MN, son of an immigrant from Norrköping. The family moved to Canada in 1913 and settled in Manitoba. See Landelius, *Swedish Place-Names,* 284.

46 Leonard Holst (1868–19?) was born in Alstad, Skåne, and immigrated to Canada around 1895. See Emigrant Institute, *"Holst Point – turisthotellet,"* 9:19:17:J; letter from Ingemar Ingers, Lund, Sweden, to Utvandrarnas hus, Växjö, 15 September 1928; see also Landelius Biography Collection, volume 2, #087.

47 Landelius, *Swedish Place-Names,* 291.

48 Algot Johnson (18?–1963) was born in Vena parish, Småland. See ibid., 273.

49 Ragnar Jonsson (ca. 1907–1988) was born in Örnsköldsvik, Ångermanland, and immigrated to Saskatchewan in 1927. He came to Nueltin Lake in 1938. See *Geographical Names of Manitoba,* 125; see also Bob Henderson, "Post in Keewatin," *Paddler* 2, no. 4 (1988) 10–11; see also Bob Lowery's five articles in the *Winnipeg Free Press* – "Lynn Lake: Veteran Trapper Sees Life in a Tent as 'Sensible Way,'" 28 April 1981; "New Flavour Given to Old Rescue Story," 6 April 1982; "Civilization Is Just Too Quick,",12 June 1982, "Trapper Finds City 'Fast' after 59 Years in North," 13 September 1982, "The Pas: North's Fabled Trapper Dies," 29 June 1988.

50 Correspondence Gerald F. Holm, Provincial Toponymist, Winnipeg, to Ted Simonson, Winnipeg, 27 February 2001; see also correspondence A.C. Roberts, Director of Surveys, Winnipeg, to Ragnar Jonsson, Lynn Lake, 15 May 1981; see also Raymond England, "In Search of Ragnar Jonsson," *Manitoba Moods* (Summer 1977): 12–13.

51 Landelius, *Swedish Place-Names*, 292.

52 Barr, "Station Names along the Canadian Pacific Railway," 6.

53 John Olof Englund was born in Sweden, and in 1892 immigrated to Ottawa, then to Kipling. See *Kipling 100*, 4.

54 Ibid., 1.

55 Landelius, *Swedish Place-Names*, 292.

56 Lars Anderson (1875–19?) was born in Lilla Harrie parish, Skåne, and immigrated to Canada in 1909. See ibid., 273.

57 Howard, *Vancouver's Svenskar*, 36.

58 Charles Arthur Lindell (1879–1952) was born in Karlstad, Värmland. In 1900 he immigrated to Manitoba and the following year moved to Edmonton, then in 1904 chose a homestead at Lindale where he was cruising timber for Walters Lumber Company. See Landelius, *Swedish Place-Names*, 262; see also Martin, *Forests to Grainfields*, 74–8, 268.

59 Landelius, *Swedish Place-Names*, 262–3; see also Sanders, *The Story behind Alberta Names*.

60 Landelius, *Swedish Place-Names*, 273–4.

61 Andrew Lindell (1846–1918) was born in Sweden. See ibid., 274.

62 Waldemar Lindgren (1860–1939) was born in Ljungby parish, Småland, graduated from Freiburg University, Germany, and emigrated to the United States in 1883. He worked for the Geological Survey from 1884 to 1912 and as a professor at the Massachusetts Institute of Technology from 1912 to 1933. See ibid., 263.

63 Charlie Lindquist (ca. 1875–1951) was born in Sweden, came to Canada at the turn of the century, and never married. See ibid., 274.

64 Barr, "Station Names along the Canadian Pacific Railway," 7.

65 Maurice Gottfred Lofquist (1886–1933) was born in Sweden, immigrated in 1904 to Port Arthur, and in 1911 moved to Nipigon, where he was elected reeve in 1930. See "Former Nipigon Reeve M.G. Lofquist Is Dead," *Port Arthur News-Chronicle*, 13 January 1933.

66 Charlie Thulin (1863–1932) was born Carl August Petersson in Tryserum, Småland, and migrated in 1886, moving to the site of Lund three years later. Fred Thulin (1873–1935) was born Fredrik Gottfrid Petersson and emigrated in 1889 to be his brother's partner. Thulins manned the post office until 1962. See Landelius, *Swedish Place-Names*, 274–5; see also UBCL SC, Seaholm Collection.

67 Johannes Lundberg (1786–1856) was born in Neu Herrnhut on the Danish island of St Thomas in the West Indies, the son of Moravian missionary Thomas Lundberg. At the age of six Johannes was sent to the Moravian children's home in Kleinwelka, Germany, and there became a teacher.

He was sent to Labrador as a missionary and became moderator of the Moravian church with headquarters at Nain. See Landelius, *Swedish Place-Names*, 287–8.

68 Ibid., 263.

69 Inga Gustava Jonsson (1860–19?) was born in Granliden, Vilhelmina, and emigrated to Minnesota in the early 1890s. There she married the Norwegian Jakob Lunde (1828–1909), and migrated to the Hay Lakes district around the turn of the century. See Ågren, "Från Vilhelmina till Wilhelmina," 24–5, 32; see also *Scandinavian Connections*, 194–5, 198–9.

70 A thousand people emigrated from Vilhelmina from 1867 to 1915. Half of them left Sweden from 1903 to 1912, many with Canada as their destination. See Ågren, "Från Vilhelmina till Wilhelmina," 22. See also Ingalena Marthin, "Swedes in Wilhelmina, Canada: A Tradition is Tested against the Records," *Swedish American Genealogist* 4 (2004): 18–19.

71 Landelius, *Swedish Place-Names*, 288.

72 Ibid., 303.

73 Ibid., 163; see also *Malmo Mission Covenant Church: Seventy-five Years 1898–1973*, 11–12; see also *Scandinavian Connections*, 254–7.

74 Landelius, *Swedish Place-Names*, 311; see also R.C. Coutts, *Yukon: Places and Names* (Sidney, BC: Gray's Publishing, 1980), 180.

75 Landelius, *Swedish Place-Names*, 284–5; see also Holm, *Geographical Names of Manitoba*, 164.

76 Sandin was born in the United States ca. 1893. See Landelius, *Swedish Place-Names*, 275.

77 *New Sweden Mission Church 1894–1994: How Great Thou Art, O Store Gud* (1994), n.p.; see also *Our Scandinavian Missions*; see also *Pioneer Pathways*, 533–4.

78 Nils Daniel Niklasson (1843–1906) immigrated from Långasjö, Småland, in 1889 directly to his farm. His wife, Johanna Matilda (1854–1916), followed in 1893 with their five children. See *En Smålandsocken emigrerar*, 200, 252–3.

79 Landelius, *Swedish Place-Names*, 297.

80 Ibid., 310.

81 Ibid., 292.

82 Oscar William Nordin (1863–19?) was born in Härnösand, Ångermanland. He eventually moved to Montreal. See ibid., 286.

83 John August Peterson (18?–1924) and his wife, Anna (18?–1936), immigrated in 1906. See *Logs and Lines*, 226–7.

84 Frans Gustaf Nordstrom (1907–19?) was born in Dalarna and immigrated to northern Saskatchewan with his brother Erik in 1924. In 1952 he sold

his farm and started a mink ranch on Buffalo Narrows in Churchill Lake. See ibid., 304.

85　Ibid., 304.

86　Ibid., 304–5.

87　UBCL SC, Matthew Lindfors Fonds, Box 2; "Hälsning från Canada," Matthew M. Lindfors. Some of these early immigrants from Offerdal were Albert and Ellen Larson (1903), Nels and Katarina Hagstrom (1904), and Erik and Karin Engstrom (1907). Thanks to Roxann Buskas, Wetaskiwin, for information about these families.

88　Carl Eric Ogren (ca. 1924–1943) was born in Elm Creek, Manitoba, the son of Harold Ogren born Gustav Harald Jonatan Ågren in Ed, Värmland, and Kristine Henriette Lund, who was born in Oslo, Norway. Thanks to Malte Nilsson, Sweden, for family information. See also Holm and Buchner, *A Place of Honour*, 319.

89　Gotthard Erick Öhrn (1860–1930) was born in Hamrånge parish, Gästrikland, and in 1879 emigrated to Ohio, where he married Matilda Eliason. Lung problems from working in a steel smelter led to a move to Pierre, South Dakota. After a period of drought the family came to Alberta in 1900. Thanks to Ralph Ohrn, Edmonton, for family information. See also *A Patchwork of Memories* (Thorsby: The Historical Society of Thorsby and District, 1979), 507–8.

90　Charles Herman Olin (1867–1930) was born in Alingsås, Västergötland, emigrated to the United States in 1886, then in 1892 came to Wetaskiwin as a carpenter and builder. A Liberal, he was elected to the Alberta Legislature in 1909 and again in 1913. See Landelius, *Swedish Place-Names*, 263–4; see also *Pioneer Pathways*, 1166; see also Landelius Biography Collection, volume 2, #075.

91　Landelius, *Swedish Place-Names*, 275–6.

92　Ibid., 292–3.

93　Ibid., 276.

94　Barr, "Station Names along the Canadian Pacific Railway," 8.

95　Linnea Kralik, Culture and Public Affairs Assistant at the Consulate General of Sweden, New York, confirmed in correspondence dated 5 December 2001 that the word "oxdrift" is "an old Swedish word no longer in use" and means approximately "ox driving," using oxen for heavy work.

96　Barr, "Station Names along the Canadian Pacific Railway," 8. The fourteen-kilometre portage connected the west arm of Wabigoon Lake to Boulder Bay on Eagle Lake, where construction materials were transferred to boats and transported to points along the north shore of

Eagle Lake, including Vermilion Bay. Thanks to John Corner, Oxdrift, for on-site information.

97 Carl Edvin "Charlie" Palmquist (1901–19?) was born in Torsås, Småland, and immigrated to Canada in 1920. See Landelius, *Swedish Place-Names*, 297.

98 Carl Emil Poignant (1868–19?) was born on the island of Värmdö, east of Stockholm, and in 1891 emigrated with his family to Illinois, moving to Wisconsin and Bellingham, Washington, before arriving in Ridgedale, British Columbia, in 1906. He was a baker by trade, and continued baking hardtack for sale in Ridgedale. See ibid., 276; see also *Wigwams to Windmills: A History of Ridgedale and Area* (Abbotsford: Ridgedale Women's Institute, 1977), 144–7.

99 Landelius, *Swedish Place-Names*, 276.

100 Ibid., 293.

101 Peter Eriksson Ringwall (1861–1933) and his wife, Gölin Skanse, were born in Överhogdal, Hälsingland, and emigrated to North Dakota in 1883. In 1900 they moved to Canada and became charter members of Malmo Mission Church. Thanks to Marion Petersson, Wetaskiwin, for family information. See also Roanna Bean Campbell, *Little Beaver Tales: Ferintosh and District* (Ferintosh: Ferintosh History Book Committee, 1986), 49.

102 Anders Johan Rosen (18?–1927) was born in Stora Tuna parish, Dalarna, and emigrated to the United States, where he worked for the Great Northern Railroad, blasting rocks. He moved to Jaffray in 1909 as a farmer, owner of a general store, and logging contractor. See Landelius, *Swedish Place-Names*, 276–7.

103 Charles Rosen (1876–1958) was born Carl Theodor Andersson in Lerbäck parish, Närke, and emigrated in 1907 to the United States, where he adopted the surname Rosen. See ibid., 276–7.

104 Olof Sandell (1873–19?) was born in Lomma, Skåne, and immigrated to the mouth of the Fraser River in 1891. See ibid., 277; see also Nilsson, *Från Lomma till Norra Amerika*, 25.

105 Landelius, *Swedish Place-Names*, 264.

106 Ibid., 277.

107 Uppland is a Swedish province. See ibid., 264; see also Baglo, *The Story of Augustana Lutherans in Canada*, 40–1. The settlers from Scandia, MN, were Albert Swenson, his brother Frank Swenson, and their brother-in-law Al Hawkinson. The first postmaster was John L. Johnson from Chicago.

108 Jens "James" Hemmingson (1858–1931) was born in Själland, Denmark, and immigrated to Canada in the early 1880s. His wife, Clara Munson, had immigrated from Sweden. See *Forest to Field*, 412.

109 Landelius, *Swedish Place-Names*, 293.

110 Charles Johnson emigrated from Långemåla, Småland, in the early 1870s, settling in Minnedosa when it was called Tanner's Crossing. He was the first mail carrier to and from Portage la Prairie. Later his brothers Fred and August joined him as farmers. See *Minnedosa Valley Views*, 446–9.

111 Thompson, *Texada Island*, 313–15.

112 Landelius, *Swedish Place-Names*, 305.

113 Daniel Solander (1735–1782), who wrote the first scientific description of the kangaroo, is regarded as the father of Pacific botany. See ibid., 277; see also *Swedish Press*, May 2002, 13.

114 Jacob Alexander Stenberg (1864–1951) was born in Lidingö, and in 1882 moved to nearby Stockholm. He and his wife, Svea Amalia Hess, immigrated to New Stockholm in 1887. Thanks to grandson Stuart Stevenson, Stockholm, for family information. See also Landelius, *Swedish Place-Names*, 305; see also Nilsson, *De sista svenska rösterna*, 150; see also Godfrey Persson, Sr, "Pioneer Settlers of New Stockholm," *The Western Producer*, March 1958, 22.

115 There were communities named Stockholm in Iowa, Kansas, Kentucky, Maine, Minnesota, Nebraska, New Jersey, New York, South Dakota, Texas, and Wisconsin, and a bay and a point on Kodiak Island in Alaska. See Alan Winquist, "Searching for Stockholm in America," *Sweden and America* (Spring 1998): 10–12.

116 Carl Stolz (1883–19?) was born in Överkalix, Norrbotten, and immigrated with his family to Prince Albert, Saskatchewan, in 1912. See *Geographical Names of Manitoba*, 264; see also Manitoba Archives C551-552, Swedish Community Oral History Collection, Oral Histories, Manitoba, Anne Richter, 1–2, 4–5.

117 Abraham Daniel Swanson, Jr (1879–1912) was born in Esmond, North Dakota, the son of Abraham Daniel Swanson, Sr, from Stockholm, Sweden. The post office closed in 1976. See Landelius, *Swedish Place-Names*, 305–6.

118 Ibid., 297.

119 Jöns Pehrsson Svedberg (1866–1915) was born in Risnäset, Ström, Jämtland, and immigrated to Nelson, British Columbia, around 1890. His partners were William Johnson and the Dane Pete Nelson. Thanks to Valerie Lawson, Winnipeg, for donating her family history *Putting it All Together: One Swedish Family in Canada* (1999), 94–103; see also Landelius, *Swedish Place-Names*, 277–8.

120 Ibid., 278.

121 Coutts, *Yukon*, 256; see also Anton Money, "Journey into the Unknown," *Alaska Sportsman*, May 1968, 15.

122 Landelius, *Swedish Place-Names*, 310; see also Coutts, *Yukon*, 256; see also Elle Andra-Warner, *Robert Service; A Great Canadian Poet's Romance with the North* (Canmore: Altitude Publishing, 2004).

123 Coutts, *Yukon*, 357.

124 Oslund, *One Hundred Years of Swedish Settlement*, 10.

125 Swedeville was home to the Nilssons, Bergstrands, four Knutson families, and Reeds and Topes, who had married Swedish girls. Living in Waterville itself were the Carlquists, Andersons, Svensons, Hansons, and Karlssons. See James Knutson, "Swedeville, A Few Memories," in *Taproot: Poetry, Prose and Images from the Eastern Townships*, ed. Brenda Hartwell (Sherbrooke, QC: Townshippers' Association, 1999), 50–1.

126 Ibid., 50. According to Jim Knutson about fifty Swedish- and Norwegian-born people are buried in Greenwood cemetery, and a significant number in the nearby towns of Sherbrooke, Lennoxville, Beebe, Hatley, and North Hatley.

127 Wonders, "Mot Canada's Nordväst," 149.

128 Barr, "Station Names along the Canadian Pacific Railway," 10. See Holm, *Geographical Names of Manitoba*, 270, which lists the locality Telford, as well as Telford Lake and Telford Pond.

129 Olov August Sahlström (1866–1931) and his nephews Karl Johan "Charlie" and August Waldemar "Walter" were born in Fryksände parish, Värmland. Two other nephews, Sten and Gustav (postmaster from 1917– 1923), returned to Sweden, but Charlie settled in Castlegar, British Columbia. Thanks to his son, Bob Sahlstrom of Castlegar, for family information. See also Landelius, *Swedish Place-Names*, 264–5.

130 Louise Smith, "Same Name, Different Places: Introducing Thorsby – Alberta, Alabama and Sweden," *Westworld Alberta* (January–February 1997): n.p.

131 Thanks to Barbro Baker, Victoria, for sending the undated articles "Anna – en värmländsk indian," "Välkommen till Sahlströmsgården!" by Bengt Sahlström, and "Torsby Herrgård: levande miljö mitt i Torsby," by Lennart Toresjö, 12–13.

132 Landelius, *Swedish Place-Names*, 278.

133 Ibid., 293–4.

134 Coutts, *Yukon*, 272.

135 Barr, "Station Names along the Canadian Pacific Railway," 10.

136 Landelius, *Swedish Place-Names*, 265.

137 Ibid.

138 Nils Hanson (1851–1920) was born in Tubbetorp, Siene parish, Västergötland. He acquired land on the Kootenay River in 1893. See ibid., 273.

139 Johan Erik Norström (1846–19?) was born in Skerike parish, Västmanland, and immigrated to Wetaskiwin in 1905 with his wife, Johanna. See ibid., 265–6; see also Erickson, *Freeway West*, 1000–1. Thanks to Roxann Buskas, Wetaskiwin, for donating George Norstrom's article "Norstrom Halfway House (Westerose)."

140 Flying Officer Fred E. Wickstrom (ca. 1921–1942) was the son of Albin and Jennie Wickstrom. See *Forest to Field*, 704–5; see also Holm and Buchner, *A Place of Honour*, 462.

Appendix 2: Firsts for Swedes in Canada

1 Sten Aminoff, database, 1861 Census of Canada.

2 Ibid.

3 Ibid., 1871 Census of Canada

4 Anders Johan Johansson (1864–19?) was born near Halmstad, Halland. In 1888 he homesteaded thirty-two kilometres north of Wolseley at Pheasant Fork, a colony of the Primitive Methodist Colonization Company, and married a daughter of his neighbour, Luther Brown, from Goodridge, Ontario. See Landelius Biography Collection, volume 2, #119-125, a series of four articles by N.C. Eriksen, Weyburn, published in *Canada-tidningen* 20 and 27 March, 10 and 17 April 1941, titled "Svensk veteran från Rielupproret berättar om gamla tider."

5 Landelius Biography Collection, volume 1, #012. Anderberg had emigrated ca. 1902 and taken up a homestead.

6 Ottawa Senators were an NHL team from 1917 to 1934, and came back to life in 1992. See Dan Diamond, ed., *Total Hockey* (Kingston, NY: Total Sports Publishing, 1998), 254, 704.

7 Landelius Biography Collection, volume 1, #076.

8 Harry Strom was elected to the Alberta legislature in 1955, serving as minister of agriculture and of municipal affairs. He represented the Social Credit Party.

Bibliography

ARCHIVES AND REPOSITORIES

Canada

Archives of Alberta, Edmonton
- Donald Carlson, "The Scandinavian Hospital in Wetaskiwin"
- *Scandinavian Centre News*, 1958–87

Archives of Ontario, Toronto
- Oral interviews, Multicultural History Society of Ontario

British Columbia Archives, Victoria
- Documents relating to the probate of Albert Blom's estate
- "The Eek Story"
- "James Olson (Swede), Tanglefoot BC, 1918"

City of Vancouver Archives
- "Sven Sherdahl's Pioneer Days in Kansas"
- Otto Nordling Fonds
- Olof Seaholm, "Sweden's Contributions to Canada"

City of Wetaskiwin Archives
- Gustav Carlson Family Fonds
- Copy of *An Act to incorporate the Scandinavian Hospital in Wetaskiwin*

Diocese of Algoma Archives, Sault Ste Marie
– Boyce Report
Ear Falls District Museum, Ontario
– Re Nels Anderson
Eastern Townships Research Centre, Sherbrooke
– James Knutson, comp., "Scandinavian Settlers: Waterville" (1999)
Evangelical Lutheran Church in Canada Archives, Saskatoon
– *Canada härald*, 1914–16
Glenbow Archives, Calgary
– CPR Land Settlement and Development 1884–1963
– John L. Edlund Fonds
– Magnuson/Anderson Family Fonds (Fogelvik Farms)
Lakehead University Library Archives, Thunder Bay
– Einar Nordstrom Collection
– Oscar Styffe Collection
Library and Archives Canada, Ottawa (LAC)
– E.A. Alm Family Fonds
– Carl Emil Berg Fonds
– Fred Burman Fonds
– Devlin Papers
– Louise de Kiriline Lawrence Fonds
– Mackenzie-Papineau Battalion Fonds
– Otto Nordling Fonds
– Carl E. Soderquist Fonds (includes his "En återblick")
– Swedish Lutheran Immigration Aid Society of Canada
Manitoba Archives, Winnipeg
– Hudson's Bay Company Archives re Jacob Fahlstrom
– Minute Book, Winnipeg branch of the Swedish Canadian League
    1926–41
– Louise Ostlin Collection
– W.J. Sisler Collection
– Swedish Community Oral History Collection
McKee Archives/Library, Brandon University
– Re Brandon College
Northwest Territories Archives
– Sven Johansson, "The Canadian Reindeer Herd" (1965)
Northwestern Ontario Sports Hall of Fame
– Re Victor Lindquist
Red Deer and District Archives
– Emanuel Cronquist Fonds

– "Andrew Edgar Hallgren"
– Biography file, Telning Family
St Mary's Museum, Ontario
– "Description Gottfrid Larson Sous Fonds"
Saskatchewan Archives, Regina and Saskatoon
– August Dahlman, "Estevan, Assiniboia, N.W.T., Canada"
– Frank Eliason, "Biography of a Swedish Emigrant"
– Kasper Persson Landine, "A Story of New Stockholm's First Church
  Activities"
– Nils Nilsson, *Swedish Ballads Sung by Sleepy and Swede*
– Carl Ian Walker, "Sven Erikson Svedberg, A Swedish Pioneer"
– Translations by Doris Paulson of newspaper articles (Stockholm Binder)
Swedes in Canada Project Compilations
– Immigrant Database
– Survey of Immigrants Since the Second World War (database)
– Ambassadors, Consuls-General, Consuls, Vice-Consuls Database
Thunder Bay Historical Museum Society
– Einar Nordstrom Fonds
– A.T. Hill, "Highlights of Labor History – Lakehead, Canada & World"
– Register, Scandinavian Boarding House
United Church Archives, Toronto
– Cobalt-Haileybury Scandinavian Presbyterian Mission
University of British Columbia Library, Special Collections (UBCL SC)
– Peter B. Anderson Fonds
– Paul Axel Boving Fonds
– Irene Howard Fonds
– Matthew Lindfors Fonds
– Olof Seaholm Collection
– Swedish Cultural Society Fonds
Yukon Archives, Whitehorse
– Otto Nordling Fonds

Sweden

Emigrant Institute, Växjö (*Emigrantinstitutet*)
– Harald Fegraeus Collection
– Landelius Biography Collection on Swedes Abroad – Canada, 3 vol-
  umes
– "Stories of Swedish Pioneers in North America" (1948)
Foreign Affairs Archives, Stockholm (*Utrikesdepartementet*)
– *Svenska och norrska consuler, 1850–1969*

– *Kungl. Utrikesdepartementets kalender 1870–2001*
Landsarkivet i Göteborg
– Sam Widenfelt's family archive
Landsarkivet i Östersund
– Gunilla Hansson Collection
National Archives, Stockholm (*Riksarkivet*)
– Utrikesdepartementet
– Konsulatet i Montreal
– Släktforskarnas hus, Leksand
– "Bror Daniel Andersson's Letters"

United States

University of Minnesota, Immigration History Research Center (UM IHRC)
– Tell Dahllöf Collection
Swenson Swedish Immigration Research Center (SSIRC)
– The Erik Norelius Papers
– Church records
Vasa National Archives

Private Collections

Elinor Barr, Scandinavian Heritage Project
– Research material for *The Scandinavian Home Society 1923–1993*
– Oscar Johnson Collection
– Minute Book IOGT Lodge *I* Räddningsbåten, 1914–17
Michael Brook, Nottingham – selected photocopies
Irene Howard, Vancouver – research notes for *Vancouver's Svenskar*
Viveka Janssen, Victoria – research material from her study of Swedes in Alberta
Lucille Szumutku, Stockholm – research material gathered by "Ohlen '86" (Stockholm Binder)
Elisabeth Thorsell, Sweden – Sten Aminoff's Census of Canada database

ARTICLES AND SPEECHES

Abbott, George M. "Rolf Wallgren Bruhn, Pioneer and Politician." *Okanagan History* 59 (1995): 87–95.

Ågren, Per-Uno. "Från Vilhelmina to Wilhelmina." *Västerbotten 1987*: 22–34.

Ainley, Marianne Gosztonyi. "In Memoriam: Louise de Kiriline Lawrence, 1894–1992." *The Auk* 109, no. 4 (1992): 909–10.

Åkerman, Sune. "The Story of the Bergsten Brothers in Canada [Peace River Valley]: Ethnic Barriers, Unfavorable Sex Ratios, and the Creation of Male Households." In *Interpreting the Promise of America: Essays in Honor of Odd Sverre Lovoll*, edited by Todd W. Nichol, 137–48. Northfield, Minnesota: Norwegian-American Historical Association, 2002.

Anderson, Alan Betts. "Scandinavian Settlements in Saskatchewan: Migration History and Changing Ethnocultural Identity." *Scandinavian-Canadian Studies* 2 (1986): 89–113.

Anderson, Arthur Antonius. "Svenskar och svenska insatser i Kanada." In *Vår svenska stam på utländsk mark: Svenska öden och insatser i främmande land*, edited by Axel Boethius, 235–57. Stockholm: Lindqvist, 1952.

– *Stoft: Dust of Our Being: A Collection of Poems*. Winnipeg: 1934. Reprinted with English translation by Ellen Boryen. Edited and published by Laurel Anderson-McCallum. Winnipeg: 2013

Attebery, Jennifer Eastman. "Swedish Immigrants and the Myth of the West." *Swedish-American Historical Quarterly* 55, no. 3 (July 2004): 179–91.

Avery, Donald. "Ethnic and Class Relations in Western Canada during the First World War: A Case Study of European Immigrants and Anglo-Canadian Nativism." In *Canada and the First World War: Essays in Honour of Robert Craig Brown*, edited by David MacKenzie, 272–99. Toronto: University of Toronto Press, 2004.

Bagge, Gösta Adolfsson. "Kanada som immigrationsland: Några anteckningar från en studieresa." In *Sociala meddelanden 1925*, n:r 8, 619–51. Stockholm: Norstedt, 1925.

Barr, Elinor. "Jacob Fahlstrom Challenge." *Swedish American Genealogist* 4 (2005): 5–8.

– "Station Names along the Canadian Pacific Railway: Fort William to Selkirk." *Canoma* [Geographical Names Board of Canada] 26, no. 2 (December 2000): 1–16.

– "Swedes at the Lakehead 1900–1930." *Papers & Records* [Thunder Bay Historical Museum Society] 20 (1992): 50–62.

– "Swedish Immigration to Canada 1923–29: The Case of Port Arthur, Ontario." *Swedish-American Historical Quarterly* 51, no. 2 (April 2000): 150–61.

– "Swedish Language Retention." *Polyphony: Thunder Bay's People* 9, no. 2 (1987): 84–6.

Barton, H. Arnold. "Editor's Introduction." *Swedish-American Historical Quarterly* 33, no. 1 (1982): 3.

– "Swedish Reactions to the Emigration Question Around the Turn of the Century." *Swedish-American Historical Quarterly* 44, no. 2 (April 1993): 84–101.

– "Why Don't We Know More about the Swedes in Canada?" *Pioneer-American Historical Quarterly* 28, no. 2 (1977): 79–81. Reprinted in *The Scandinavian Canadian Businessman* (April 1977): 11–12.

Beijbom, Ulf. "A Decade with the Emigrant Institute." In *Perspectives on Swedish Immigration: Proceedings of the International Conference on the Swedish Heritage in the Upper Midwest, April 1–3, 1976, University of Minnesota, Duluth*, edited by Nils Hasselmo, 311–24. Chicago: Swedish Pioneer Historical Society, 1978.

Bengston, Henry. "Upplevelser Östanhavs och Västanhavs." *Bryggan/The Bridge* (1970–72). Original manuscript translated by his daughter Margit Fredrickson as "Autobiography."

Bergstrom, Ingrid. "Mary Berglund: Backwoods Nurse." *The Canadian Nurse* 72, no. 9 (1976): 44–9.

Biggs, Rae. "Vasa Lodges of Alberta." *Heritage* [Alberta Culture] 4, no. 6 (November–December 1976): 5.

Bjork, Kenneth O. "Scandinavian Migration to the Canadian Prairie Provinces, 1893–1914." *Norwegian-American Studies* 26 (1974): 3–30.

Bjork, Ulf Jonas. "The Dangerous Prairies of Texas: The Western Dime Novel in Sweden, 1900–1908." *Swedish-American Historical Quarterly* 55, no. 3 (July 2004): 165–78.

– "Nils F:son Brown and the Decline of the Swedish-American Press, 1910–1940." *Swedish American Genealogist* 19, nos. 2–3 (June–September 1999): 221–32.

– "Swedish Ethnicity and Labor Socialism in the Work of Nils F:son Brown, 1919–1928." *The Historian* 56, no. 4 (Summer 1997): 759–75.

– "A Swedish-American View of Sweden: The Journalism of Nils F. Brown, 1910–1953." *Swedish-American Historical Quarterly* 44, no. 1 (January 1993): 21–38.

Brook, Michael. "Scandinavians." In *The Immigrant Labor Press in North America, 1840s–1970s: An Annotated Bibliography*, edited by Dirk Hoerder, 85–117. New York: Greenwood Press, 1987.

– "Swedes." In *The Immigrant Labor Press in North America, 1840s–1970s: An Annotated Bibliography*, edited by Dirk Hoerder, 139–80. New York: Greenwood Press, 1987.

Brorson, Alf. "Ett Piece of Canada in Sven Delblanc's Authorship." *Bryggan/ The Bridge* 4 (2008): 8–9.

– "On the Stage of History." *Bryggan/The Bridge* 3 (2008): 12–13. About Jacob Fahlstrom.

Carlson, Axel J. "The Swedes in Canada." *Scandinavia: A Monthly Magazine Devoted to the Interests of Scandinavians Everywhere* 1, no. 5 (May 1924): 30–2, 70.

Carlsson, Sten. "Why Did They Leave?" In *Perspectives on Swedish Immigration: Proceedings of the International Conference on the Swedish Heritage in the Upper Midwest, April 1–3, 1976, University of Minnesota, Duluth*, edited by Nils Hasselmo, 25–35. Chicago: Swedish Pioneer Historical Society, 1978.

Dahlie, Jörgen. "The Ethnic Press as a Cultural Resource: *Canada Skandinaven* and the Norwegian-Swedish Community in B.C., 1910–1930." *Scandinavian-Canadian Studies* 1 (1983): 15–26.

– "No Fixed Boundaries: Scandinavian Responses to Schooling in Western Canada." In *Frontières Ethniques en Devenir/Emerging Ethnic Boundaries*, edited by Danielle Juteau Lee, 7:117–29. Ottawa: Canadian Ethnic Studies Association, 1979.

– "Scandinavian Immigration, Assimilation and Settlement Patterns in Canada: Large Landscape, Limited Impact?" In *Finns in North America: Proceedings*, edited by Edward W. Laine, Olavi Koivukangas, and Michael G. Karni, 9–12. Turku, Finland: Siirtolaisuusinstituutti, 1988.

Dejke, Inger. "Guldgrävare – kanotkonstruktör – författare." *Minnesbilder från Ljungskilebygden. Ljungskileortens hembygdsförening* 12 (1995): 42–51. About Harry Macfie.

Delafenêtre, David G.. "The Scandinavian Presence in Canada: Emerging Perspectives." *Canadian Ethnic Studies* 27, no. 2 (1995): 34–58.

Delblanc, Sven. "A Storyteller's Story." *Saturday Night* 102, no. 12 (December 1987): 70–2.

Duncan, Hal G. "Sleepy and Swede." *Western People*, 13 December 1984, 10–11.

Elfving, Folke. "Minnen från Resteröd." *Minnesbilder från Ljungskilebygden. Ljungskileortens hembygdsförening* 12 (1995): 9–21. About the Wallgren family.

Eneberg, Kaa. "Recruitment of Swedish Immigrants to Soviet Karelia." In *Karelian Exodus: Finnish Communities in North America and Soviet Karelia during the Depression Era*, edited by Ronald Harpelle, Varpu Lindström, and Alexis E. Pogorelskin. Special Issue of the *Journal of Finnish Studies* 8, no. 1 (August 2004): 189–200.

Enhörning, Louise. "SWEA History." *SWEA bladet, Commemorative Issue Celebrating the Official Visit to Toronto of Their Majesties King Carl XVI Gustaf and Queen Silvia of Sweden* (1988): 3–4.

Erickson, Lesley. "Interplay of Ethnicity and Gender: Swedish Women in Southeastern Saskatchewan." In *Other Voices: Historical Essays on Saskatchewan Women*, 27–40. Regina: University of Regina, Canadian Plains Research Centre, 1995.

Forssell, Lars. *Flickan i Montréal*. In Lars Forssell, *Upptåg*. Stockholm: Bonnier, 1967. Play.

Fur, Gunlög. "The Making of a Legend: Joe Hill and the I.W.W." *Swedish-American Historical Quarterly* 40, no. 3 (1989): 101–13.

– "Romantic Relations. Swedish Attitudes towards Indians during the Twentieth Century." *Swedish-American Historical Quarterly* 55, no. 3 (July 2004): 145–64.

Gates, Paul W. "Official Encouragement to Immigration by the Province of Canada." *The Canadian Historical Review* 15, no. 1 (March 1934): 24–38.

Guernsey, A.H. "Folk-Life in Sweden 1871." *Swedish American Genealogist* 23, no. 2 (June 2003): 65–84. Reprinted from *Harper's New Monthly Magazine* (January 1871).

Gustafson, Ralph. "A Preface and Some Poems: Canada's Kinship with Scandinavia." *Northward Journal* 18–19 (1980): 75–7.

Håkanson, Mikael. "The Svenskybybo-people in Canada – A Dying Culture?" *Bryggan/The Bridge* 15, no. 4 (1983): 104–9.

Hale, Christopher S. "Ethnic Minorities on the Canadian Prairies in the Writings of Aksel Sandemose and Sven Delblanc. *Scandinavian-Canadian Studies* 8 (1985): 37–55.

– "Swedes." In *Encyclopedia of Canada's Peoples*, edited by Paul Robert Magocsi, 1218–33. Toronto: University of Toronto Press, 1999.

Halldin, David. "Pioneering in Alberta's Peace River Country." *Swedish-American Historical Quarterly* 33, no. 1 (1982): 43–61.

Hanson, Henry. "The Vasa Order of America: Its Role in the Swedish-American Community: 1896–1996." *Swedish-American Historical Quarterly* 47, no. 4 (1996): 236–44.

Harvey, Anne-Charlotte, and Richard H. Hulan. "'Teater, visafton och bal': The Swedish-American Road Show in its Heyday." *Swedish-American Historical Quarterly* 37, no. 3 (1986): 126–41.

Hedblom, Folke. "The Gammalsvenskby People: Swedish-Canadian Immigrants from South Russia." *Swedish-American Historical Quarterly* 34, no. 1 (1983): 32–48.

Hildeman, Nils-Gustav. "Swedish Strikes and Emigration." *Swedish Pioneer Historical Quarterly* 8, no. 3 (1957): 87–93.

Hjelm, Jonny. "Forest Work and Mechanization: Changes in Sweden and Canada During the Post-War Period." *Polhem: Tidskrift för teknikhistoria* 12, no. 3 (1994): 260–88.

Hokanson, Nels. "Swedes and the I.W.W." *Swedish Pioneer Historical Quarterly* 23, no. 1 (1972): 25–35.

Holloway, Sam. "The Two Stories of Charley Anderson." *The Yukon Reader* 2, no. 2 (n.d.): 13–18.

Howard, Irene. "Pete Larson, North Vancouver Hotelman." *North Shore Historical Society Newsletter* 1, no. 7 (October 1976): 3–5.

– "Vancouver Swedes and the Loggers." *Swedish Pioneer Historical Quarterly* 21, no. 3 (1970): 163–82.

Hvidt, Kristian. "Emigration Agents: The Development of an Industry and its Methods." *Scandinavian Journal of History* 3, no. 2 (1978): 179–203.

Innis, Donald Q. "Sweden – An Example for Canada." *Queen's Quarterly* 71, no. 1 (Spring 1964): 95–102.

Isaacson, John A. "American-Swedish History of Many, Illustrated by Experience." *Swedish Pioneer Historical Quarterly* 26, no. 4 (October 1975): 247–59. About the Calgary-Edmonton area.

Jalava, Mauri I. "The Scandinavians as a Source of Settlers for the Dominion of Canada: The First Generation, 1867–1897." *Scandinavian-Canadian Studies* 1 (1983): 3–14.

Janssen, Viveka. "Swedish Settlement in Alberta, 1890–1930." *Swedish-American Historical Quarterly* 33, no. 2, (April 1982): 111–29.

Jensen, Adolph. "Migration Statistics of Denmark, Norway and Sweden." In *International Migrations*, edited by Walter F. Willcox, 2:283–312. New York: National Bureau of Economic Research, 1931.

Johnson, Emeroy. "Was Oza Windib a Swede?" *Swedish-American Historical Quarterly* 35, no. 3 (1984): 207–20. About Jacob Fahlstrom.

Jordan, Robert Paul, ed. "When the Rus [Swedish Vikings] Invaded Russia: Viking Trail East." *National Geographic* 167, no. 3 (1985): 278–317.

Kealey, Gregory S. "State Repression of Labour and the Left in Canada, 1914–1920: The Impact of the First World War." In *A Nation of Immigrants: Women, Workers, and Communities in Canadian History*, edited by Franca Iacovetta and Robert Ventresca, 384–412. Toronto: University of Toronto Press, 1998.

Knutson, Jim. "Swedeville, A Few Memories." In *Taproot: Poetry, Prose and Images from the Eastern Townships*, edited by Brenda Hartwell, 50–2. Sherbrooke: Townshippers' Association, 1999.

Lager, C.H. "Svenskarna i Canada." In *Svenskarna i Amerika: Populär historisk skildring i ord och bild av svenskarnas liv och underbara öden i Forenta Staterna och Canada*, edited by Karl Hildebrand and Axel Fredenholm, 2:334–50. Stockholm: Historiska Förlaget, 1925.

Lanken, Dane. "Scene Setter." *Canadian Geographic* (July–August 2003): 56–64. About Clarence Tillenius.

Larsen, H.K. "Swedish Planning: A Lesson for Canada." *Queen's Quarterly* 82, no. 1 (Spring 1975): 98–106.

Larson, Nels T.A. "Life in Saskatchewan, 1918–1925: A Story of a Pioneering Missionary Family," edited by Samuel Chell. *Swedish-American Historical Quarterly* 36, no. 1 (1985): 39–55.

Leppard, Henry M. "The Settlement of the Peace River Country." *The Geographical Review* 25 (1935): 62–78.

Liljewall, Britt. "Emigration, Literacy, and Networks or Letters from the Lost Land." *Swedish-American Historical Quarterly* 56, nos. 2–3 (April–July 2005): 141–57.

Limberg, Lennart. "Almost a Century's Work: Preserving Swedishness Outside of Sweden." In *Scandinavians in Old and New Lands: Essays in Honor of H. Arnold Barton*, edited by Philip J. Anderson, Dag Blanck, and Byron J. Nordstrom, 125–57. Chicago: The Swedish-American Historical Society, 2004. About Riksförening för svenskhetens bevarande i utlandet, now called Riksföreningen Sverigekontakt.

Lindfors, M.M. "The Swedes." In *Strangers Entertained: A History of the Ethnic Groups of British Columbia, 1971*, edited by John Norris, 130–2. Vancouver: British Columbia Centennial '71 Committee, 1971.

Lindman, Kerstin. "Finland's Swedes: An Introduction and a Bibliography." *Scandinavian Studies* 35, no. 2 (May 1965): 123–31.

Lindquist, Emory. "Appraisals of Sweden and America by Swedish Emigrants: The Testimony of Letters in *Emigrationsutredningen* (1907)." *Swedish Pioneer Historical Quarterly* 17, no. 2 (April 1966): 78–95.

Ljungmark, Lars. "Canada: An Alternative for Swedish Emigration to the New World, 1873–1875." *Swedish-American Historical Quarterly* 35, no. 3 (July 1984): 253–66.

– "Canada's Campaign for Scandinavian Immigrants 1880–1895." In *Canada and the Nordic Countries: Proceedings from the Second International Conference of the Nordic Association for Canadian Studies, University of Lund, 1987*, edited by Jørn Carlsen and Bengt Streijffert, 215–25. Lund: University of Lund, 1988.

– "Canada's Campaign for Scandinavian Immigration, 1873–1876." *Swedish-American Historical Quarterly* 33, no. 1 (January 1982): 21–42.

- "Hans Mattson's Minnen: A Swedish-American Monument." *Swedish Pioneer Historical Quarterly* 29, no. 1 (1978): 57–68.
- "Northern Neighbor: Winnipeg, The Swedish Service Station in the 'Last Best West', 1890–1950." In *Swedes in the Twin Cities: Immigrant Life and Minnesota's Urban Frontier*, edited by Philip J. Anderson and Dag Blanck, 91–103. Minneapolis: Minnesota Historical Society Press, 2001.
- "On Emigration, Social Mobility, and the Transfer of Capital." *Swedish-American Historical Quarterly* 41, no. 3 (1990): 155–64.
- "Push- and Pull-Factors Behind the Swedish Emigration to America, Canada, and Australia." In *European Expansion and Migration: Essays on the Intercontinental Migration from Africa, Asia, and Europe*, edited by P.C. Emmer and M. Mörner, 79–103. New York: Berg, 1992.
- "Snusboulevarder och snusandet i Svensk-Amerika," edited by Per Clemensson, Lennart Limberg, and Lars Ljungmark. *Göteborgs-Emigranten* 5 (1996): 114–40.
- "Swedes in Winnipeg up to the 1940s: Inter-Ethnic Relations." In *Swedish Life in American Cities*, edited by Dag Blanck and Harald Runblom, 44–71. Uppsala: Centre for Multiethnic Research, 1991. An abridged version of the same title was published in Ulf Beijbom, ed., *Swedes in America: Intercultural and Interethnic Perspectives on Contemporary Research: A Report of the Symposium Swedes in America: New Perspectives, 67–77.* Växjö: Emigrant Institute, 1993.
- and Hans Åkerman. "The Unknown Emigration – Swedes in Canada 1870–1970." *Arkiv i Norrland* 16 (1998): 81–125.
Lodge, Linnea. "Scandinavian Studies Association." *Vasa Star* (May–June 2008): 25.
- "The Vasa Order in Canada." *Vasa Star* (1971): 10–11.
Macfie, Dougald. "Så minns jag Harry!" *Minnesbilder från Ljungskilebygden. Ljungskileortens Hembygdsförening* 12 (1995): 36–41.
McKnight, Roger, trans. and ed. "Anders Olsson in British Columbia: Six Letters, 1906–1908." *Swedish Pioneer Historical Quarterly* 30, no. 2 (1979): 94–102.
Magnuson, Bruce. "Bruce Magnuson." In *Dangerous Patriots: Canada's Unknown Prisoners of War*, edited by William Repka and Kathleen M. Repka, 121–6, 228–30. Vancouver: New Star Books, 1982.
Mårald, Elisabeth. "A Postmodern Geographical Analysis of the Canadian Wilderness as Documented in Harry Macfie's Texts." Paper delivered at a 2004 conference in Riga. An abridged version of the same title was published in *Släktkrönikan: Tidning för medlemmar av Släktföreningen Thorburn-Macfie* 68 (December 2004): 24–5.

Marthin, Ingalena. "Swedes in Wilhelmina, Canada: A Tradition Is Tested against the Records." *Swedish American Genealogist* 24, no. 4 (2004): 18–19.

Mattisson, Jane. "Outside of Things: Swedish Emigrants, the English Language and the Canadian Prairie Dream." Paper delivered at the 8th Nordic Conference for English Studies, Göteborg University, 24–26 May 2001.

Mead, W.R. "A Northern Naturalist, Pehr Kalm, Disciple of Carl Linnaeus." *The Norseman* 12 (1954): 98–106, 182–8.

Mohr, Merilyn. "To Whom the Wilderness Speaks: The Remarkable Life of Louise de Kiriline Lawrence." *Harrowsmith* 83 (January–February 1989): 72–81.

Montero, Gloria. "Einar: Part and Parcel of Canada." In Gloria Montero, *The Immigrants*, 213–17. Toronto: James Lorimer, 1977. About Einar Nordstrom.

Moser, Isobel. "Why Is This Man Wearing His Suitcase? Hint: He's Not Making a Fashion Statement." *The Western Producer* (1 April 1993), quoting an article in *Scientific American*.

Myhrman, Anders. "The Finland-Swedes in America," translated by H. Arnold Barton. *Swedish Pioneer Historical Quarterly* 31, no. 1 (1980): 16–33.

Nelson, Helge. "The Interior Colonization in Canada at the Present Day, and its Natural Conditions." *Geografiska annaler* (1923): 244–308.

– "Kolonisation och befolkningsförskjutning inom Kanadas prärieprovinser." *Ymer* (1934): 161–80.

Olin, Johan Otto. "We Went to the Klondike in 1898." *Swedish Pioneer Historical Quarterly* 10, no. 3 (July 1959): 91–104.

Olljum, Irene. "The Swedish Cultural Society." Speech delivered at the fiftieth anniversary banquet, Vancouver, 6 June 2001.

Olsson, Nils William. "Naming Patterns among Swedish-Americans." *Swedish American Genealogist* 14, no. 2 (June 1994): 83–100.

– "Per Kalm and the Image of North America." James Ford Bell Lecture #7, 1970, 3–15.

Pearson, Helge V. "Canada-Tidningen: Swedish Canada News." In *The Multilingual Press in Manitoba*, edited by Joyce Bowling and M.H. Hykawy, 86–8. Winnipeg: Canada Press Club, 1974.

– "Norrona." In *The Multilingual Press in Manitoba*, edited by Joyce Bowling and M.H. Hykawy, 139–41. Winnipeg: Canada Press Club, 1974.

Person, Henry A. "The Swedes and Their Family Names." *Scandinavian Studies* 39, no. 3 (August 1967): 209–48.

Persson, Godfrey Sr. "Pioneer Settlers of New Stockholm." *The Western Producer* (March 1958): 22, 26.

Peterson, Ruth. "Vasa Children's Clubs Keep Swedish Traditions and Heritage Alive." *Bryggan/The Bridge* 18, no. 3 (1986): 86–7.

Plym, Albin. "Tolv år i Canadas vildmarker." In *Från Calmare Nyckel till Leif Viking: Ett samlingsverk för in- och utvandrare, svenskar ute och hemma*, edited by C. Österberg, 64–74. Stockholm: Riksinstitutet för släkt- och bygdeforskning, 1959.

Repo, Satu. Ivar [Einar] Nordstrom as told to Satu Repo. "Lakehead in the Thirties: A Labour Militant Remembers." *This Magazine* 13, no. 3 (July/ August 1979).

Roinila, Mika. "Finland-Swedes in Canada: Discovering Some Unknown Finnish Facts." *Siirtolaisuus – Migration* 1 (1997).

Rönnqvist, Carina. "Bröder och rivaler: Svenskarna, norrmännen och den skandinaviska identiteten i Canada, 1905–1945." In *Hembygden och världen: Festskrift till Ulf Beijbom*, edited by Lars Olsson and Sune Åkerman, 329–45. Växjö: Emigrantinstitutet, 2002.

– "Från ett framtidsland till ett annat: 1900-talsutvandringen från Norrbotten till Kanada." *Oknytt* 3–4 (2002): 50–72.

– "Scattered Swedes and Single Settlers: On Ethnic Identity Reflected in Nationalistic Sentiments, Gender and Class in 20th-century Canada." In *Swedishness Reconsidered: Three Centuries of Swedish-American Identities*, edited by Daniel Lindmark, 91–119. Umeå: Kulturgräns norr, 1999.

Rösiö, Bengt, Consul General of Sweden. "Letter from Montreal." *The Swedish-Canadian Chamber of Commerce Newsletter* 13 (December 1988): 6.

Rudling, Per Anders. "Ukrainian Swedes in Canada: Gammalsvenskby in the Swedish-Canadian Press, 1929–1931." *Scandinavian-Canadian Studies* 15 (2004–5): 62–91.

– "Scandinavians in Canada: A Community in the Shadow of the United States." *Swedish-American Historical Quarterly* 57, no. 3 (July 2006): 151–94.

Runblom, Harald. "Svenskarna i Canada. En studie i låg etnisk medvetenhet." In *Historieforskning på nya vägar: studier tillägnade Sten Carlsson*, edited by Lars-Göran Tedebrand, 213–28. Lund: Studentlitt, 1977.

– "The Swedes in Canada: A Study of Low Ethnic Consciousness," translated by Raymond Jarvi. *Swedish-American Historical Quarterly* 33, no. 1 (January 1982): 4–19.

St Jean, Eva. "En karlakarl bland karlar: Brev av ensamhet och trånad från svenska immigranter i Kanada, 1900–1930." In *Hembygden och världen: Festskrift till Ulf Beijbom*, edited by Lars Olsson and Sune Åkerman, 315–28. Växjö: Emigrant Institute, 2002.

– "From Defiance to Defence: Swedish-Canadian Ethnic Awareness during the Two World Wars." *American Studies in Scandinavia* 34 (2002): 54–84.

– "'Letters from the Promised Land': The Ambiguous Radicalization of a Swedish Immigrant, 1928–1934." *Labour/Le Travail* 53 (Spring 2004): 203–21.

Sandberg, L. Anders. "Literature as Social History: A Swedish Novelist in Manitoba." *Prairie Forum* 13, no. 1 (Spring 1988): 83–98. About Sven Delblanc.

Scott, Franklin D. "Sweden's Constructive Opposition to Emigration." *The Journal of Modern History* (September 1965): 307–35.

Shervill, R. Lynn. "Olof 'Tie' Hanson." *Whistle Punk* (Spring 1986): 17–21.

Sidenius, Oscar. "Making Sweden Known in America." *Scandinavia: A Monthly Magazine Devoted to the Interest of Scandinavians Everywhere* 1, no. 5 (May 1924): 55–6.

Sillanpää, Lennard. "Participating in Canada's Victory: The Finnish Community in Canada During World War II." *Siirtolaisuus-Migration* 2 (2004): 3–14.

Skarin, Ada. "Emil Rikard Thure Skarin, 1882–1970." In *Bjurträsk och Söderby byar i Lycksele socken*, edited by Ossian Egerbladh, 70–4 (1976).

Smistad, Alice Jean. "History of Branting Lodge." Speech delivered at the seventy-fifth anniversary celebration of Branting Vasa Lodge, Calgary, 19 April 1997.

Spafford, Mary. "Swede Girls for Canadian Homes." *The Canadian Magazine* (April 1907): 545–9.

Stenberg, Peter. "Nordic Languages and Programmes at Canadian Universities in Comparison with US Universities." In *Rediscoveriong Canada: Culture and Politics*, edited by Gudrun Björk Gudsteins and John Erik Fossum, 200–6. Aarhus, Denmark, and Reykjavik, Iceland: Nordic Association for Canadian Studies #19, 2002.

Streijffert, Bengt. "Karl Gunnarson's Canada." In *Canada and the Nordic Countries in Times of Reorientation: Literature & Criticism*, edited by Jørn Carlsen, 202–6. Aarhus, Denmark: Nordic Association for Canadian Studies #12, 1998.

Strid, Artur. "Från Södra Hulta till Lake Temiskaming: Några emigrantöden." *Osby Hembygdsförenings årsbok* (1989): 49–56.

Sundmark, Pat. "Clanwilliam Settlers, John and Hanna Sundmark." *Generations: Journal of the Manitoba Genealogical Society* 29, no. 3 (2004): 24–5.

Svensson, Roland. "Lars-Janne: Den störste av Gustavas folkrörelsepionjärer." *Gustavabygden* (2005): nr. 47, 14–16; nr. 48, 4–7; *Gustavabygden* (2006): nr. 49, 7–8.

"Swedes." In *Notes on the Canadian Family Tree*, 121–5. Ottawa: Department of Citizenship and Immigration, 1960.

Tedebrand, Lars-Göran. "Strikes and Political Radicalism in Sweden and Emigration to the United States." *Swedish Pioneer Historical Quarterly* 34, no. 3 (July 1983): 194–210.

Tornblom, Rolf. "Coming Home." *Green Mantle*, 27 November 1996, 5–7.

Tracie, C.M. "Land of Plenty or Poor Man's Land: Environmental Perception and Appraisal Respecting Agricultural Settlement in the Peace River Country, Canada." In *Images of the Plains: The Role of Human Nature in Settlement*, edited by Brian W. Blouet and Martin P. Lawson, 115–22. Lincoln: University of Nebraska Press, 1975.

Vennerström, Ivar. "Den skandinaviske Canadapressen: Stipendieberättelse." In *Publicistklubbens årsberättelse 1929*, 1–7.

Von Born, Heidi. "Promoting Canadian Literature in Sweden." In *Canada and the Nordic Countries: Proceedings from the Second International Conference of the Nordic Association for Canadian Studies, University of Lund, 1987*, edited by Jørn Carlsen and Bengt Streijffert, 65–73. Lund: University of Lund, 1988.

Wedin, Walter F. "Seeds and Swedes: Emigrant Clover from Alsike." *Swedish-American Historical Quarterly* 57, no. 1 (January 2006): 33–59.

Welsh, Dolores. "Familjen Ståhl i Canada." In *Bodsjöboken*, translated by Lennart Brunfelt, 13–14. Jämtland: Bodsjö hembygdsförening, 1999.

Westerberg, Kermit B. "In Private and Public: The Dialogue of Libraries, Immigrants, and Society." In *Scandinavian Immigrants and Education in North America*, edited by Philip J. Anderson, Dag Blanck, and Peter Kivisto, 190–204. Chicago: Swedish-American Historical Society, 1995.

Wijkman, The Honourable Per. "Sweden's Relationship with the British Empire and with Canada in Particular." In *The Empire Club of Canada Speeches 1944–1945*, 98–111. Toronto: The Empire Club of Canada, 1945.

Williams, P.O. George, as told by Geoffrey Hewelcke. "The Swedes Are our Friends." *Maclean's* (15 September 1944): 13, 26, 28, 30, and 32.

Wilson, J. Donald, and Jorgen Dahlie. "Introduction." *Canadian Ethnic Studies, Special Issue: Ethnic Radicals* 10, no. 2 (1978): 1–8.

Wonders, William C. "Mot Kanadas Nordväst: Pioneer Settlement by Scandinavians in Central Alberta." *Geografiska annaler* 65B (1983): 129–52.

– "Scandinavian Homesteaders." *Alberta History* 24, no. 3 (Summer 1976): 1–4.

– "Scandinavian Homesteaders in Central Alberta." In *The New Provinces: Alberta and Saskatchewan 1905–1980*, edited by H.B. Palmer and D.B. Smith, 131–71. Vancouver: Tantalus Research, 1980.

Wright, Rochelle. "Delblanc's *Kanaans land* and Moberg's Emigrant
Tetralogy: Intertextuality and Transformation." *Scandinavian-Canadian
Studies* 5 (1992): 81–93.

Zoumer, Rudolf. "Ett brev från Kanada." *Bryggan/The Bridge* 3, no. 3 (1971):
68–9.

BOOKS, THESES, AND REPORTS

Abella, Irving. *The Canadian Labour Movement, 1902–1960.* Booklet No. 28.
Ottawa: The Canadian Historical Association, 1975.

Alm, Edwin A. *I Never Wondered: An Autobiography.* Vancouver: Evergreen
Press, 1971.

Anderson, Alan Betts. "Assimilation in the Bloc Settlements of North-
Central Saskatchewan: A Comparative Study of Identity Change among
Seven Ethno-religious Groups in a Canadian Prairie Region." PhD
dissertation, University of Saskatchewan, Saskatoon, 1972.

Anderson, Ivah M. *Other Days Around Me: My Life in the Rainy River District.*
Devlin, ON, 1992.

Andersson, Per, and Johan Lindhardt. *Långarydssläkten: Länsman Anders
Jönssons i Långaryd ättlingar under tre sekel.* 4 vols. Stockholm: Draking, 2006.

Arnoldsson, Kjell. *Amerika-emigranterna från Örkened 1861–1961.* Lönsboda,
1961.

Austin, Paul Britten. *On Being Swedish: Reflections Towards a Better
Understanding of the Swedish Character.* London, UK: Secker & Warburg,
1968.

Avery, Donald. *"Dangerous Foreigners": European Immigrant Workers and Labour
Radicalism in Canada, 1896–1932.* Toronto: McClelland & Stewart, 1979.

Barr, Elinor. *A Capsule History, Norrskenet* [Northern Lights], *Swedish Sick
Benefit Society Est. 1905, Thunder Bay, Canada: 90th Anniversary, 2 April
1995.*

– *The Scandinavian Home Society 1923–1993: A Place to Meet, A Place to Eat.*
Thunder Bay: The Society, 1996.

– [Berglund]. *The Swedish Experience in Canada: An Annotated Bibliography.*
Växjö: Emigrant Institute, 1991.

Barton, H. Arnold. *A Folk Divided: Homeland Swedes and Swedish Americans,
1840–1940.* Carbondale: Southern Illinois University Press, 1994.

– ed. *Letters from the Promised Land: Swedes in America, 1840–1914.*
Minneapolis: University of Minnesota Press, 1975.

– *Search for Ancestors: A Swedish-American Family Saga*. Carbondale: Southern Illinois University Press, 1979.

Becker, Ethel Anderson. *Klondike '98: Hegg's Album of the 1898 Alaska Gold Rush*. 2nd ed. Portland, OR: Binfords & Mort, 1958.

Beijbom, Ulf. *Amerikabilder: Från utställningen Drömmen om Amerika och andra samlingar*. Växjö: Emigrantinstitutets vänner, 2002.

– *Guldfeber: En bok om guldrusherna till Kalifornien och Klondike*. Stockholm: Natur och kultur, 1979.

– *Uppbrott från stenriket: Utvandring från Kronoberg och kronobergare bortom haven*. Växjö: Emigrantinstitutets vänner, 2000.

Bengston, Henry. *On the Left in America: Memoirs of the Scandinavian-American Labor Movement*. Edited and introduction by Michael Brook. Translated by Kermit B. Westerberg. Carbondale: Southern Illinois University Press, 1999.

Benson, Adolph B., ed. *The America of 1750: Peter Kalm's Travels in North America*. 2 vols. 2nd ed. New York: Dover, 1966.

Bergen, N.J.L. *Nya sånger för folket*. Wetaskiwin, 1923.

Bergman, Hans. *British Columbia och dess svenska innebyggare. Historia, topografi, klimat, resurser, biografi, med 5 färgtrycksplanscher och 150 illustrationer därav 68 porträtt*. Victoria, 1923.

Bergren, Myrtle. *Bough of Needles: Eleven Canadian Short Stories*. Toronto: Progress Books, 1964.

– *Tough Timber: The Loggers of British Columbia – Their Story*. Toronto: Progress Books, 1966.

Bicha, Karel Denis. *The American Farmer and the Canadian West 1896–1914*. Lawrence, KS: Coronado Press, 1968.

Bjorkquist, Connie. *Bjorkquist Family History* [Birch Branch]. Jasper, 2005.

Black, Carol. *Härjedalsgillet*. North Vancouver, 1983.

Blanck, Dag. *Becoming Swedish-American: The Construction of an Ethnic Identity in the Augustana Synod, 1860–1917*. Uppsala, 1997. Reprinted with an added index as *The Creation of an Ethnic Identity: Being Swedish American in the Augustana Synod, 1860–1917*. Carbondale, IL: Southern Illinois University Press, 2006.

Blue, John. *Alberta, Past and Present, Historical and Biographical*. 3 vols. Chicago: Pioneer Historical Publishing Company, 1924.

Bogusis, Ruth, comp. *Checklist of Canadian Ethnic Serials: Swedish/Suedois*. Ottawa: National Library of Canada, Newspaper Division, Public Services Branch, 1981.

Bolander, Knud Graah. *Det nya Canada i ett möjligheternas land*. Stockholm: Ljus, 1947.

Burnet, Jean R., with Howard Palmer. *Coming Canadians: An Introduction to a History of Canada's Peoples*. Toronto: McClelland & Stewart, 1988.

Carlson, Emma Hall. *We Come to Canada and Our First Ten Years*. Erickson, MB, 1954.

Carlsson, Ragnar Emmanuel. *Män av gamla stammen: Historier från Brittiska Columbia*. Stockholm: Seelig, 1942.

– *Ung man gick west: Ett prärireportage*. Västervik: Rese Förlag, 1961.

Carlsson, Sten Carl Oscar. *Swedes in North America, 1638–1988: Technical, Cultural, and Political Achievements*. Stockholm: Streiffert, 1988.

Clemensson, Per, and Kjell Andersson. *Your Swedish Roots: A Step by Step Handbook*. Provo, UT: MyFamily.com, Inc. and Genline AB, 2004. Genealogy.

Daun, Åke. *Swedish Mentality*. Translated by Jan Teeland. Foreword by David Cooperman. Philadelphia: Pennsylvania State University Press, 1996.

Delblanc, Sven. *Kanaans land*. Stockholm: Bonnier, 1984.

– *Kritik och essäistik 1958–1991*. Edited by Lars Ahlbom. Introduction by Karl Erik Lagerlöf. Eslöv: B. Östlings bokförlag Symposion, 2007.

– *Minnen från Kanada*. Booklet published by Månadens Bok, 1984. Reprinted in *Swedish Press*, March 1988, 36–42.

– and Alice Boychuk. *Kära Alice: Sven Delblancs brev till sin syster i Canada kommenterade av henne själv* [Dear Alice: Sven Delblanc's letters to his sister in Canada with her own comments]. Edited and translated by Lars Helander. Sveriges Radio förlag, 1995. Swedish and English.

Ekberg, Percy, ed. *Årsbok 1931, Utgiven till Midsommartinget: Wadena, Sask. den 26, 27 och 28 juni, 1931*. Svenska förbundet i Canada/Swedish Canadian League, 1931.

Eldstrom, Herb. *Reflections and Recollections: A Collection of Memories*. Saskatchewan, 1995.

Emigrationsutredningen. Vol. 7, *Utvandrarnes egna uppgifter: Upplysningar inhemtade genom Emigrationsutredningens agenter äfvensom bref från svenskar i America*. Stockholm: Nordiska bokhandel, 1908.

En Smålandssocken emigrerar: En bok om emigrationen till Amerika från Långasjö socken i Kronobergs län. Växjö: Långasjö emigrantcirkel, 1967.

Epp, A. Ernest. *Nordic People in Canada: A Study in Demography 1861–2001*. Thunder Bay: A Lakehead Social History Institute Report, 2004.

Ericson, E. *Tänker du emigrera? Råd och upplyssningar för utvandrare.* Karlskoga: J.E. Ericsons förlag, 1924.

Fabbe, Harry F:son. *I slagbjörnens spår med bröderna Utterström: Bland indianer och storvilt.* Stockholm: Bonnier, 1932.

Flood, David. *Med gott humör i bagaget.* Uppsala: J.A. Lindblad, 1941.

Flygare, Hälle. *Buffelmarker.* Kungsbacka: Elander, 1975.

– *Sir Alexander Mackenzie Historic Waterways in Alberta: A Map/guide for River Travel on the Clearwater, Athabasca, Slave, Peace Rivers.* In cooperation with Recreation, Parks and Wildlife Foundation of Alberta: Canmore, AB, 1983.

– *Storvilt i Canada.* Stockholm: Bonnier, 1970.

– and John Woodworth. *In the Steps of Alexander Mackenzie: Trail Guide.* Sponsored by the Nature Conservancy of Canada. rev. ed. Kelowna: Sunbird Press, 1987.

Foster, Thelma Hofstrand. *Wild Daisies: A Novel.* Saskatoon: Modern Press, 1977.

Friesen, Gerald. *The Canadian Prairies: A History.* Toronto: University of Toronto Press, 1984.

Gibbon, John Murray. *Canadian Mosaic: The Making of a Northern Nation.* Toronto: McClelland & Stewart, 1938.

Gillén, C.W. *Minnen från mina resor genom Norra Amerikas Förenta Stater och Canada.* Örebro, 1897.

Giöbel-Lilja, Ingrid. *Erik for till Canada.* Stockholm, 1985.

Godtemplarordens Sångbok utgiven av Sveriges Storloge af I.O.G.T. Stockholm: Oskar Eklund, 1924.

Grenke, Arthur. *The German Community in Winnipeg: 1872–1919.* New York: AMS Press, 1991.

Grove, Frederick Philip. *Settlers of the Marsh.* Toronto: McClelland & Stewart, 1925, 1966.

Gunnarson, Karl, pseud. *Åter i Kanada som cowboy och pälsjägare.* Stockholm: Medén, 1941.

– *Kamratliv och äventyr på Kanadas prärier.* Stockholm: Hökerberg, 1931.

– *Som emigrant i Kanada.* 2nd. ed. Stockholm: Hökerberg, 1949.

– *Somranchägare bland indianer.* Stockholm: Hökerberg, 1945.

Gyllenhaal, Lars, and Lennart Westberg. *Svenskar i krig, 1914–1945.* Lund: Historiska Media, 2004.

Hacquoil, Andrew J. "'Let Us All Be Optimistic from Now On.' Oscar Styffe Limited 1927–1945: The Middleman of Northwestern Ontario and the

Pulp and Paper Trade." Master's thesis, Lakehead University, Thunder Bay, 1994.

Hagglund, Ruth E. "Building a Home in Fort William: The Origins and Development of the John Hagglund Lumber and Fuel Company." HBA thesis, Lakehead University, Thunder Bay, 1984.

Halliwell, Gladys M., and M. Zetta D. Persson. *Three Score and Ten, 1886–1956: A Story of the Swedish Settlement of Stockholm and District.* Yorkton, 1959.

Hansen, Marcus Lee, and John Bartlet Brebner. *The Mingling of the Canadian and American Peoples.* Vol. 1, *Historical.* Toronto: Ryerson Press, 1940.

Hedman, Irina. *Canada.* Stockholm, 1976.

Hedman, Jörgen. *Gammalsvenskby – The True Story of the Swedish Settlement in Ukraine.* Stockholm, 2005.

– *Svenskbysläkter: Släktförteckningar över familjerna från Gammalsvenskby i Ukraina.* Visby: Ödin, 1994.

– and Lars Åhlander. *Historien om Gammalsvenskby och svenskarna i Ukraina.* Stockholm: Dialogos, 2003. Appendix titled "Svenskbyborna i Canada: De första emigranterna (1885–1926)."

Hirsch, Stina. "The Swedish Maid, 1900–1915." Master's thesis, De Paul University, Chicago, 1985.

Hoerder, Dirk. *Creating Societies. Immigrant Lives in Canada.* Montreal: McGill-Queen's University Press, 2000.

Holm, Gerald F. *Geographical Names of Manitoba.* Winnipeg: Manitoba Geographical Names Program, 2001.

– and Anthony P. Buchner. *A Place of Honour – Manitoba's War Dead Commemorated in its Geography.* Winnipeg: Manitoba Geographical Names Program, 2002.

Houser, George J. *The Swedish Community at Eriksdale, Manitoba.* Ottawa: National Museum of Man, 1976.

Howard, Irene. *Gold Dust on His Shirt: The True Story of an Immigrant Mining Family.* Toronto: Between the Lines, 2008.

– *Vancouver's Svenskar: A History of the Swedish Community in Vancouver.* Vancouver: Vancouver Historical Society, 1970.

Karlson, Knute E. *A Swedish Immigrant in Canada 1911–1971.* New York: Vantage Press, 1977.

Kastrup, Allan. *Swedes in Canada.* New York: Swedish Information Service, 1967. Ten typescript pages.

– *The Swedish Heritage in America: The Swedish Element in America and American-Swedish Relations in Their Historical Perspective.* Minneapolis: Swedish Council of America, 1975.

Kerkkonen, Martti. *Peter Kalm's North American Journey: Its Ideological Background and Results*. Helsinki: Finnish Historical Society, 1959.

Kirkconnell, Watson. *Canadian Overtones: An Anthology of Canadian Poetry Written Originally in Icelandic, Swedish, Norwegian, Hungarian, Italian, Greek, and Ukrainian, and Now Translated and Edited with Biographical, Historical, Critical and Bibliographical Notes*. Winnipeg, 1935.

Knowles, Valerie. *Strangers at Our Gates: Canadian Immigration and Immigration Policy, 1540–1990*. Toronto: Dundurn Press, 1992.

Kristiansson, Gunnar, and Karin Färnström. *Framtidslandet Kanada*. Stockholm: Natur och kultur, 1954.

Landelius, Otto Robert. *Swedish Place-Names in North America*. Translated by Karin Franzén. Edited by Raymond Jarvi. Chicago: Swedish-American Historical Society, 1985.

Lawrence, Louise de Kiriline. *Another Winter, Another Spring: A Love Remembered*. Toronto: Natural Heritage, 1987. Previously published by McGraw-Hill.

Lindal, Walter Jacobson. *The Contribution Made by the Scandinavian Ethnic Groups to the Cultural Enrichment of Canada: Draft: Final Report*. Winnipeg: Royal Commission on Bilingualism and Multiculturalism, 1966.

Lindell, Lucy B. *Rites of Passage: Our Story*. Eriksdale, MB: Christian Press, 2000.

Ljungmark, Lars. *Svenskarna i Winnipeg: Porten till prärien 1872–1940*. Växjö: Emigrantinstitutets vänner, 1994.

– *Swedish Exodus*. Translated by Kermit Westerberg. Carbondale: Southern Illinois University Press, 1979. Revised translation of *Den stora utvandringen*, 1965.

Lodge, Linnea. *Skandia [Vasa Lodge No. 549, Edmonton]: 60 Years in Review: 1929–1978*. Edmonton, 1978.

Loewen, Royden. *Ethnic Farm Culture in Western Canada*. Booklet No. 29. Ottawa: Canadian Historical Association, 2002.

Loken, Gulbrand. *From Fjord to Frontier: A History of the Norwegians in Canada*. Toronto: McClelland & Stewart, 1980.

Loov, Edvin Anders William. *Twenty-Five Years Away From Home: Experiences of a Swedish Immigrant in Canada 1927–1952*. Translated by Robert Loov with Verner Loov and Solveig Penner. Calgary, 1995.

Macfie, Harry. *Farväl Falcon Lake*. Stockholm: Bonnier, 1943.

– *Lägereldar längesen*. Stockholm: Bonnier, 1936.

– *Norrskenets män: En berättelse om den canadensiska vildmarkens polis*. Stockholm: Bonnier, 1938.

– and Hans G. Westerlund. *Wasawasa: äventyr som trapper och guldgrävare i Canada och Alaska*. Stockholm: Bonnier, 1935.

– *Wasa-Wasa: A Tale of Trails and Treasure*. Translated from the Swedish by F.H. Lyon. London, UK: Allen & Unwin, 1951.

Magee, Joan. *A Scandinavian Heritage: 200 Years of Scandinavian Presence in the Windsor-Detroit Border Region*. Toronto: Dundurn Press, 1985.

Magnuson, Bruce. *The Untold Story of Ontario's Bushworkers: A Political Memoir*. Toronto: Progress Books, 1990.

Marshall, Denis. *Sawdust Caesars and Family Ties in the Southern Interior Forests*. Salmon Arm Branch: Okanagan Historical Society, 2003. Includes business biography of Rolf Wallgren Bruhn.

McCloy, William. *Scandinavians in Europe and in Canada*. Presbyterian Church in Canada: Board of Home Missions, 1913.

Mikkelsen, Mai Klaerke, Robert Christian Thomsen, and Peter Bakker, eds. *NACS/ANEC: Chronicle of Activities and Publications 1997–2007*. Århus, Denmark: Nordic Association for Canadian Studies, 2007.

Molin, Adrian. *Några drag af kolonisationen i Canada*. Stockholm: Geber, 1913.

Morgan, Murray Cromwell. *One Man's Gold Rush: A Klondike Album, Photographs by E.A. Hegg*. Seattle: University of Washington Press, 1967.

Murray, Joan, ed. and intro. *Letters Home 1859–1906: The Letters of William Blair Bruce*. Moonbeam, ON: Penumbra Press, 1982.

Nelson, Carl G. *Memoarer och reseskildringar*. San Diego: 1971.

Nelson, Helge. *Canada: Nybyggarlandet*. Stockholm: Bergvall, 1922.

– *Nordamerika: Natur, bygd och svenskbygd*. 2 vols. Stockholm: Bergvall, 1926.

– *Swedes and the Swedish Settlements in North America*. 2 vols. Lund: Gleerup, 1943.

Nilsson, Axel V. *Brända vingar*. Ystad: Aurora, 1947.

Nilsson, Birgitta. *Från Lomma till Norra Amerika*. Bjärred, Skåne: 2005.

Nilsson, Gunnar. *De sista svenska rösterna: Resa bland emigranter i Kanada*. Stockholm: Carlsson, 1995.

Norman, Hans, Harald Runblom, Ann-Sofie Kälvemark, and Lars-Göran Tedebrand. *Amerika-emigrationen*. Uddevala: Cikada, 1980.

Olafson, Karl. *A Sentimental Journey: A Memoir*. Winnipeg, 2006. A memoir about growing up along the railway line.

Österberg, C., ed. *Från Calmare Nyckel till Leif Viking: Ett samlingsverk för in- och utvandrare, svenskar ute och hemma*. Stockholm: Riksinstitutet för släkt- och bygdeforskning, 1959. Interviews with immigrants who returned to Sweden.

Österlund-Pötzsch, Susanne. *American Plus: Etnisk identitet hos finlandssvenska ättlingar i Nordamerika.* Helsinki: Svenska litteratursällskapet i Finland, 2003. Includes a summary in English.

Øverland, Orm, ed., trans., and intro. *Johan Schrøder's Travels in Canada, 1863.* Montreal: McGill-Queen's University Press, 1989.

Pearson, John, and Lorne Pearson. *The Valley of the Fraser: A True Historic Narrative from Surrey's Formative Years.* Surrey, BC: City of Surrey, 2005. About Eric Anderson, 1872 immigrant.

Person, Lloyd H. *Growing up in Minby.* Saskatoon: Western Producer Prairie Books, 1976.

Petrou, Michael. *Renegades: Canadians in the Spanish Civil War.* Vancouver: University of British Columbia Press, 2008.

Plym, Albin. *Rallare och guldgrävare.* Stockholm: Arbetarkultur, 1952.

– *Rallarliv i Canada.* Stockholm: Arbetarkultur, 1950.

Rasmussen, Mildred E. *A Swedish Girl, En Svenska Flicka.* Edmonton: Teddington Lock, 2000.

Ringstrom, Emma. *Riding Mountain Yesterday and Today.* Winnipeg: Prairie Publishing, 1981.

Roinila, Mika. *Finland-Swedes in Canada: Migration, Settlement and Ethnic Relations.* Turku, Finland: Institute of Migration, 2000.

Rönnqvist, Carina. *Svea folk i Babels land: Svensk identitet i Kanada under 1900-takets första hälft.* Umeå: Kulturgräns norr, 2004. English summary pages 319–25.

Sahlin, Claes. *Från Canada till Mexico: Reseskildring.* Chicago: Skandinaviska Socialistförbundet i America, 1916.

St Jean, Eva. "Swedes on the Move: Politics, Culture, and Work among Swedish Immigrants in British Columbia, 1900-1950." PhD dissertation, University of Victoria, Victoria, 2004.

Scandinavian Connections: A Guide to Sites in Alberta: Denmark, Finland, Iceland, Norway, Sweden. Edmonton: Scandinavian Trade and Cultural Society, 2007.

Scott, Franklin D. *Sweden: The Nation's History.* Minneapolis: University of Minnesota Press, 1977.

Skagegård, Lars-Åke. *The Remarkable Story of Alfred Nobel and the Nobel Prize.* Translated by George Varcoe. Uppsala: Konsultförlaget, 1994.

Stenindustrins historia i Örkened åren 1890–1980. Hässleholm: Nord-Skåne, 1981.

Stone, C.G., and F. Joan Garnett. *Brandon College: A History, 1899–1967.* Brandon: Brandon University, 1969.

Styffe, John. *Oscar R. Styffe, 1885–1943: The Man and His Companies.* Thunder Bay: Lakehead University Library, 1985.

Sundbeck, Carl. *Svensk-amerikanerna, deras materiella och andliga sträfvanden: Anteckningar från en resa i Amerika.* Rock Island: Augustana Book Concern, 1904.

Svedberg, Staffan. *Expedition Canada: Kanotexpedition över canadansiska tundran.* Translated by Anne-Marie Axelsson and Rolf Esko as *A Report of the Swedish Canoe Expedition Across the Canadian Barrens.* Kiruna, 1972.

Swanson, Roy. *Swanee's Cabins 1933–1967.* Mississauga: R. Swanson, 1993.

Swanson, Swan. *Swan Swanson – Immigrant, 1867–1900.* Edited by Roy Swanson. Mississauga: R. Swanson, 1992.

– *The Forgotten Army, 1900–1933.* Mississauga: R. Swanson, 1992.

Taylor, C. James, Edward Mills, and Pat Buchik. *Riding Mountain National Park of Canada: Built Heritage Resource Description and Analysis.* Calgary: Parks Canada, Western Service Centre, 2001.

Taylor, Philip. *The Distant Magnet: European Immigration to the U.S.A.* New York: Harper & Row, 1971.

Thomeus, Edwin. *Letters of a Swedish Homesteader: Life in Magnolia 1905–1912.* Translated by Harold Anderson. Stony Plain, AB: Multicultural Heritage Centre, 1983.

Thompson, John Herd. *Ethnic Minorities during Two World Wars.* Ottawa: Canadian Historical Association, 1991.

Tolvanen, Ahti. *Finntown: A Perspective on Urban Integration: Port Arthur Finns in the Inter-War Period 1918–1939.* Helsinki: Yliopistopaino, 1985.

Troper, Harold Martin. *Only Farmers Need Apply: Official Canadian Government Encouragement of Immigration from the United States, 1896–1911.* Toronto: Griffin House, 1972.

Tyman, John Langton. *By Section, Township and Range: Studies in Prairie Settlement.* Brandon: Assiniboine Historical Society, 1972.

Uddén, Svante. *Från Canada.* Rock Island: Augustana Book Concern, 1898.

Utterström, John. *Pälsjägarliv: Med kamera och bössa på canadensiska jaktstigar.* Stockholm: Wahlström & Widstrand, 1932.

– *Straws in the Wind.* New York: Vantage Press, 1962.

Vasa Order of America: A Swedish-American Fraternal Organization: Centennial 1896–1996. Bishop Hill, IL: Vasa Order of America, 1996.

Vennerström, Ivar. *Kanada och Kanadasvenskarna: Studier och reseintryck.* Stockholm: Tiden, 1926.

Viksten, Adolf. *Bland jägare och guldgrävare i Canada*. Laholm: Settern, 1979.

Viksten, Albert. *Guds eget land*. Stockholm: Bonnier, 1938.

– *I guldjägares spår: resan till Yukon och Alaska*. Stockholm: LT, 1951.

– *Pälsjägarnas paradis*. Stockholm: LT, 1959.

– *Vilda vägar västerut*. Stockholm: Bonnier, 1938.

Viksten-Koerner, Karin. *Albert Viksten: A Portrait of My Father: A Selection of My Father's Writings*. Translated by Ann-Charlotte Berglund. Victoria: Trafford, 2005.

Visit to Canada of Their Majesties King Carl XVI Gustaf and Queen Silvia of Sweden. Ottawa: Parliamentary Relations Secretariat, 1988.

Waldenström, Paul Peter. *Genom Canada: Reseskildringar från 1904*. Stockholm: Norman, 1905.

Werner, Gunnar. *Från Gotland till Nordamerika: Några drag ur en gotländsk emigranthistorik 1884–ca1900*. Linköping: 1979.

Wickström, Victor Hugo. *Genom sju konungariken: Reseminnen*. Östersund: 1904.

Wonders, William C. "Norden and Canada – A Geographer's Perspective, A Theme Paper presented at the Triennial Conference 'Canada and the Nordic Countries' of the Nordic Association for Canadian Studies, Lund University, Sweden, 11–14 August, 1987."

Woodsworth, James S. *Strangers Within our Gates or Coming Canadians*. Toronto: Missionary Society of the Methodist Church, 1909.

LOCAL HISTORIES

Along the Burnt Lake Trail: A History of Shady Nook, Burnt Lake, Centerville, Pine Hill, Marianne, Kuusamo and Evarts. Red Deer, AB: Burnt Lake History Society, 1977.

Between Long Lake and Last Mountain: Bulyea, Duval, Strasbourg. 2 vols. Strasbourg, SK, 1982.

Caldwell, Gary. *Waterville 1876–2001*. Sherbrooke, QC: Éditions Louis Bilodeau, 2000.

Campbell, Roanna Bean. *Little Beaver Tales: Ferintosh and District*. Ferintosh, AB, 1986.

Centennial Tribute: Broadview, Percival, Oakshela 1892–1992. Broadview, SK: Broadview Pioneer Historical Society, 1982.

Chronicles of Canwood and Districts: Moose Valley, Sugar Hill, Moonbeam, Boro Green, Sandy Lake, Stump Lake, Balsamdale, Silver Cliff, Dry Creek, Silent

Call, Nestledown, Summit Prairie, Blue Heron, Canwood. Canwood, AB, 1981.

Closson, George. *Freedhome: 70 Years*. Stockholm, SK, 1978.

Crowsnest and Its People. Coleman, AB: Crowsnest Historical Society, 2000.

Edstrom, Sylvia, and Florence Lundstrom, comps. *Memoirs of the Edberg Pioneers*. Edmonton, AB: Douglas Printing, 1955.

Enarson, Amy. "Highland Park." In *Memory Opens the Door: New Norway and District*, 86–107. Edmonton, AB, 1978.

Footsteps to Follow: A History of Young, Zelma and Districts. Young, SK, 1981.

Forest to Field: Centennial History of Rural Municipality of Clanwilliam and Village of Erickson, Manitoba, Canada. Erickson, MB, 1984.

Golden Memories: Warburg and District. Warburg, AB, 1977.

Halliwell, Gladys M., and M. Zetta Persson. *Three Score and Ten 1886–1956: A Story of the Swedish Settlement of Stockholm and District*. Yorkton, SK: Redeemers' Voice Press, 1959.

Helander, Otto, and Judith Johnson. "Swedish Colony of Norris Lake." In *Rockwood Echoes: 90 Years of Progress 1870–1960: A History of the Men and Women who Pioneered the Rockwood Municipality*, edited by R.A. Quickfall. Stonewall, MB: Rockwood-Woodlands Historical Society, 1960.

History of Compton County: And Sketches of the Eastern Townships, District of St. Francis and Sherbrooke County. Belleville, ON: Mika, 1975.

Interlake Beckoned: A History of Inwood and Surrounding Districts. Inwood, MB, 1980.

Kipling 100, 1893–1993. Kipling, ON, 1993.

Larson, Annie. "The Influence of Swedish Settlers in the District of Young." *Nya svenska pressen*, 15 January 1965.

Leaves Green and Gold: Weldon, Shannonville, Windermere. Weldon, SK: Weldon and District Historical Society, 1980.

Lewisville Pioneers. Malmo, AB: Malmo Women's Institute History Committee, 1963.

Lindell, Lucy, comp. *Memory Opens the Door: History as Told by Pioneers of the Central West-Interlake Area*. Eriksdale, MB, 1970.

Livelong Legacies. Livelong, SK: Livelong Historical Society, 1981.

Logs & Lines from the Winnipeg River: A History of the Lac du Bonnet Area. Lac du Bonnet, MB, 1980.

MacDonald, Linda E.T., and Lynette R. Bleiler, comps. *Gold & Galena: A History of the Mayo District*. Mayo, YK: Mayo Historical Society, 1999.

Magnolia: The First Hundred Years. Entwhistle, AB: Magnolia Press, 2000.

Martin, Isobel, ed. *Forests to Grainfields*. Berrymoor, AB: Berrymoor/Canwood Historical Society, 1977.

Meadows: Centennial 1970. Meadows, MB, 1970.

Mecca Glen Memories. 2nd ed. Ponoka, AB, 2001.

Mingling Memories. Red Deer, AB: Red Deer Historical Society, 1979.

Minnedosa Valley Views: Minnedosa's 100th Anniversary. Winnipeg, MB, 1982.

Mitchell, Helen A. *Diamond in the Rough: A History of Campbell River*. Alder Grove, BC: Frontier Publishing, 1966, 1975.

Nespor, Vivian, and Ray (Sonny) Burnside. *Caviar and Venison: Memories of Lettonia and Newcombe*. Winnipeg, MB, 1991.

Norquay Nostalgia: 1912–1982. Norquay, SK, 1982.

100 Years of History: Rockwood Municipality. Stonewall, MB, 1982.

Oslund, Christopher. *One Hundred Years of Swedish Settlement in Timiskaming*. Haileybury, ON: Rosanne Fisher, 1996.

Pages from the Past: A History of Paswegin and School Districts Harrow, North Quill, Quill City, Tiger Lily and Wooler. Wadena, SK, 1982.

A Patchwork of Memories. Thorsby, AB: The Historical Society of Thorsby and District, 1979.

Pioneer Pathways: Rural Wetaskiwin. 2 vols. Wetaskiwin, AB, 1981.

Pioneers and Progress: Calmar and District. Calmar, AB, 1980.

Prairie Echoes: Precious Memories of the Former Hillcrest Municipality: Metiskow, Cadogan, Cairns. Cadogan, AB: Hillcrest Heritage Society, 1976.

Quarter Stake Echoes. Shaunavon, SK, 1981.

Remembering Times: Wadena and Area Dating Back to 1882. 2 vols. Wadena, SK, 1992.

Richthammer, John E. *The End of the Road: A History of the Red Lake District*. Red Lake, ON: Red Lake District Festival Days Association, 1985.

Rock, Fur, Forest, Lakes: A History. Wabigoon, ON, 1988.

Scandia Since Seventeen. Scandia, AB, 1978.

Stout, Clarence Howard. *From Frontier Days in Leduc and District: 65 Years of Progress: 1891–1956*. Leduc, AB: Leduc Historical Society, 1956, 1980.

Taylor, Harry, comp. *Powell River's First Fifty Years: 1910–1960*. Powell River, BC: A.H. Alsgard, 1960.

Thompson, Bill. *Texada Island*. Powell River, BC, 1997.

Water under the Bridge: History of the Little Grassy River, McCrosson-Tovell, 1893–1993. Sleeman, ON, 1994.

Where the Red Willows Grew: Valleyview and Surrounding Districts. Valleyview, AB, 1980.

Where the Wheatlands Meet the Range. Claresholm, AB, 1974.

Wickstrom, Ella Forssell, Karin Edberg-Lee, and Linda Eide Kask. *Recollections of Silverhill: An Informal History of an Immigrant Settlement.* Vancouver, BC, 1990.

Wigwams to Windmills: A History of Ridgedale and Area. Abbotsford, BC: Ridgedale Women's Institute, 1977.

Wilderness to Wildlife: Chatfield, Fishlake, Narcisse, Sandridge, Clematis, Willowview, Neveton, Markland, Wheathill. Selkirk, MB, 1981.

Yesterday and Today. 2 vols. Ponteix, SK, 1991.

RELIGIOUS MATERIALS

Anderson, Bruce William. *Pioneer Missionary: Lars Petter Lundgren and Wife Alma: The True Life Story of a Pioneer Ministry in Minnesota's Last Frontier, North Dakota, and Canada 1892–1923.* Niles, MI: The Author, 2004.

Anderson, E. Earl. *"Si Gud's Lam/*Behold the Lamb of God: The Story of the Swedish Evangelical Lutheran Bethesda Congregation, Kenora, Ontario, 1894–1994." Thesis, Lutheran Theological Seminary, Gettysburg, PA, 1999.

Anderson, W.B. *The Covenant Church in Canada 1904–1994: A Time to Remember.* Prince Albert, SK: Evangelical Covenant Church of Canada, 1995.

Arden, G. Everett. *Augustana Heritage: A History of the Augustana Lutheran Church.* Rock Island: Augustana Press, 1963.

Årsbok för svenska baptistförsamlingarna inom Amerika. Chicago: Svenska Baptisternas i Amerika allmänna konferens. Missionary reports from Canada, 1905–1914.

Baglo, Ferdinand Eugene. *The Story of Augustana Lutherans in Canada.* Saskatoon: Canada Conference of the Augustana Lutheran Church, 1962.

– general ed. *Faithfully Yours: Otto A. Olson (1920–1976): A Devotional Biography of the First President of the Central Canada Synod, Lutheran Church in America (1963–1976).* Winnipeg: Central Canada Synod, Lutheran Church in America, 1978.

Bergendoff, Conrad John Immanuel. "Augustana in America and Sweden." *Swedish Pioneer Historical Quarterly* 24, no. 4 (1973): 238–41.

– *The Augustana Ministerium: A Study of the Careers of the 2,504 pastors of the Augustana Evangelical Lutheran Synod/Church, 1850–1962.* Rock Island: Augustana Historical Society, 1980.

Bethesda Lutheran Church, Kenora, ON, Fiftieth Anniversary, 1894–1944.

– Ninetieth Anniversary, 1894–1984.

Bethlehem Lutheran Church, Erickson-Scandinavia, Manitoba, 1891–1941.

– *Erickson, Manitoba, 75th Anniversary, 1891–1966.*

Bethlehem Lutheran Church, Wetaskiwin, Alberta, Seventy-Fifth Anniversary, 1898–1973.

Boegh, Beth. *Immanuel Evangelical Lutheran Church, 1906–2006: 100 Years of Faith and Fellowship.* Thunder Bay, 2006.

Brandt, E. "Swedish Baptists." In *Pioneering in Western Canada: A Story of the Baptists,* edited by Colin C. McLaurin, 357–80. Calgary, 1939.

Brockington Mission Covenant Church [Saskatchewan], Fiftieth Anniversary 1913–1963.

Brorson, Alf. "Fryksande, Minnesota." *Bryggan/The Bridge* 38, no. 2 (2006): 8–10.

– "Fryksende i Kanada." *Siriklockan: Fryksände pastorats kyrkoblad* 16, no. 3 (2005): 10–11.

– *Något om Fryksande och Lekvatten i ett nordamerikanskt perspektiv.* Vol. 11, *Skrifter från Fryksände.* Torsby: Fryksände församling, 2004.

Burgess, Thomas. *Swedish Folk Within Our Church: The Rise, Normal Decline and Glorious Results of Half a Century's Work.* New York: [Episcopal] Church Missions House, Foreign-Born Americans Division, 1929.

Calvary Lutheran Church, 1898–1973, 75th Anniversary. Wetaskiwin, 1973. Originally Svea Lutheran Church.

– *Wetaskiwin, Alberta, 1898–1998, 100th Anniversary.*

"Canadamissionen: Dess uppkomst och bedrivande inom provinserna Ontario, Manitoba, Saskatchewan och Alberta till år 1913, då Canada-konferensen bildades." In Emil Lund, *Minnesota-Konferensens av Augustana-Synoden och dess församlingars historia,* 91–101. Rock Island: Augustana Book Concern, 1920.

Carlson, G. William. *"God Knows What Is Best": Poems by Signe Olson Peterson.* Swedish poems edited and read by Jean Hanslin. Bethel College Library, 7 October 2000.

– "The Pietist Poetry of Signe Olson Peterson: 'The Letter Started on' Understanding the Immigrant Experience." *The Baptist Pietist Clarion* 6, no. 1 (June 2007): 12–15.

Cronmiller, Carl Raymond. *A History of the Lutheran Church in Canada.* Vol 1. Kitchener, ON: Evangelical Lutheran Synod of Canada, 1961.

Dahlberg, J.G. "Canada-missionen." In *Korsbaneret: Kristlig kalender för året 1914,* edited by O.V. Holmgrain, 59–105. Rock Island: Augustana Book Concern, 1914.

Dahlhielm, Erik, ed. *Covenant Memories: Swedish Evangelical Mission Covenant 1885–1935: Golden Jubilee.* Chicago: Covenant Book Concern, 1935.

Days of Our Years: Golden Jubilee of the Evangelical Mission Covenant of Canada: A History in Commemoration of Fifty Years, 1904–1954. Prince Albert, SK: Evangelical Mission Covenant of Canada, 1954.

Evangelical Covenant Church of Minnedosa, Manitoba [Smoland Mission Covenant Church], 50th Anniversary 1908–1958.

Evangelical Covenant Church, Minnedosa, Manitoba, 1908–1983.

Fihn, L.J. "Canada Missionen." In *Minnesskrift 1858–1908 tillegnad Minnesota-Konferensens af Ev. Luterska Augustana-Synoden 50-års Jubileium,* edited by F. M. Eckman, 207–17. Rock Island, IL.

Fremling, J. "L.G. Almén." In *Korsbaneret: Kristlig kalender för året 1914,* edited by O.V. Holmgrain, 166–77. Rock Island: Augustana Book Concern, 1914.

Fullerton, Keith C., ed. *One Hundred Years: The Evangelical Covenant Church in Canada.* Winnipeg: Evangelical Covenant Church of Canada, 2004.

Granquist, Mark A. "The Augustana Synod and the Episcopal Church." *Lutheran Quarterly* 14 (2000): 173–92.

– "Smaller Religious Groups in the Swedish-American Community." *Swedish-American Historical Quarterly* 44, no. 4 (October 1992): 217–29.

Grant Memorial Baptist Church: Historical Highlights 1894–1994.

– *A History of: Vision Unlimited: Prepared on the Occasion of Our 90th Anniversary Year 1895–1984.*

Heckman, Warren L. *History of the Fellowship of Christian Assemblies.* Kankakee, IL: Olivet Nazarene University, 1994.

Highland Park Evangelical Free Church [Alberta], 60th Anniversary, 1961.

Hilltop Baptist Church [Manitoba], 100th Anniversary, 1896–1996.

Johnson, Emeroy. *God Gave the Growth: The Story of the Lutheran Minnesota Conference 1876–1958.* Minneapolis: Denison, 1958.

Lyttkens, Carl Henrik. *The Growth of Swedish-Anglican Intercommunion between 1833 and 1922.* Lund: Gleerup, 1970.

Malmo Mission Covenant Church [Alberta]: Seventy-five Years, 1898–1973.

Minnesskrift: Första skandinaviska kristna missionsförsamlingen, Winnipeg, Canada: Femtio år1885–1935, Femtioårs-jubileet den 25 januari 1935. Winnipeg, 1935.

Munholland, Lois Knudson. *Pulpits of the Past: A Record of Closed Lutheran Churches in Saskatchewan up to 2003.* Strasbourg, SK: Three West Two South Books, 2004.

Murray, Robert, ed. *The Church of Sweden, Past and Present.* Translated by Nils G. Sahlin. Malmö: Swedish Bishops' Conference, 1960.

Nelson, Edward O. "Recollections of the Salvation Army's Scandinavian Corps." *Swedish Pioneer Historical Quarterly* 29, no. 4 (October 1978): 257–76.

New Stockholm Lutheran Church [Saskatchewan] 1889–1989: A Century of Faith.

New Sweden Mission Church [Alberta]: 1894–1994: How Great Thou Art, O Store Gud.

Olson, Adolf. *A Centenary History: As Related to the Baptist General Conference of America: A Century of God's Grace 1852–1952.* Chicago: Baptist Conference Press, 1952.

Our Scandinavian Missions, Alberta, N.W.T. Sherbrooke, QC: Canada Congregational Missionary Society, 1904.

Renhard, Carl J. *Fifty Years of the Columbia Conference 1893–1943: Historical Glimpses of Lutheran Mission Work in the Pacific Northwest under the Auspices of the Columbia Conference of the Lutheran Augustana Synod.* Edited by Carl H. Sandgren. Rock Island: Augustana Book Concern, 1943.

St Mark's Lutheran Church, Winnipeg, 100th Anniversary, 1990.

Salem Lutheran Church, Scandia, Alberta: 75th Anniversary Celebrations, 1994.

Sjoberg, Donald W. "Augustana in Canada – People and Places." Speech delivered at the Augustana Heritage Association Gathering, St Peter, MN, 26 June 2004.

Swedish Baptist Churches of America for 1942–1943. Part II, Statistics and addresses. Chicago: Swedish Baptist General Conference of America, 1943.

Taylor, Bruce W. *Pioneer Ministry: St. Andrew's Presbyterian Church, New Liskeard, Ontario: Centennial History 1895–1995.* New Liskeard, 1995.

Thompson, Margaret E. *The Baptist Story in Western Canada.* Calgary: Baptist Union of Western Canada, 1975.

"Vårt missionsarbete i de britiska provinserna Manitoba, Assiniboia och Alberta i N. Amerika." In *Korsbaneret: Kristlig kalender för 1894,* edited by Erik Norelius, 46–70. Rock Island: Augustana Book Concern, 1894.

Wilhelmina Evangelical Lutheran Church: Fifty Years of Grace, 1908–1958: Golden Jubilee June 27–29, 1958.

Wilhelmina Lutheran Church, Hay Lakes, Alberta: Living in God's Grace: 1908–2008.

SELECTED UNPUBLISHED WORKS
FROM PRIVATE COLLECTIONS

Anderson, Olga. "Olga's Essay about our Family" (1974).

Anderson, Viola. "The Gift: Memoirs of Viola Anderson."

Bowman, Edward L. "Family Tree for Karin Margareta Randin" (1987).

Buskas, Roxann. "Malmas Memories."

Carlson, Ed. "Some Memories from Logan Ave. in the Dirty Thirties."

Carlson, Erick. "History of My Life in Canada."

Carlson, Ingrid. "From Earth to Glory: Mom Carlson's Life Story 1906–1986."

Clark, Erika M. "Swedish Immigrant Women" (1994).

Cook, Arthur. "The Frejd Family Tree."

"Diary of Dan Ericson, 29 March 1918–19 June 1919" (transcribed by Leslie Daniel Ericson).

Domier, K.W. "History of the Scandinavian Studies Association" (2006).

Ericson, Ottilia Carolina. "Tillie's Triumphs" (1967).

Fahlstrom, Lars. "Emil Skarin (1882–1970)" (2003).

Fitzsimmons, Sharon. "The Peterson Family Story" (1988).

Goodyear, Roland C. "Lewis Miller and Harry J. Crowe" (1968).

Graydon, Karin. "The Hammarstrand Family."

Gusdal, Patricia. "The Johnson-Gusdal Family and Riding Mountain National Park" (1983).

Hautala, Vi. "Eric Ericson, My Father" (1999).

Havel, J.E. "Anne Marie Havel born Luhr" (2003).

Hedvall, Per. "History of Scandinavian Baptist Church in Port Arthur, 25th Anniversary" (1930).

Kelley, Marta (Setterlund). "Anna Maria (Persson) Setterlund."

Larson, Verna, comp. "Family Life Lines."

Lawson, Valerie. "Putting it all Together: One Swedish Family in Canada" (1999).

Lind, Luella. "Memoirs of Ernest (Ernie) Waldemar Lind/Ernst Valdemar Lind."

Lodge, Linnea. "A Profile of the Scandinavian Communities in Edmonton" (1992).

Lundman, Martha Larson. "Beginnings" (1984).

"Lundstrom Family History: Sweden to Canada: Their Family Remembers" (2005).

McGill, Earl. "John Anderson: A Tribute" (1940).

Nelson, Anton A. "Treasured Reflections: An Autobiography" (1984).

Nordstrom, Gary. "A Brief History of Peter and Inga Nordstrom and their Family" (2001).

Olson, Elof. "And So it Happened: The Olson History" (1987).

Osterlind, Lennart. "President's Report, Scandinavian Community Centre Society" (1996).

Persson, William S. "Memoir" (1971).

Quarnstrom, Leonard, & Harriett Quarnstrom Swanson. "Gustaf Aaron Quarnstrom, 1875–1953."

Runesson, Anna. "Svenska kyrkan i Toronto: en historik" (2006).

Sargent, Margo E. (Swanson). "All the Way from Sweden" (1979).

Shanner, Carol, comp. "Anderson Family History 1844–1985" (1985).

Silver, Vernon, comp. "Gerhard Hilarius Silver (Thord Bjorke, pseud) and his Family."

Simmons, Elsie Kvarnberg. "Andrew and Kerstin Kvarnberg & Family" (1989).

Sjoberg, Donald W. "The Sillen Family in Sweden and Canada" (2002).

– "The Sjoberg Family in Sweden and Canada" (2005).

Swanson, Ben. "A little Bit of Sweden Comes to Canada" (c1995).

Symes, Bill. "Chronicles of the Swedish Canadian Social Group" (Victoria).

"Translation of letters from Nils Dahl and Jon Persson to their younger sister Maria Setterlund, 1880–1901."

Trygg, Karen. "History of the Swedish-Canadian Rest Home" (Vancouver).

Virding, Tor. "The History of Roald Amundsen Centre" (1997).

Personal Names Index

General Index

The author, Elinor Barr, teaching her dog to dance the hambo.